Chomsky

on Democracy & Education

Social Theory, Education, and Cultural Change

Series Editors:
Carlos Alberto Torres
Raymond Allen Morrow

Globalization and Education
Critical Perspectives
edited by Nicholas C. Burbules and Carlos Alberto Torres

Critical Theories in Education
Changing Terrains of Knowledge and Politics
edited by Thomas S. Popkewitz and Lynn Fendler

Chomsky on Democracy and Education
by Noam Chomsky, edited by C. P. Otero

Chomsky

on Democracy & Education

Noam Chomsky

edited by C. P. Otero

RoutledgeFalmer   New York and London

Published in 2003 by
RoutledgeFalmer
29 West 35th Street
New York, New York 10001
www.routledge-ny.com

Published in Great Britain by
RoutledgeFalmer
11 New Fetter Lane
London EC4P 4EE
www.routledgefalmer.com

RoutledgeFalmer is an imprint of the Taylor & Francis Group.

10   9   8   7   6   5   4   3   2   1

Library of Congress Cataloging-in-Publication Data

Chomsky, Noam.
    Chomsky on democracy and education / Noam Chomsky ; edited by C. P. Otero.
        p. cm. — (Social theory, education, and cultural change)
    Includes bibliographical references and index.
    ISBN 0–415–92631–9 — ISBN 0–415–92632–7 (pbk.)
        1. Education—Philosophy. 2. Democracy. 3. Critical pedagogy. 4. Language and languages. I. Otero,
Carlos. II. Title. III. Series.

LB885.C5215 C46 2002
370.11'5—dc21
                                                                    2001051058

Contents

Acknowledgments

The writings collected in this volume are published here by the kind permission of Noam Chomsky, which we gratefully acknowledge. We are also grateful to Black Rose Books (the publisher of Chomsky's *Radical priorities* and *Language and politics*, where seven of the following selections were first collected by the present editor), to Alternative Radio (which first made available tape recordings of four of our selections), to Pisa's Scuola Normale Superiore, and to the periodicals where some of the selections included here first appeared (in particular, *Z Papers, Profession 2000, Nicaraguan Perspectives, The Pedagogic Reporter, Language, Northeast Conference on the Teaching of Foreign Languages, The English Magazine,* and *Journal of Advanced Composition*). See the Editor's Notes at the end of the volume for details.

Foreword

This is the first anthology of Chomsky's writings concerned with questions of democracy or of education, many of them little known, if at all (some are published here for the first time). Its purpose is to bring together a highly representative and fairly extensive collection of interviews, talks, and articles that provide support for his views on these two closely interrelated topics, which are at the root of his libertarian social philosophy. Most of the pieces included (in particular the five interviews that open or close the book) are among the most concise and readable ones in Chomsky's now-voluminous output. Thus the collection may serve as a user-friendly and wide-ranging introduction to some of the most powerful ideas of "arguably the most important intellectual alive"—possibly "one of the more powerful thinkers that ever lived" (*New York Times Book Review*, February 25, 1979). It is accessible, informative, and compelling, and, arguably, essential reading for anyone truly concerned with the current and future course of the country and of the world at large. An essential part of that course is the present and future of the educational system. No wonder education typically tops the list of politically salient issues in the United States, ranking above crime, unemployment, and even the economy as a whole, at the beginning of the new millennium.

The importance of these writings can hardly be exaggerated. A case can be made that Chomsky's approach to both democracy and education is one of the most, if not the most, principled and best-founded available. As the Introduction suggests, from the limited perspective of this domain of inquiry Chomsky can be seen as the natural successor of two of the greatest social philosophers of the twentieth century (one American, one British): John Dewey and Bertrand Russell. It is important, however, to keep in mind that, in sharp contrast with Dewey's and Russell's epistemological philosophies, which in fact undermine their respective views of education and democracy rather than provide a solid foundation for them, Chomsky's theory of knowledge, and above all the epoch-making scientific discoveries that underlie it, furnishes a much needed basis for a truly principled conception of democracy and education. In fact, the science of human language that he initiated in the mid-1950s, which is the first and still the most advanced of the cognitive natural sciences, is at the very core of the study of everything human.

The collection of articles, lectures, talks, and interviews brought together here provides an underlyingly unified and interconnected discussion of a broad range of fundamental questions by a rare and unsurpassed example of a systematic thinker and scientist—one with a rare and hard-to-match commitment to truth and justice. Its scope extends from current scientific knowledge about central aspects of the human mind/brain to a description of all-important aspects of the cultural environment and a vision of a higher level of culture—and many other questions in between. What is more, the new conception of the specifically human genetic endowment of the mind/brain suggests a specific type of social organization and a closely related kind of education.

Among the questions that come up for discussion are the following:

- the extent of the comprehensibility of the natural world
- rationality/science and ideology (against all current post-this-or-that)
- the language organ as a product of biological evolution
- linguistics as a model for human studies
- the creative aspect of language use (not just in literature)
- analysis of several notions of equality, freedom, and social organization
- technology and self-management, cultural level and social change
- the ideological subversion of science, technology, and scholarship (with reference to an unsurpassed and still unassimilated discussion of race and IQ)
- scholarship and commitment in the 1960s and now
- media propaganda and control of the public mind under freedom ("an American invention")
- the responsibility of individuals and communities
- the function of the university and the schools, and the choice of curriculum (actual and potential)
- self-teaching and the capacity to discover

No attempt has been made to eliminate redundancy and repetition, and this is for a number of reasons. An important one is that the somewhat varying formulations of essential points may prove helpful, particularly to those unfamiliar with Chomsky's extensive, varied, and sometimes quite demanding work: even the simplest and most basic points discussed in these interviews continue to be misunderstood. It is also helpful, and sometimes instructive, to relate an answer to its context, and the contexts are quite different in the different papers and interviews—as it is helpful to see which issues are taken up again and again, and which are never mentioned. Last but not least, it is often the case that we have to be told something ten times before we can really hear it.

The texts, most of which are conversational in style (not an easy thing for someone who, seemingly without effort, can formally lecture on a broad range of subjects as if reading from a carefully argued and crafted book), have been edited as lightly as possible, often not at all, though some punctuation has been silently supplied when it seemed that it might be of help as well as additional paragraphing throughout. Practically all the subheadings in the table of contents (corresponding to those inserted in the articles and the interviews) have been added, as have some titles (in some cases, a title has been modified or replaced, as is made clear in the Editor's Notes). The material in the Editor's Notes should help readers look for what they want to find or pursue—and to continue the dialogue, if they so wish. The Introduction attempts to provide a unifying perspective on Chomsky's thought and action against his personal background and his moral and intellectual development as an individual, particularly as it relates to his views on democracy and education.

The References section at the end of the book provides the necessary bibliographic information for the writings briefly identified in the Introduction and the Editor's Notes or directly relevant to the discussion, together with additional references (reflecting a variety of viewpoints) that may be of help to the reader.

I am greatly indebted to Noam Chomsky, not just for making the collection possible (in more ways than one) but also for his work and his standards, and for the help and encouragement he has, most generously, provided me over the years. I am sure I am not alone in recognizing that he has brought about or inspired some of the best thought and action of the second half of the twentieth century (the half century of programming "languages" and DNA structure, of the 1960s, of the growing solidarity movements on behalf of less fortunate people everywhere, of animal rights, and of the World Wide Web, among other things), and no doubt will continue to be a major source of creation and widespread inspiration in years to come.

Thanks are also due to David Barsamian for his invaluable contribution to making a good part of the oral output of Chomsky and others available, for promptly sharing his last addition to his set of interviews with me, and for welcoming the inclusion in this book of several pieces from his archives; to Black Rose Books, and in particular Dimitri Roussopoulos, for welcoming the reprinting of a number of pieces from the two books by Chomsky that I edited for them; to Wayne O'Neil, and to Louis Kampf and Richard Ohmann, for a few much-needed precise references; to Carlos Torres for having taken the all-important first step (and the no less decisive more recent ones); to Catherine Fountain, for her research assistance; and to Octavio Pescador for his help with correspondence related to the permissions. As always, Judith Strozer's daily supply of what's most valuable, Daniel Otero's warm and stimulating presence, and David Otero's long-distance nearness, have made all the difference.

Carlos-Peregrín Otero
May 2001

Introduction

Chomsky's education-for-democracy: enlightening mental growth

by C. P. Otero

Democracy and education are central topics in the work of Noam Chomsky. This is not surprising. His parents, who were both teachers, provided a very stimulating and thought-provoking environment at home and sent him to a Deweyite experimental school (Oak Lane Country School) run by Temple University from the time he was two until he was about twelve, that is, roughly from early 1931 to 1943.[1]

These two complementary experiences (at home and at school) were perhaps the most decisive ones in Chomsky's life. To this day he remembers them vividly and fondly. In contrast, he barely remembers anything about his years in high school (a sort of "black hole" in his life, he has repeatedly said—with easily detectable abhorrence), although the high school he attended was considered to be the best in Philadelphia, his hometown. As for his experience at the University of Pennsylvania, where he did his undergraduate work (and ended up doing his early graduate work), after one year or so he was more than ready to drop out. It was a connection with an outstanding professor of linguistics who shared his political views (Zellig Harris) that luckily came to the rescue. The rest, as they say, is history.

Not only was his father, William Chomsky, a teacher and outstanding scholar ("one of the world's foremost Hebrew grammarians"—obituary in the *New York Times*, July 22, 1977), but his main field of interest was education (for most of his life he served as a college professor of Hebrew and Jewish education), and his writings all had an educational purpose.[2] Naturally enough, he was "very much influenced" by John Dewey, the major American intellectual figure of his time and "the greatest American social philosopher" (Selection 15 below), one of whose central interests was democracy and education: "[the elder Chomsky's] own main work (pedagogy), both teaching and writing, was explicitly Deweyite," and so was "his general point of view about the world, mostly," in the words of his oldest son (personal communication)—a likely heir apparent of Dewey's mantle, it will be suggested below. In fact, shortly before his death, William Chomsky described the major objective of his life, echoing Dewey, as "the education of individuals who are well integrated, free and independent in their thinking, concerned about improving and enhancing the world, and eager to participate in making life more meaningful and worthwhile for all."[3] And he appears to have been thoroughly successful in at least one case: it is hard to improve on his words as a description of his oldest son as an individual.

However, the roots of Noam Chomsky's interest in education go well beyond his formative experiences—even beyond his experiences as an educator and, more generally, beyond his work as a student of culture and as an activist. They are at the very core of his inquiries as a scientist and a philosopher. One of the most important consequences of his investigations into the nature of language and the human mind/brain is that, as we will see, they provide the most decisive evidence and argument available in favor of one of the two main traditional stances on the nature of democracy and the nature of education: the one that takes democracy to be self-management, and education to be very largely self-education.

It might be helpful, then, to consider Chomsky's contribution to what he sees as democracy-for-everyone and education-for-democracy under three headings: (1) the educator, (2) the scientist and the epistemologist and philosopher of mind, and (3) the student of culture (contemporary or centuries old, in particular intellectual history) and the activist.

1. The educator

It is the approach that takes education to be very largely self-education that underlies Chomsky's practice, in particular his phenomenal success as an educator in the broadest sense of the term—an educator at large, if you will (he regularly gives talks and lectures all over the world to a variety of audiences, which generally find them unusually enlightening—and then he writes up as many as time allows). For many of us Chomsky is, above all, a dedicated educator and mentor—"by all odds a dedicated teacher," Norman Mailer wrote in his perceptive "history as a novel" in "the year of the first March on the Pentagon, 1967," after spending one night in the bunk next to Chomsky's in some kind of detention center the police had set up somewhere, before Chomsky was transferred to a Washington, D.C., prison (where he was able to see the incredible conditions for the real prisoners). Actually, he has been reputed to be a superb educator and mentor since the time he began to tutor his classmates in the early 1940s, as his high school yearbook for 1945 attests.

There is little doubt that, as an educator, he has been exceptionally successful (far more than John Dewey or Bertrand Russell—or Albert Einstein or Richard Feynman, to zero in on four of his true peers). He has officially supervised over four score doctoral dissertations, something unheard of (to the best of my knowledge), and has contributed to the supervision of many others, within and outside the Massachusetts Institute of Technology (MIT), where his professional ascent was nothing short of meteoric: he became a full professor in 1961 (at thirty-two), attained an endowed chair in 1966, since 1976 has held the coveted position of Institute Professor (a rank reserved for about a dozen scholars of special distinction, most of them Nobel laureates), and in 1991–1992 was given the Killian Faculty Achievement Award, perhaps the most prestigious faculty award, which recognizes "extraordinary professional accomplishments by full-time members of the MIT faculty." Many of the most distinguished contemporary linguists and other cognitive scientists were his advisees, and numerous others were registered students or auditors in his classes—or else students of his students or coworkers. There are also many who are keen students of his prolific writings, unfailingly insightful and inspiring, as I believe the small and circumscribed sample brought together between the covers of this book shows.

What is more, there is often something very special about the guidance he regularly provides to his students in a broad sense, as many acknowledgments in doctoral dissertations and books suggest. (In an even broader sense, no inquiring student of the mind/brain can, in our day and age, escape being his student—among those who really know what they are doing.) It is generally recognized that anybody working in the field of generative grammar and, more generally, cognitive psychology owes him a special intellectual debt. In the case of those who are lucky enough to share the "unique experience" of his classes and his "being so accessible for individual discussions," that debt can become "incalculable," particularly for beginners with "no official status whatsoever at MIT," who seek his opinion and often discover, not without surprise, that he treats them as if they had official or quasi-official status there (the quotations are from dissertation acknowledgments). The even more special experience of being one of Chomsky's doctoral advisees has been described by more than one of them. I'll pick out just three, with very different backgrounds (one American, one Chinese, and one French) but comparable straightforwardness:[4]

> Working with Noam Chomsky . . . is a privilege few can hope for, and even four
> years after arriving here, I feel sometimes that it must be a dream. About Noam

Chomsky much has been said, and I agree with all of it that is good. His inspiring classes, brilliant insights, and his sharp involvement in the work of his students are just three facets of the experience of working with him. His quick reaction to any problem is such that one of my proudest moments here was when he actually had to think silently for several minutes in order to come up with an argument against me. Thursdays, the day of his class and of my appointments with him, will never be so good again.

—Diana Massam

Noam Chomsky, whose influence on me can be seen throughout the following pages, has given me invaluable advice on every aspect of the thesis and of the other aspects of linguistics and life. The extent to which he has made himself available to me and the amount of thought he has put into my work go well beyond what I or anyone else can reasonably expect. His confidence in me and interest in my work has also kept me up during the past years.

—Cheng-Teh James Huang

As the inventor of modern syntactic theory and as its most brilliant exponent, Noam Chomsky has already contributed more to this thesis than perhaps is in it. In working directly with him, I have profited crucially from the unmatched rapidity of comprehension and the immensity of theoretical imagination he routinely brings to bear on the subjects of his attention.

—Jean-Roger Vergnaud, who also knows what it is
like to get a doctoral degree in Paris

2. The scientist and the epistemologist and philosopher of mind

When considering democracy-for-everyone and education-for-democracy, as when considering other aspects of human endeavor, the most fundamental question unavoidably focuses on the interaction of "nature" and "nurture" or, less misleadingly, the interaction between the genetic endowment of an individual and a particular cultural environment. This, of course, takes for granted that, in a literal sense, the disjunction "nature or nurture" makes no sense at all. It should be immediately obvious than both the genetic endowment of an individual and the particular cultural environment will have to play a role in the mental development of any human being (in fact, of any animal). After all, not everyone speaks Armenian, or Basque, or Catalan . . . or Vietnamese, or Welsh, or Xhosa, or Yaqui, or Zhuang—and no one's temper is indistinguishable from her or his temperament (in the use of these terms that takes the temperament of an individual to be made up of innate characteristics, and his or her temper to involve qualities acquired through experience). What has to be discovered, then, is the relative importance or weight of the respective contributions of the human brain and the environment.

It does not take a genius to see that it is not the environment that accounts for the fact that a human cannot fly like an eagle nor an eagle speak like a five-year-old child. But not everyone can readily see, even less help others see, that the environment cannot possibly provide a sufficient basis for any of the seemingly miraculous things a five-year-old can do. A quick look at what children have to know to be able to do what they do without giving it a second thought immediately shows that their knowledge goes well beyond what the environment can provide. This is also true of the adult, of course.

A simple pair of expressions is enough to give an inkling of what is involved. Consider the following two (call them E1 and E2), which, obviously, are identical except for the three initial words of the second one:

(E1) Leslie expects to educate herself
(E2) I wonder who Leslie expects to educate herself

If we rely on what the environment has to offer, it is natural to conclude that the female who educates herself is the same in both E1 and E2, since the words after *Leslie* are the same, in the same order, in both cases. However, to our great surprise, this expectation turns out to be wrong. To begin with, in E1 we understand that Leslie is a female, while in E2 we are left in the dark about Leslie's sex. We also understand that in E1 it is Leslie who expects to educate herself, while in E2 it is not Leslie but some other female who expects to educate herself: every speaker of English would find it perfectly natural (perhaps without hesitation, perhaps after giving it a moment's thought) if the answer to the question implicit in E2 was something like: "You don't really know? Laura, that's who." In other words, if "Laura" is the right answer to the question implicit in E2, we understand that Leslie (male or female, we don't know) expects Laura to educate herself. In more technical terms this means that the "value" the hearer or reader has to "calculate" or compute for the "variable" *herself* to be able to understand E2 is not the same as the value computed for *herself* in E1—even though E2 contains all the words E1 contains, in the very same order. Every speaker of English "instinctively" knows that, which goes to show that the environment is too "poor" to account for those and other facts (presumably uncountably many) never actually "observed" by speakers who are not moderately competent linguists.

The crucial question now is: How do you, say, as a speaker of English, come to know this, being, as it is, radically at odds with what the information provided by the environment suggests? Did your mother or your peers tell you? Did your teacher tell you? Just kidding. Since no one was aware of it until, a few years ago, Chomsky first had the "aha!" experience, how could anyone tell you? Does everyone discover it on their own by luckily coming across the right expression (a probability tending to zero), unconsciously realizing what's going on, and remaining forever unaware of their mind-blowing discovery?

If the answer to these and similar questions is no, there are only two possible ways out of the impasse: (1) it is a miracle that can, in principle, occur again and again every minute of the day, or (2) the knowledge that allows every speaker of English (necessarily human) to understand the two expressions differently comes from the inside of the individual human, is simply part of the genetic endowment of the individual, part of being human; it is, in other words, an example of the "innate" knowledge discussed in some detail in Selection 1.

A more sustained exploration along these lines suggests that, actually, the better part of our knowledge comes from inside, not from the environment, even though the environment often makes a non-negligible contribution (to begin with, there is no physical growth, non-mental or mental, without appropriate "food"). If true, as it seems to be, this can only mean that in many of its uses the term "learning" (or "teaching," necessarily understood with reference to "learning") can be applied to the knowledge resulting from mental development or growth only colloquially, the way we speak about the sun "setting," a question discussed in Selection 25.

It is easy to see now, after Chomsky made it plain, that the evidence in support of these conclusions provides much valuable fodder for the epistemologist, since it unequivocally suggests that it is the epistemological philosophy of Plato and Descartes, not that of Aristotle and the British empiricists, that is on the right track.[5]

In the context of this book we may take these barely outlined findings and their implications as the gist of the so-called cognitive revolution of the 1950s, the emergence of the cognitive sciences as we know them, spearheaded by Chomsky's profound discoveries about human language and the human mind/brain—the first to extend the range of the Galilean-Newtonian style of research to the study of the human sciences in a strict sense, rarely used and even more rarely applicable. But we should keep in mind that it's just the initial gist. The full, ongoing attempt at explanation of the human language organ as a unique major component of the human mind/brain now encompasses hundreds of tightly reasoned pages, some of which make ample use of a precise and sometimes forbidding symbolism (in particular many pages of Chomsky's first monumental study of 1955, almost one thousand pages long). Given the centrality of language in our genetic endowment (language is generally taken to be a, if not *the*, defining property of humanness), the resulting new understanding, which is certainly Chomsky's most important intellectual contribution to the accumulated cultural wealth of humankind, cannot fail to be epoch-making. One not-insignificant bonus is that this precise theory of human language provides a suggestive model for other cognitive sciences (the first such naturalistic model in the history of civilization, still far from adequately put to work in other investigations of cognition).

The significance of this model for a conception, far from wholly unsupported, of democracy and education derives from the fact that it strongly suggests that cultural advance, hence cultural level, which is at the root of democracy and defines the outer limits of education, is a function of individual enlightenment. And, as Chomsky never tires of emphasizing, the fuller mental development that brings about individual enlightenment is just a very special kind of physical growth, namely, growth of the mind/brain—particularly before puberty, during the natural course of maturation.[6] Seen from this illuminating perspective, the aim of education-for-democracy is to foster enriching mental growth in the individual, growth self-directed toward enlightenment, hence self-enlightening mental growth. Enlightening in precisely what sense or direction? Unfortunately, this is not a question with a scientific answer (at least, as of now). We return to it in the next section.

Perhaps a word should be added here about another (related) question that science has not been able to address: the emergence of the human brain (with a unique capacity for language). From the perspective just sketched it is not very hard to see that there is a strong parallelism between the (ontogenetic) development of language in the individual human and the (phylogenetic) development of language in the human species. Even the leading behaviorist of his time, B. F. Skinner, was able to see this parallelism (in his own terms, of course).[7] Thus, in a 1966 article on the topic in *Science* he takes such a parallelism for granted, so at least he was consistent, something that cannot be said of a number of contemporary (neo-)Darwinians. What he also failed to see is that, just as there is no environmentalistic solution to the wonder of the growth of language in the mind of a normal child, there is no environmentalistic solution to the mystery of human evolution either.

It should be immediately obvious to anyone relatively free of prejudice that the environment (a.k.a. natural selection) can no more account for the emergence of human cognition in the species than for the growth of language

in the child. The reason in either case is that the environment is just too des-
titute: it entirely lacks the complex cognitive mental structures that any serious investigation of the human mind/brain must postulate. Understood in
these terms, it is much easier to make sense of the objections of the creationists
than of the dogmatic pronouncements of some self-defined (neo-)Darwinians.

For starters, there seems to be no way to establish the unsupported claim
that you can get evolutionary rabbits out of the environment's magician's hat.
In contrast, it is easy enough to turn the creationists' claim into a reasonable
one: all that is needed is to substitute for it Spinoza's formula *Natura sive
Deus*, "Nature or God/Divinity/Creator" (a formula much celebrated, for
example, by Goethe, who was no fool), where, of course, *sive* (as opposed to
aut) is an identifier, not the disjunctive "or" of elementary mathematical logic.
Spinoza's formula, in turn, can be taken to be an early way of saying that "it
may be that the whole of evolution is shaped by physical processes in a deep
sense, yielding many properties that are casually attributed to selection," as
Chomsky has recently put it.[8]

3. The student of culture and history and the activist

Chomsky's scientific and epistemological investigations provide, then, the
most decisive evidence and argument available in favor of one of the two
main traditional stances on the nature of education: the one that privileges
the genetic endowment over the environment, particularly the cultural environment (which, it bears repeating, is not to say that the environment cannot
make a significant contribution). This is, of course, the stance best represented by Plato and his modern heirs, a lineage that runs from Descartes to
Chomsky through the British Platonists, in particular Ralph Cudworth
(1617–1688), and Leibniz, to both of whom Kant was heavily indebted. The
great classical liberal Wilhelm von Humboldt, a major theorist not only of
language but also of democracy and education (he was "the architect of the
Prussian educational system and the founder of the University of Berlin,"
which was consciously selected as a model by a number of modern universities), brought to the fore in Chomsky's work on intellectual history, was
(unwittingly) very much in line with this Cartesian tradition in essential
respects (see Selections 7, 9, 10).[9]

One instructive way of looking at Chomsky's conception of education is
to try to see it as a natural outgrowth of a streamlined and enriched form of
Cartesian mentalism he has related to the centuries-old tradition, and
arguably the current culmination of the Enlightenment phase of this tradition. But this is a sort of reconstructed historical idealization. What actually

happened was that he made his discoveries in blissful ignorance of their partial antecedents and then searched for predecessors.[10]

From this updated and vastly enriched Cartesian perspective, "e-ducation" (literally "out-drawing"), understood as the process of drawing out something latent in a human mind or just helping it "flourish" in the proper "soil" under the "sunlight" (perhaps providing "water" or "food" when necessary), is always to be preferred to "in-struction" or, worse still, "in-doctrination" (even to gently indoctrinating persuasion, still analogous to pouring some concoction into a human mind as one may pour a liquid into a vessel). The terms education and instruction are not usually opposed in this way, but the insight has, of course, very old roots ("Teachers open the door, but you must enter by yourself," says a venerable Chinese proverb). It is not hard to see that, for an aspiring democracy, the likely benefits of striving to bring about this kind of educational practice (a "practice of freedom" and creativity, as emphasized by the Brazilian educator Paulo Freire) could hardly be overestimated—if our incipient understanding of the human mind/brain is on the right track. (See Selection 25.)[11]

Thus Chomsky cites with approval Russell's characterization of the goal of education as being "to give a sense of the value of things other than domination, to help create wise citizens of a free community, to encourage a combination of citizenship with liberty, individual creativeness, which means that we regard a child as a gardener regards a young tree, as something with an intrinsic nature which will develop into an admirable form given proper soil and air and light." (See Selection 9.) Chomsky also feels, as "Dewey seems to have felt for much of his life (later he was more skeptical)," that "reforms in early education could be in themselves a major lever of social change; they could lead the way to a more just and free society, a society in which, in Dewey's words, 'the ultimate aim of production [is not production of goods but] the production of free human beings associated with one another on terms of equality.'" And he goes on to emphasize Dewey's view that it is "illiberal and immoral" to train children to work "not freely and intelligently, but for the sake of the wage earned," because in such case their activity "is not free because not freely participated in."[12]

The quotes are from the Prologue, an important and little-known 1994 talk. Chomsky begins by contrasting two completely different traditions of Western thought about the ideas of democracy, freedom, and justice that have developed since the French and American revolutions. One tradition, with roots in Enlightenment values, stems from the nineteenth-century working class press and organizations, evolves through left libertarian and socialist movements, and is enriched and given much needed support in Chomsky's conception of democracy-for-everyone and education-for-democracy. This tradition, he writes in the Prologue,

> included progressive liberals of the John Dewey variety, independent socialists like Bertrand Russell, the leading elements of the Marxist mainstream (mostly anti-Bolshevik), and of course libertarian socialists of various anarchist movements, not to speak of major parts of the labor movement and other popular sectors.[13]

Although Chomsky passes over it in silence, presumably because it is not the appropriate occasion to take up the matter, the libertarian views of "the two leading thinkers of the twentieth century in the West" (in his opinion), are really undermined by the empiricistic epistemology that underlies them. It is true that classical British empiricism, which "arose in often healthy opposition to religious obscurantism and reactionary ideology" and "offers a vision of limitless progress," is historically "closely associated with classical liberal thought,"as indeed it is in the cases of Dewey and Russell.[14] But "a deeper look will show that the concept of 'empty organism,' plastic and unstructured, apart from being false, also serves naturally as the support for the most reactionary social doctrines," as Chomsky writes in his *Reflections on language.*

This is not an entirely new idea. To mention a well-known antecedent: Kant's critique of certain aspects of empiricist doctrines "is not simply an epistemological quibble, but a far-reaching argument about the nature of human freedom," Ellen Wood suggests in her 1972 book (a revised version of her UCLA doctoral dissertation). The reason, as she points out, is that whether the human mind is "a responsive cog in the mechanism of nature," as in empiricist doctrine, or "a creative, determinative force" is a crucial question underlying all-important social choices.[15]

From this perspective it is easier to understand Chomsky's concern, from day one, with empiricist—in particular, behaviorist—concepts of human nature, which he felt and feels are essentially manipulative and coercive. Like the Bolsheviks and other authoritarians (including many postclassical liberals), the behaviorists conceived of the brain as virtually a blank tablet upon which a particular type of consciousness may be imprinted by superior minds and farsighted leaders ("Leninist" in Leningrad at one time, "(neo-)liberal" or "conservative" or something else in either of the two Cambridges). Not surprisingly, Chomsky has always been rather concerned about these developments—particularly for political reasons, since the whole complex of ideas seemed to him to be linked to potentially quite dangerous social currents.

For him, to be well founded, a vision of a social order must be anchored in the enduring strain of the Cartesian tradition, which has consistently argued for a conception of the human mind that is the polar opposite of the notion of the tabula rasa. Moreover, for him, as for Descartes, there is no essential variation among humans (no "degrees of humanness") apart from superficial physical aspects: a creature is either human or it is not. Thus racism, sexism, and other inegalitarian tendencies are a logical impossibility under his essentially Cartesian conception—if consistently applied.[16] This renewed and deepened egalitarian vision, which his technical linguistic work shores up to some extent, is at the root of his more general studies of human nature and society, in particular of his conception of education. Hence the importance of the results of Chomsky's scientific and epistemological investigations, the unrivaled modern contribution toward a resolution of the centuries-old philosophical debate about the nature of the human mind.

If we have strong reasons to believe that the mind/brain, far from being empty at birth, is highly structured and rich, reasonable people concerned with democracy and education would naturally ask what, if any, is the role of the environment. It is easy to see that people grow in every sense of the word and that a high level of intellectual and moral growth cannot be all biologically inherited. What is inborn (innate) is the genetic constitution of an individual, including the basic structure of the mind/brain and the principles that determine its properties and development. The fact that the *course* of development is largely internally determined "does not mean that it will proceed without care, stimulation, and opportunity." All human development, including the development of moral judgment, "is heavily determined by the nature of the environment, and may be severely limited unless the environment is appropriate": "a stimulating environment is required to enable natural curiosity, intelligence and creativity to develop, and to enable our biological capacities to unfold." Not surprisingly, "if a child is placed in an impoverished environment, innate abilities simply will not develop, mature and flourish" (see Selection 3).[17]

Needless to say, these and related conclusions involve questions of fact concerning human nature, for which there is some evidence, and "there are certain conclusions that one may draw from these factual judgments with respect to educational theory and practice, social theory, and the activism which naturally flows from a conscientious commitment to the conclusions of that theory." It is, then, important to make the effort required to make these judgments thoughtfully rather than "mindlessly in conformity to prevailing ideology," tacitly accepting most of "the judgments which prevail in our society" (Selection 9).

The next question, then, is: What kind of mental growth is to be fostered in the individual? In the previous section, the idea was tentatively advanced that the aim of education-for-democracy is to foster growth self-directed toward enlightenment, hence self-enlightening mental growth. Since enlightenment should come along the two basic dimensions of our human makeup, namely, intellectual and moral, we are in fact talking about the free development of intellectual and moral knowledge and insight—hopefully not wanting in wisdom. At this point we can turn to the question left unanswered before: What kind of knowledge and insight would be the hallmark of a successful self-education?

The intellectual part of the question is relatively easy to answer for a child of the Enlightenment with a capital E (the eighteenth-century aftermath of the Galilean-Newtonian scientific revolution): knowledge can be attained only through rational inquiry based on (logical) argument alone, as in the formal sciences, or based in both (factual) evidence and argument, as in the natural sciences (the deepest and most reliable repository of knowledge humans are in the process of attaining), or, at a less deep level, in the most serious investigations of animal behavior and human cultural endeavors. (See Selection 5.)[18] Insight can come both from the sciences and "parasciences" (the humanities and the social and anthropological disciplines) and from the arts (in the broadest sense of the term).

Our understanding of the moral part of the question is much thinner, at least as of now. But, as Chomsky never tires of repeating, underlying it all is the truism that everyone is fully responsible for the foreseeable consequences of their actions—or inactions, as the case may be. It is also fairly clear that there can be morally retarded people (moral morons, if you will), as there are intellectually retarded people (intellectual morons).

Truly educated people would agree in at least that much, it would seem. But the specifics are something else. Like Russell, Chomsky stresses that "in the absence of compelling reasons to the contrary, one should be quite cautious about trying to control someone else's life and character and mode of thought," a hypothesis with "political and social as well as pedagogic consequences for the educator and teacher." There are, then, "significant consequences to one's thinking or thoughtlessness about these issues, and a corresponding personal and professional responsibility." For example, in a certain sense, "control of behavior" of the type generally advocated before he wrote his 1959 review of Skinner's book "will be abhorrent to the person who accepts the humanistic conception of education" (Selection 9).

There are many things no one can prove. One directly relevant in this

connection is that it cannot be proved that some system of authority and domination, whether it is patriarchy, slavery, feudalism, "modern" private corporatism, or other authoritarian institutions, including schools, is unnecessary.
This being the case, what matters is that the burden of proof is on those who
claim it is necessary, as Chomsky has made abundantly clear. Reasonable questions about human concerns can be answered only by experiment, but the initial negative assumption (what the statistician calls the null hypothesis) about
any state autocrat or town autocrat or school autocrat or any other species of
autocrat is that they are not needed: no one should be able to dictate any solutions. The reason is that no one knows enough about human affairs to predict
the best outcome in advance with much confidence. There is no substitute for
wide-ranging discussion and analysis. This is why, for Chomsky, the first thing
is to remain very skeptical. As he told an interviewer in February 1999:

> The world's a complicated place. Anything you look at, whether it's a molecule or
> international society, there are many different perspectives you can take, and you'll
> get very different answers depending on which perspective you take. That's a stan-
> dard problem in the sciences. Why do people do experiments? Doing experiments
> is a creative act, an effort to try to peel away things that you believe, rightly or
> wrongly, are irrelevant to determining the fundamental principles by which things
> are operating and see if you can find something simplified enough that those prin-
> ciples will actually be apparent and then try to rebuild some picture of complex
> reality from that, never getting anywhere near it because reality is just too much of
> a mess, too many intervening factors and so on. Any experiment in the hard sci-
> ences is attempting to discover a perspective which will be illuminating. That
> approach is all the more necessary when you look at things as poorly understood,
> as complex, as human affairs. You have to discover a perspective from which inter-
> esting things seem to appear, recognizing that at best you'll capture one significant
> aspect of a highly complex reality. You hope it's an important one.

There is another respect in which Chomsky's contribution to a better
understanding of a crucial question, closely related to his essentially
Cartesian conception of a (libertarian) social order and deepened egalitarian
vision, is teeming with consequences, in this case for the immediate possibility of truly revolutionary cultural and social advance. The question at issue is
the genetic relation between two forms of organization, for him both tyrannical (See selection 7):

- state socialism/fascism of the totalitarian variety
- state (private) "corporatism," U.S.-style

Most people would now agree that the Bolshevik system brought about by Lenin and Trotsky, sometimes referred to as "really existing socialism" by both admirers and critics, was "turned into an even greater monstrosity by Stalin," and that (at the time) actually existing fascism/Nazism, which had been brought about a few years later by Mussolini and Hitler and their nanoclones (all the way down to Franco), deserved no less high marks in the realm of monstrous inhumanity. But not many people unfamiliar with Chomsky's thought will be prone to see what we might call "really existing capitalism" (since it isn't really capitalism in the earlier sense of the term) or, more transparently, state (private) corporatism, as a tyrannical system.[19]

From the perspective of Chomsky's updated Cartesian conception of the human mind, the two, Bolshevism/fascism and U.S.-style private corporatism, are actually similar in fundamental ways. Russell had observed early on the "extreme similarity between the Bolshevik [commissar] and the [corporate] magnate," to which Chomsky was quick to add the similarity of their ideologically biased doctrines, more or less blindly derived from empiricist assumptions (cf. Section 2 above). This is one of the main points he tried to make in his very first "non-professional" book, *American power and the new mandarins* (1969), where he attempted to show that "Bolshevism and American liberalism are basically manifestations of the same thing." A few years later he cited with approval the observation that "Lenin, in such pamphlets as *What is to be done?*, conceived of the proletariat as a *tabula rasa* upon which the 'radical' intelligentsia must imprint a socialist consciousness . . . to the masses from the outside" and "organize and control society in order to bring 'socialist structures' into existence" (never mind what the vast majority of the people, a.k.a. the "masses," might think or want).[20] And if we substitute "democratic structures" for "socialist structures," so do the traders in wares and votes of our consumption-oriented huckster societies, where the "masses" (Alexander Hamilton's "great beast") have to swim against the current of sort of preprogrammed permissible thoughts. From this perspective, the overgrown and still growing virtual Big Brother of the media (not to mention current or sought after "spy centers") makes a mockery of the much less sophisticated Bolshevik one.

In Chomsky's insightful analysis, the two systems fall together into a single tradition (profoundly at odds with the libertarian one), which finds cultural expression in "actually existing industrial democracies" and in their media and their educational institutions. Both tyrannical forms (totalitarianism and neo-liberalism) are very sharply and dramatically opposed to genuine libertarian values, and "both were, and one of them remains, deeply authoritarian in fundamental commitment," as he writes in the Prologue.

At this point an intriguing series of questions arises. Where does this "modern" (read: recent) conception of private corporation, the dominant institution in contemporary industrial societies, come from? What is the intellectual soil that nourishes it? What are its underlying assumptions? The answers to these questions shed a great deal of light on our current predicament and suggest a course of action with epoch-making potential, in Chomsky's view.

To proceed to answer them, a good place to begin is with the emergence of the U.S.-style private corporation little more than a century ago, as a "collectivist legal entity" (in legal-history terminology), a new monstrous creature under the sun. How did it happen? How have the private companies and institutions of an earlier era come to arrogate rights and privileges which inhere in individual persons? On the basis of appropriate legislation? Not at all. Largely by the sleight of hand of courts and lawyers that supported by an elite intellectual community. Courts and lawyers introduced the vast changes into the legal system that granted these tyrannical "collectivist legal entities" ("as they are properly called") the rights they now enjoy, a radical and uncalled-for break with the past. In fact, the nineteenth century was characterized by "an entirely different moral climate," as Chomsky often reminds us: "wage labor was considered hardly different from slavery by such folks as Abraham Lincoln, the Republican Party, and the *New York Times*—not to speak of working people." It was only toward the end of the nineteenth century that steps were first taken that departed radically from the enduring tradition.[21] As he pointed out in a 1998 interview in *Citizenship Studies:*

> The process began from the 1880s [cf. *Powers and prospects* (1996), p. 74], but it took some time for the system to be really institutionalized. It was sharply condemned by conservatives, already then a vanishing breed that has now virtually disappeared (apart from the name, typically taken over by statist reactionaries). The reason was that these radical innovations undermined traditional "natural rights" doctrine as well as markets. These developments reflected very significant changes in the economy, and were supported by an intriguing range of opinion: corporate power, for obvious reasons, but also "progressive opinion."

Surprising as it may seem, the intellectual root of these unparalleled innovations is the until-then-preposterous idea that "organic entities," over and above individuals, have the rights of persons. This is of course a neo-Hegelian doctrine, in Chomsky's view. Recall that "organic form," an ancient metaphor ("organic unity" was first discussed by Plato and later defined by Aristotle), was a preoccupation of the German Romantics, no doubt related to their unbounded admiration for the "glory that was Greece." So, for example, Wilhelm von Humboldt's concept of the "organic form" of language (parallel to Goethe's much earlier *Urform*), "must be considered against the background of the intensive discussion during the Romantic period of the distinction between 'mechanical form' and 'organic form.'"[22] But at the time, apparently, most people did not lose track of the fact that to say that a form freely created by humans was "organic" was just a way of making a point and that the expression was not to be taken literally: metaphoric "organicism" was not to be confused with biological organicism (as in the case of the biological organic form of human language).[23] In other words, most people did not attribute a biological existence, or the characteristics of biological organisms, to non-biological "organisms" (in particular, to a state or a society).

One notable exception (not just on this) was Hegel, "a person of quite appalling ignorance" in Chomsky's considered opinion (and "an egregious racist" to boot), who, for some reason that not everyone can understand, was for some time, and in some quarters still is, greatly respected across the spectrum.[24] For Hegel, an entity such as the state, which in his view expresses the identity of the community, is an "organic entity" or social "organism" (literally, we are to believe) with a life of its own: it logically and actually precedes the individual constituents of the community. In other words, for Hegel the whole is logically and actually prior to the parts, and "cultures, practices, institutions, and so on should be seen as products of a progressively emerging historical process." That's why he rejects even the "misleading philosophical fiction" of the "social contract" as the source of legitimacy for the (for him always absolutist) state.[25]

It is not hard to see that this doctrine is not unlike the dogmas underlying Bolshevism and fascism/Nazism, the two generally recognized main forms of modern totalitarianism. What is perhaps less obvious is that similar neo-Hegelian dogmas underlie the conception of twentieth-century U.S.-style private corporatism, since a corporation has the "organic" status of a "person" before the law.[26] This is no small matter if indeed a U.S.-style private corporation is, in Chomsky's words, "as totalitarian an institution as humans have managed so far to contrive": "those inside their hierarchical command structure take orders from above and send orders down below."[27] The fact that "such terms as 'fascist' and 'totalitarian' are restricted to political entities" makes no difference. As he goes on to say, echoing Dewey, "Terminology is crafted to avoid the substance behind the shadow." What matters is that "the similarity in character is unmistakable." This is, in his view, one of the reasons why genuine conservatives (classical liberals among them) were strongly opposed to this attack on human ("natural") rights principles and on markets (corporations are also a radical attack on markets, he underscores)—and, by the same token, one of the reasons why (postclassical) "liberals" and "progressives" tended to support the epoch-making legal decisions to grant corporations the rights of "immortal persons" of exorbitant power.

Revealingly, this assault on human rights is sometimes seen as a legacy of "individualism" when in fact it is a sharp attack against individualism; more precisely, an attack against the until-then taken-for-granted doctrine that rights inhere in "persons," by which classical liberals meant, as was standard for most of historical time, persons of flesh and blood, not "collectivist legal entities." After all, in our day a typical private corporation, let alone a mega-corporation, is a kind of absolutist state-like institution, sometimes in fact bigger and more powerful and autocratic than some of the foreign states it "does business" with. Once one accepts the doctrine that a "corporate entity" is an "organic entity," a social "organism," their "rights" (especially their right of "freedom of speech" in marketing, advertising, and other types of deception) in practice go far beyond those of persons, both because of the huge differences of scale and because private corporations are immortal (as also stipulated by the courts), features that Chomsky has brought to the fore more than once. (See Selection 15.)[28]

What has never been changed, fortunately for the great majority of the population, is one of the traditional restrictions generally imposed on a corporation: it has to be chartered by a state. This is a sort of Achilles' heel whose significance should not be underestimated: since the charter can be taken away, a private American corporation "exists at the whim of the public."[29] Thus the private corporate structure, the major (tyrannical) power system in the West, is weak, in Chomsky's view, appearances not withstanding. Given that "half of the population thinks that both parties should be disbanded" and "over 80 per cent regard the economic system as 'inherently unfair' and the government 'run for the benefit of the few' . . . , not the people," once a certain level of understanding and commitment is reached, "a democratically organized public could simply take away the charter of any corporation and place it under worker control or community control."[30] It hasn't been done for a long time (perhaps since the 1880s), but the mechanisms are there, ready to be triggered. If so, the fact that this system of centralized, autocratic, and unaccountable power not only has not yet succumbed, as its twin brothers, fascism/Nazism and Bolshevism, did, but is increasing its sway and dominance all over the world does not mean that all the possibilities of historical development have already been exhausted. The latter two misshapen monstrosities were expected by their leaders to last a thousand years yet succumbed within a minute fraction of that time. The seemingly overwhelming power of the surviving current incarnations of autocracy is also "based upon social policies with particular goals that are not graven in stone or founded in law of nature or society, any more than the human institutions from which they arise."[31]

At this point it's a short step from an illuminating analysis by a superb intellectual historian to an educational program—and, beyond that, to a suggestive and potentially effective program for action. Since "the first step is always to penetrate the clouds of deceit and distortion and learn the truth about the world," our schools and colleges have part of their work cut out for them. Their responsibility on this score is not slight: it should be abundantly clear by now that "there has rarely been a time in history when the choice carried such dramatic human consequences."[32] No wonder education is the top political issue for the American people at the beginning of the new millennium.

The frank and open discussion in our schools, colleges, and universities (as well as in the local and national media, we may add) of truly significant questions such as the ones just illustrated—crucial not just for the advance but for the very survival of human civilization, perhaps for the survival of our species (and certainly for the survival of many other species)—is a fair measure of a decisive aspect of any program of education-for-democracy within a genuinely democratic (political and economic) order, as Chomsky understands it. Only when any truly significant question can be routinely discussed in an open and honest way in our schools and universities within a multifaceted curriculum can we begin to entertain the idea that we are out of the doldrums of our current stupor and may be on our way to at least the glimmerings of a truly advanced industrial society.

Moreover, a society that has attained at least the intellectual and moral level reached by the eighteenth-century Enlightenment would make this kind of education freely available to every one of our children and our teenagers—in fact, to everyone, at any age. (See Selection 10.) "Freedom without opportunity is a devil's gift, and the refusal to provide such opportunities is criminal," we read at the beginning of "Market democracy in a neoliberal order" (1997). This is certainly the case when what is at stake is the intellectual and moral growth of the more vulnerable among us (mostly children). Indeed, "the fate of the more vulnerable offers a sharper measure of the distance from here to something that might be called 'civilization.'"[33]

Notes

1. Recall that John Dewey published "Progressive education and the science of education" and became honorary president of the Progressive Education Association (PEA) in 1928, the very year Chomsky was born, and published his last book on education, *Experience and education*, the centerpiece of which was an indictment of much "progressive" education (more on this later), in 1938.

2. See my introduction to N. Chomsky's *Language and politics* (1988). (Reminder: a list of references for the writings mentioned in this Introduction and in the Editor's Notes to the selections, or relevant to the discussion, appears at the end of the book.)

3. Kinsman (ed.), *Contemporary authors* (1975–1978), s.v. Chomsky.

4. For more on the topic and a broader sample of representative testimonials, see Otero 1986/1994.

5. This conclusion, and Chomsky's epistemology more generally, is often misunderstood, perhaps because it goes so much against the grain of common sense (as the dismissal of geocentrism did—and still does for a large number of people). A relevant example in this context is the chapter "Human Learning" by D. W. Hamlyn in *The philosophy of education* (1973), ed. by R. S. Peters. Of necessity Hamlyn was unfamiliar with *Language and learning: the debate between Jean Piaget and Noam Chomsky* (1980), ed. by M. Piattelli-Palmarini, especially Chomsky's reply to Piaget, which may very well spare poorly informed and misguided critics from grossly misunderstanding what is at issue.

6. Before puberty as a rough first approximation. The "critical ages" are obviously not the same along every developmental dimension (every subcourse of maturation). Even within one specific course, say, the development of language, it seems to be necessary to distinguish more than one "critical age." Cf. Strozer, *Language acquisition after puberty* (1994).

7. His terms are generally understood as pitifully inadequate ones since Chomsky's rightly celebrated 1959 review of Skinner's book on "verbal behavior," after which "Chomsky's star began to rise" and "generative grammar became the thing." The controversy was really over then and there (Skinner never attempted to defend his position), which is not to say there are no diehards left. Perhaps the latest book-length "reappraisal" is Richelle's *B. F. Skinner* (1993). Skinner's explanation for not answering Chomsky, cited at length on page 122, from which the last two quotations in the text are taken, is not without interest. See also Chomsky, "Psychology and ideology" (1972) in his *For reasons of state* (1973), reprinted in part in *The Chomsky reader*.

8. "An interview on Minimalism" (conducted by Adriana Belletti and Luigi Rizzi), University of Siena, November 8–9, 1999, included in Chomsky's *Of Nature and language* (2002), as well as in the Italian edition (2001); cf. *Science and creationism* (1984), ed. A. Montagu. Extended discussion of these questions can now be found in Jenkins, *Biolinguistics* (2000), and in his review of Calvin and Bickerton, *Lingua ex machina: reconciling Darwin and Chomsky with the human brain* (2000) in *Mind and Language* 16:4 (September 2001). See also Wesson, *Beyond natural selection* (1991) together with Lewin's *Complexity* (1992, 1999), Waldrop's *Complexity* (1992), and in particular Kaufmann's *At home in the universe* (1995), and references in these works.

9. The quote is from Burrow's introduction to his (1969) edition of Humboldt's *The limits of state action* (1792), p. vii. The richer single source of information on the great classical liberal (a category not to be confused with that of contemporary "liberal," as the term is generally understood today, let alone with that of "neo-liberal") is perhaps Sweet's *Wilhelm von Humboldt: a biography* (1978–1980). Ch. 8, covering the years 1808 to 1810

(in case it helps: Darwin and Lincoln were both born in 1809), is mostly on "the reluctant educational reformer." See also Viertel, "The concept of 'diversity' in Humboldt's
thought" (1973).

10. Understandably, the highly original and innovative character of his work made it hard
    for many to see that he is more traditional and conservative than most—as conservative
    as the really enduring tradition allows him to be. In fact, as has occasionally been sug-
    gested, and Chomsky is fond of showing, it is not truly revolutionary developments, but
    reactionary gambits, that tend to depart sharply and irresponsibly from enduring tradi-
    tional values. Cf. MacIntyre, *A short history of ethics* (1966), ch. 17.

11. Cf. Spring, *Wheels in the head: educational philosophies of authority, freedom, and culture
    from Socrates to Paulo Freire* (1994).

12. Cf. Chomsky, *World orders old and new* (1994, 1996), 2.1, in particular the sentence in
    note 4 about the articulation of these themes by Adam Smith (and other classical liber-
    als of the Enlightenment). With respect to children's free participation, it should be kept
    in mind that Dewey was against not just those who still failed to "connect the subject
    matter of the curriculum to the interest and activities of the child," but also (something
    less generally known) against some advocates of "progressive" child-centered education
    for their failure to "connect the interests and activities of the child to the subject matter
    of the curriculum" (Westbrook, pp. 99; see also pp. 502f.).

13. Elsewhere he identifies those "leading elements of the Marxist mainstream" as Rosa
    Luxemburg, Arthur Rosenberg, Anton Pannekoek, Karl Korsch and (his late friend)
    Paul Mattick, and the two outstanding "libertarian socialists of various anarchist move-
    ments," as Mihail Bakunin and Rudolf Rocker, and adds that "Russell's views were
    rather similar, in this regard" (*Powers and prospects* [1996], p. 76; cf., e.g., Chomsky,
    American power [1969], p. 363 [*Chomsky reader*, p. 413]; *Language and responsibility*
    [1979], p. 74; *Language and politics* [1988], pp. 167–69.) Among the important refer-
    ences for the "popular sectors" he may have in mind are Ware's *The industrial worker
    1840–1860* (1924) and David Montgomery's *Citizen worker* (1993) and *The fall of the
    house of labor* (1987).

14. Although each adheres to a form of empiricism (Russell more self-consciously than
    Dewey), there are important differences between the two thinkers. Thus, in Chapter 30
    of his history of Western philosophy (1945), after describing Dewey as "a man of the
    highest character, liberal in outlook, generous and kind in personal relations, indefatiga-
    ble in work" with most of whose opinions he is "in almost complete agreement," Russell
    proceeds to refute what he considers Dewey's most important work "from a strictly
    philosophical point of view": "his criticism of the traditional notion of 'truth,' which is
    embodied in the theory of what [Dewey] calls 'instrumentalism.'" Dewey's instrumental-
    ism, and pragmatism more generally, is as alien to Chomsky as it is to Russell—and just
    as alien to Chomsky is Russell's empiricism. No less significant is the fact that neither
    Russell nor Chomsky had a lapse in judgment comparable to Dewey's. Cf. Chomsky,
    American power (1969), pp. 6, 317 (a page included in Selection 16).

15. The quotes are from Chomsky's *Reflections on language* (1975), pp. 128f. (see also
    Selection 12). No less relevant is the rest of the chapter, which cannot be discussed fur-
    ther here for limitations of space.

16. See Harry Bracken, *Mind and language: essays on Descartes and Chomsky* (1984), where
    these ideas are developed.

17. See also *Language and problems of knowledge* (1986), 171–76 and last page. For other

related references, see Corson's "Chomsky on education" (1980) and Barsky (forthcoming), Ch. 5. Cf. Rai (1995), Ch. 8, on his view of the function of the university.

As is to be expected, Chomsky's view is totally at odds with current trends, in particular the current attempt to privatize the educational system, that is, the attempt of the corporations to take over the educational system as they took over most of the health system and part of the prison system in order to make them sources of large profits. In other words, the educational analog of HMOs will be EMOs, Chomsky suspects. This is "the direction that financial capital wants to move in. . . . The next big target of public money that [investors] can go after in the parasitic fashion of the rich is the education system" ("U.S. to world: get out of the way," 1999). In his view, it is just part of the general assault of the last quarter century on solidarity, democracy, social welfare, and anything that interferes with private power and profit making. For a recent special report on the trend, see the ranking of "the top U.S. universitites in their quest for intellectual property, commercial partners and profits" in Rebecca Zacks, "The TR university research scorecard," in the July-August 2000 isssue of the *Technology Review*, "MIT's Magazine of Innovation" (not surprisngly, the University of California emerges as undisputed number one in both "campus patenting" and "tech transfer riches," with MIT a distant second in the first category and tenth in the second category); see also Buderi, "From the ivory tower to the bottom line," in the same isssue. Cf. R. Solomon and J. Solomon, *Up the university: re-creating higher education in America* (1993), Soley, *Leasing the ivory tower: the corporate takeover of academia* (1995), Masao, "Ivory tower in escrow" (2000), for critiques of higher education as big business, with bloated university administrations vying for research grants and lucrative profits, having lost sight of teaching as the university's mission; also, Hewlett, *Child neglect in rich societies* (1993) and Hewlett and West, *The war against parents* (1998), for a related aspect of the general issue.

18. There's no reason to be any less rational in the study of human affairs than in any other study: if a rational approach is essentially not allowed to run its course, institutional structure is likely to be blocking the way. On the other hand, since the high point of the scientific revolution in the seventeenth century, most knowledgeable people agree that there is no such thing as indubitable knowledge or absolute certainty about empirical matters. See Popkin, *The history of scepticism from Erasmus to Spinoza* (1979).

19   The term *corporatism* is first documented in English in 1890 (the date is significant). The qualification "private" is necessary to distinguish it from public corporatism. Both types can be found in both fascist regimes and "liberal" democracies.

Interestingly, current studies of corporatism usually pay no attention to private corporatism of the U.S. variety ("big business"). The object of their attention is public or communal corporatism, particularly in fascist or formerly fascist states (see, e.g., *The corporate state: corporatism and the state tradition in Western Europe* [1988], ed. Cox and O'Sullivan). So when an American specialist on the topic writes in a comparative overview that

> In fact, we do not like to talk about corporatism very much in the United States. It is not mentioned in polite company, in part because of its association with fascism. . . . We like to think of ourselves as a free and democratic country. We do not like to think that we are like . . .

he, in sharp contrast with Chomsky's analysis, is not thinking of the private corporation (which the fascist regimes tried to rein in somewhat), but rather of public measures, as the following passage makes clear:

> Nevertheless, whenever we talk about private groups (such as business, labor, teachers) being *incorporated* into the political system; whenever we have government-sponsored group entitlements, set-asides, quotas, or group favoritism; whenever we discuss health care reform, industrial policy, reforming Medicare or Medicaid, welfare or Social Security reform—then corporatism, or elements of corporatism, are almost always involved. (Wiarda, *Corporatism and comparative politics,* 1997, pp. 129, 130)

An explicit lame justification offered for a usage quite different from Chomsky's usage (or from the one attributed to the "New Left" below) is the following:

> The "New Left" has used the term "corporate state" to signify a state in which business corporations have important or decisive influence. If this usage were generally adopted, we would be at a loss to have an English equivalent for the German *Ständestaat* ["'corporate state' in the old sense"]. The French and Italian, of course, speak of *ordre corporatif* or *stato corporativo* in the same sense in which we use the term here. (Landauer, *Corporate state ideologies: historical roots and philosophical origins,* 1883, p. 1)

20. *Problems of language and freedom* (1971), p. 63f.; *Language and responsibility* (1979), p. 90. The quote about one of the main points in *American power* is from *Language and politics* (1988), p. 181.
21. The quotes are from answers by Chomsky to questions posed to him in the Znet Forum; cf. his *World orders old and new* (1994, 1996), p. 86. See, among others, Sklar, *The corporate reconstruction of American capitalism, 1890–1916* (1988); Sellers, *The market revolution* (1991), Montgomery, *Citizen worker* (1993); also, Veblen, *The higher learning in America: a memorandum on the conduct of universities by business men* (1918); Spring, *Education and the rise of the corporate state* (1971); Smith, *Who rules the universities?* (1974). (See n. 16 above.) The real picture is quite different from familiar doctrine. For example, Sklar reveals that the story of the Sherman Antitrust Act, currently facing one more trying challenge, is quite different from what casual inspection suggests.
22. Chomsky, *Cartesian linguistics* (1966), p. 22f. He also suggests that the emphasis on language as "un système où tout se tient" and "un tout organique" of Saussurean structuralism "is, conceptually at least, a direct outgrowth" of Humboldt's concept.
23. See *Organic form* (1972), ed. Rousseau, in particular Orsini's "The ancient roots of a modern idea" and Wimsatt's "Questions about a metaphor."
24. For some telling examples from his most mature work (his lectures on philosophy of history), see the "outlandish and astonishingly ignorant racist ravings, shocking even by the (not particularly lovely) standards of the day" (Znet Forum) quoted in Chomsky, *Year 501* (1993), pp. 4–5, 119–20, 226, 230.
25. See Boucher and Kelly (eds.), *The social contract from Hobbes to Rawls* (1994), Chapter 8 (by B. Haddock).
26. As Chomsky has pointed out, the neo-Hegelian doctrines and their place in the intellectual history of Bolshevism, fascism, and private corporatism, an extremely interesting topic, which should be illuminating as well, have not been studied in any depth (it's not a favorite topic anywhere on the political spectrum), although there are intimations here and there. Some, perhaps among the earliest, can be found in an outstanding study (*Business as a system of power,* 1943) by Robert Brady, "a very important Veblenite political economist" whom Chomsky has quoted now and then. The major source on legal history appears to be *The transformation of American law, 1870–1960* (1992) by Morton Horwitz, a Harvard law professor and a leading legal historian, who gives a detailed and

interesting history of relevant judicial decisions at the root of contemporary corporate law. As he writes, such a "judicial personification of the corporation . . . radically enhanced the position of the business corporation in American law" (p. 67). In the preface he points out that "historical thinkers as varied as Hegel and Marx, or Whig historians like McCauley, or conservatives like Sir Henry Maine, sought to find the general laws of history, change and social progress," mimicking the natural sciences, we may add, and more or less consciously assuming that some cultural entities are no less "organic" than a human organism. See also pp. 52, 222, and "The natural entity theory," pp. 100f.

27. *Powers and prospects* (1996), p. 72.

28. As Chomsky points out, in the mislabeled "free trade agreements" (NAFTA, WTO, etc.) corporations are granted rights far beyond persons: for example, NAFTA's Chapter 11 grant of the right to bring suit against sovereign states for actions "tantamount to expropriation" (e.g., regulations that might interfere with future profits), or "national treatment," which can be demanded by General Motors in Mexico but not by a Mexican of flesh and blood in New York.

29. See Robert W. Benson, *Challenging corporate rule: the petition to revoke Unocal's charter as a guide to citizen action* (1999), a very good account of an effort (proceeding through the courts at the time of writing) to compel the attorney general of California to rescind the charter of Unocal, for crimes committed in Burma and in California. This book also provides good background and a guide to citizen action elsewhere. See also Dean Ritz (ed.), *Defying corporations, defining democracy: A book of history and strategy* (2001).

30. Chomsky, *Powers and prospects* (1996), p. 113, and "The system is weak" (1996), respectively.

31. Chomsky, *Powers and prospects* (1996), Ch. 4; see also "Rollback III" (April 1995); "Propaganda and control of the public mind" (Feb. 1997), of which Selection 20 is an excerpt; and "Market democracy in a neoliberal order: doctrine and reality" (1997), excerpted in *Profits over people* (1999), among other writings.

32. *Powers and prospects* (1996), p. 131.

33. For a wide range of comments on a variety of aspects of Chomsky's work, see *Noam Chomsky: critical assessments* (1994), ed. by C. P. Otero, and references there, in particular those in the introduction to each of the four volumes; for overviews of his work, see the monographs by Lyons (1970, 1991), Leiber (1975), Salkie (1990), Haley and Lundsford (1994), Wilkin (1997), Barsky (1997, fothcoming), McGilvray (1999), Smith (1999), and Otero (forthcoming a, b). There is also a *Chomsky for beginners* (1996) by Cogswell and, in the same vein, *Introducing Chomsky* (1997) by Maher and Groves.

Prologue

Democracy and education (October 1994)

The topic that was suggested, which I'm very happy to talk about, is "Democracy and Education." The phrase *democracy and education* immediately brings to mind the life and work and thought of one of the outstanding thinkers of the past century, John Dewey, who devoted the greater part of his life and his thought to this array of issues. I guess I should confess a special interest. It just happened that his thought was, for various reasons, a strong influence on me in my formative years—in fact, from about age two on, for a variety of reasons that I won't go into but are real. For much of his life (later he was more skeptical) Dewey seems to have felt that reforms in early education could be in themselves a major lever of social change. They could lead the way to a more just and free society, a society in which, in his words, "The ultimate aim of production is not production of goods, but the production of free human beings associated with one another on terms of equality."

This basic commitment, which runs through all of Dewey's work and thought, is profoundly at odds with the two leading currents of modern social intellectual life: one, strong in his day (he was writing in the 1920s and 1930s about these things), is associated with the command economies in Eastern Europe in that day, the systems created by Lenin and Trotsky and turned into an even greater monstrosity by Stalin; the other, the state capitalist industrial society being constructed in the U.S. and much of the West, with the effective rule of private power. These two systems are actually similar in fundamental ways, including ideologically. Both were, and one of them remains, deeply authoritarian in fundamental commitment, and both were very sharply and dramatically opposed to another tradition, the left libertarian tradition, with roots in Enlightenment values, a tradition that included progressive liberals of the John Dewey variety, independent socialists like Bertrand Russell, the leading elements of the Marxist mainstream (mostly anti-Bolshevik), and of course libertarian socialists of various anarchist movements, not to speak of major parts of the labor movement and other popular sectors. (Dewey and Russell were perhaps the two leading thinkers of the twentieth century in the West, in my opinion.)

This independent left, of which Dewey was a part, has strong roots in classical liberalism. It grows right out of it, in my opinion, and it stands in sharp opposition to the absolutist currents of state capitalist and state socialist institutions and thought, including the rather extreme form of absolutism that's now called conservative in the U.S., a terminology that would have amused Orwell and would have caused any genuine conservative to turn over in his grave—if you could find one.

I need not stress that this picture is not the conventional one, to put it rather mildly, but I think it does have one merit, at least, namely the merit of accuracy. I'll try to explain why.

Let me return to one of Dewey's central themes, that the ultimate aim of production is not production of goods but the production of free human beings associated with one another on terms of equality. That includes, of course, education, which was a prime concern of his. The goal of education, to shift over to Bertrand Russell, is "to give a sense of the value of things other than domination, to help create wise citizens of a free community, to encourage a combination of citizenship with liberty, individual creativeness, which means that we regard a child as a gardener regards a young tree, as something with an intrinsic nature which will develop into an admirable form given proper soil and air and light."

In fact, much as they disagreed on many other things, as they did, they did agree on what Russell called the humanistic conception, with its roots in the Enlightenment: the idea that education is not to be viewed as something like filling a vessel with water, but rather assisting a flower to grow in its own way (in other words, providing the circumstances in which the normal creative patterns will flourish). It's an eighteenth-century view which they revived.

Dewey and Russell also shared the understanding that these leading ideas of the Enlightenment and classical liberalism had a revolutionary character, and they retained it right at the time they were writing, in the early half of this century. If implemented, these ideas could produce free human beings whose values were not accumulation and domination but rather free association on terms of equality and sharing and cooperation, participating on equal terms to achieve common goals which were democratically conceived. There was only contempt for what Adam Smith called the "vile maxim of the masters of mankind, all for ourselves, and nothing for other people." The guiding principle that nowadays we're taught to admire and revere as traditional values have eroded under unremitting attack, the so-called conservatives leading the onslaught in recent decades.

It's worth taking time to notice how sharp and dramatic is the clash of values between, on the one hand, the humanistic conception that runs from the Enlightenment up to leading twentieth century figures like Russell and Dewey and, on the other hand, the prevailing doctrines of today, the doctrines that were denounced by Adam Smith as the "vile maxim" and also denounced by the lively and vibrant working-class press of a century ago, which condemned what it called the "new spirit of the age, gain wealth, forgetting all but self" (Smith's vile maxim). The quote is from 1850 or so, from the working class press in the U.S.

It's quite remarkable to trace the evolution of values from a pre-capitalist thinker like Adam Smith, with his stress on sympathy and the goal of perfect equality and the basic human right to creative work, to contrast that and move on to the present, to those who laud the new spirit of the age, sometimes rather shamelessly invoking Adam Smith's name. For example, Nobel prize–winning economist James Buchanan, who writes that "what each person seeks in an ideal situation is mastery over a world of slaves." That's what you seek, in case you hadn't noticed—something that an Adam Smith would have regarded as simply pathological. The best book I know of on Adam Smith's actual thought *(Adam Smith and his legacy for modern capitalism* [1991]) is written by a professor here at Loyola, Patricia Werhane. That's Adam Smith's actual views. Of course, it's always best to read the original.

One of the most dramatic illustrations of this new spirit of the age and its values is the commentary that's now in the press on the difficulties we face in uplifting the people of Eastern Europe. As you know, we're now extending to them, our new beneficiaries, the loving care that we've lavished on our wards elsewhere in Latin America and the Philippines and so on; with the consequences that are dramatically clear and consistent in these horror chambers, but also are miraculously free of any lessons about who we are and what we do. One might ask why. In any event, we are now proceeding to uplift the people liberated from communism as we've in the past liberated Haitians and Brazilians and Guatemalans and Filipinos and Native Americans and African slaves and so on.

The *New York Times* is currently running an interesting series of articles on these different problems. They give some interesting insight into the prevailing values. There was an article on East Germany, for example, written by

Steven Kinzer. It opens by quoting a priest who was one of the leaders of the popular protests against the communist regime in East Germany. He describes the growing concerns there about what's happening to the society. He says: "Brutal competition and the lust for money are destroying our sense of community, and almost everyone feels a level of fear or depression or insecurity" (as they master the new spirit of the age in which we instruct the backward peoples of the world).

The next article, written by Jane Perlez, turned to what we regard as the showplace, the real success story, Poland. The headline reads "Fast and Slow Lanes on the Capitalist Road." The structure of the story is that some are getting the point, but there are also some who are still backwards. She gives one example of a good student and one example of a slow learner. The good student is the owner of a small factory which is a "thriving example of the best in modern capitalist Poland." "It produces intricately designed wedding gowns sold mostly to rich Germans and to that tiny sector of super-rich Poles." This is in a country where poverty has more than doubled since the reforms were instituted, according to a World Bank study last July, and incomes have dropped about 30 percent. However, the people who are hungry and jobless can look at the intricately designed wedding gowns in the store windows, appreciating the new spirit of the age, so it's understandable that Poland is hailed as the great success story for our achievements. This good student explains that "people have to be taught to understand they must fight for themselves and can't rely on others." She is describing a training course she's running that's trying to instill American values among people who are still brainwashed with slogans like, "I'm a miner. Who else is better?" They have got to get that out of their heads. A lot of people are better, namely people who can design wedding gowns for rich Germans.

That's the chosen illustration of the success story of American values. Then there are the failures, still on the slow lane on the capitalist road. Here she picks one as her example, a forty-year-old coal miner who "sits in his wood-paneled living room admiring the fruits of his labor under communism: a TV set, comfortable furniture, a shiny, modern kitchen, and he wonders why he's at home, jobless and dependent on welfare payments," having not yet absorbed the new spirit of the age (gain wealth, forgetting all but self, and not "I'm a miner. Who else is better?"). The series goes on like that. It's interesting to read and to see what's taken for granted.

What's happening in Eastern Europe recapitulates what's gone on in our Third World domains for a long time and falls into place in a much longer story. It's very familiar from our own history and the history of England before us. There's a recent book, by a distinguished Yale University labor historian, David Montgomery, in which he points out that modern America was created over the protests of its working people. He's quite right. Those protests were vigorous and outspoken, particularly in the working class and community press that flourished in the U.S. from the early nineteenth century up until the 1930s, when it was finally destroyed by private power, as its counterpart in England was about thirty years later. The first major study of this topic was in 1924 by Norman Ware. It stills makes very illuminating reading. It was published here in Chicago and reprinted very recently by Ivan Dee, a local publisher. It's very much worth reading. It's a work that set off a very substantial study in social history.

What Ware describes, looking mostly at the labor press, is how the value system that was advocated by private power had to be beaten into the heads of ordinary people, who had to be taught to abandon normal human sentiments and to replace them with the new spirit of the age, as they called it. He reviews the mainly mid-nineteenth-century working class press, often, incidentally, run by working class women. The themes that run through it are very constant for a long period. They are concerned with what they call "degradation" and "loss of dignity and independence, loss of self-respect, the decline of the worker as a person, the sharp decline in cultural level and cultural attainments as workers were subjected to" what they called "wage slavery," which they regarded as not very different from chattel slavery, which they had fought to uproot during the Civil War. Particularly dramatic and quite relevant to today's problems was the sharp decline in what we call "high culture," reading of classics and contemporary literature by the people who were called the factory girls in Lowell and by craftsmen and other workers. Craftsmen would hire somebody to read to them while they were working because they were interested and had libraries. All that had to go.

What they described, quoting from the labor press, is "when you sell your product, you retain your person. But when you sell your labor, you sell yourself, losing the rights of free men and becoming vassals of mammoth establishments of a monied aristocracy that threatens annihilation to anyone who questions their right to enslave and oppress. Those who work in the mills ought to own them, not have the status of machines ruled by private despots who are entrenching monarchic principles on democratic soil as they drive downwards freedom and rights, civilization, health, morals and intellectuality in the new commercial feudalism." Just in case you're confused, this is long before Marxism. This is American workers talking about their experiences in the 1840s.

The labor press also condemned what they called the "bought priesthood," referring to the media and the universities and the intellectual class, that is, the apologists who sought to justify the absolute despotism that was the new spirit of the age and to instill its sordid and demeaning values. One of the early leaders of the AFL (American Federation of Labor), about a century ago, late nineteenth century, expressed the standard view when he described the mission of the labor movement as "to overcome the sins of the market and to defend democracy by extending it to control over industry by working people."

All of this would have been completely intelligible to the founders of classical liberalism, people like Wilhelm von Humboldt, for example, who inspired John Stuart Mill, and who, very much like his contemporary Adam Smith, regarded creative work freely undertaken in association with others as the core value of a human life. So if a person produces an object on command, Humboldt wrote, "we may admire what he did but we will despise what he is" (not a true human being who acts on his own impulses and desires).

The bought priesthood have the task of undermining these values and destroying them among people who sell themselves on the labor market. For similar reasons, Adam Smith warned that in any civilized society governments would have to intervene to prevent the division of labor from turning people into "creatures as stupid and ignorant as it's possible for a human being to be." He based his rather nuanced advocacy of markets on the thesis that if conditions were truly free, markets would lead to perfect equality (that was their moral justification). All of this has been forgotten by the bought priesthood, who have a rather different tale to tell.

Dewey and Russell are two of the leading twentieth-century inheritors of this tradition, with its roots in the Enlightenment and classical liberalism. Even more interesting is the inspiring record of struggle and organization and protest by working men and women since the early nineteenth century, as they sought to win freedom and justice and to retain the rights that they had once had as the new despotism of state-supported private power extended its sway.

The basic issue was formulated with a good deal of clarity by Thomas Jefferson around 1816. This was before the Industrial Revolution had really taken root in the former colonies, but you could begin to see the developments. In his later years, observing what was happening, Jefferson had rather serious concerns about the fate of the democratic experiment. He feared the rise of a new form of absolutism that was more ominous than what had been overthrown in the American Revolution, in which he was of course a leader.

Jefferson distinguished in his later years between what he called "aristocrats" and "democrats." The aristocrats are "those who fear and distrust the people, and wish to draw all powers from them into the hands of the higher classes." The democrats, in contrast, "identify with the people, have confidence in them, cherish and consider them as the honest and safe depository of the public interest, if not always the most wise." The aristocrats of his day were the advocates of the rising capitalist state, which Jefferson regarded with much disdain, clearly recognizing the quite obvious contradiction between democracy and capitalism, or more accurately what we might call really existing capitalism, that is, guided and subsidized by powerful developmental states, as it was in England and the U.S. and indeed everywhere else.

This fundamental contradiction is enhanced as new corporate structures were granted increasing powers, not by democratic procedures but mainly by courts and lawyers who converted what Jefferson called the "banking institutions and monied incorporations," which he said would destroy freedom, and which he could barely see the beginnings of in his day. They were converted, mainly through courts and lawyers, into "immortal persons" with powers and rights beyond the worst nightmares of pre-capitalist thinkers like Adam Smith or Thomas Jefferson. Half a century earlier, Adam Smith already warned against this, though he could barely see the beginnings of it.

Jefferson's distinction between aristocrats and democrats was developed about a half a century later by Bakunin, the anarchist thinker and activist (actually one of the few predictions of the social sciences ever to have come true; it ought to have a place of honor in any serious academic curriculum in the social sciences and the humanities for this reason alone). Back in the nineteenth century, Bakunin predicted that the rising intelligentsia of the nineteenth century would follow one of two parallel paths. One path would be to exploit popular struggles to take state power, becoming what he called a "Red bureaucracy that will impose the most cruel and vicious regime in history." That's one strain. The other strain, he said, will be those who discover that real power lies elsewhere, and they will become its "bought priesthood" (in the words of the labor press), serving the real masters in the state-supported private system of power, either as managers or apologists who "beat the people with the people's stick" (as he put it) in the state capitalist democracies.

The similarities are pretty striking, and they run right up to the present. They help account for the rapid transitions that people make from one to the other position. It looks like a funny transition, but in fact it's a common ideology. We're seeing it right now in Eastern Europe with the group that's sometimes called the nomenclatura capitalists (the old communist ruling class), now the biggest enthusiasts for the market enriching themselves as the societies become standard Third World societies. The move is very easy, because it's basically the same ideology. A similar move from Stalinist commissar to "celebration of America" is quite standard in modern history, and it doesn't require much of a shift in values, just a shift in judgment as to where power lies.

Independently of Jefferson and Bakunin, others were coming to the same understanding in the nineteenth century. One of the leading American intellectuals was Charles Francis Adams, who in 1880 described the rise of what is now called the "post-industrial society" by Daniel Bell and Robert Reich and John Kenneth Galbraith and others (this is 1880, remember), a society in which, Adams says, "the future is in the hands of our universities, our schools, our specialists, our scientific men and our writers and those who do the actual work of management in the ideological and economic institutions." Nowadays they're called the "technocratic elite" and the "action intellectuals" or the "new class" or some other similar term. Adams, back in 1880, concluded that "the first object of thinking citizens, therefore, should be not to keep one or another political party in power, but to insist on order and submission to law"—meaning that the elites should be permitted to function in what's called "technocratic isolation" by the World Bank (I'm being a little anachronistic here, that's modern lingo), or, as the London *Economist* puts the ideal today, "policy should be insulated from politics." That's the case in free Poland, they assure their readers, so they don't have to be concerned about the fact that people are calling for something quite different in free elections. They can do what they like in the elections, but since policy is insulated from politics and technocratic insulation proceeds, it really doesn't matter. That's democracy.

A decade earlier, in 1870, Adams had warned (they were worried then about universal suffrage, people were fighting for the right to vote), he warned that universal suffrage would "bring the government of ignorance and vice, with power in the hands of the European and especially Celtic proletariat on the Atlantic coast," those horrible Irish people, "an African proletariat on the shores of the Gulf and a Chinese proletariat on the Pacific." Adams didn't foresee the sophisticated techniques that would be developed in the twentieth century to ensure that policy remains insulated from politics as the franchise was extended through popular struggle and to guarantee that the general public would remain marginalized and disaffected, subdued by the new spirit of the age and coming to see themselves not as free people who have a right to dignity and independence but as atoms of consumption who sell themselves on the labor market, at least when they're lucky.

Adams was in fact expressing an old idea. Eighty years earlier Alexander Hamilton had put it clearly. He said there was the idea that your people are a "great beast" and that the real disease is democracy. That's Hamilton. These ideas have become ever more entrenched in educated circles, as Jefferson's fears and Bakunin's predictions were increasingly realized. The basic attitudes coming into this century were expressed very clearly by Woodrow Wilson's secretary of state, Robert Lansing, attitudes that led to Wilson's "Red scare," as it was called, which destroyed labor and independent thought for a decade. Lansing warned of the danger of allowing the "ignorant and incapable mass of humanity" to become "dominant in the earth," or even influential, as he believed the Bolsheviks intended. That's the hysterical and utterly erroneous reaction that's pretty standard among people who feel that their power is threatened. Those concerns were articulated very clearly by progressive intellectuals of the period, maybe the leading one being Walter Lippman in his essays on democracy, mainly in the 1920s. (Lippmann was also the dean of American journalism and one of the most distinguished commentators on public affairs for many years.)

He advised that "the public must be put in its place so that the responsible men may live free of the trampling and the roar of a bewildered herd" (Hamilton's "beast"). In a democracy, Lippman held, these "ignorant and meddlesome outsiders" do have a "function." Their function is to be "interested spectators of action," but not participants. They are to lend their weight periodically to some member of the leadership class (that's called elections), and then they are supposed to return to their private concerns.

In fact, similar notions became part of mainstream academic theory at about the same time. In the presidential address to the American Political Science Association in 1934, William Shepard argued that government should be in the hands of "an aristocracy of intellect and power," while the "ignorant, the uninformed and the anti-social elements" must not be permitted to control elections, as he mistakenly believed they had done in the past. One of the founders of modern political science, Harold Lasswell (one of the founders of the field of communications, in fact), wrote in the *Encyclopedia of Social Sciences* in 1933 or 1934 that modern techniques of propaganda, which had been impressively refined by Wilsonian liberals, provided the way to keep the public in line. Lasswell described Wilson as "the great generalissimo on the propaganda front." Wilson's World War I achievements in propaganda impressed others, including Adolf Hitler (you can read about it in *Mein*

Kampf), but crucially they impressed the American business community. That led to a huge expansion of the public relations industry, which was dedicated to "controlling the public mind," as advocates used to put it in more honest days, just as, writing in the *Encyclopedia of Social Sciences* in 1934, Lasswell described what he was talking about as propaganda. We don't use that term. We're more sophisticated.

As a political scientist, Lasswell advocated more sophisticated use of this new technique of control of the general public that was provided by modern propaganda. That would, he said, enable the intelligent men of the community, the natural rulers, to overcome the threat of the great "beast," who may undermine order because of, in Lasswell's terms, "the ignorance and superstition of the masses." We should not succumb to "democratic dogmatisms about men being the best judges of their own interests." The best judges are the elites (Jefferson's aristocrats, in other words), who must be ensured the means to impose their will for the common good.

Lippmann and Lasswell represent the more liberal, progressive fringe of opinion, which grants the "beast" at least a spectator role. At the reactionary end you get those who are mislabeled conservatives in contemporary newspeak. So the Reaganite statist reactionaries thought that the public, the "beast," shouldn't even have the spectator role. That explains their fascination with clandestine terror operations, which were not secret to anybody except the American public, certainly not to their victims. Clandestine terror operations were designed to leave the domestic population ignorant. They also advocated absolutely unprecedented measures of censorship and agitprop and other measures to ensure that the powerful and interventionist state that they fostered would serve as a welfare state for the rich and not troubled by the rabble.

The huge increase in business propaganda in recent years, the recent assault on the universities by right-wing foundations, and other tendencies of the current period, are other manifestations of the same concerns. These concerns were awakened by what liberal elites had called the "crisis of democracy" that developed in the 1960s, when previously marginalized and apathetic sectors of the population, like women and young people and old people and working people and so on, when they sought to enter the public arena, where they have no right to be, as all right-thinking aristocrats understand.

John Dewey was one of the relics of the Enlightenment classical liberal tradition who opposed the rule of the wise, the onslaught of the Jeffersonian aristocrats, whether they found their place on the reactionary or the liberal part of this very narrow ideological spectrum. Dewey understood clearly that "politics is the shadow cast on society by big business," and as long as this is so, "attenuation of the shadow will not change the substance"—meaning, reforms are of limited utility: democracy requires that the source of the shadow be removed, not only because of its domination of the political arena, but because the very institutions of private power undermine democracy and freedom. Dewey was very explicit about the anti-democratic power that he had in mind. To quote him: "Power today" (this is the 1920s) "resides in control of the means of production, exchange, publicity, transportation and communication. Whoever owns them rules the life of the country," even if democratic forms remain: "business for private profit through private control of banking, land, industry, reinforced by command of the press, press agents and other means of publicity and propaganda"—that is the system of actual power, the source of coercion and control, and until it's unraveled we can't talk seriously about democracy and freedom. Education, he hoped, of the kind he was talking about ("the production of free human beings"), would be one of the means of undermining this absolutist monstrosity.

In a free and democratic society, Dewey held, workers should be "the masters of their own industrial fate," not tools rented by employers. He agreed on fundamental issues with the founders of classical liberalism and with the democratic and libertarian sentiments that animated the popular working-class movements from the early Industrial Revolution until they were finally beaten down by a combination of violence and propaganda. In the field of education, therefore, Dewey held that it is "illiberal and immoral" to train children to work "not freely and intelligently, but for the sake of the wage earned," in which case their activity "is not free because not freely participated in" (again the conception of classical liberalism and the workers' movements). Therefore, Dewey held, industry must also change "from a feudalistic to a democratic social order" based on control by working people and free association (again, traditional anarchist ideals with their source in classical liberalism and the Enlightenment).

As the doctrinal system has narrowed under the assault of private power, particularly in the past few decades, these fundamental libertarian values and principles now sound exotic and extreme, perhaps even anti-American, to borrow one of the terms of contemporary totalitarian thought in the West. Given these changes, it's useful to remember that the kinds of ideas that Dewey was expressing are as American as apple pie. They have origins in straight American traditions, right in the mainstream (not influenced by any dangerous foreign ideologies), in a worthy tradition that's ritually lauded, though it's commonly distorted and forgotten. And all of that is part of the deterioration of functioning democracy in the current age, both at the institutional and at the ideological level, in my opinion.

Education is, of course, in part a matter of schools and colleges and the formal information systems. That's true whether the goal of education is education for freedom and democracy, as Dewey advocated, or education for obedience and subordination and marginalization, as the dominant institutions require. The University of Chicago sociologist James Coleman, one of the main students of education and effects of experience on children's lives, concludes from many studies that "the total effect of home background is considerably greater than the total effect of school variables in determining student achievement." Actually, about twice as powerful in effect, he concludes from a lot of studies. So it's therefore important to have a look at how social policy and the dominant culture are shaping these factors (home influences and so on).

That's a very interesting topic. The inquiry is much facilitated by a UNICEF study published a year ago called *Child Neglect in Rich Nations*, written by a well-known American economist, Sylvia Ann Hewlett. She studies the preceding fifteen years, the late 1970s up through the early 1990s, in the rich nations. She's not talking about the Third World but about the rich countries. She finds a sharp split between the Anglo-American societies, on the one hand, and continental Europe and Japan, on the other hand. The Anglo-American model, spearheaded by the Reaganites and Thatcher, has been a disaster for children and families, she says. The European model, in contrast, has improved their situation considerably, from a starting point that was already considerably higher—despite the fact that the European societies lack the huge advantages of the Anglo-American societies. The U.S. has unparalleled wealth and advantages, and while the United Kingdom, Britain, has severely declined, particularly under Thatcher, it has the economic advantage, at least, of being a U.S. client as well as being a major oil exporter in the Thatcher years. That's something that makes the economic failure of Thatcherism even more dramatic, as authentic British conservatives like Lord Ian Gilmour have shown.

Hewlett describes the Anglo-American disaster for children and families as attributable "to the ideological preference for free markets." Here she's only half right, in my opinion. Reaganite conservatism opposed free markets. It did advocate markets for the poor, but it went well beyond even its statist predecessors in demanding and winning a very high level of public subsidy and state protection for the rich. Whatever you choose to call this guiding ideology, it's unfair to tarnish the good name of conservatism by applying it to this particular form of violent and lawless and reactionary statism. Call it what you like, but it's not conservatism, it's not the free market.

However, Hewlett is quite right in identifying the free market for the poor as the source of the disaster for families and children. And there isn't much doubt of the effects of what Hewlett calls the "anti-child and anti-family spirit that's loose in these lands" (in the Anglo-American lands, most dramatically in the U.S., but also Britain), this "neglect-filled Anglo-American model based on market discipline for the poor has largely privatized child rearing while making it effectively impossible for most of the population to rear children." That's been the combined goal and policy of Reaganite conservatism and the Thatcherite analogue. The result is, of course, a disaster for children and families.

Continuing, Hewlett points out, "in the much more supportive European model, social policy has strengthened rather than weakened support systems for families and children." It's no secret, except of course as usual to readers of the press. As far as I'm aware, this 1993 study, rather critically relevant to our current concerns, has yet to be reviewed anywhere. It's not been, say, featured in the *New York Times*, although the *Times* did devote last Sunday's book review section largely to this topic, with somber forebodings about the fall of IQ, the decline of SAT scores, and so on, and what might be causing it, say, in the city of New York, where the social policies that have been pursued and backed by the *Times* have driven about 40 percent of the children below the poverty level, so that they're suffering malnutrition, disease, and so on.

But it turns out that is irrelevant to the decline in IQ, as is anything that Hewlett discusses in this Anglo-American neglect-filled model. What's relevant, it turns out, is bad genes. Somehow people are getting bad genes, and then there are various speculations about why this is. For example, maybe it's because black mothers don't nurture their children, and the reason is maybe they evolved in Africa, where the climate was hostile. So those are maybe the reasons, and this is really serious, hardheaded science, and a democratic society will ignore all this at its peril, the reviewer says. Well-disciplined commissars know well enough to steer away from the obvious factors, the ones rooted in very plain and clear social policy. They are perfectly evident to anybody with their head screwed on, and happen to be discussed in considerable detail by a well-known economist in a UNICEF study that's not likely to see the light of day around here.

The facts are no secret. A blue-ribbon commission of the state boards of education and the American Medical Association reported: "Never before has one generation of children been less healthy, less cared for, and less prepared for life than their parents were at the same age." That's a big shift in an industrial society. It's only in the Anglo-American societies where this anti-child, anti-family spirit has reigned for fifteen years under the guise of conservatism and family values. That's a real triumph for propaganda. It's one that would very much have impressed even "generalissimo" Woodrow Wilson, or probably Stalin and Hitler.

A symbolic expression of this disaster is that when Hewlett wrote her book, a year ago, 146 countries had ratified the international convention on the rights of the child, but one had not: the U.S. That's a standard pattern for international conventions on human rights. However, just for fairness, it's only proper to add that Reaganite conservatism is catholic in its anti-child, anti-family spirit, so the World Health Organization voted to condemn the Nestlé Corporation for aggressive marketing of infant formula, which kills plenty of children. The vote was 118 to 1. I'll leave you to guess the one. However, this is quite minor compared with what the World Health Organization calls the "silent genocide" that's killing millions of children every year as a result of the free-market policies for the poor and the refusal of the rich to give any aid. Again, the U.S. has one of the worst and most miserly records among the rich societies.

Another symbolic expression of this disaster is a new line of greeting cards by the Hallmark Corporation. One of them says: "Have a super day at school." That one, they tell you, is to be put under a box of cereal in the morning, so that when the children go off to school it says: "Have a super day at school." Another one says, "I wish I had more time to tuck you in." That's one that you stick under the pillow at night when the kid goes to sleep alone. There are other such examples.

In part, this disaster for children and families is the result simply of falling wages. State corporate policy has been designed for the last years, especially under the Reaganites and Thatcher, to enrich small sectors and to impoverish the majority, and it succeeded. It's had exactly the intended effect. That means that people have to work much longer hours to survive. For much of the population both parents have to work maybe fifty to sixty hours merely to provide necessities. Meanwhile, incidentally, corporate profits are zooming. *Fortune* magazine talks about the "dazzling" profits reaching new heights for the Fortune 500 even though sales are stagnating.

Another factor is job insecurity, what economists like to call "flexibility in the labor markets," which is a good thing under the reigning academic theology, but a pretty rotten thing for human beings, whose fate doesn't enter into the calculations of sober thinking. Flexibility means you better work extra hours or else. There are no contracts and no rights. That's flexibility. We've got to get rid of market rigidities. Economists can explain it. When both parents are working extra hours, and for most on falling incomes, it doesn't take a great genius to predict the outcome. The statistics show them. You can read them in Hewlett's UNICEF study if you like. It's perfectly obvious, without reading them, what's going to happen. Contact time, that is, actual time spent by parents with children, has declined 40 percent in the last twenty-five years in the Anglo-American societies, mostly in recent years. That's actually ten to twelve hours a week of eliminating contact time, and what they call "high-quality time," when you're not just doing something else, is virtually disappearing. Of course that leads to the destruction of family identity and values. It leads to sharply increased reliance on television for child supervision. It leads to what are called "latchkey children," kids who are alone, a factor in rising child alcoholism and drug use and in criminal violence against children by children and other obvious effects in health, education, ability to participate in a democratic society, even survival, of course decline in SATs and IQs, but you're not supposed to notice that. That's bad genes, remember.

None of these things are laws of nature. These are consciously selected social policies designed for particular goals, namely enrich the Fortune 500 but impoverish others. In Europe, where conditions are more stringent but policy is not guided by the same anti-family, anti-child spirit, the tendencies are in the opposite direction, and the standards for children and families are much better.

It's worth mentioning, and let me stress, that this is not just true in the Anglo-American societies themselves. We're a big, powerful state. We have influence. It's very striking to notice what happens when other countries within the range of our influence try to undertake policies that benefit families and children. There are several striking examples.

The region that we control most completely is the Caribbean and Central America. There are two countries there that did undertake such policies: Cuba and Nicaragua, and with considerable success, in fact. Something which should surprise no one is that those are the two countries that were primarily targeted for U.S. assault. And it succeeded. So in Nicaragua, the rising health standards and the improvement in literacy and the reduction in child malnutrition have been reversed thanks to the terrorist war that we fought in Nicaragua, and now it's proceeding to the level of Haiti.

In the case of Cuba, of course, the terrorist war has been going on a lot longer. It was launched by John F. Kennedy. It had nothing to do with communism. There weren't any Russians around. It had to do with things like the fact that these people were devoting resources to the wrong sectors of the population. They were improving health standards. They were concerned with children, with malnutrition. Therefore we launched a huge terrorist war. A bunch of CIA documents were just released recently, filling in some of the details of the Kennedy period, which was bad enough. It continues up to the present. Actually, there was another assault just a couple of days ago. On top of that, there's an embargo to try to ensure that they'll really suffer. For years the pretext was that this had to do with the Russians, which is completely fraudulent, as you can see by what was going on when the policies were instituted and as is demonstrated conclusively by what happened after the Russians disappeared. Here was a real job for the "bought priesthood." They have to not notice that after the Russians disappeared we *harshened* the attack against Cuba. Kind of odd if the reason for the attack was that they were an outpost of communism and the Russian empire. But we can handle that.

So after the Russians disappeared from the scene and it really became possible to strangle them, the conditions got harsher. A proposal was sent through Congress by liberal Democrats, led by Representative Torricelli, calling for a cutoff of any trade with Cuba by any subsidiary of any American corporation or any foreign corporation that used any parts produced in the U.S. That is so obviously in violation of international law that George Bush vetoed it. However, he was forced to accept it when he was outflanked from the right by the Clintonites in the last election, so he did then allow it to go through. That went right to the United Nations, where the U.S. position was denounced by just about everybody. In the final vote, the U.S. could pick up only Israel, which is automatic, and they got Rumania for some reason. Everyone else voted against it. The U.S. position was defended by no one. It is an obvious violation of international law, as even Britain and others pointed out. But it doesn't matter. It's extremely important to carry out our anti-child, anti-family spirit and our insistence on highly polarized societies everywhere we can go. If any foreign country under our control tries to go that way, we'll take care of them, too.

That's now continuing. It's the kind of thing you can actually do something about if you like. In Chicago there is the Pastors for Peace, and the Chicago-Cuba Coalition has another caravan going to Cuba to try to undermine the embargo and bring humanitarian aid, medicines, medical books, powdered milk for infants, and other assistance. They're in the phone book under Chicago-Cuba Coalition. You can look them up. Anyone who is interested in countering the anti-child, anti-family spirit that reigns here and that we're exporting by violence elsewhere can do that, just as they can do plenty of things at home.

I should say that the effects of this latest Democratic proposal, which went through, to strangle Cuba have recently been reviewed in this month's issues, October, of two leading American medical journals, *Neurology* and the *Florida Journal of Medicine,* which simply review the effects. They point out the obvious thing. It turns out that about 90 percent of the trade that was cut off by the Clinton-Torricelli bill was food and humanitarian aid—food, medicine, and things like that. For example, one Swedish company which was trying to export a water filtration device to create vaccines was blocked by the U.S. because there's some part in it that's American-made. We really have to strangle them badly. We have to make sure that plenty of children die. One effect is a very sharp rise in infant mortality and child malnutrition. Another is a rare neurological disease that's spread over Cuba that everyone pretended they didn't know the reasons for (but of course they did, and now it's conceded: it's malnutrition), a disease which hasn't been seen since Japanese prison camps during the Second World War. So we're succeeding in that one. The anti-child, anti-family spirit is not just directed against kids in New York, but much more broadly.

I stress again that the difference in Europe (it is different in Europe, and there are reasons for it), one of the differences, is the existence of a strong trade union movement. That's one aspect of a more fundamental difference, namely, the U.S. is a business-run society to quite an unparalleled degree and, as a result, the vile maxim of the masters prevails to an unprecedented extent, pretty much as you'd expect. These are among the means that allow democracy to function formally, although by now most of the population is consumed by what the press calls "anti-politics," meaning hatred of government, disdain for political parties and the whole democratic process. That, too, is a great victory for the aristocrats in Jefferson's sense, that is, those who fear and distrust the people and wish to draw all power from them into the hands of the higher classes—by now that means into the hands of transnational corporations and the states and quasi-governmental institutions that serve their interests.

Another victory is the fact that the disillusionment, which is rampant, is anti-politics. A *New York Times* headline on this reads: "Anger and Cynicism Well Up in Voters as Hope Gives Way. Mood Turns Ugly as More People Become Disillusioned with Politics." Last Sunday's magazine section was devoted to anti-politics (notice: *not* devoted to opposition to power and authority, to the easily identifiable forces that have their hands on the lever of decision-making and that cast their shadow on society as politics, as Dewey put it; they have to be invisible). The *Times* has a story today again about this topic where they quote some uneducated person who doesn't get the point. He says, "Yeah, Congress is rotten, but that's because Congress is big business, so of course it's rotten." That's the story you're *not* supposed to see. You're supposed to be anti-politics. The reason is that whatever you think about the government, it's the one part of the system of institutions that you *can* participate in and modify and do something about (by law and principle, you can't do anything about investment firms or transnational corporations). Therefore nobody better see that. You've got to be anti-politics. That's another victory.

Dewey's observation that politics is the shadow cast on society by big business, which was incidentally also a truism to Adam Smith, has now become invisible. The force that casts the shadow has been pretty much removed by the ideological institutions and is so remote from consciousness that we're left with anti-politics. That's another severe blow to democracy and a grand gift to the absolutist and unaccountable systems of power that have reached levels that a Thomas Jefferson or a John Dewey could scarcely imagine.

We have the usual choices. We can choose to be democrats in Thomas Jefferson's sense or we can choose to be aristocrats. The latter path is the easy one. That's the one that the institutions are designed to reward. It can bring rich rewards, given the locus of wealth and privilege and power and the ends that they very naturally seek. The other path, the path of the Jeffersonian democrats, is one of struggle, often defeat, but also rewards of a kind that can't even be imagined by those who succumb to "the new spirit of the age, gain wealth, forgetting all but self." It's the same now as it was 150 years ago, when there was an attempt first to drive it into the heads of the factory girls in Lowell and the craftsmen in Lawrence and so on. Today's world is very far from Thomas Jefferson's. The choices it offers, however, have not changed in any fundamental way.

Part I
Science: the genetic endowment

Chapter 1
Things no amount of learning can teach (November 1983)

Why do you believe that language behavior critically depends on the existence of a genetically preprogrammed language organ in the brain?
There's a lot of linguistic evidence to support this contention. But even in advance of detailed linguistic research, we should expect heredity to play a major role in language because there is really no other way to account for the fact that children learn to speak in the first place.

What do you mean?
Consider something that everyone agrees to is due to heredity—the fact that humans develop arms rather than wings. Why do we believe this? Well, since nothing in the fetal environments of the human or bird embryo can account for the differences between birds and men, we assume that heredity must be responsible. In fact, if someone came along and said that a bird embryo is somehow "trained" to grow wings, people would just laugh, even though embryologists lack anything like detailed understanding of how genes regulate embryological development.

[A close parallel to embryology]
Is the role of heredity as important for language as it is for embryology?
I think so. You have to laugh at claims that heredity plays no significant role in language learning, because exactly the same kinds of genetic arguments hold for language learning as hold for embryological development.

I'm very much interested in embryology, but I've got just a layman's knowledge of it. I think that recent work, primarily in molecular biology, however, is seeking to discover the ways that genes regulate embryological development. The gene-control problem is conceptually similar to the problem of accounting for language growth. In fact, language development really ought to be called *language growth*, because the language organ grows like any other body organ.

Is there a special place in the brain and a particular kind of neurological structure that comprises the language organ?

Little enough is known about cognitive systems and their neurological basis, so caution is necessary in making any direct claims. But it does seem that the representation and use of language involve specific neural structures, though their nature is not well understood.

But clearly, environment plays some role in language development. What's the relationship between heredity and environment for human language?

The language organ interacts with early experience and matures into the grammar of the language that the child speaks. If a human being with this fixed endowment grows up in Philadelphia, as I did, his brain will encode knowledge of the Philadelphia dialect of English. If that brain had grown up in Tokyo, it would have encoded the Tokyo dialect of Japanese. The brain's different linguistic experience—English versus Japanese—would modify the language organ's structure.

Roughly the same thing goes on in animal experiments, showing that different kinds of early visual experience can modify the part of the brain that processes visual information. As you may know, cats, monkeys, and humans have hierarchically organized brain-cell networks connected to the retina in such a way that certain cells fire only when there is a horizontal line in the visual field; other hierarchies respond only to vertical lines. But early experience can apparently change the relative numbers of horizontal- and vertical-line detectors. MIT psychologists Richard Held and Alan Hein showed some time ago, for example, that a kitten raised in a cage with walls covered by bold, black vertical lines will display good sensitivity to vertical lines as an adult but poor horizontal-line sensitivity. Lack of stimulation apparently causes the horizontal-line detectors to atrophy.

An even closer analogy exists between language growth and the growth that occurs in human beings *after* birth—for example, the onset of puberty. If someone came along and said, "Kids are trained to undergo puberty because they see other people," once again everybody would laugh. Would we laugh because we know in great detail the gene mechanisms that determine puberty? As far as I can tell, no one knows much of anything about that. Yet we all assume that puberty is genetically determined.

Still, as your own example shows, environmental factors do play a major role in physiological growth.

And it goes without saying that the onset of puberty may well vary over quite a range depending on childhood diet and all kinds of other environmental influences. Nonetheless, everyone takes for granted that the fundamental processes controlling puberty are genetically programmed. This is probably true of death as well. You may be genetically programmed to die at roughly a certain point; it's a reasonable theory.

Look, all through an organism's existence, from birth to death, it passes through a series of genetically programmed changes. Plainly language growth is simply one of these predetermined changes. Language depends upon genetic endowment that's on a par with the ones that specify the structure of our visual or circulatory systems, or determine that we have arms instead of wings.

What about the linguistic evidence? What have you learned from studying human languages to corroborate your biological viewpoint?
The best evidence involves those aspects of a language's grammar that are so obvious, so intuitively self-evident to everyone, that they are quite rightly never mentioned in traditional grammars.

You mean that school grammars fill in the gaps left by heredity? They teach every-thing about French or Russian, for example, that can't be taken for granted by virtue of the fact that you're human?
That's right. It is precisely what seems self-evident that is most likely to be part of our hereditary baggage. Some of the oddities of English pronoun behavior illustrate what I mean. Take the sentence, "John believes he is intel-ligent." Okay, we all know that *he* can refer either to John or to someone else, so the sentence is ambiguous. It can mean either that John thinks he, John, is intelligent, or that someone else is intelligent. In contrast, consider the sen-tence, "John believes him to be intelligent." Here the pronoun *him* can't refer to John; it can refer only to someone else.

Now, did anyone teach us this peculiarity about English pronouns when we were children? It would be hard to even imagine a training procedure that would convey such information to a person. Nevertheless, everybody knows it—knows it without experience, without training, and at quite an early age. There are any number of other examples that show that we humans have explicit and highly articulate linguistic knowledge that simply has no basis in linguistic experience.

There's just no way that children can pick up this kind of information by listening to the grown-ups around them?
Precisely. But let me give you another example. English contains grammati-cal constructions that are called parasitic gaps. In these constructions, you can

drop a pronoun and still understand the sentence in the same way as when the sentence contains a pronoun. Consider the sentence, "Which article did you file without reading it?" Notice that you can drop the pronoun it without changing meaning or grammaticality. You can say, "Which article did you file without reading?" But you can't say, "John was killed by a rock falling on," when you mean, "John was killed by a rock falling on him." This time omitting the pronoun destroys both meaning and grammaticality.

Constructions of this type—where you can or cannot drop the pronoun—are very rare. In fact, they are so rare that it is quite likely that during the period a child masters his native language (the first five or six years of life), he never hears any of these constructions, or he hears them very sporadically. Nonetheless, every native speaker of English knows flawlessly when you can and can't drop pronouns in these kinds of sentences.

So we're faced with a mystery. How could anyone possibly learn enough about the English language to possess the rich and exotic grammatical knowledge that we all seem to possess by the time we are five or six years old?
There's an obvious answer to that: the knowledge is built in. You and I can learn English, as well as any other language, with all its richness because we are designed to learn languages based upon a common set of principles, which we may call universal grammar.

What is universal grammar?
It is the sum total of all the immutable principles that heredity builds into the language organ. These principles cover grammar, speech sounds, and meaning. Put differently, universal grammar is the inherited genetic endowment that makes it possible for us to speak and learn human languages.

Suppose that somewhere else in the universe intelligent life has evolved. Could we, with our specialized language organ, learn the aliens' language if we made contact with them?
Not if their language violated the principles of our universal grammar, which, given the myriad ways that languages can be organized, strikes me as highly likely.

Maybe we shouldn't call it universal, then. But please explain what you mean.
The same structures that make it possible to learn a human language make it impossible for us to learn a language that violates the principles of universal grammar. If a Martian landed from outer space and spoke a language that violated universal grammar, we simply would not be able to learn that language the way that we learn a human language like English or Swahili. We

should have to approach the alien's language slowly and laboriously—the way that scientists study physics, where it takes generation after generation of labor to gain new understanding and to make significant progress. We're designed by nature for English, Chinese, and every other possible human language, but we're not designed to learn perfectly usable languages that violate universal grammar. These languages would simply not be within our range of abilities.

How would you assess current research about universal grammar?
In the last three or four years there's been a major conceptual change in the underlying theory. We now assume that universal grammar consists of a collection of preprogrammed subsystems that include, for example, one responsible for meaning, another responsible for stringing together phrases in a sentence, a third one that deals, among other things, with the kinds of relationships between nouns and pronouns that I discussed earlier. And there are a number of others.

These subsystems are not genetically preprogrammed down to the last detail. If they were, there would be only one human language. But heredity does set rather narrow limits on the possible ways that the rules governing each subsystem's function can vary. Languages like English and Italian, for example, differ in their choice of genetically permitted variations that exist as options in the universal grammar. You can think of these options as a kind of linguistic menu containing mutually exclusive grammatical possibilities.

For example, languages like Italian have chosen the "null subject" option from the universal-grammar menu: In Italian you can say *left* when you mean "He left" or "She left." English and French have passed up this option and chosen instead the rule that requires explicit mention of the subject.

What are some other grammatical options on the universal-grammar menu?
In English the most important element in every major grammatical category comes first in its phrase. In simple sentences, for example, we say "John hit Bill," not "John Bill hit." With adjectives we say "proud of John" not "John of proud"; with nouns we say "habit of drinking wine," not "drinking wine of habit"; and with prepositions we say "to John," not "John to." Because heads of grammatical categories always come first, English is what is called a head-initial language.

Japanese is a head-final language. In Japanese you say "John Bill hit." And instead of prepositions, there are postpositions that follow nouns: "John to," rather than "to John." So here's another parameter the child's got to learn from experience: Is the language head-initial or head-final?

These grammatical parameters are interconnected. You can't pick them any more freely than, say, a wine fanatic who insists on white wine with fish and red wine with meat is free to choose any main dish once he's decided on his wine. But grammars are even more sensitive than this culinary example might suggest. A slight change in just one of the universal grammar's parameters can have enormous repercussions throughout the language. It can produce an entirely different language.

Again, there's a close parallel to embryology, where a slight shift in the gene mechanisms regulating growth may be all that separates a fertilized egg from developing into a lion rather than a whale.

So what exactly would you say is *the grammar of English?*
The grammar of English is the collection of choices—head-initial rather than head-final, and null subject forbidden, for example—that define one of a limited number of genetically permitted selections from the universal-grammar menu of grammatical options. And of course there are all the lexical facts. You just have to learn your language's vocabulary. The universal grammar doesn't tell you that *tree* means "tree" in English.

But once you've learned the vocabulary items and fixed the grammatical parameters for English, the whole system is in place. And the general principles genetically programmed into the language organ just churn away to yield all the particular facts about English grammar.

It sounds as if your present research goal is to reach the point where you can define every human language's grammar simply by specifying its choices from the universal grammar's menu of options.
That's the kind of work you would hope would soon be done: to take a theory of universal grammar, fix the parameters one way or another, and then deduce from these parameters the grammar of a real human language—Japanese, Swahili, English, or whatnot.

This goal is only on the horizon. But I think that it is within our conceptual grasp. Undoubtedly the principles of universal grammar that we currently theorize are wrong. It would be a miracle if we were right this early along. But the principles *are* of the right type, and we can now begin to test our present system with complex examples to see what is wrong and to make changes that will improve our theory.

Judging from what you've said about language and heredity, it sounds as if you must be sympathetic to the aims of sociobiology. Is that a fair assumption?
Well, I think that in some respects the sociobiologists are on the right track.

I think it's true that a good deal of our personal behavior, social behavior, reactions, and so on are the reflection of genetic programs, and I think that it's a worthwhile enterprise to discover what these programs are. But while I think the general idea behind sociobiology is right, I also think that sociobiologists should be extremely cautious about the specific conclusions they draw from their research. Unfortunately, they often draw conclusions that are remote from evidence or theory.

Many sociobiologists would dispute your note of caution. They claim that science has already gained enough information about the relationships between genes and behavior to permit some shrewd guesses about some of the ways heredity influences human social behavior. What do you say to these claims?

I'm very skeptical. I haven't really studied the newer research in enough detail to make any informed judgment. But as for the earlier work—for example, E. O. Wilson's *Sociobiology*—well, about 90 percent of the book was on non-primates, and that looked interesting. There was a little bit on primates, which was more questionable. And there was a final chapter on humans that was completely empty. I don't think Wilson understood what he was talking about in that final chapter. There were real errors in what he did describe in any detail. I don't even understand why the chapter on humans was tacked onto the book. It didn't seem to belong.

What do you think about the claim made by Wilson and others that there's an innate incest taboo in human beings?

Sorting out what is and what is not genetically preprogrammed in human behavior is a very difficult task. As I said, I agree with the *general* approach of sociobiology. I think it's a reasonable approach. But it's important to be very cautious in making any claims about the role of heredity in human affairs—especially claims that would have social consequences if they were true. Science is held in such awe in our culture that every scientist has a special responsibility to make clear to the lay audience where his expert knowledge actually yields scientifically verifiable results and where he is guessing, indulging in sheer speculation, or expressing his own personal hopes about the success of his research. This is an important task because the lay audience is in no position to make these distinctions.

[Piaget versus Skinner]

Moving on to another controversial area in the behavioral sciences, how do you think your views differ from B. F. Skinner's behaviorist theory of language, learning, and mind?

Skinner used to take a relatively extreme position. At one point he held that, apart from the most rudimentary functions, essentially nothing of importance was genetically programmed in the human brain. Skinner agreed that humans were genetically programmed to see and hear, but that's about all. Accordingly he argued that all human behavior was simply a reflection of training and experience. This view can't possibly be correct. And, in fact, Skinner's approach has led absolutely nowhere in this area. It has yielded no theoretical knowledge, no non-trivial principles as far as I am aware—thus far, at any rate.

Why is that?
Because Skinnerian behaviorism is off the wall. It's as hopeless a project as trying to explain that the onset of puberty results from social training. But I really don't know whether Skinner still maintains this extreme position.

What about the late Jean Piaget? Where do you stand on his theories of the child's mental development?
Piaget's position is different: it's more complex than Skinner's. Piaget held that the child passes through cognitive states. According to my understanding of the Piagetian literature, Piaget and his supporters were never really clear about what produced a new stage of cognitive development. What they could have said—though they seemed to shy away from it—is that cognitive development is a genetically determined maturational process like puberty, for example. That's what the Piagetians ought to say. They don't like this formulation, but it seems right to me.

In other words, Piagetians place much more emphasis on the role of experience in cognitive development than you do. Are there other differences as well?
Yes. Piagetians maintain that the mind develops as a whole rather than as a modular structure with specific capacities developing in their own ways. This is a possible hypothesis, but in fact it seems to be extremely wrong.

How do you mean?
Well, consider the properties that determine the reference of pronouns that we talked about earlier. Once you ferret out these rules for pronouns, they seem to have nothing in common with the logical operations that Piagetians single out as being typical of the early stages of the child's mental development.

In other words, a four-year-old who may not realize that the amount of water stays the same when you pour the contents of a low, wide glass into a tall, thin container nevertheless displays sophisticated logical abilities in his grasp of the complex rules of English grammar?

Yes. And these abilities are independent of the logical capacities measured by tests. There's just no resemblance between what a child does with blocks and the kind of knowledge that he displays of English grammar at the same age. In fact, I think it's sort of quixotic to expect tight interconnections between language development and growth in other mental domains. By and large, body systems develop in their own ways at their own rates. They interact, but the circulatory system doesn't wait until the visual system reaches a certain stage of organization before proceeding to imitate the visual system's organizational complexity. Cognitive growth shouldn't be different in this respect either. As far as we know, it isn't.

[A riddle: free will]

What about the problem of free will? If genes play a crucial role in structuring the mind's abilities, is free will an illusion?
Well, that's interesting. Here, I think I would tend to agree with Descartes. Free will is simply an obvious aspect of human experience. I know—as much as I know that you're in front of me right now—that I can take my watch and throw it out the window if I feel like it. I also know that I'm not going to do that, because I want the watch. But I could do it if I felt like it. I just know this.

Now, I don't think that there's any scientific grasp, any hint of an idea, as to how to explain free will. Suppose somebody argues that free will is an illusion. Okay. This could be the case, but I don't believe that it's the case. It *could* be. You have to be open-minded about the possibility. But you're going to need a very powerful argument to convince me that something as evident as free will is an illusion. Nobody's offered such an argument or even pretended to offer such an argument.

So where does that leave us? We're faced with an overwhelmingly self-evident phenomenon that *could* be an illusion even though there's no reason to believe that it is an illusion. And we have a body of scientific knowledge that simply doesn't appear to connect with the problem of free will in any way.

Do you think that science will ever solve the problem of free will?
Personally, I don't think so. People have been trying to solve the problem of free will for thousands of years, and they've made zero progress. They don't even have *bad* ideas about how to answer the question. My hunch—and it's no more than a guess—is that the answer to the riddle of free will lies in the domain of potential science that the human mind can never master because of the limitations of its genetic structure.

Can you spell out what you mean?

We can laugh at a rat that always fails a complicated maze. We can say, "The rat is always going to fail because it can't look at the maze in the right way. It's doomed to fail this test forever."

Similarly, some other intelligence, organized along hereditary lines different from our own, could look at the human race and say, "Those humans are always formulating the problem of free will in the wrong way. And the reason they don't understand the problem has something to do with their biological nature."

It could well turn out that free will is one maze that we humans will never solve. We may be like the rat that simply is not designed to solve a certain type of maze and will never do so even if it works on it for ten million years. Look, in principle, there are almost certainly true scientific theories that our genetically determined brain structures will prevent us from ever understanding. Some of these theories may well be ones that we would like to know about.

That's a discouraging prospect.

I don't see it as much of a reason to despair. In fact, I kind of like the conclusion. I'm not sure that I want free will to be understood.

[The new work in art and science: a crisis of modernism?]

Do you think that any other human abilities fall into the same mysterious category as free will?

In my opinion all of them do.

All of them?

Take, for example, the aesthetic sense. We like and understand Beethoven because we are humans, with a particular, genetically determined mental constitution. But that same human nature also means there are other conceivable forms of aesthetic expression that will be totally meaningless to us. The same thing is as true for art as it is for science: the fact that we can understand and appreciate certain kinds of art has a flip side. There must be all kinds of domains of artistic achievement that are beyond our mind's capacities to understand.

Do you think genetic barriers to further progress are becoming obvious in some areas of art and science?

You could give an argument that something like this has happened in quite a few fields. It was possible in the late nineteenth century for an intelligent person of much leisure and wealth to be about as much at home as he wanted to be in the arts and sciences. But forty years later that goal had become hopeless. Much of the new work in art and science since then is meaningless to the ordinary person.

Take modern music—post-Schoenbergian music. Many artists say that if you don't understand modern music it's because you just haven't listened enough. But modern music wouldn't be accessible to me if I listened to it forever. Modern music is accessible to professionals and maybe to people with a special bent, but it's not accessible to the ordinary person who doesn't have a particular quirk of mind that enables him to grasp modern music, let alone make him want to deal with it.

And you think that something similar has happened in some scientific fields?
I think it has happened in physics and mathematics, for example. There's this idea, which goes back to the French mathematicians known collectively as Bourbaki, that the development of mathematics was originally the exploration of everyday intuitions of space and number. That is probably somewhat true through the end of the nineteenth century. But I don't think it's true now. As for physics, in talking to students at MIT, I notice that many of the very brightest ones, who would have gone into physics twenty years ago, are now going into biology. I think part of the reason for this shift is that there are discoveries to be made in biology that are within the range of an intelligent human being. This may not be true in other areas.

You seem to be saying two things. First, that whatever defines our common human nature will turn out to be a shared set of intuitions that owe much of their strength and character to our common genetic heritage—our species genotype. Second, that the exhaustion of these intuitions in many areas is producing a peculiar kind of artistic and scientific specialization. Further progress in music or mathematics, for example, requires a scientist or artist with an unusual heredity.
Well, it's a different mental constitution—something like being a chess freak or a runner who can do a three-and-one-half-minute mile. It's almost a matter of logic that this change is going to occur sooner or later. Has it happened already? That's a matter of judgment. It's a matter of looking at, say, the twentieth century and seeing whether there are signs of this change. Is it the case, for example, that contemporary work in the arts and sciences is no longer part of our common aesthetic and intellectual experience? Well, there are signs. But whether the signs are realistic or whether we are just going through a sort of sea change, and something will develop, who knows? Maybe a thousand years from now we'll know.

Do these possibilities ever make you feel that you're living in a time of creative stagnation?
I don't really feel that. I think that there are too many possibilities. There's too much human potential that hasn't as yet been realized. And don't forget that the vast majority of the human race hasn't even entered into the world that we're claiming may be finished. Who knows what the Third World will contribute to mankind's store of science and art when it does catch up with the industrialized nations? We are well short of real stagnation or termination, but that doesn't rule out the possibility that one might be able to perceive signs of such a change, or even be able to gain some insight into the ultimate limits to our intelligence by examining these signs.

How do these ideas fit into your choice of linguistics as a career?
My choice of linguistics was like most people's choice of work. It was an accident that depended on whom I met, where I was, and that sort of thing. Linguistics, however, was a fortunate choice for me because I think that linguistics is an area where it is possible to construct a very rich science.

[One major scientific revolution with a lot of outgrowths]
How would you assess your own contributions to linguistics?
They seem sort of pre-Galilean.

Like physics before the scientific revolution in the seventeenth century?
Yes. In the pre-Galilean period, people were beginning to formulate problems in physics in the right way. The answers weren't there, but the problems were finally being framed in a way that in retrospect we can see was right.

How "pre-" do you mean? Are you saying that linguistics is about where physics was in the sixteenth century? Or are we going back still further, to Aristotle and to other Greek ideas about physics?
We don't know. It depends, you see, on when the breakthrough comes. But my feeling is that someday someone is going to come along and say, "Look, you guys, you're on the right track, but you went wrong here. It should have been done this way." Well, that will be it. Suddenly things will fall into place.

And then we'll have a scientific revolution in linguistics?
I would think so, although to speak of scientific revolutions occurring outside a small core of the natural sciences is rather misleading. In fact, there was one major scientific revolution in the seventeenth century, and there have been a lot of outgrowths from it since then, including biochemistry and molecular

biology. But that's it. Nothing remotely resembling a scientific revolution has ever occurred in the social sciences.

How should a scientist exercise responsibility for the uses of his research?
The same way that any human does in any area of life.

Do you think that there are areas in science so potentially vulnerable to social misuse that they should not be pursued?
I think there are. For example, research on how to build more effective nuclear weapons. I don't think that should be pursued.

What about fundamental research—say, basic research in molecular biology that might conceivably give the weapons makers of the next generation a new set of destructive tools?
There's no simple answer to that question. Human beings are responsible for the predictable consequences of their actions. I would stop doing what I was doing if I discovered that I was engaged in an area of scientific research that I thought, under existing social conditions, would lead to, say, oppression, destruction, and pain.

An anachronistic question, then: if you were a physicist in 1929, would you have done basic work in nuclear physics even though there was already speculation about the possibility of someday building an atom bomb?
It's not an easy question. It's tempting to say, "Yes, because we have to understand the world." On the other hand, it could be that basic research in nuclear physics will lead to the extinction of the human race or to something close to that. So I don't think a glib answer is possible. Still, if you ask me specifically, I'm sure that my answer would have been yes. I would have done the work just out of interest and curiosity and with the hope that things would somehow work out. But whether that would have been the morally responsible path is not clear.

Chapter 2

Language as a key to human nature and society (1975)

You represent an anthropological approach to linguistics. Do you think that linguistics can contribute to the understanding of philosophical problems of human nature and culture?

My feeling is that a human being or any complex organism has a system of cognitive structures which develop much in the way the physical organs of the body develop. That is, in their fundamental character they are innate; their basic form is determined by the genetic nature of the organism. Of course, they grow under particular environmental conditions, assuming a specific form that admits of some variation. Much of what is distinctive among human beings is a specific manner in which a variety of shared cognitive structures develop.

Perhaps the most intricate of these structures is language. In studying language we can discover many basic properties of this cognitive structure, its organization, and also the genetic predispositions which provide the foundation for its development.

So in this respect, linguistics, first of all, tries to characterize a major feature of human cognitive organization. And secondly, I think it may provide a suggestive model for the study of other cognitive systems. And the collection of these systems is one aspect of human nature.

[Is anything really "learned"?]

Language, then, is a key to human nature?

In Western scientific thought of the last several centuries there has been a tendency to assume that human nature is limited to the immediate observable physical structure of the organism. And that for other aspects of human nature, specifically for behavior, there are no genetically determined structures of comparable complexity to the directly observable physical organization of the body. So human physical structures and intellectual structures are generally studied in different ways. The assumption is that physical structures are genetically inherited and intellectual structures are learned.

I think that this assumption is wrong. None of these structures is learned. They all grow, they grow in comparable ways; their ultimate forms are heavily dependent on genetic predispositions. If we understood, as we do not, the physical bases for these structures, I have little doubt that we would find structures in the brain for social interaction, or language, or analysis of personality—a whole variety of systems developed on the basis of specific biological endowment.

Do you mean that all behavior is innate, genetically determined?
No. But the basic structures for our behavior are innate. The specific details of how they grow would depend on interaction with the environment.

[Thought without language]
Supposing that linguistics could describe one of such structures, would the findings apply to all our intellectual activity? Do we think only in language, or do there exist non-linguistic forms of thinking too?
The analysis of linguistic structures could help in understanding other intellectual structures. Now, I don't think that there is any scientific evidence about the question whether we think only in language or not. But introspection indicates pretty clearly that we don't think in language necessarily. We also think in terms of visual images, we think in terms of situations and events, and so on, and many times we can't even begin to express in words what the content of our thinking is. And even if we are able to express it in words, it is a common experience to say something and then to recognize that it is not what we meant, that it is something else.

What does this mean? That there is a kind of non-linguistic thought going on which we then are trying to represent in language. And that we know that sometimes we fail.

I've read several times that we think in language but "feel" in a non-linguistic way. I know that it is false of me, at least if "language" refers (in my case) to English, and I assume that it is false of everyone else. I don't think that you would have any trouble at all in deciding that you are thinking of some event and then visualizing it happening with its consequences, and constructing a rational analysis of it without being able to verbalize adequately anything like its full complexity.

You used the expression "rational analysis." Do you believe that all our thinking is rational and linear?

I don't think that all thinking is a kind of rational structure. But I don't think that it is correct to identify the rational/non-rational dichotomy with the linguistic/non-linguistic dichotomy.

Can language be non-rational?

Yes. So those are two dimensions that do not correlate. It's true that language is in a sense linear, but that is as obvious as that perceptual space is three-dimensional.

[Language without communication]

As I understand it, language has an innate biological basis. Its use, however, is social. What do you think of the social functions of language? Is it primarily an instrument of communication?

I think that a very important aspect of language has to do with the establishment of social relations and interactions. Often, this is described as communication. But that is very misleading, I think. There is a narrow class of uses of language where you intend to communicate. Communication refers to an effort to get people to understand what one means. And that, certainly, is one use of language and a social use of it. But I don't think that is the only social use of language. Nor are social uses the only uses of language. For example, language can be used to express or clarify one's thoughts with little regard for the social context, if any.

I think that the use of language is a very important means by which this species, because of its biological nature, creates a kind of a social space, to place itself in interaction with other people. It doesn't have much to do with communication in a narrow sense, that is, it doesn't involve transmission of information. There is much information transmitted, but it is not the content of what is said that is transmitted. There is undoubtedly much to learn about the social use of language, for communication or for other purposes that are important. But at present there is not much in the way of a theory of sociolinguistics, of social uses of language, as far as I am aware.

What, then, in the field of linguistics are the greatest achievements?

I think that the most important work that is going on has to do with the search for very general abstract features of what is sometimes called universal grammar: general properties of language which reflect a kind of biological necessity rather than logical necessity, that is, properties of language which are not logically necessary for such a system but which are essential invariant properties of human language and are known without learning. We know these properties but we don't learn them. We simply use our knowledge of these properties as the basis for learning.

Do we genetically inherit this knowledge?
Yes, we must. In fact, by universal grammar I mean just that system of principles and structures which are the prerequisite for acquisition of language, and to which every language necessarily conforms.

Does it mean that this genetic basis of language is universal?
Yes, that's right. But we are only one species. You can imagine a different world in which a number of species developed with different genetically determined linguistic systems. It hasn't happened in evolution. What has happened is that one species has developed, and the genetic structure of this species happens to involve a variety of intricate abstract principles of linguistic organization which, therefore, necessarily constrain every language, and, in fact, create the basis for learning language as a way of organizing experience rather than constituting something learned from experience.

Would such knowledge also be helpful in understanding human nature?
It would, in two respects. For one thing, it is by itself a part of a study of human intelligence which is, perhaps, the central aspect of human nature. And, secondly, I think, it is a good model for studying other human properties, which ought to be studied by psychologists in the same way.

Do you mean that psychology could benefit from linguistics? Could you explain how?
One thing that you and I know is language. Another thing that you and I know is how objects behave in perceptual space. We have a whole mass of complex ways of understanding what is the nature of visual space. A proper part of psychology ought to be, and in recent years has been, an effort to try to discover the principles of how we organize the visual space. I would say that the same is true of every domain of psychology, of human studies. To understand, for example, how people organize social systems, we have to discover the principles that we create to make some societies intelligible.

I understand that we could have a kind of "universal grammar" of non-linguistic forms of human behavior as well. But if, as you say, our behavior and language are heavily guided by universal principles, why, then, do they differ so much all around the world?

I don't think they differ so much. I think that as human beings we quite naturally take for granted what is similar among human beings and then pay attention to what differentiates us. That makes perfect sense for us as human beings. I suppose that frogs pay no attention to being a frog. They take it for granted. What interests a frog are differences among frogs. From our point of view they are all more or less the same, from their point of view they are all radically different.

Similarly with us. For us, we all are very different, our languages are very different, and our societies are very different. But if we could extract ourselves from our point of view and sort of look down at human life the way a biologist looks at other organisms, I think we could see it a different way. Imagine an extra-human observer looking at us. Such an extra-human observer would be struck precisely by the uniformity of human languages, by the very slight variation from one language to another, and by the remarkable respects in which all languages are the same. And then he would notice, observing us, that we do not pay attention to that because for the purpose of human life it is quite natural and appropriate just to take for granted everything that is common. We don't concern ourselves with that, all we worry about are differences.

[Limited scientific capacity]

Would this extra-human observer think the same way about our symbols, ideas, needs, and values?

Absolutely. I think he would be struck with the uniformity of human societies in every aspect. And there is more than that. Let's imagine again an observer looking at us without any preconceptions. I think he would be struck by the fact that although human beings have the capacity to develop scientific knowledge, it must be a very limited capacity because it is done only in very narrow and specific domains. There are huge areas where the human mind is apparently incapable of forming sciences or at least has not done so. There are other areas—so far, in fact, one area only—in which we have demonstrated the capacity for true scientific progress.

Physics?

Physics and those parts of other fields that grow out of physics: chemistry, the structure of big molecules—in those domains there is a lot of progress. In many other domains there is very little progress in developing real scientific understanding.

Isn't because humans want to exercise control over the physical world?

I don't think so. I think that probably reflects something very special about the nature of our minds. There is no evolutionary pressure to create minds capable of forming sciences; it just has happened. Evolutionary pressure has not led to higher rates of reproduction for people capable of solving scientific problems or creating new scientific ideas. So if, in fact, the science-forming capacities evolved for other reasons, it would not be too surprising if those particular structures that have developed proved to be rather special in their nature, reflecting the contingencies of their evolution or the working of physical law.

Do you mean that we may, by virtue of this accidental origin of science, be capable of development of some disciplines of science and incapable of others, and that we are not conscious of that?

Yes. As human beings, we are not too conscious of that because we naturally assume that our mental structures are universal. But I suppose an outside biologist looking at us would see something very different. He would see that, like other organisms, we have a narrow sphere within which we are very good, but that sphere is very limited. And that, in fact, the very achievements that we can have within that sphere are related to lack of achievements in other spheres.

To construct a scientific theory from the data and to be able to recognize that it is a reasonable theory is possible only if there are some very sharp restrictive principles that lead you to go in one direction and not in another direction. Otherwise you wouldn't have science at all, merely randomly chosen hypotheses. Then human genius may have limitless opportunities to develop in one direction, but at the same time this genius will not go in other directions. And those two considerations are related. The very properties of the human mind that provide an enormous scope for human genius in some domains will serve as barriers to progress in other domains, just as the properties that enable each child to acquire a complex and highly articulated human language block the acquisition of other imaginable linguistic systems.

[A condition of (temporary) ignorance?]

What domains do you consider the most backward and neglected?

I think that we have basically nothing in the field of human behavior. Maybe that is just a condition of temporary ignorance. But it may be that we are simply not intellectually equipped to develop such a theory.

Do you mean that not only do we not have tools to develop such a theory but we are not capable of creating the necessary tools?

Yes. Intellectual tools. Our minds are specifically adapted to developing certain theories, and we have a science if the theories which are available to our minds happen to be close to true. Well, there is no particular reason to suppose that the intersection of true theories and theories that are accessible to the mind is very large. It may not be very large.

Can we know at least how large it is?

It is a question of biology how large that intersection is. And if humans are organisms like every other organism, which they are, then we would expect precisely that if there are some domains where real scientific progress is possible, then there are others where it is not.

Chapter 3

A really new way of looking at language (November 1987)

Dr. Chomsky, many of our teachers are unfamiliar with your work, because the study of linguistics is not required in their professional training. It would be helpful and would arouse some interest in this field if you answered the following questions.

[Four central questions: innate knowledge and its creative use]

Your 1957 publication entitled Syntactic structures *presented a completely new way of looking at language. What was it that started you on this exploration?*

One may be interested in language for many different reasons and from many different points of view. My own interest has been dominated by several central questions: (1) What is it that we know when we know a language? (2) How is this knowledge acquired? (3) How is this knowledge put to use? (4) What is the physical basis, in neural mechanisms, for systems of knowledge and use of language? The fourth question remains on the horizons of research. Let us keep, then, to the first three.

In the early 1950s, typical answers to these questions would have been something like this. (1) A language is a certain system of habits and skills; to know a language is to have mastered these skills. (2) Knowledge of language is acquired by such mechanisms as conditioning, association, practice in exercising skills, et cetera. (3) Use of language is exercise of the skills that have been mastered. Within psychology, the dominant framework of thinking was one or another variety of behaviorism. Within linguistics, the dominant assumptions were structuralist. As a theoretical discipline, linguistics was devoted to devising principles of analysis that could be used to provide an organized and systematic account of the elements of a language, their relations, the orders in which they appear, the way they are grouped into larger elements, and so on.

It seemed to me clear that these approaches were entirely inadequate—in fact, that the entire conception was completely wrong. Normal use of language is not an exercise of any habit or skill. Typically, use of language is creative in the sense that it constantly involves the production and interpretation of new forms—new in the experience of the language user or even in the history of language. This is not an exotic phenomenon, but rather the norm. Thus readers of these sentences may not have seen any of them before, or anything like them, yet they have no difficulty recognizing them as sentences of their language and assigning to them a specific meaning. They do this in the same way as other speakers of (similar varieties of) English. If these sentences were modified in some arbitrary way—say, in reverse order—they would be equally novel for the reader, but they would be gibberish. It is easy to show that speakers of a language, even young children, assign specific and precise meanings to very simple sentences that are entirely new in their experience.

Consider, for example, the following sentences to illustrate what is in fact the norm in language use:

(1) We expect to like each other
(2) John wonders who [we expect to like each other]
(3) John is too clever to catch Bill
(4) John is too clever to expect anyone to catch Bill
(5) John is too clever to catch
(6) John is too clever to expect anyone to catch
(7) John is too clever to meet anyone who caught

In case 1, we know that the sentence means, roughly, that each of us expects that we will like the others of us. In case 2, the very same sentence is embedded in the context "John wonders who———," yet we interpret it quite differently. The reciprocal phrase "each other" does not relate to *we*, but rather the more remote phrase *who*. The meaning is something like "John wonders which people are such that we expect that each of those people will like the others of those people." In example 3, we understand that John is to do the catching; in 4, John is to do the expecting. But in 5 and 6, which differ from 3 and 4 only by the deletion of the final noun, the meaning is quite different: it is not John who is to do the catching and expecting, but someone else, maybe us; John is the person to be caught. (To understand sentence 6 often takes a moment's reflection, whatever that means exactly.) Sentence 7 appears to be of the same complexity and roughly the same form as 6, but it is complete gibberish unless we understand *catch* quite differently, as in "he catches for the Yankees."

These are very short and simple sentences. We understand them in a precise and explicit way even though they may be novel in our experience and unlike others that we have heard (in fact, we typically have no idea what sentences we have heard, apart from conventional greetings and the like). Children are not instructed to interpret these sentences in the ways they do, nor are foreigners learning English. Examples such as these do not appear in grammar books or teaching texts, and would only confuse people if they did appear; in fact, the properties of these sentences were not even noticed until recently. The sentences seem familiar, but that is not because we have come across others resembling them.

In fact, inspection of actual texts would show that such constructions are quite rare. Plainly, we cannot be carrying out these accomplishments by habit, and there is no mere skill involved. Our inability to associate "each other" with "we" in 2 is not a lack of ability; it is not that we haven't practiced enough, or that we are too weak, or that we should try harder. Furthermore, such examples show that no notion of "analogy" or "similarity" will be of any help at all in explaining the core properties of language. Thus the phrase given within brackets in 2 is identical with 1, and thus is surely analogous to it in any reasonable sense of analogy, but it is interpreted quite differently. Such examples also show that the entire framework of behaviorist psychology is simply irrelevant to normal linguistic behavior, though to demonstrate this point, much simpler observations suffice, as they suffice to demonstrate the irrelevance of behaviorist doctrine to behavior generally, apart from its peripheral aspects.

Attention to the facts shows that the answers to the three questions posed must be entirely different from those that were conventional at the time. Recognition of such facts as these in various domains, and ideas as to how to account for them, led to the "cognitive turn" in psychology in the mid-1950s and to the development of generative grammar within linguistics, one primary factor in this "cognitive revolution," as it is sometimes called. It seems that the right answers to the three questions are something like this: (1) to know a language is to have mastered a system of rules and principles; (2) the child acquires this knowledge on the basis of a very rich biological endowment that determines, quite precisely, the kinds of systems that can develop in language growth; (3) use of language is rule-governed behavior. At the heart of language, and much of human action and thought, is a system of mental representations and computations. The goal of linguistics, then, is to discover these systems, and more deeply, to discover the fixed, invariant biological endowment that enables each child to develop a very rich and highly articulated system of knowledge on the basis of quite fragmentary and limited evidence.

These ideas were by no means entirely novel. In fact, they recall a rich tradition that had long been forgotten by the mid-1950s and is still little known.

[A system of mental computations]

For those of us who are not linguists, how would you state the basic idea of your generative transformational theory?

The basic idea is that knowledge of language involves a system of rules and representations, of mental computation, linked to the motor and perceptual apparatus; and that much of this system is fixed and invariant, just as the essential form and organization of the human body is fixed and invariant, determined by our biological endowment. To develop these ideas further would lead us to the principles that determine the form and meaning of sentences. Phenomena such as those illustrated above are common to the languages of the world, so far as we know. Notice that in all of these examples certain elements are missing in the physical form, but understood. Thus in 1 and 2 the subject of *like* is not expressed but is understood; it is understood differently in the two cases. The same is true in the other examples. The principles of language determine where these missing elements must appear, and how they must be understood. They are missing only in the sense that they are not pronounced: the mind "sees" them and uses them in its mental computations, and they are just as real as the elements *John, we,* et cetera, which happen to be linked to the vocal apparatus in the system of mental computation.

Languages of course differ; English is not Japanese. But it seems that languages differ only in their lexical choices and in selection of certain options that are not fully determined by the fixed principles of our biological endowment. Thus in every language, verbs take objects; but the object may follow the verb, as in English, or precede it, as in Japanese. This option holds not only for verb phrases, but for all phrases. Thus English has prepositions, while Japanese has postpositions. Japanese in many ways seems a mirror image of English, and seems superficially to differ in many other respects as well. But the systems are cast from the same mold. The same is true of other languages, so far as we know, however different they may seem superficially. Indeed, we know that this must be the case, or children would never be able to learn any of these languages. A language can be acquired, in all of its richness and complexity, because the child basically already knows it as part of its biological endowment. The same is true much more broadly, in every domain of human achievement.

[The most complex and intricate biological system]

You have written that a major contribution of the study of language is in under-standing of the character of mental processes, i.e., "Language is a mirror of the mind." At the present point in your work, what important reflections are in this mirror?

The idea that language is a mirror of mind is a traditional one which has received expression in various ways over the centuries. I have never felt that this metaphor should be taken too literally. Rather, it seems that language is one essential component of the human mind. The human brain is the most complex and intricate biological system we know. When we study its proper-ties and manifestations, we are studying what we call "mind." The human mind appears to consist of different systems, each intricate and highly spe-cialized, with interactions of a kind that are largely fixed by our biological endowment; in these respects it is like all other known biological systems— the physical organs of the body below the neck, for example.

One of these systems is the human language faculty. It is particularly interesting because it is a common property of humans, with little if any vari-ation apart from quite serious impairment, and it appears to be unique to the human species; contrary to much mythology, other organisms appear to lack even the most rudimentary features of the human language faculty, a fact that has been shown quite dramatically in recent studies of apes. Thus human lan-guage appears to be a true "species property," and one that enters in a central way into thought and understanding. But it is not, in my view, a "mirror of mind"; rather, an essential component of the human mind, a crucial element of the human essence.

[A very radical departure from the tradition]

In Language and mind, *you wrote in essence that as research in grammar contin-ues, we may expect boundaries that seem clear today to shift for a new basis for organization of grammar. Now, in 1987, which, if any, have shifted?*

There have been many changes in our conception of the nature of language over the past thirty years. Early work in generative grammar, as in *Syntactic structures,* was in some respects similar to traditional grammar. Specifically, it involved rules that were specific to particular constructions and to particular languages. Thus the rule for forming questions in English, or passives in English, was language-particular and construction-particular, just as in a traditional grammar there will be a chapter on passives, one on questions, and so on. The so-called rules of traditional grammars are really only hints, understandable to an intelligent reader who already knows the language, just as the rules in a teaching grammar presuppose that the learner already knows the basic structure of language. Generative grammar, in contrast, attempted to make explicit what is presupposed—indeed, what was not even recognized to exist—in traditional and pedagogic grammar. But apart from this crucial distinction, the rule systems of early generative grammar had a rather familiar look to them.

More recent work has led to the conclusion that the rules of traditional and early generative grammar are an artifact, not real elements of the mind/brain. There appear to be no construction-particular rules, but rather very general principles, such as the principles for interpreting missing elements, that are common to all languages and all constructions. Languages differ in the manner indicated earlier, but not by selection of different rules. There is thus, in recent work, a very radical departure from the tradition of study of language over the past several thousand years.

Reading teachers are concerned with language acquisition, since oral language provides a basis for reading. In your writings, you state that at birth, children are genetically programmed to acquire language and that it is innate. Is then the heavy emphasis placed on language development by nursery schools and kindergartens justified?

There is little doubt that the basic structure of language and the principles that determine the form and interpretation of sentences in any human language are in large part innate. But it does not follow that emphasis on language development is misplaced. If a child is placed in an impoverished environment, innate abilities simply will not develop, mature, and flourish. To take an extreme case, a child who wears a cast on its legs for too long will never learn to walk, and a child deprived of appropriate nutrition may undergo puberty only after a long delay, or never, though there is no doubt that walking and sexual maturation are innately determined biological properties. Similarly, a child brought up in an institution may have ample experience and nutrition but still may not develop normally, either physically or mentally, if normal human interaction is lacking.

It is a traditional insight that teaching is not like filling a cup with water, but more like enabling a flower to grow in its own way; but it will not grow and flourish without proper care. Language development, like all human development, will be heavily determined by the nature of the environment, and may be severely limited unless the environment is appropriate. A stimulating environment is required to enable natural curiosity, intelligence, and creativity to develop, and to enable our biological capacities to unfold. The fact that the course of development is largely internally determined does not mean that it will proceed without care, stimulation, and opportunity.

We realize that linguistics is the scientific study of language and not a recipe for language instruction. But if teachers in primary grades were familiar with your work, what kind of changes or even emphasis might they make in reading instruction? What general suggestions would help them?

I'm hesitant even to suggest an answer to this question. Practitioners have to decide for themselves what is useful in the sciences and what is not. As a linguist, I have no particular qualifications or knowledge that enables or entitles me to prescribe methods of language instruction. As a *person,* I have my own ideas on the topic, based on my own experience (in part as a teacher of language to children), introspection, and personal judgment, but these should not be confused with some kind of professional expertise, presented from on high. My own feeling, for what it is worth, is that at any level, from the nursery to graduate school, teaching is largely a matter of encouraging natural development. The best "method" of teaching is to make it clear that the subject is worth learning, and to allow the child's—or adult's—natural curiosity and interest in truth and understanding to mature and develop. That is about 90 percent of the problem, if not more. Methods of instruction may influence the residue.

[Problems of the society at large]

Many of the early beliefs concerning the nature of language of "disadvantaged children" have been disproven by research, i.e., that Black English is deficient or inferior; that it fails to provide an adequate basis for abstract thinking. Yet speakers of Black English want their children to learn standard English. Is this best done by direct instruction or by osmosis?

Anyone who was familiar with language took for granted, or should have taken for granted, that so-called Black English is simply a language on a par with my urban Philadelphia dialect of English, the English of [the] high table at Oxford, Japanese, Greek, et cetera. If race, class, and other power relations were to change, Black English might emerge as the standard language, and what I speak would be regarded as defective. None of this has anything to do with the nature of the languages. The idea that Black English, or my urban dialect, or any other language fails to provide an adequate basis for abstract thinking is utterly implausible, and I think one should be extremely skeptical about claims to the contrary. Typically, they are based on gross misunderstanding.

Questions nevertheless arise about what should be taught in the schools. If speakers of Black English came to dominate and control American society, so that my speech would be regarded as nonstandard and defective, then it might be argued that my children should be taught the language of the dominant culture, Black English, not the particular variety of English that I speak. The decision would not be based on characteristics of the language, or on some ludicrous beliefs about how certain languages stand in the way of abstract thought, but rather on other considerations. Thus one would have to ask whether my children would suffer in the real world of power, authority, inequality, and coercion if they were not to acquire relevant features of the dominant culture. Surely this consideration would have to be given weight if the welfare of my children were to be taken into account. On the other hand, if my children were to be instructed in what amounts to a foreign language, their intellectual development might be inhibited; there is little doubt, for example, that it would be harder for them to learn to read if the language of instruction were Black English, which is not the language that they acquired in their pre-school environment. The same questions would arise if I had moved to Italy when my children were young. Exactly how these factors should be balanced is not a simple question, and there is no reason to believe that there is any uniform answer to them; too many factors vary.

My own personal judgment, for what it is worth, is that speakers of a language that is not that of groups that dominate some society should probably be taught in their own languages at least at very early stages, until basic skills are acquired, and should be taught in the dominant language at later stages, so that they can enter the society without suffering disadvantages that are rooted in prevailing power, privilege, and domination. One might hope to modify these features of the dominant society, but that is another question. Children have to be helped to function in the world that exists, which does not mean, of course, that they—or others—should not try to change it to a better world.

I am not presuming to express any firm judgments or to offer general proposals. There are a great many factors to consider, and the answers will surely not be the same for every person or every circumstance. We have to do here not with the problems of language but of the society at large, and they have to be confronted in these terms.

Chapter 4

Perspectives on language and mind (October 1999)

It would only be appropriate to begin with some of the thoughts of the master, who does not disappoint us, even though the topics I want to discuss are remote from his primary concerns. Galileo may have been the first to recognize clearly the significance of the core property of human language, and one of its most distinctive: the use of finite means to express an unlimited array of thoughts. In his *Dialogo*, he describes with wonder the discovery of a means to communicate one's "most secret thoughts to any other person . . . with no greater difficulty than the various collocations of 24 little characters upon a paper." This is the greatest of all human inventions, he writes, comparable to the creations of a Michelangelo—of whom Galileo himself was a virtual reincarnation, according to the mythology constructed by his student and biographer Viviani, memorialized in Kant's image of the reincarnation of Michelangelo in Newton through the intermediary of Galileo.

[A product of biological evolution: discrete infinity]
Galileo was referring to alphabetic writing, but the invention succeeds because it reflects the nature of the language that the little characters are used to represent. Shortly after his death, the philosopher-grammarians of Port Royal took that further step, referring to the "marvellous invention" of a means to construct "from 25 or 30 sounds that infinity of expressions, which bear no resemblance to what takes place in our minds, yet enable us to reveal [to others] everything that we think, and all the various movements of our soul." The "infinity of expressions" is a form of discrete infinity, similar to that of the natural numbers. The Port Royal theorists recognized that "the marvellous invention" should be the central topic of the study of language, and pursued the insight in original ways, developing and applying ideas that became leading topics of inquiry only much later. Some were revived and

reshaped in Frege's concept of *Sinn* and *Bedeutung*, others in the phrase structure and transformational grammars of the latter part of this century.

From a contemporary point of view, the term *invention* is of course out of place, but the core property of language that Galileo and his successors identified is no less marvelous as a product of biological evolution, proceeding in ways that lie well beyond current understanding.

The same property of human language, and its apparent biological isolation, also intrigued Charles Darwin when he turned his attention to human evolution. In his *Descent of man*, Darwin wrote that with regard to understanding of language, dogs appear to be "at the same stage of development" as one-year-old infants, "who understand many words and short sentences but cannot yet utter a word." There is only one difference between humans and other animals in this regard, Darwin held: "man differs solely in his almost infinitely larger power of associating together the most diversified sounds and ideas." This "association of sounds and ideas" is the "marvellous invention" of seventeenth-century commentators, which Darwin hoped would somehow be incorporated within the theory of evolution.

The theory of *evolution*, not necessarily the workings of natural selection; and surely not these alone, since, trivially, they operate within a physical channel, the effects of which are to be discovered, not stipulated. It is also worth recalling that Darwin firmly rejected the hyperselectionism of his close associate Alfred Russell Wallace, which has been revived in some contemporary popular versions of so-called neo-Darwinism. Darwin repeatedly emphasized his conviction "that natural selection has been the main but not the exclusive means of modification," taking explicit note of a range of possibilities, including non-adaptive modifications and unselected functions determined from structure—all topics that are alive in contemporary theory of evolution.

[The faculty of language as a "language organ"]

An interest in the nature and origins of the "marvellous invention" leads to investigation of the component of the human brain that is responsible for these unique and indeed wondrous achievements. This language organ or faculty of language, as we may call it, is a common human possession, varying little across the species as far as we know, apart from very serious pathology. Through maturation and interaction with the environment, the common language faculty assumes one or another state, apparently stabilizing in several stages, finally at about puberty. A state attained by this faculty resembles what is called a language in ordinary usage, but only partially: we are no longer sur-

prised when notions of common sense find no place in the effort to understand and explain the phenomena they deal with in their own ways, another
achievement of the Galilean revolution, now taken for granted in the hard sciences but still considered controversial beyond—inappropriately, I think.

The internal language, in the technical sense, is a state of the faculty of
language. Each internal language has the means to construct the mental
objects that we use to express our thoughts and to interpret the limitless array
of overt expressions that we encounter. Each of these mental objects relates
sound and meaning in a particular structured form. A clear understanding of
how a finite mechanism can construct an infinity of objects of this kind was
reached only in this century, in work in the formal sciences. These discoveries made it possible to address in explicit ways the task that was identified by
Galileo, the Port Royal theorists, Darwin, and some others—a scattering of
others, as far as I have been able to discover. For the past half century, a good
part of the study of language has been devoted to the investigation of such
mechanisms—called "generative grammars" in the study of language—an
important innovation in the long and rich history of linguistics, though, as
always, there are precedents, in this case tracing back to ancient India.

Darwin's formulation is misleading in several respects. It is now understood that the linguistic achievements of infants go far beyond what Darwin
attributed to them, and that non-human organisms have nothing like the linguistic capacities he assumed. Furthermore, association is not the appropriate
concept. And his phrase "differs solely" is surely inappropriate, though "primarily" might be defensible: the property of discrete infinity is only one of
many essential differences between human language and animal systems of
communication or expression—for that matter, other biological systems
rather generally. And of course the phrase "almost infinite" must be understood to mean "unbounded," that is, "infinite" in the relevant sense.

Nonetheless, Darwin's point is basically correct. Essential characteristics
of human language, such as the discrete-infinite use of finite means that
intrigued him and his distinguished predecessors, appear to be biologically
isolated and a very recent development in human evolution, millions of years
after the separation from the nearest surviving relatives. Furthermore, the
"marvellous invention" must be present in Darwin's one-year-old, indeed in
the embryo, even if not yet manifested, just as the capacity for binocular
vision or undergoing puberty is part of the genetic endowment, even if manifested only at a particular stage of maturation and under appropriate environmental conditions. Similar conclusions seem highly plausible in the case
of other aspects of our mental nature as well.

The concept of mental nature underwent an important revision in the Galilean era. It was formulated in a novel way, in fairly clear terms—and, I think it can be argued, for the last time: the concept soon collapsed, and nothing has replaced it since. The concept of mind was framed in terms of what was called "the mechanical philosophy," the idea that the natural world is a complex machine that could in principle be constructed by a skilled artisan. "The world was merely a set of Archimedian simple machines hooked together," Galileo scholar Peter Machamer observes, "or a set of colliding corpuscles that obeyed the laws of mechanical collision." The world is something like the intricate clocks and other automata that excited the scientific imagination of that era, much as computers do today—and the shift is, in an important sense, not fundamental, as Alan Turing showed sixty years ago.

Within the framework of the mechanical philosophy, Descartes developed his theory of mind and mind-body dualism, still the *locus classicus* of much discussion of our mental nature—a serious misunderstanding, I believe. Descartes himself pursued a reasonable course. He sought to demonstrate that the inorganic and organic world could be explained in terms of the mechanical philosophy. But he argued that fundamental aspects of human nature escape these bounds and cannot be accommodated in these terms. His primary example was human language: in particular, that "marvellous invention" of a means to express our thoughts in novel and limitless ways that are constrained by our bodily state but not determined by it; that are appropriate to situations but not caused by them, a crucial distinction; and that evoke in others thoughts that they could have expressed in similar ways—a collection of properties that we may call the creative use of language.

More generally, Descartes held, "free will is in itself the noblest thing we can have" and all that "truly belongs" to us. As his followers expressed the thesis, humans are only "incited and inclined" to act in certain ways, not "compelled" (or random). In this respect they are unlike machines—a category that includes the entire non-human world, they held.

For the Cartesians generally, the creative aspect of ordinary use of language was the most striking illustration of our noblest gift. It relies crucially on the "marvellous invention," the mechanisms responsible for providing the infinity of expressions for expressing our thoughts and for understanding other people, though it relies on far more than that.

That we ourselves have these noble qualities of mind we know by reflection; we attribute them to others, in the Cartesian model, by best-theory arguments, as they are now called: only in this way can we deal with the problem of "other minds." Body and mind are two substances, one an extended substance, the other a thinking substance, *res cogitans*. The former falls within the mechanical philosophy, the latter not.

Adopting the mechanical philosophy, "Galileo forged a new model of intelligibility for human understanding," Machamer argues plausibly, with "new criteria for coherent explanations of natural phenomena" based on the picture of the world as an elaborate machine. For Galileo, and leading figures in the early modern scientific revolution generally, true understanding requires a mechanical model, a device that an artisan could construct. Thus he rejected traditional theories of tides because we cannot "duplicate [them] by means of appropriate artificial devices."

[Incomprehensibility of the natural world]

The Galilean model of intelligibility has a corollary: when mechanism fails, understanding fails. The apparent inadequacies of mechanical explanation for cohesion, attraction, and other phenomena led Galileo finally to reject "the vain presumption of understanding everything." Worse yet, "there is not a single effect in nature . . . such that the most ingenious theorist can arrive at a complete understanding of it." For mind, the Galilean model plainly fails, as Descartes convincingly showed. Though much more optimistic than Galileo about the prospects for mechanical explanation, Descartes neverthe- less speculated that the workings of *res cogitans* may lie beyond human under- standing. He thought that we may not "have intelligence enough" to understand the creative aspect of language use and other manifestations of mind, though "there is nothing that we comprehend more clearly and per- fectly" than our possession of these capacities, and "it would be absurd to doubt that of which we inwardly experience and perceive as existing within ourselves, just because we do not comprehend a matter which from its nature we know to be incomprehensible." He goes too far in saying that we "know" the matter to be incomprehensible, but anyone committed to the belief that humans are biological organisms, not angels, will recognize that human intel- ligence has specific scope and limits, and that much of what we seek to understand might lie beyond these limits.

The fact that *res cogitans* escapes the model of intelligibility that ani- mated the modern scientific revolution is interesting, but in a way not impor- tant. The reason is that the entire model quickly collapsed, confirming Galileo's worst fears. Newton demonstrated, to his dismay, that nothing in nature falls within the mechanical model of intelligibility that seemed to be the merest common sense to the creators of modern science. Newton regarded his discovery of action at a distance, in violation of the basic principles of the mechanical philosophy, as "so great an Absurdity that I believe no Man who has in philosophical matters a competent Faculty of thinking, can ever fall into it." Nonetheless, he was forced to conclude that the absurdity "does really exist." "Newton had no physical explanation of it at all," two contemporary scholars observe, a deep problem for him and eminent contemporaries who "accused him of reintroducing occult qualities" with no "physical, material substrate" that "human beings can understand" (Betty Dobbs and Margaret Jacob). In the words of one of the founders of modern Galilean studies, Alexander Koyré, Newton demonstrated that "a purely materialistic or mechanistic physics" is "impossible."

To the end of his life, Newton sought to escape the absurdity, as did Euler, D'Alembert, and many since, but in vain. Nothing has lessened the force of David Hume's judgment that by refuting the self-evident mechanical philosophy, Newton "restored [nature's] ultimate secrets to that obscurity in which they ever did and ever will remain." Later discoveries, introducing still more extreme absurdities, only entrenched more deeply the realization that the natural world is not comprehensible to human intelligence, at least in the sense anticipated by the founders of modern science.

While recognizing the absurdity, Newton defended himself vigorously against the criticism of continental scientists—Huygens, Leibniz, and others—who charged him with reintroducing the "occult qualities" of the despised Scholastic philosophers. The occult qualities of the Aristotelians were vacuous, Newton wrote, but his new principles, while unfortunately occult, nevertheless had substantive content. "To derive two or three general Principles of motion from Phaenomena, and afterwards to tell us how the properties and Actions of all corporal Things follow from those manifest Principles, would be a very great step in Philosophy," Newton wrote, "though the Causes of those Principles be not yet discover'd." Newton was formulating a new and weaker model of intelligibility, one with roots in what has been called the "mitigated skepticism" of the British scientific tradition, which had abandoned as hopeless the search for the "first springs of natural motions" and other natural phenomena, keeping to the much more modest effort to develop the best theoretical account we can.

The implications for the theory of mind were immediate, and immediately recognized. Mind-body dualism is no longer tenable, because there is no notion of body. It is common in recent years to ridicule Descartes's "ghost in the machine" and to speak of "Descartes's error" in postulating a second substance: mind, distinct from body. It is true that Descartes was proven wrong, but not for those reasons. Newton exorcised the machine; he left the ghost intact. It was the first substance, extended matter, that dissolved into mysteries. We can speak intelligibly of *physical* phenomena (processes, etc.), as we speak of the *real* truth or the *real* world, but without supposing that there is some other truth or world. For the natural sciences, there are mental aspects of the world, along with optical, chemical, organic, and others. The categories need not be firm or distinct, or conform to commonsense intuition, a standard for science that was finally abandoned with Newton's discoveries along with the demand for intelligibility as conceived by Galileo and early modern science rather generally.

In this view, mental aspects of the world fall together with the rest of nature. Galileo had argued that "at present we need only . . . investigate and demonstrate certain of the properties of motion which is accelerated," putting aside the question of "the cause of the acceleration of natural motion." After Newton, the guiding principle was extended to all of science. The eighteenth-century English chemist Joseph Black recommended that "chemical affinity be received as a first principle, which we cannot explain any more than Newton could explain gravitation, and let us defer accounting for the laws of affinity, till we have established such a body of doctrine as [Newton] has established concerning the laws of gravitation." Chemistry proceeded along that course. It established a rich body of doctrine, achieving its "triumphs . . . in isolation from the newly emerging science of physics," a leading historian of chemistry points out (Arnold Thackray). Well into this century, prominent scientists regarded molecules and chemical properties as basically calculating devices; understanding of these matters was then vastly beyond anything known about mental reality. Unification was finally achieved sixty-five years ago, but only after physics had undergone radical revision, departing even more from commonsense intuitions.

Notice that it was unification, not reduction. Chemistry not only *seemed* irreducible to the physics of the day, but indeed was.

[Important lessons for the cognitive sciences]

All of this conveys important lessons for the study of mind. Though they should be far more obvious to us today, they were already clear after Newton's demolition of the mechanical philosophy. And they were drawn at once, pursuing John Locke's suggestion that God might have chosen to "superadd to matter a *faculty of thinking*" just as he "annexed effects to motion which we can in no way conceive motion able to produce." In Newton's words, defending his postulation of innate active principles in matter, "God, who gave animals self-motion beyond our understanding, is, without doubt, able to implant other principles of motion in bodies, which we may understand as little." Motion of the limbs, thinking, acts of will—all are "beyond our understanding," though we can seek to find "general principles" and "bodies of doctrine" that give us a limited grasp of their fundamental nature. Such ideas led naturally to the conclusion that properties of mind arise from "the organization of the nervous system itself," that those properties "termed mental" are the result of the "organical structure" of the brain just as matter "is possessed of powers of attraction and repulsion" that act at a distance (La Mettrie, Joseph Priestley). It is not clear what might be a coherent alternative.

A century later, Darwin expressed his agreement. He asked, rhetorically, "Why is thought, being a secretion of the brain, more wonderful than gravity, a property of matter?" Essentially Locke's suggestion, as elaborated by Priestley and others. It is well to remember, however, that the problems raised by the Cartesians were never addressed. There is no substantial "body of doctrine" about the ordinary creative use of language or other manifestations of our "noblest" quality. And lacking that, questions of unification cannot be seriously raised.

The modern cognitive sciences, linguistics included, face problems much like those of chemistry from the collapse of the mechanical philosophy until the 1930s, when the bodies of doctrine that chemists had developed were unified with a radically revised physics. Contemporary neuroscience commonly puts forth, as its guiding idea, the thesis that "things mental, indeed minds, are emergent properties of brains," while recognizing that "these emergences are not regarded as irreducible but are produced by principles that control the interactions between lower level events—principles we do not yet understand" (Vernon Mountcastle). The thesis is often presented as an "astonishing hypothesis," "the bold assertion that mental phenomena are entirely natural and caused by the neurophysiological activities of the brain," a "radical new idea" in the philosophy of mind that may at last put to rest Cartesian dualism, some believe, while others express doubt that the apparent chasm between body and mind can really be bridged.

These are not, however, the proper ways to look at the matter. The thesis is old, not new; it closely paraphrases Priestley and others two centuries ago. It is, furthermore, a virtual corollary of the collapse of mind-body dualism as Newton undermined the concept of matter, in any intelligible sense and left science with the problems of constructing "bodies of doctrine" in various domains of inquiry and seeking unification.

How unification might take place, or whether it can be achieved by human intelligence or even in principle, we will not know until we know.

Speculation is as idle as it was in chemistry early in this century. And chemistry is hard science, just beyond physics in the misleading hierarchy of reductionism. Integration of mental aspects of the world with others appears to be a distant goal. Even for insects—the so-called language of the bees, for example—problems of neural realization and evolution are barely at the horizon. It is perhaps surprising to find that such problems are lively topics of speculation for the vastly more complex and obscure systems of human higher mental faculties, language and others, and that we regularly hear confident pronouncements about the mechanisms and evolution of such faculties—for humans, not for bees; for bees the problems are understood to be too hard. Commonly the speculations are offered as solutions to the mind-body problem, but that can hardly be, since the problem has had no coherent formulation for three hundred years.

For the present, the study of language and other higher human mental faculties is proceeding much as chemistry did, seeking to "establish a rich body of doctrine," with an eye to eventual unification, but without any clear idea of how this might take place.

[An idea surprising in its implications]

Some of the bodies of doctrine that are under investigation are rather surprising in their implications. Thus it now seems possible to take seriously an idea that a few years ago would have seemed outlandish: that the language organ of the brain approaches a kind of optimal design. For simple organic systems, conclusions of this sort seem very reasonable, and even partially understood. If a very recent emergent organ that is central to human existence in fact does approach optimal design, that would suggest that in some unknown way it may be the result of the functioning of physical and chemical laws for a brain that has reached a certain level of complexity. And further questions arise for general evolution that are by no means novel, but that have been somewhat at the margins of inquiry until fairly recently. I am thinking of the work of D'Arcy Thompson and Alan Turing, to mention two of the most prominent modern figures.

Similar conceptions, now emerging in a certain form in the study of language, also had a central place in Galileo's thought. In studying acceleration, he wrote, "we have been guided . . . by our insight into the character and properties of nature's other works, in which nature generally employs only the least elaborate, the simplest and easiest of means. For I do not believe that anybody could imagine that swimming or flying could be accomplished in a simpler or easier way than that which fish and birds actually use by natural instinct." In a more theological vein, he held that God "always complies with the easiest and simplest rules, so that His power could be all the more revealed through his most difficult ways." Galileo was guided by the onto- logical principle that "nature is perfect and simple and creates nothing in vain," historian of science Pietro Redondi observes.

The theory of evolution adopts a more complex picture. Evolution is a "tinkerer," in François Jacob's often-quoted phrase. It does the best it can with the materials at hand, but the best may be convoluted, a result of path- dependent evolution, and under physical constraints and often conflicting adaptive demands. Nonetheless, the conception of the perfection of nature remains a vital component of contemporary inquiry into organic nature, at least in its simpler aspects: the polyhedral shells of viruses, cell division into spheres, the appearance of the Fibonacci series in many phenomena of nature, and other aspects of the biological world. How far this goes is a mat- ter of speculation and debate.

Very recently, the issues have come to the fore in the study of language. It has become possible to pose in a productive way the question of "perfec- tion of language": specifically, to ask how closely human language approaches an optimal solution to design conditions that the system must meet to be usable at all. To the extent that the question receives a positive answer, we will have found that nature has—in Galileo's words—"employed the least elabo- rate, the simplest and easiest of means," but in a domain where this would hardly be expected: a very recent and apparently isolated product of evolu- tion, a central component of the most complex organic object known, a com- ponent that is surely at the core of our mental nature, cultural achievement, and curious history.

Perhaps I might add one final remark about the limits of understanding. Many of the questions that inspired the modern scientific revolution are not even on the agenda. These include issues of will and choice, which were taken to be at the heart of the mind-body problem before it was undermined by Newton. There has been very valuable work about how an organism executes a plan for integrated motor action—how a cockroach walks, or a person reaches for a cup on the table. But no one even raises the question of why this plan is executed rather than some other one, apart from the very simplest organisms. Much the same is true even for visual perception, sometimes con- sidered to be a passive or reflexive operation. Recently two cognitive neuro- scientists published a review of progress in solving a problem posed in 1850 by Helmholtz: "even without moving our eyes, we can focus our attention on different objects at will, resulting in very different perceptual experiences of the same visual field." The phrase "at will" points to an area beyond serious empirical inquiry. It remains as much of a mystery as it was for Newton at the end of his life, when he was still seeking some "subtle spirit" that lies hidden in all bodies and that might, without absurdity, account for their properties of attraction and repulsion, the nature and effects of light, sensation, and the way "members of animal bodies move at the command of the will"—all comparable mysteries for Newton, perhaps even "beyond our understanding," like the "principles of motion."

It has become standard practice in the last few years to describe the problem of consciousness as the "hard problem," others being within our grasp, now or imminently. I think there are good reasons to treat such pronouncements with at least mitigated skepticism, particularly when we recognize how sharply understanding declines beyond the simplest systems of nature. History also suggests caution. In the Galilean era, the nature of motion was the "hard problem." "Springing or Elastic Motions" are the "hard rock in Philosophy," Sir William Petty observed, proposing ideas that resemble those soon developed much more richly by Newton. The "hard problem" was that bodies that seem to our senses to be at rest are in a "violent" state, with "a strong endeavor to fly off or recede from one another," in Robert Boyle's words. The problem, he felt, is as obscure as "the Cause and Nature" of gravity, thus supporting his belief in "an intelligent Author or Disposer of Things." Even the skeptical Newtonian Voltaire argued that the ability of humans to "produce a movement" where there was none shows that "there is a God who gave movement" to matter. To Henry More, the transfer of motion from one body to another was an ultimate mystery: if a blue ball hits a red ball, the motion is transferred, but not the color, though both are qualities of the moving blue ball.

These "hard problems" were not solved; rather, abandoned as science turned to its more modest post-Newtonian course. That has been recognized by leading historians of science. Friedrich Lange, in his classic scholarly history of materialism a century ago, observed that we have simply "accustomed ourselves to the abstract notion of forces, or rather to a notion hovering in a mystic obscurity between abstraction and concrete comprehension," a "turning-point" in the history of materialism that removes the doctrine far from the "genuine Materialists" of the seventeenth century and deprives it of much significance. Their "hard problems" disappeared, and there has been little noticeable progress in addressing the other "hard problems" that seemed no less mysterious to Descartes, Newton, Locke, and other leading figures, including the "free will" that is "the noblest thing" we have, manifested most strikingly in normal language use, they believed, for reasons that we should not lightly dismiss.

For some of these mysteries, extraordinary bodies of doctrine have been developed in the past several hundred years, some of the greatest achievements of the human intellect. And there have been remarkable feats of unification as well. How remote the remaining mountain peaks may be, and even just where they are, one can only guess. Within the range of feasible inquiry, there is plenty of work to be done in understanding mental aspects of the world, including human language. And the prospects are surely exciting. We would do well, however, to keep in some corner of our minds Hume's conclusion about "nature's ultimate secrets" and the "obscurity in which they ever did and ever will remain," and particularly the reasoning that led him to that judgment, and its confirmation in the subsequent history of the hard sciences. These are matters that are sometimes too easily forgotten, I suspect, and that merit serious reflection—possibly, someday, even constructive scientific inquiry.

Part II
Anthropology: the cultural environment (vision and reality)

Chapter 5
Rationality/science and post-this-or-that (October 1992)

This discussion [in *Z Papers*] involves people with a large range of shared aspirations and commitments; in some cases at least, friends who have worked and struggled together for many years. I hope, then, that I can be quite frank. And personal, since, to be honest, I don't see much of independent substance to discuss.

[A self-destructive perversion of the values of rational inquiry]

I don't want to mislead, and therefore should say at once that I am not all sure that I am taking part in the discussion. I think I understand some of what is said in the six papers [in the same issue of *Z Papers*], and agree with much of it. What I don't understand is the topic: the legitimacy of "rationality," "science," and "logic" (perhaps modified by "Western")—call the amalgam "rational inquiry" for brevity. I read the papers hoping for some enlightenment on the matter, but, to quote one contributor, "my eyes glaze over and thanks, but I just don't want to participate." When Mike Albert asked me to comment on papers advocating that we abandon or transcend rational inquiry, I refused, and probably would have been wise to keep to that decision. After a good deal of arm-twisting, I will make a few comments, but, frankly, I do not really grasp what the issue is supposed to be.

Many interesting questions have been raised about rational inquiry. There are problems about justification of belief, the status of mathematical truth and of theoretical entities, the use to which rational inquiry is put under particular social and cultural conditions, and the way such conditions, influence its course, and so on. These, however, are not the kinds of topics we are to address; rather, something about the legitimacy of the entire enterprise. That I find perplexing, for several reasons.

First, to take part in a discussion, one must understand the ground rules.

In this case, I don't. In particular, I don't know the answers to such elementary questions as these: Are conclusions to be consistent with premises (maybe even follow from them)? Do facts matter? Or can we string together thoughts as we like, calling it an "argument," and make facts up as we please, taking one story to be as good as another? There are certain familiar ground rules: those of rational inquiry. They are by no means entirely clear, and there have been interesting efforts to criticize and clarify them; but we have enough of a grasp to proceed over a broad range. What seems to be under discussion here is whether we should abide by these ground rules at all (trying to improve them as we proceed). If the answer is that we are to abide by them, then the discussion is over: we've implicitly accepted the legitimacy of rational inquiry. If they are to be abandoned, then we cannot proceed until we learn what replaces the commitment to consistency, responsibility to fact, and other outdated notions. Short of some instruction on this matter, we are reduced to primal screams. I see no hint in the papers here of any new procedures or ideas to replace the old, and therefore remain perplexed.

A second problem has to do with the allusions to "science," "rationality," et cetera, throughout these papers. These targets are sharply criticized, but they are not clearly identified. True, they are assigned certain properties. But these are either irrelevant to the issue raised or unrecognizable to me; in many cases, the properties attributed to rational inquiry are antithetic to it, at least as I have always understood this endeavor.

Perhaps my failure to recognize what is called here "science," et cetera, reflects personal limitations. That could well be, but I wonder. For some forty years, I've been actively engaged in what I, and others, regard as rational inquiry (science, mathematics); for almost all of those years, I've been at the very heart of the beast, at MIT. When I attend seminars, read technical papers in my own or other fields, and work with students and colleagues, I have no problem in recognizing what is before me as rational inquiry. In contrast, the descriptions presented here scarcely resemble anything in my experience in these areas, or understanding of them. So there is a second problem.

With regard to the first problem, I'm afraid I see only one way to proceed: by assuming the legitimacy of rational inquiry. Suppose that such properties as consistency and responsibility to fact are old-fashioned misconceptions, to be replaced by something different—something to be grasped, perhaps, by intuition that I seem to lack. Then I can only confess my inadequacies and inform the reader in advance of the irrelevance of what follows. I recognize that by accepting the legitimacy of rational inquiry and its canons, I am begging the question; the discussion is over before it starts. That is unfair, no doubt, but the alternative escapes me.

With regard to the second problem, since what is called "science," et cetera, is largely unfamiliar to me, let me replace it by X and see if I understand the argument against X. Let's consider several kinds of properties attributed to X, then turn to the proposals for a new direction; quotes below are from the papers criticizing X.

First category. X is dominated by "the white male gender." It is "limited by cultural, racial and gender biases" and "establishes and perpetuates social organization [with] hidden political, social and economic purposes." "The majority in the South has waited for the last four hundred years for compassionate humane uses of X," which is "outside and above the democratic process." X is "thoroughly embedded in capitalist colonialism" and doesn't "end racism or disrupt the patriarchy." X has been invoked by Soviet commissars to bring people to "embrace regimentation, murderous collectivization, and worse"; though no one mentions it, X has been used by Nazi ideologists for the same ends. X's dominance "has gone unchallenged." It has been "used to create new forms of control mediated through political and economic power." Ludicrous claims about X have been made by the "state system," which "used X for astoundingly destructive purposes . . . to create new forms of control mediated through political and economic power as it emerged in each system."

Conclusion: there is "something inherently wrong" with X. We must reject or transcend it, replacing it by something else, and we must instruct poor and suffering people to do likewise. It follows that we must abandon literacy and the arts, which surely satisfy the conditions on X, as well as science. More generally, we must take a vow of silence and induce the world's victims to do likewise, since language and its use typically have all these properties, facts too well known to discuss.

Even more obviously, the crafts and technology should be utterly abolished. It is surprising that several of these critiques appear to be lauding the "practical logical thinking" of "technologists" who concentrate on "the mechanics of things," the "T-knowledge" that is "embedded in practice" and rooted in "experience"; that is, the kind of thinking and practice which, notoriously, have been used for millennia to construct tools of destruction and oppression, under the control of the white males who dominate them (I say "appear to be" because the intent is not entirely clear). The inconsistency is startling, though admittedly, if consistency is to be abandoned or transcended, there is no problem.

Plainly, what I've reviewed can't be the argument; these cannot be the properties of rational inquiry that lead us to abandon (or transcend) it. So let us turn to a second category of properties attributed to X.

[The "two cultures" and their respective limits: no coherent alternative]

X is "E-knowledge" "obtained by logical deduction from firmly established first principles." The statements in X must be "provable"; X demands "absolute proofs." The "most distinctive component of Western E-knowledge" may be its "elaborate procedures for arriving at acceptable first principles." These are among the few attempts here to define or identify the villain.

Furthermore, X "claims to a monopoly of knowledge." It thus denies, say, that I know how to tie my shoes, or know that the sky is dark at night or that walking in the woods is enjoyable, or know the names of my children and something about their concerns, et cetera; all such aspects of my (intuitive) knowledge are far beyond what can be "obtained by logical deduction from firmly established first principles," indeed, well beyond the reach of rational inquiry now and perhaps ever, and are therefore mere "superstition, belief, prejudice," according to advocates of X. Or, if not denying such knowledge outright, X "marginalizes and denigrates" it. X postulates dogmatically that "a predictable end point can be known in advance as an expression of X-achieved truth," and insists upon "grounding values in [this] objective truth." It denies the "provisional and subjective foundations" of agreement in human life and action, and considers itself "the ultimate organizing principle and source of legitimacy in the modern society," a doctrine to which X assigns "axiomatic status." X is "arrogant" and "absolutist." What doesn't fall "within the terms of its hegemony . . . —anger, desire, pleasure, and pain, for example—becomes a site for disciplinary action." The varieties of X are presented as "charms to get us through the dark of a complex world" providing a "resting place" that offers a "sure way of 'knowing' the world or one's position in it." The practitioner of X "screens out feeling, recreating the Other as object to be manipulated," a procedure "made easier because the subjective is described as irrelevant or un-X." "To feel was to be anti-X." "By [the] mid-twentieth century the phrase 'it works' came to be enough for X-ists," who no longer care "why it worked," and lost interest in "what its implications" are. And so on.

I quite agree that X should be consigned to the flames. But what that has to do with our topic escapes me, given that these attributions scarcely rise to the level of a caricature of rational inquiry (science, etc.), at least as I'm familiar with it.

Take the notion of "E-knowledge," the sole definition of science presented here. Not even set theory (hence conventional mathematics) satisfies the definition offered. Nothing in the sciences even resembles it. As for "provability" or "absolute proofs," the notions are foreign to the natural sciences. They appear in the study of abstract models, which are part of pure mathematics until they are applied in the empirical sciences, at which point we no longer have "proof." If "elaborate procedures," or any general procedures, exist "for arriving at acceptable first principles," they have been kept a dark mystery.

Science is tentative, exploratory, questioning, largely learned by doing. One of the world's leading physicists was famous for opening his introductory classes by saying that it doesn't matter what we cover, but what we *dis-cover*—maybe something that will challenge prevailing beliefs if we are fortunate. More advanced work is to a large extent a common enterprise in which students are expected to come up with new ideas, to question and often undermine what they read and are taught, and to somehow pick up, by experience and cooperative inquiry, the trick (which no one begins to comprehend) of discerning important problems and possible solutions to them. Furthermore, even in the simplest cases, proposed solutions (theories, large or small) "outrun empiricism," if by "empiricism" we mean what can be derived from experience by some procedure; one hardly has to move to Einstein to exhibit that universal trait of rational inquiry.

As for the cited properties of X, they do hold of some aspects of human thought and action: elements of organized religion, areas of the humanities and "social sciences" where understanding and insight are thin and it is therefore easier to get away with dogmatism and falsification, perhaps others. But the sciences, at least as I am familiar with them, are as remote from these descriptions as anything in human life. It is not that scientists are inherently more honest, open, or questioning. It is simply that nature and logic impose a harsh discipline: in many domains, one can spin fanciful tales with impunity or keep to the most boring clerical work (sometimes called scholarship); in the sciences, your tales will be refuted and you will be left behind by students who want to understand something about the world, not satisfied to let such matters be "someone else's concern." Furthermore, all of this seems to be the merest truism.

Other properties are attributed to X, including some that are presumably intended as caricature: for instance, that practitioners of X claim "that seventeenth-century Europe answered all the basic questions of humankind for all times to come. . . . "

I've tried to select a fair sample, and apologize if I've failed. As far as I can see, the properties assigned to rational inquiry by the critics fall into two categories. Some hold of human endeavor rather generally and are thus irrelevant to the issue (unless we mean to abandon language, the arts, etc. as well); they clearly reflect the social and cultural conditions that lead to the outcome that is properly deplored. Others do not hold of rational inquiry, indeed, are flatly rejected by it; where detected, they would elicit internal critique.

Several writers appear to regard Leninist-Stalinist tyranny as an embodiment of science and rationality. Thus "the belief in a universal narrative grounded in truth has been undermined by the collapse of political systems that were supposed to [have] produced the New Socialist Man and the New Postcolonial Man." And the "state systems" that "used positive rationality for astoundingly destructive purposes" were guided by "socialist and capitalist ideologies"—a reference, it appears, to radically anti-socialist (Leninist) and anticapitalist (state-capitalist) ideologies. Since "scientific and technological progress were the watchword of socialist and capitalist ideologies," we see that their error and perversity is deep, and we must abandon them, along with any concern for freedom, justice, human rights, democracy, and other "watchwords" of the secular priesthood who have perverted Enlightenment ideals in the interests of the masters.

["White male science" as the struggle to understand hard questions]

Some of the commentary is more familiar to me. One contributor calls for "plural involvement and clear integration in which everyone sits at the table sharing a common consciousness," inspired by "a moral concept which is linked to social trust and affection in which people tell what they think they see and do and allow the basic data and conclusions to be cross examined by peers and non-peers alike"—not a bad description of many seminars and working groups that I've been fortunate enough to be part of over the years. In these, furthermore, it is taken for granted that "knowledge is produced, not found, fought for—not given," a sentiment that will be applauded by anyone who has been engaged in the struggle to understand hard questions, as much as to the activists to whom it is addressed.

There is also at least an element of truth in the statement that the natural sciences are "disembedded from the body, from metaphorical thought, from ethical thought and from the world"—to their credit. Though rational inquiry is rife with metaphor and (uncontroversially) embedded in the world, its intent is to understand, not to construct doctrine that accords with some ethical or other preferences or that is confused by metaphor. Though scientists are human, and cannot get out of their skins, they certainly, if honest, try to overcome the distortions imposed by "body" (in particular, human cognitive structures, with their specific properties) as much as possible. Surface appearances and "natural categories," however central to human life, can mislead, again uncontroversially; we "see" the sunset and the moon illusion, but we have learned that there is more to it than that.

It is also true that "reason separates the 'real' or knowable . . . and the 'not real,'" or at least tries to (without identifying "real" with "knowable")—again, to its credit. At least, I know that I try to make this distinction, whether studying questions that are hard, like the origins of human knowledge, or relatively easy, like the sources and character of U.S. foreign policy. In the latter case, for example, I would try, and urge others to try, to separate the real operative factors from the various tales that are spun in the interests of power and privilege. If that is a fault, I plead guilty, and will compound my guilt by urging others to err in the same way.

Keeping to the personal level, I have spent a lot of my life working on questions such as these, using the only methods I know of—those condemned here as "science," "rationality," "logic," and so on. I therefore read the papers with some hope that they would help me "transcend" these limitations, or perhaps suggest an entirely different course. I'm afraid I was disappointed. Admittedly, that may be my own limitation. Quite regularly, "my eyes glaze over" when I read polysyllabic discourse on the themes of poststructuralism and postmodernism; what I understand is largely truism or error, but that is only a fraction of the total word count. True, there are lots of other things I don't understand: the articles in the current issues of math and physics journals, for example. But there is a difference. In the latter case, I know how to get to understand them, and have done so in cases of particular interest to me; and I also know that people in these fields can explain the contents to me at my level, so that I can gain what (partial) understanding I may want. In contrast, no one seems to be able to explain to me why the latest post-this-and-that is (for the most part) other than truism, error, or gibberish, and I do not know how to proceed. Perhaps the explanation lies in some personal inadequacy, like tone-deafness. Or there may be other reasons. The question is not strictly relevant here, and I won't pursue it.

Continuing with my personal quest for help in dealing with problems to which I have devoted a large part of my life, I read here that I should recognize that "there are limits to what we know" (something I've been arguing, in accord with an ancient rationalist tradition, for many years). I should advance beyond "panopticized rationality" (which I might happily do, if I knew what it was) and should not be "transferring God into knowable nature" (thanks). Since "it is now obvious" that its "very narrow and surface idea of rationality and rationalism" has undermined "the canon of Western thought," I should adopt "a new notation system which laid out moral and historical propositions" in a "rationality [that is] deepened" (thanks again). I should keep to "rebuttable axioms," which means, I take it, hypotheses that are taken to be open to question—the practice adopted without a second thought in all scientific work, unless the intent is that I should drop *modus ponens* and the axioms of arithmetic; apparently so, since I am also to abandon "absolutism or absolute proofs," which are unknown in science but, admittedly, sometimes assumed with regard to the most elementary parts of logic and arithmetic (a matter also subject to much internal controversy in foundational inquiries).

I should also follow the lead of those who "assert that there is a common consciousness of all thought and matter," from human to "vegetable or mineral," a proposal that should impinge directly on my own attempts for many years to understand what Hume called "the secret springs and origins, by which the human mind is actuated in its operations"—or might, if I had the slightest idea of what it means. I am also enjoined to reject the idea that "numbers are outside of human history" and to regard Goedel's incompleteness theorem as "a situation of inability" of the twentieth century, which to my old-fashioned ear sounds like saying that the irrationality of the square root of two—a disturbing discovery at the time—was "a situation of inability" of classical Greece. How human history or the way rationality "is presently defined" impinges on these truths (or so I thought them to be), I again fail to see.

I should regard "truth" not "as an essence" but "as a social heuristic," one "predicated on intersubjective trust and story telling whether through narrative or numbers and signs." I should recognize that "scientific endeavor is also in the world of story and myth creation," no better or worse than other "stories and myths"; modern physics may "have more funding and better PR" than astrology but is otherwise on a par. That suggestion does in fact help solve my problems. If I can just tell stories about the questions that I've been struggling with for many years, life will indeed be easier; the proposal "has all the advantages of theft over honest toil," as Bertrand Russell once said in a similar connection.

I should also "favor particular directions in scientific and social inquiry because of their likely positive social outcomes," thus joining the overwhelming mass of scientists and engineers—though we commonly differ on what are "positive social outcomes," and no hints are given here as to how that issue is to be resolved. The implication also seems to be that we should abandon "theories or experiments" favored "because of their supposed beauty and elegance," which amounts to saying that we should abandon the effort to understand the mysteries of the world; and by the same logic, presumably, should no longer be deluded by literature, music, and the visual arts.

I'm afraid I didn't learn much from these injunctions. And it is hard for me to see how friends and colleagues in the "non-white world" will learn more from the advice given by "a handful of scientists" who inform them that they should not "move on the tracks of Western science and technology," but should prefer other "stories" and "myths"—which ones, we are not told, though astrology is mentioned. They'll find that advice a great help with their problems, and those of the "non-white world" generally. I confess that my personal sympathies lie with the volunteers of Tecnica.

In fact, the entire idea of "white male science" reminds me, I'm afraid, of "Jewish physics." Perhaps it is another inadequacy of mine, but when I read a scientific paper, I can't tell whether the author is white or is male. The same is true of discussion of work in class, the office, or somewhere else. I rather doubt that the non-white, non-male students, friends, and colleagues with whom I work would be much impressed with the doctrine that their thinking and understanding differ from "white male science" because of their "culture or gender and race." I suspect that "surprise" would not be quite the proper word for their reaction.

[A common human attribute providing means of emancipation and liberation]

I find it depressing, frankly, to read learned left discourse on science and technology as a white male preserve, and then to walk through the corridors at MIT and see the significant results of the efforts to change that traditional pattern on the part of scientists and engineers, many of them very remote from the understanding of "positive social outcomes" that we largely share. They have dedicated serious and often successful efforts to overcome traditional exclusiveness and privilege because they tend to agree with Descartes (as I do) that the capacity for understanding in the "profoundest sciences" and "high feeling" are a common human attribute, and that those who lack the opportunity to exercise the capacity to inquire, create, and understand are missing out on some of life's most wonderful experiences. One contributor condemns this humane belief for labeling others as "defective." By the same logic, we should condemn the idea that the capacity to walk is a common human possession over a very broad range.

Acting on the same belief, many scientists, not too long ago, took an active part in the lively working-class culture of the day, seeking to compensate for the class character of the cultural institutions through programs of workers' education or by writing books on mathematics, science, and other topics for the general public. Nor have left intellectuals been alone in such work, by any means. It strikes me as remarkable that their left counterparts today should seek to deprive oppressed people not only of the joys of understanding and insight, but also of tools of emancipation, informing us that the "project of the Enlightenment" is dead, that we must abandon the "illusions" of science and rationality—a message that will gladden the hearts of the powerful, delighted to monopolize these instruments for their own use. They will be no less delighted to hear that science (E-knowledge) is intrinsically a "knowledge system that legitimates the authority of the boss," so that any challenge to such authority is a violation of rationality itself—a radical change from the days when workers' education was considered a means of emancipation and liberation. One recalls the days when the evangelical church taught not-dissimilar lessons to the unruly masses as part of what E. P. Thompson called "the psychic processes of counter-revolution," as their heirs do today in peasant societies of Central America.

I'm sorry if the conclusion sounds harsh; the question we should consider is whether it is correct. I think it is.

It is particularly striking that these self-destructive tendencies should appear at a time when the overwhelming majority of the population regards the economic system as "inherently unfair" and wants to change it. Through the Reagan years, the public continued its drift toward social democratic ideas, while the shreds of what existed were torn away. Furthermore, belief in the basic moral principles of traditional socialism is surprisingly high: to mention merely one example, almost half the population considers the phrase "from each according to his ability, to each according to his need" to be such an obvious truth that they attribute it to the U.S. Constitution, a text taken to be akin to holy writ. What is more, with Soviet tyranny finally overthrown, one long-standing impediment to the realization of these ideals is now removed. With limited contribution by left intellectuals, large segments of the population have involved themselves in urgent and pressing problems: repression, environmental concerns, and much else. The Central American solidarity movements of the 1980s are a dramatic example, with the direct involvement in the lives of the victims that was a novel and remarkable feature of protest and activism. These popular efforts have also led to a good deal of understanding of how the world works, again, with very limited contributions from left intellectuals, if we are to be honest.

Particularly noteworthy is the divergence of popular attitudes from mainstream ideology. After twenty-five years of unremitting propaganda, including ten years of Reaganism, over 70 percent of the population still regard the Vietnam War as "fundamentally wrong and immoral," not a "mistake." Days before the U.S.-UK bombing began in the Gulf, the population, by two to one, favored a negotiated settlement with "linkage" rather than war. In these and numerous other cases, including domestic affairs and problems, the thoughts are individual and private; people have rarely if ever heard them publicly expressed. In part, that reflects the effectiveness of the system of cultural management; in part, the choices of left intellectuals.

Quite generally, there is a popular basis for addressing the human concerns that have long been part of "the Enlightenment project." One element that is lacking is the participation of left intellectuals.

However meritorious motives may be, the abandonment of these endeavors, in my opinion, reflects yet another triumph for the culture of power and privilege, and contributes to it. The same abandonment makes a notable contribution to the endless project of creating a version of history that will serve the reigning institutions. During periods of popular activism, many people are able to discern truths that are concealed by the cultural managers, and to learn a good deal about the world; Indochina and Central America are two striking recent examples. When activism declines, the commissar class, which never falters in its task, regains command. As left intellectuals abandon the field, truths that were once understood fade into individual memories, history is reshaped into an instrument of power, and the ground is laid for the enterprises to come.

The critique of "science" and "rationality" has many merits, which I haven't discussed. But as far as I can see, where valid and useful the critique is largely devoted to the perversion of the values of rational inquiry as they are "wrongly used" in a particular institutional setting. What is presented here as a deeper critique of their nature seems to me based on beliefs about the enterprise and its guiding values that have little basis. No coherent alternative is suggested, as far as I can discern; the reason, perhaps, is that there is none. What is suggested is a path that leads directly to disaster for people who need help—which means everyone, before too long.

APPENDIX
Comment on the Kansas school curriculum decision (September 1999)

In the ZNet Sustainer's Forum System Chomsky was asked whether he was "perturbed" by the Kansas school curriculum decision against teaching natural selection. His answer follows.

Very much. Also by the decision to eliminate the Big Bang—that is, to get rid of fundamentals of physics as well as the fundamentals of biology from the basic curriculum. More generally, this is another long step in the project of redesigning the school curriculum in ways that will reduce the possibility that students will have the intellectual tools to escape the fundamentalist fanaticism that the designers of the new curriculum prefer. One should not be fooled by the rhetoric that is used to disguise what they are doing, for example, the pretense that anyone is still allowed to do as they like. Technically true, but the pressures to conform will, of course, be substantial. And we can guess how much attention students and teachers will give to material that is placed under a cloud and is excluded from the core curriculum and examinations.

This is, as intended, a serious blow to integrity and honesty. If it were taking place in Andorra, maybe one could just laugh, although that would be unfair to Andorrans. They deserve much better than the rule of superstitious hysterics and extreme authoritarians, who try to instill obedience to their holy texts and chosen divinities—and we should not fail to see that the terms are appropriate, if anything too kind. But when this is happening in the richest and by far the most powerful country in the world, with a huge capacity for destruction and harm, it's no laughing matter. And it's not just Kansas. This is just one part of a wave of astonishing irrationality and fanaticism; other states have introduced similar measures. Recall as well a simple fact about the economics of the textbook industry. Publishers want to have a mass market, furthermore undifferentiated. It's expensive to produce and market separate texts for different parts of the country. Accordingly, there is a tendency, sometimes very strong, to move to the lowest common denominator. If a text won't sell in Kansas for reasons X, Y, Z, then cut out the "offending material" for the whole country. The consequences are obvious and doubtless just what are intended by the authoritarian extremists who seek to impose their religious doctrines on the population at large.

There have for years been comparative studies of religious fanaticism and factors that correlate with it. By and large, it tends to decline with increasing industrialization and education. The United States, however, is off the chart, ranking near devastated peasant societies. About half the population believes the world was created a few thousand years ago: the justification for the belief is that that is what they were ordered to believe by authority figures to whom they were taught one must subordinate oneself. And on and on. One can easily understand why great efforts should be made to keep the public at an extremely low cultural and intellectual level, subordinated to power and blind obedience to authority. But it is something that should elicit very great concern.

It's also worth noting the hypocrisy. The same newspaper stories showed pictures of the Ten Commandments posted on walls of classrooms (a version of them, at least). Apart from the obvious questions of establishing a particular choice of religious doctrine within the public school system, have a look at what children are to be taught to believe—on the (admittedly weak) assumption that anyone is expected to take the words seriously. Thus the self-designated chief of the gods orders them not to worship any of the other gods before him: in this polytheistic system, he is top dog. They are told not to make "graven images" (which means statues, pictures, etc.)—that is, they are taught that all the priests, ministers, teachers, and other authority figures are liars and hypocrites. There's more—all familiar in the seventeenth and eighteenth centuries, now to be driven from the mind by the autocrats who hope to gain control of the cultural system and demolish the threat of independent thought and rational analysis and discussion.

No slight matter, in my opinion.

Chapter 6

Equality: language development, human intelligence,

and social organization (March 1976)

I would like to comment on three notions of equality, namely, equality of rights, equality of condition, and equality of endowment—and more generally, the nature of that endowment, or briefly, human nature and its variety. The last of these questions is essentially a matter of fact, poorly understood, but plainly in the domain of the natural sciences, to be answered, as best we can, by unprejudiced inquiry. The first two questions raise serious questions of value. All of these notions demand careful analysis, far beyond anything I can attempt here.

If the discussion of equality of rights and condition is to be at all serious—in particular, if it is to pertain to choice of action—then questions of fact inevitably intrude. Discussion becomes socially irrelevant, whatever interest it may retain as an intellectual exercise, to the extent that relevant facts are not accurately presented. In much current discussion of problems of equality, they are not accurately presented.

[Government programs in an inegalitarian society]

Consider, for example, a series of articles on "egalitarianism" by John Cobbs in *Business Week* (December 1975), which is not untypical of current debate over these issues. Cobbs takes as his starting point the factual assumption that "in one way or another, all the government's social programs are equalizers" (although, he adds, federal programs do "not always achieve this result"). Does this factual premise even approximate the truth? A strong case can be made to the contrary. Subsidies to higher education, for example, tend to be roughly proportional to family income. The enormous federal highway program has been in large measure a subsidy to commercial trucking (and, arguably, has indirectly raised the cost of living) and to major corporations that make their profits from petroleum and from modes of transportation that carry a substantial social cost. Nor can the government housing programs of the past thirty years be readily described as "equalizers." For example, the programs that in my own city destroyed "a low-income, predominantly Italian neighborhood" on Beacon Hill and replaced it with "high-income apartment towers financed with government-insured loans"—I quote from MIT professor of architecture Robert Goodman in a review of federal housing programs that he describes as an "effective way of exploiting the poor."[1]

Or consider the government subsidies to arms producers and agribusiness, the latter in part through subsidy of research into agricultural technology designed for the interests of large corporations, which is undertaken in government-supported universities. Or consider the vast government expenditures to ensure a favorable international climate for business operations. In a highly inegalitarian society, it is most unlikely that government programs will be equalizers. Rather, it is to be expected that they will be designed and manipulated by private power for its own benefits; and to a significant degree the expectation is fulfilled. It is not very likely that matters could be otherwise in the absence of mass popular organizations that are prepared to struggle for their rights and interests. An effort to develop and implement government programs that really were equalizers would lead to a form of class war, and in the present state of popular organization and distribution of effective power, there can hardly be much doubt as to who would win—a fact that some "populists," who rightly deplore the government programs that benefit private economic power, sometimes tend to ignore.

Discussion of the role of the state in a society based on the principle of private power must not neglect the fact that "generally speaking, capitalism must be regarded as an economy of unpaid costs, 'unpaid' insofar as a substantial proportion of the actual costs of production remain unaccounted for in entrepreneurial outlays; instead they are shifted to, and ultimately borne by, third persons or by the community as a whole."[2] A serious analysis of the government's social programs—not to speak of its programs of economic intervention, military force, and the like—will assess the function of these programs in paying social costs that cannot realistically be relegated to a footnote. There may be a residual sense to the notion that the state serves as an equalizer, in that without its intervention the destructive forces of capitalism would demolish social existence and the physical environment, a fact that has been well understood by the masters of the private economy, who have regularly called upon the state to restrain and organize these forces. But the common idea that the government acts as a social equalizer can hardly be put forth as a general principle.

[Egalitarian efficiency and egalitarian freedom]

As a second example, consider the widely held doctrine that moves toward equality of condition entail costs in efficiency and restrictions of freedom. The alleged inverse relation between attained equality and efficiency involves empirical claims that may or may not be true. If this relation holds, one would expect to find that worker-owned and -managed industry in egalitarian communities is less efficient than matched counterparts that are privately owned and managed and that rent labor in the so-called free market.

Research on the matter is not extensive, but it tends to show that the opposite is true.[3] Harvard economist Stephen Marglin has argued that harsh measures were necessary in early stages of the industrial system to overcome the natural advantages of cooperative enterprise, which left no room for masters, and there is a body of empirical evidence in support of the conclusion that "when workers are given control over decisions and goal setting, productivity rises dramatically."[4] From another point of view, Cambridge economist J. E. Meade has argued that efficiency and equitable distribution of income can be reconciled if measures are taken "to equalize the distribution of the ownership of private property and to increase the net amount of property which was in social ownership."[5] In general, the relation between equality and efficiency is hardly a simple or well-established one, despite many facile pronouncements on the matter.

Turning to the relation between equality and freedom, allegedly inverse, we also find non-trivial questions. Workers' control of production certainly increases freedom along some dimensions—extremely important ones, in my judgment—just as it eliminates the fundamental inequality between the person compelled to sell his labor power to survive and the person privileged to purchase it, if he so chooses. At the very least, we should bear in mind the familiar observation that freedom is illusion and mockery when conditions for the exercise of free choice do not exist. We only enter Marx's "realm of freedom" when labor is no longer "determined by necessity and mundane considerations,"[6] an insight that is hardly the precept of radicals and revolutionaries alone. Thus Vico observed that there is no liberty when people are "drowned . . . in a sea of usury" and must "pay off their debts by work and toil."[7] David Ellerman puts the issue well in an important essay:

> It is a veritable mainstay of capitalist thought (not to mention so-called "right-wing libertarianism") that the moral flaws of chattel slavery have not survived in capitalism since the workers, unlike the slaves, are free people making voluntary wage contracts. But it is only that, in the case of capitalism, the denial of natural

rights is less complete so that the worker has a residual legal personality as a free "commodity-owner." He is thus allowed to voluntarily put his own working life to traffic. When a robber denies another person's right to make an infinite number of other choices besides losing his money or his life and the denial is backed up by a gun, then this is clearly robbery even though it might be said that the victim is making a "voluntary choice" between his remaining options. When the legal system itself denies the natural rights of working people in the name of the prerogatives of capital, and this denial is sanctioned by the legal violence of the state, then the theorists of "libertarian" capitalism do not proclaim institutional robbery, but rather they celebrate the "natural liberty" of working people to choose between the remaining options of selling their labor as a commodity and being unemployed.[8]

Considering such questions as these, we can hardly rest comfortably with the assumption that freedom declines as equality—for example, in control over resources and means of production—increases. It may be true that equality is inversely related to the freedom to dispose of and make use of property under the social arrangements of capitalism, but the latter condition is not to be simply identified as "freedom."

I do not even consider here the immeasurable loss incurred when a person is converted to a tool of production, so that, as Adam Smith phrased it, he "has no occasion to exert his understanding, or to exercise his invention" and "he naturally loses, therefore, the habit of such exertion and generally becomes as stupid and ignorant as it is possible for a human creature to become," his mind falling "into that drowsy stupidity which, in a civilized society, seems to benumb the understanding of almost all the inferior ranks of people."[9] What is the loss in "efficiency" and social product resulting from this enforced stupidity? What does it mean to say that a person driven to such "drowsy stupidity" by his conditions of work still remains "free"?

[A theory of justice]

When we ask ourselves what would be a just and decent society, we are faced by conflicting intuitions, standards that are imprecise and poorly formulated, and significant questions of fact. Relying on some of these intuitions to the exclusion of others, we may seem to escape complexity and conflict, but at the risk of pursuing a mere logical exercise, and not a very interesting one at that. The hazards are well illustrated by some contemporary discussion. Consider, for example, the "entitlement theory of justice," now enjoying a certain vogue. According to this theory, a person has a right to whatever he has acquired by means that are just. If, by luck or labor or ingenuity, a person acquires such-

and-such, then he is entitled to keep it and dispose of it as he wills, and a just society will not infringe on this right.

One can easily determine where such a principle might lead. It is entirely possible that by legitimate means—say, luck supplemented by contractual arrangements "freely undertaken" under pressure of need—one person might gain control of the necessities of life. Others are then free to sell themselves to this person as slaves, if he is willing to accept them. Otherwise, they are free to perish. Without extra question-begging conditions, the society is just.

The argument has all the merits of a proof that 2 + 2 = 5. Presented with such a proof, we may be sufficiently intrigued to try to find the source of error in faulty reasoning or incorrect assumptions. Or we may disregard it and proceed to more important matters. In a field with real intellectual substance, such as mathematics, it may be interesting, and has in the past proven really fruitful, to pursue such questions. In considering the problems of society and human life, the enterprise is of dubious value. Suppose that some concept of a "just society" is advanced that fails to characterize the situation just described as unjust, to an extreme (however the outcome may have come about). Then one of two conclusions is in order. We may conclude that the concept is simply unimportant and of no interest as a guide to thought or action, since it fails to apply properly even in such an elementary case as this. Or we may conclude that the concept advanced is to be dismissed in that it fails to correspond to the pre-theoretical notion that it intends to capture in clear cases. If our intuitive concept of justice is clear enough to rule social arrangements of the sort described as grossly unjust, then the sole interest of a demonstration that this outcome might be "just" under a given "theory of justice" lies in the inference by reductio ad absurdum to the conclusion that the theory is hopelessly inadequate. While it may capture some partial intuition regarding justice, it evidently neglects others.

The real question to be raised about theories that fail so completely to capture the concept of justice in its significant and intuitive sense is why they arouse such interest. Why are they not simply dismissed out of hand on grounds of this failure, which is so striking in clear cases? Perhaps the answer is, in part, the one given by Edward Greenberg in a discussion of some recent work on the entitlement theory of justice. After reviewing empirical and conceptual shortcomings, he observes that such work "plays an important function in the process of . . . 'blaming the victim,' and of protecting property against egalitarian onslaughts by various nonpropertied groups."[10] An ideological defense of privileges, exploitation, and private power will be welcomed, regardless of its merits.

These matters are of no small importance to poor and oppressed people here and elsewhere. Forms of social control that sufficed to ensure obedience in an expanding economy have lost their efficacy in times of stagnation. Ideas that circulate in the faculty club and executive suite can be transmuted into ideological instruments to confuse and demoralize. Furthermore, in 1976 we can hardly ignore the fact that the power of the American state has been employed, on a massive scale, to impose capitalist social forms and ideological principles on unwilling and resisting victims throughout the world. Academic ideologists and political commentators in the media may choose to interpret history in other terms, but the business press is considerably more accurate in observing that the "stable world order for business operations," "the international economic structure, under which U.S. companies have flourished since the end of World War II," has been dependent on the organized violence of the state: "No matter how negative a development, there was always the umbrella of American power to contain it," though in the world after Vietnam, they fear, this may no longer be so.[11]

I once visited a village in Laos in the midst of which there was a pleasant lake that had, at one time, served as the water supply for the village and a place where villagers could relax and enjoy themselves. One powerful individual had succeeded in gaining control of all access to the lake, now fenced off. To obtain water, villagers had to trudge several miles. They could see the lake beyond the fence, but it was no longer available to them. Suppose that ownership of that lake had been attained by means that were "just," as certainly might have been the case in principle.[12] Would we then conclude that the village was a "just society" in this respect? Would we seriously urge the villagers to accept this consequence as only right and just? The government backed—it would be more accurate to say imposed—by the United States implicitly took that position. The Pathet Lao organized the peasants of Laos to overcome such forms of "justice." So substantial was their success that the United States government undertook to demolish much of rural Laos in a war that was "secret," in that the free press in our free society freely chose to keep it secret for a long period while thousands of peasants were murdered and dispossessed. We now freely choose to forget what has happened and erase it from history, or to dismiss it as an unfortunate though minor incident, an example of our "blundering efforts to do good," our "good intentions" mysteriously transmuted into "bad policy" through our ignorance, error, and naïveté.[13] In fact, the question of "justice," in crucial cases such as this one, is by no means abstract and remote, and we would do well to think seriously about it.

Similar questions arise in a stark form in our own society, one that has a substantial degree of freedom by world standards. For example, we have free access to information, in principle. In the case of the secret war in Laos, it was possible to ascertain the facts—much too late—by visiting the country, speaking to people in refugee camps, and reading reports in the foreign press and ultimately even our own. But freedom of that sort, though important for the privileged, is socially rather meaningless. For the mass of the population of the United States, there was no possibility, in the real world, to gain access to that information, let alone to comprehend its significance. The distribution of power and privilege effectively limits the access to information and the ability to escape the framework of doctrine imposed by ideological institutions: the mass media, the journals of opinion, the schools and universities.

The same is true in every domain. In principle, we have a variety of important rights under the law. But we also know just how much these mean, in practice, to people who are unable to purchase them. We have the right of free expression, though some can shout louder than others by reason of power, wealth, and privilege. We can defend our legal rights through the courts—insofar as we understand these rights and can afford the costs. All of this is obvious and hardly worth extended comment. In a perfectly functioning capitalist democracy, with no illegitimate abuse of power, freedom will be in effect a kind of commodity; effectively, a person will have as much of it as he can buy. We readily understand why the powerful and the privileged often rise to the defense of personal freedom, of which they are the chief beneficiaries in practice, though they manage to look the other way when, for example, the national political police become involved in political assassination and destruction of political groups that attempt to organize among the poor, as happened in Chicago not very long ago, to the resounding silence of the national press and journals of opinion.[14]

[Human nature and social order]

I have only barely touched on some of the questions that arise when we consider problems of equality and freedom. I have as yet said nothing at all about the third notion of equality, namely, "equality of endowment." Here, too, there is a widely held doctrine that deserves examination. Again, it is expressed clearly by John Cobbs. He poses what he takes to be "the great intellectual dilemma of the egalitarians," namely, that "a look at the real world demonstrates that some men are smarter than others." Is it fair to insist, he asks, that "the fast and slow . . . should all arrive at the same condition at the same time?" Is it fair to insist on equality of condition achieved, when natural endowment so plainly varies?

Presumably it is the case that in our "real world" some combination of attributes is conducive to success in responding to "the demands of the economic system." Let us agree, for the sake of discussion, that this combination of attributes is in part a matter of native endowment.

Why does this (alleged) fact pose an "intellectual dilemma" to egalitarians? Note that we can hardly claim much insight into just what the relevant combination of attributes may be. I know of no reason to believe, and do not believe, that "being smart" has much to do with it. One might suppose that some mixture of avarice, selfishness, lack of concern for others, aggressiveness, and similar characteristics plays a part in getting ahead and "making it" in a competitive society based on capitalist principles. Others may counter with their own prejudices. Whatever the correct collection of attributes may be, we may ask what follows from the fact, if it is a fact, that some partially inherited combination of attributes tends to lead to material success. All that follows, so far as I can see, is a comment on our particular social and economic arrangements. One can easily imagine a society in which physical prowess, willingness to murder, ability to cheat, and so on, would tend to bring success; we hardly need resort to imagination. The egalitarian might respond, in all such cases, that the social order should be changed so that the collection of attributes that tends to bring success will no longer do so. He might even argue that in a more decent society, the attributes that now lead to success would be recognized as pathological, and that gentle persuasion might be a proper means to help people to overcome their unfortunate malady. Again we return to the question: What is a just and decent social order? The "egalitarian" faces no special "intellectual dilemmas" distinct in character from those that confront the advocates of a different social order.

A standard response is that it is just human nature to pursue power and material interest by any means so long as one can get away with it. Let us suppose that human nature is such that under given social conditions these admirable traits manifest themselves or, more accurately, that people with such tendencies will prosper. Suppose further that wealth and power, once attained, can be employed to extend and protect such privilege, as has been the case under industrial capitalism. The obvious question, of course, is whether other social arrangements might be brought into being that would not encourage these tendencies but would rather be conducive to the flourishing of other traits that are no less part of our common nature: solidarity, concern, sympathy, and kindness, for example.

Discussion of egalitarian views is often misleading, in that the criticism of such views is commonly directed against a straw-man opponent, as egalitarians have been quick to point out.[15] In fact, "equality of condition," much deplored by contemporary ideologists, has rarely been the express goal of reformers or revolutionaries, at least on the left. In Marx's utopia, "the development of human energy" is to be taken as "an end in itself" as humans escape the "realm of necessity" so that questions of freedom can be seriously raised. The guiding principle, reiterated to the point of cliché, is "from each according to his abilities, to each according to his needs." The principle of "equality of condition" is nowhere invoked. If one person needs medical treatment and another is more fortunate, they are not to be granted an equal amount of medical care, and the same is true of other human needs.

Libertarian socialists who objected to the theory of proletarian dictatorship also saw little merit in "egalitarianism" as such and in fact condemned "authoritarian Socialism" for failing to comprehend that "Socialism will be free or it will not be at all":

> In the prison, in the cloister, or in the barracks one finds a fairly high degree of economic equality, as all the inmates are provided with the same dwelling, the same food, the same uniform, and the same tasks. The ancient Inca state in Peru and the Jesuit state in Paraguay had brought equal economic provision for every inhabitant to a fixed system, but in spite of this the vilest despotism prevailed there, and the human being was merely the automaton of a higher will on whose decisions he had not the slightest influence. It was not without reason that Proudhon saw in a "Socialism" without freedom the worst form of slavery. The urge for social justice can only develop properly and be effective when it grows out of a man's sense of freedom and responsibility, and is based upon it.[16]

For Rocker, anarchism was "voluntary socialism," and "freedom is not an abstract philosophical concept, but the vital concrete possibility for every human being to bring to full development all capacities and talents with which nature has endowed him, and turn them to social account." Marx would not have disagreed, and the basic conceptions can be traced back to earlier libertarian thought.[17] These ideas deserve close attention as the most serious expression, in my view, of a concept of a just and decent society that incorporates serious and critical principles while attending to significant social and historical facts.

Note that for such socialists as Marx, Bakunin, Rocker, and others of the left, there is no "intellectual dilemma" arising from inequality of endowment. Libertarian socialists, at least, looked forward to a "federation of free communities which shall be bound to one another by their common economic and social interests and arrange their affairs by mutual agreement and free contract," "a free association of all productive forces based upon co-operative labor, which would have for its sole purpose the satisfying of the necessary requirements of every member of society."[18] In such a society, there is no reason why rewards should be contingent on some collection of personal attributes, however selected. Inequality of endowment is simply the human condition—a fact for which we may be thankful; one vision of hell is a society of interchangeable parts. It carries with it no implications concerning social rewards.

In a socialist society, as envisioned by the authentic left, a central purpose will be that the necessary requirements of every member of society be satisfied.[19] We may assume that these "necessary requirements" will be historically conditioned in part, and will develop along with the expansion and enrichment of material and intellectual culture. But "equality of condition" is no desideratum, as we approach Marx's "realm of freedom." Individuals will differ in their aspirations, their abilities, and their personal goals. For some person, the opportunity to play the piano ten hours a day may be an overwhelming personal need; for another, not. As material circumstances permit, these differential needs should be satisfied in a decent society, as in healthy family life. In functioning socialist societies such as the Israeli kibbutzim, questions of this sort constantly arise. I cannot imagine that it is possible to formulate very strong general principles to resolve conflicts and measure individual opportunity against social demands. Honest people will differ in their assessments and will try to reach agreement through discussion and sympathetic consideration of the needs of others.

The problems are not exotic ones; they arise constantly in functioning social groups, such as the family. We are not accustomed to think beyond such small groups, given the inhuman and pathological premises of competitive capitalism and its perverse ideology. It is no wonder that "fraternity" has traditionally been inscribed on the revolutionary banner alongside "liberty" and "equality." Without bonds of solidarity, sympathy, and concern for others, a socialist society is unthinkable. We may only hope that human nature is so constituted that these elements of our essential nature may flourish and enrich our lives, once the social conditions that suppress them are overcome. Socialists are committed to the belief that we are not condemned to live in a society based on greed, envy, and hate. I know of no way to prove that they are right, but there are also no grounds for the common belief that they must be wrong.

The distinction between equality of condition and equality of rights loses its apparent sharpness when we attend to it more closely. Suppose that individuals, at each stage of their personal existence, are to be accorded their intrinsic human rights; in this sense, "equality of rights" is to be upheld. Then conditions must be such that they can enjoy these rights. To the extent that inequality of condition impairs the exercise of these rights, it is illegitimate and is to be overcome in a decent society. What, then, are these rights? If they include the right to develop one's capacities to the fullest, to realize what Marx calls the "species character" of "free conscious activity" and "productive life" in free associations based on constructive, creative work, then conditions must be equalized at least to the rather considerable extent required to guarantee these rights, if equality of rights is to be maintained. The vision of the left, then, blurs the distinction between equality of rights and condition, denies that inequality of endowment merits or demands corresponding inequality of reward, rejects equality of condition as a principle in itself, and sees no intellectual dilemma in the conflict between egalitarian principles, properly understood, and variability of endowment. Rather, we must face the problems of a repressive and unjust society, emerging with greater clarity as we progress beyond the realm of necessity.

Criticism of egalitarianism misfires when directed against at least this segment of the left. But one may legitimately raise other questions. Thus it might be argued that the intuitions that lead to this vision of a decent and just society conflict with others: for example, the belief that one must pay for one's sins or errors. Or it might be argued that all of this is utopian nonsense and that wage slavery and authoritarian structures such as the modern business enterprise are an inescapable necessity in a complex society. Or one may consider a more limited time frame and work for "more equality" and "more justice," putting aside the question of further goals and the principles that inspire them.

Here we enter the grounds of legitimate and useful controversy. For example, if an argument can be constructed that advanced industrial societies cannot survive unless some people rent themselves to others, some people give orders while others march to the beat of a drum, then it should be taken seriously. If correct, it undermines the socialist vision. But the burden of proof rests on those who insist that some fundamental conditions of repression, exploitation, or inequality are inescapable. To say merely that things have never been otherwise is not very convincing. On these grounds, one could have demonstrated, in the eighteenth century, that capitalist democracy is an impossible dream.

Can we seriously raise the question "What is human nature?" Can we make some progress toward the understanding of human nature? Can we develop a theory of intrinsic human needs, of the nature of human capacities and their variation in the species, of the forms these capacities will assume under varied social conditions—a theory that will have some consequences or at least be suggestive with regard to questions of human and social import? In principle, we enter at this point into the domain of scientific inquiry, though it is potential rather than actual science.

The proposition that humans differ in fundamental respects from other organisms in the natural world is hardly open to serious dispute. If a Martian scientist were to study earthly matters, he would have little doubt on this score. The conclusion would be particularly obvious if he were to observe changes in the life of organisms over an extended period. The humans of today are, with at most minor modifications, of the same genetic constitution as their forebears many millennia ago, but patterns of life have changed remarkably, particularly in the past few hundred years. This is not true of other organisms, except as a result of human intervention. A Martian observer would also be struck by the fact that at any moment of history there are remnants of earlier ways, even of Stone Age conditions, among humans who do not differ significantly in genetic constitution from those whose mode of life has changed most radically. He would note, in short, that humans are unique in the natural world in that they have a history, cultural diversity, and cultural evolution. In these respects, our hypothetical Martian might well be intrigued by the question "Why is this so?"

The same question has, of course, been raised in one or another form since the earliest recorded origins of human thought. That is natural enough. Humans naturally seek to define their place in the world of nature. The question "What is human nature?"—what is the collection of attributes that so radically distinguishes the human species from the rest of the organic world— is a profound and essentially unanswered question of science. It has been held to lie beyond the range of scientific inquiry, in that the specific difference of humans lies in their possession of an immortal soul that cannot be further understood by the methods of science. We might note that the inaccessibility of the soul to study is no essential conclusion of dualist theory. One might argue, say, on Cartesian grounds, that humans and humans alone possess some non-material quality—Cartesian mind; and yet one might maintain, as I think the Cartesians would have done, that there can be a science of mind. But putting this issue aside, there are quite unique properties of human intelligence, elements of distinctive human nature. Assuming no a priori limits to inquiry, it is an empirical question, a question of science, to determine what human nature may be.

The puzzlement of our hypothetical Martian observer, with regard to the uniqueness of the human species, would perhaps mount if he knew a little modern biology. Thus it seems to be the case that the quantity of DNA in the fertilized egg is not very different for a mouse, a cow, a chimpanzee, or a person. Structural differences revealed only at a more refined level of analysis are evidently responsible for the precise course and character of embryological development. In a complex and intricate system, small differences in initial condition may have major consequences for the form, size, structure, and function of the resulting organism and its components. The same phenomenon is a commonplace in the natural sciences. It can also be easily demonstrated in the investigation of a system of the intricacy of human language. Given a linguistic theory of sufficient range and complexity, it is easy to show that small modifications in general conditions imposed on rules may lead to very curious and varied changes among predicted phenomena, because of the complex interactions that take place as a sentence is generated by a system of rules operating under these conditions.

Assuming that modern biology is essentially on the right track, it must be that natural selection gave rise somehow to a particular quality of genetic complexity, producing "a new force: the human mind," a "unique instrument [that] gave for the first time to a biological species the power to alter its relation to the environment . . . by conscious manipulation of the surrounding world," as well as the means for expression of thought and emotion, for creation of art and science, for planning actions and assessing their consequences over a hitherto inconceivable range. It is often assumed, quite plausibly, that in the development of this unique instrument, the human mind, "the critical step must have been the invention of language."[20] In some manner that is still poorly understood, genetic endowment was modified to produce a creature that grows a human language as part of a system of "mental organs," a creature that can then proceed to create the conditions under which it will live to an extent without significant analogue in the natural world, so far as we know.

The question "What is human nature?" has more than scientific interest. As we have noted, it lies at the core of social thought as well. What is a good society? Presumably, one that leads to the satisfaction of intrinsic human needs, insofar as material conditions allow. To command attention and respect, a social theory should be grounded on some concept of human needs and human rights, and in turn on the human nature that must be presupposed in any serious account of the origin and character of these needs and rights. Correspondingly, the social structures and relations that a reformer or revolutionary seeks to bring into existence will be based on a concept of human nature, however vague and inarticulate.

Suppose that at the core of human nature lies the propensity to truck and barter, as Adam Smith alleged. Then we will work to achieve an early capitalist society of small traders, unhindered by monopoly, state intervention, or socially controlled production. Suppose, in contrast, that we take seriously the concepts of another classical liberal thinker, Wilhelm von Humboldt, who contends that "to inquire and to create—these are the centers around which all human pursuits more or less directly revolve," and who further maintains that true creation can take place only under conditions of free choice that goes beyond "instruction and guidance," in a society in which social fetters have been replaced by freely created social bonds. Or suppose that we assume further with Marx that "only in a state of community with others has each individual the means to develop his predispositions in all directions; only in a state of community will personal freedom thus become possible"—where personal freedom presupposes abolition of the alienation of labor that Humboldt condemned as well, the condition of labor that "casts some of the workers back into barbarous kind of work and turns others into machines."[21] On such assumptions about human needs we derive a very different conception of a social order that we should work to create.

Some Marxists have taken the view that "man has no essence apart from his historical existence,"[22] that "human nature is not something *fixed by nature*, but, on the contrary, a 'nature' which is *made by man* in his acts of 'self-transcendence' as a natural being."[23] This interpretation derives from Marx's dictum that "the nature which comes to be in human history—the genesis of human society—is man's real nature," and other similar remarks.[24] Even if we adopt this view, it still remains true that the next step in social change should seek to provide the conditions for the "real nature" that can be expressed at a given stage of historical and cultural evolution.

Is it true that human nature is in no way "fixed by nature"? Evidently it is not true of the physical components of human nature. When a modern Marxist thinker such as Antonio Gramsci, for example, argues that "the fundamental innovation introduced by Marxism into the science of politics and history is the proof that there does not exist an abstract, fixed and immutable 'human nature' . . . but that human nature is the totality of historically determined social relations," he is referring, of course, not to human physical organs in general but to one specific organ: the human brain and its creations.[25] The content of this doctrine must be that at least so far as the higher mental functions are concerned, the human brain is unique among the systems known to us in the natural world in that it has no genetically determined structure, but is, in effect, a tabula rasa on which the totality of historically determined social relations is then inscribed. For some segments of the left, there has been an extraordinary compulsion to adopt some such view. In a report on a recent discussion at the American Association for the Advancement of Science, Walter Sullivan writes:

> The most extreme view, expressed by some members of the audience, was that human brains were "uncoupled" from any genetic influences whatsoever—that, like computers built to a standard design, their relative levels of performance were completely determined by programming.[26]

As scientific hypotheses, these assumptions, which are familiar from radical behaviorism as well, seem to me to have little to recommend them. On these assumptions, it would be quite impossible to account for the richness and complexity of human cognitive systems and the uniformity of their growth, not to speak of the remarkable qualitative differences as compared with other species. Surely, no evidence or argument has been adduced in support of the belief that the human brain is so markedly distinct from every other structure known to us in the natural world, and it is perhaps a bit ironic that such views are proposed, not only on the left, as if they were an outgrowth of some kind of scientific naturalism. Exactly the contrary seems to me to be the case. The human brain is unique in many respects, and the mental structures that grow under the boundary conditions set by experience—the cognitive structures that are "learned," to employ the common and I think rather misleading locution—also provide humans with a "unique instrument." But it is difficult to imagine that this uniqueness resides in the total absence of structure, despite the antiquity of such a belief and its remarkable grip on the modern imagination.

What little we know about the human brain and about human cognitive structures suggests a very different assumption: a highly constrained genetic program determines the basic structural properties of our "mental organs," thus making it possible for us to attain rich and intricate systems of knowledge and belief in a uniform manner on the basis of quite limited evidence. I might add that such a view comes as no surprise to biologists, particularly as regards human language.[27] And I believe it would generally be regarded by neurophysiologists as entirely natural, if not almost obvious.

We need not rest with qualitative and vague remarks such as these. In the study of human language, at least, there are substantive hypotheses, which I believe have considerable force and explanatory power, as to the general character of the genetic program that provides for the growth of the capacity for language and the particular forms that it assumes. I see no reason to doubt that the same will prove true in other domains as we come to understand the structure of human cognitive capacity. If so, we may think of human nature as a system of a sort familiar in the biological world: a system of "mental organs" based on physical mechanisms that are now largely unknown, though not beyond investigation in principle, a system that provides for a unique form of intelligence that manifests itself in human language; in our unique capacity to develop a concept of number and abstract space,[28] to construct scientific theories in certain domains, to create certain systems of art, myth, ritual, and so on, to interpret human actions, to develop and comprehend certain systems of social institutions, and so on.

[The variability of human talents: remuneration, IQ, and race]

On an "empty organism" hypothesis, human beings are assuredly equal in intellectual endowments. More accurately, they are equal in their incapacity to develop complex cognitive structures of the characteristically human sort. If we assume, however, that this biologically given organism has its special capacities like any other, and that among them are the capacities to develop human cognitive structures with their specific properties, then the possibility arises that there are differences among individuals in their higher mental functions. Indeed, if cognitive faculties such as the language faculty are really "mental organs," it would be surprising if there were not. People obviously differ in their physical characteristics and capacities; why should there not be genetically determined differences in the character of their mental organs and the physical structures on which they are based?

Inquiry into specific cognitive capacities such as the language faculty leads to specific and I think significant hypotheses concerning the genetically programmed schematism for language, but gives us no evidence concerning variability. Perhaps this is a result of the inadequacy of our analytic tools. Or it may be that the basic capacities are truly invariant, apart from gross pathology. We find that over a very broad range, at least, there are no differences in the ability to acquire and make effective use of human language at some level of detail, although there may be differences in what is acquired, as there are evidently differences in facility of use. I see no reason for dogmatism on this score. So little is known concerning other cognitive capacities that we can hardly even speculate. Experience seems to support the belief that people do vary in their intellectual capacities and their specialization. It would hardly come as a surprise if this were so, assuming that we are dealing with biological structures, however intricate and remarkable, of known sorts.

Many people, particularly those who regard themselves as within the left-liberal political spectrum, find such conclusions repugnant. It may be that the empty-organism hypothesis is so attractive to the left in part because it precludes these possibilities; there is no variability in a null endowment. But I find it difficult to understand why conclusions of this sort should be at all disturbing. I am personally quite convinced that no matter what training or education I might have received, I could never have run a four-minute mile, discovered Gödel's theorems, composed a Beethoven quartet, or risen to any of innumerable other heights of human achievement. I feel in no way demeaned by these inadequacies. It is quite enough that I am capable, as I think any person of normal endowments probably is, of appreciating and in part understanding what others have accomplished, while making my own personal contributions in whatever measure and manner I am able to do.

Human talents vary considerably within a fixed framework that is characteristic of the species and that permits ample scope for creative work, including the creative work of appreciating the achievements of others. This should be a matter for delight rather than a condition to be abhorred. Those who assume otherwise must be adopting the tacit premise that people's rights or social reward are somehow contingent on their abilities. As for human rights, there is an element of plausibility in this assumption in the single respect already noted: in a decent society, opportunities should conform as far as possible to personal needs, and such needs may be specialized and related to particular talents and capacities. My pleasure in life is enhanced by the fact that others can do many things that I cannot, and I see no reason to want to deny these people the opportunity to cultivate their talents, consistent with general social needs. Difficult questions of practice are sure to arise in any functioning social group, but I see no problem of principle.

As for social rewards, it is alleged that in our society remuneration correlates in part with IQ. But insofar as that is true, it is simply a social malady to be overcome, much as slavery had to be eliminated at an earlier stage of human history. It is sometimes argued that constructive and creative work will cease unless it leads to material reward, so that all of society gains when the talented receive special rewards. For the mass of the population, then, the message is: "You're better off if you're poor." One can see why this doctrine would appeal to the privileged, but it is difficult to believe that it could be put forth seriously by anyone who has had experience with creative work or workers in the arts, the sciences, crafts, or whatever. The standard arguments for "meritocracy" have no basis in fact or logic, to my knowledge; they rest on a priori beliefs, which, furthermore, do not seem particularly plausible. I have discussed the matter elsewhere and will not pursue it here.[29]

Suppose that inquiry into human nature reveals that human cognitive capacities are highly structured by our genetic program and that there are variations among individuals within a shared framework. This seems to me an entirely reasonable expectation and a situation much to be desired. It has no implications with regard to equality of rights or condition, so far as I can see, beyond those already sketched.

Consider finally the question of race and intellectual endowments. Notice again that in a decent society there would be no social consequences to any discovery that might be made about this question. Individuals are what they are; it is only on racist assumptions that they are to be regarded as an instance of their race category, so that social consequences ensue from the discovery that the mean for a certain racial category with respect to some capacity is such-and-such. Eliminating racist assumptions, the facts have no social consequences whatever they may be, and are therefore not worth knowing, from this point of view at least. If there is any purpose to investigation of the relation between race and some capacity, it must derive from the scientific significance of the question.

It is difficult to be precise about questions of scientific merit. Roughly, an inquiry has scientific merit if its results might bear on some general principles of science. One doesn't conduct inquiries into the density of blades of grass on various lawns or innumerable other trivial and pointless questions. But inquiry into such questions as race and IQ appears to be of virtually no scientific interest. Conceivably, there might be some interest in correlations between partially heritable traits, but if someone were interested in this question, he would surely not select such characteristics as race and IQ, each an obscure amalgam of complex properties. Rather, he would ask whether there is a correlation between measurable and significant traits, say, eye color and length of the big toe. It is difficult to see how the study of race and IQ, for example, can be justified on any scientific grounds.

Since the inquiry has no scientific significance and no social significance, apart from the racist assumption that individuals must be regarded not as what they are but rather as standing at the mean of their race category, it follows that it has no merit at all. The question then arises, Why is it pursued with such zeal? Why is it taken seriously? Attention naturally turns to the racist assumptions that do confer some importance on the inquiry if they are accepted.

In a racist society, inquiry into race and IQ can be expected to reinforce prejudice, pretty much independent of the outcome of the inquiry. Given such concepts as "race" and "IQ," it is to be expected that the results of any inquiry will be obscure and conflicting, the arguments complex and difficult for the layman to follow. For the racist, the judgment "Not proven" will be read, "Probably so." There will be ample scope for the racist to wallow in his prejudices. The very fact that the inquiry is undertaken suggests that its outcome is of some importance, and since it is important only on racist assumptions, these assumptions are insinuated even when they are not expressed. For such reasons as these, a scientific investigation of genetic characteristics of Jews would have been appalling in Nazi Germany. There can be no doubt that the investigation of race and IQ has been extremely harmful to the victims of American racism. I have heard black educators describe in vivid terms the suffering and injury imposed on children who are made to understand that "science" has demonstrated this or that about their race, or even finds it necessary to raise the question.

We cannot ignore the fact that we live in a profoundly racist society, though we like to forget that this is so. When the *New York Times* editors and U.N. ambassador [Daniel Patrick] Moynihan castigate Idi Amin of Uganda as a "racist murderer," perhaps correctly, there is a surge of pride throughout the country and they are lauded for their courage and honesty. No one would be so vulgar as to observe that the editors and the ambassador, in the not very distant past, have supported racist murder on a scale that exceeds Amin's wildest fantasies. The general failure to be appalled by their hypocritical pronouncements reflects, in the first place, the extremely powerful ideological controls that prevent us from coming to terms with our acts and their significance and, in the second place, the nation's profound commitment to racist principle. The victims of our Asian wars were never regarded as fully human, a fact that can be demonstrated all too easily, to our everlasting shame. As for domestic racism, I need hardly comment.

The scientist, like anyone else, is responsible for the foreseeable consequences of his acts. The point is obvious and generally well understood; consider the conditions on the use of human subjects in experiments. In the present case, an inquiry into race and IQ, regardless of its outcome, will have a severe social cost in a racist society, for the reasons just noted. The scientist who undertakes this inquiry must therefore show that its significance is so great as to outweigh these costs. If, for example, one maintains that this inquiry is justified by the possibility that it may lead to some refinement of social science methodology, as argued by Boston University president John Silber (*Encounter,*

August 1974), he provides an insight into his moral calculus: the possible contribution to research methodology outweighs the social cost of the study of race and IQ in a racist society. Such advocates often seem to believe that they are defending academic freedom, but this is just a muddle. The issue of freedom of research arises here in its conventional form: does the research in question carry costs, and if so, are they outweighed by its significance? The scientist has no unique right to ignore the likely consequences of what he does.

Once the issue of race and IQ is raised, people who perceive and are concerned by its severe social cost are, in a sense, trapped. They may quite properly dismiss the work on the grounds just sketched. But they do so in a racist society in which, furthermore, people are trained to consign questions of human and social importance to "technical experts," who often prove to be experts in obfuscation and defense of privilege—"experts in legitimation," in Gramsci's phrase. The consequences are obvious. Or they may enter the arena of argument and counterargument, thus implicitly reinforcing the belief that it makes a difference how the research comes out, and thus tacitly supporting the racist assumption on which this belief ultimately rests. Inevitably, then, by refuting alleged correlations between race and IQ (or race and X, for any X one selects), one is reinforcing racist assumptions. The dilemma is not restricted to this issue. I have discussed it elsewhere in connection with debate over murder and aggression.[30] In a highly ideological society, matters can hardly be otherwise, a misfortune that we may deplore but cannot easily escape.

We exist and work in given historical conditions. We may try to change them but cannot ignore them, either in the work we undertake, the strategies for social change that we advocate, or the direct action in which we engage or from which we abstain. In discussion of freedom and equality, it is very difficult to disentangle questions of fact from judgments of value. We should try to do so, pursuing factual inquiry where it may lead without dogmatic preconception, but not ignoring the consequences of what we do. We must never forget that what we do is tainted and distorted, inevitably, by the awe of expertise that is induced by social institutions as one device for enforcing passivity and obedience. What we do as scientists, as scholars, as advocates, has consequences, just as our refusal to speak or act has definite consequences. We cannot escape this condition in a society based on concentration of power and privilege. There is a heavy responsibility that the scientist or scholar would not have to bear in a decent society, in which individuals would not relegate to authorities decisions over their lives or their beliefs. We may and should recommend the simple virtues: honesty and truthfulness, responsibility and concern. But to live by these precepts is often no simple matter.

APPENDIX
Some elementary comments on the rights of freedom of expression
(October 11, 1980)

The remarks that follow are sufficiently banal so that I feel that an apology is in order to reasonable people who may happen to read them. If there is, nevertheless, good reason to put them on paper—and I fear that there is—this testifies to some remarkable features of contemporary French intellectual culture.

Before I turn to the subject on which I have been asked to comment, two clarifications are necessary. The remarks that follow are limited in two crucial respects. First: I am concerned here solely with a narrow and specific topic, namely, the right of free expression of ideas, conclusions, and beliefs. I have nothing to say here about the work of Robert Faurisson or his critics, of which I know very little, or about the topics they address, concerning which I have no special knowledge. Second: I will have some harsh (but merited) things to say about certain segments of the French intelligentsia, who have demonstrated that they have not the slightest concern for fact or reason, as I have learned from unpleasant personal experience that I will not review here. Certainly, what I say does not apply to many others, who maintain a firm commitment to intellectual integrity. This is not the place for a detailed account. The tendencies to which I refer are, I believe, sufficiently significant to merit attention and concern, but I would not want these comments to be misunderstood as applying beyond their specific scope.

Some time ago I was asked to sign a petition in defense of Robert Faurisson's "freedom of speech and expression." The petition said absolutely nothing about the character, quality, or validity of his research, but restricted itself quite explicitly to a defense of elementary rights that are taken for granted in democratic societies, calling upon university and government officials to "do everything possible to ensure the safety [of Faurisson] and the free exercise of his legal rights." I signed it without hesitation.

The fact that I had signed the petition aroused a storm of protest in France. In the *Nouvel Observateur*, an ex-Stalinist who has changed allegiance but not intellectual style published a grossly falsified version of the contents of the petition, amidst a stream of falsehoods that merit no comment. This, however, I have come to regard as normal. I was considerably more surprised to read in *Esprit* (September 1980) that Pierre Vidal-Naquet found the petition "scandaleuse," citing specifically that fact that I had signed it (I omit the discussion of an accompanying article by the editor that again merits no comment, at least among people who retain a commitment to elementary values of truth and honesty).

Vidal-Naquet offers exactly one reason for finding the petition, and my act of signing it, "scandaleuse": the petition, he claims, presented Faurisson's " 'conclusions' comme si elles étaient effectivement des découvertes [as if they had been, in fact, discoveries]." Vidal-Naquet's statement is false. The petition simply stated that Faurisson had presented his "findings," which is uncontroversial, stating or implying precisely nothing about their value and implying nothing about their validity. Perhaps Vidal-Naquet was misled by faulty understanding of the English wording of the petition; that is, perhaps he misunderstood the English word *findings*. It is, of course, obvious that if I say that someone presented his findings, I imply nothing whatsoever about their character or validity; the statement is perfectly neutral in this respect. I assume that it was indeed a simple misunderstanding of the text that led Vidal-Naquet to write what he did, in which case he will, of course, publicly withdraw that the accusation that I (among others) have done something "scandaleuse" in signing an innocuous civil rights petition of the sort that all of us sign frequently.

I do not want to discuss individuals. Suppose, then, that some person does indeed find the petition "scandaleuse," not on the basis of misreading, but because of what it actually says. Let us suppose that this person finds Faurisson's ideas offensive, even horrendous, and finds his scholarship to be a scandal. Let us suppose further that he is correct in these conclusions—whether he is or not is plainly irrelevant in this context. Then we must conclude that the person in question believes that the petition was "scandaleuse" because Faurisson should indeed be denied the normal rights of self-expression, should be barred from the university, should be subjected to harassment and even violence, et cetera. Such attitudes are not uncommon. They are typical, for example of American communists and no doubt their counterparts elsewhere. Among people who have learned something from the eighteenth century (say, Voltaire) it is a truism, hardly deserving discussion, that the defense of the right of free expression is not restricted to ideas one approves of, and that it is precisely in the case of ideas found most offensive that these rights must be most vigorously defended. Advocacy of the right to express ideas that are generally approved is, quite obviously, a matter of no significance. All of this is well understood in the United States, which is why there has been nothing like the Faurisson affair here. In France, where a civil libertarian tradition is evidently not well established and where there have been deep totalitarian strains among the intelligentsia for many years (collaborationism, the great influence of Leninism and its offshoots, the near-lunatic character of the new intellectual right, etc.), matters are apparently quite different.

For those who are concerned with the state of French intellectual culture, the Faurisson affair is not without interest. Two comparisons immediately come to mind. The first is this. I have frequently signed petitions—indeed, gone to far greater lengths—on behalf of Russian dissidents whose views are absolutely horrendous: advocates of ongoing U.S. savagery in Indochina, or of policies that would lead to nuclear war, or of a religious chauvinism that is reminiscent of the dark ages. No one has ever raised any objection. Should someone have done so, I would regard this with the same contempt as is deserved by the behavior of those who denounce the petition in support of Faurisson's civil rights, and for exactly the same reason. I do not read the Communist Party press, but I have little doubt that the commissars and apparatchiks have carefully perused these petitions, seeking out phrases that could be maliciously misinterpreted, in an effort to discredit these efforts to prevent the suppression of human rights. In comparison, when I state that irrespective of his views, Faurisson's civil rights should be guaranteed, this is taken to be "scandaleuse" and a great fuss is made about it in France. The reason for the distinction seems obvious enough. In the case of the Russian dissidents, the state (our states) approves of supporting them, for its own reasons, which have little to do with concern for human rights, needless to say. In the case of Faurisson, however, defense of his civil rights is not officially approved doctrine—far from it—so that segments of the intelligentsia, who are ever eager to line up and march off to the beat of the drums, do not perceive any need to take the stance accepted without question in the case of Soviet dissidents. In France, there may well be other factors: perhaps a lingering guilt about disgraceful behavior of substantial sectors under Vichy, the failure to protest the French wars in Indochina, the lasting impact of Stalinism and more generally Leninist doctrines, the bizarre and dadaistic character of certain streams of intellectual life in postwar France (which makes rational discourse appear to be such an odd and unintelligible pastime), the currents of anti-Semitism that have exploded into violence.

A second comparison also comes to mind. I rarely have much good to say about the mainstream intelligentsia in the United States, who generally resemble their counterparts elsewhere. Still, it is very illuminating to compare the reaction to the Faurisson affair in France and to the same phenomenon here. In the United States, Arthur Butz (whom one might regard as the American Faurisson) has not been subjected to the kind of merciless attack leveled against Faurisson. When the "no Holocaust" historians hold a large international meeting in the United States, as they did some months ago, there is nothing like the hysteria that we find in France over the Faurisson affair. When the American Nazi Party calls for a parade in the largely Jewish city of Skokie, Illinois—obviously, pure provocation—the American Civil Liberties Union defends their rights (though of course, the American Communist Party is infuriated). As far as I am aware, much the same is true in England or Australia, countries which, like the United States, have a live civil libertarian tradition. Butz and the rest are sharply criticized and condemned, but without any attack on their civil rights, to my knowledge. There is no need, in these countries, for an innocuous petition such as the one that is found "scandaleuse" in France, and if there were such a petition, it would surely not be attacked outside of limited and insignificant circles. The comparison is, again, illuminating. One should try to understand it. One might argue, perhaps, that Nazism and anti-Semitism are much more threatening in France. I think that this is true, but it is simply a reflection of the same factors that led to the Leninism of substantial sectors of the French intelligentsia for a long period, their contempt for elementary civil libertarian principles today, and their current fanaticism in beating the drums for crusades against the Third World. There are, in short, deep-seated totalitarian strains that emerge in various guises, a matter well worth further consideration, I believe.

Let me add a final remark about Faurisson's alleged "anti-Semitism." Note first that even if Faurisson were to be a rabid anti-Semite and fanatic pro-Nazi—such charges have been presented to me in private correspondence that it would be improper to cite in detail here—this would have no bearing whatsoever on the legitimacy of the defense of his civil rights. On the contrary, it would make it all the more imperative to defend them since, once again, it has been a truism for years, indeed centuries, that it is precisely in the case of horrendous ideas that the right of free expression must be most vigorously defended; it is easy enough to defend free expression for those who require no such defense. Putting this central issue aside, is it true that Faurisson is an anti-Semite or a neo-Nazi? As noted earlier, I do not know his work very well. But from what I have read—largely as a result of the nature of the attacks on him—I find no evidence to support either conclusion. Nor do I find credible evidence in the material that I have read concerning him, either in the public record or in private correspondence. As far as I can determine, he is a relatively apolitical liberal of some sort. In support of the charge of anti-Semitism, I have been informed that Faurisson is remembered by some schoolmates as having expressed anti-Semitic sentiments in the 1940s, and as having written a letter that some interpret as having anti-Semitic implications at the time of the Algerian war. I am a little surprised that serious people should put such charges forth—even in private—as a sufficient basis for castigating someone as a longtime and well-known anti-Semite. I am aware of nothing in the public record to support such charges. I will not pursue the exercise, but suppose we were to apply similar standards to others, asking, for example, what their attitude was toward the French war in Indochina, or to Stalinism, decades ago. Perhaps no more need be said.

Notes

1. Robert Goodman, *After the planners* (New York: Simon and Schuster, 1971).
2. K. William Kapp, *The social cost of private enterprise* (New York: Schocken Books, 1971), p. 231.
3. Cf. Seymour Melman, "Industrial efficiency under managerial versus cooperative decision-making," *Review of Radical Political Economics*, spring 1970; reprinted in B. Horvat, M. Markovic, and R. Supek, eds., *Self-governing socialism*, vol. 2 (White Plains, N.Y.: International Arts and Sciences Press, 1975). See also Melman, *Decision-making and productivity* (Oxford: Blackwell, 1958); and Paul Blumberg, *Industrial democracy: the sociology of participation* (New York: Schocken Books, 1969).
4. Stephen A. Marglin, "What do bosses do?" *Review of Radical Political Economics*, summer 1974; Herbert Gintis, "Alienation in capitalist society," in R. C. Edwards, M. Reich, and T. E. Weiskopf, *The capitalist system* (Englewood Cliffs, N.J.: Prentice-Hall, 1972)
5. J. E. Meade, *Efficiency, equality and the ownership of property* (Cambridge, Mass.: Harvard University Press, 1965).
6. Karl Marx, *Capital*, vol. 3 (Moscow: Foreign Languages Publishing House, 1959).
7. Giambattista Vico, *The new science*, trans. T. C. Bergin and M. H. Fisch (Garden City, N.Y.: Anchor Books, 1961).
8. David Ellerman, "Capitalism and workers' self-management," in G. Hunnius, G. D. Garson, and J. Case, eds., *Workers' control* (New York: Random House, 1973), pp. 10–11.
9. Adam Smith, *Wealth of nations*, cited by Marglin, "What do bosses do?"
10. Edward S. Greenberg, "In defense of avarice," *Social Policy*, Jan.-Feb. 1976, p. 63.
11. "The fearful drift of foreign policy," commentary, *Business Week*, April 1975.
12. In fact, in this case, sheer robbery backed by state power is a more likely explanation.
13. On the interpretation of the "lessons of Vietnam" by academic scholars and liberal commentators as the war ended, see my "Remaking of history," *Ramparts*, September 1975 (reprinted in *Towards a new cold war* [New York: Pantheon Books, 1982]), and "The United States and Vietnam," *Vietnam Quarterly*, no. 1 (winter 1976).
14. For a discussion of this topic, see my introduction to N. Blackstock, ed., *Cointelpro* (New York: Vintage Books, 1976).
15. See, for example, Herbert J. Gans, "About the equalitarians," *Columbia Forum*, spring 1975.
16. Rudolf Rocker, "Anarchism and anarcho-syndicalism," in P. Eltzbacher, ed., *Anarchism* (London: Freedom Press, 1960), pp. 234–35.
17. I have discussed some of the roots of these doctrines elsewhere, e.g., *For reasons of state* (New York: Pantheon Books, 1973).
18. Rocker, "Anarchism and anarcho-syndicalism," p. 228. Rocker is characterizing the "ide-

ology of anarchism." Whether Marx would have welcomed such a conception is a matter of conjecture. As a theoretician of capitalism, he did not have very much to say about the nature of a socialist society. Anarchists, who tended to the view that the workers' organizations must create "not only the ideas but also the facts of the future itself" within capitalist society (Bakunin), correspondingly provided a more extensive theory of postrevolutionary society. For a left-Marxist view of these questions, see Karl Korsch, "On Socialization," in Horvat, Markovic, and Supek, eds., *Self-governing socialism*, vol. 1.

19. Evidently there is a value judgment here, for which I do not apologize.

20. Quotes are from Salvador E. Luria, *Life: the unfinished experiment* (New York: Scribner's Sons, 1973).

21. For references and discussions, see note 17; also, Frank F. Manuel, "In memoriam: critique of the Gotha Program, 1875–1975," *Daedalus*, winter 1976.

22. Fredy Perlman, *Essay on commodity fetishism*, 1968, reprinted from *Telos*, no. 6 (Somerville, Mass.: New England Free Press, 1968).

23. Istvan Meszaros, *Marx's theory of alienation* (London: Merlin Press, 1970).

24. Cited in ibid.

25. See my *Reflections on language* (New York: Pantheon Books, 1975) for reference and discussion.

26. Walter Sullivan, "Scientists debate question of race and intelligence," *New York Times*, Feb. 23, 1976, p. 23. His account may well be accurate; I have often heard and read similar comments from left-wing scientists.

27. Cf., for example, the remarks on language in Luria, *Life: the unfinished experiment*; Jacques Monod, *Chance and necessity* (New York: Alfred A. Knopf, 1971); and François Jacob, *The logic of life* (New York; Pantheon Books, 1973). For some recent discussion of this issue, see my *Reflections on language*.

28. It is extremely misleading to argue, as some do, that certain birds have an elementary "concept of number" as revealed by their ability to employ ordinal and visually presented systems up to some finite limit (about 7). The concepts 1, 2 . . . 7 are not to be confused with the concept of natural number, as formally captured, e.g., by the Dedekind-Peano axioms and intuitively understood, without difficulty, by normal humans, as an infinite system.

29. Cf. my *For reasons of state*, Ch. 7.

30. *American power and the new mandarins* (New York: Pantheon Books, 1969), introduction.

Chapter 7

Two conceptions of social organization (February 16, 1970)

I think it's useful to set up as a framework for discussion four somewhat idealized positions with regard to the role of the state in an advanced industrial society. I want to call these positions (1) classical liberal, (2) libertarian socialist, (3) state socialist, and (4) state capitalist, and I want to consider each in turn. Also I'd like to make clear my own point of view in advance so you can evaluate and judge what I'm saying.

I think that the libertarian socialist concepts—and by that I mean a range of thinking that extends from left-wing Marxism through anarchism—are fundamentally correct, and that they are the proper and natural extension of classical liberalism into the era of advanced industrial society. In contrast, it seems to me that the ideology of state socialism, that is, what has become of Bolshevism, and of state capitalism (the modern welfare state) of course are dominant in the industrial societies, but I believe they are regressive and highly inadequate social theories, and a large number of our really fundamental problems stem from a kind of incompatibility and inappropriateness of this social forms to a modern industrial society.

[Four points of reference]

Well, then, let me consider these four points of reference in sequence, beginning with the classical liberal point of view.

Classical liberalism asserts as its major idea an opposition to all but the most restrictive and minimal forms of state intervention in personal or social life. This conclusion is quite familiar. However, the reasoning that leads to it is less familiar, and I think a good deal more important than the conclusion itself.

One of the earliest and most brilliant expositions of this position is in Wilhelm von Humboldt's *Limits of state action,* which was written in 1792, though not published [in full] for sixty or seventy years after that [in 1851, as a book—CPO]. In his view, the state tends to "make man an instrument to serve its arbitrary ends, overlooking his individual purposes," and since a human being is in his essence a free, searching, self-perfecting being, it follows that the state is a profoundly anti-human institution, that is, its actions, its existence, are ultimately incompatible with "the full harmonious development of human potential in its richest diversity," hence incompatible with what Humboldt and in the following century Marx, Bakunin, Mill, and many others see as the true end of man. And, for the record, I think that this is an accurate description.

The modern conservative tends to regard himself as the lineal descendant of the classical liberal in this sense, but I think that can be maintained only from an extremely superficial point of view, as one can see by studying more carefully the fundamental ideas of classical libertarian thought as expressed, in my opinion in its most profound form, by Humboldt. I think the issues are of really quite considerable contemporary significance, and if you don't mind what may appear to be a somewhat antiquarian excursion, I'd like to expand on them.

For Humboldt, as for Rousseau, and before him the Cartesians, man's essential attribute is its freedom: "To inquire and to create, these are the centers around which all human pursuits more or less directly revolve." But, he goes on to say, "all moral culture springs solely and immediately from the inner life of the soul, and can never be produced by external and artificial contrivances. The cultivation of the understanding as of any of man's other faculties is generally achieved by his own activity, his own ingenuity, or his own methods of using the discoveries of others."

Well, from these assumptions quite obviously an educational theory follows, and he develops it, but I won't pursue it. But also far more follows. Humboldt goes on to develop at least the rudiments of a theory of exploitation and of alienated labor that suggests, in significant ways, I think, the early Marx. So Humboldt in fact continues the comments that I quoted about the cultivation of understanding through spontaneous action in the following way:

> Man never regards what he possesses as so much his own as what he does, and the laborer who tends a garden is perhaps in a truer sense its owner than the listless voluptuary who enjoys its fruits.

And since truly human action is that which flows from inner impulse,

> it seems as if all peasants and craftsmen might be elevated into artists, that is, men who love their labor for its own sake, improve it by their own plastic genius and inventive skill, and thereby cultivate their intellect, ennoble their character and exalt and refine their pleasures. And so humanity would be ennobled by the very

things which now, though beautiful in themselves, so often tend to degrade it.
Freedom is undoubtedly the indispensable condition without which even the pursuits more congenial to individual human nature can never succeed in producing
such salutary influences. Whatever does not spring from a man's free choice, or is
only the result of instruction and guidance, does not enter into his very being, but
remains alien to its true nature: he does not perform it with truly human energies,
but merely with mechanical exactness.

And if a man acts in a mechanical way, reacting to external demands or
instruction rather than in ways determined by his own interests and energies
and power, we may admire what he does, but we despise what he is.

For Humboldt, then, man is born to inquire and create. And when a man
or a child chooses to inquire or create out of his own free choice, then he
becomes in his own terms an artist rather than a tool of production or a well-
trained parrot.

This is the essence of his concept of human nature. And I think it's very
revealing and interesting to compare it with the early Marx manuscripts, in
particular Marx's account of the "alienation of labor when work is external to
the worker, . . . not part of his nature . . . [so that] he does not fulfill himself
in his work, but denies himself . . . [and is] physically exhausted and mentally
debased, this alienated labor that casts some of the workers back into a barbarous kind of work, and turns others into machines, thus depriving man of
his species character, of free conscious activity and productive life."

Recall also Marx's well-known and often-quoted reference to a higher
form of society in which labor has become "not only a means of life but also
the highest want in life." Recall also his repeated criticism of the specialized
labor which "mutilates the worker into a fragment of a human being,
degrades him to become a mere appurtenance of the machine, makes his
works such a torment that its essential meaning is destroyed, estranges from
him the intellectual potentialities of the labor process in varied proportion to
the extent to which science is incorporated into it as an independent power."

Robert Tucker, for one, has rightly emphasized that Marx sees the revolutionary "more as a frustrated producer than as a dissatisfied consumer." And
this far more radical critique of capitalist relations of production flows
directly, often in the same words, from the libertarian thought of the
Enlightenment. For this reason, I think, one must say that classical liberal
ideas—in their essence, though not in the way they developed—are profoundly anti-capitalist. The essence of these ideas must be destroyed for them
to serve as an ideology of modern industrial capitalism.

[From classical liberalism to libertarian socialism]

Writing in the early 1790s, Humboldt had no conception of the forms that industrial capitalism would take. Consequently, in this classic of classical liberalism he stresses the problem of limiting state power and is not overly concerned with the dangers of private power. The reason is that he believes in, and speaks of, the essential equality of condition of private citizens. Of course he has no idea, writing in 1791–1792, of the ways in which the notion "private person" would come to be reinterpreted in the era of corporate capitalism. He did not foresee (I now quote the anarchist historian Rudolf Rocker) that "democracy, with its motto of equality of all citizens before the law, and liberalism, with its right of man over its own person, both would be wrecked on the realities of capitalist economy."

Humboldt did not foresee that in a predatory capitalist economy state intervention would be an absolute necessity to preserve human existence, to prevent the destruction of the physical environment (I speak optimistically, of course). As Karl Polanyi for one has pointed out, the self-adjusting market "could not exist for any length of time without annihilating the human and natural substance of society; it would have physically destroyed man and transformed his surroundings into a wilderness." I think that's correct.

Humboldt also did not foresee the consequences of the commodity character of labor, the doctrine (again in Polanyi's words) that "it is not for the commodity to decide where it should be offered for sale, to what purpose it should be used, at what price it would be allowed to change hands, in what manner it should be consumed or destroyed." But the commodity in this case is of course a human life, and social protection was therefore a minimal necessity to constrain the irrational and destructive workings of the classical free market.

Nor did Humboldt understand in 1790 that capitalist economic relations perpetuated a form of bondage which long before that—in fact, as early as 1767—Simon Linguet had declared to be even worse than slavery, writing,

> It is the impossibility of living by any other means that compels our farm laborers to till the soil whose fruits they will not eat, and our masons to construct buildings in which they will not live; it is want that drags them to those markets where they await masters who will do them the kindness of buying them; it is want that compels them to go down on their knees to the rich man in order to get from him permission to enrich him. . . . What effective gain has the suppression of slavery brought him? . . . He's free, you say. Ah! That is his misfortune. . . . These men, it is said, have no master—they have one, and the most terrible, the most imperious of masters, that is, *need*. It is this that reduces them to the most cruel dependence.

And if there is something degrading to human nature in the idea of bondage, as every spokesman for the Enlightenment would insist, then it would follow that a new emancipation must be awaited, what Fourier referred to as the third and last emancipatory phase of history, the first having made serfs out of slaves, the second wage earners out of serfs, and the third, which will transform the proletariat into free men by eliminating the commodity character of labor, ending wage slavery, and bringing the commercial, industrial, and financial institutions under democratic control.

These are all things that Humboldt in his classical liberal doctrine did not express and didn't see. But I think he might have accepted these conclusions. He does, for example, agree that state intervention in social life is legitimate if freedom would destroy the very conditions without which not only freedom but even existence itself would be inconceivable, which are precisely the circumstances that arise in an unconstrained capitalist economy. And he does, as in the remarks that I quoted, vigorously condemn the alienation of labor. In any event, his criticism of bureaucracy and the autocratic state stands as a very eloquent forewarning of some of the most dismal aspects of modern history, and the important point is that the basis of his critique is applicable to a far broader range of coercive institutions than he imagined, in particular to the institutions of industrial capitalism.

Though he expresses a classical liberal doctrine, Humboldt is no primitive individualist in the style of, for example, Rousseau. Rousseau extols the savage who lives within himself. But Humboldt's vision is entirely different. He sums up his remarks as follows:

> The whole tenor of the ideas and arguments unfolded in this essay might fairly be reduced to this: that while they would break all fetters in human society, they would attempt to find as many new social bonds as possible. The isolated man is no more able to develop than the one who is fettered.

And he in fact looks forward to a community of free association, without coercion by the state or other authoritarian institutions, in which free men can create and inquire, achieve the highest development of their powers. In fact, far ahead of his time, he presents an anarchist vision that is appropriate perhaps to the next stage of industrial society.

We can perhaps look forward to a day when these various strands will be brought together within the framework of libertarian socialism, a social form that barely exists today, though its elements can perhaps be perceived, for example in the guarantee of individual rights that has achieved so far its fullest realization (though still tragically flawed) in the Western democracies, or in the

Israeli kibbutzim, or in the experiments with workers' councils in Yugoslavia, or in the effort to awaken popular consciousness and to create a new involvement in the social process which is a fundamental element in the Third World revolutions, coexisting uneasily with indefensible authoritarian practice.

So let me summarize this first point. The first concept of the state that I want to set up as a point of reference is classical liberal. Its doctrine is that the state function should be drastically limited. But this familiar characterization is a very superficial one. More deeply, the classical liberal view develops from a certain concept of human nature, one that stresses the importance of diversity and free creation. Therefore this view is in fundamental opposition to industrial capitalism, with its wage slavery, its alienated labor, and its hierarchic and authoritarian principles of social and economic organization. At least in its Humboldtian form, classical liberal thought is opposed as well to the concepts of possessive individualism which are intrinsic to capitalist ideology. So it seeks to eliminate social fetters, but to replace them by social bonds, not by competitive greed, not by predatory individualism, not of course by corporate empires, state or private. Classical libertarian thought seems to me therefore to lead directly to libertarian socialism, or anarchism, if you like, when combined with an understanding of industrial capitalism.

The second point of reference that I want to discuss is the libertarian socialist vision of the state. A French writer rather sympathetic to anarchism once wrote that "anarchism has a broad back, like paper it endures anything." There are many shades of anarchism, and I'm concerned here only with one, namely, the anarchism of Bakunin, who wrote in his anarchist manifesto of 1865 that to be an anarchist one must first be a socialist. I'm concerned with the anarchism of Adolf Fischer, one of the martyrs of the Haymarket affair in 1886, who said that "every anarchist is a socialist, but not every socialist is necessarily an anarchist."

A consistent anarchist must oppose private ownership of the means of production. Such property is indeed, as Proudhon's famous remark asserted, a form of theft. But a consistent anarchist will also oppose "the organization of production by government":

> It means state socialism, the command of state officials over production and the command of managers, scientists, shop officials in the shop. The goal of the working class is liberation from exploitation, and this goal is not reached, and cannot be reached, by a new directing and governing class, substituting itself for the bourgeoisie. It is only realized by the workers themselves being masters over production by some form of workers' councils.

These remarks, it so happens, are quoted from the left-wing Marxist Anton Pannekoek, and in fact radical Marxism, what Lenin once called "infantile ultra leftism," merges with anarchist currents. This is an important point, I think.

Let me give one further illustration of this convergence between left-wing Marxism and socialist anarchism.

Consider the following characterization of revolutionary socialism:

> The revolutionary socialist denies that state ownership can end in anything other than a bureaucratic despotism. We have seen why the state cannot democratically control industry. Industry can only be democratically owned and controlled by the workers electing directly from their own ranks industrial administrative committees. Socialism will be fundamentally an industrial system. Its constituencies will be of an industrial character. Thus those carrying on the social activity and industries of society will be directly represented in the local and central councils of social administration. In this way the powers of such delegates will flow upwards from those carrying on the work and conversant with the needs of the community. When the central administrative industrial committee meets, it will represent every phase of social activity, hence the capitalist, political, or geographical state will be replaced by the industrial administrative committee of socialism. The transition from one social system to the other will be the social revolution. The political state throughout history has meant the government of men by ruling classes. The republic of socialism will be the government of industry administered on behalf of the whole community. The former meant the economic and political subjection of the many, the latter will mean the economic freedom of all. It will be therefore a true democracy.

These remarks are taken from a book called *The state: its origins and function* written by William Paul in early 1917, just prior to Lenin's *State and revolution*, which is his most libertarian work. William Paul is one of the founders of the British Communist Party, later the editor of the British Communist Party journal. And it's interesting that his critique of state socialism resembles very closely, I think, the libertarian doctrine of the anarchists, in particular in its principle that the state must disappear to be replaced by the industrial organization of society in the course of the social revolution itself. Proudhon in 1851 wrote that "what we put in place of the government is industrial organization," and many, many similar comments can be cited. That, in a sense, is the fundamental idea of anarchist revolutionaries.

What is more important than the fact that many such statements can be cited is that these ideas have been realized in spontaneous revolutionary action several times, for example, in Germany and Italy after the first World War, in Catalonia in 1936. One might argue, or at least I would argue, that council communism in this sense (in the sense of the long quotation that I read) is the natural form of revolutionary socialism in an industrial society. It reflects the intuitive understanding that democracy is largely a sham when the industrial system is controlled by any form of bureaucratic elite, whether of owners, managers, technocrats, a vanguard party, state bureaucracy, or whatever. Under these conditions of authoritarian domination, the classical liberal ideals, which are expressed also by Marx and Bakunin and all true revolutionaries, cannot be realized. A human being, in other words, will not be free to inquire and create, to develop their own potentialities to their fullest; the worker will remain a fragment of a human being, degraded, a tool in the productive process directed from above.

The ideas of revolutionary libertarian socialism in this sense have been submerged in the industrial societies of the past half century. The dominant ideologies have been those of state socialism and state capitalism. But there's been an interesting resurgence in the last couple of years. In fact, the theses that I quoted from Anton Pannekoek were taken from a recent pamphlet by a radical French workers' group, and the quotation that I read from William Paul on revolutionary socialism was taken from a paper by Walter Kendall at the National Conference on Workers' Control in Sheffield, England, last March. Both of these groups, the French and the English one, represent something significant. The workers' control movement in England, in particular, has developed into a, I think, remarkably significant force in the last few years. It includes some of the largest trade unions, for example the Amalgamated Engineers Federation, which I think is the second largest trade union in England, and which has taken these principles as its fundamental ideas. It's had a series of successful conferences, putting in an interesting pamphlet literature. And on the continent there are parallel developments. May 1968 in France of course accelerated the growing interest in council communism and similar ideas, other forms of libertarian socialism, in France and Germany, as it did in England.

Given the general conservative cast of our highly ideological society, it's not too surprising that the United States is relatively untouched by these currents. But that, too, may change. The erosion of the cold war mythology at least makes it possible to discuss some of these questions. And if the present wave of repression can be beaten back, if the left can overcome its more suicidal tendencies and build on the achievements of the past decade, the problem of how to organize industrial society on truly democratic lines, with democratic control in the workplace as well as in the community, should become the dominant intellectual issue for those who are alive to the problems of contemporary society. And as a mass movement for revolutionary libertarian socialism develops, as I hope it will, speculation should proceed to action.

It may seem quixotic to group leftist Marxism and anarchism under the same rubric, as I've done, given the antagonism throughout the past century between Marxists and anarchists, beginning with the antagonism between Marx and Engels on the one hand and, for example, Proudhon and Bakunin on the other. In the nineteenth century, at least, their difference with regard to the question of the state was significant, but in a sense it was tactical. The anarchists were convinced that capitalism and the state must be destroyed together. Engels, in a letter of 1883, expressed his opposition to this idea as follows:

> The anarchists put the thing upside down. They declare that the proletarian revolution must *begin* by doing away with the political organization of the state, but to destroy it at such a moment would be to destroy the only organism by means of which the victorious proletariat can assert its newly conquered power, hold down its adversaries and carry out that economic revolution of society without which the whole victory must end in a new defeat and in a mass slaughter of the workers, similar to those after the Paris commune.

The Paris commune, I think it's fair to say, did represent the ideas of libertarian socialism, of anarchism, if you like, and Marx of course wrote about it with great enthusiasm. In fact, the experience of the commune led him to modify his concept of the role of the state, as you can see, for example, by looking at the introduction to the *Communist Manifesto,* the edition that was published in 1872, and to take on something like a more anarchist perspective of the nature of the social revolution.

The commune was, of course, drowned in blood, as the anarchist communes of Spain were destroyed by fascist and communist armies. And it might be argued that more dictatorial structures would have defended the revolution against such forces. But I doubt this very much. At least in the case of Spain, it seems to me that a more consistent libertarian policy might have provided the only possible defense of the revolution. Of course, this can be contested, and is a long story, which I don't want to go into here. But at the very least it's clear that one would have to be rather naive, after the events of the past half century, to fail to see the truth in Bakunin's repeated warnings that the Red bureaucracy would prove "the most vile and terrible lie of the century." He once said (in 1870):

Take the most radical revolutionary and place him on the throne of all the Russias or give him dictatorial power, and before a year is past he'll become worse than the czar himself.

I'm afraid that in this respect Bakunin was all too perceptive, and this kind of warning was repeatedly voiced from the left. For example, the anarcho-syndicalist Fernand Pelloutier asked in the 1890s:

Must even the transitory state to which we have to submit necessarily and fatally be the collectivist jail? Can it consist in a free organization limited exclusively by the need of production and consumption, all political institutions having disappeared?

I don't pretend to know the answer to that question, but I think it is tolerably clear that unless the answer is positive, the chances for a truly democratic revolution that will achieve the humanistic ideals of the left are perhaps rather slight. I think Martin Buber put the problem quite succinctly when he said: "One cannot in the nature of things expect a little tree that has been turned into a club to put forth leaves."

For just this reason, it's essential that a powerful revolutionary movement exist in the United States if there are to be any reasonable possibilities for democratic social change of a radical sort anywhere in the capitalist world. And comparable remarks, I think, undoubtedly hold for the Russian empire. Lenin till the end of his life stressed the idea that "it is an elementary truth of Marxism that the victory of socialism requires the joint effort of workers in a number of advanced countries." At the very least it requires that the great centers of world imperialism be impeded by domestic pressures from counterrevolutionary intervention. Only such possibilities would permit any revolution to overthrow its own coercive state institutions as it tries to bring the economy under direct democratic control.

Let me summarize briefly again. I mentioned so far two reference points for discussion of the state: classical liberalism and libertarian socialism. They are in agreement that the functions of the state are repressive and that state action must be limited. The libertarian socialist goes on to insist that state power must be eliminated in favor of the democratic organization of industrial society, with direct popular control over all institutions by those who participate in, as well as those who are directly affected by, the workings of these institutions. So one might imagine, then, a system of workers' councils, consumers' councils, commune assemblies, regional federations, and so on, with the kind of representation that is direct and revocable in the sense that representatives are directly answerable to, and return directly to, the well-defined and integrated social group for which they speak in some higher-order organization, something obviously very different than our system of representation.

It might very well be asked whether such a social structure is feasible in a complex, highly technological society. There are counterarguments, and I think they fall into two main categories: the first is that such an organization is contrary to human nature, and the second says roughly that it's incompatible with the demands of efficiency. I'd like to briefly consider each of these.

Consider the first, that a free society is contrary to human nature. It's often asked: Do humans really want freedom? Do they want the responsibility that goes with it? Or would they prefer to be ruled by a benevolent master? Consistently, apologists for the existing distribution of power have held to one or another version of the idea of the "happy slave." Two hundred years ago Rousseau denounced the sophistic politicians and intellectuals who search for ways to obscure the fact (so he maintained) that "the essential and defining property of man is his freedom":

> They attribute to man a natural inclination to servitude, without thinking that it is the same for freedom as for innocence and virtue: their value is felt only as long as one enjoys them oneself, and the taste for them is lost as soon as one has lost them.

As proof of this doctrine, he refers to the marvels done by all free peoples to guard themselves from oppression. "True," he says,

> those who have abandoned the life of a free man do nothing but boast incessantly of the peace and repose they enjoy in their chains. But when I see the others sacrifice pleasures, repose, wealth, power, and life itself for the preservation of this sole good, which is so disdained by those who have lost it, when I see multitudes of entirely naked savages scorn European voluptuousness and endure hunger, fire, the sword, and death to preserve only their independence, I feel that does not behoove slaves to reason about freedom

—a comment to which we can perhaps give a contemporary interpretation.

Rather similar thoughts were expressed by Kant forty years later. He cannot, he says, "accept the proposition that certain people are not ripe for freedom," for example, the serfs of some landlord. "If one accepts this assumption," he writes,

> freedom will never be achieved, for one cannot arrive at the maturity for freedom
> without having already acquired it. One must be free to learn how to make use of
> one's powers freely and usefully. The first attempts will surely be brutal and will
> lead to a state of affairs more painful and dangerous than the former condition
> under the dominance but also the protection of an external authority. However one
> can achieve reason only through one's experiences and one must be free to be able
> to undertake them. To accept the principle that freedom is worthless for those
> under one's control, and that one has the right to refuse it to them forever, is an
> infringement of the right of God himself, who has created man to be free.

This particular remark is interesting because of its context as well. Kant on
this occasion was defending the French revolution during the Terror against
those who claimed that showed the masses to be unready for the privilege of
freedom. And his remarks too, I think, have obvious contemporary relevance.
No rational person would approve of violence and terror, and in particular the
terror of the post-revolutionary state, which has fallen into the hands of a
grim autocracy, has more than once reached undescribable levels of savagery.
At the same time, no person of understanding or humanity will too quickly
condemn the violence that often occurs when long-subdued masses rise
against their oppressors or take the first steps toward liberty and social reconstruction.

Humboldt, just a few years before Kant, had expressed a view very similar to that. He also said that "freedom and variety are the preconditions for
human self-realization":

> Nothing promotes this ripeness for freedom so much as freedom itself. This truth
> perhaps may not be acknowledged by those who so often use this unripeness as an
> excuse for continuing repression, but it seems to me to follow unquestionably from
> the very nature of man. The incapacity for freedom can only arise from a want of
> moral and intellectual power. To heighten this power is the only way to supply the
> want, but to do so presupposes the freedom which awakens spontaneous activity.
> And those who do not comprehend this may justly be suspected of misunderstand-
> ing human nature and wishing to make men into machines.

Rosa Luxemberg's fraternal, sympathetic critique of Bolshevik ideology
and practice was given in very similar terms. Only the active participation of
the masses in self-government and social reconstruction could bring about
what she described as the "complete spiritual transformation of the masses
degraded by centuries of bourgeois class rule," just as only their creative experience and spontaneous action can solve the myriad problems of creating a

libertarian socialist society. She went on to say that "historically, the errors committed by a truly revolutionary movement are infinitely more fruitful than the infallibility of the cleverest Central Committee."

I think that these remarks can be translated immediately for the somewhat parallel ideology of the "soulful corporation," which is now fairly popular among American academics, for example, Karl Kassem, who writes:

> No longer the agent of proprietorship seeking to maximize return on investment, management sees itself as responsible to stockholders, employees, customers, the general public, and perhaps more important the firm itself as an institution. There is no display of greed or graspingness, there is no attempt to push off on the workers of the community at least part of the social cost of the enterprise. The modern corporation is a soulful corporation.

Similarly, the vanguard party is a soulful party. In both cases, those who urge that humans submit to the rule of these benevolent autocracies may, I think, justly be accused of wishing to make humans into machines.

Now the correctness of the view which is expressed by Rousseau and Kant and Humboldt and Luxemburg and innumerable others, I don't think the correctness of this is for the moment susceptible to scientific proof. One can only evaluate it in terms of experience and intuition. But one can also point out the social consequences of adopting the view that men are born to be free or that they are born to be ruled by benevolent autocrats.

What of the second question, the question of efficiency? Is democratic control of the industrial system down to the smallest functional units incompatible with efficiency? This is very frequently argued on several grounds. Some say, for example, that centralized management is a technological imperative. But I think the argument is exceedingly weak when one looks into it. The very same technology that brings relevant information to the board of managers can bring it, at the time that it is needed, to everyone in the workforce. The technology that's now capable of eliminating the stupefying labor that turns humans into specialized tools of production permits in principle the leisure and the educational opportunities that make them able to use this information in a rational way. Furthermore, even an economic elite which is "dripping with soulfulness," to use Ralph Milliband's phrase, is constrained by the system in which it functions to organize production for certain ends (power, growth, profit) but not, in the nature of the case, human needs, needs that, to an ever more critical degree, can be expressed only in collective terms. It's surely conceivable, and perhaps even likely, that decisions made by the collective itself would reflect these needs and interests as well as those made by various soulful elites. In any event, it's a bit difficult to take seriously arguments about efficiency in a society that devotes such enormous resources to waste and destruction. As everyone knows, the very concept of efficiency is dripping with ideology. Maximization of commodities is hardly the only measure of a decent existence. The point is familiar, and no elaboration is necessary.

[State socialism and state capitalism: two parallel ideologies]

Let me turn finally to the two final points of reference, the Bolshevik or state socialist and the state capitalist. As I tried to suggest, they have points in common. And in interesting respects they diverge from the classical liberal ideal or its later elaboration in libertarian socialism.

Since I'm concerned with our society, let me make a few rather elementary observations about the role of the state, its likely evolution, and the ideological assumptions that accompany, and sometimes disguise, this phenomenon.

It's obvious to begin with that we can distinguish two systems of power: the political system and the economic system. The former consists in principle of elected representatives of the people who set public policy; the latter, in principle, is a system of private power, a system of private empires that are free from public control except in the remote and indirect ways in which even a feudal nobility or a totalitarian dictatorship must be responsive to the public will.

There are several immediate consequences of this organization of society. The first is that in a subtle way an authoritarian cast of mind is induced in a very large mass of the population, which is subject to arbitrary decree from above. I think this has a great effect on the general character of the culture (the belief that one must obey arbitrary dictates and accede to authority). I think in fact that a remarkable and exciting fact about the youth movement in recent years is that it's challenging and beginning to break down some of these authoritarian patterns.

The second fact that is important is that the range of decisions that are in principle subject to public democratic control is quite narrow. For example, it excludes, in law and in principle, the central institutions in any advanced industrial society, that is, the entire commercial, industrial, and financial system.

And the third fact is that even within the narrow range of issues that are submitted in principle to democratic decision making, the centers of private power of course exert an inordinately heavy influence in perfectly obvious ways: through control of the media, through control of political organizations, or in fact by the simple and direct means of supplying the top personnel for the parliamentary system itself, as they obviously do. Dick Barnet, in his recent study of the top four hundred decision makers in the postwar national security system, reports that most "come from executive suites and law offices within shouting distance of each other in fifteen city blocks in five major cities." And every other study shows the same thing.

In short, the democratic system at best functions within a very narrow range in a capitalist democracy, and even within this narrow range its functioning is enormously biased by the concentrations of private power and by the authoritarian and passive modes of thinking that are induced by autocratic institutions such as corporations. It's a truism, but one that must be constantly stressed, that capitalism and democracy are ultimately quite incompatible, and a careful look at the matter merely strengthens this conclusion. There are perfectly obvious processes of centralization and control taking place in both the political and the industrial system.

As far as the political system is concerned, in every parliamentary democracy, not only ours, the role of parliament in policy formation has been declining in the years since World War II, as everyone knows and political commentators repeatedly point out. The executive, in other words, is becoming increasingly more powerful as the planning functions of the state become more significant. The House Armed Services Committee a couple of years ago described the role of Congress as that of "a sometimes querulous but essentially kindly uncle who complains while furiously puffing on his pipe but who, finally, as everyone expects, gives in and hands over the allowance." And careful study of civil military decisions since World War II show that this is quite an accurate perception. Senator Vanderberg twenty years ago expressed his fear that the American chief executive would become "the number one war lord of the earth" (his phrase). That has since occurred. The clearest example is the decision to escalate in Vietnam in February 1965, in cynical disregard of the expressed will of the electorate.

This incident reveals, I think, with perfect clarity the role of the public in decisions about peace and war—the role of the public in decisions about the main lines of public policy in general. And it also suggests the irrelevance of electoral politics to major decisions of national policy. Unfortunately, you can't "vote the rascals out," because you never voted them in in the first place. The corporate executives and the corporation lawyers and so on, who overwhelmingly staff the executive, assisted increasingly by a university-based mandarin class, remain in power no matter whom you elect.

Furthermore, it's interesting to note that this ruling elite is pretty clear about its social role. As an example, take Robert McNamara, who is a person widely praised in liberal circles for his humanity, his technical brilliance, and his campaign to control the military. His views of social organization, I think, are quite illuminating. He says, "Vital decision making in policy matters as well as business must remain at the top. That is partly, though not completely, what the top is for." He goes on to suggest that this is apparently a divine imperative:

> God is clearly democratic. He distributes brain power universally. But He quite
> justifiably expects us to do something efficient and constructive with that priceless
> gift. That's what management is all about. Management is in the end the most cre-
> ative of all the arts for its medium is human talent itself. The real threat to democ-
> racy comes from under management. The under management of a society is not
> the respect of liberty; it is simply to let some force other than reason shape reality.
> If it is not reason that rules man, then man falls short of his potential.

So reason, then, is to be identified as the centralization of decision making at the top in the hands of management. Popular involvement in decision making is a threat to liberty, a violation of reason. Reason is embodied in autocratic, tightly managed institutions. Strengthening these institutions, within which man can function most efficiently, is, in his words, "the great human adventure of our time." All of this has a faintly familiar ring to it, and I think it is the authentic voice of the liberal technical intelligentsia, the technocratic corporate elite in a modern society.

There is a parallel process of centralization in economic life. A recent FTC [Federal Trade Commission] report notes that the two hundred largest manufacturing corporations now control about two-thirds of all manufacturing assets. At the beginning of World War II, the same amount of power was spread over one thousand corporations. The report says that "a small industrial elite of huge conglomerate companies is gobbling up American business and largely destroying competitive free enterprise." Furthermore, "these 200 corporations are partially linked with each other and with other corporations in ways that may prevent or discourage independent behavior in market decisions." What is novel about such observations is only their source: the FTC. They are familiar to the point of cliché among left-liberal commentators on American society.

The centralization of power also has an international dimension. It's been pointed out (in *Foreign Affairs*) that "on the basis of the gross value of their output, U.S. enterprises abroad in the aggregate comprise the third largest country in the world, with a gross product greater than that of any country except the United States and the Soviet Union." American firms control over half of the automobile industry in England, almost 40 percent of petroleum in Germany, over 40 percent of the telegraphic, telephone, and electronic and business equipment in France, 75 percent of the computers. Within a decade, given present trends, more than half of British exports will be from American-owned companies. And furthermore these are highly concentrated investments. Forty percent of direct investment in Germany, France, and Britain is by three American firms.

George Ball has explained that the project of constructing an integrated world economy dominated by American capital (an empire, in other words) is no idealistic pipe dream but a hardheaded prediction. It's a role, he says, into which we are being pushed by the imperatives of our own economy, the major instrument being the multinational corporation, which George Ball describes as follows:

> In its modern form the multinational corporation or one with world-wide operations and markets is a distinctly American development. Through such corporations it has become possible for the first time to use the world's resources with maximal efficiency. But there must be greater unification of the world economy to give full play to the benefits of multinational corporations. These multinational corporations are the beneficiary of the mobilization of resources by the federal government and its world-wide operations and markets are backed ultimately by American military force now based in dozens of countries.

It's not difficult to guess who will reap the benefits from the integrated world economy, which is the domain of operation of these American-based international economic institutions.

At this stage in the discussion one has to mention the specter of communism. What is the threat of communism to this system? For a clear and cogent answer one can turn to an extensive study of the Woodrow Wilson Foundation, the National Planning Association, called *The political economy of American foreign policy,* a very important book, which is compiled by a representative segment of the tiny elite that largely sets public policy whoever is technically in office. In effect, it's as close as you can come to a manifesto of the American ruling class. Here they define the primary threat of communism as "the economic transformation of the Communist powers in ways which reduce their willingness or ability to complement the industrial economies of the West." That is the primary threat of Communism. Communism, in short, reduces the willingness and ability of the underdeveloped countries to function in the world's capitalist economy in the manner of, for example, the Philippines, which has developed a colonial economy of the classic type after seventy-five years of American tutelage and domination. It's this doctrine which explains why the British economist Joan Robinson describes the American crusade against communism as a crusade against development.

The cold war ideology and the international communist conspiracy function, in an important way, as essentially a propaganda device to mobilize support, at a particular historical moment, for this longtime imperial enterprise. In fact, I believe that this is probably the main function of the Cold War. It serves as a useful device for the managers of American society and their counterparts in the Soviet Union to control their own populations and their own respective imperial systems. I think that the persistence of the Cold War can be in part explained by its utility for the managers of the two great world systems.

[An escape from contemporary barbarism]

There's one final element that has to be added to this picture, namely, the ongoing militarization of American society. How does this enter in?

To see, I think, one has to look back to World War II and to recall that prior to World War II, of course, we were deep in the Depression. World War II taught an important economic lesson. It taught the lesson that government-induced production in a carefully controlled economy, centrally controlled, could overcome the effects of the Depression. I think that this is what Charles E. Wilson [then president of General Electric] had in mind in 1944 when he proposed that we have a "permanent war economy" in the postwar world. Of course, the trouble is that in a capitalist economy there are only a number of ways in which government intervention can take place: it can't be competitive with the private empires, for example, which is to say that it can't be any useful production. In fact, it has to be the production of luxury goods, not capital, not useful commodities, which would be competitive. And unfortunately there is only one category of luxury goods that can be produced endlessly, with rapid obsolescence, quickly wasting, and no limit on how many of them you can use. We all know what that is.

This whole matter is described pretty well by the business historian Alfred Chandler. He describes the economic lessons of World War II as follows:

> The government spent far more than the more enthusiastic New Dealer had ever proposed. Most of the output of the expenditures was destroyed or left on the battlefields of Europe and Asia. But the resulting increase demand sent the nation

into a period of prosperity the like of which had never before been seen. Moreover, the supplying of huge armies and navies, fighting the most massive war of all time, required a tight centralized control of the national economy. This effort brought corporate managers to Washington to carry out one of the most complex pieces of economic planning in history. That experience lessened the ideological fears over the government's role in stabilizing the economy.

(This is a conservative commentator, I might point out.)

It may be added that the ensuing cold war carried further the depoliticization of American society and created the kind of psychological environment in which the government is able to intervene in part through fiscal policies, in part through public work and public services, but very largely, of course, through "defense" spending. In this way, to use Alfred Chandler's words, "the government acts as a coordinator of last resort" when "managers are unable to maintain a high level of aggregate demand." As another conservative business historian, Joseph Monsen, writes: "Enlightened corporate managers, far from fearing government intervention in the economy, view the new economics as a technique for increasing corporate viability."

Of course, the most cynical use of these ideas is by the managers of the publicly subsidized war industries. There was a remarkable series in the *Washington Post* about this about a year ago by Bernard Nossiter. For example, he quoted Samuel Downer, financial vice president of LTV Aerospace Corporation, one of the big new conglomerates, who explains why "the postwar world must be bolstered by military orders":

> It's basic. Its selling appeal is defense of the home. This is one of the greatest appeals that politicians have for adjusting the system. If you're the President and you need a control factor in the economy, and you need to sell this factor, you can't sell Harlem and Watts, but you can sell self-preservation, a new environment. We are going to increase defense budgets as long as those bastards in Russia are ahead of us. The American people understand this.

Of course, those bastards aren't exactly ahead of us in this deadly and cynical game, but that's only a minor embarrassment to the thesis. In times of need we can always follow Dean Rusk, Hubert Humphrey, and other luminaries and appeal to the billion Chinese, armed to the teeth and setting out on a world conquest.

Again, I want to emphasize the role in this system of the cold war as a technique of domestic control, a technique for developing a psychological climate for paranoia and psychosis in which the taxpayer will be willing to provide an enormous, endless subsidy to the technologically advanced sectors of American industry and the corporations that dominate this increasingly centralized system.

Of course, it's perfectly obvious that Russian imperialism is not an invention of American ideologists. It's real enough to the Hungarians and the Czechs, for example. What is an invention is the uses to which it's put, for example by Dean Acheson in 1950, or Walt Rostow a decade later, when they pretend that the Vietnam War is an example of Russian imperialism. Or by the Johnson administration in 1965, when it justifies the Dominican intervention with reference to the Sino-Soviet military block; or by the Kennedy intellectuals, who, as Townsend Hopes put it in an article in the *Washington Monthly* last month, were "conditioned by the tensions of the Cold War years" and could not perceive that the triumph of the national revolution in Vietnam would not be "a triumph for Moscow and Peking"—a most remarkable degree of delusion on the part of presumably literate men. Or, for example, by Eugene Rostow, who, in a recent book that was very widely praised by liberal senators and academic intellectuals, outlines a series of challenges to world order in the modern era as follows: Napoleon, Kaiser Wilhelm, Hitler, and, continuing in the postwar world, general strikes in France and Italy, the civil war in Greece, and the attack on South Vietnam, where, he writes in 1968, Russia "has put us to severe tests" in its efforts to spread communism by the sword. That's a very interesting series of challenges to world order: Napoleon, Kaiser Wilhelm, Hitler, general strikes in France and Italy, the civil war in Greece, and the Russsian attack on South Vietnam. If one thinks it through, he can reach some pretty interesting conclusions about modern history.

One can continue with this indefinitely. I mean to suggest that the cold war is highly functional, both to the American elite and its Soviet counterpart, who, in a perfectly similar way, exploit Western imperialism, which they did not invent, as they send their armies into Czechoslovakia. It's important in both cases in providing an ideology for empire and for the government-subsidized system here of military capitalism. It's predictable, then, that challenges to this ideology will be bitterly resisted, by force if necessary.

In many ways American society is indeed open, and liberal values are preserved. However, as poor people and black people and other ethnic minorities know very well, the liberal veneer is pretty thin. Mark Twain once wrote that "it is by the goodness of God that in our country we have those three unspeakable precious things: freedom of speech, freedom of conscience, and the prudence never to practice either of them." Those who lack the prudence may well pay the cost.

Roughly speaking, I think it's accurate to say that a corporate elite of managers and owners governs the economy and the political system as well, at least in very large measure. The people, so-called, do exercise an occasional choice among those who Marx once called "the rival factions and adventurers of the ruling class." Those who find this characterization too harsh may prefer the formulations of a modern democratic theorist like Joseph Schumpeter, who describes modern political democracy, favorably, as "a system in which the deciding of issues by the electorate is secondary to the election of the men who are to do the deciding." "A political party," he says, accurately, "is a group whose members propose to act in concert in the competitive struggle for political power; if that were not so it would be impossible for different parties to adopt exactly or almost exactly the same program." That's all the advantages of political democracy as he sees it.

This program that both parties adopt, more or less exactly, and the individuals who compete for power express a narrow conservative ideology, basically the interests of one or another element in the corporate elite, with some modifications. This is obviously no conspiracy. I think it is simply implicit in the system of corporate capitalism. These people and the institutions they represent are in effect in power, and their interests are the "national interests." It's this interest that is served primarily and overwhelmingly by the overseas empire and the growing system of military state capitalism at home. If we were to withdraw the consent of the governed, as I think we should, we're withdrawing our consent to have these men, and the interests they represent, govern and manage American society and impose their concept of "world order" and their criteria for political and economic development on much of the world. Although an immense effort of propaganda and mystification is carried on to conceal these facts, nonetheless facts they remain.

We have today the technical and material resources to meet man's animal needs. We have not developed the cultural and moral resources, or the democratic forms of social organization, that make possible the humane and rational use of our material wealth and power. Conceivably, the classical liberal ideas as expressed and developed in their libertarian socialist form are achievable, but if so, only by a popular revolutionary movement, rooted in wide strata of the population and committed to the elimination of repressive and authoritarian institutions, state and private.

To create such a movement is the challenge we face and must meet if there's to be an escape from contemporary barbarism.

APPENDIX
On the "national interest" (January 28, 1977)

The concept "national interest" has been so debased by propagandists that it is probably best abandoned. Nevertheless, it is conceivable that it might be rehabilitated as a useful term for the analysis of international affairs in a world of nation-states. In such a world, it might on occasion be the case that in the welter of individual, class, and other group interests, some concerns might be identified that are largely shared by citizens of a particular nation-state: the interest in not being overrun by foreign force, for example. In practice, the "nation" will be divided even on this elemental issue: no occupying army has lacked collaborators to perform its filthy work. Still, at the level of vagueness and generality characteristic of terminology of social and political analysis, one might resurrect a reasonable notion of "national interest" along these lines.

But the exercise is academic, even deceptive. Within the nation-state, the "national interest" will be articulated by those who control the central economic and political institutions. There is no reason to suppose that the "national interest," so articulated, will have any relation to such common interests as might be generally shared within a society.

It is often held that rejection of "national interest" in favor of "class interest" is a radical stance, but that is incorrect. It is common enough outside of radical circles, though the point is often presented in a somewhat different way and remains implicit.

Consider, for example, the work of Hans Morgenthau, who has written extensively and often perceptively on the national interest, perhaps more than any other American political analyst. In the most recent presentation of his views (*New Republic*, January 22, 1977), he states that the national interest underlying a rational foreign policy "is not defined by the whim of a man or the partisanship of party but imposes itself as an objective datum upon all men applying their rational faculties to the conduct of foreign policy." He then cites as illustrations such commitments as support for South Korea, containment of China, and upholding of the Monroe Doctrine. He further observes that "the concentrations of private power which have actually governed America since the Civil War have withstood all attempts to control, let alone dissolve them . . . [and] have preserved their hold upon the levers of political decision."

True, no doubt. Under such circumstances, do we expect the "national interest" as actually articulated and pursued to be simply the outcome of the application of rational faculties to objective data, or to be an expression of specific class interests? Obviously the latter, and a serious investigation of the cases Morgenthau cites, which is beyond the scope of these remarks, will demonstrate that the expectation is amply fulfilled. The real interests of Americans were in no way advanced by the crushing of popular forces in South Korea in the late 1940s and the imposition of a series of dictatorial regimes, to cite just one of his examples. But it can be argued that the interests of the "concentrations of private power" in the United States that effectively dominate the world capitalist system were advanced by this pursuit of the "national interest." The same holds quite generally. The idea that foreign policy is derived in the manner of physics is sheer myth.

Or consider a recent analysis by Walter Dean Burnham in *Trialogue* (fall 1976), the journal of the Trilateral Commission. He notes that the "basic functions" of the state are "the promotion externally and internally of the basic interests of the dominant mode of production and the need to maintain social harmony." Radicals would not disagree, in essence, though they would observe that the formulation is highly misleading. In the first place, these "basic functions" of the state are not a matter of metaphysical necessity, but arise from specific causes. Furthermore, the "dominant mode production" does not have interests; rather, those individual groups who participate in it have interests, often conflicting ones. And since those who own and manage this system are also in effective control of the state apparatus—a fact that should be sufficiently obvious to those familiar with the Trilateral Commission, which dominates the new administration in a most remarkable way—the "basic interests" pursued will be theirs. There are no grounds in history or logic to suppose that these interests will coincide to any significant extent with the interests of those who participate in the dominant mode of production by renting themselves to its owners and managers.

Concepts such as "socialism" and "democracy" have been no less debased in contemporary political discourse. To libertarian socialists, at least, socialism and freedom are inseparable. There is no socialism worthy of the name under a party dictatorship. And democracy is an empty pretense to the extent that production, finance, and commerce—and along with them, the political processes of the society as well—are under the control of "concentrations of private power." The "national interest" as articulated by those who dominate the state-capitalist or state-socialist societies will be their special interests. Under these circumstances, talk of "national interest" can only contribute to mystification and oppression.

If libertarian socialist forces develop on any significant scale, they will be compelled, at the outset at least, to adapt themselves to the system of nation-states, and will undertake to dissolve these systems of class dominance from within while working in solidarity with others across national lines to reconstruct international society as well. Short of this, authoritarian states, whether they call themselves "socialist" or "democratic" (or both), will act to perpetuate the particular interests of those who are in a position to organize the resources and productive institutions of the society. It is futile to ask whether the United States or the Soviet Union, or for that matter lesser powers, might undertake a commitment to general interests of their own populations or others on any significant scale. In the interest of preserving order ("social harmony"), it may be necessary to pursue such policies in any society—feudal, fascist, state socialist, democratic capitalist, or whatever. And by sheer historical accident, policies undertaken in the interest of ruling groups may on occasion have such effects. But power will work for its own purposes, whatever the rhetoric employed to disguise or legitimate it.

Chapter 8
Some tasks for responsible people (August 1969)

Dire warnings with regard to the state of American society are hardly confined to the left these days. Senator Fulbright has recently warned that the United States is "already a long way toward becoming an elective dictatorship." If we continue on our present course, "the future can hold nothing for us except endless foreign exertions, chronic warfare, burgeoning expense and the proliferation of an already formidable military-industrial-labor-academic complex—in short, the militarization of American life. . . . If, in short, America is to become an empire, there is very little chance that it can avoid becoming a virtual dictatorship as well."[1]

Senator Fulbright was commenting on an attempt to combat the erosion of the constitutional system, typical of all Western parliamentary democracies as centralization of power in the executive continually increases. The attempt is embodied in a "sense of the Senate" resolution that was proposed by the Senate Committee on Foreign Relations. Its report (April 16, 1969) notes that the chief executive "now exercises something approaching absolute power over the life or death of every living American—to say nothing of millions of other people all over the world." It warns that in consequence the American people are threatened "with tyranny or disaster."

["Internal aggression" and "national defense"]
The committee's report recalls the fears expressed by Abraham Lincoln when President Polk "precipitated the clash which began the Mexican War": "Kings had always been involving and impoverishing their people in wars, pretending generally, if not always, that the good of the people was the object. This our Convention undertook to be the most oppressive of all kingly oppressions; and they resolved to so frame the Constitution that no one man should hold the power of bringing oppression upon us." The report notes further

that there are 50,000 American troops in Thailand, many "engaged in military support operations against insurgency." It cites a classified memorandum asserting "that the presence of American Armed Forces in Spain constitutes a more significant security guarantee to Spain than would a written agreement." Since the only attack that threatens Spain is what is nowadays called "internal aggression," it is clear what form of "security" is guaranteed by these secret agreements.

The Senate committee is surely accurate in remarking that domestic tyranny is a likely concomitant to the effort by the "kingly oppressor" to protect such delightful regimes as those of Spain and Thailand (and Saigon, and Greece, and Brazil) from "internal aggression." We can expect, with fair confidence, that any serious domestic challenge to American global management or its ideological underpinnings will call forth the repressive force and ultimately the violence of the state. What we may expect, then, is voluntary submission to the coercive ideology of Pax Americana and its repressive practices or the overt use of force to compel obedience; in either case, a form of domestic tyranny.

The attempt to construct an integrated global economy dominated by American capital is one major theme of postwar history. Though there have been setbacks, the project proceeds apace along many paths, and no one can predict the degree to which it will succeed. Evidently, only certain forms of national development are compatible with this aim, and American foreign policy has endeavored to block all others. In practice this has often meant, in Joan Robinson's words, that "the United States' crusade against Communism is a campaign against development. By means of it the American people have been led to acquiesce in the maintenance of a huge war machine and its use by threat or actual force to try to suppress every popular movement that aims to overthrow ancient or modern tyranny and begin to find a way to overcome poverty and establish national self-respect."[2]

The maintenance of the huge war machine has deeper social roots than the need to protect the regimes of Greece, Spain, and Brazil from internal aggression. Even if American military support were not needed to preserve these bastions of freedom, the militarization of American society would be unlikely to abate. The particular form of state-subsidized capitalism evolving in the United States demands substantial government support for technologically advanced segments of American industry. Under existing social conditions, with public policy largely determined by private empires, it is naturally preparation for war to which the public subsidy is diverted. With the best of will, it is not easy to devise alternative forms of government intervention in the economy that will not conflict with the interests of these private empires but will rather enhance them. Furthermore, a public subsidy must be tolerable to the population at large. Even a totalitarian state must win some measure of popular support for its policies and expenditures, and "defense of the home" is invariably the last resort. A challenge to the system of preparation for war is not likely to be tolerated.

Such a challenge has arisen in the United States in the last few years, largely from the student movement and the black liberation movements. The rising wave of repression should therefore come as no surprise. The editors of *Monthly Review* have quite correctly noted the analogy to the postwar repression that helped to impose the narrow conservatism that has dominated American life for the past two decades. It is typical of repressive regimes throughout the world that they place their harshest and most reactionary figures in control of the ministries of war and interior. The Nixon administration has adopted this familiar practice (Laird and Mitchell). A bill now before Congress proposes the establishment of a crime of peacetime treason, with severe punishments for those who give "aid and comfort" to "any foreign nation or armed group which is engaged in open hostilities" with American armed forces. The implications are clear. But even without such "legal" authorization, there are many early signs of what might ultimately become a police state, perhaps with extensive popular support: coordinated counterinsurgency operations, as in Berkeley; criminal police violence against Black Panthers; harassment by quasi-judicial means; punitive sentencing for minor violations; congressional investigation of universities, and so on.

Twenty years ago, the contribution of American liberalism to the repression was not small. One of the first acts of the Americans for Democratic Action was "to use guilt-by-association tactics by printing in major urban newspapers the names of the Progressive Party's principal contributors and then listing the organizations on the Attorney-General's list of subversive groups to which these contributors belonged—or had belonged"—this well before McCarthy got into the act.[3] The hysterical reaction, in some quarters, to the revival of politics in the 1960s suggests that history may repeat. In these circumstances, even the defense of civil liberties has a radical content.

[A vision of a future social order]
The best way to defend civil liberties is to build a movement for social change with a positive program that has a broad-based appeal, that encourages free and open discussion and offers a wide range of possibilities for work and action. The potential for such a movement surely exists. Whether it will be

realized remains an open question. External repression is one serious threat. Factional bickering, dogmatism, fantasies, and manipulative tactics are probably a considerably greater danger.

A movement of the left should distinguish with clarity between its long-range revolutionary aims and certain more immediate effects it can hope to achieve. Specifically, for us today there is no priority higher than bringing the Vietnam War to a quick end with the withdrawal of all American military force. This may be a feasible goal. It would entail the abandonment of a policy that has been pursued for twenty years as part of a more general strategy for constructing an integrated world empire compatible with the perceived needs of American capital and organized in accordance with the dominant principles of American ideology. Nevertheless, this particular venture could no doubt be "liquidated" without too severe a blow to the system—fortunately for the people of Vietnam and Laos, for if this were not true, their future would be dim indeed. I continue to believe that nonviolent resistance provides the best means for achieving this goal.

But in the long run, a movement of the left has no chance of success, and deserves none, unless it develops an understanding of contemporary society and a vision of a future social order that is persuasive to a large majority of the population. Its goals and organizational forms must take shape through their active participation in political struggle and social reconstruction. A genuine radical culture can be created only through the spiritual transformation of great masses of people, the essential feature of any social revolution that is to extend the possibilities for human creativity and freedom.

There is no doubt that we can learn from the achievements and the failures of revolutionary struggles in the less-developed countries, and it would be as foolish to fail to do so as it would be criminal not to help where we can. It is evident, however, that their experiences cannot be mechanically transferred to a society such as ours. In an advanced industrial society it is, obviously, far from true that the mass of the population have nothing to lose but their chains, and there is no point in pretending otherwise. On the contrary, they have a considerable stake in preserving the existing social order.

Correspondingly, the cultural and intellectual level of any serious radical movement will have to be far higher than in the past, as Andre Gorz, for one, has correctly emphasized. It will not be able to satisfy itself with a litany of forms of oppression and injustice. It will have to provide compelling answers to the question of how these evils can be overcome by revolution or large-scale reform. To accomplish this aim, the left will have to achieve and maintain a position of honesty and commitment to libertarian values. It must not succumb to the illusion that a "vanguard party," self-designated as the repository of all truth and virtue, can take state power and miraculously bring about a revolution that will establish decent values and truly democratic structures as the framework for social life. If its only clearly expressed goals are to smash and destroy, it will succeed only in smashing and destroying itself.

Furthermore, if a radical movement hopes to be able to combat imperialism or the kinds of repression, social management, and coercion that will be developed by the evolving international economic institutions, it too will have to be international in its organizational forms as well as in the cultural level it seeks to attain. To construct a movement of this sort will be no mean feat. It may well be true, however, that success in this endeavor is the only alternative to tyranny and disaster.

The threat of tyranny and disaster, or even their early manifestations, does not itself provide a sufficient basis for the creation of a significant radical mass movement. In fact, this threat may induce a conservative defensive reaction. For a person to commit himself to a movement for radical social change, with all of the uncertainty and hazard that this entails, he must have a strong reason to believe that there is some likelihood of success in bringing about a new social order.

This is not merely a matter of satisfaction of personal material needs, of narrow self-interest in the sense cultivated by capitalist ideology. There is, to be sure, a justification for radical politics even in terms of self-interest in this narrow sense. The enormous waste of resources that are far from boundless and the race toward mutual annihilation on the part of the great powers provide a sufficient reason for a rational man to seek actively for some far-reaching alternative. Beyond this, it is by now widely realized that the economist's "externalities" can no longer be consigned to footnotes. No one who gives a moment's thought to the problems of contemporary society can fail to be aware of the social costs of consumption and production, the progressive destruction of the environment, the utter irrationality of the utilization of contemporary technology, the inability of a system based on profit or growth maximization to deal with needs that can only be expressed collectively, and the enormous bias this system imposes toward maximization of commodities for personal use in place of the general improvement of the quality of life.

All of these are factors in modern life that should lead to the growth of a vigorous left that seeks to replace contemporary barbarism by some form of libertarian socialism. But there is something insufferably arrogant about the belief that "we" are radical because we are humane and that "they" will join us when they see that it is in their self-interest to do so. Compassion, solidarity, friendship are also human needs. They are driving needs, no less than the desire to increase one's share of commodities or to improve working conditions. Beyond this, I do not doubt that it is a fundamental human need to take an active part in the democratic control of social institutions. If this is so, then the demand for industrial democracy should become a central goal of any revitalized left with a working-class base.

[Technology and self-management: from autocracy to acracy]

In fact, in France and England there has been a renewed interest in industrial democracy and workers' control after a lapse of quite a few years.[4] This is a most welcome development. It is often argued that the formation of enormous planning units—the centralized state bureaucracy, immense corporations, or both acting in concert—is a technological imperative, a requirement for economic health and proper utilization of resources in a complex advanced industrial society. I have yet to see an argument that advanced technology requires centralized autocratic management. The same technology that can strengthen the authority of a narrow elite of owners, managers, or technocrats might also be used to extend industrial democracy. In its early stages, the industrial system required the kind of specialized labor which, as Adam Smith pointed out, turned men into imbeciles, mere tools of production. Now this is no longer true. With modern technology, tools can be tools and men can be men. The need for managers is a corollary to the specialization of the labor force. It diminishes as the opportunities increase for each participant in the workforce to obtain relevant information when it is needed for decision making and to achieve the cultural level that enables him to take part in global decisions. Simulation makes it possible to carry out certain experiments without suffering the cost of failure. Automation may provide the possibility to eliminate mind-destroying drudgery. To develop these possibilities in a concrete and detailed form is the proper task for the left. It is a task that can be carried out only by direct participation of manual and intellectual workers; it should lead to blurring, perhaps to the disappearance, of the distinction between these social categories.

What can be plausibly argued is that planning is a necessity in an advanced industrial society. One must, however, bear in mind an observation that is put very well by Ken Coates in introducing a recent symposium on workers' control: "If planning has become a crucial need, then it has also become transparently clear that none of the most basic and elementary liberal values can survive such planning upon such a scale, unless it is arranged along lines which are inherently and profoundly democratic."[5] The problem of how to combine planning with democracy, and so to preserve and significantly extend and enrich liberal values, will not be solved on paper, but only through a combination of practical experience and intellectual analysis. Almost by definition, this is a task for a revitalized movement of the left, a movement that will combine the highest level of science and technology with serious inquiry into the sources and social conditions for creativity and freedom.

Questions of this sort barely exist in the academic social sciences. For example, the leading textbook on modern economics describes the range of possible economic systems as falling on a spectrum with complete laissez-faire and "totalitarian dictatorship of production" as the polar cases: "the relevant choice for policy today is not a decision between these extremes, but rather the degree to which public policy should do *less or more* in modifying the operation of particular private economic activities."[6] Evidently, basic questions are begged by describing the spectrum of possible systems in these terms. There is quite another spectrum that can be imagined, with democratic and autocratic control of the system of production as the polar cases. Along this dimension, both of Samuelson's polar opposites fall at the same extreme point: both "ideal" private capitalism and "totalitarian dictatorship of production" are forms of autocratic control, to be contrasted with popular democratic control of the economy through workers' councils, commune assemblies, and other forms of popular organization that can be imagined. Similarly, in a recent symposium of the American Academy of Arts and Sciences devoted to "Perspectives on Business," there is much discussion of the matter of management- vs.-ownership control (and the effect of technology on this distribution of power), but no mention of the possibility that the economic system might be brought under popular democratic control.[7]

The assumptions that guide the mass of scholarship hardly differ from those expressed in manifestos of the American ruling elite, for example, the report of the study group on *Political economy of American foreign policy*, which identifies Western civilization with capitalist forms (as contrasted to the collectivist denial of freedom, initiative, and progress) and defines "the aim of economic activity in the West [as] the maximization of money income—in one or another of its forms—by individuals through the investment of capital or of labor on one's own account or for, and under the direction of, others."[8] The document goes on, characteristically, to describe this particular perversion in terms of universal ideals. We cannot be merely an "impartial arbiter . . . maintaining world order" but must be an active leader in the struggle to save Western civilization and the "universal ideals of human freedom, individual growth, and economic justice" which are expressed ("however imperfectly") in the capitalist institutions of the West.

Surely this concept of economic man is a psychological absurdity which leads to untold suffering for those who try to mold themselves to this pattern, as well as for their victims. "Look out for number one" is a prescription for demoralization, corruption, and ultimately general catastrophe, whatever value it may have had in the early stages of industrialization. Cooperation for the common good and concern for the rights and needs of others must replace the dismal search for maximization of personal power and consumption if the barbarism of capitalist society is to be overcome.

[A large-scale "cultural revolution"]

The left has the inestimable advantage that it can hope to speak for humane values in opposition to the barbarous irrationality of a competitive society and to the autocratic rule of private economic empires, state bureaucracies, vanguard parties, technocratic-meritocratic elites, or whatever other monstrosities the future may hold. It will have to exploit this advantage if there is to be any hope for a serious anti-imperialist, anti-militarist movement with a broad base in the advanced societies.

Consider again the manifesto cited above. It defines the primary threat of communism, perceptively, in the following terms:

> It has meant: (1) A serious reduction of the potential resource base and market opportunities of the West owing to the subtraction of the communist areas from the international economy and their economic transformation in ways which reduce their willingness and ability to complement the industrial economies of the West.[9]

Evidently, this interpretation of the communist threat (which goes a long way toward explaining Joan Robinson's judgment, quoted above, that the American crusade against Communism is a campaign against development) will be quite compelling to the rich, who will easily understand why our goal must be to assist "the millhands of Calcutta, the peasants of Egypt and the Indians of Guatemala [to] become politically more reliable and economically more cooperative members of the free world community," able to exercise "the capacity for self-control, for rational and morally valid choices and for responsible actions." American dominance of the world requires such political reliability, cooperativeness, and moral responsibility. For the wealthy and privileged, it is easy to identify American dominance of the world's resources with "the continued existence of human freedom and humane society everywhere." This dominance is threatened by forms of national independence or international cooperation that appropriate resources for the benefit of those who now "complement the industrial economies of the West."

This kind of "threat" should be welcomed and encouraged by the left, as should its domestic analogue. An international movement of the left should aim, of course, to reduce inequity. But this is to say that participants in such a movement, in the advanced countries, must be motivated by compassion and brotherhood rather than mere personal greed. In the long run, there is no reason why an equitable distribution of the earth's resources should lead to a decline of standard of living in the advanced countries if it is combined with an end to the irrational waste and destruction of resources characteristic of the advanced industrial societies. Once again, however, it is clear that a large-scale "cultural revolution" is a prerequisite—or better, a necessary concomitant—for a movement of the left with solid roots in technologically advanced societies.

The same considerations hold when we consider the urgent matter of bringing the arms race to an end. In the near future it will no doubt be exceedingly difficult to organize a campaign against militarism with support among workers, technicians, engineers, and scientists who are heavily dependent on the military budget for their employment. When radical students at MIT succeeded in raising a serious challenge to military research, the first reaction of the labor union in the university laboratories was to enter a suit in the federal courts to prevent MIT from dropping military work. The response was not irrational; the New England economy provides no alternative sources of employment. Similar factors will make it quite difficult for engineers and many scientists to dissociate themselves from the commitment to war and waste.

If a radical movement hopes to make any progress among skilled workers, engineers, and scientists, it will have to persuade them that their short-run interest is outweighed by other factors, among them the personal interest of every rational man in the conversion of intellectual and material resources to reasonable ends, more specifically in halting the preparation for war that may well lead to a final catastrophe. The task for radicals, in this case, is to develop concrete alternatives and to show how they could be realized under different conditions of social organization. Furthermore, they must combat the psychotic worldview that has been constructed to rationalize the race to destruction. They must try to bring about a fundamental change of values, a commitment to general goals that will, once achieved, spell an end to imperial domination, militarism, and oppression.

A decade ago, only a visionary would have been able even to contemplate these questions. Now they are lively and exciting ones. The revisionist historians have succeeded in shattering the illusions that dominated postwar scholarship. Groups such as the North American Conference on Latin America, the Committee of Concerned Asian Scholars, the Union for Radical Political Economics, and many others have the potential to revitalize the professions and to create a radical intellectual culture with a broad base in the universities and colleges, with effects that will extend through the media—perhaps newly created for this purpose—the schools, communities, and activist organizations of many sorts.

Of course, these professional groups have been riding the crest of a wave of political activism. Inquiry that is free from the narrow ideological constraints imposed by dominant social institutions will be severely inhibited and easy to disregard unless the general political climate is conducive to challenge and innovation. In the absence of an alive and healthy radical political movement, the "softer" disciplines will easily be subverted by social pressures, as has so often been the case. At the same time, a movement of the left condemns itself to failure and irrelevance if it does not create an intellectual culture that becomes dominant by virtue of its excellence and that is meaningful to the masses of people who, in an advanced industrial society, can participate in creating and deepening it.

[The university and the future]

The prospects seem to me good that the small groups that now exist can grow and interact with one another and with a political movement of the left that is rooted in many strata of American society. I think that, for the present, the universities are a natural and relatively favorable place for such growth and interaction. There is sure to be opposition to the development of scholarship and teaching that is not constrained by the dominant conservative ideology. There will undoubtedly be an effort to repress the activism that is a natural outgrowth of serious inquiry. The universities have been highly politicized by the influence of the dominant social institutions, the national state, and the great corporations to which it is closely linked. The natural conservatism of the faculty will combine with the political conservatism imposed by external pressures to set up barriers to free inquiry. Examples of repression can easily be cited. Nevertheless, they should not be exaggerated. It should be recognized that in any field there is resistance to innovation on the part of those who have achieved a certain status and prestige. This natural resistance, easy to document, provides a kind of baseline in terms of which one must assess the actual political repression that exists in the universities. My personal feeling is that by this measure, which is the correct one, repression on political grounds is not extensive at the moment. It may grow, but that is not to say that it will necessarily succeed. For the present, there is no strong reason for pessimism in this regard.

Of particular significance, I think, are certain efforts undertaken in the past year among scientists and engineers. For example, at MIT a handful of graduate students succeeded, within a few months, in organizing a one-day research strike that spread to some fifty colleges and that led to the formation of active and continuing organizations of students and faculty. This initiative grew out of a sanctuary for an AWOL [absent without leave] soldier, Mike O'Conner, which was held at MIT last fall and dramatically changed the political climate on the campus.

["Radical" culture and social change]

In some ways, the creation of a radical movement of scientists and engineers is analogous to the organization of GI resistance. American imperial dominance is based as much on technique as on mass military force. As Franz Schurmann has rightly pointed out, "it is not likely that, barring a major emergency, the United States could again foot a massive army," and "aside from a few puppet states such as South Korea, no country has been willing to provide the U.S. militarists with the manpower necessary to fight 'limited wars' distant from America's shores. . . . Thus [the U.S.] must depend on technology to fight its wars."[10]

Furthermore, scientists and engineers are well aware of the corruption of intelligence imposed by a system so irrational that the majority of engineers are forced to accept employment with NASA, the AEC [American Energy Commission] (in essence, a weapons-producing agency), and the Defense Department. There is, therefore, symbolic significance in the fact that a successful movement of scientists and engineers has developed, in part, from an expression of solidarity with a GI resister. By means of such organization of scientists and engineers, the system of subsidy to technologically advanced segments of industry and achievement of global dominance through a subverted technology can be threatened at its most vulnerable point, its personnel. Scientists and engineers can make the same key contribution to a radical culture—ultimately, a successful movement for significant social change—that they now make to militarism and repression.

As already noted, it is inconceivable that the left can achieve real success in an advanced industrial society unless it develops the intellectual resources to provide plausible, concrete solutions to the problems of our society. Those who believe that these problems can be met only when social institutions are reconstructed along democratic lines have the task of showing that this is so. Potential solutions to these problems are of limited interest when they merely appear in technical monographs (though even this would be a far from negligible accomplishment). They must become ingrained in the consciousness of those who will implement them and live under the conditions that they bring into existence.

There are many kinds of interaction among scientists, engineers, technicians, and skilled workers, the blue-collar workforce, professionals and other white-collar workers, and writers and artists, among all of those who must contribute to a vital movement of the left. Some of these connections I have already mentioned; specifically, the application of modern technology to creating the conditions for industrial democracy and the rational and humane use of resources is one major task that lies on the immediate horizon. A serious mass movement of the left should involve all of these segments of American society. Its politics and understanding must grow out of their combined efforts to build a new world.

Notes

1. *Boston Globe,* June 20, 1969.
2. Joan Robinson, "Contrasts in economic development: China and India," in Neal Houghton, ed., *Struggle against history* (New York: Simon and Schuster, 1968).
3. Walter Lafeber, *America, Russia and the cold war* (New York: Wiley, 1967), p. 73. See Christopher Lasch, *The agony of the American left* (New York: Knopf, 1969) for a perceptive discussion of the "cultural cold war" of the 1950s.
4. See, for example, the new French journal *Autogestion* and the publications of the Institute for Workers' Control, 91 Goldsmith St., Nottingham, England.
5. Ken Coates, ed., *Can the workers run industry?* (London: Sphere Books and the Institute for Workers' Control, 1968).
6. Paul Samuelson, *Economics,* 6th ed. (New York: McGraw-Hill, 1964).
7. *Daedalus,* winter 1969.
8. Woodrow Wilson Foundation and National Planning Association, *Political economy of American foreign policy* (New York: Holt, 1955). Our humane values are illustrated further in this important document in many ways. Thus "constructive wage and social welfare policies are obviously needed." Why? "To mitigate industrial unrest." At the same time it is necessary to combat the excessive egalitarianism and social welfare legislation undertaken under leftist and socialist governments. The capitalist elite might agree with Stalin that egalitarianism is "a reactionary petty-bourgeois absurdity worthy of some sect of ascetics" (17th Party Congress). The document goes on to insist that we must preserve the right to intervene in support of "older ruling groups" who see "that their future independence lies in alliance with the West" unless the responsible middle-class elements have achieved dominance. We must continue to ensure that Western Europe and

Japan refrain from "neutralism and pacifism"—in the case of Japan, by making "possible greater Japanese participation in the development of Southern Asia"—a non-negligible factor in the Vietnam War, incidentally. We must combat irrational, communist-inspired land redistribution, as in Guatemala, where (as in Iran) "nationalistic totalitarian or crypto-communist regimes have nearly succeeded in consolidating their rule" (the reference is to Arbenz and Mossadegh). And so on.

9. There are three other aspects to this threat: "a planned disruption of the free world economies," the higher growth rate of Soviet heavy industry (N.B., the date is 1955), and "the fact that Soviet communism threatens not merely the political and economic institutions of the West but the continued existence of human freedom and humane society everywhere."

10. Franz Schurmann, "The Nixon administration and the Vietnam War," paper submitted to the Stockholm Conference on Vietnam, May 1969.

Chapter 9
Toward a humanistic conception of education (April 1971)

I had the very great personal honor to deliver some memorial lectures for Bertrand Russell at Trinity College, Cambridge, and in the course of thinking about and preparing for them I had the pleasure of reading and rereading a fair amount of his work written over many years.[1]

Russell had quite a number of things to say on educational topics that are no less important today than when he first discussed them. He regularly took up—not only discussed but also tried to carry out—very interesting and provocative ideas in the field of educational theory and practice. He claimed throughout his years of interest in this area that the primary goal of education is to elicit and fortify whatever creative impulse man may possess. And this conclusion, which he formulated in many different ways over a period of years, derives from a particular concept of human nature that he also expressed in many different forms. It grows from what he called a "humanistic conception," which regards a child as a gardener regards a young tree, that is, as "something with a certain intrinsic nature, which will develop into an admirable form, given proper soil and air and light."

Elsewhere he pointed out that "the soil and the freedom required for a man's growth are immeasurably more difficult to discover and to obtain. . . . And the full growth which may be hoped for cannot be defined or demonstrated; it is subtle and complex, it can only be felt by a delicate intuition and dimly apprehended by imagination and respect." Therefore he argued that education should be guided by "the spirit of reverence" for "something sacred, indefinable, unlimited, something individual and strangely precious, the growing principle of life, an embodied fragment of the dumb striving of the world."

This is one view of the nature of education, based on a certain conception of human nature that Russell called the humanistic conception.

According to this conception, the child has an intrinsic nature, and central to it is a creative impulse. Pursuing that line of thinking, the goal of education should be to provide the soil and the freedom required for the growth of this creative impulse; to provide, in other words, a complex and challenging environment that the child can imaginatively explore and, in this way, quicken his intrinsic creative impulse and so enrich his life in ways that may be quite varied and unique. This approach is governed, as Russell said, by a spirit of reverence and humility: reverence for the precious, varied, individual, indeterminate growing principle of life; and humility with regard to aims and with regard to the degree of insight and understanding of the practitioners.

Because he was well acquainted with modern science, Russell was also well aware of how little we really know about the aims and purposes of human life. Therefore the purpose of education, from this point of view, cannot be to control the child's growth to a specific, predetermined end, because any such end must be established by arbitrary authoritarian means; rather, the purpose of education must be to permit the growing principle of life to take its own individual course, and to facilitate this process by sympathy, encouragement, and challenge, and by developing a rich and differentiated context and environment.

This humanistic conception of education clearly involves some factual assumptions about the intrinsic nature of man and, in particular, about the centrality to that intrinsic nature of a creative impulse. If these assumptions, when spelled out properly, prove to be incorrect, then these particular conclusions with regard to educational theory and practice will not have been demonstrated. On the other hand, if these assumptions are indeed correct, much of contemporary American educational practice is rationally as well as morally questionable.

[Libertarian educational theories: the nature of work]

The humanistic conception of man leads to what might be called libertarian educational theories. It also leads in a natural and direct way to libertarian concepts of social organization that incorporate closely related ideas concerning, for example, the central and essential concept of the nature of work. In this context Russell quoted a remark by Kropotkin that "overwork is repulsive to human nature—not work. Overwork for supplying the few with luxury—not for the well-being of all. Work, labor is a physiological necessity, a necessity of expanding accumulated bodily energy, a necessity which is health and life itself."[2]

Elaborating on this theme, Russell pointed out that "if man had to be tempted to work instead of driven to it, the obvious interest of the community would be to make work pleasant," and social institutions would be organized to this end. They would provide the conditions, in other words, under which productive, creative work would be freely undertaken as a part of normal, healthy life. To place these particular remarks in an appropriate historical context, one who conceives of the "species character" of man as "free, conscious activity" and "productive life," in the words of the early Marx, will also seek to create the higher form of society that Marx envisioned, in which labor has become not only a means of life, but also the highest want in life.[3]

There is a contrasting and more prevalent view of the nature of work, namely, that labor is a commodity to be sold on the market for maximal return, that it has no intrinsic value in itself; its only value and immediate purpose is to afford the possibility to consume, for on this account humans are primarily concerned with maximizing consumption, not with producing creatively under conditions of freedom. They are unique and individual not by virtue of what they make, what they do for others, or how they transform nature; rather, individuality is determined by material possessions and by consumption: I am what I am because of what I own and use up. Thus on this view the primary aim of life must be to maximize the accumulation of commodities, and work is undertaken almost solely for this aim. The underlying assumption, of course, is that work is repulsive to human nature—contrary to Kropotkin, Russell, Marx, and many others—and that leisure and possession, rather than creative labor, must be the goal of humankind.

Again, the issue involves factual assumptions. On this conception of human nature the goal of education should be to train children and provide them with the skills and habits that will fit them in an optimal way for the productive mechanism, which is meaningless in itself from a human point of view but necessary to provide them with the opportunity to exercise their freedom as consumers, a freedom that can be enjoyed in the hours when they are free from the onerous burden of labor. Such an idea is, of course, repugnant to one who accepts Russell's humanistic conception of human nature, but it bears repeating that between these contrasting views of work and education there is a factual judgment involved with regard to intrinsic human nature.

This question, in short, is whether creative work can be the highest want of life or whether labor is a burden and idleness and consumption of commodities the highest want and goal of life.

It may be that the humanistic conception expressed by Russell, Kropotkin, Marx, and many others is wrong. I believe it is correct, but in either case there are direct consequences with regard to social organization as well as education.

This possibility has been recognized by social critics who tried to elaborate the humanistic conception and draw appropriate conclusions from it. For example, Russell quoted a pamphlet of the National Guilds League, a British working-class radical socialist organization of the early part of the century, which tried to develop a point of view rather like the humanistic one outlined above. In the course of speaking about what Russell called the humanistic conception of man, it admits that "there is a cant of the Middle Ages and a cant of 'joy in labor.'" But it goes on to declare that "it were better, perhaps, to risk that cant" than to accept a philosophy that makes "work a purely commercial activity, a soulless and joyless thing."

Again, my personal bias is toward Russell and the medieval cant, but I am not directly concerned to defend this position here so much as I want to suggest a connection between the concomitant view of human nature—specifically with regard to creativity and productive work—and certain questions concerning educational practice, namely, whether it should be oriented toward freedom and challenge or toward guidance, direction, and control.

[Implications for social theory and educational practice]

This debate between the positions did not originate in the present century. To mention one case of considerable historical importance, Wilhelm von Humboldt, an extremely important and too-neglected thinker whose works have only been made readily available in the last few years, wrote about educational practice and its foundation in a certain concept of human nature, along the lines of the humanistic conception we have been considering. He said that "to inquire and to create—these are the centers around which all human pursuits more or less directly revolve." "All moral culture," he wrote, "springs solely and immediately from the inner life of the soul and can only be stimulated in human nature, and never produced by external and artificial contrivance. . . . Whatever does not spring from a man's free choice, or is only the result of instruction and guidance, does not enter into his very being, but remains alien to his true nature; he does not perform it with truly human energies, but merely with mechanical exactness." If a man acts in this way, he says, we may "admire what he does, but despise what he is."[4]

This view has implications for educational practice similar to Russell's, and, of course, related implications for social theory. Again, one who regards human nature in this light will proceed to search for social forms that will encourage the truly human action that grows from inner impulse. In this case,

Humboldt writes,

> All peasants and craftsmen might be elevated into artists; that is, men who love
> their labor for its own sake, improve it by their own plastic genius and inventive
> skill, and thereby cultivate their intellect, ennoble their character, and exalt and
> refine their pleasures. And so humanity would be ennobled by the very things
> which now, though beautiful in themselves, so often tend to degrade it.[5]

Humbolt was an important educational theorist as well as a practitioner.
He was one of the founders of the modern university system, and at the same
time he was a great libertarian social thinker who directly inspired and in
many ways anticipated John Stuart Mill. His rationalistic conception of
human nature, emphasizing free creative action as the essence of that nature,
was developed further in the libertarian social thought of the industrial period,
specifically in nineteenth-century libertarian socialist and anarchist social theory and their accompanying doctrines concerning educational practice.

Let me reiterate the point that these views involve questions of fact concerning human nature and that there are certain conclusions that one may
draw from these factual judgments with respect to educational theory and
practice, social theory, and the activism which naturally flows from a conscientious commitment to the conclusions of that theory.

Judgments about these matters are, in fact, very often determined not so
much by evidence as by ideological commitment. This is not particularly surprising, though it is not too happy a state. It is not surprising because there is very little evidence that bears on these issues, yet we cannot avoid making judgments on
them. We may, and commonly do, tacitly accept most of the judgments which prevail in a given society. In other words, we make these judgments rather mindlessly
in conformity to prevailing ideology. It requires effort to make them thoughtfully,
recognizing the inadequacy of the evidence. But there are no other alternatives.

In this kind of situation the null hypothesis would be the point of view
that Bertrand Russell expressed. That is, in the absence of conflicting evidence, the proper course should be to approach these problems with the reverence and humility that Russell suggested in discussing his "humanistic
conception." In the absence of compelling reasons to the contrary, one should
be quite cautious about trying to control someone else's life and character and
mode of thought. The acceptance or rejection of the null hypothesis has
political and social as well as pedagogic consequences for the educator and
teacher. There are, in other words, significant consequences to one's thinking
or lack of thinking about these issues and a corresponding personal and professional responsibility.

To become somewhat more concrete, consider the matter of control of behavior. In a certain sense this will be abhorrent to the person who accepts the humanistic conception of education. There is no doubt that control of behavior can be carried out to some degree. Effective techniques of conditioning and control exist that have been investigated experimentally in great detail. But it would surely be a mistake to consider that these investigations have significantly advanced our understanding of learning processes [i.e., mental growth processes in Chomskian terms—CPO]. For example, there are numerous results on the effects of various schedulings of reinforcement on the frequency of simple responses. Have we learned that learning takes place through conditioning, by the application of such methods in a natural or contrived environment? Of course we have not learned anything of the sort. Learning involves the interplay of an innate endowment, innately determined maturational processes, and a process of interaction with the environment. The pattern of this interaction and the nature of the various factors are largely unknown, as any honest investigator will concede.

In some domains—language is an example—such evidence as is available seems to indicate that the innate component is extremely significant and that, in considerable detail, the form and character of what is learned is determined by an innate schematism of mind. In fact, precisely those characteristics of language that make it an effective instrument for free thought and expression seem to have their origins in this innately determined structure. It is fairly clear that language cannot be seriously regarded as a system of habits and skills acquired through training. Rather it must be understood as an elaborate mental structure largely determined by innate properties of mind. This point of view may be right or wrong when it is spelled out in detail, but there is no inherent mystery about it. One could make it quite precise and quite explicit; it is in no sense mysterious. What is mysterious, perhaps, is the biological or neurophysiological basis for these (and other) mechanisms of mind, but that is another question entirely.

There is a point of confusion that might be mentioned here, a confusion that one finds among many linguists who have identified the free creative use of language with the system of rules that permit that free creative use, that is, with the recursive property of grammars that permits arbitrarily many utterances to be constructed. These two notions, although related, are not to be confused. To do so would be a category mistake, a confusion of performance and competence. There are rules that permit an indefinite range of possible expression. Such rules are an indispensable component in the creative use of language. But a computer that produced sentences randomly would not be acting creatively. There is an interplay, a complex relationship between constraints and rules and creative behavior. If there is no system of rules, no system of constraints, no set of forms, then creative behavior is quite unthinkable. Someone who is throwing paints at a wall in an arbitrary fashion is not acting creatively as an artist. Similarly, some system of constraints and forms and principles and rules is presupposed as a basis for any kind of creative action. But creative action has to be understood in different terms, with this being only one fundamental component.[6]

Returning to the question of what has been learned from the study of conditioning, it could not be true that these investigations have demonstrated that learning results from conditioning for the very simple reason that the fundamental problem of learning theory has barely been posed, let alone answered, within the theory of learning as it has developed over the years. There is an important conceptual gap in the theory of learning which makes it very difficult to pose this fundamental question and therefore casts a good deal of doubt on the significance of any results that are achieved, however interesting they may be in their own terms. The conceptual gap is basically this: the theory of learning is concerned with situation and action; that is, it is concerned with stimulus and response. But there really is no concept of what is learned. The fundamental problem of learning theory, properly understood, is to determine how what is learned is related to the experience on the basis of which it is learned. We can study, if we like, the relation between stimulus and response, but it is very unlikely that such a study will contribute to solving the problem because that relationship is surely mediated by the system of knowledge and belief that has been acquired, by what has been learned.

Take again the case of language, which is perhaps the clearest example we can consider. Stimuli impinge upon the organism, which carries out certain "verbal behavior." It is perfectly obvious that the person's behavior as a speaker of a language is affected by what he knows as a speaker of this language, by the system of rules that is mentally represented in some fashion, which provides the framework within which the largely free, creative behavior takes place. If we want to study learning of language, we are going to have to study the relationship between experience and what is learned, between experience and knowledge, experience and this internally represented system of rules. We can then go ahead to study behavior, that is, interaction among many factors, including immediate stimuli, mediated through the already known system of rules. We can study the relationship between these factors and behavior. But to try to study the relationship between stimuli and responses directly is a sure road to triviality.

We could not expect to find a direct connection between experience and action, omitting any reference to what is learned. Nor could we even pose the questions of learning theory with that concept—what is learned, what is known—missing. To pose the problem of learning theory in the first place, one must face the task of systematizing what it is a person knows or believes, or has acquired or learned, at a certain stage in his or her development. (The same is true of animal learning, for that matter.) Later we can ask how that system of knowledge or belief arose from the various factors that enter into it—experience, maturational processes, and so on. But to avoid any concern for the nature of what is known and what is learned is simply to condemn the enterprise to barrenness in the first place.

When we pose the question of what is learned, the few tentative answers that seem plausible are remote from the tacit and generally unargued assumptions of many learning theorists. The belief that conditioning is an important feature of learning may conceivably be true, but at the moment it stands as a kind of dogma. And if, in fact, the humanistic conception of human nature, work, and education mentioned earlier is correct, then the theory of conditioning may be a dangerous and possibly pernicious dogma. Recall again Humboldt's remark that "whatever does not spring from a man's free choice, or is only the result of instruction and guidance, does not enter into his very being but remains alien to his true nature; he does not perform it with truly human energies, but merely with mechanical exactness."[7]

The fact that this observation was made by a profound social critic does not make it correct, of course, but there is not any scientific evidence to suggest that it is false. Indeed, I think that our own experience and the insights that arise from it—which are not to be discounted in areas where scientific evidence is so sparse—lend a certain credibility to this view. At an experimental level there is some evidence that voluntary, self-willed action plays a very significant role in learning and acquiring knowledge. This work supports the observations and guesses concerning the intrinsic, self-willed character of anything of real human significance that is acquired by a child in the course of learning—or an adult as well, for that matter.

What about the concomitant idea that knowledge is acquired in small, incremental steps? Consider a teaching program for geometry. Again, there are inherent dangers in any such approach. Perhaps the dangers are even greater if the approach begins to work. To educate a mathematician, you do not train him to face problems which are just on the border of what he has already learned to do. Rather, he must learn to deal with new situations, to take imaginative leaps, to act in a creative fashion. If he is going to be a good mathematician, he must have a good imagination and use it frequently.

We really do not understand what is involved in taking such imaginative, creative leaps in mathematics or in any other domain. But it is plausible to suppose that the ability to undertake these essentially creative efforts is acquired through the experience of coming to grips with interesting, complex problems that are challenging and which attract one's attention but are not at all closely related in any incremental fashion to the skills that one has achieved and acquired. Programs that work quite successfully in teaching some fixed domain through small incremental steps may precisely deprive persons of the opportunity to develop these poorly understood abilities that enable them to act in a normal human fashion, occasionally with genius; and perhaps much the same is true of normal human behavior.

[Well-planned schools and challenging environments]

The schools have taken quite a beating in recent years, and I do not want to join in the pummeling. Personally, I do not really agree with the more radical critics like Paul Goodman or Ivan Illich, who imply that the solution to the problem of the schools is virtually to eliminate them. (On the humanistic conception of education, it is important to provide the richest and most challenging of environments for children so that the creative impulse will have maximum utilization, and a well-planned school should be able to provide just that environment.) But I think one cannot discount a good deal of what Goodman and Illich say. A close friend of mine came from Europe at age fifteen and went to an American high school in New York. He was struck immediately by the fact that if he came to school three minutes late he had to go to the principal's office to be properly chastised, but if he did not do his work in a particularly intelligent fashion or if he was not creative or original, then people might not be too happy about it but at least he did not have to go to the principal's office. And quite generally, punctuality and obedience were very highly valued and were the values that definitely had to be instilled. As to originality or achievement, well, that was nice too, but it obviously was not of paramount importance.

An approach to education which emphasizes such values as punctuality and obedience is very well suited for training factory workers as tools of production. It is not suited at all to the humanistic conception of creative and independent individuals, which brings us back again to those assumptions concerning human nature and the social forces and educational practices that give due regard to intrinsic human capacities.

[Immense potential for good and for evil]

The consideration of assumptions of this kind is particularly important in a rich and powerful country with immense potential for good and for evil. The early experiences of citizens of this country are a matter of enormous human significance. It is a cliché to say that the responsibility of the teacher to the student, like that of the parent to the child, is beyond calculation, but it is further amplified to the extent that this child can affect history.

Here in the United States we are clearly dealing with that situation. One of the worst forms of control, developed to very dangerous extremes in totalitarian states, is indoctrination of children. We very rightly deplore it elsewhere. We rarely recognize it at home. I do not pretend to be well versed in this matter, but I do have several children in school and I look over their shoulders occasionally. Some of the kinds of indoctrination that face them are, to state it frankly, frightening. I went through an issue of the *Weekly Reader*, a children's newspaper, which discussed the problem of American prisoners in North Vietnam. It said, "A war is going on in Vietnam. The war has been going for many years. North Vietnam and South Vietnam are fighting each other. Americans are fighting on the side of South Vietnam. Many Americans have been taken prisoner by North Vietnam." Then it talked about some American children: "The children sent their letters to the president of North Vietnam. The children asked him to set American prisoners of war free and to let the men come home to the United States."[8] There is also a teachers' edition which goes along with the paper, which explains how the teacher is supposed to elicit the appropriate answers.

Look at what the *Weekly Reader* was telling these impressionable young children: first that there was a war between North Vietnam and South Vietnam. That is of course totally false. Anybody in the government knows that that was false. They know perfectly well that it began as a war between the United States and the peasant societies of Indochina, in particular South Vietnam. It never was a war between the North and the South. If you ask when the first regular units of the North Vietnamese Army were discovered in South Vietnam, you get the curious answer that it was in late April 1965—one battalion of four hundred men, approximately two and a half months after the start of regular bombardment of North Vietnam and South Vietnam, approximately eight months after the first bombing of strategic targets—at a time when there were thirty-five thousand American troops deployed. In fact, U.S. military forces had been engaged in direct military actions for four or five years. So it is hardly a war between North Vietnam and South Vietnam.

Second, the impression that the *Weekly Reader* tries to convey is that the pilots were captured while defending South Vietnam from North Vietnam. There is not a word about what the pilots were doing when they were captured. What they were doing, of course, was destroying everything in North Vietnam outside of the central population centers, a fact which is still not admitted in the United States. There is also not a word about prisoners captured by the United States and South Vietnam, for example, those who were dropped to their death from helicopters or those who were tortured or those who found their way to the tiger cages in Con Son Island. And there is no particular explanation in the *Weekly Reader* as to why prisoners should be released while the United States continued to drop seventy thousand tons of bombs on Indochina, as it did during the month in which this article appeared, January 1971.[9] But worst of all, there is not a word about what the United States soldiers have been doing in South Vietnam and in Laos. These countries, of course, have borne the main brunt of the American aggression in Indochina, not North Vietnam.

Now, this kind of distortion, which we see in the *Weekly Reader,* continues to pound on children through most of their adult lives as well. The corruption of the media in this respect is extreme.

Children have to be spared indoctrination, but they also have to be trained to resist it in later life. This is a very serious problem in our society and every other society. Let me give another example. I have a daughter in junior high school, and in looking at her history book on the topic of the countries of the communist bloc, I came across the following:

> In no case did a revolution merely happen. The shift to Communism was skillfully brought about by groups of dedicated, Moscow-trained revolutionaries.

In China and Cuba, for example? This is certainly nonsense, but it is pernicious nonsense, and when it is drilled into people constantly, day after day, week after week, throughout their lives, the effects are overwhelming.

This section of the book goes on to discuss peaceful coexistence. It says,

> We all believe first in the existence of different systems of government and society, and second in the right of every people to settle independently all the political and social problems of their country. We have always had respect for the sovereignty of other nations and have adhered to the principle of non-interference in internal affairs. And we strongly believe in and practice the policy of trying to settle all international questions by negotiations.

Then the book turns to the leaders of the Soviet Union. It says that "they claim they want to end the cold war," and so on. Before this can happen, the book continues, "we have to learn to trust each other"; but

> Such actions as those the Soviet Union has taken in North Korea, in North
> Vietnam and in Cuba, in which Soviet-trained communists have taken over the
> reins of government have given the United States ample cause to doubt the sincer-
> ity of Mr. Khrushchev's pronouncements about peaceful co-existence.[10]

There was often good reason to doubt the sincerity of Mr. Khrushchev's pronouncements, but on the basis of Soviet actions in North Vietnam, such doubt would be difficult to defend, particularly since this book was written in 1963, when there were no Soviet actions in Indochina. There were, however, plenty of American actions: in that year a substantial part of the population of South Vietnam was forcibly removed by the U.S.-imposed regime to what we would call concentration camps if any other country had built them.

Let me give a third example, also from the textbook of one of my own daughters—this one in the fourth grade. It is a social science reader called *Exploring New England*. The book has a protagonist, a young boy named Robert who is told about the marvels of colonial times. In the course of the narrative the extermination of the Pequot tribe by Captain John Mason is described as follows:

> His little army attacked in the morning before it was light and took the Pequots by
> surprise. The soldiers broke down the stockade with their axes, rushed inside, and
> set fire to the wigwams. They killed nearly all the braves, squaws, and children, and
> burned their corn and other food. There were no Pequots left to make more trou-
> ble. When the other Indian tribes saw what good fighters the white men were,
> they kept the peace for many years.
>
> "I wish I were a man and had been there," thought Robert.

That is the last that Robert hears or speaks about this matter. Nowhere does he express or hear any second thoughts.[11]

I think it is very important to consider such passages and to take them seriously—I do not know how prevalent they are—especially in the light of My Lai or the many incidents like it.

Even more important, perhaps, than direct and gross indoctrination is the general pattern of authoritarianism that one finds in the schools, and the associated pattern of the technocratic, problem-solving mode of thought combined with a great awe of expertise—quite natural in an advanced industrial society. In some areas of our lives this latter pattern has reached dimensions that can really only be described as pathological.

To take only one dangerous example, the domain of counterinsurgency theory has been developed into an effective technique of mystification during the last decade. The idea is to formulate the problems of repression of popular movements in purely technical terms. Thus, two experts in counterinsurgency writing in *Foreign Affairs* explain to us that all the dilemmas of counterinsurgency are "practical and as neutral in an ethical sense as the laws of physics."[12] In short, the situation is a very simple one. We have the goal of establishing the rule of certain social groups in the society that is selected for the experiment in counterinsurgency. A number of methods are available, ranging from rural development and commodity import programs to B-52s and crop destruction. And the policy maker faces the task of combining these methods in such a manner as to maximize the probability of success. Quite obviously, only a hysteric or a self-flagellating moralist could see an ethical problem in this situation; it is just like an experiment in physics.

Academic terminology can be put to very mischievous use in this connection, and it often is. For example, driving people into government-controlled cities by firepower and chemical destruction is called "urbanization," which is then taken as a key index of the modernization of the society. We carry out what are called "experiments with population control measures." We should learn, one RAND Corporation theorist tells us, to disregard such mystical notions as attitudes; rather, we should control behavior by appropriate arrangements for positive and negative reinforcements such as "confiscation of chickens, razing of houses, or destruction of villages." Or consider, for example, "the offer of food in exchange for certain services. . . . If this has in the past been a strong stimulus, it can probably be weakened by increasing local agricultural production. If it has been a weak or neutral stimulus, it can probably be strengthened by burning crops." This is from a publication of the American Institute for Research, 1967.[13] Whatever such experts may be, they are not scientists, and the concept of science suggested by such pronouncements is not one that Russell—or any other honest commentator—could endorse.

Christopher Lasch once pointed out that one of the dominant values of the modern intellectual is his acute sense of himself as a professional with a vested interest in technical solutions to political problems. The schools to a large extent are training professionals, and they are training the general population to accept the values and the ideological structures that are developed by professionals. All of this is particularly important in a postindustrial or advanced industrial society where the intelligentsia are increasingly associated with the exercise of power. This is, of course, not a criticism of professionalism or of technology or science, but rather of the subversion of intellectual values as part of a new coercive ideology that seeks to remove decision making even further from popular control by exploiting the aura of science and technology, by pretending that social planning is much too complex for the common man and must therefore be the domain of experts who claim to be value-free technicians, but who in fact quite generally accept without question the most vulgar forms of official ideology as a basis for their planning.

If you have read serious social science journals or foreign policy journals over the last few years, you have seen that it is very common to counterpose the "emotional approach" of certain people with the "rational response" of others. For example, the people who worry about the slaughter of peasant populations—these people are overcome by emotion. On the other hand, those who talk about arranging inputs to realize a certain outcome are "reasonable" commentators. This is an interesting development, the counterposing of emotion to reason, because it departs significantly from the Western intellectual tradition. For example, David Hume wrote that "reason is and ought to be the slave of the passions." And Russell, commenting on the observation, noted that every reasonable man subscribes to this dictum. He surely would be an "unreasonable" commentator by the standards of today. Reason is concerned with the choice of the right means to an end that you wish to achieve, taking emotional and moral factors into consideration. Unfortunately, too many modern technocrats, who often pose as scientists and scholars, are really divorcing themselves from traditional science and scholarship and excluding themselves from the company of reasonable persons in the name of a kind of reason that is perverted beyond recognition.

All of these are matters that require the most careful attention of teachers. We have to learn to adopt the questioning and iconoclastic approach that is highly valued and carefully nurtured in the physical sciences, where an imaginative worker will very often hold up his basic assumptions to searching analysis. We have to adopt this approach as teachers, and also as citizens who must be social critics, recognizing that in the domain of social criticism the normal attitudes of a scientist are feared and deplored as a form of subversion or as dangerous radicalism.

[A real potential for revolutionary social change]
I have been discussing the negative potential of American power. There is also a positive side, one that should make the work of teachers particularly demanding but highly exciting. The United States has a real potential for revolutionary social change to a libertarian democratic society of the form that probably cannot be achieved anywhere else in the world. As compared with other societies, libertarian instincts are reasonably strong in the United States. There is also very little class prejudice as compared with most other

societies. But most of all, in an advanced industrial society the rational and humane use of resources and technology provides the possibility to free people from the role of tools of production in the industrial process. It provides the possibility, perhaps for the first time in modern history, to free human beings from the activities that, as Adam Smith pointed out, turn them into imbeciles through the burden of specialized labor. This, then, is the real challenge of the twentieth century in the United States: to create social forms that will realize the humanistic conception of man. And it is the responsibility of teachers, of citizens, and of ourselves to liberate the creative impulse and to free our minds and the minds of those with whom we deal from the constraints of authoritarian ideologies so that this challenge can be faced in a serious and an open-minded way.

Notes

1. Published as *Problems of knowledge and freedom* (Pantheon: New York, 1971). Unless otherwise noted, all specific references to Russell's writings are given in that volume.
2. "Anarchist communism." Quoted by Russell in *Proposed roads to freedom: anarchy, socialism and syndicalism* (New York: Henry Holt, 1919), p. 100.
3. Specifically taken up in the *Economic and philosophical manuscripts*.
4. Wilhelm von Humboldt, *The limits of state action*, ed. J. W. Burrow (Cambridge: Cambridge University Press, 1969), pp. 76, 63, 28.
5. Ibid., p. 27.
6. These linguistic themes are taken up in more detail in *Problems of knowledge and freedom*, pp. 3–51.
7. Humboldt, *The limits of state action*, p. 28.
8. *Weekly Reader,* January 1971; fourth-grade edition.
9. For a fuller, non–*Weekly Reader* account, see Noam Chomsky, *At war with Asia* (New York: Pantheon, 1969).
10. C. Kohn and D. Drummond, *The world today* (New York: McGraw-Hill, 1963).
11. Harold B. Clifford, *Exploring New England* (Chicago: Follett, 1961). The example and precedent set by Mason was not forgotten by later soldiers. It was, for example, cited by General Leonard Wood while justifying the army's killing of six hundred Moro men, women, and children in the Philippines in 1906: "The renegades had from 3 to 6 months supply on the mountain, with an abundance of water. There was nothing to do but take the place. . . . I believe that some of our hard-praying ancestors dealt with the Pequot Indians in a somewhat similar manner, and on a great deal less provocation." Quoted in R. O'Connor, *Pacific destiny* (Boston: Little, Brown, 1969), p. 295. The analogy is actually fairly accurate; like the Pequots, the native Moros were armed with bows, spears, and rocks (against Wood's machine guns, bombs, and howitzers).
12. George Tanham and Dennis Duncanson, "Some dilemmas of counterinsurgency," *Foreign Affairs* 48, 1 (1969): 113–22.
13. See also Chomsky, *American power and the new mandarins* (New York: Pantheon, 1969).

Chapter 10

The function of the university in a time of crisis (1969)

Writing 150 years ago, the great liberal reformer and humanist Wilhelm von Humboldt defined the university as "nothing other than the spiritual life of those human beings who are moved by external leisure or internal pressures toward learning and research." At every stage of his life, a free man will be driven, to a greater or lesser extent, by these "internal pressures." The society in which he lives may or may not provide him with the "external leisure" and the institutional forms in which to realize this human need to discover and create, to explore and evaluate and come to understand, to refine and exercise his talents, to contemplate, to make his own individual contribution to contemporary culture, to analyze and criticize and transform this culture and the social structure in which it is rooted. Even if the university did not exist formally, Humboldt observes, "one person would privately reflect and collect, another join with men of his own age, a third find a circle of disciples. Such is the picture to which the state must remain faithful if it wishes to give an institutional form to such indefinite and rather accidental human operations."[1]

[One measure of the level of civilization]

The extent to which existing institutional forms permit these human needs to be satisfied provides one measure of the level of civilization that a society has achieved. One element in the unending struggle to achieve a more just and humane social order will be the effort to remove the barriers—whether they be economic, ideological, or political—that stand in the way of the particular forms of individual self-fulfillment and collective action that the university should make possible.

It is the great merit of the student movement of the 1960s to have helped shatter the complacency that had settled over much of American intellectual life, both with regard to American society and to the role of the universities within it. The renewed concern with university reform is in large measure a consequence of student activism. A great deal of energy has been directed to problems of "restructuring the university": democratizing it, redistributing "power" in it, reducing constraints on student freedom as well as the dependence of the university on outside institutions. I suspect that little can be achieved of real substance along these lines. Formal changes in university structure will have little effect on what a student does with his life, or on the relation of the university to the society. To the extent that reform does not reach the heart of the university—the content of the curriculum, the interaction between student and teacher, the nature of research, and, in some fields, the practice that relates to theory—it will remain superficial. But it is doubtful that these matters will be significantly affected by the kinds of structural reforms that are now being actively debated on many campuses.

It is pointless to discuss the "function of the university" in abstraction from concrete historical circumstances, as it would be a waste of effort to study any other social institution in this way. In a different society entirely different questions might arise as to the function of the university and the problems that are pressing. To one who believes, as I do, that our society must undergo drastic changes if civilization is to advance—perhaps even to survive—university reform will appear an insignificant matter except insofar as it contributes to social change. Apart from this question, improvements in the university can no doubt take place within the framework of the presently existing institutional forms, and drastic revision of these forms will contribute little to it.

It is never an easy matter to determine to what extent deficiencies of a particular institution can actually be overcome through internal reform and to what extent they reflect characteristics of society at large or matters of individual psychology that are relatively independent of social forms.

[Sharing of discovery and mutual assistance]

Consider, for example, the competitiveness fostered in the university, in fact, in the school system as a whole. It is difficult to convince oneself that this serves an educational purpose. Certainly it does not prepare the student for the life of a scholar or scientist. It would be absurd to demand of the working scientist that he keep his work secret so that his colleagues will not know of his achievements and not be helped by his discoveries in pursuing their own studies and research. Yet this demand is often made of the student in the classroom. In later life, collective effort with sharing of discovery and mutual assistance is the ideal; if it is not the norm, we rightly interpret this as an inadequacy of those who cannot rise above personal aggrandizement and to this extent are incompetent as scholars and teachers. Yet even at the most advanced level of graduate education, the student is discouraged by university regulation from working as any reasonable man would certainly choose to do: individually, where his interests lead him; collectively, when he can learn from and give aid to his fellows. Course projects and examinations are individual and competitive. The doctoral dissertation not only is required to be a purely individual contribution; beyond this questionable requirement, there is a built-in bias toward insignificance in the requirement that a finished piece of work be completed in a fixed time span. The student is obliged to set himself a limited goal and to avoid adventuresome, speculative investigation that may challenge the conventional framework of scholarship and, correspondingly, runs a high risk of failure. In this respect, the institutional forms of the university encourage mediocrity.

Perhaps this limitation is one reason why it is so common for a scholar to devote his career to trivial modifications of what he has already done. The patterns of thinking imposed in his early work, the poverty of conception that is fostered by too-rigid institutional forms, may limit his imagination and distort his vision. That many escape these limitations is a tribute to the human ability to resist pressures that tend to restrict the variety and creativity of life and thought. What is true even at the most advanced levels of graduate education is far more significant at earlier stages, as many critics have eloquently demonstrated. Still, it is not evident, even in this case, to what extent the fault is one of the universities and to what extent it is inherent in the role assigned them in a competitive society, where pursuit of self-interest is elevated to the highest goal.

Some of the pressures that impoverish the educational experience and distort the natural relation of student and teacher clearly have their origin in demands that are imposed on the school. Consider, for example, the sociological problem defined by Daniel Bell: "Higher education has been burdened with the task of becoming a gatekeeper—perhaps the only gatekeeper to significant place and privilege in society; . . . it means that the education system is no longer geared to teaching but to judging."[2] Jencks and Riesman make a similar point: "College is a kind of protracted aptitude test for measuring certain aspects of intelligence and character." The result: "Reliance on colleges to preselect the upper-middle class obviously eliminates most youngsters born into lower-strata families, since they have 'the wrong attitudes' for academic success."[3] The effect is that the university serves as an instrument for ensuring the perpetuation of social privilege.

[Open to any person, at any stage of life]

The same, incidentally, holds for later life. To achieve the Humboldtian ideal, a university should be open to any man, at any stage of life, who wishes to avail himself of this institutional form for enhancing his "spiritual life." In fact, there are programs for bringing corporate executives or engineers from industry to the university for specialized training or simply for broadening their cultural background, but none, to my knowledge, for shoemakers or industrial workers, who could, in principle, profit no less from these opportunities. Evidently, it would be misleading to describe these inequities merely as defects of the university.

In general, there is little if any educational function to the requirement that the university be concerned with certification as well as with education and research. On the contrary, this requirement interferes with its proper function. It is a demand imposed by a society that ensures, in many ways, the preservation of certain forms of privilege and elitism.

Or consider the often-voiced demand that the universities serve the needs of the outside society—that its activities be "relevant" to general social concerns. Put in a very general way, this demand is justifiable. Translated into practice, however, it generally means that the universities provide a service to those existing social institutions that are in a position to articulate their needs and to subsidize the effort to meet these needs. It is not difficult for members of the university community to delude themselves into believing that they are maintaining a "neutral, value-free" position when they simply respond to demands set elsewhere. In fact, to do so is to make a political decision, namely, to ratify the existing distribution of power, authority, and privilege in the society at large, and to take on a commitment to reinforce it. The Pentagon and the great corporations can formulate their needs and subsidize the kind of work that will answer to them. The peasants of Guatemala or the unemployed in Harlem are in no position to do so, obviously. A free society should encourage the development of a university that escapes the not-too-subtle compulsion to be "relevant" in this sense. The university will be able to make its contribution to a free society only to the extent that it overcomes the temptation to conform unthinkingly to the prevailing ideology and to the existing patterns of power and privilege.

[A center of intellectual stimulation: ("subversive") challenges of orthodoxy]

In its relation to society, a free university should be expected to be, in a sense, "subversive." We take for granted that creative work in any field will challenge prevailing orthodoxy. A physicist who refines yesterday's experiment, an engineer who merely seeks to improve existing devices, or an artist who limits himself to styles and techniques that have been thoroughly explored is rightly regarded as deficient in creative imagination. Exciting work in science, technology, scholarship, or the arts will probe the frontiers of understanding and try to create alternatives to the conventional assumptions. If, in some field of inquiry, this is no longer true, then the field will be abandoned by those who seek intellectual adventure.

These observations are clichés that few will question—except in the study of man and society. The social critic who seeks to formulate a vision of a more just and humane social order and is concerned with the discrepancy—more often, the chasm—that separates this vision from the reality that confronts him is a frightening creature who must "overcome his alienation" and become "responsible," "realistic," and "pragmatic." To decode these expressions: he must stop questioning our values and threatening our privilege. He may be concerned with technical modifications of existing society that improve its efficiency and blur its inequities, but he must not try to design a radically different alternative and involve himself in an attempt to bring about social change. He must, therefore, abandon the path of creative inquiry as it is conceived in other domains. It is hardly necessary to stress that this prejudice is even more rigidly institutionalized in the state socialist societies.

Obviously, a free mind may fall into error; the social critic is no less immune to this possibility than the inventive scientist or artist. It may be that at a given stage of technology, the most important activity is to improve the internal combustion engine, and that at a given stage of social evolution, primary attention should be given to the study of fiscal measures that will improve the operation of the state capitalism of the Western democracies. This is possible but hardly obvious in either case. The universities offer freedom and encouragement to those who question the first of these assumptions but more rarely to those who question the second. The reasons are fairly clear. Since the dominant voice in any society is that of the beneficiaries of the status quo, the "alienated intellectual," who tries to pursue the normal path of honest inquiry—perhaps falling into error on the way—and thus often finds himself challenging the conventional wisdom tends to be a lonely figure. The degree of protection and support afforded to him by the university is, again, a measure of its success in fulfilling its proper function in a free society. It is, furthermore, a measure of the willingness of the society to submit its ideology and structure to critical analysis and evaluation, and a measure of the willingness to overcome inequities and defects that will be revealed by such critique.

Such problems as these—which will never cease to exist, so long as human society continues—have become somewhat more critical in the last few years for a number of reasons. In an advanced industrial society, the linkage between the university and external social institutions tend to become more tight and intricate because of the utility of the "knowledge that is produced" (to use a vulgar idiom) and the training that is provided.

This is a familiar insight. Half a century ago, Randolph Bourne noted that the world war had brought to leadership a liberal, technical intelligentsia "immensely ready for the executive ordering of events, pitifully unprepared for the intellectual interpretation or the idealistic focussing of ends," pragmatic intellectuals who "have absorbed the secret of scientific method as applied to political administration" and who readily "lined up in the service of the war technique." Turning to the university, and taking Columbia University as the prototype, he described it as "a financial corporation, strictly analogous, in its motives and responses, to the corporation which is concerned in the production of industrial commodities. . . . The university produces learning instead of steel or rubber, but the nature of the academic commodity has become less and less potent in insuring for the academic workman a status materially different from that of any other kind of employee." The trustees, he claimed, define their obligation in this way: "to see that the quality of the commodity which the university produces is such as to seem reputable to the class which they represent," "Under trustee control," Bourne went on, "the American university has been degraded from its old, noble ideal of a community of scholarship to a private commercial corporation."[4]

Bourne's characterization of the university can be questioned in many respects, but it nevertheless has an unpleasant ring of authenticity, today even more than at the time when he wrote. It will not escape the reader that the student movement of the past few years has—quite independently—developed a very similar critique, often with the same rhetoric. Again, one can point to exaggerations and even flights of fancy, but it would be a mistake to overlook the kernel of truth within it.

A further reason why the problems of the universities have become a more urgent concern than heretofore is that the universities have, on an unprecedented scale, come to be the center of intellectual life. Not only scientists and scholars but also writers and artists are drawn to the academic community. To the extent that this is true, to the extent that other independent intellectual communities disappear, the demands on the university increase. Probably this is a factor in the university crises of the past few years.

With the depoliticization of American society in the 1950s and the narrowing of the range of social thought, the university seems to have become, for many students, almost the only center of intellectual stimulation. Lionel Trilling, in a recent interview, pointed out that he cannot draw on his own experience as a student to help him comprehend the motivation of the "militant students" at Columbia:

> Like all my friends at college, I hadn't the slightest interest in the university as an institution: I thought of it, when I thought of it at all, as the inevitable philistine condition of one's being given leisure, a few interesting teachers, and a library. I find it hard to believe that this isn't the natural attitude.[5]

This is an apt comment. In the past, it was for the most part the football and fraternity crowd who had an interest in the university as such. But in this respect there have been substantial changes. Now it is generally the most serious and thoughtful students who are concerned with the nature of the universities and who feel hurt and deprived by its failings. Twenty years ago [in 1949], these students—in an urban university at least—would have looked elsewhere for the intellectual and social life that they now expect the university to provide.

Personally, I feel that the sharp challenges that have been raised by the student movement are among the few hopeful developments of these troubled years. It would be superficial, and even rather childish, to be so mesmerized by occasional absurdities of formulation or offensive acts as to fail to see the great significance of the issues that have been raised and that lie beneath the tumult. Only one totally lacking in judgment could find himself offended by "student extremism" and not, to an immensely greater extent, by the events and situations that motivate it. A person who can write such words as the following has, to put it as kindly as possible, lost his grasp of reality:

> Quite a few of our universities have already decided that the only way to avoid on-campus riots is to give students academic credit for off-campus rioting ("fieldwork" in the ghettos, among migrant workers, etc.).[6]

Consider the assumptions that would lead one to describe work in the ghettos or among migrant workers as a form of "rioting," or, for that matter, to regard work of this sort as necessarily inappropriate to a college program—as distinct, say, from work on biological warfare or counterinsurgency, which is not described in these terms. Less extreme, but still seriously distorted, is the perception of the student movement expressed by George Kennan, who is concerned with what he sees as the extremely disturbed and excited state of mind of a good portion of our student youth, floundering around as it is in its own terrifying wilderness of drugs, pornography, and political hysteria.[7]

Again, it is striking that he is so much less concerned with the "extremely disturbed and excited state of mind" of those responsible for the fact that the tonnage of bombs dropped on South Vietnam exceeds the total expended by the U.S. Air Force in all theaters of World War II, or with those responsible for the anti-communist "political hysteria" of the 1950s, or, for that matter, with that great mass of students who are still "floundering around" in the traditional atmosphere of conformism and passivity of the colleges and whose rioting is occasioned by football victories.

The irrationality which has been all too characteristic of the response to the student movement is itself a remarkable phenomenon, worthy of analysis. More important, however, is the effort to take the challenge presented by the student movement as a stimulus to critical thinking and social action, perhaps of a quite radical nature—a necessity in a society as troubled as ours, and as dangerous.

Since World War II we have spent over a trillion dollars on "defense" and are now expending billions on an infantile competition to place a man on the moon. Our scientists and technologists are preparing to construct an antiballistic missile system [ABM] at an ultimate cost of many billions of dollars though they know that it will contribute nothing to defense, that in fact it will raise a potentially suicidal arms race to new heights. At the same time, our cities crumble, and millions suffer hunger and want, while those who try to publicize these conditions are investigated by the FBI. It is intolerable that our society should continue to arrogate to itself—in part for consumption, in part for unconscionable waste—half of the far-from-limitless material resources of the world. There are simply no words to describe our willingness to destroy, on a scale without parallel in the contemporary world, when our leaders detect a threat to the "national goals" that they formulate, and that a passive and docile citizenry accepts.

It may appear to be an extreme judgment when a social scientist, a native of Pakistan, asserts that "America has institutionalized even its genocide," referring to the fact that the extermination of the Indians "has become the object of public entertainment and children's games."[8] A look at school texts confirms his assessment, however. Consider the following description in a fourth-grade reader of the extermination of the Pequot tribe by Captain John Mason:

His little army attacked in the morning before it was light and took the Pequots by surprise. The soldiers broke down the stockade with their axes, rushed inside, and set fire to the wigwams. They killed nearly all the braves, squaws, and children, and burned their corn and other food. There were no Pequots left to make more trouble. When the other Indian tribes saw what good fighters the white men were, they kept the peace for many years.

"I wish I were a man and had been there," thought Robert.[9]

A child who acquires such attitudes in the schools will become the man who can behave in the way described by a British eyewitness:

I asked one American who had just ordered a strike on some huts and some sampans (blowing the latter to bits with parts of the boat and the bodies flying in all directions) if air attacks like that did not kill many harmless civilians. "But people shouldn't continue to live here," he said.[10]

[Critical analysis of our institutions and ideology]

It is hardly necessary to add that attitudes created in the schools are supported by the mass media, not only directly but by their encouragement of a general passivity. There is much truth in the observation of Paul Lazarsfeld and Robert Merton that

these media not only continue to affirm the *status quo* but, in the same measure, they fail to raise essential questions about the structure of society. Hence by leading toward conformism and by providing little basis for a critical appraisal of society, the commercially sponsored mass media indirectly but effectively restrain the cogent development of a genuinely critical outlook.[11]

This is not the place for an extended discussion; it is enough to point out that, for reasons suggested by these few remarks, it is a matter of great urgency, for ourselves and for world society, that our institutions and ideology be subjected to serious critical analysis. The universities must be a primary object of such analysis and, at the same time, must provide the "institutional form" within which it can be freely conducted. In these specific historical circumstances, it is useful to recall a remark of Bertrand Russell:

Without rebellion, mankind would stagnate, and injustice would be irremediable. The man who refuses to obey authority has, therefore, in certain circumstances, a legitimate function, provided his disobedience has motives which are social rather than personal.[12]

It is these historical circumstances that define the context for a study of the function of the university and the current challenge to the university.

Reactions to the recent wave of student unrest throughout the world have varied widely. Nathan Glazer asks "whether the student radicals fundamentally represent a better world that can come into being, or whether they are not committed to outdated and romantic visions that cannot be realized, that contradict fundamentally other desires and hopes they themselves possess, and that contradict even more the desires of most other people." He tends toward the latter view; the student radicals remind him "more of the Luddite machine smashers than the Socialist trade unionists who achieved citizenship and power for workers."[13] Consider, in contrast, the reaction of Paul Ricoeur to the massive rebellion of French students in May 1968:

> The signs are now eloquent. The West has entered into a cultural revolution which is distinctively its own, the revolution of the advanced industrial societies, even if it echoes or borrows from the Chinese revolution. It is a cultural revolution because it questions the world-vision, the conception of life, that underlie the economic and political structures and the totality of human relations. This revolution attacks capitalism not only because it fails to bring about social justice but also because it succeeds too well in deluding men by its own inhuman commitment to quantitative well-being. It attacks bureaucracy not only because it is burdensome and ineffectual, but because it places men in the role of slaves in relation to the totality of powers, of structures and hierarchical relations from which they have become estranged.
> Finally, it attacks the nihilism of a society which, like a cancerous tissue, has no purpose beyond its own growth. Confronted with a senseless society, this cultural revolution tries to find the way to the creation of goods, of ideas, of values, in relation to their ends. The enterprise is gigantic; it will take years, decades, a century.[14]

Glazer (like Brzezinski—see note 7) sees the student rebels as Luddites, displaced and unable to find their role in the new society of advanced technology and complex social management. They "come from the fields that have a restricted and ambiguous place in a contemporary society."[15] Ricoeur, on the other hand, expresses a very different perception: in the advanced industrial societies in the coming years there will be a sharp conflict between the centralizing force of a technical bureaucracy, managing society for dubious ends, and the forces that seek to reconstruct social life on a more human scale on the basis of "participation" and popular control. Both interpretations sense that a major historical process is under way. They differ in their judgment as to where they expect (and no doubt hope) it will end, and correspondingly, in the interpretation they give of student dissidence and rebellion. Both expect the university to be at the center of the conflict. Optimists may hope that it will be in the eye of the hurricane—but it is more realistic to expect that it will continue to be caught up in controversy and turmoil.

It is hardly in doubt that we are in the midst of a historical process of centralization and bureaucratization not only in the economy but also in politics and social organization. The crisis of parliamentary institutions is a worldwide phenomenon.[16] Reactions can be seen not only in the university rebellions but also in the search for forms of community organization and control—which have forced their way onto the front pages in recent months—and even, it seems, in tentative gropings toward more direct worker control, often in opposition to the highly bureaucratized trade unions that are increasingly more remote from the day-to-day concerns of those whom the leadership claims to represent.[17] In Eastern Europe there are somewhat analogous developments.

[Commitment to a "free marketplace of ideas"]

The student movement must, I believe, be understood in this more general context. The universities will not be able to isolate themselves from the profound social conflict that appears likely, though its course can hardly be guessed. The linkage of the universities to other social institutions, noted earlier, guarantees this. In fact, there may be very serious questioning, in coming years, of the basic assumption of modern society that development of technology is inherently a desirable, inevitable process; and with it, a critique of the role of the university in advancing knowledge and technique and putting it to use. When students in Western Europe take as their war cry the chant "Ho, Ho, Ho Chi Minh," they are not merely protesting the Vietnam War and the crushing of the poor by the rich that it symbolizes; they are also reacting against the values of industrial society, protesting the role assigned to them as managers of this society, and rejecting the kind of rationality uninformed by any sense of justice, which—as they see it, with considerable accuracy—translates into practice as the knowledge how to preserve privilege and order but not how to meet human needs. The American student movement is also animated in part by such concerns.

In many respects, the university is a legitimate target for protest. The unflattering portrait given by such critics as James Ridgeway may be overdrawn, but it is basically realistic, and quite properly disturbing to the concerned student.[18] Recognition of these characteristics of the university leads to revulsion and often militancy. Nevertheless, the problems brought to the surface may be irresoluble within the framework of the university itself.

Consider, for example, the matter of government contracts for research. It is a classical liberal ideal, echoed also by Marx, that "government and church should . . . be equally excluded from any influence on the school."[19] On the other hand, there is little doubt that government research contracts provide a hidden subsidy to the academic budget by supporting faculty research which would otherwise have to be subsidized by the university. Furthermore, it is quite probable that the choice of research topics, in the sciences at least, is influenced very little by the source of funds, at least in the major universities. It is doubtful that scientific education can continue at a reasonable level without this kind of support. Radical students will certainly ask themselves why support from the Defense Department is more objectionable than support from capitalist institutions—ultimately, from profits derived by exploitation—or support by tax-free gifts that in effect constitute a levy on the poor to support the education of the privileged.[20]

It is impossible to escape the fact that the university is ultimately a parasitic institution from an economic point of view. It cannot free itself from the inequities of the society in which it exists. At the same time, it is dependent for its existence as a relatively free institution on values that are upheld in the society at large. When, for example, Senator Fulbright criticizes the universities for having "betrayed a public trust" by associating themselves with the military-industrial complex instead of acting as an independent critical institution, he is expressing the values that permit the university to function as a free institution to the extent that it does. It is not impossible that these values will be a casualty of the domestic turmoil that is itself in part a consequence of American militarism. It would be foolish to remain blind to these dangers.

One legacy of classical liberalism that we must fight to uphold with unending vigilance, in the universities and without, is the commitment to a "free marketplace of ideas." To a certain extent, this commitment is merely verbal. The task, however, is to extend, not to limit, such freedom as exists— and this freedom is not inconsiderable. Students are right to ask why faculty members should be permitted to contribute to the weapons cult or to work on counterinsurgency. They also point out, with much justice, that it is unreasonable to claim that this is simply a freely undertaken commitment. Access to funds, power, and influence is open to those who undertake this work, but not, say, to those who would prefer to study ways in which poorly armed guerrillas might combat an enemy with overwhelming technological superiority. Were the university truly "neutral and value-free," one kind of work would—as noted earlier—be as well supported as the other.

190 Chomsky on Democracy and Education

The argument is valid but does not change the fact that the commitment is nevertheless undertaken with eagerness and a belief that it is right. Only coercion could eliminate the freedom to undertake such work. Once the principle is established that coercion is legitimate in this domain, it is rather clear against whom it will be used. And the principle of legitimacy of coercion would destroy the university as a serious institution; it would destroy its value to a free society. This must be recognized even in the light of the undeniable fact that the freedom falls far short of ideal.

In certain respects, the specific issue of Defense Department funding of research is a misleading one. Research on chemical and biological warfare or counterinsurgency would be no more benign if funded by the National Institutes of Health or the Social Science Research Council, just as work on high-energy physics is not corrupted if funding comes through the Department of Defense. The important question is the nature of the work and the uses to which it is likely to be put, not the bureaucratic issue of the source of the funding. The latter is of some significance, insofar as one might argue that the Pentagon gains respectability and power by its support of serious research. For American society as a whole, this development is a very minor symptom of a real tragedy, the ongoing and perhaps irreversible militarization of American society. But in the particular case of the universities, these considerations seem to me marginal. Another side issue, in my opinion, is the question of a campus base for military research. In fact, the Vietnamese care very little whether the counterinsurgency technology that is used to destroy and repress them is developed in the halls of the university or in private spin-offs on its periphery.[21] And to the victims of the endless arms race—the present victims of the waste of resources, material and intellectual, that are desperately needed elsewhere, or the possible future victims of a devastating catastrophe—it is of little interest whether their fate is determined in a Department of Death on the university campus or in Los Alamos or Fort Detrick, hundreds of miles away. To move such work off campus is socially irrelevant. It might, in fact, even be a regressive step. It might be argued that as long as such work continues, it would be preferable for it to be done on campus, where it can become a focus for student activism and protest that may not only impede such work but also contribute to growing public awareness.

One of the most hopeful signs, in my opinion, is the increase in concern among students over the problem of the uses of research. There are few today who would agree with the judgment of Edward Teller that "we must trust our social processes" to make the best use of technological advance and "must not be deterred by arguments involving consequences or costs."[22] The question of the uses of technology is multifaceted: it involves complex historical and political judgments as well as technical issues. Properly, it should be faced by students at a time in life when they are free to explore the many dimensions of the problems and supported by a community with like concerns, rather than isolated in a competitive job market. For such reasons the problems of campus-based military research seem to me rather complex.

[Goals of university reform]

Those who believe that radical social change is imperative in our society are faced with a dilemma when they consider university reform. They want the university to be a free institution, and they want the individuals in it to use this freedom in a civilized way. They observe that the university—or to be more precise, many of its members—is "lined up in the service of the war technique" and that it often functions in such a way as to entrench privilege and support repression.

Given this largely correct observation, it is easy to move to some serious misconceptions. It is simply false to claim—as many now do—that the university exists only to provide manpower for the corporate system, or that the university (and the society) permit no meaningful work, or that the university merely serves to coerce and "channel" the student into a socially accepted lifestyle and ideology, even though it is true that the temptation to make choices that will lead in these directions is very great. To an overwhelming extent, the features of university life that rightly are offensive to many concerned students result not from trustee control, not from defense contracts, not from administrative decisions, but from the relatively free choices of faculty and students. Hence the dilemma noted above. "Restructuring of the university" is unlikely to be effective in eliminating the features of the institution that have sparked student criticism. In fact, many of the concrete proposals that I have seen are, I suspect, likely to have the opposite effect; namely, they may lead toward a system of enforceable regulations that may appear democratic on paper but will limit the individual freedom that exists in an institution that is highly decentralized and rather loose in its structure of decision making and administration, hence fairly responsive to the wishes of its members.

It is possible to imagine useful reforms; I suspect, however, that they will have at best a small effect on the way the university functions. The real problem is a much deeper one: to change the choices and personal commitment of the individuals who make up the university. This is much harder than modification of formal structures and is not likely to be effected by such restructuring in any very serious way.

More to the point, I believe, is the view expressed in the Port Huron Statement of 1962, more or less the founding document of SDS [Students for a Democratic Society]:

> The university is located in a permanent position of social influence. Its educational function makes it indispensable and automatically makes it a crucial institution in the formation of social attitudes. In an unbelievably complicated world, it is the central institution for organizing, evaluating, and transmitting knowledge. . . . Social relevance, the accessibility to knowledge, and internal openness—these together make the university a potential base and agency in the movement of social change.
>
> Any new left in America must be, in large measure, a left with real intellectual skills, committed to deliberativeness, honesty, and reflection as working tools. The university permits the political life to be an adjunct to the academic one, and action to be informed by reason.[23]

University reform, in my opinion, should be directed toward such goals as these: not toward imposing constraints, but rather toward lessening them; not toward enjoining the work that now is often dominant—much of which I personally find detestable—but toward opening up alternatives. This can be done, I think, though it will require a degree of intellectual commitment that has, by and large, been lacking on the part of those concerned with university reform.

The university should compensate for the distorting factors introduced by external demands, which necessarily reflect the distribution of power in extra-university society, and by the dynamics of professionalization, which, though not objectionable in itself, often tends to orient study toward problems that can be dealt with by existing techniques and away from those that require new understanding. The university should be a center for radical social inquiry, as it is already a center for what might be called radical inquiry in the pure sciences. For example, it should loosen its institutional forms even further, to permit a richer variety of work and study and experimentation, and it should provide a home for the free intellectual, for the social critic, for the irreverent and radical thinking that is desperately needed if we are to escape from the dismal reality that threatens to overwhelm us. The primary barrier to such a development will not be the unwillingness of administrators or the stubbornness of trustees. It will be the unwillingness of students to do the difficult and serious work required and the fear of the faculty that its security and authority, its guild structure, will be threatened.

These, I think, are the real barriers to serious reform and innovation in the universities as matters now stand, though new barriers may arise if these are successfully overcome. These are the primary problems that should motivate and direct efforts to change the university. In general, I think that the so-called new left has a task of historic importance; and I think that this task was formulated quite fittingly in the Port Huron statement when it spoke of the necessity for "a left with real intellectual skills, committed to deliberativeness, honesty, and reflection as working tools," committed to a political life in which "action is informed by reason."

These are goals that can easily be forgotten in the heat of conflict, but they remain valid ones, and one can only hope that they will be continually resurrected as a guide to positive action.

Notes

1. Wilhelm von Humboldt, "On the inner and outer organization of the higher institutions of learning in Berlin," parts translated in Marianne Cowan, ed., *Humanist without portfolio* (Detroit: Wayne State University Press, 1963).
2. Daniel Bell, "The scholar cornered," *American Scholar* 37, 3 (1968): 401–6.
3. Christopher Jencks and David Riesman, *The academic revolution* (New York: Doubleday, 1968), pp. 104, 100.
4. *The world of Randolph Bourne*, ed. Lillian Schlissel (New York: E. P. Dutton, 1965), pp. 198, 85, 87. I do not intend my citation of these remarks to suggest approval of what is asserted or implied—as that universities were once a noble community of scholarship, or that the "academic workman" should have a status different from other employees. The "academic workman" is not the only one who should be freed from serving as a tool of production.
5. *Partisan Review* 35, 2 (1968).
6. Irving Kristol, "A different way to restructure the university," *New York Times Magazine*, Dec. 8, 1968. No less revealing is his next sentence: "And at Harvard—of all places!—there is now a course (Social Relations 148) which enrolls several hundred students and is given for credit, whose curriculum is devised by the SDS, whose classes are taught by SDS sympathizers, and whose avowed aim is 'radicalization' of the students." Why, in fact, is it so scandalous that Harvard ("of all places!") should have a student-initiated course offering a radical critique of American society and its international behavior?
7. George Kennan, speech to the International Association for Cultural Freedom on Dec. 2, 1968, at Princeton, N.J.; *New York Times*, Dec. 4, 1968. Zbigniew Brzezinski, who interprets the student movement as basically "Luddite," describes Kennan as "in a mood of rage at the young."
8. Eqbal Ahmad, in *No more Vietnams?* ed. Richard M. Pfeffer (New York: Harper and Row, 1968), p. 18.
9. Harold B. Clifford, *Exploring New England* (Chicago: Follett, 1961), p. 11.
10. Richard West, *Sketches from Vietnam* (London: Jonathan Cape, Ltd., 1968), pp. 97–8.
11. Paul Lazarsfeld and Robert Merton, "Mass communication, popular taste and organized social action," in W. L. Schramm, ed., *Mass communications* (Urbana: University of Illinois Press, 1949); quoted by D. W. Smythe and H. Wilson in a study in which they

conclude that "the principal function of the commercially supported mass media in the United States is to market the output of the consumer goods industries and to train the population for loyalty to the American economic-political system"("Cold War-mindedness and the mass media," in *Struggle against history,* ed. N. D. Houghton [New York: Washington Square Press, 1908], pp. 71–72).

12. *Power* (New York: W. W. Norton, 1938), p. 252. He concludes his essay with these words (p. 305): "just as we teach children to avoid being destroyed by motor cars if they can, so we should teach them to avoid being destroyed by cruel fanatics, and to preserve, as far as possible, the instinctive joy of life that is natural to healthy children. This is the task of a liberal education: to give a sense of the value of things other than domination, to help to create wise citizens of a free community, and through the combination of citizenship with liberty in individual creativeness to enable men to give to human life that splendor which some few men have shown that it can achieve."

13. Nathan Glazer, "'Student power' in Berkeley," *Public Interest* 13 (1968).

14. *Le Monde,* June 9–10, 1968.

15. Glazer, "'Student power' in Berkeley."

16. For some illuminating discussion, see Michael Kidron, *Western capitalism since the war* (London: George Weidenfeld and Nicholson, 1968).

17. Ibid.

18. James Ridgeway, *The closed corporation* (New York: Random House, 1968).

19. Karl Marx, *Critique of the Gotha Programme* (1875).

20. Cf. ibid.: "If in some states of [the United States] the higher education institutions are also 'free,' that only means in fact defraying the cost of the education of the upper classes from the general tax receipts."

21. As it continues to be. For example, one of the initiators of Project Cambridge at MIT, Professor Ithiel Pool, states that this $7.6 million project will "strengthen" research in counterinsurgency (*Scientific Research,* September 15, 1969). At the same time, he characterizes student protests that this will be the case as "a lot of hogwash."

22. "Teller urges strong nuclear management," *Aviation Week and Space Technology,* April 23, 1963. We must push "scientific advancements to the limit," Teller urges, "the military requirements will soon follow." Concerns over "the best human use of the advances already achieved" is in his view "an extremely grave symptom," which threatens the "whole dynamic civilization of the West, for which America is the spearhead."

23. Students for a Democratic Society, Port Huron Statement (1962), reprinted in Mitchell Cohen and Dennis Hale, eds., *The new student left,* rev. ed. (Boston: Beacon Press, 1967).

Chapter 11

Scholarship and commitment, then and now (December 1999)

If my memory is correct, the last time I spoke at the MLA [Modern Language Association] was thirty-one years ago, at a session that was similar to this one in some important ways, different in others that are no less important. The main similarity is the topic: scholarship and commitment. The difference is the formal structure. The meeting in December 1968 was informal, a lively overflow session but not on the program, organized by a group called the "radical caucus." The fact that this evening's session is within the formal framework of the conference is a reflection of significant changes that have taken place in the intervening years. The difference has both positive and negative aspects, which perhaps merit some reflection, but I'll put that question aside.

The 1968 meeting grew out of extensive educational and organizing efforts within the profession, in the universities more broadly, and well beyond; and it contributed to inspiring other such efforts, which gave a very different cast to the general culture and the character and place of the universities within it.

On the changes within the profession, I would not presume to offer any detailed comment: you know much better than I. At a very general level, the profession was opened up to far wider concerns and constituencies. Traditional commitments remain, but no longer to the virtual exclusion of a range of others. By now it occasions no surprise that an issue of *PMLA* [Publications of the Modern Language Association of America] is devoted to working-class literature. There have been explorations of novel curricula, along with outreach to community colleges and high schools, and commitment to the principle that serious literary expression, either access to it or its creation, is not the special province of privileged sectors.

[The liberating function of the university]

The 1968 side session of the MLA was one of many like it. Throughout much of the academic world there were similar expressions of concern over the subordination of intellectual life and its institutions to external structures of power, and the abandonment of what many felt to be the primary responsibility of the universities, and their social function as well in free communities: to be liberating for all participants, and to have that impact on the broader society as well.

These developments were, of course, an expression of initiatives and challenges that were arising throughout the broader society in which the universities and the academic professions find their place. The immediate driving factors were the civil rights and anti-war movements, and while there is no need to rehearse the tremendous obstacles that remain, nonetheless in both domains changes have undoubtedly been large in scale—and salutary, I think most of us would agree.

Among the outcomes were a much heightened sensitivity to oppression and injustice, an enriched respect for other cultures, and the substantial growth of popular activism committed to human and civil rights, sometimes even reflected in congressional legislation and court decisions, and imposed with varying success on an often unwilling executive branch. A related outcome has been much reduced tolerance for state violence and terror. Not long after the December 1968 meeting, some 70 percent of the population came to condemn the Indochina wars as "fundamentally wrong and immoral," not "a mistake," a stand that has remained unshaken to the present—a remarkable fact, given that such judgments receive virtually no support from articulate opinion and are ignored or misinterpreted in elite commentary. No U.S. president [now] could launch a major war as JFK did in 1961, with scarcely a whisper of protest for many years; internal documents ruefully recognize these constraints on state violence. The popular movements that evolved in the years that followed—feminist, environmental, anti-nuclear, solidarity, and others—have dramatically changed the social and political culture, and intellectual life as well.

One illustration of these remarkable developments, only one of many, is that for the first time it has become possible at least to face the "original sin" of U.S. history: the fate of the indigenous population. It is sometimes hard to remember that thirty years ago school texts still celebrated the glorious massacres that cleared New England of the native scourge, as I recall from the experience of my own children in a progressive, largely professional community, or that a leading liberal scholarly history could cheerily explain that after winning their independence, Americans were free to "concentrate on the task of felling trees and Indians and of rounding out their natural boundaries." Nothing of the sort would be imaginable today—only one indication of the generally civilizing effect of the turmoil of the period, though there is a long way to go before we might be able to regard the outcome with much satisfaction or self-respect.

In that ferment, students and young faculty often had a prominent role. It was natural and appropriate that they should turn their attention as well to their own institutions. This was the context for the activities within the professional associations and universities—like others of the day, chaotic and complex, sometimes constructive and sometimes not, but broadly, I think, healthy and positive in the consequences to which they contributed, including a more vibrant and engaged concern for committed scholarship: committed not only to truth, but also to humane values.

These are matters of no slight importance. It is common to describe modern history in terms of a transition from mainly agriculture-based to manufacturing-based economies, and more recently to a new phase in which knowledge is the driving force. The description has merit and is likely to be even more true of the world of tomorrow. In that context universities have come to occupy an increasingly prominent place.

While the shift toward a knowledge-based society is described with admiration and hopeful expectations, there are aspects that are dubious. The questions "Knowledge for what?" and "Knowledge for whom?" should always be in the forefront, and the answers are often not too attractive. The entire concept is defective in a more fundamental way. However rich, knowledge is quite different from true understanding, including some insight into our proper place in the material and social world. If there is no transition to an understanding-based society in something like this sense, then the prospects may be dim for the kind of world in which a decent person would want to live.

[A difference between the sciences and the humanities]

Throughout intellectual history there has been a distinction between inquiry into what the world is and how it works, and into how a decent life should be lived. Intellectual and cultural traditions have, of course, differed in the relative emphasis they give to these concerns. As the world moves toward an intellectual and social order based on knowledge—or, we may hope, on understanding—the responsibilities of the universities are likely to increase in both respects. They should seek to develop the thinking, the ideas, the insights into science and human life, the knowledge, and the broad understanding that are needed to help us find our way toward a more human future. To contribute to this end, they must be free from external pressures. Furthermore, that freedom must be distributed. It is not for administrators or professors, but for all of those who take part in the life of the university: students, faculty, staff. That goal may be hard to reach but should remain as an ideal to be actively sought.

In a fundamental sense, the social and intellectual role of the university should be subversive in a healthy society. In the sciences, that is more or less taken for granted, if not in these words. It is understood that science survives by constant challenge to established thinking. Successful education in the sciences seeks to encourage students to initiate such challenges and to pursue them. Individuals and society at large benefit to the extent that these liberatory ideals extend throughout the educational system—in fact, far beyond.

But the responsibilities are undertaken in the shadow of dilemmas that are not easy to resolve in the real world of highly concentrated power. Naturally, the reigning institutions, state and private, use their power to try to shape the social and intellectual world in their own interests. Universities are economically parasitic, relying on external support. To maintain this support while serving their proper liberating function poses problems that verge on contradiction. In practice, universities face a constant struggle to maintain their integrity, their fundamental social role in a healthy society, in the face of external pressures. The problems are heightened with the expansion of private power in every domain, in the course of the vast state-corporate social engineering projects designed to shift decision-making authority from the public sphere, with all of its extreme deficiencies, to private power that is unaccountable in principle—projects often called "neo-liberal," a highly misleading term: they are not new and would have scandalized classical liberals.

The effects can be seen in the natural sciences. A pharmaceutical corporation, for example, may be reluctant to sponsor university research in fundamental biology, which may yield an economic payoff but at some uncertain time and with benefits freely available. It is more likely to fund applied projects, with controls to ensure that it has a prior claim to results and even publication. The likely effects, the topic of considerable current concern, are greater secrecy and a shift to short-term applied research geared to commercial success, as compared with the days when university research was primarily government-funded, including Pentagon funding, which was commonly free and unconstrained though radically undemocratic in the way resources are allocated, a complicated issue that I will have to put aside. The problems that have always existed are becoming more serious today in the context of the general attack on substantive democracy that has been under way for the past thirty years, tendencies that should not be obscure to those with eyes open.

The problems take a different form beyond the natural sciences, in the domains that are expected to construct an intellectual culture and a framework of attitudes and beliefs that are conducive to the needs of external power systems. Here the contradiction between the parasitic character of the university and the liberatory function it should carry out in a free and healthy society is more severe than in the hard sciences. One reason is that the results of inquiry that is truly free and unconstrained can rarely be taken over to enhance private power, as is commonly the case in the sciences. A second is that the universities, at the core of the intellectual culture, are expected to take part in the task of "regimenting the public mind every bit as much as an army regiments the bodies of its soldiers," to borrow the words of one of the founders and leading figures of the public relations industry, a respected Wilson-Roosevelt-Kennedy liberal. He was expressing views that have long been a familiar doctrine of elite opinion, particularly so in this century as popular struggles have succeeded in expanding the realm of freedom, leading to the recognition that control of attitude and belief must replace the reliance on force that is no longer so readily available, a critical distinguishing feature of modern industrial democracies.

Such concerns are always latent and regularly receive overt and often impassioned expression when the "ignorant and meddlesome outsiders" threaten the authority and tranquility of the "responsible men" who are to conduct public affairs undisturbed in a well-run democracy, in which the "bewildered herd," the general public, are to be "spectators" and not "participants in action." I happen to be quoting Walter Lippmann's rendition of Wilsonian liberalism, but the ideas are a standard feature of intellectual opinion, with a distinguished history.

[Two kinds of intellectuals]

The dangerously civilizing tendencies of the 1960s were no exception in this regard. A strong backlash was to be expected from the ranks of privilege, and it was forthcoming at once, pretty much across the spectrum of respectable opinion and, more important, in policies undertaken to contain and destroy the threat. Toward the liberal end, the fears of privilege were given lucid expression in a study that should be a well-known classic, the first report of the Trilateral Commission, representing liberal internationalist opinion in the three main centers of industrial democracy: North America, Europe, and Japan. In the U.S., the Carter administration was drawn almost entirely from its ranks.

The report was devoted to the "crisis of democracy" that arose throughout the industrial democracies as large sectors of the population that had been passive and marginalized sought to enter the public arena to defend and advance their interests. The naive might mistake this to be a step toward democracy, but the participants in the study understood that it is a crisis of democracy that must be overcome. Failure of the "ignorant and meddlesome outsiders" to understand their place as "spectators," not "participants," is "excessive democracy," an ominous change from the days when "Truman had been able to govern the country with the cooperation of a relatively small number of Wall Street lawyers and bankers," as the U.S. rapporteur, a distinguished political scientist, commented with apparent nostalgia if a little exaggeration. Then we had proper "moderation in democracy."

The commission was particularly concerned by the rise of "value-oriented intellectuals," who "devote themselves to the derogation of leadership, the challenging of authority, and the unmasking and deligitimation of established institutions," including the institutions that are responsible for "the indoctrination of the young"—the schools, the churches, and the universities. It contrasted these sinister groupings with the "technocratic and policy-oriented intellectuals," the "responsible men" whom we label "commissars" and "apparatchiks" in the societies of official enemies, though values are of course reversed at home, in the standard way. The "responsible men" on our side are not distracted by romantic ideas about justice and freedom but keep to serious pursuits: managing the world within the framework of "established institutions" that are subject to no challenge and that serve the needs of power and privilege, including doctrinal management, in particular, "the indoctrination of the young" in proper modes of thought and understanding.

[A serious threat]

The task of restoring discipline and obedience has been a major theme of the years since. This is not the place to review the successes and failures. It should never be forgotten, however, that the modalities employed for the traditional victims have been extremely brutal, primarily for the poor and defenseless but for intellectuals as well. Nor should we allow ourselves to overlook the reaction of the privileged. We have just witnessed a harrowing and, I think, highly instructive example: the tenth anniversary of the assassination of six leading Latin American intellectuals, including the rector of the Jesuit university in San Salvador, by elite state terrorist forces fresh from more training sessions by U.S. Green Berets, the same forces that had compiled an awesome record of atrocities during the grim Salvadoran phase of the global restoration of approved behavior; the list of church martyrs alone that is being sent to the Vatican by Salvadoran bishops for the jubilee year 2000 runs to over one hundred pages, and that is a fraction of the toll. We should also not forget that along with the countless other victims, the intellectuals who had disturbed good order by their commitment to the voiceless and oppressed were doubly assassinated: first murdered, then forgotten. The tenth anniversary passed without a single mention of their names in the U.S. press. Few literate Westerners would even know their names or would have read a word they had written, in sharp contrast to dissidents in the camp of the official enemy, who suffered severe repression, but in the post-Stalin period nothing like the treatment meted out within the free world. I am omitting the most depraved element of the reaction of Western intellectuals to these atrocities, but perhaps this is enough to suggest some questions that might be high on the agenda, not only in a discussion of scholarship and commitment.

Within the rich industrial societies, the attempt to restore discipline and obedience takes more subtle forms, which young people in particular understand very well. One aspect is corporatization of the universities, a serious threat to the liberatory and subversive function that it is their responsibility to undertake in a free and healthy society. To defend the integrity of the universities and their proper commitments is an honorable and difficult task in itself, but our sights should hardly be set that low. Particularly in the societies that are more privileged, many choices are available, including fundamental institutional change if that is the right way to proceed, and surely including scholarship that contributes to and draws from the never-ending struggles for freedom and justice. We need not quietly accept the suffering and oppression that are all around us, and the prospect, which is not slight, that human beings will prove to be an "evolutionary error," appearing very recently in the evolutionary record and disappearing quickly, causing great damage along the way.

Chapter 12

The mechanisms and practices of indoctrination (December 1984)

How is [the] remarkable collective historical amnesia [of the American elite] achieved? To better understand the system, let us first take a look at the way the process works in a totalitarian society, poles apart from our own in its internal order.

[A rare specimen of newscaster]

In May 1983, a remarkable incident occurred in Moscow. A courageous newscaster, Vladimir Danchev, denounced the Soviet invasion of Afghanistan in five successive radio broadcasts. This aroused great admiration in the West. The *New York Times* commented accurately that this was a departure from the "official Soviet propaganda line," that Danchev had "revolted against the standards of doublethink and newspeak."

Danchev was taken off the air and sent to a psychiatric hospital. He was returned to his position last December. A Soviet official was quoted as saying that "he was not punished, because a sick man cannot be punished." In the West, all of this was understood as a glimpse into the world of Orwell's *1984*. Danchev was admired for his courage, for a triumph of the human will, for his refusal to be cowed by totalitarian violence. In Paris, a prize was established for a "journalist who fights for the right to be informed."

What was remarkable about Danchev's radio broadcasts was not simply that he expressed opposition to the Soviet invasion and called for resistance to it, but that he called it an "invasion." In Soviet theology, there is no such thing; rather, there is a Russian *defense* of Afghanistan against bandits operating from Pakistani sanctuaries and supported by the CIA and other warmongers.

Implicit in the coverage of the Danchev affair by Western media was a note of self-congratulation: It couldn't happen here. No American newscaster has been sent to a psychiatric hospital for calling an American invasion an "invasion" or for calling on the victims to resist.

We might, however, inquire further into just why this has never happened. One possibility is that the question has never arisen because no American journalist would ever mimic Danchev's courage or could even perceive that an American invasion of the Afghan type is in fact an invasion or that a sane person might call on the victims to resist. If this were the cue, it would signify a stage of indoctrination well beyond any achieved under Soviet terror, well beyond anything Orwell imagined.

[Astonishing subservience to the doctrinal system]

Consider the following facts: in 1962, President Kennedy sent the U.S. Air Force to attack rural South Vietnam, where more than 80 percent of the population lived, as part of a program intended to drive several million people to concentration camps (called "strategic hamlets") where they would be surrounded by barbed wire and armed guards and "protected" from the guerrillas whom, we conceded, they were willingly supporting.

The direct U.S. invasion of South Vietnam followed our support for the French in their attempt to reconquer their former colony, our disruption of the 1954 "peace process," and a terrorist war against the South Vietnamese population that had already left some seventy-five thousand dead. In the following years, the United States resisted every attempt to arrive at a peaceful settlement. In 1964 it began to plan a ground invasion of South Vietnam, which took place in early 1965, accompanied by bombing of North Vietnam and intensified bombing of the South. The United States also extended the war to Laos and then to Cambodia.

The United States protested that it was invited in, but as the London *Economist* recognized in the case of Afghanistan (never in the case of Vietnam), "an invader is an invader unless invited in by a government with a claim to legitimacy," and outside the world of newspeak, the client regime established by the United States had no more legitimacy than the Afghan regime established by the Soviet Union. Nor did the United States regard this government as having any legitimacy; in fact, it was regularly overthrown and replaced when its leaders appeared to be insufficiently enthusiastic about U.S. plans to escalate the terror, or when they were feared to be considering a peaceful settlement.

The United States openly recognized throughout that a political settlement was unacceptable, for the simple reason that the "enemy" would win handily in a political competition. The conflict had to be restricted to the military dimension, where the United States could hope to reign supreme. In the words of Douglas Pike, now head of the Indochina archives at Berkeley and much revered in mainstream journalism as one of a new breed of "non-ideological" scholars, the South Vietnamese enemy "maintained that its contest with the U.S.-installed government and the United States should be fought out at the political level and that the use of massive military might was in itself illegitimate" until forced by the U.S. "to use counterforce to survive."

For the past twenty-two years, I have been searching for some reference in mainstream journalism or scholarship to an American invasion of South Vietnam in 1962 (or ever), or an American attack against South Vietnam, or American aggression in Indochina—without success. There is no such event in history. Rather, there is an American *defense* of South Vietnam against terrorists supported from outside (namely, from Vietnam), a defense that was unwise, the doves maintain.

In short, there are no Danchevs here. Within the mainstream, there is no one who can call an invasion an "invasion," or even perceive the fact; it is unimaginable that any American journalist would have publicly called upon the South Vietnamese to resist the American invasion. Such a person would not have been sent to a psychiatric hospital, but he would surely not have retained his professional position and standing. Even today, those who refer to the U.S. invasion of South Vietnam in 1962, intensified in 1965, are regarded with disbelief; perhaps they are confused, or perhaps quite mad. Note that here it takes no courage to tell the truth, merely honesty. We cannot plead fear of state violence, as followers of the party line can in a totalitarian state.

Just to add a personal note: in a book I wrote shortly after the Russian invasion of Afghanistan, I compared it to the U.S. invasion of South Vietnam, and discussed more generally the responsibility of both superpowers for the cold war system of conflict and intervention. American reviewers were unable to see the words, and complained that while there might be something to what I wrote, it would be more convincing if the story had been told "a little more evenhandedly" (Christopher Lehmann-Haupt in the *New York Times*) or that I was guilty of a "double moral standard" (James Fallows in the *Atlantic Monthly*). The same book was reviewed in the communist press, which dismissed my "far-fetched and groundless concept that both powers have a vested interest in the Cold War" (James West of the American Communist Party Political Bureau, in the *World Marxist Review*), offering arguments that this was solely an American affair. What is of interest is that the communist commentary, while incorrect, is at least rational, while the mainstream U.S. commentary reflects the kind of incapacity to perceive or think about simple issues that is sometimes found in the more fanatical religious cults.

It is common now to deride any analogy between the Soviet invasion of Afghanistan and the U.S. invasion of Grenada, and indeed they differ radically in scale and character. A comparison to the U.S. invasion of South Vietnam would be more appropriate but is inconceivable within the mainstream. We incidentally see here another typical device of the well-indoctrinated intellectual (a somewhat redundant locution): select or concoct some weak criticism of the holy state and dismiss it with contempt, thus displacing rational critical analysis and dispelling the threat of understanding.

[Spurious tasks of an educational system]

In their important study *Demonstration elections*, Edward Herman and Frank Brodhead include a photograph of Notre Dame president Theodore Hesburgh contemplating a ballot box while he was serving as an observer during the 1982 election in El Salvador, much heralded as a step toward something that we call "democracy." The caption reads: "The Rev. Theodore Hesburgh, 'observing' the Salvadoran election, but not 'seeing' the transparent voting box," plainly shown in the photograph. One of the central tasks of a successful educational system is to endow its victims with the capacity to observe but not to see, a capacity that is the hallmark of the "responsible intellectual."

There did, of course, develop a kind of opposition to the Vietnam War in the mainstream, but it was overwhelmingly "pragmatic," as the critics characterized it with considerable self-adulation, distinguishing themselves from the "emotional" or "irresponsible" opponents who objected to the war on principled grounds. The "pragmatic" opponents argued that the war could not be won at an acceptable cost, or that there was unclarity about goals, or duplicity, or errors in execution. On similar grounds, the German general staff was no doubt critical of Hitler after Stalingrad.

Public attitudes, incidentally, were rather different. As recently as 1982, over 70 percent of the population held that the war was "fundamentally wrong and immoral," not merely a "mistake," a position held by far fewer "opinion leaders" and by virtually none of the articulate intelligentsia, even at the height of opposition to the war in 1970.

How has this remarkable subservience to the doctrinal system been achieved? It is not that the facts were unavailable, as is sometimes the case. The devastating bombing of northern Laos and the 1969 bombing and other attacks were suppressed by the media, a fact that is suppressed within the mainstream until today (these are called "secret wars," meaning that the government kept the secret—as it did, with the complicity of the media). But in the case of the American attack against South Vietnam, sufficient facts were always available. They were observed, but not seen.

American scholarship is particularly remarkable. The official historian of the Kennedy administration, Arthur Schlesinger, regarded as a leading dove, does indeed refer to aggression in 1962. "1962 had not been a bad year," he writes in his history *A Thousand Days:* "aggression [was] checked in Vietnam." That is, the year in which the U.S. undertook direct aggression against South Vietnam was the year in which aggression was *checked* in Vietnam. Orwell would have been impressed.

Another respected figure in the liberal pantheon, Adlai Stevenson, intoned at the United Nations that in Vietnam we were combating "internal aggression," another phrase that Orwell would have admired; that is, we were combating aggression by the Vietnamese against us in Vietnam, just as we had combated aggression by the Mexicans against us in Mexico a century earlier. We had done the same in Greece in the late 1940s, Stevenson went on to explain, intervening to protect Greece from "the aggressors" who had "gained control of most of the country," these "aggressors" being the Greeks who had led the anti-Nazi resistance and whom we succeeded in removing, with an impressive display of massacre, torture, expulsion, and general violence, in favor of the Nazi collaborators of our choice. The analogy was, in fact, more apt than Stevenson—apparently a very ignorant man—was likely to have known. As always, the American posture is defensive, even as we invade a country halfway around the world after having failed to destroy the political opposition by large-scale violence and terror.

A closer look at the debate that did develop over the Vietnam War provides some lessons about the mechanisms of indoctrination. The debate pitted the hawks against the doves. The hawks were those, like journalist Joseph Alsop, who felt that with a sufficient exercise of violence we could succeed in our aims. The doves felt that this was unlikely, although, as Arthur Schlesinger explained, "We all pray that Mr. Alsop will be right," and "we may all be saluting the wisdom and statesmanship of the American government" if the United States succeeds (contrary to his expectations) in a war policy that was turning Vietnam into "a land of ruin and wreck." It was this book that established Schlesinger as a "leading war opponent," in the words of Leslie Gelb.

[The spectrum of mainstream thinkable thought]

It is, of course, immediately evident that there is a possible position omitted from the fierce debate between the hawks and the doves, which allegedly tore the country apart during these trying years, namely, the position of the peace movement, a position in fact shared by the large majority of citizens as recently as 1982: the war was not merely a "mistake," as the official doves allege, but was "fundamentally wrong and immoral." To put it plainly: war crimes, including the crime of launching aggressive war, are wrong, even if they succeed in their "noble" aims. This position does not enter the debate, even to be refuted; it is unthinkable within the ideological mainstream.

It should be emphasized that departures from orthodoxy were very rare among the articulate intelligentsia. Few journalists were more critical of the war than Anthony Lewis, who summed up his attitude in 1975 by explaining that the war began with "blundering efforts to do good," though by 1969 (1969!) it was clear that it was a "disastrous mistake."

In mainstream academic circles, it would have been difficult to find a more committed critic of the war than John King Fairbank of Harvard, the dean of American Asian scholars who was considered so extreme as to be a "comsymp," or worse, in McCarthyite terminology. Fairbank gave the presidential address to the American Historical Society in December, 1968, a year after the Tet offensive had converted most of the corporate elite and other top planning circles to dovedom. He was predictably critical of the Vietnam War, in these terms: this is "an age when we get our power politics overextended into foreign disasters like Vietnam mainly through an excess of righteousness and disinterested benevolence": "our role in defending the South after 1965" was based on analytic errors, so that "we had great trouble in convincing ourselves that it had a purpose worthy of the effort."

The doves felt that the war was "a hopeless cause," we learn from Anthony Lake, a leading dove who resigned from the government in protest against the Cambodia invasion. All agree that it was a "failed crusade," "noble" but "illusory" and undertaken with the "loftiest intentions," as Stanley Karnow puts it in his best-selling companion volume to the PBS TV series, highly regarded for its critical candor. Those who do not appreciate these self-evident truths, or who maintain the curious view that they should be supported by some evidence, simply demonstrate thereby that they are emotional and irresponsible ideologues, or perhaps outright communists. Or more accurately, their odd views cannot be heard; they are outside the spectrum of thinkable thought. Few dictators can boast of such utter conformity to Higher Truths.

All of this illustrates very well the genius of democratic systems of thought control, which differ markedly from totalitarian practice. Those who rule by violence tend to be "behaviorist" in their outlook. What people may think is not terribly important; what counts is what they do. They must obey, and this obedience is secured by force. The penalties for disobedience vary depending on the characteristics of the state. [In a totalitarian state], the penalties may be psychiatric torture, or exile, or prison under harsh and grim conditions. In a typical U.S. dependency such as El Salvador the dissident is likely to be found in a ditch, decapitated after hideous torture; and when a sufficient number are dispatched we can even have elections in which people march toward democracy by rejecting the Nazi-like D'Aubuisson in favor of Duarte, who presided over one of the great mass murders of the modern period (the necessary prerequisite to democratic elections, which obviously cannot proceed while popular organizations still function), and his minister of defense Vides Casanova, who explained in 1980 that the country had survived the massacre of 30,000 peasants in the 1932 Matanza, and "today, the armed forces are prepared to kill 200,000–300,000, if that's what it takes to stop a Communist takeover."

Democratic systems are quite different. It is necessary to control not only what people do, but also what they think. Since the state lacks the capacity to ensure obedience by force, thought can lead to action, and therefore the threat to order must be excised at the source. It is necessary to establish a framework for possible thought that is constrained within the principles of the state religion. These need not be asserted; it is better that they be presupposed, as the unstated framework for thinkable thought.

The critics reinforce this system by tacitly accepting these doctrines and confining their critique to tactical questions that arise within them. To achieve respectability, to be admitted to the debate, they must accept without question or inquiry the fundamental doctrine that the state is benevolent, governed by the loftiest intentions, adopting a defensive stance, not an actor in world affairs but only reacting to the crimes of others—sometimes unwisely because of personal failures, naïveté, the complexity of history, or an inability to comprehend the evil nature of our enemies. If even the harshest critics tacitly adopt these premises, then, the ordinary person may ask, who am I to disagree? The more intensely the debate rages between hawks and doves, the more firmly and effectively the doctrines of the state religion are established. It is because of their notable contribution to thought control that the critics are tolerated, indeed honored—that is, those who play by the rules.

This is a system of thought control that was not perceived by Orwell, and is never understood by dictators who fail to comprehend the utility for indoctrination of a class of critics who denounce the errors and failings of the leadership while tacitly adopting the crucial premises of the state religion.

These distinctions between totalitarian and democratic systems of thought control are only rough first approximations. In fact, even a totalitarian state must be concerned about popular attitudes and understanding, and in a democracy, it is the politically active segments of the population, the more educated and privileged, who are of prime concern. This is obvious in the United States, where the poor tend not even to vote, and more significant forms of political participation—the design and formulation of political programs, candidate selection, the requisite material support, educational efforts, or propaganda—are the domain of relatively narrow, privileged elites. Three-quarters of the population may support a nuclear freeze, and some of them may even know that this is official Soviet policy as well, but that has no impact on the policy of massive government intervention to subsidize high-technology industry through a state-guaranteed market for armaments, since no serious alternative is available in the system of political economy

Mass popular resistance to military aggression does serve as an impediment to the planners, as has been evident in the last few years with regard to Central America. But such resistance, while sometimes effective in raising the costs of state violence, is of limited efficacy as long as it is not based on understanding of the forces at work and the reasons for their systematic behavior, and it tends to dissipate as quickly as it arises.

At the same time, a frightened and insecure populace, trained to believe that Russian demons and Third World hordes are poised to take everything they have, is susceptible to jingoist fanaticism. This was shown dramatically by the popular response to the Grenada invasion. The U.S. is again "standing tall," Reagan proclaimed after six thousand elite troops managed to overcome the resistance of a handful of Cuban military men and a few Grenadan militiamen, winning 8,700 medals for their valor, and eliciting a reaction here that cannot fail to awaken memories of other great powers that won cheap victories not too many years ago.

[Less subtle methods of indoctrination]

The more subtle methods of indoctrination just illustrated are considerably more significant than outright lying or suppression of unwanted fact, though the latter are also common enough. Examples are legion.

Consider, for example, the current debate as to whether there is a "symmetry" between El Salvador and Nicaragua in that in each case rebels supported from abroad are attempting to overthrow the government. The administration claims that in one case the rebels are "freedom fighters" and the government is an illegitimate tyranny, while in the other case the rebels are terrorists and the government is a still somewhat flawed democracy. The critics question whether Nicaragua is really supporting the guerrillas in El Salvador or whether Nicaragua has already succumbed to totalitarianism.

Lost in the debate is a more striking symmetry. In each country, there is a terrorist military force that is massacring civilians, and in each country we support that force: the government of El Salvador, and the contras.

This is the real symmetry between Nicaragua and El Salvador. Its significance is lost as we debate the accuracy of the government cases, meanwhile continuing to labor under the mysterious collective amnesia that prevents us from seeing that there is little here that is new[, and from understanding why this should be so].

Or to turn to another part of the world, consider what is universally called "the peace process" in the Middle East, referring to the Camp David agreements. Israeli-run polls reveal that the population of the territories under Israeli military occupation overwhelmingly oppose the "peace process," regarding it as detrimental to their interests. Why should this be so? Surely of all the people in the region, they are among those who must be yearning the most for peace. But no journalist seems to have inquired into this strange paradox.

The problem is easily solved. The "peace process," as was evident at the time and should be transparent in retrospect, was designed in such a way as to remove the major Arab military force, Egypt, from the conflict, so that Israel would then be free, with a huge and rapidly expanding U.S. subsidy, to intensify settlement and repression in the conquered territories and to attack its northern neighbor—exactly as it did, at once and unremittingly since. It is hardly a cause for wonder that the victims of the "peace process" overwhelmingly condemn and reject it, though it is perhaps a little surprising that such elementary truths, obvious enough at the outset, cannot be seen even today. Meanwhile, we must continue to support the "peace process." Who can be opposed to peace?

In this case, too, it would be salutary to overcome our mysterious collective amnesia about the facts of recent history. There is no time here to review the diplomatic record, but anyone who troubles to do so will quickly learn that there have been possibilities for peace with a modicum of justice for about fifteen years, blocked in every instance by U.S.-Israeli rejectionism. In the early 1970s, this rejectionist stance was so extreme as to block even Arab initiatives (by Egypt and Jordan) to attain a general peace settlement that entirely ignored Palestinian national rights.

Since the international consensus shifted to adherence to a two-state settlement a decade ago, any such possibility has consistently been barred by the U.S. and Israel, which persist in rejecting any claim by the indigenous population to the rights that are accorded without question to the Jewish settlers who largely displaced them, including the right to national self-determination somewhere within their former home. Articulate American opinion lauds this stance, urging the Palestinians to accept the Labor Party program that denies them any national rights and regards them as having "no role to play" in any settlement ([according to] Labor dove Abba Eban). There is no protest here, or even mere reporting of the facts, when the U.S. government blocks a UN peace initiative, stating that it will accept only negotiations "among the parties directly concerned with the Arab-Israeli dispute," crucially excluding the Palestinians, who are not one of these parties. Analogous rejectionist attitudes on the part of Libya and the minority PLO Rejection Front are condemned here as racist and extremist; the quite comparable U.S.-Israeli stance, obviously racist in essence, is considered the soul of moderation.

I will not proceed with further examples. The crucial point is that the pattern is pervasive, persistent, and overwhelmingly effective in establishing a framework of thinkable thought.

[The manufacture/engineering of consent, otherwise known as "agitprop"]

Over sixty years ago, Walter Lippmann discussed the concept of "manufacture of consent," an art that is "capable of great refinements" and that may lead to a "revolution" in "the practice of democracy." The idea was taken up with much enthusiasm in business circles—it is a main preoccupation of the public relations industry, whose leading figure, Edward Bernays, described "the engineering of consent" as the very essence of democracy. In fact, as Gabriel Kolko notes, "from the turn of the century until this day, [the public mind] was the object of a cultural and ideological industry that was as unrelenting as it was diverse: ranging from the school to the press to mass culture in its multitudinous dimensions." The reason, as an AT&T vice president put it in 1909, is that "the public mind . . . is in my judgment the only serious danger confronting the company."

The idea was also taken up with vigor in the social sciences. The leading political scientist Harold Lasswell wrote in 1933 that we must avoid "democratic dogmatisms," such as the belief that people are "the best judges of their own interests." Democracy permits the voice of the people to be heard, and it is the task of the intellectual to ensure that this voice endorses what far-sighted leaders know to be the right course. Propaganda is to democracy what violence is to totalitarianism. The techniques have been honed to a high art, far beyond anything that Orwell dreamt of. The device of feigned dissent, incorporating the doctrines of the state religion and eliminating rational critical discussion, is one of the more subtle means, though more crude techniques are also widely used and are highly effective in protecting us from seeing what we observe, from knowledge and understanding of the world in which we live.

It should be stressed again that what the Communists call "agitprop" is far more important in the democracies than in states that rule by violence, for reasons already discussed, and is therefore more refined and possibly more effective. There are no Danchevs here, except at the remote margins of political debate.

For those who stubbornly seek freedom, there can be no more urgent task than to come to understand the mechanisms and practices of indoctrination. These are easy to perceive in the totalitarian societies, much less so in the system of "brainwashing under freedom" to which we are subjected and which all too often we serve as willing or unwitting instruments.

APPENDIX
The media as a mirror of society—not quite in the usual sense (October 1984)

What credence, if any, is there to the proponents of the media's view that news is a mirror of society, that if we blame the news media, we are actually blaming the medium for the message?

Well, there is a lot of truth, I think, to the idea that the media are a mirror of society, but not quite in that sense. It's not that they accurately portray social reality. Rather I think the truth in the contention lies in the fact that the media tend to present and interpret social reality within a framework that is very largely set by domestic power. That's true in any society, but in our society that means, ultimately, the corporate system and the closely related state executive, the very extensive and elaborate ideology system (which includes large parts of the mainstream intelligentsia, the schools, and so on). That forms a framework that we could properly call a system of indoctrination, which does reflect social power, and the media operate very effectively within it, often unconsciously.

Do news organizations lend themselves to any sort of systematic analysis or do individual idiosyncrasies and judgments varying from operation to operation prevent any sort of general logic?

Oh, I think there is a very general logic. There is something that you might call a kind of party line. Well, first of all there are differences. For example, a local reporter, say, working on police corruption, is certainly subjected to some kinds of influences, like maybe a city editor knows a local businessman or something, but, basically, he is pretty free to do what he wants. That is, the pressure of indoctrination is not very heavy.

On the other hand, when you move to issues of more fundamental concern, to what is real power in the country—questions of foreign policy, questions of national military policy and so on, or general questions of national economic policy, policies that really affect people with real power—in that case one finds that the pressure of the system of indoctrination, of the party line, becomes very heavy, and there are very few people who deviate from it or who even perceive it. They think they're being quite objective, but you can easily demonstrate that they are operating within a framework of shared assumptions that is very far from obvious and often very far from true.

Let me give you an example of how subtle this can be. In the October 7 Sunday *Times* magazine there was a rather interesting article by Thomas Friedman, who is a very good reporter, one of the best. It was extremely interesting to read for students of propaganda. This was an article about the danger of extremism in the Middle East. And he said there is this moderate center where the hope lies, but then there are extremist fringes which are slowly taking over. They believe in violence and so on and so forth.

Well, okay. Terms like *moderate* and *extremist* are not very well defined; it depends where you stand. Everybody regards themselves as a moderate and everyone else is an extremist. So it's interesting to see how the terms were used. That's what tells you what the implicit assumptions are. Well, the terms were used as you'd expect. The extremists are the Khomeinis, the Shiite terrorists who bombed the marines, and in Israel, Kahane. The moderates are the Israeli Labor Party, the United States of course. The PLO, incidentally, are extremists. Arafat is an extremist but the moderates are the Israeli Labor Party and the Reagan administration.

Well, now that's interesting because that tells you what the implicit assumptions are. The implicit assumptions are that the people who reject the possibility of a political settlement based on the principle that the two peoples there have the right to national determination, both Israel and the

Palestinians, the people who reject that are the moderates; the people who advance that position, like the PLO, are the extremists.

Now, all that makes sense if you accept the deeply racist assumption that the Palestinians don't have the human rights we accord the Jews. If you believe that Palestinians and Jews are human beings with the right to national self-determination, and that the indigenous population at least has that right, then it is the PLO position which is the moderate one and [the] American and Labor Party [position] which is the extremist. In fact, even groups in Israel like Peace Now don't go as far as the PLO does in advocating a two-state political settlement. So implicit in the discussion was a real racist assumption. Also implicit in the discussion was the even more crucial assumption that facts are totally irrelevant. For example, the fact that the PLO had come forth with a two-state settlement was considered irrelevant, the fact that the United States had rejected it and the Labor Party had rejected it was considered irrelevant.

Also interesting is the use of the term *terrorist* or *extremist* with regard to people carrying out violent acts in Lebanon. From their point of view it's not terrorism, it's resistance. It's very rare that attacks on an occupying army are called terrorism. It's called that only by occupying armies. So, for example, when we call the attack on the marines in Lebanon "terrorism," that expresses assumptions that can certainly be questioned. I mean, for much of the population, the marines were there just to consummate the Israeli invasion. The acts taken against them are resistance. But these are all questions that can't even be raised in the American press.

What is interesting about the Friedman article is that it is a very persuasive article and it gives the impression of moderation and it implicitly incorporates principles which are deeply racist and which assume the crucial irrelevance of any historical fact. That's the way propaganda really works. That's much more effective than beating people over the head with a bludgeon.

Let me give you another example. Turn to Central America. The big news this week is that Duarte made this offer to have negotiations. So there is headline after headline in the paper about Duarte's dramatic offer and so on.

Well, the fact of the matter is slightly different. What actually happened is that Duarte *accepted* an offer. The offer for negotiations had been a long-standing guerrilla offer, and in fact it had been repeated insistently since last May, and Duarte finally, for whatever reasons, decided to go along with it. Well, that's a rather different picture. And in fact, if you really read carefully, you can sometimes see it—again, not in the *New York Times,* I haven't seen anything about it in the *New York Times.* But in the AP report on Duarte's offer, at least the one that was published in the *Boston Globe,* when you get down to the twenty-third paragraph of the report (literally), you find a remark saying that Radio Venceremos, the guerrilla radio, announced that Duarte had accepted the guerrillas' offer. Well, okay, if you're really a fanatic reader of the press, you can see that the whole story is being put on its head. But for most people, and for history, it's going to be Duarte's magnificent offer.

Actually that reminds me of another example. The alleged arms flow from Nicaragua to El Salvador was recently dealt a pretty severe blow by a former CIA officer.
Yeah, David MacMichael. Even the ambassador said that he was convinced that by early 1981 the arms flow had reduced to a trickle.

But you see, there is even something deeper here. Notice the way the question is framed. This shows you something about the press. I mean, look, we have Argentine proxies, Israeli arms, German, we've got sanctuaries in Honduras. I mean, all of this is going on openly. In fact, we're fighting a war against Nicaragua. But the only question you're allowed to ask is whether the Nicaraguans are in fact sending some arms to the guerrillas.

Now the fact of the matter is if the Nicaraguans aren't sending arms to the guerrillas, it's because they've been intimidated. They should be sending arms to the guerrillas. Everybody should be sending them arms. Just as you should send arms to the Afghan guerrillas. Imagine we were in the Soviet Union and there was a big debate going on about whether there are actually CIA arms coming in through Pakistan to the Afghan guerrillas. Well, the answer is there ought to be. You ought to give people arms to defend themselves against a gang of thugs supported by a foreign power who are trying to massacre them. But you couldn't raise that question in the Soviet Union, and you can't raise this question here. So even the doves are caught in it. Even the doves are trapped into arguing about whether the Nicaraguans are or are not giving them arms. The fact of the matter is that it would be quite proper to give them arms.

There seems to be a pervasive philosophy of hedonism in this country, the desire to be entertained rather than informed. Do you think the media is responsible for creating this hedonism or is it something that developed naturally?
Well, my feeling is that there has been a major effort, a concentrated major effort, especially directed against the youth, since about 1970, to try to convince people that they're hedonists. And narcissists. There has been a huge effort to try to convince young people that they're narcissists. So there is all

sorts of stuff of the cult of narcissism, and everybody is "me first," and so on and so forth.

Well, you know, such tendencies always exist, but opposing tendencies also exist—tendencies for sympathy, solidarity, and care and so on. And it's been very important to drive that out of people's consciousness. In fact, the net effect of this propaganda campaign has probably been to convince young people that if they are not narcissists, they're weird. So even if they have feelings of concern and sympathy, they had better suppress them because that's not what their generation is. And I think that's been effective.

Undoubtedly people are interested in their own welfare, but human beings are complicated creatures, they have a lot of drives and interests. And these are the ones that have been emphasized. It's interesting the way this campaign has been presented. It's been presented as if it's a descriptive fact. But really what it is is an attempt at persuasion and inducement. There were a lot of people who were really quite scared in the sixties when people did begin to show concern and political activism and so on. That's dangerous.

And the media has been effective?
Oh, I think they have been very effective. And I think much of the left has contributed to this with all its talk of narcissism and so on. There is a story going on that the left contributes to as well, saying that activism died in the seventies. That isn't true. There was probably more activism in the seventies than there was in the sixties: you have the feminist movement, the ecological movement, and all these things. These are creatures of the seventies, but they're dangerous, so therefore you want to pretend they don't exist.

And this is basically a concerted effort?
Well, I don't mean to suggest it's a conspiratorial effort. It's just that a lot of shared interests lie behind it.

Chapter 13

The task of the media: Central America as a test case (April 1989)

On assumptions that are not really controversial, one would expect U.S. political life and the media to be dominated by the interests of corporate ownership and management. That this is so is readily confirmed. On major issues, political life rarely escapes tactical debates among sectors of corporate power. The media that set the basic agenda are themselves major corporations, and many other factors also influence them to produce a picture of the world that reflects the interests of owners, advertisers, and privileged elements that occupy the managerial positions.

[Basic presuppositions of the propaganda system]

With respect to the Third World, as outlined in high-level planning documents, U.S. foreign policy has been dedicated to barring "nationalistic regimes" that are responsive to popular demands for "improvement in the low living standards of the masses" and production for domestic needs, and that interfere with U.S. access to their resources. Internal documents explain that the U.S. must encourage "a political and economic climate conducive to private investment of both foreign and domestic capital," including the "opportunity to earn and in the case of foreign capital to repatriate a reasonable return." Since such policies will have little public support, it is understood that the U.S. will have to rely ultimately on force: preferably, the domestic military, or if it is incompetent or unreliable, U.S. subversion, terror, or aggression.

A society can qualify as a "democracy" only if it is in the hands of local elements responsive to U.S. elite interests. "Nationalistic regimes" are depicted as a "virus" or a "cancer" that might spread, "infecting" others. Capitalist democracy, right-wing military regimes, and governments of the left all qualify as cancers that must be excised if they succumb to independent nationalism that might impede the right of exploitation. More rational planners understand that the mechanisms by which "the rot may spread" is the demonstration effect of successful independent development. The public image is that the villain targeted for elimination is on the warpath and must be stopped before he takes what we have, as Lyndon Johnson warned.

The task of the media is to convey these images while portraying the U.S. as the guardian of virtue, sometimes erring in its benevolent naïveté. Where there is tactical disagreement among elites, the media will encourage debate, but not beyond. The liberal media provide a particularly important service. They establish the limits: thus far, and no further. These limits incorporate the basic presuppositions of the propaganda system: the U.S. is committed to peace, justice, human rights, democracy, and other noble causes, and seeks only to defend these values against their enemies. That the media adhere to these conditions generally has been documented beyond serious question. Coverage of Central American affairs provides a textbook example.

[A textbook example]

Until the late 1970s, U.S. elite interests were not seriously challenged. Accordingly, the region received little media attention, and the problem of establishing "democracy" did not arise. The one major exception was Guatemala, where the U.S. overthrew the democratic capitalist regime for the familiar reasons. The CIA coup was presented as an indigenous uprising to foil the efforts of "the world Bolshevik conspiracy to take over the country" (Arthur Krock, the leading thinker of the *New York Times*). The media spouted a variety of idiocies and lies concocted by the state propaganda services and the public relations industry, which has long been dedicated to controlling "the public mind." The regular U.S. intervention since to maintain the Guatemalan charnel house is also not a legitimate topic. Thus a *New York Times Magazine* story (March 26, 1989) by Stephen Kinzer concedes that "democracy" in Guatemala is not very attractive, but without a word on the U.S. role in terminating Guatemala's democratic interlude thirty-five years ago or its interventions since, apart from a vague reference to lack of sufficient commitment to our noble ideals. This is standard practice.

By the late 1970s, alarm bells were ringing in Washington and New York. Throughout the region, new popular organizations offered the general population a way to escape from misery and repression and take part in political life, and in Nicaragua the tyrant who provided the U.S. with its major base of power was unable to suppress a broad popular revolution. Concerns mounted as the Sandinistas took power and, despite the vast destruction, began to institute social reforms and development programs that seemed dangerously successful. Washington and the media reacted exactly as would be expected.

In Guatemala, the military regime launched a program of large-scale slaughter, supported tacitly during the Carter administration, then enthusiastically under Reagan as the massacre approached near-genocide with heavy reliance on U.S. mercenary states. The media looked the other way.

In El Salvador, the media barely noted the rising state terror in the final year of the Carter administration. They suppressed the first large-scale massacre at the Sumpul River in May 1980 and largely avoided the Honduran refugee camps, where a congressional delegation, which violated the rules, discovered that peasants were fleeing "a systematic campaign of terrorism" conducted by the U.S.-backed forces, including "murder, torture, rape, the burning of crops in order to create starvation conditions, and a program of general terrorism and harassment." Its report passed virtually without notice. Rather, readers were assured that "there is no real argument that most of the estimated 10,000 political fatalities in 1980 were victims of government forces or irregulars associated with them" (*Washington Post*); the argument was overwhelming, as quietly conceded later. Extensive reports of extermination of peasants in the foreign press were also suppressed, and the public did not hear the successor of the assassinated archbishop condemn the armed forces' "war of extermination and genocide against a defenseless civilian population" (Bishop Rivera y Damas, October 1980).

There was a brief period of actual reporting as the terror reached Pol Pot levels under the Reagan administration, particularly when it seemed that the U.S. might be drawn into a conflict harmful to its interests. But coverage dropped when Washington's program of traumatizing the population by violence appeared to be successful and "demonstration elections" were held for the benefit of the home front, while the media suppressed polls showing that some 10 percent of the population saw signs of a "democratic process" in the "fledgling democracy" they hailed. European media coverage of the elections was radically different, recognizing that elections are merely farcical when conducted in "an atmosphere of terror and despair, grisly rumor and macabre reality" (Lord Chitnis, who observed the elections for the British Parliamentary Human Rights Group).

After the Esquipulas II Accord of August 1987, state terror increased in both Guatemala and El Salvador. The facts were largely suppressed, sometimes mentioned as a response to guerrilla terror (James LeMoyne of the *New York Times*). The assigned task at the time was to concentrate on alleged Nicaraguan failures to live up to the accords under the interpretation stipulated by

Washington and to highlight alleged Sandinista crimes that rarely approached the regular lesser abuses of the U.S. terror states, let alone their frequent atrocities. The media performed on cue, as extensively documented elsewhere.

Throughout, the horrifying reports of human rights groups were given little notice; the *Times* did not even mention the October 1988 Amnesty International study describing the Salvadoran government policy of death squad terror. The message was inconsistent with the official line that the U.S. was sponsoring democracy and reform. In both of Washington's terror states, the media helped implement the policies of torture, rape, mutilation, massacre, and general savagery—if truth be told.

[The limits of debate]

Nicaragua, in contrast, was made the villain of the piece, following the script of the State Department Office of Latin American Public Diplomacy, an illegal covert propaganda operation committed to "demonizing the Sandinistas" and mobilizing support for Washington's terror states. Its doctrines were accepted by most of the liberal opposition, with some tactical reservations. Studies of editorials and opinion columns reveal debate over the wisdom of contra aid, reflecting the fact that by 1986 leadership groups overwhelmingly opposed the contra option as too costly and disruptive at home, preferring other measures available to a superpower to strangle a tiny dependent country and reverse its social and economic programs. The media encouraged debate over the best way to return Nicaragua to the "Central American mode" (*Washington Post*) and to ensure that Nicaragua would submit to a "regional arrangement . . . enforced" by such worthy allies as El Salvador and Guatemala (Tom Wicker, at the outer limits of dissent). The fact that, unlike the U.S. clients, Nicaragua does not slaughter its citizens is unmentioned in hundreds of opinion pieces surveyed; mention of Nicaragua's social reforms before the government-media campaign restored the "regional standard" of starvation and misery is at the level of statistical error. These omissions reflect the importance of mass slaughter and brutal oppression in our political culture when U.S. elites and their clients are the agents and beneficiaries. With regard to Central America as a whole, debate was limited to the means for achieving U.S. goals, described as fostering democracy and human rights while Washington dedicated its energies to demolishing any hope that they might be realized—another fact that escapes the proper limits.

The news columns kept to the same conditions. Studying the *New York Times*, Jack Spence found that the U.S. government provided most of the sources on Nicaragua. The U.S. proxy forces ranked second, with almost twice as many citations as the government, a discrepancy that was increased by broad coverage of the U.S.-backed internal opposition. Coverage of the U.S. clients was largely favorable; only one of thirty-three stories on the contras in early 1986 focused on human rights abuses, and there were a few other references to atrocities that were by then reaching a remarkable scale. Like the State Department and Congress, the media preferred what human rights investigators described as "intentional ignorance."

Readers of the *Times* could plausibly conclude that support for the Sandinistas is virtually nonexistent, outside of the government itself. In the first fifty Stephen Kinzer articles after the signing of the Esquipulas Accords, there are two references to the possible existence of such people—though we do read of store owners, banana vendors, laborers, truck drivers, et cetera, all bitterly anti-Sandinista: in short, the people, united, rising up against their oppressors. Given the poll results (which the *Times* did not report) indicating that support for all opposition parties combined amounts to 9 percent, less than one-third of the support for the Sandinistas (and much less than the personal approval for President Ortega), one might suppose that there would be some other attitudes, but they are unreported.

In El Salvador, the pattern was sharply reversed. Here, the guerrillas were Marxist terrorists, and the official line, as laid forth in *New York Times* editorials, was that things were improving under the democratic government of "the honorable Mr. Duarte," "the honest, reform-minded Christian Democrat," who is trying to lead his people to a better life while "beset by implacable extremes," though he may have been "less than rigorous in bringing death squad operatives to judicial account" (in translation: he has done nothing to curb the security forces he praises for their "valiant service alongside the people against subversion" while conceding quietly that "the masses were with the guerrillas" when he assumed the role of front man for the war against the population). News reporting was similar in style. Duarte was portrayed as a victim, not as the willing agent whose role was to ensure adequate congressional funding for the state terrorists whom he protected.

["All the news that's fit to print"]

In editorials reviewed over six and a half years, the *Times* never mentioned such matters as the assassination of Archbishop Romero; the destruction and closure of the university by the army, with many killed; the physical destruction of the independent media; or the Salvadoran state of siege from March 1980, when Duarte joined the junta, under which the atrocities were conducted with his backing and constant apologetics. In contrast, when

Nicaragua declared a state of siege on October 15, 1985, the *Times* bitterly condemned this demonstration of Nicaragua's lack of "respect for democracy and human rights"; the renewal of El Salvador's far more draconian state of siege two days later received no mention. The events ignored in the editorials were also largely suppressed or falsified in the news columns. The political opposition had been murdered by Duarte's security forces or had fled the country, so there was no need to report or comment on their problems. Similarly, no second thoughts were aroused by the selection of one of the leading murderers to be Duarte's minister of defense; as director of the National Guard, he had coolly explained that "the armed forces are prepared to kill 200,000–300,000, if that's what it takes to stop a Communist takeover," acting accordingly. When he was named defense minister, this mass murderer and torturer was described by the *New York Times* as "a soft-spoken, amiable man who has a reputation as an excellent administrator." Conceding that the guard under his command had been responsible for horrible atrocities, including the rape and murder of four American churchwomen and the assassination of two U.S. labor advisors, the *Times* adds that "in his defense, others contend that under his command the National Guard's reputation has improved to the point where it is no longer considered the most abusive of Salvador's three security forces"—an impressive achievement, doubtless.

With regard to Nicaragua, the pattern was for the state propaganda services to concoct some charge that the media would then prominently and uncritically relay. Occasionally, when the charges were recognized to be too outlandish, a mild disclaimer might appear on the inside pages. Often the charges persisted even when they were acknowledged to be groundless or sheer fabrication: State Department fabrications about "revolution without borders" and Sandinista support for Colombian guerrillas (repeated, with further fabrications, after the Colombian government issued its—suppressed—denial of the charges), miraculously undetectable weapons flows from Nicaragua to El Salvador, et cetera.

The official line is that there are four democracies in Central America with elected presidents and one dictatorship that never had an election meeting the high standards of the U.S. terror states. Media obedience is virtually exceptionless. The astonishing media distortion of the Central American elections of the 1980s has been extensively documented. The chief diplomatic correspondent of the *Times* even refers to "the diplomatic initiative opened by the leaders of Costa Rica, Guatemala, El Salvador, and Honduras"—and opposed only by the totalitarian Sandinistas, the reader is to understand (Thomas Friedman). No level of absurdity is too great once the state has spoken.

The standard device is endless repetition of the government line that, to meet our high standards, Nicaragua must "permit true elections, end support for 'subversion' elsewhere in Central America and not permit the establishment of Soviet bases" (*Washington Post,* discussing the bipartisan accord of March 1989). The technique succeeds in establishing that Nicaragua alone has had no elections, that the Salvadoran guerrillas are a foreign implant (thus legitimizing the contras), and that the U.S. is facing a major threat to its existence; and in establishing further that the U.S. is in favor of freedom, democracy, an end to subversion, peace, and security.

[Dramatic insight into media priorities]

In a properly functioning propaganda system, such doctrines are not asserted, merely presupposed as the foundation for rational discourse. It is then unnecessary to deal with the fact that they are demonstrably false. The media can plead that they are only being "objective," reporting the views of Washington. *Pravda* could make the same claim. And the media do not choose to report regularly (or at all) the views of the professional association of Latin American scholars, human rights and development organizations, or even the leading figure of Central American capitalist democracy, José Figueres, excluded from the media because of his harsh critique of U.S. policies and his conclusion that "for the first time, Nicaragua has a government that cares for its people."

Treatment of freedom of the press provides dramatic insight into media priorities. In Guatemala, one editor returned from exile to test the new "democracy" in 1988, braving death threats. After a few issues, his small journal was firebombed by elements of the security forces, and he left the country after declaring in a press conference that freedom of expression is obviously impossible in the "fledgling democracy." Neither of the two national dailies found the matter worthy of reporting, just as "censorship by assassination" had not been their concern in earlier years. In El Salvador, the security forces of the "moderate centrist" Duarte quickly took care of the independent media by murdering the editor of one and destroying the facilities of the second, driving the owners into exile. These events merited not a single word in the *New York Times* news columns or editorials, then or since.

It is not that freedom of the press is unimportant to the media. The tribulations of *La Prensa* in Nicaragua have aroused enormous outrage, probably more—and surely more irate—coverage than all other issues of freedom of press combined worldwide in the 1980s. This massive coverage (over a story a week in the *New York Times* for a four-year period surveyed) manages

to avoid the fact that *La Prensa* is a unique phenomenon; there is no counterpart in the history of the Western democracies to a major journal openly
supporting the overthrow of the government by foreign-run terrorist forces,
funded by the superpower organizing the attack. Nothing remotely similar
was true of the media destroyed by state violence in the U.S. terror states,
arousing no interest here. Or consider the leading U.S. client, lauded as a stel-
lar democracy and "the symbol of human decency" (*New York Times*). Israel
closes newspapers and expels and jails editors for far lesser provocation
(within Israel proper, not only in the occupied territories), a matter that
passes in silence in the U.S. media, which also do not report the extreme censorship over TV (a state monopoly) and the press. The comparative coverage
demonstrates unequivocally that concern over *La Prensa* is not attributable to
sudden libertarian passions, but to the dictates of the state authorities.

The media have also had to deal with Washington's commitment to bar
all efforts to remove the conflict from the arena of violence, where the U.S.
reigns supreme, to that of diplomacy, where it is very weak. The U.S. blocked
Nicaraguan efforts to monitor the borders, undermined the Contadora negotiations, rejected the World Court decision condemning it for "unlawful use
of force" and an illegal embargo, vetoed a Security Council resolution calling
on all states to observe international law, et cetera—all with the acquiescence,
or silence, of the major media. None of this suggested that the U.S. was not
the leading peace-loving state.

In August 1987, to the discomfiture of Washington, the Central
American presidents agreed to the Esquipulas II Accord. The U.S. at once
dedicated all efforts to undermining it. The CIA stepped up its illegal supply
flights to the contras, which had already reached the phenomenal level of one
a day, virtually tripling them in the following months in an effort to increase
the level of violence—successfully. The media cooperated by suppressing the
facts. Washington also rejected the "symmetry" on which the accords were
based, since this would require the U.S. client states to adhere to the conditions on democracy and human rights, an evident impossibility. Also unacceptable was the international monitoring, a threat to the U.S. intent to
undermine the accord and to the constant violations of the U.S. terror states.
By January 1988, U.S. pressure had succeeded in entirely dismantling the
accord, eliminating the international monitoring and narrowing its application to Nicaragua alone. The media cooperated throughout, another remarkable contribution to terror and repression in the service of power.

In March 1988, a cease-fire was reached in Nicaragua. The agreement
designated Secretary General Soares of the OAS [Organization of American

States] as the official in charge of monitoring the agreement, and stipulated that aid to the contras must be limited to neutral carriers, delivered only in cease-fire zones (within Nicaragua) and in accord with the Esquipulas II agreements. Congress voted at once to provide aid to the contras in violation of all these conditions, while declaring that it was adhering to the terms of the cease-fire. Soares wrote an official letter to Secretary of State George Shultz, unreported to my knowledge, condemning these violations of the cease-fire agreements. The media adhered to the Washington version that the only problem was whether the treacherous Sandinistas would agree to permit "humanitarian" aid to reach the suffering resistance fighters; that the aid did not qualify as "humanitarian" by any standards had already been determined explicitly by the World Court, to the usual media silence.

In February 1989, the Central American presidents reached another agreement, largely observing U.S. demands: the accords were limited to Nicaragua, and its request for international monitoring was rejected. But their obedience was insufficient: the agreement called for dismantling the contras and stipulated that any aid to them must conform to the Esquipulas II Accord, which barred aid of any form ("military, logistical, financial, propagandistic"), excepting aid for "demobilization, repatriation or relocation." Congress voted at once to violate these terms by providing $4.5 million per month to maintain the contras as a military force in Honduras as a threat against Nicaragua. On the eve of the congressional vote, the *Times* observed that "on its face, the Administration proposal to keep the contras in place would seem to be inconsistent with the spirit of the regional peace agreement, which calls for their relocation"—meaning that the proposal is flatly inconsistent with the terms of the agreement; "but Administration officials say there is no inconsistency" (Robert Pear). These reservations quickly disappeared, and the media cooperated by lauding the historic agreement "committing the Administration and Congress to aid for the Nicaraguan rebels and support for the Central American peace efforts" (Bernard Weinraub), while a *Times* editorial solemnly intoned that U.S. goals are now "consistent with the regional pact." In this case, the media advanced to cheerful tolerance for outright self-contradiction in place of the standard practice of mere suppression and falsification in the service of power.

We find much the same wherever we turn. Responsible insiders obey and do their work. The torment of the tortured and suffering victims elsewhere is not their concern. We need not dwell on the historical precedents, which are not hard to find.

Chapter 14

Propaganda and control of the public mind (February 1997)

The war against working people should be understood to be a real war. It's a new war, it's an old one. Furthermore, it's a perfectly conscious war everywhere, but specifically in the U.S., a very free country, but one which has a highly class-conscious business class, so you have a lot of information about it. They talk; you have their records. They have long seen themselves as fighting a bitter class war, except they don't want anybody else to know about it.

Occasionally someone else gets the news. A rather famous case is Doug Fraser, about twenty years ago (1978, I think), when he pulled out of the Labor Management Council and condemned business leaders for having decided to fight a one-sided class war against working people, the poor, the unemployed, minorities, even members of the middle class, and for having torn up the fragile social compact that had been achieved during a period of growth and prosperity which in fact (although he didn't say this) had been achieved primarily through very militant struggle under harsh conditions back in the 1930s.

The only thing wrong with his statement is that it was way too late. That war that he's talking about was initiated, and very openly, as soon as the fragile social compact was established back in the 1930s. You don't have to go to secret records to find out about it. Nor do you have to have been at the wrong end of the clubs when the strikes were broken up in the late 1930s to know about it. It was completely public. The reason it's not well known is because neither the educational system nor scholarship, like Harvard, pay any attention to it. It's not a topic that's studied.

[One of the major issues of twentieth-century U.S. history]
There's no doubt that one of the major issues of twentieth-century U.S. history is corporate propaganda. It's a huge industry. It extends over, obviously,

the commercial media, but includes the whole range of systems that reach the public: the entertainment industry, television, a good bit of what appears in schools, a lot of what appears in the newspapers, and so on. A huge amount of that comes straight out of the public relations industry, which was established in this country early in this century and developed mainly from the 1920s on. It's now spreading over the rest of the world, but it's primarily here.

Its goal from the beginning, perfectly openly and consciously, was to "control the public mind," as they put it. The public mind was seen as the greatest threat to corporations, from early in the century. Business power was strong. As it's a very free country (by comparative standards), it's hard, not impossible, to call upon state violence to crush people's efforts to achieve freedom, rights, and justice. Therefore it was recognized early on that it's going to be necessary to control people's minds. I should say that's not a new insight. You can read it in David Hume in the Enlightenment, where it was already recognized. Go back to the early stirrings of democratic revolution in England in the seventeenth century: already there was concern that we're not going to be able to control people by force, and we therefore have to control them by other means—controlling what they think, what they feel, their attitudes toward one another. All sorts of mechanisms of control are going to have to be devised which will replace the efficient use of force and violence. That use was available to a much greater extent earlier on, and has been, fortunately, declining—although not uniformly—through the years.

You don't have to move very far from the Cambridge elite to learn about it. The leading figure of the public relations industry is a highly regarded Cambridge liberal, a Roosevelt-Kennedy liberal who died recently: Edward Bernays. He wrote the standard manual of the public relations industry back in the 1920s, which is very much worth reading. I'm not talking about the right wing here. This is way over at the left-liberal end of American politics. His book is *Propaganda*.

(I should mention that terminology changed during the Second World War. Prior to World War II, the term *propaganda* was used, quite openly and freely, for controlling the public mind. It got bad connotations during the Second World War because of Hitler, so the term was dropped. Now there are other terms used. But if you read the literature in the social sciences and the public relations industry back into the 1920s and 1930s, they describe what they're doing as "propaganda.")

Bernays's *Propaganda* is a manual for the rising public relations industry. He opens by pointing out that the conscious manipulation of the organized habits and opinions of the masses is the central feature of a democratic soci-

ety. It's the "essence of democracy," as he later pointed out. He said: we have
the means to carry this out, the means to regiment people's minds as efficiently as armies regiment their bodies. And we must do this. First of all, it's
the essential feature of democracy. But also (as a footnote) it's the way to
maintain power structures, and authority structures, and wealth, and so on,
roughly the way it is. . . .

[Protecting the minority of the opulent from the majority]

What's called the industrial capitalist system today is one in which private
power overwhelms government by its combinations and is bribed by its
largesse. That's a pretty good description of 1997. With all the changes that
have taken place since 1792, there's a good deal of stability to all this, including the commitment to the principle enunciated by James Madison that the
primary goal of government is to protect the minority of the opulent from the
majority. . . . The increasingly, overwhelmingly significant idea, particularly
among liberals (like, say, Bernays), is that it is necessary to control people's
minds because they're too much of a danger.

Take a look at, say, the *Encyclopedia of Social Sciences*, a big encyclopedia
from 1933, still pre–Second World War. There actually is an entry on propaganda. Remember, *propaganda* was a usable term then. The entry is written
by a very distinguished liberal political scientist, Harold Lasswell, one of the
founders of modern political science and communications. He says (these are
paraphrases, but they're pretty close to quotes): We must not succumb to
democratic dogmatisms about people being the best judges of their own
interests; they are not. *We*'re the best judges of *their* interests, we smart guys.
And *we* must therefore ensure that those idiots out there don't get into trouble by actually using their theoretical right to vote to interfere where they
don't belong, like in the public arena. So we've got to keep them out of the
public arena somehow and make sure that it's just us smart guys who are in
there. It's for their good, of course: you don't let your three-year-old grand-
child run across the street. She may want to run across the street, but it would
be improper to let her have that choice. The same is true about the masses.
They have to be controlled at the workplace, they have to be kept out of the
political arena, and they're not going to understand the need to protect the
opulent minority against the majority. They're going to have all these strange
leveling impulses and will do all kinds of things that will mess the world up
in all sorts of horrible ways.

So for *their* benefit *we* have to regiment their minds the way an army regiments their bodies, and ensure that they're under control—make it very clear

that they don't participate in workplace management, and certainly not in the political arena. They're to be outside somewhere.

The dedication with which this task has been pursued is pretty awesome. Right after the fall of the "house of labor" in the 1920s, when American labor really was smashed, people were privatized and they tried to accommodate individually to "a most undemocratic America" (as David Montgomery and others have pointed out). That was a time when there was great awe about the end of history and the utopia of the masters: "It's all over. Us good guys have won. Everybody else is at our feet." Kind of like some of the stuff you read today. . . .

A few years later the whole thing collapsed, and there was militant working-class struggle and other popular activism. There had to be an accommodation of some kind to these unwashed masses who were getting out of line with sit-down strikes. There was this fragile social compact that Doug Fraser referred to, meaning labor laws and the limited social system. It was established. It wasn't a gift. It was won through struggle. (In fact, American workers in the 1930s began to get the rights that had been standard long before, even in much more brutal societies. Read the right-wing British press over the early part of this century; they can't believe how badly American workers were treated.) . . .

[The "Mohawk Valley formula"]

But by the 1930s the United States was brought into the mainstream of industrial society in these matters to a limited extent. That caused hysteria among the masters by 1936 or 1937. (Again, these are things which in a really free society everybody would study in elementary school, because they're important to give the real framework of the society.) In the business press, they were talking about the hazard facing industrialists and the rising political power of the masses, and how we [meaning, they] must do something to save ourselves or our way of life will be gone; we don't have a lot of time to do it. They started right away.

By the late 1930s a big anti-labor campaign had been built up with new techniques. There was still use of force, but it was understood that this was not going to work the way it had. So there was a shift to more propaganda. The main idea was called the "Mohawk Valley formula," designed by a lot of public relations hotshots around 1936 or 1937, during some of the steel strikes, to have what they called "scientific" methods of strikebreaking: We [meaning, they] don't just come in with clubs and shoot people and smash their heads; we do it the scientific way, because the old way didn't work anymore.

The "scientific" methods of strikebreaking were in fact drawn from public relations ideas of the kind that I talked about. The main idea was to mobilize the community against the strikers and the union activists, to present a
picture which is by now so standard. You can hardly turn on the tube without seeing it. It's just poured out in streams ever since then.

The basic idea is to present a picture of the world that looks kind of like
this: There's "us," a big happy family in the community. The honest workman
going off every morning with his lunch box, his loyal wife making the meals
and taking care of the kids, the hardworking executive who's toiling day and
night in the interests of his workers and the community, the friendly banker
running around looking for people to lend money to. That's us. We're all in
harmony. (*Harmony* was a big word.) We're all together. It's Americanism.

You might take a look at that word "Americanism," an unusual term. It's
the kind of term that you only find in totalitarian societies, as far as I know.
So in the Soviet Union, "anti-Sovietism" was considered the gravest of all
crimes. And the Brazilian generals had a concept like that, "anti-Brazilian."
But try publishing a book on, say, "anti-Italianism" and see what happens in
the streets of Rome and Milan. People won't even bother laughing. It's a ludicrous idea. The idea of "Italianism" or "Norwayism" would be the object of
ridicule in societies that have some kind of residue of democratic culture
inside people's heads (I don't mean in the formal system). But in totalitarian
societies it is used, and as far as I know the U.S. is the only free society that
has such a concept. "Americanism" and "anti-Americanism" and "un-
Americanism" are concepts which go along with "harmony" and getting rid
of those "outsiders."

Another part is simply to induce hatred and fear among people. It's a
diverse society—if you go to Europe, most places are pretty uniform—so it's
easy for propagandists to get people to hate the guy next door because he
looks a little different. Huge campaigns go on to instigate divisions among
people. But these are very natural techniques of social control.

Going back to the Mohawk Valley formula, the idea was to move into a
community where there's a strike going on, flood it with propaganda, take
over the media, the churches, the schools; pour in this propaganda about
"harmony" and those "bad guys" out there who are trying to disrupt our "harmonious" lives. Like that union organizer—he's probably a "communist" or
an "anarchist" anyway, and probably "un-American." He's trying to destroy all
these wonderful things we have. We've got to band together and kick him
out. We have to defend our way of life against this.

A lot of religion gets thrown in. Remember that the United States is an extremely fundamentalist country. You look at comparative statistics: usually religious fundamentalism declines as industrialization goes up. It's a very close correlation. The U.S. is off the chart. It ranks with devastated peasant societies. It's probably more fundamentalist than Iran. Why this is so is a complicated question. But one factor is that it was certainly consciously fomented by business leaders, way back in the nineteenth century. John D. Rockefeller's favorite evangelist, who he poured a lot of money into, was a guy who said that people ought to have more enlightened ideas than labor agitation. The "more enlightened ideas" are: go to church, listen to orders, do what they tell you, and shut up. It's a really interesting case, because Mohawk Valley was the model that was later used for strikebreaking and destruction of the labor movement in the postwar period.

Incidentally, I don't know of any literature on this, do you? These are untouchable topics. You can almost say that anything that's important, that's going to matter for people's lives, is off the agenda. And it sort of makes sense. You don't want people to know about it. You don't want people to know the "wrong" kind of thing. It's not a conspiracy, it's just common sense. If you have a certain degree of power and authority and privilege, you just don't want people to know things that might be "harmful" to them. They're really like children. "We"'re the ones who have to make the decisions for them.

Enormous amounts of money and effort go into this. . . . It's another technique of trying to create the marginalization of people, removing people from the actual social and political struggles that might make their lives better, and to keep them from working with one another by dividing them up in all sorts of ways. . . .

A couple of days ago, I put myself through the pain of reading the *New York Times* every day for some masochistic reason which I won't try to explain. But they've got a big chief correspondent, sort of the main thinker, a guy named Thomas Friedman, who had an article three or four days ago, a big think piece, in which he said: The Cold War's over, so the breakdown isn't hawks and doves any more; it is between integrationists and anti-integrationists. That means [according to Friedman] people who are in favor of more globalization and what they call free trade (which isn't free trade), and people who want to slow it down or end it. That's one breakdown. The other is between people who are in favor of a safety net and those who think that everybody ought to "be on your own" and "get what you can." . . .

[Newt Gingrich] is put in the corner that says "integrationist" and everybody for themselves, devil take the hindmost. It's testable that that's Gingrich's position. For example, on the question of whether Gingrich is an integrationist, in favor of free trade, we can ask how he reacted when the Reagan administration instituted the greatest wave of protectionism since the 1930s. That's just straight protectionism, alongside of a huge increase in public subsidies to private power, to industry—along with the biggest nationalization in American history, the takeover of Continental Illinois Bank. That's all radically anti-integrationist. How did Newt Gingrich react? We can ask that question. The answer is he thought it was great.

What about the safety net story? Gingrich is in favor of people being out there on their own, rugged entrepreneurs. You can check that, too. He represents Cobb County, Georgia, and he happens to hold the national championship in bringing federal subsidies to his rich constituents. To be precise, among suburban counties in the U.S., Cobb County ranks third in federal subsidies, right after Arlington, Virginia, which is part of the federal government, so they get a lot of federal subsidies—the Pentagon's there—and Brevard County, Florida, which is the home of the space center, so it's another part of the federal government. But if you move outside of the federal government itself, Gingrich's district is number one. They get more federal subsidies than anybody. The biggest employer in Cobb County is Lockheed, which is a publicly subsidized, private for-profit corporation. They sell commercial planes. But, everyone knows, the way the system is designed, technology is developed under the guise of the military, and then handed over to private power when it works. That's true of everything: airplanes, computers, the Internet, you name it. Cobb County is right at the center of it.

He's in favor of being out on your own and fighting in this harsh world? Ridiculous. He's the biggest welfare freak in the country. That's literally true. Except that he wants the welfare to go to very rich people. . . . The way our economy works—take just about any dynamic sector of it you know, at least that I know and have studied, and you find that it's based on massive public subsidies and privatization of profit—the public pays the costs and takes the risks, and private systems make the profit if there is any. Cobb County is just an extreme example of this. . . .

You cannot be a good propagandist unless it's in your bones. It's extremely hard to lie. I think we all know that from personal experience. It's hard to lie to people. Every one of us lies to people all the time, unless we're some kind of crazy angels. But the way we do it, and I'm sure you know this, is that you first convince yourself that what you're saying is true. You're an eight-year-old kid and you steal a toy from your brother. Your mother comes in and yells at you. Don't say: I wanted a toy and he had it so I took it because I'm stronger than him. What you say is: It really wasn't his, and besides, he'd taken a toy of mine, and anyway, I needed it more than he did, so it was right for me to take it. If people haven't had that experience, they're some other species.

[Selection for obedience in the schools]

That kind of experience goes all the way up to being a hotshot journalist for the *New York Times*. You don't even make it into those circles unless you're already so deeply overwhelmed by doctrine and propaganda that you can't even think in other terms. So when people talk like this, you'll read liberal columnists in the *New York Times* very angrily saying, "Nobody tells me what to write. I write anything I feel like." Which is absolutely true. If people with real power weren't sure that they were going to say the right things, they wouldn't be in a position to say anything they feel like.

How does that work? It starts from childhood, in kindergarten, on television. There's selection for obedience from the very first moment. When I think about my own school experience or any other school experience I know about, there was selection for obedience. I ended up going to fancy colleges like this place. The way I did it was by shutting up. If I thought that the high school teacher was a horse's ass, which I did most of the time, I didn't say so (sometimes I did and got thrown out of class). I learned not to say anything, to say okay, I'll do the next stupid assignment because I know that's the way I'll get ahead and ultimately I'll do this and that. If you have whatever ability it takes to do this kind of thing and are sufficiently disciplined and passive, you make it through up to the higher echelons.

There are people who don't. They get into trouble. They're called "behavior problems," or "disruptive," or you stick drugs in them because they're just too independent, and people who are independent are a pain in the neck. They disrupt the system. They're going to be cut off one way or another. . . .

When you watch television, some sitcom, you don't think, "I'm being exposed to the Mohawk Valley formula." But you are. That's the picture of life that's presented, day after day after day.

People have personal problems, but nothing that would bring them together to struggle against the new spirit of the age. When was the last time you saw a sitcom about that? What you get is this stuff that flows out of the PR industry, very consciously.

[A major theme of modern history]

A major element in the huge public relations propaganda after the Second World War was strictly demonizing labor. And the labor movement knew that. There was a fairly substantial labor press, even then. As late as the 1950s there were still about eight hundred labor newspapers, which were reaching maybe twenty or thirty million people a week. Not commercial media, but pretty substantial. And they're interesting reading, too. I'm not talking about anything radical, no left-wing press, just labor newspapers, the conservative American labor movement. They were talking about developing antidotes to the poisons of the "kept press," the commercial media, who were demonizing labor at every opportunity and trying to undermine our achievements and glossing over the crimes of the corporate rulers who run the society.

There's a good book on this one, too. This tells you something about American academic life. The first study that I've ever heard of in the U.S. on this major theme of modern history just appeared in the University of Illinois Press, called *Selling Free Enterprise*, by Elizabeth Fones-Wolf. It's kind of apolitical. She doesn't have any special point of view. But the material in it is pretty revealing.

Remember that the U.S. came out of the Second World War pretty social democratic, like most of the world. An awful lot of people in the U.S. too, like maybe half, thought that there ought to be popular control over industry in some fashion. There was enormous support for social programs. That had to be beaten out of people's heads, and fast. The leaders of the public relations industry said: We have three to five years to save our way of life. We have to fight, and quickly win [what they called] the everlasting battle for the minds of men and indoctrinate people with the capitalist story so fully that they can repeat it on every opportunity.

They weren't kidding around. For example, about a third of the material in American elementary schools was coming straight out of corporate propaganda offices by the early 1950s. Sports leagues were taken over. The churches were taken over. The universities were attacked. It was an across-the-board major effort to try to win the everlasting battle for the minds of men. And it's still going on. . . .

It's particularly harmful to democracy when media systems are in the hands of private tyrannies. . . . Here's this huge system, built at public expense. Most media analysts with their heads screwed on see, and even report, that it's very likely going to end up in the hands of a half-dozen mega-corporations internationally. That's worse than the oligopolies that run steel and computers, because here we're talking about a new mode of information and communication being handed over to private power.

We've heard about the Telecommunications Act of 1996, the big legislative achievement of the last Congress, but it wasn't discussed as a public interest issue. It was discussed as a business issue. Most of the reporting was in the business pages. . . . It's not supposed to be a question of public interest whether major systems of information and interchange are handed over as gifts to Rupert Murdoch. The only thing that was discussed was: Do you give it to six corporations or twelve, or do it this way or that way? That's effective indoctrination, when these things don't even occur to people. . . . This is worse than the handing over of decision-making power to private tyrannies, because in this case it's also handing over the things that they're going to use for the control of the public mind. These systems could also be used to liberate people. . . .

[Marketing as a form of manipulation and deceit]

This is very much a business-run society. The last figures I saw, about one out of six dollars in the whole economy is spent on marketing. It's an extremely inefficient use of funds. Marketing doesn't produce anything, any public good. But marketing is a form of manipulation and deceit. It's an effort to create artificial wants, to control the way people look and think about things. A lot of that marketing is straight propaganda, advertising. Most of it is tax-free . . . which means, the way our system works, you pay for the privilege of being propagandized, of having all this stuff dumped on you. Those are not small figures. I think it was a trillion dollars a year in 1992. When you've got that much of a commitment to controlling minds and manipulating desires, and doing all the things they talk about in the public relations literature (I'm not making it up; you can read it there) and the social science literature (because this is also standard academic talk), when you've got those stakes, you're going to work on it hard. And it's going to be hard to fight against. That's what makes organizing tough. You have to break through a lot of psychic resistance.

The whole history of the labor movement tells you that. This was well understood by mill hands in Lowell 150 years ago. But it's a big battle. And you're not just struggling against somebody who calls it a "right-to-work act." You're struggling against five hours a day of television and the movie industry and the books and the schools and everything else. The scale of the efforts to win the battle for men's minds is enormous. I thought I knew something about this, but when I read Elizabeth Fones-Wolf's book, I was pretty shocked just to see the scale of the efforts and the frenzied dedication to winning this everlasting battle. It's really impressive. Although if you think of the stakes, it's not too surprising.

Chapter 15

Prospects for democracy (March 1994)

I'll begin with a few simple observations. The title is "Prospects for democracy." To evaluate the prospects for democracy, we have to first of all carry out some kind of assessment of where the world is heading. That's the "prospects" part. And, crucially, we have to decide what we mean by "democracy," which is a term that is used in a wide variety of ways.

[Conception of a good society: enriching popular participation]
If we look at the present scene, we find an apparent clash between doctrines that are widely and, in fact, proudly proclaimed and social and political realities that appear to conflict with them very sharply. The leading doctrine is that the wave of the future is democracy and markets, a future for which America is "the gatekeeper and the model." I happen to be quoting from the *New York Times*, but if you sample almost at random, you'll hear the same thing in more or less the same words.

That's the doctrine. The reality is that the world, including our own society, is moving toward a more autocratic and absolutist structure. The scope of the public arena is narrowing. The opportunities for popular participation in it are also declining. In short, the realities are that democracy is under attack. There are also parallel attacks on free markets, and there are expanding forms of market distortion. It's an interesting topic, but I'll put it aside and keep to the question of democracy, the other half of the story.

I've said that the doctrine and the reality are apparently in conflict, that is, the doctrine that the wave of the future is democracy and we're the gatekeeper and the model, and the reality, which I think is rather the opposite. So there's at least an apparent conflict. But in fact the conflict can be resolved, namely, by attenuating the concept of democracy and reducing it to pretty much an empty shell, to various forms with little meaning. And I think that

that's exactly what is happening. Of course in that case the doctrine will be true, and I think if we look that's pretty much what we see. The same is true of the talk about markets, but again I'll put that aside.

The currently prevailing concepts of democracy, which have been narrowing and becoming more restricted and impoverished over the years—democracy and liberty as well—these concepts would, I think, have utterly appalled someone like, say, Thomas Jefferson and other great figures of classical liberalism, for whom, incidentally, democracy and even liberty were part of something broader. They were part of the conception of a good society, which would be measured and evaluated by how well it freed individuals and their creative powers. It's to that end that democracy was considered an appropriate means.

If we turn to a more modern period, I think that the currently prevailing and increasingly narrowing concepts of democracy would also have appalled contemporary, twentieth-century thinkers. A crucial example is John Dewey, who was the greatest American social philosopher and whose thoughts focused primarily on the problem of enriching democracy, which he understood pretty much in the classical sense. He, incidentally, was appalled by the narrowing of the scope of meaningful democracy both in practice and in the rising democratic theories of his era, mainly the 1920s, 1930s, and 1940s, the progressive intellectuals of the Wilsonian period who laid pretty much the basis for the modern form of the impoverishment and the attenuation of democratic theory, helped out by the then-rising fields of the academic political sciences. There's little doubt in my mind that Dewey, like Thomas Jefferson, would find today's scene, a half century later, even more ominous and depressing.

These are pretty important issues in contemporary intellectual history. They have very broad implications. There's a reality beneath them that is even more portentous. These are very large topics, actually topics for an ongoing seminar and not for a talk. I'll try to say a few words about them, but they're going to be inadequate, I'm afraid.

To begin with, notice that just about every contemporary society calls itself "democratic." Actually, every contemporary society also calls itself "egalitarian." The question is: Equality of what?, as is discussed in an interesting book by Harvard economist Amartya Sen that came out recently. So in our doctrinal system you're supposed to insist upon equality of opportunity. It's one particular form of equality. Others call for other forms of equality. I stress ideology, where the reality is something else, as usual.

Take, say, the old Soviet Union. It consisted of countries that were called "people's democracies" and in fact described themselves as the highest form of democracy. We laugh at that, for good reasons. It's useful to have a look at the reasons. It's not that they didn't have elections. In fact, they did have elections. They could have even made the elections free in the sense that anybody who wanted to could say, I'm a candidate, and could even be listed on the ballot. Nothing significant would have changed.

The reasons were several. The primary reason was that the basic decisions, the most important decisions about how the society worked, were not in the public arena at all. So it didn't matter much who voted and who ran. The basic decisions were made by a military, bureaucratic elite, including crucial decisions over the economy, decisions over what was invested, what was produced, commercial interactions, and so on. In fact, the basic decisions that are at the core of any modern society were out of the public arena entirely. That had a lot of consequences. One consequence was that information was quite narrowly controlled by the very same hands, namely, by those who had the resources and the power to impose decisions on how they were used.

A side comment: The population of the Soviet Union apparently had very wide access to information and used that access. There were interesting U.S. government-funded studies done by American Russian research centers and others in the 1970s who concluded that it appeared that over three-quarters of the population were listening regularly to foreign broadcasts (about 95 percent of the most educated sectors of the population). *Samizdat* (underground newspapers, technically illegal but all over the place) were read by about half of the relatively educated part of the population and by about 15 percent of blue-collar workers, according to these studies. Those are phenomenal figures for dissident literature, incomparably beyond anything that we can imagine.

Returning to the reasons why we laugh at "Soviet people's democracies," another was that there was very little in the way of popular organizations that were able to function in the political sphere. Public participation in proposing, crafting, and formulating public policy was extremely slight, and there weren't any organizational structures around that enabled people to take part in it. Finally, most people were so busy just trying to survive that they were unable to participate in any meaningful way in the public arena and wouldn't have been able to even if opportunities had existed. Under such conditions, democracy is at best a very thin reed.

[The autocratic structures of twentieth-century absolutism]
You'll have noticed, I'm sure, that I'm describing our society. The basic point, the crucial point about the concentration of resources and decision-making power, is not quite the same as in the Soviet Union. Basic decision making

here too is out of the public arena—in fact, entirely out of it, almost. But it's not in the hands of a military, bureaucratic elite. It's in the hands of private power, like corporations, financial institutions, and the like, which operate in secret without any public scrutiny, virtually no public input. They are almost completely unaccountable. In fact, they determine the basic things that happen in life. They are now increasingly transnational.

It's been the case over a long period that governing structures—things that become government—tend to coalesce around concentrations of power. In the last couple of centuries that means primarily economic power, so national economies led to and were integrated with national governments: the increase in and rapid escalation of transnational corporations, banking institutions, financial institutions, and so on. Around them there is also coalescing a network of structures of governance, what the world's leading business newspaper, the London *Financial Times*, describes as a "de facto world government," with its own institutions: the IMF, the World Bank, the new World Trade Organization (WTO), the GATT, the G-7 executive, the executive branches of the seven rich countries. That's a kind of framework of world government that also operates very remotely, in secret, without scrutiny, without accountability. Its primary constituents are in fact precisely the transnational corporations and the financial institutions. It reflects their interests.

The new trade agreements—which is a rather misleading term, in my opinion—are accelerating this transfer of effective power to these absolutist, unaccountable institutions on a vast scale. Corporations themselves are absolutist institutions. Power lies in the hands of owners and managers. The only debate is about how you divvy out the shares. Big literature about that. There's a fairly strict authority structure in a corporation. An individual can sometimes enter into the hierarchy, which means you essentially take orders from above and transfer orders down below. It's a fairly strict hierarchy, as much as any we know of in any institution. If you're an outsider, you're not part of it. You have basically nothing to say. You're allowed to rent yourself to it. That's called "getting a job." You can buy what they sell, if you like. You can watch—you can't see very much because they operate mostly in secret. Now that they're remote enough to be transnational and have their governing institutions in Brussels and Geneva and so on, they are even more operating in secret.

This is all well-known and old stuff. About ten years ago I was at a conference in Switzerland on international affairs. One of the participants was a Swiss diplomatic historian. In fact, he told me he was *the* Swiss diplomatic historian from the University of Geneva. We got kind of friendly. We were out having a beer one night. He told me that the worst job in the world is to be a Swiss diplomatic historian. The reason for that is quite simple: Diplomatic historians are people who look at archival materials primarily. They try to figure out what's going on by looking at the archives.

In most countries there's a sort of buffer between private power, which basically rules, and policy. The buffer is called the government. Governments do leave a kind of paper trail. We're pretty good in that respect by comparative standards. If you wait thirty or thirty-five years, sometimes even earlier, you get some kind of a record, in fact, often quite an interesting and complete record, of what the government was up to. But in Switzerland they don't bother with the buffer. The corporations just rule straight. They make the decisions (the banks and transnationals and so on). Corporations don't leave any paper trail at all. They are secret societies. They are secret, absolutist organizations. If you learn anything about them, it's because the Multinational Operations Committee in Congress in the mid-1970s, under the pressure of the popular movements of the 1960s, in fact, got subpoena power and released some information about them. Occasionally you find something out in other ways. But basically you learn nothing. So being a Swiss diplomatic historian, without this kind of intervening level, leaves you with not a lot to do, he was complaining. Well, we have something to do because there is this transmission belt. But the picture is not all that different, if you think about it—if you think about where power actually is, how decisions are made and how much you can find out about the centers of power.

This has its consequences, naturally—for example, the other aspects of deficiencies of democracy (I can't even use the word), the absurdity of using the term *democracy* to refer to the Soviet system of tyranny. In various respects we also have the same features. Information is very narrowly concentrated in pretty much the same hands as other decision making. The major media are just huge corporations, selling people like you, selling audiences, to other businesses, to advertisers. That sets the framework within which most of the rest operates. Actually, it's a different information system and all sorts of different properties. One of the properties is that people here have much less access (they have access; they don't seek access to other sources of information). So the proportion of the population here that listens to foreign broadcasts is minuscule. Publications that are outside the very narrow and rigid ideological framework reach a statistically insignificant part of the population. Nothing like, say, the Soviet *samizdat*. There are reasons for that, and they are interesting ones, but again, that's another topic.

With regard to popular organizations that permit the people to function in the political sphere, they're very limited. We don't have functioning political parties. We don't have political clubs. There's very little. And furthermore, most people are indeed so busy trying to survive that even if such organizations existed, and even if information were readily available, there would be a limited amount that they could do with it. Under such conditions, again, democracy is a fairly thin reed. I don't want to suggest that here it's like under Soviet tyranny, but some of the structural properties are quite similar and worth thinking about.

[Liberty as a bridge to equality]

These are the kinds of reasons why classical democrats and libertarians were so hostile to corporate power. They didn't really see it. They were in the classical period (people like Thomas Jefferson). They were only witnessing the very early, incipient moments of what was going on, but enough to see it and not to like it. So Thomas Jefferson in 1816 expressed his fear that "the country was moving toward a single and splendid government of an aristocracy founded on banking institutions and monied incorporations." If that tendency, which was just beginning, continued, he said, "it would be the end of democracy and freedom. The few would be riding and ruling over the plundered plowmen and the beggared yeomanry."

That was 1816. A decade later, during the Jacksonian democracy, Jefferson was a little more optimistic. But right before his death, in fact I think hours before his death, he spoke at the fiftieth anniversary of the Declaration of Independence. In speaking there, he made a crucial distinction which is worth paying careful attention to. He distinguished between "those who fear and distrust the people and wish to draw all powers from them into the hands of the higher classes," that's one category, and the others are those who "identify with the people, have confidence in them, cherish and consider them as the most honest and safe depository of the public interest, even though not the most wise." That's the second category of people. He was hoping that the second category would be in the ascendancy.

Looking now—that was 1826—it's clear, it should be clear to any observer, that Thomas Jefferson's worst fears have been realized. Effective power is indeed in the hands of the higher classes. The early institutions, banking institutions and monied incorporations, that he was concerned about are now vast in power and control and dominate the decision-making system, essentially in secret. Modern democratic theory, interestingly, has veered very sharply from Jeffersonian ideas and in fact is precisely based on fear and distrust of the people, who must not be allowed to determine public policy or enter into the public arena because, as contemporary thinkers put it, they are too "stupid and ignorant." They agree with Jefferson only on one point: that the people are perhaps not the "most wise." But they disagree with him on everything else. That's rather important. I'll return to that.

If we go back, say, a half century earlier, to Adam Smith, he was describing a world that is very different from ours, so much so that the descriptions and the explanations really don't carry over very well, but the ideas do. He lived too early to see the autocratic structures of modern industrial capitalism. He didn't anticipate their development. But he was already, at that period, very much opposed to joint stock companies, what we nowadays call corporations. He was particularly opposed to them if, as he feared might happen, they would become personified and made permanent, that is, they would gain the status of "immortal persons," in effect, with all the right of persons, except immortal.

That in fact is exactly what happened in the nineteenth century. One of the major parts of American nineteenth-century history is the creation of corporate power by government decision and the turning of corporations, which used to be sort of public interest groups (to build a bridge, etc.) into immortal persons with the rights of persons, which, if you have corporate power, means vast rights, well beyond any real person. That didn't happen through the democratic process. It happened primarily through judicial decision, decision by lawyers and judges and so on, as part of the effort to create a developmental state, a powerful interventionist state that would introduce a high level of protectionism and direct public resources to private power and in that way enable development to take place.

Incidentally, that's the only way in history that development has ever taken place, from England up to South Korea and Taiwan. There are some lessons there, too. The prescriptions that contemporary economic ideologues offer to underdeveloped societies have the interesting property that they are refuted 100 percent of the time. If you can find one case in history of a society that's developed by those rules, or even marginally using them, it would be interesting to hear about it. There are cases of societies that *have* followed those rules, and they're mostly basket cases. Again, something worth looking at when you read primers on free trade and so on on the front pages of the *New York Times*. Again, that's another topic I'm not talking about.

The judiciary in the nineteenth century did create the immortal persons that Adam Smith was so concerned about. Again, his worst fears were realized, though again it's a very different world that he was describing and the arguments that were true for his world don't hold for ours, nevertheless the ideas are interesting and the beliefs are worth paying attention to. This is part of the system of classical liberal thought, the basis for modern libertarian theories of freedom and democracy. He held that markets could function properly only under conditions of relative equality. He also thought and gave a long argument to try to show that liberty would lead to equality, either absolute perfect liberty would lead to either absolute equality or to continual tendencies toward equality. Insofar as we don't attain that state of equality, or near equality, insofar as that's not realized, that simply indicates that we have not attained the state of liberty, of perfect liberty.

Of course, the discrepancies are vast and growing. That gives you a measure of how far we are from liberty in any sense that someone like Adam Smith would have recognized. He held, in fact, that only under conditions of relative equality and tendencies toward equality would market competition be efficient or fair and thus able to contribute to its further ends. The market was no end in itself for people like Adam Smith. The further ends were realization of human capacities and potentialities. A market could contribute to those ends insofar as the outcomes were relatively equal. That, he thought, would happen under conditions of liberty. Otherwise you don't have liberty.

The very foundation of liberty, in Adam Smith's view, and this is standard Enlightenment thinking, is the right of every workman to the fruits of his own labor. That, he said, is sacred and inviolable. It's a crucial element in fulfillment, as another major classical liberal thinker, Wilhelm von Humboldt (who very much inspired John Stuart Mill) put it: if a craftsman creates something beautiful but does it on external command, by the orders of someone else and under coercion, we may admire what he does but we will despise what he is, because he's not human; he's a machine. Adam Smith held the same view.

Coming to the present, John Dewey, who again was one of the increasingly lone voices speaking for democracy and freedom in twentieth-century America—although he was very much in the mainstream intellectual and political culture of his day, the first half of the twentieth century, increasingly marginalized, by now is viewed as almost unrecognizable—he held (and I'm reading it because I think it's basically correct, incidentally), he held that "politics is the shadow cast on society by big business, and as long as that is so, the attenuation of the shadow will not change the substance." In other words, reforms are basically pointless. The reason is that democracy requires that the shadow of big business simply be removed so that the political system can function. The very institutions of private power, he stressed, undermine freedom and democracy.

He was very explicit about the anti-democratic power that he was talking about. To quote Dewey, "it resides in control of the means of production, exchange, publicity, transportation, and communication." Whoever owns them rules the life of the country; even if under democratic forms, we act under the shadow that big business casts. "Big business for private profit, through private control of banking, land, industry, reinforced through command of the press, press agents, and other means of propaganda," he said, is the system of actual power, the source of coercion. Unless it's unraveled, we cannot seriously talk about democracy and freedom. In a free and democratic society, workers have to "be masters of their own industrial fate."

That's a classical liberal doctrine. You find it right through classical liberalism, Adam Smith, Humboldt, Thomas Jefferson, of course, and the rest. It's "illiberal and immoral" to train children to work "for the sake of the wage earned," not "freely and intelligently" under their own control. Hence industry must be changed if democracy is to exist. It must be changed "from a feudalistic to a democratic social order." All of these are, or at least should be, truisms. Indeed, they were very common coin. They were common ideas among uneducated working people not all that long ago, during the century, for example, when working people called for an end to what was standardly called "wage slavery," which they regarded as not very different from chattel slavery.

I stress that all of this is as American as apple pie. It has nothing to do with Marxism, Leninism, or any of the other scare words that are concocted by the contemporary commissars. And it's all completely down the tubes as the system has become more feudalistic in Dewey's sense, more fundamentally illiberal, and more closed to the ideals of human freedom that were held, and indeed rightly held, by classical libertarians, those who we profess to honor but in fact constantly kick in the face and whose ideas are simply disappearing from sight.

As the system has itself become more feudalistic, absolutist, unaccountable, narrow, remote, secret in essentially the classical liberal sense, running right up to Dewey and others of the time, as it has become narrower, the doctrinal system has also correspondingly become narrower. That's what universities are about, in fact, to narrow it and exclude the thinking that in fact inspired classical liberalism and democratic action and thought. The fundamental libertarian principles—which, as I say, were even common coin among the general population, let alone libertarian thinkers—now sound very exotic and extreme. I just gave you a sample of them. In fact, they're often called "anti-American," an interesting term that can be used only in cultures where there are really deep totalitarian strains. For example, in the Soviet Union the worst crime was to be "anti-Soviet." In the U.S., people like professors at the University of Massachusetts published books called *The anti-Americans*, which people don't laugh about. They're highly regarded. You get several reviews in the *New York Times* and so on. You might ask yourself, as a sort of thought experiment, what would happen if somebody, say, in Italy were to publish a book called *The anti-Italians,* or anti-Italianism, or anti-Norwegianism, and ask what the reaction would be on the streets of Milan or Oslo, or in fact any political culture that had not succumbed to totalitarian doctrine and still had a memory of what freedom and democracy were about. The very fact that we're able to use terms like that is quite striking, particularly if you consider our own history, of which I've just barely given a sample, but it's a real sample, of major figures.

[Brainwashing under freedom: an American invention]

These are very important features of the deterioration of democracy in the current period, not only at the institutional level but also in the doctrinal support for power that accompanies it. I want to stress that this fear of democracy is a very old story and very deep-seated. The first modern democratic revolution was in England in the seventeenth century. The popular democratic forces were bitterly condemned for seeking, as the leading intellectuals of the day put it, to "raise the rascal multitude . . . against the men of best quality" and for making the people "so curious and so arrogant that they will not submit to a civil rule." There was a civil war going on, as you learned in high school, between king and Parliament. But what often isn't taught is that the rabble, the "rascal multitude," were opposed to both sides in the civil war. Their pamphlets said that they did not want to be ruled by king *or* Parliament, rather, as they put it, "by countrymen like ourselves that know our wants" and "know the people's sores."

Incidentally, that same call was reiterated by rebellious farmers right here after the American Revolution, when they learned that they would continue to be ruled by the "men of best quality" and not by "countrymen like themselves," as the revolutionary pamphlets had claimed. We're back to the distinction that Thomas Jefferson drew in 1826 that I quoted earlier. Actually, that's true of *every* social upheaval and revolution, at least to my knowledge. The official story is that there are two sides fighting. The reality, quite typically, is that there are three sides: the two sides that are officially fighting one another for a share of the power, or all of it, and then the general population, which wants to be free of both of them and quite often gets crushed. That, I think, if you look, is the *real* history of social upheaval and revolution, including the American Revolution, if you look closely.

Over time the rabble has won rights. They have won rights through struggle. They're not gifts from above. The rights include, for example, the franchise, the right to vote, which has expanded. So in the U.S. half the population was disenfranchised until the 1920s, for example, but it finally won the vote. In the 1960s the vote extended effectively to the black population, which hadn't really had it before. So these are all victories for democracy, it extends the franchise, extends something.

These victories brought with them renewed fears of the rascal multitude and new and more sophisticated devices to control and marginalize them. As the power of the state to coerce gradually declined over the years, these modes of coercion and control and marginalization shifted more and more to propaganda. Propaganda is naturally in the hands of the powerful, not for surprising reasons. In our own business-run autocracies, that means primarily business propaganda. That includes media propaganda, the media just being big businesses. That's a huge phenomenon, some of it direct, like what comes out of the public relations industry (an American creation, not surprising in a uniquely business-run society with a highly class-conscious business community that is always fighting a bitter class war and knows it). And then there are its outlets, including a good part of the media and the academic profession and so on.

The leading student of twentieth-century business propaganda, an Australian, Alex Carey, who has written very interesting things about the U.S. and is unknown here, opens some of his work with the following comment, which I think is quite accurate: "The twentieth century has been characterized by three developments of great political importance. The first is the growth of democracy. The second is the growth of corporate power. The third is the growth of corporate propaganda as a means of protecting corporate power against democracy." That's quite right, and that's in fact the new version of the methods of the fear of the rascal multitude and the methods of controlling. And we see that if we look at recent American history.

Start with, say, the First World War, which was important. The First World War taught quite important lessons in this regard. Woodrow Wilson created the first official government propaganda agency, the Creel Commission, designed to try to drive what was in fact a very pacifist country into war. He was particularly aided by the people who modestly called themselves the "most intelligent members of the society," the liberal intellectuals, who took pride in the fact that for the first time in history a population had been driven into war not by generals and rotten people, but by the smart guys, who perceived that it was the right thing to do. In fact, what they were doing was disseminating fabrications concocted by the British Ministry of Information about Belgian babies with their arms ripped off and various other propaganda that was designed by the British, as they put it, to "try to control the thought of the world." The ones who they were most easily able to control were the most intelligent members of the society here, self-designated, namely, the serious intellectuals, who propounded all of this stuff with great sobriety and later took great credit for what they had achieved.

This was quite successful, this business propaganda. It impressed people. Woodrow Wilson himself was called the "Great Generalissimo of the Propaganda" on the propaganda front, a phrase that was used by Harold Lasswell, one of the leading figures in contemporary political science, the founder of the modern field of communications, who began a very influential career by studying wartime propaganda. The success of the Generalissimo was substantial and it impressed several audiences. One first audience that it impressed was the most important one, the American business community. It gave a big shot in the arm to the public relations industry, which had existed, but it really took off, very much influenced by the successes of the Generalissimo. In fact, the Generalissimo of corporate propaganda, Edward Bernays, who lived here, was in the Wilson propaganda agency and learned a lot from it. He developed the ideas which he later propounded, which were that the essence of democracy is propaganda, what he sometimes called the "engineering of consent." It's quite obvious who's going to do the engineering, obvious but unsaid, because that's not one of the things you're supposed to say.

Another person who was quite impressed by the successes of Anglo-American propaganda was Adolf Hitler. If you read *Mein Kampf,* you'll notice that he thinks Germany's defeat in the First World War was in large part due to the inability of autocratic, authoritarian Germany to compete on the propaganda front with the democratic societies, which carried out thought control much more efficiently and effectively. He's actually quite right about that. In *Mein Kampf* he promised next time around they'd have their own propaganda agencies. Whether they succeeded equally to ours or not is another question, but again we'll put that one aside.

A third group, an audience that was deeply impressed, were American intellectuals, people like Harold Lasswell, for example. They were not particularly cognizant of the fact that they were the main victims of the propaganda, which was true, but you don't want to think that about yourself.

Lasswell was the author in the *Encyclopedia of the Social Sciences* in 1933 or 1934 of an article called "Propaganda." In those days people were a little more honest. We don't use the term now. We use other terms, like *journalism*, or something like that. But in those days they were pretty straight and just called it propaganda. He recognized that propaganda is necessary in any society and more necessary in a society that's more free.

The logic is sort of obvious. If you can control people with a whip, you don't really care all that much what they think. That's probably part of the reason why the Soviet Union wasn't very repressive with regard to, say, *samizdat* and foreign broadcasts. They were to an extent, but nowhere near what they could have been. It really didn't matter all that much. They had a bludgeon over people's heads. Here it matters a lot more what people think, so propaganda has to be far more sophisticated and much more intensive, as Lasswell and others realized. "Propaganda," he wrote back in the 1930s, "is a new technique of control" of the general public, who are a threat because of what he called "the ignorance and superstition [of] the masses. We must not succumb to democratic dogmatisms about men being the best judges of their own interests." We are the best judges. That you'll recognize from the two alternatives that Jefferson counterposed in 1826—notice that Jefferson's worst fears became the credo of the modern liberal intellectuals, in fact, of the intellectual community rather generally.

Bolshevism is a subcase of this (not very different, if you think it through), a fact which was long noted by libertarian, by anarchist thinkers, and in fact predicted by Bakunin long before the Bolshevik Revolution. He predicted that there would be two forms of modern intellectuals, what he called the "Red bureaucracy," who would use popular struggles to try to take control of state power and institute the most vicious and ruthless dictatorships in history, and the other group, who would see that there isn't going to be an access to power that way and would therefore become the servants of private power and state capitalist democracy, where they would, as Bakunin put it, "beat the people with the people's stick," talk about democracy but beat the people with it. That's actually one of the few predictions in the social sciences that's come true, to my knowledge, and a pretty perceptive one.

That's the credo of twentieth-century intellectual life to quite a remarkable extent. It shows how much we have declined since Jefferson's day. Jefferson was hoping that the alternative would turn out to be true; this is what *did* turn out to be true, his worst fears. This should be part of intellectual history in a free society, the kind of thing that you ought to learn in elementary school. Jefferson's distinction applies with precision to the modern age, except everything has been reversed and forgotten. This is also pretty standard in the academic culture. So, for example, the president of the American Political Science Association in 1934, Harold Lasswell, in his presidential address, right in the period of the big ferment in the Depression, workers' struggles, everybody uprising, said, "We must exclude the ignorant, the uninformed and antisocial elements from the political arena." That's almost everybody, if you look at what he's talking about. "What we need is an aristocracy of intellect and character. The men of brains must seize the torch" (the action intellectuals of the Kennedy period, for example). There's an unspoken assumption in all of this, unspoken and possibly unnoticed, since it's not nice to see yourself in a mirror. The unspoken assumption is that these guys can seize the torch insofar as they keep well within the shadow that's cast by big business that we call "politics." If they move a little bit beyond that shadow or even to its margins, they forfeit their place within the aristocracy of intellect and character. As I say, that's not much discussed, though an obvious truth.

The leading thinker, the leading exponent of these doctrines and one of the most influential ones, was Walter Lippmann, who was the leading figure in American journalism for half a century, a major commentator on foreign affairs, and also a highly regarded progressive political theorist. He made a distinction between what he called the "responsible men," a small number— he was of course one of them; everyone who presents the views is always within the group of the men of best quality, the aristocracy of intellect and character and so on—so there are the "responsible men" on the one side, and then there are the "ignorant and meddlesome outsiders," who are the population. It's a democracy, so the ignorant and meddlesome outsiders have a role or a function, as he put it. Their function in a democracy is to be spectators, not participants, but they are allowed to, as he put it, "lend their weight" periodically to one or another member of the responsible men, the men of best quality. That's called an "election." Then they're supposed to go home and watch the Super Bowl, or whatever the equivalent was in the 1920s.

[A recurrent pattern through American history]

I'm talking about the center. This is the liberal, pragmatic mainstream. The spectrum extends in both directions. Toward the more libertarian end, it extends in his day, for example, to John Dewey, with his roots in classical liberalism. Toward the more reactionary end, it includes the mainstream business community (which has enormous fear of the rascal multitude) and its explicit political representatives, for example, say, the Wilson political system and, in the ideological sphere, the Reaganites, the people who are funding those journals that were mentioned before. Their view is that the population shouldn't even be spectators. That's too much. They should be completely outside.

That's one reason why the Reaganites were so committed to protecting an increasingly powerful state, because they were statist reactionaries and believe in an extremely powerful and interventionist state intervening in the economy and overseas. But it should also be protected. So they instituted an unprecedented censorship, the first government propaganda agency since Wilson, this time illegal, because the laws had changed. They went for clandestine operations; big, huge clandestine operations reached new peaks. Clandestine operations are operations undertaken targeting the domestic population. Everybody else knows about them. It's just the domestic population that doesn't. That's the respect in which they're clandestine. There are very interesting counterparts to this in corporate propaganda. I'll read you a couple of examples if you're interested. They're kind of interesting to look at, rather well crafted. But I'll put it aside, time being tight.

That's basically the spectrum. At the libertarian end you have the extremists like Thomas Jefferson, Adam Smith, and John Dewey. That end has been pretty much sawed off. The rest of the spectrum lies between the Generalissimo of propaganda and his administration (that's kind of like the center), Lippman, Bernays, Lasswell, the concept of engineered consent and elite control. Then you go all the way off to the right like, for example, the Reaganites, who think even a spectator role is too much. They're basically Stalinists adapted to our political system.

At the end of World War I the Generalissimo had some work to do. There was a lot of ferment, labor organizing, strikes, political thought, and so on. That had to be squashed. So the liberal Wilson administration conducted a very violent and repressive Red scare, with the support of the liberal press. That worked quite well. It led to a decade of quiescence and subordination to business control. That's when these mainstream views of the Lippmann, Lasswell, and Bernays type flourished.

In the 1930s, during the Great Depression, the quiescence broke. People became active again and fought to enter the political arena, began to organize. They actually won some victories in 1935. Labor finally won the rights that European labor had won half a century before, namely, the Wagner Act, the right to organize. That victory for working people and democracy sent a real chill through the business community. The National Association of Manufacturers, the major business association, in its publications described the "hazard facing industrialists in the newly realized political power of the masses." This must be reversed and their thinking directed to more proper channels, or we are definitely headed for adversity [the industrialists thought]. They indeed began a huge corporate propaganda offensive to block this incipient threat of democracy and human rights. The world war came along and put it on hold for a while. But right after the war it took off: huge corporate propaganda offensives. That's one of the reasons why the U.S. is essentially off the spectrum of industrial societies on things like health, social contract, labor rights, and so on. The right to organize was essentially destroyed by 1948, and by then the game was pretty much over. This is, incidentally, all pre-McCarthy. McCarthy was kind of a latecomer. This was led by a spectrum of liberal Democrats attacking independent thought and people further over to the right undermining unions and social policy. McCarthy picked it up and turned it into something obscene, but it was bad enough before. Essentially it was all over by the late 1940s.

The labor victories were reversed and there was a major attack on independent thought. That led to the 1950s, which were very quiescent, rather similar to the 1920s. Incidentally, this has been a recurrent pattern through American history: democratizing tendencies, repression, quiescence, and then things blow up again.

At that time there was a lot of new technology that helped, and that has a lot of bearing on the present day. So in the 1920s and 1930s radio was coming into existence. Radio, everybody recognized, is a public resource. It's not like shoes. There's a fixed band that's got to be regulated. Everyone knew that. The question was, where will it go? Will radio be assigned to the public interests, meaning public radio, hence democratic to the extent that the society is democratic? That's one option. The other option is just to hand it over to private absolute power and turn it into a device for propaganda and profit making by the private sector. Just about every country in the world, maybe every one, I don't offhand know of an exception, went the first way, toward making it a public resource. The U.S. went the second way. It became a virtual private monopoly. A college could have a little radio station that you could hear for three blocks away, but this issue was struggled about. Labor groups, church groups, other public interest groups sought to put the U.S. within the mainstream of Western society, and they lost. They lost flat out. That's a reflection of a lot of other things, the extent to which we are indeed an unusual society with a highly class-conscious business community always fighting a vicious class war and very well aware of it. These quotes that I read from the National Association of Manufacturers are quite typical.

That was radio. By the time television came along it wasn't even an issue. The world went one way, the U.S. went the other way. That's coming along right today. We're right in the middle of it with the question of this information highway business. Again, there is a question: Is it going to be a public interest resource, serving a democratic, democratizing function, as the technology certainly allows, or is it simply going to become another instrument of corporate power and corporate propaganda and thought control and concocting artificial wants and so on? The answer to that depends on the balance of forces. The way things now stand, you can predict it's just going to be another instrument of thought control and corporate power, but it doesn't have to be. These are questions of how people react. Other countries not very different from us, in fact very much like us, went the other way with radio and television, and we could have, too. It's a question of organizing and activism and awareness. One of the reasons for the intensive propaganda is to keep people from thinking about these things. To some extent it has succeeded.

The 1950s were quiescent, very much like the 1920s. In the 1960s it broke again, rather like the 1930s. There was a lot of ferment, and it aroused the usual fear. Ever since then, from the early 1970s, there has been a major attempt to carry out another Red scare, essentially, to beat back the population to conformity and quiescence. It's kind of interesting that this time it hasn't worked. That's really the first time in American history where the cycle hasn't really worked out. It's a rather interesting phenomenon with a lot of consequences. There's not much time to talk about it. That's what we're right in the middle of.

[The attack on democracy: a key to understanding policy]
The new slogan in the early 1970s is what was called by the liberals the "crisis of democracy." As the chairman of the political science department at Harvard put it, the Eaton professor of the science of government—I love that title—speaking for the science of government, he deplored the "crisis of democracy" and the fact that societies were becoming "ungovernable," essentially because the rabble was trying to enter the public arena. That made it ungovernable. Unspoken in all of these discussions is that somebody is allowed into the public arena. Who? You're not allowed to say that bad word. But the public is not allowed. Samuel Huntington almost gave it away. He referred nostalgically to the Truman period, when Truman, as he put it, "had been able to govern the country with the help of a few Wall Street lawyers and financiers." (That's a little on the vulgar Marxist side—it wasn't quite that— but you get the idea.) He had the general idea correct. In those days there was

no "crisis of democracy": that's exactly the way things were supposed to be. But now there was a crisis: women, blacks, young people, old people, farmers, all these bad types were trying to enter the public arena and press their demands, and that just made the society "ungovernable." It had been fine when you had a couple of Wall Street lawyers and financiers doing it.

That's the struggle we're right in the middle of. The efforts to restore passivity have been a mixed success, not completely by any means. We're right in the middle of it now, and the lines that are drawn are the usual ones, quite currently, in fact.

Take, say, the NAFTA debate. It's very revealing in this respect. NAFTA was a major issue for the corporate world, such a major issue that the media, which usually pretend to be above the struggle, abandoned the pretense, and their class commitments became very explicit. In fact, the *New York Times* actually used the phrase "class lines" at one point. That's like a no-no: you're not allowed to refer to that. But it was just too obvious to conceal, as were the commitments of the media. There was a real frenzy about NAFTA. Unusual, in fact. That tells you something really important was at stake, because it was.

A lot of what was important was the attack on democracy, which is accelerated by these so-called trade agreements. Right at the end, it looked like not such a clear thing. The frenzy mounted to a fever pitch and focused on one thing primarily: the fact that labor, working people, were attempting to lobby their representatives. That was considered an absolute scandal. Clinton made all kinds of speeches, which were headlined all over the place, in which he denounced what he called the "naked pressure" and the "raw muscle of labor" which even descended to "pleading based on friendship, threatening based on money and work in campaigns": total outrage to approach your representatives and say, look, we'd like you to do something. This went all the way over to what's considered the left in the media, say, Anthony Lewis (about as far out as you can imagine and still be in respectable society), who denounced the "backward, unenlightened labor movement with its crude, threatening tactics and its fear of change."

The whole thing was real hysteria. It was quite interesting. The *New York Times* the last day had an editorial which had a box in which they listed people in the New York area who were planning to vote against NAFTA. They listed their contributions from labor. They said it was ominous, that it raises serious questions about whether they were being honest and so on. The *Washington Post* did the same thing.

That was interesting. As everybody knew but didn't say until afterward, when they came clean on it—in fact, they came clean the day after the vote—

corporate lobbying was hugely greater than labor lobbying, by an overwhelming factor, as always. Nobody worried about that. They weren't having
"crude, threatening tactics" and all this bad stuff. There's a good reason for
that: corporate lobbying is not a problem. They are the men of best quality.
They are the ones who are supposed to rule. And the responsible intellectuals are their good and loyal servants. Therefore there's nothing to say about
corporate lobbying. They won't object to it. It's when the rascal multitude
tries to get in the act that everyone starts foaming at the mouth. They are
supposed to submit in silence to the rule of the aristocracy of wealth and, of
course, the aristocracy of intellect and character, the smart guys who do the
work for them.

Actually very little has changed since the seventeenth century. If you look
at the hysteria in the seventeenth century, among seventeenth-century intellectuals, which I just gave a couple of quotes from (I have a lot more elsewhere if you like), it's very similar to the hysteria today, say, if working people
dare to lobby their representatives. The reason it's the same is the issues are
the same. You can call it a new world order, if you like, but it's the same class
war: the intellectuals playing the same service role, the ones who are within
the shadow cast by big business, that is, and therefore granted respectability.
Departures from this do exist, but they're very slight.

All of this helps to explain the enthusiasm for NAFTA and GATT. The
primary thing about them is that they vest far more power in private, absolutist institutions which are completely unaccountable to the public and
operate in secret, spawning the de facto world government that the business
press openly talks about. All of that moves us back to that spectrum on
democracy. This moves us toward the reactionary end, the Reaganite end, in
which the population are not even spectators. Insofar as power is shifted to
the transnational arena with its own de facto world government, you're not
even a spectator, because only the real experts and specialists have any idea
what's going on in the IMF. That's a great achievement in the destruction of
democracy, and that helps explain the tremendous enthusiasm for NAFTA,
GATT, and other such profoundly anti-democratic developments—also
anti-market developments, but as I say, that's another story.

Finally, just a couple of words on how this stuff works out in our depend-
encies. Sometimes it's described with considerable candor. One of the clearest voices these days is a former Reaganite insider, a guy named Thomas
Carothers, who was part of the "democracy enhancement" programs, as they
were called, within the State Department in the 1980s. These were hailed
with great pride that makes us the beacon of the future. He has written a

book and a couple of articles about this, and they're informative and honest, rather rueful. He says that the policies were sincere, but he thinks they failed.

On the contrary, in my opinion they succeeded quite brilliantly. But putting aside that judgment, what he describes is entirely accurate. It's just interesting to have it said from the inside. He points out that there was a correlation between democracy in the hemisphere and U.S. influence, namely, a negative correlation. Where U.S. influence was least, the steps toward democracy were greatest, primarily in the Southern Cone of Latin America, where, as he points out, speaking from the inside, the Reagan administration strongly opposed the moves toward democracy, tried to back the autocratic governments, which are in fact a residue of the Kennedy liberals, I should say, who were very close to the Reaganites in their picture of the world, remarkably close.

The Reagan Administration sought to preserve these neo-Nazi states in the Southern Cone, but they failed and there was democracy. Then of course they took credit for what happened afterward. That in fact happened all over the place: where U.S. influence was the greatest, in Central America and the Caribbean, the effects were worst. He recognizes that but doesn't draw any conclusions from it. But in fact it's something that generalizes on human rights as well (it's another one of those lessons you're not supposed to learn). He then points out what happened. Here is his description (from the inside), which he opposes as a bad thing. He says,

> Washington sought only limited, top-down forms of democratic change that did not risk upsetting the traditional structures of power with which the U.S. has long been allied. It sought to maintain the basic order of quite undemocratic societies because of the deep fear of populace-based change with all its implications for upsetting established economic and political orders and heading off in a leftist direction.

What's a "leftist direction"? That's a direction of some "leftist extremist" that holds that "the mass of mankind has not been born with saddles on their backs, nor a favored few, booted and spurred, ready to ride them." It is the view that we should oppose "a single and splendid government founded on banking institutions and monied incorporations." I'm quoting that "leftist extremist" Thomas Jefferson in the early days of the corporate state-capitalist absolutism that he despised and feared and that has come into existence.

Carothers is quite correct. His picture of what happened is accurate, generalizes very broadly. It applies at home as well. It is the key to understanding policy.

[Lessons still not taught in elementary school]

Again, these are truths that would be taught in elementary school in a free society. Major efforts have to be made in the educational system, way up to the elite universities, to prevent people from seeing that 2 + 2 = 4. But that's the answer: it does. It's not very hard to figure out. If you look not even very profoundly, you see it all over the place. It's quite systematic. The policy is that the traditional structures of power must remain. They have to be protected from the "populace-based changes." That's true abroad and that's true at home. Democracy is a fine thing, but only if it has the right outcome. Democracy is defined not by process but by outcome. The right guys have to win, otherwise it's not democracy. The "right guys" means Thomas Jefferson's "banking institutions and monied incorporations" and their modern inheritors and the aristocracy of intellect and character that serves them and labors to conceal the reality of the world from the rascal multitude. People like you, if you get properly trained. You have to be willing to accept the training, of course. And if you do, a lot of privilege and power comes with that submission to power, a lot of advantages.

We can see the Thomas Carothers thesis of the 1980s, which is just a chapter of history right before our eyes today. In fact, it's playing itself out with really brilliant clarity right in front of us in Haiti. There couldn't be a clearer example. In Haiti, the U.S. made a mistake. We had been supporting dictators and murderers and everything was all great. But there was a mistake: they allowed a free election. It was assumed that the U.S.-backed candidate, a World Bank official, would win easily. He had all the resources. But unknown to the "men of best quality" there and here, there had been a lot of ferment in Haiti. There was a lot of popular organizing. Many popular organizations had developed, with nobody paying attention to them. They had been very effective, and in fact the wrong guy won with an overwhelming majority in the first free election in the history of the country, namely President Aristide, with two-thirds of the vote.

The trouble is, it was the wrong two-thirds of the population. As it was described by Americas Watch, the leading human rights group, he was swept into power by a remarkably advanced array of popular organizations that gave the vast majority of the population a share in local and national politics. Totally the wrong thing. Completely wrong from every point of view. He was quickly overthrown by violence, and that was the end to Haiti's democracy. As the *New York Times* put it in a headline right afterward, "Haiti's Democracy, Such as It Was." That contemptuous comment means "not much." That just symbolically means the rabble that voted for him. We read regularly that President Aristide has meager democratic credentials. He is opposed by what the *New York Times* calls "civil society," which fears that he supports class-based violence. He even blamed the rich for the poverty of the masses. That's an absolute outrage, to tell elementary truths in public. Maybe in secret somewhere, but not in public.

That happens to be the *New York Times,* but it's standard, again. Pick at random, that's the story. So therefore Aristide must "broaden his government." That's the current phrase. Unlike Clinton, whose government is broad enough—just take a look at the average income in his cabinet. So that's broad enough, but Aristide must "broaden" his cabinet. That's a code word which everyone understands. It means that he must broaden his cabinet to exclude the huge mass of the population, because they don't belong there, and he must extend it to the "democratic" elements, which are called the "moderates" in the military and the business community. Power has to be shifted into their hands.

Who are the "moderates"? The "moderates" are the ones who don't think everyone should just be exterminated. That's why they're moderates. Rather, they think that people should be allowed to work for $0.14 an hour in U.S.-owned assembly plants—which, incidentally, is a very useful weapon against poor people and working people at home: it's a way to lower standards of living and wages throughout the world, in the rich societies, an extremely important thing. So that's the "moderates." Also, they're allowed to produce food for export. Right now, under Clinton (although I haven't seen any headlines about it), food exports from Haiti are increasing. This is a starving country, remember. Food exports are increasing not by a small factor. They increased by a factor of thirty-six last year (a big number), under Clinton, thanks to the liberal Democrats. That's fruits, nuts, melons—from a starving island. That's for the benefit of U.S. agribusiness and yuppie markets.

In fact, all trade with Haiti is increasing rather substantially under what is laughably called an embargo. The reason is because the embargo has an exception. It has an exception for U.S.-owned assembly plants. When that's mentioned, it's always explained as a "humanitarian gesture." You have to understand that Haitians suffer only when U.S.-owned plants don't export and import. When others don't export and import, they don't suffer. Also, like children in Cuba, fortunately, they don't suffer when they starve, so you don't have to worry about embargoes there. But we have to have a very carefully crafted embargo in Haiti which excludes U.S.-owned assembly plants, whose trade is increasing (in fact, total trade is increasing), which allows export of food, which doesn't happen to notice that the Dominican border is completely porous. The rich can get anything they feel like. The U.S. is totally impotent to control the Dominican army, which it runs. The U.S. is known for having been able to exert influence in places, but not over a superpower like the Dominican Republic, so they can't do anything about that.

The Haitian military, as everyone knows, lives primarily on narcotrafficking. Take a look. The U.S. Navy and Coast Guard have been able to pick up just about every fishing boat that escapes Haiti with some terrified refugees. That's a totally illegal blockade, incidentally. It's as if Libya, say, were to block all commercial air traffic out of the U.S. But we're a terrorist state, so we do what we feel like. We've been able to pick up every refugee, just about, but not a single narcotrafficking boat. It's amazing, isn't it?

This was asked by the Black Caucus. They got an answer. They were told the problem in stopping narcotrafficking in Haiti is that the Haitian military, who we worked with and still work with, don't have radar. So they can't pick up the planes and boats. And of course the U.S. Navy and Air Force, because of these terrible Pentagon budget cuts, can't figure out a way to remedy this deficiency. So therefore what can we do? We'd like to stop it but we can't.

All this is going on. The end result is perfectly predictable and has been predictable from the beginning. For example, it was predictable when Warren Christopher, the secretary of state, had his confirmation hearings. The incoming liberal Democrats asked him (if you looked at the small print), What do you think about Haiti? He said, We think that President Aristide definitely has a place in the final settlement, but we haven't quite determined yet what that place is. With that ringing endorsement of democracy, the Clinton administration took it over and has succeeded in harshening the policies of the Bush administration, which Christopher attacked, including what I've just described. The end result is, of course, that the government is to be "broadened" to include the "moderates" of the kind that I've described. Aristide either doesn't get back at all, or maybe he gets back and has a kind of symbolic presence, which means that the population has a symbolic presence.

Meanwhile, the population is terrorized and intimidated. A year ago, when the Americas Watch report came out, they pointed out, already at the beginning of the Clinton term, that if this goes on, it won't matter much whether Aristide gets back or not. The popular organizations will have been decimated. People will be intimidated and terrified. Then you can even run a vote, like the way we're doing in El Salvador. And then you'll be fine. If you intimidate and demoralize people enough, if you crush them, if you eliminate any hope, make it clear to them that if they get out of line they're going to be slaughtered, then you can even run an election. Then you'll get Anthony Lewis to talk about this "romantic era," like Thomas Jefferson, as he did after we succeeded in doing precisely that in Nicaragua. That's called "democracy," and we're now watching it play out before our eyes in the case of Haiti.

That formula that Carothers described is it. If after sufficient terror, intimidation, destruction of popular organizations, and so on, you can ensure that power stays in the hands of the right power groups, the ones linked up to U.S. corporations and banking institutions and the others who basically run this society, then that's democracy and everybody's happy and we praise ourselves for our glory. As I say, the same thing's going on in El Salvador right now. We saw it in Nicaragua, and we're going to see it again. It has nothing to do with the cold war, zero. That was just a pretext for things that happened before and continue without change since.

So what are the prospects for democracy? Again, that depends on what we mean by "democracy." If we mean what Thomas Jefferson hoped for, then the prospects are gloomy and declining significantly. If we mean the official theory that's been taken over, that has in fact taken over our increasingly impoverished and authoritarian intellectual culture, then the prospects are just as grand as we're told every day by respectable authorities who sing odes to the new world order for which *we* (meaning *they*) are the gatekeepers and the model.

That, of course, is not the whole story. The real prospects for authentic democracy depend on something else. They depend on how the people in the rich and privileged societies learn some other lessons, for example, the lessons that are being taught right now by Mayans in Chiapas, Mexico, who are among the most impoverished, oppressed sectors on the continent, but unlike us they retain a vibrant tradition of liberty and democracy, a tradition that we have allowed to slip out of our hands or simply be stolen from us. Unless people here and in the other rich and privileged societies can recapture and revitalize that tradition, the prospects for democracy are indeed dim.

Part i

The educational institutions

Chapter 16

Some thoughts on intellectuals and the schools (June 1966)

In happier times, I would have liked to approach this topic in a rather technical and professional way, asking how students might best be exposed to the leading ideas and the most stimulating and penetrating thought in the fields that particularly interest me, how they might be helped to experience the pleasures of discovery and of deepening insight and given an opportunity to make their own individual contribution to contemporary culture. At this particular historical moment, however, there are other, more pressing matters.

[The schools, civilization, and justice]

As I write, the radio is bringing the first reports of the bombings of Hanoi and Haiphong. In itself, this is no atrocity by contemporary standards—surely no atrocity, for example, compared with the American assault on the rural population of South Vietnam for the past year. But the symbolism of this act casts its shadow over any critique of American institutions. When the bombings of North Vietnam began, Jean Lacouture commented aptly that these acts, and the documents produced to justify them, simply reveal that the American leaders regard themselves as having the right to strike where and when they wish. They reveal, in short, that these leaders regard the world as an American preserve, to be governed and organized in accordance with superior American wisdom, and to be controlled, if necessary, by American power. At this moment of national disgrace, as American technology is running amuck in Southeast Asia, a discussion of American schools can hardly avoid noting the fact that these schools are the first training ground for the troops that will enforce the muted, unending terror of the status quo in the coming years of a projected American century; for the technicians who will be developing the means for extension of American power; for the intellectuals who can be counted on, in significant measure, to provide the ideological justification for this particular form of barbarism and to decry the irresponsibility and lack of sophistication of those who will find all of this intolerable and revolting.

Thirty years ago, Franz Borkenau concluded a brilliant study of the crushing of the popular revolution in Spain with this comment:

> In this tremendous contrast with previous revolutions one fact is reflected. Before these latter years, counter-revolution usually depended upon the support of reactionary powers, which were technically and intellectually inferior to the forces of revolution. This has changed with the advent of fascism. Now, every revolution is likely to meet the attack of the most modern, most efficient, most ruthless machinery yet in existence. It means that the age of revolutions free to evolve according to their own laws is over.[1]

It would have taken a fair amount of foresight, at that time, to realize that the prediction would be proven accurate with the substitution of "liberal imperialism" for "fascism," and that the United States would, in a generation, be employing the most efficient and most ruthless machinery in existence to ensure that revolutionary movements will not evolve according to their own laws, to guarantee that its own particular concept of civilization and justice and order will prevail. And it would have required considerable insight, in the late 1930s, to realize that before too long a reformist American administration with a "welfare state" domestic orientation would be doing its utmost to prove the correctness of Marx's grim observation about this concept of civilization and justice and order:

> The civilization and justice of bourgeois order comes out in its lurid light whenever the slaves and drudges of that order rise against their masters; then this civilization and justice stand forth as undisguised savagery and lawless revenge.

It is conceivable that American actions in Vietnam are simply a single outburst of criminal insanity, of no general or long-range significance except to the miserable inhabitants of that tortured land. It is difficult, however, to put much credence in this possibility. In half a dozen Latin American countries there are guerrilla movements that are approaching the level of the second Vietnamese war, and the American reaction is, apparently, comparable. That is, American arms are used to attack guerrilla forces and to "dry up the sea in which they swim," in the Maoist terminology affected by the military; and American "advisers" guide and train the troops, which, as Latin American liberals observe, are needed only to occupy their own country in the interests of domestic ruling classes and American capital.

In these countries it has not yet become necessary, as in Vietnam, to convert the fact of communist involvement into the myth of communist aggression in justification of open United States control of the counterrevolutionary forces, nor has the time yet arrived for application of the full arsenal of terror in support of the regime selected as most favorable to American interests. But it seems that this next step is fully expected. In *Le Nouvel Observateur*, the peasant organizer Francisco Julião was recently quoted as certain of United States intervention when rebellion breaks out in the Brazilian northeast provinces. Others, less well known, have expressed themselves similarly. There is little basis, in history or logic, for supposing them to be wrong—little basis, that is, apart from the kind of sentimentality that sees the United States, alone among nations, as a selfless (if rather oafish) public benefactor, devoted only to projects of "international goodwill," though frequently blundering in an excess of warmhearted generosity. One should, no doubt, take seriously the insistence of administration spokesmen that one purpose of the present violence is to prove that wars of national liberation cannot succeed— to demonstrate, that is, in the clearest and most explicit terms, that any revolutionary movement that we—unilaterally, as in Vietnam—designate as illegitimate will face the most efficient and ruthless machinery that can be developed by modern technology.

In minor ways, world opinion can serve as some kind of brake on full-scale utilization of the technology of terror and destruction. There has, as yet, been no use of nuclear weapons in Vietnam, and although rural populations are considered fair game for any sort of military attack, urban areas, where the butchery would be more evident to the outside world, are still relatively immune. Similarly, the use of gas attacks and chemical warfare has been extended only slowly, as habituation permits each gradual increment to pass unnoticed.[2] But ultimately, the only effective brake can be popular revulsion on a mass scale in the United States itself. Consequently, the level of culture that can be achieved in the United States is a life-and-death matter for large masses of suffering humanity. This too is a fact that must color any discussion of contemporary American institutions.

[A program of intellectual self-defense]
It is easy to be carried away by the sheer horror of what the daily press reveals and to lose sight of the fact that this is merely the brutal exterior of a deeper crime, of commitment to a social order that guarantees endless suffering and humiliation and denial of elementary human rights. It is tragic that the United States should have become, in Toynbee's words, "the leader of a

world-wide anti-revolutionary movement in defense of vested interests." For American intellectuals and for the schools there is no more vital issue than this indescribable tragedy.

No one would seriously propose that the schools attempt to deal directly with such contemporary events as the American attack on the rural population of Vietnam or the backgrounds in recent history for the atrocities that are detailed in the mass media. No sane person would have expected the schools in France, for example, to explore the character of and justification for the Algerian war, or the schools in Russia to have dealt honestly with the crushing of the Hungarian revolution, or the schools in Italy to have analyzed the invasion of Ethiopia in an objective way, or the schools in England to have exposed the contemporary suppression of Irish nationalism. But it is perhaps not ridiculous to propose that the schools might direct themselves to something more abstract, to an attempt to offer students some means for defending themselves from the onslaught of the massive government propaganda apparatus, from the natural bias of the mass media, and—to turn specifically to our present topic—from the equally natural tendency of significant segments of the American intellectual community to offer their allegiance not to truth and justice but to power and the effective exercise of power.

It is frightening to observe the comparative indifference of American intellectuals to the immediate actions of their government and its long-range policies, and their frequent willingness—often eagerness—to play a role in implementing these policies. This is not the place to illustrate in detail; in any event, I do not command the rhetoric to speak, in the only accurate and appropriate terms, of the actual conduct of the war and the way it has been tolerated at home. But more superficial examples make the point well enough.

Only marginal groups of American academics have reacted to the fact that while the United States stands in the way of the only sort of meaningful negotiations, namely, negotiations among indigenous South Vietnamese political forces to the exclusion of the foreign invaders from the United States and Korea, and (on a vastly different scale) from North Vietnam, it nevertheless is able to persist in its pretense of interest in a "negotiated settlement" with no outcry of protest against this farce. When Secretary Rusk openly admits that we cannot accept the North Vietnamese proposals of April 1965 because they require that the Saigon government be supplanted by a broad, national democratic coalition representing existing political forces in the country, there is no public denunciation of the cynicism of the position he upholds. When the press reports that the electoral law commission in South

Vietnam faces the "awesome task" of running "honest elections" while making sure that the communists do not win and that no communists or "neutralists whose actions are advantageous to the communists" appear on the ballot, there is little editorial comment, few letters to the editor, no general dismay.

There is little point in multiplying examples. One can only be appalled at the willingness of American intellectuals, who, after all, have access to the facts, to tolerate or even approve of this deceitfulness and hypocrisy. Instead of shocked denunciations, we hear and read mock-serious discussions of the rationality of the American attempt to drive the North Vietnamese by force toward the negotiations that they had been demanding; of the sincere American desire to permit the South Vietnamese people to elect freely the government of their choice (now that the domestic opposition has been crushed and all communist and neutralist candidates excluded); of the "great complexity" of international affairs (which, strangely, did not seem to justify Russian domination of Eastern Europe or the Japanese attempt to impose a new order in Asia); of the judicious restraint of the administration, presumably, in refraining from genocide at a single stroke; and so on. Or, what is worse, we read of the "bedrock vital interest of the United States" in demonstrating that its military power, once committed for whatever reason, cannot be forced to withdraw—a viewpoint which, had it been accepted by the world's second superpower as well, would have brought the history of Western civilization to a close in 1962, and which, if consistently pursued, must lead either to a Pax Americana or to a devastating world conflict.

Traditionally, the role of the intellectual, or at least his self-image, has been that of a dispassionate critic. Insofar as that role has been lost, the relation of the schools to intellectuals should, in fact, be one of self-defense. This is a matter that should be seriously considered. It is, to be sure, ridiculous to propose that the schools, in any country, deal objectively with contemporary history—they cannot sufficiently free themselves from the pressures of ideology for that. But it is not necessarily absurd to suppose that in Western democracies, at least, it should be possible to study in a fairly objective way the national scandals of the past. It might be possible in the United States to study, let us say, the American occupation of the Philippines, leaving implicit its message for the present.

[A central part of any civilized curriculum]
Suppose that high school students were exposed to the best of current American scholarship, for example, George Taylor's recent study for the

Council on Foreign Relations, *The Philippines and the United States*. Here they would learn how, half a century after the bloody suppression of the native independence movement at a cost of well over 100,000 lives, the country achieved nominal independence and the surface forms of democracy. They would also learn that the United States is guaranteed long-term military bases and unparalleled economic privileges; that for three-fourths of the population, living standards have not risen since the Spanish occupation; that 70 percent of the population is estimated to have tuberculosis; that profits flowing to the United States have exceeded new investment in each postwar year; that the democratic forms give a new legitimacy to an old elite, allied now to American interests. They would read that "colonial policy had tended to consolidate the power of an oligarchy that profited . . . from the free trade relationship and would be likely to respect, after independence, the rights and privileges of Americans"; that economically, "the contrast between the small upper class and the rest of the population . . . [is] one of the most extreme in Asia"; that the consequences of American colonial policy were "that little was done to improve the lot of the average Filipino and that the Philippine economy was tied to the American to the advantage of the few"; and so on. They would then read the book's final recommendation, that we go on with our good work: "In spite of our many shortcomings, the record shows that we are more than equal to the task." It is at least possible that to a young mind, still uncontaminated by cant and sophistry, such a study can teach a revealing lesson, not only about what American dominance is likely to mean, concretely, in the Third World, but also about the way in which American intellectuals are likely to interpret this impact.

In general, the history of imperialism and of imperialist apologia, particularly as seen from the point of view of those at the wrong end of the guns, should be a central part of any civilized curriculum. But there are other aspects to a program of intellectual self-defense that should not be overlooked. It is inevitable, in an age of science and technology, that their prestige will be employed as an ideological instrument—specifically, that the social and behavioral sciences will, in various ways, be made to serve in defense of national policy or as a mask for special interest.

It is not merely that intellectuals are strongly tempted, in a society that offers them prestige and affluence, to take what is now called a "pragmatic attitude" (in a perverse sense of pragmatism which is, sad to say, not without some historical justification, as shown in the Dewey-Bourne interchange during the First World War), that is, an attitude that one must accept, not critically analyze or struggle to change, the existing distribution of power, domestic or international, and the political realities that flow from it, and must work only for slow measures of improvement in a technological, piecemeal manner. It is not merely that having taken this position (conceivably, with some justification, at a particular historical moment), one is strongly tempted to provide it with an ideological justification of a very general sort. Rather, what we must also expect is that political elites will use the terminology of the social and behavioral sciences to protect their actions from critical analysis—the nonspecialist does not, after all, presume to tell physicists and engineers how to build an atomic reactor. And for any particular action, experts can certainly be found in the universities who will solemnly testify as to its appropriateness and realism. This is not a matter of speculation; thus we already find, in congressional testimony, the proposal by a leading political scientist that we try to impose mass starvation on a quarter of the human race if their government does not accept our dictates. And it is commonly argued that the free-floating intellectual of the past has no business questioning the conclusions of the professional expert, equipped with the tools of modern science.

This situation again carries a lesson for the schools, one to which teachers, in particular, should be quite sensitive, bombarded as they have been in recent years by authoritative conclusions about what has been "demonstrated" with regard to human learning, language, and so on. The social and behavioral sciences should be seriously studied not only for their intrinsic interest (their contribution, though meager, is not without value), but also so that the student can be made quite aware of exactly how little they have to say about the problems of man and society that really matter. They should, furthermore, be studied in the context of the physical sciences, so that the student can be brought to appreciate clearly the limits of their intellectual content. This can be an important way to protect a student from the propaganda of the future, and to put him in a position to comprehend the true nature of the means that are sure to be used to conceal the real significance of domestic or international policy.

[Level of culture as a life-and-death matter]

Suppose, however, that contrary to all present indications, the United States will stop short of using its awesome resources of violence and devastation to impose its passionately held ideology and its approved form of social organization on large areas of the world. Suppose, that is, that American policy ceases to be dominated by the principles that were crudely outlined by President Truman almost twenty years ago when he observed in a famous and important speech that "all freedom is dependent on freedom of enterprise," that "the whole world should adopt the American system," that "the American system can survive in America only if it becomes a world system." It would, nevertheless, remain true that the level of culture that can be achieved in the United States is a matter of overwhelming importance for the rest of the world.

If we want to be truly utopian, we may consider the possibility that American capital resources might be used to alleviate the terrorism that seems to be an inevitable correlate of modernization, if we can judge from past and present history. We can conceive of the possibility that the schools, or the intellectuals, might pay serious attention to questions that have been posed for centuries, that they might ask whether society must, indeed, be a Hobbesian *bellum omnium contra omnes*, and might inquire into the contemporary meaning of Rousseau's protest that it is contrary to natural right that "a handful of men be glutted with superfluities while the starving multitude lacks necessities." They might raise the moral issue faced, or avoided, by one who enjoys his wealth and privilege undisturbed by the knowledge that half of the children born in Nicaragua will not reach five years of age, or that only a few miles away there is unspeakable poverty, brutal suppression of human rights, and almost no hope for the future; and they might raise the intellectual issue of how this can be changed. They might ask, with Keynes, how long we must continue to "exalt some of the most distasteful of human qualities into the position of the highest virtues," setting up "avarice and usury and precaution . . . [as] our gods," and pretending to ourselves that "fair is foul and foul is fair, for foul is useful and fair is not."

If American intellectuals will be preoccupied with such questions as these, they can have an invaluable civilizing influence on society and on the schools. If, as is more likely, they regard them with disdain as mere sentimental nonsense, then our children will have to look elsewhere for enlightenment and guidance.

APPENDIX
On staying informed and intellectual self-defense (March 1999)

There's no way to be informed without devoting effort to the task, whether we have in mind what's happening in the world, physics, major league baseball, or anything else. Understanding doesn't come free. It's true that the task is somewhere between awfully difficult and utterly hopeless for an isolated individual. But it's feasible for anyone who is part of a cooperative community—and that's true about all of the other cases too. Same holds for "intellectual self-defense." It takes a lot of self-confidence—perhaps more self-confidence than one ought to have—to take a position alone because it seems to you right, in opposition to everything you see and hear. There's even evidence about this: under experimental conditions people deny what they know to be true when they are informed that others they have reason to trust are doing so (Solomon Asch's classic experiments in social psychology, which were often held to show that people are conformist and irrational, but can be understood differently, to indicate that people are quite reasonable and use all the information at hand).

More important than any of this is that a community—an organization—can be a basis for action, and while understanding the world may be good for the soul (not meant to be disparaging), it doesn't help anyone else, or oneself very much either for that matter, unless it leads to action. There are also many techniques for penetrating the veil of propaganda that should become second nature in dealing with the output of doctrinal institutions (media, journals of opinion, scholarship). For example, it is quite common for the basic framework of an article or news report to be hopelessly misleading, conforming to doctrinal requirements. But within it one can often discover hints that something else is going on. I often recommend reading the mainstream press beginning with the final paragraphs. That's no joke. The headline, the framing, the initial paragraphs, are designed (consciously—you learn these things in journalism school) to give the general picture and the whole story for almost all readers, who aren't going to take the trouble to look at the small print, to think much about it, and to compare it with yesterday's tales. One discovers this all the time.

To illustrate, I happen to have just read Sunday's *New York Times* [March 14, 1999]. There's an interesting article in the Week in Review section by Ralph Blumenthal called "Comparing the Unspeakable to the Unthinkable." It summarizes his long article (with Judith Miller) on March 4 concerning Japan's horrendous World War II record of biological warfare, both experimentation and use—quite comparable to Mengele, as the articles correctly points out. They discuss the horrifying Unit 731 and General Ishii, who ran it. The framework is "How could such evil exist?" "Japan rebuffs requests for information," "How could the Japanese be so awful?" et cetera, a familiar and useful genre, which I've often discussed, comparing it with self-examination, a useful and revealing exercise.

The original article condemns Japan for refusing inquiries from the U.S. Justice Department, which is seeking to expose these terrible crimes, and to bar suspected (Japanese) participants from entering the United States.

A careful reader, who has been following all of this for years, will notice hints about something else, carefully sanitized in the article and review, and properly hidden. Here are a few examples, keeping mostly to today's summary article.

The article states that "in the early 1980s, American and British scholars and journalists rediscovered the germ war issue, adding new details of American involvement in covering up the crimes." Shows how wonderful and fearless "American and British scholars and journalists" are. The truth, as Blumenthal can hardly fail to know, is that the U.S. government (and mainstream scholars and journalists) were *not* covering the story (and arguably, covering it up), including the nature and extent of U.S. involvement—and that he and his colleagues are continuing along that path. The facts were revealed not "in the early 1980s" by "American and British scholars and journalists," but in October-December 1980, in the *Bulletin of Concerned Asian Scholars*. That is one of the journals that grew out of sixties dissidence and critique of mainstream scholarship and ideology, and this article is one example of its success in exposing material that the mainstream—surely the *New York Times*—wanted hidden. The author of that article, who provided extensive detail, was John Powell, who had been hounded by congressional committees, denied employment, indicted for sedition, his China journal closed, et cetera. This is highly relevant to the Blumenthal/Miller stories, but to tell the truth, which they surely know, would not help create the proper image of adulation of our free institutions and the courage and integrity of their leaders and participants.

The *Times* article states that the "delay" in recognizing Japanese war crimes "illustrates the West's Eurocentric view of wartime suffering as well as striking differences in the willingness of the two former Axis allies to come to terms with their past," and throws a "harsh light on cold-war rivalries." The "delay" in fact illustrates something radically different: it resulted from the fact that the U.S. took over the whole hideous operation and protected the Mengeles who it now claims to be so eager to reveal, and used their work as the basis for the huge U.S. biological and bacteriological warfare program. By 1949 the Joint Chiefs had incorporated the results into first-strike plans, and that was given official authorization in 1956.

As for the lame reference to the cold war, that's a standard—virtually reflexive—device for covering up past crimes; it's being invoked right now in the case of Central America, in ways that are as cowardly as they are shameful. One should always look more closely when the ritual phrase "cold war" is invoked. But crucially, the delay has little to do with what is mentioned, and a great deal to do with what is *very* conveniently ignored.

The *Times* article states that Soviet trials of Japanese for biological war crimes were "largely ignored or dismissed in the West as Communist propaganda" and that the United States prosecuted no one for these crimes. True, and a true picture of the *New York Times,* for example (as might have been pointed out in an honest report), but far from the whole story. The Soviet trials of Japanese Mengeles were ridiculed as part of the need to cover up the protection the United States was offering them and its takeover of their criminal activities. One finds a hint of what the *Times* knows full well in the phrase, toward the end, that the U.S. was able to "snare General Ishii's data." The fuller story is as just indicated.

And that's only a small part of it. As the *Times* can hardly fail to know, a year ago [1998] Indiana University Press published a scholarly study of all of these matters, based on newly available Chinese and U.S. archives (Endicott and Hagerman, *The US and Biological Warfare*). The story goes far beyond what I've just mentioned, which is bad enough. The *Times* article refers to new evidence from Chinese researchers about the victims of Japanese biological/bacteriological warfare. True, but as the *Times* also must know, and Endicott and Hagerman document, these Chinese researchers are also bringing out evidence about the victims of *U.S.* use of what it learned from Ishii and Unit 731, in North Korea and China in the early fifties. Furthermore, what's appearing in Chinese documents and by Chinese researchers has disturbing correlations with information from U.S. archives, as Endicott and Hagerman discuss. In the past, I'd always dismissed charges of U.S. bacteriological/biological warfare in North Korea/China. It's less easy now. In fact, this is one of the few nontrivial revelations coming out from newly released communist archives and research, a fact that also merits headlines. The charges are not proven, but they surely merit a much closer examination and can no longer simply be dismissed as communist propaganda (as I'd done myself, in fact).

The *Times* articles do cite scholarly research but studiously omit what they know to be the most recent and most important study, the only one to use recently available Chinese archives and Chinese research as well as newly declassified U.S. archives. It would take remarkable incompetence to have investigated this topic and to have "failed to discover" the most important and most recent scholarly work, not to speak of the original breakthrough, unmentionable for reasons that are not hard to guess.

The true story, surely known to those who are presenting it, continues along these lines. An honest report would not only have emphasized all of this instead of concealing hints here and there and telling a very different tale up front. It would also have drawn the obvious implications concerning current matters: for example, U.S. fulmination about the dangers of "weapons of mass destruction"—a category that does not exist, according to official U.S. policy from the early postwar period, perhaps still operative—and the horrors of biological/bacteriological weapons and their potential use by terrorists and rogue states. Very much on the front pages, and surely worth discussing—including its origins in Unit 731, the U.S. takeover and development of all of this (including possible experimentation in the field), and the way the whole story has been handled and is being handled.

And will be handled. It's likely that someday the *Times* will run a long article on all of this, after it has had time to frame the story the right way. It will be framed by official denials, irrelevant but useful apologetics about the cold war, much ranting on the (inevitable) errors that appear in the scholarly work that has revealed what has long been suppressed, et cetera. (No doubt they are there, but it will be surprising if they amount to a fraction of the revelations about what is considered highly respectable history when it serves doctrinal needs.) There will also be hints scattered around that the careful reader may find, which could lead him to the truth—with considerable effort.

The truth is not only ugly, but highly pertinent and timely. That's the way the story would be framed and presented in a free press, if such existed. With considerable effort, one can discern hints that will lead one to the true picture in the existing press. But it takes effort, and a little familiarity with how these things typically work.

I might add that the *Boston Globe*—a journal that is directed (in part) to the leading figures in the "Athens of America"—has an editorial on the topic, denouncing crimes "so despicable that no statute of limitations should ever be applied to them, and no veil of forgetfulness should be allowed to hide them away from future generations." Even the few hints scattered through the *Times* reports are excised from the editorial, which denounces Tokyo because it "has even refused to give the United States the names of Japanese veterans who belonged to a biological warfare unit." How dare they impede our dedication to reveal every scrap of truth about the Japanese Mengeles—and how they were received by those we are taught to worship.

That's a single example. I could have used have a dozen other examples from the same day's newspapers. I used to write regular articles about these things for a now defunct journal called *Lies of Our Times*—I presume it wasn't called *Lies of the Times* because of fear of libel suits. Many of them are collected in a book called *Letters from Lexington* (Common Courage); the title is because they were written informally, as letters. There are far more detailed analyses in print. I think they might give some hints on "intellectual self-defense," but ultimately, it's no different from physics or baseball. If you want to learn something, it'll take work. And the chances of success, or useful success, are greatly magnified by cooperative interchange and effort.

Notes

1. *The Spanish cockpit* (1938; reprint, Ann Arbor: University of Michigan Press, 1963), pp. 288–89.
2. This essay was written in June 1966; it now goes to press again in May 1968. On the use of gas in Vietnam, see Seymour Hersh, "Poison gas in Vietnam," *New York Review of Books*, May 9, 1968. On current plans for chemical warfare, *Science*, May 24, 1968, contains the following note (p. 863):

> Expanded Chemical Warfare: The Air Force has told Congress that it will spend $70.8 million on 10 million gallons of chemicals used for Vietnam defoliation and crop-killing in the fiscal year beginning 1 July, a $24.9 million increase over this year's figure. Next year's expanded efforts are in line with the continuing increase in the U.S. chemical warfare program in Vietnam. In the first 9 months of 1967, 843,606 acres in Vietnam were drenched with defoliants and 121,400 acres with crop-killing chemicals, a figure which slightly exceeded the totals for the whole of 1966.

In its issue of May 10, 1968, *Science* carries a letter by Thomas O. Perry of the Harvard University Press, who comments as follows on chemical warfare (p. 601):

> The DOD [Department of Defense] can raise the red herring of "long-term" effects, but there can be no doubt about the short-term effects: 2,4–D and 2,4,5–T kill the green vegetation. When followed by fire bombs, the dead foliage and twigs burn, as they did on some 100,000 acres (about 40,000 hectares) in the "Iron Triangle" last spring.
>
> Through the simple process of starvation, a land without green foliage will quickly become a land without insects, without birds, without animal life of any form. News photographs and on-the-spot descriptions indicate that some areas have been sprayed repeatedly to assure a complete kill of the vegetation. There can be no doubt that the DOD is, in the short run, going beyond mere genocide to biocide. It commandeered the entire U.S. production of 2,4,5–T for 1967 and 1968 [some 13 to 14 million pounds (6.36 million kilos) according to U.S. Tariff Commission reports]. If one combines this with the other chemicals the DOD concedes it is using, there is a sufficient amount to kill 97 percent of the aboveground vegetation on over 10 million acres of land (about 4 million hectares)—an area so big that it would require over 60 years for a man to walk on each acre.
>
> The long-term effects of spraying such an area may be imponderable, but the short-term effects of using these chemicals are certain: a lot of leaves, trees, rice plants, and other vegetation are dead or dying; and a lot of insects, birds, animals, and a few humans have either migrated or died of starvation. The North Vietnamese are fortunate—they have only bombs to contend with.

Chapter 17

The responsibility of a university community (May 31, 1969)

As the report of the [MIT Commission on MIT Education] Review Panel states at the outset, "the members of the Panel are in substantial agreement with this report except as otherwise indicated in the additional statements attached hereto." In this appended statement, I would like to indicate in what respects, and for what reasons I find myself in disagreement with this report. The nature of these disagreements is such that I cannot sign the report as it stands.

Although I concur in a general way with the short-term recommendations of the Panel, I have various reservations with regard to the general framework of assumptions within which these conclusions were reached. I will try to make clear these differences, in the hope that the work of the Panel will be only the first stage in a continuing review of the problems of technology and society in general and of the way in which the Institute should conceive its "public service" function.

Any act undertaken by MIT in its public service function is a political act and must be considered with great care. Those who develop science and technology have in their hands a powerful instrument of destruction, and a set of tools and techniques for overcoming at least some of the problems of contemporary society. They cannot ultimately control the social use of knowledge, but they also cannot remain blind to the question of how their contributions are likely to be put to use, under given social conditions. It is possible, of course, to adopt uncritically the concept of "national interest" and "public service" that is defined by those in a position to allocate funds and determine public policy. To do so is, in effect, to make a particular political judgment, namely, to support the existing structure of power and privilege and the particular ideological framework that is associated with it. This decision may or may not be correct. It must be recognized clearly, however, that it is a political decision, and must not be disguised by the pretense that it is no political decision at all, but simply the non-ideological, value-free pursuit of knowledge for its own sake.

In an institution largely devoted to science and technology, we do not enjoy the luxury of refusing to take a stand on the essentially political question of how science and technology will be put to use, and we have a responsibility to take our stand with consideration and care. Those who find this burden intolerable are simply complaining of the difficulties of a civilized life. To exercise this responsibility, scientists must continually make political and historical judgments. This is true of the work of an individual. It is far more important when the university makes an institutional commitment to the support or organization of research. Such commitments must involve careful and dispassionate deliberation on the part of the university community as a whole, for two reasons: first, so that the decision itself will be a thoughtful and considered one, and second, so that the members of the university community will rise to the level of citizens in the true sense, that is, men who are conscious of their responsibilities and prepared to exercise them. This is true of every person in a democratic society, but is particularly important in the case of scientists and engineers, because the social consequences of their acts are potentially so great.

The point is not academic. In the specific cases of weapons research and development, it is clear that there are, in our society, powerful and convergent forces that are impelling us onward to an endless and potentially suicidal arms race. Furthermore, quite apart from the shameful waste of resources, the technology that is developed is in fact put to use for the specific ends of those who set national policy. To mention just two cases discussed in the report of the Panel, the MIT project was initiated by the DOD [Department of Defense] for the purpose of counterinsurgency and has been used in Vietnam to further American war aims; and the VTOL [Vertical Take-Off/Landing (vehicles)] project, if successful, will undoubtedly be used for repressing domestic insurgency in countries subject to our influence or control. Indeed, it is fair to suppose that this will be the primary result of the project. There are in our society few countervailing forces that may inhibit or reverse the arms race or the use of technology for repression of popular movements. One such force, potentially at least, is the organized community of scientists. They may refuse to act as a countervailing force—a civilizing force, in my opinion. They may choose, instead, to add their independent contribution to waste, destruction, and repression. They may do this after having decided, consciously and explicitly, that this is the part they wish to play, or they may make this political decision thoughtlessly through passive acquiescence in policies determined elsewhere. They are not free, however, simply to avoid the problem.

The commitment to weapons research can be justified only in terms of specific views concerning modern history and the international role of the United States. We must not merely drift into tacit acceptance of this framework of assumptions. Rather, it must be a matter of intensive and continuing inquiry. In my personal opinion, a serious inquiry will show these conceptions to be indefensible, and will lead to the conclusion that military work should be drastically scaled down, not only in the university but in government laboratories and industry as well. However this may be, what is clear and beyond doubt is that any decision taken in this regard will express controversial political and historical judgments. There is no way to avoid this dilemma.

[The major contribution of a university to a free society]

The major contribution that a university can make to a free society is by preserving its independence as an institution committed to the free exchange of ideas, to critical analysis, to experimentation, to exploration of a wide range of ideas and values, to the study of the consequences of social action or scientific progress and the evaluation of these consequences in terms of values that are themselves subject to careful scrutiny. The university betrays its public trust—in Senator Fulbright's apt phrase—if it merely adopts and limits itself to policy determined elsewhere, on whatever grounds. Academic freedom is violated, not ensured, when the university merely bends to the will of outside forces and, in effect, ratifies the existing distribution of power in the society by simply meeting the demands that are articulated by the institutions that are in a position both to articulate their needs and to support the work that answers to them. This point cannot be emphasized too strongly. The idea that a university preserves its neutrality and remains "value-free" when it simply responds to requests that originate from without is an absurdity.

In the light of these general remarks, I would like to turn to the question of the special laboratories and the Panel Report. Although individuals may indeed be quite free when they work in the laboratories, there is, nevertheless, an essentially political criterion for association with them. This subpart of the university community is restricted to participants who share a particular political ideology, and in this way, the laboratories contribute to a dangerous and unwelcome politicization of the university. The constraint is a necessary consequence of the requirement that one can be associated with the special laboratories only if his work can be funded by particular government agencies, primarily the DOD, and the fact that one can work comfortably in the laboratory only if he is willing to undergo clearance procedures. Obviously, it is going to be difficult to avoid this kind of politicization, but we should, I believe, recognize its drastic character and express our principled opposition to it, our determination to struggle incessantly against it. The concept of a political criterion for association is intolerable for a university.

I do not think that the Panel Report deals adequately with the general problems raised above. It asserts, correctly, that the university should preserve "a commitment to the concept of academic freedom and free exchange of ideas, jealously protected from inhibiting restriction." It does not, however, stress the inevitable conclusion that the special laboratories are presently organized in such a way as to violate this commitment. The statement that work on "important defense-related problems" is quite appropriate for the university expresses a political judgment that I do not personally share, but that, in any event, was taken without sufficient consideration of the political and historical issues that are relevant to this judgment. The statement that a "significant reduction in defense work . . . might be undesirable from the standpoints of both the Department of Defense and the laboratory staff engaged in defense projects" might be read as implying that such a reduction would be unwarranted and improper.

I wish to dissociate myself from any such conclusion. Such a reduction would, I believe, be highly desirable; it would increase the probability that civilization will survive, and would contribute to freedom by diminishing our capacities for aggression, as in Vietnam. The willingness to tolerate "classification of project descriptions," even if "severely limited," also seems to me unacceptable, since as the report states, "this practice prevents the MIT community as a whole from knowing even the nature of some of MIT's activities," and since it is a fair assumption that such work is directed toward military ends that would, indeed, be intolerable to at least part of the Institute community were these ends known.

Still more seriously in error, in my opinion, is the statement with regard to "collective judgments on military and strategic policy," namely, that "such judgments are inappropriate for any official group at the Institute to make," including, by implication, the group empowered to review projects to which the Institute commits its resources. I think that the statement is false; that is, such judgments are entirely appropriate, indeed, inescapable. In fact, the statement is inconsistent with the thesis expressed in the Panel Report that war-related research (some of a sort that will remain unknown to the Institute community) is desirable and appropriate. Acceptance of such research implies support for particular judgments on military and strategic policy, for reasons already noted. Hence this statement is false in itself and inconsistent with the body of the report.

[Guidelines for (socially useful) technology]

I agree with the conclusion of the Panel that we should not sever the connection with the special laboratories but should, rather, attempt to assist them in directing their efforts to "socially useful technology" and away from war-related research. At the same time, I feel that we should try to establish certain guidelines for the work that the laboratories undertake, recognizing that these guidelines cannot be very precise and that they will change through time and with circumstances.

In my opinion, the special laboratories should not be involved in any work that contributes to offensive military action. They should not be involved in any form of counterinsurgency operations, whether in the hard or soft sciences. They should not contribute to unilateral escalation of the arms race. They should not be involved in the actual development of weapons systems. They should be restricted to research on systems of a purely defensive and deterrent character. Such guidelines as these must take into account not only the intrinsic character of the technology that is being studied and developed but also the political context in which the technology will be put to use.

The decision as to whether a technical capability, or even a specific weapon, is offensive or defensive in nature is a historical as well as a technical decision, and must be clearly recognized as such. These are delicate and uncertain judgments, but they cannot be avoided. They must be made seriously, and as explicitly as possible. As I understand these recommendations, they would, under present circumstances, rule out not only CBW but also development of MIRV [Multiple Independently Targetable Reentry Vehicles], and steps toward deployment of ABM [antiballistic missile system] and similar systems.

We should positively encourage the kind of research that leads toward arms control and de-escalation of the arms race. We should immediately abandon all work relating to counterinsurgency, including social science research that is likely to be used, primarily, for repression of popular movements and interference in the internal affairs of other nations, and perhaps for domestic repression as well. Evaluation of such projects, in these terms, seems to me an obligation for a responsible community of scientists. This, incidentally, is a recommendation that relates to the Institute as a whole, not merely the special laboratories. I think we should propose an immediate moratorium on MIRV and should urge that arms control negotiations be undertaken forthwith, on a large scale, and with great seriousness.

We must, furthermore, establish a procedure by which guidelines for research are administered. The ultimate responsibility for work that receives institutional support lies in the hands of the faculty, the staff, and the student body. The matter of research of an institutional character should be handled in the way that academic affairs are handled. A new department or program can be initiated only with faculty authorization. This is as it should be, and the same principle should be extended to research that exceeds a certain scale. An individual should be free to do what he wants (though even here there are limits—no principles that I can imagine are absolute). But a research project that exceeds a certain size should be subject to review in terms of the loose guidelines that we set, guidelines that should themselves be subject to review.

This review should be carried out by a student-faculty-staff committee which is elected by the faculty, the staff, and the student body, and is directly responsive to them. The committee should report back to the bodies that it represents, and should see its function as dual: first, ensuring that the work that is carried out with Institute authorization and support meets the loose guidelines that have been established; second, educating the Institute community by bringing relevant information to it and encouraging discussion and debate of the underlying issues, which—I repeat—are far too important to be left to the casual procedures that may have seemed adequate in the past. I think that the faculty should have the dominant role in this committee. I would expect that it would rarely exercise its authority, since the usual informal measures of mutual adaptation should, for the most part, suffice. But it should have a very visible "presence" and should, as a matter of course, review all contracts that exceed a certain size—perhaps about $50,000 a year might be a reasonable minimum. The committee should also seek to engage itself in the educational role just mentioned with diligence and care.

[The university and national goals]

In this respect, too, I find my views somewhat at variance with those of the Panel, which recommended that such a committee should have only an advisory capacity, residual authority resting with the administration. Let me make clear that my dissatisfaction with this plan does not result from any lack of confidence in the administration. On the contrary, to be quite frank, I would not be much surprised to discover that decisions taken by the administration would often be more in accord with my personal hopes and wishes than those taken by such a committee. But I think that it is improper procedure for this authority to rest in the hands of any group other than the Institute community as a whole—the faculty, the students, and the staff—for reasons already mentioned: the general requirements of democratic procedure, and the beneficial effect, on the Institute community as a whole, of the demand that it face these problems, both technical and political-historical, in a serious way. I do not find the reasoning of the Panel convincing in this regard.

The strongest argument that I have heard for maintaining Lincoln Laboratories in roughly its present form is that it provides objective and independent evaluation of weapons systems. I remain skeptical about this. Although I do not doubt the integrity or competence of the laboratory staff, nevertheless the fact remains that they represent a limited range of opinion. Furthermore, evaluation cannot be dissociated from political-historical judgments, and I do not feel that these are adequately represented, for reasons already mentioned. What is more, I find it hard to believe that the evaluation is not constrained by the total financial dependence of the laboratory on the DOD. A much more constructive and useful evaluation could be given if the labs were free from the constraint of security clearance and reliance on the executive branch, specifically, the DOD.

The suggestion was made, in testimony before the Panel, that the laboratory should be responsible to Congress and funded independently of the DOD. Perhaps Congress might be receptive to such a suggestion. It would be quite important for Congress, and the public at large, to have its own independent source of technical information, and its independent facilities for research and evaluation. Furthermore, the university can provide a truly objective and broad-ranging service in the evaluation of weapons systems—and, more generally, national goals and the political context in which weapons systems are developed—if it is free from the constraints now imposed. This seems to me an important matter. These are goals that cannot be realized immediately. But I think that a firm statement of principle and intent, on our part, coupled with specific measures to realize this intent, might have a useful effect on public opinion and on Congress.

[A primary task for the university]

We must emphasize that the role of the university in evaluation is not limited to providing technical information and advice. For example, in the case of the ABM or the MIRV systems, the university should not only provide information as to whether it will work, what its effects will be on arms control negotiations, and so on, but should also attempt to provide the best possible analysis of the political and historical context in which these programs are proposed.

It has been charged, for example, that the ABM is motivated more by the needs of the electronics industry and aerospace for a continuing public subsidy—in part to counteract the technologically regressive impact of the Vietnam War on government spending—than by any military or strategic objectives (objectives which, in any event, I do not think acceptable). Whether or not this is correct, it is clearly a relevant question to be raised in evaluating these systems.

A primary task for the university is the study of decision making in American society and the international role of the United States. Obviously, we cannot expect much agreement about this. But we should not contribute to the illusion that the government merely expresses the national will, independently formulated, and that it simply uses the best technical advice to achieve objectives determined by an informed citizenry. This is a caricature, and a dangerous one. We must emphasize that political and historical judgments are critical even in what appear to be technical matters, that there are no experts qualified to deal with these general issues, and that public policy is a reflection, to a very significant extent, of economic power that is entirely removed from the democratic process. The university must not become a party to a perversion of democratic ideals or to the perpetuation of social myths. Its function, in a free society, is to act in independence of powerful social institutions, and the ideology they seek to impose, to the fullest degree that it can. Again, this is an ideal that may not be fully realizable, but we must be constantly struggling to achieve it.

I would like finally to express my personal appreciation to the students in SACC [Science Action Coordinating Committee] for their serious and conscientious efforts over the past few months, efforts which led directly to the formation of the Panel and the review of policy it has conducted. The Institute as a whole owes them a debt of gratitude.

Chapter 18

Remarks before the MIT Commission on MIT Education (November 11, 1969)

I want to talk about some of the problems that I think MIT and other universities are probably going to face with increasing severity over the next couple of years. These problems are related, I think, to some very critical problems within our society. This view comes from a certain judgment about the nature of the problems of American society in the coming years and the way in which they will be reflected in and reflect upon the university.

My own feeling is that American society is headed for a very severe social crisis that's implicit in a sort of a contradiction or problem that exists in our society. We are on the one hand aggressive, imperialistic, becoming increasingly militaristic, in a sense almost overcome by a kind of military socialism at home, and have an apparently quite unchangeable policy of military intervention in the affairs of other countries. That's one aspect of our society which I think is real and very hard to change. It is coupled with something else, namely, a great deal of openness at home. The universities, despite all the criticism, are pretty open for people within them to do and say what they want. In fact, in general, they are fairly free institutions and provide a lot of opportunity for self-expression. Furthermore, we have a high degree of affluence, which means that young people in particular have the opportunity to think; they are not constrained by the demands of survival to work steadily for a living.

This fact has not been lost on people like Irving Kristol, for example, who have argued that the way to stop student unrest is to make the kids work for a living and pay for their education. Well, in a sense I think he's right. That is, if people really had to work to avoid starvation, if they had to worry about security, then they probably wouldn't have time to think, and they might be much more apathetic and conforming. However, that's not the case at the moment. They do have time to think; they are relatively free. This is something rather new in the sixties; that is, the Depression is not hanging over them as a spur to maintain their conformist and authoritarian attitudes. As a result, when people stop to think and look at reality (if the reality is the way I described it and I think it to be), they are likely to be appalled and to try to do something about it. This reaction is student unrest, of course. There's a great deal written about student unrest, but it strikes me that there is a pretty simple explanation; it is really just the reaction of any person who has time to think about what's going on.

This is my conception of the present general social framework. There are, as a reflection or perhaps as part of this, a number of things going on in the universities which I expect will continue and probably increase in intensity. One of these is that, on a personal level, a number of students are developing a kind of revulsion against science, against technology, and in fact against professional work in any field, on the grounds that, at best, it's a kind of cop-out, and at worst, it is increasing the destructive potential of an already rather dangerous society.

You can see this everywhere; my particular hall in RLE [Research Laboratory of Electronics] happens at the moment to have sprouted with signs, such as "Are you going to be dominated by science?" and "Are you going to be a machine working for the technologists?" and so on. These reflect something in student attitudes that will continue, and something incidentally which I feel myself, so that I can understand why others feel it. At the same time, although I feel it and can understand it, I think it's extremely dangerous, because at this point the other side of my recently developed schizophrenic personality enters with my commitment and interest in science and my belief in intellectual values and in the value of approaching social problems from the point of view of the highest level of rationality, intellectual understanding, and utilization of technology. So I feel a kind of schizophrenia, and I suspect this is also true of many students.

[The universities as instruments of state policy]

Now the other parallel process, perhaps the collective analogue to this individual one, is a recognition of the fact that the universities are unquestionably, and MIT paramount among them, instruments of state policy, for reasons that are not terribly obscure. They have been repeated so often that by now it's almost a cliché to say it again, but it is undeniable that the distribution of power and force and wealth in the society affects what is done in the universities in a very significant fashion.

To a significant extent, in the universities we don't simply do research that we dream up; we do the kind of research that answers to needs that are articulated elsewhere, that are compatible with an ideology that's set elsewhere, and that can be supported by outside institutions that have their own interests. Although that's not 100 percent the case, there's obviously an enormous bias in this direction, which I think no sane person would deny. An individual who recognizes this bias and is appalled by and actively opposed to the tendency toward militarization of the society at home, the concentration of power at home, and the uses of this power overseas and at home, will pretty naturally be led to the belief that he ought to try to smash the universities.

Again I can see what lies behind such a belief, and one side of my own personality has a certain great accord with that. If smashing the universities could, in fact, prevent endless escalation of the arms race, prevent militarization of American society, prevent the increasing concentration of political and economic power in the society, and prevent the extension and consolidation of the American empire and imperialist wars, then I think this would be a very justifiable action. At this point, however, the other side of my personality reacts and says that that's a pretty senseless approach because the universities are probably the most free and open institutions in the society, and precisely because they are relatively free and open they are also the weakest and the most easily attacked. Furthermore, the effect of such an attack on the universities would probably be to smash the universities as relatively free and open institutions only to have them replaced by more authoritarian, more repressive institutions which would be even more fully and irremediably instruments of a general oppressive state policy. And I think there's some likelihood that that's exactly what's going to happen over the next few years. These are general tendencies that are very serious and not likely to change, but rather to intensify as the social crisis intensifies.

There is a third and, I think, more reasonable voice than these two opposing ones, for those people who believe, as I do, that radical social change is going to be necessary in the United States if American society is going to survive in any decent fashion and if it's not going to destroy a good part of the world along with itself. This voice suggests that the universities can, because of their relative openness and the possibility of free debate and discussion within them, become a basis for some kind of social change.

[The time scale for social change]
At this point some judgments come in about the time scale within which it's reasonable to think about social change, and it is here that I differ very much from many of the people in the student movement, for I think their time scale

for social change is very wrong. I don't think that there's any chance for dealing with the kinds of problems I've been talking about in a short time scale.
Whether the solutions be reformist or revolutionary, they will not succeed
unless they are backed by the overwhelming majority of the population,
unless they are based on a social movement that's rooted very broadly and
deeply in many strata of the population. Yet anybody who isn't completely
fantasizing has to recognize that we're nowhere near that position today. In
fact, it has only recently become possible to raise certain questions in this
country about the nature of our society, about the problems of capitalism, and
about the question of imperialism.

These issues were just out of the range of discussion for a long time in
the United States, although not in the other Western democracies. The spectrum of discussion and opinion in the United States is beginning to broaden
slightly and become somewhat more compatible with what exists throughout
the West; it is not so sharply skewed to the conservative part of the spectrum
of opinion as it has been for the last twenty years. The questions can be discussed now, and my feeling is that it's possible to win this debate on intellectual grounds and perhaps to persuade the mass of the population that
contemporary capitalism is an unviable system out of which will flow endless
imperialist aggression unless significantly modified. The place I would like to
see this discussion go on is in part within the universities, in the classroom
and in study. I would also like to see activist programs flow out from this.
This is my point of view, and if it is right, it ought to stand up in debate and
ought to follow from honest, open scholarship, and I would like to see honest, open scholarship and debate continue.

Since I do think that the time scale for this kind of change is long, I
would like to see the many individuals and students who are committed to
radical social change find their roots in present-day society. I don't think that
there is much of a role for professional revolutionaries in American society.
This role may seem plausible to students, but when they get a little bit older
it just turns them toward irrationality, deprives them of any relation to any
kind of an ongoing social process, and separates them from the active working part of the population, which is where any kind of social change will have
to be rooted.

Therefore, because of this long time scale, and because there are tremendous personal benefits to be gained by scientific work (not necessarily in the
pure sciences but in any field), I would like somehow for students to have a
foot in both camps, that is, to combine a professional career with ongoing
political commitment. That's a very hard thing to do, but I don't believe that

it's possible to be both sane and responsible in the future world without combining the two.

[Open debate, (self-)education, and contempt as the best weapons]

This leads to some possibilities for change in the universities, but none that are terribly dramatic. It seems to me that the major need in the universities is to open up more options.

I'm very much out of sympathy with the idea that things ought to be stopped by force; I'd like to see them stopped by the weapon of persuasion and often contempt, and I think they can be stopped in that fashion. If there's ever going to be any real change in the universities, it will have to be because the mass of students and faculty decide to do different things; there will be no other way to achieve change. The only method for this is continued effort at education, recognizing that education is very largely self-education.

These deep and very important problems have to be handled with the same humility that a scientist will automatically take to his own problems, recognizing both the difficulty of arriving at highly verified, highly plausible insights and understandings and the tremendous benefits of open debate, no matter what the problem. Anything of this sort that can be said for the sciences can be said with far greater force for the social sciences. In fact, these intellectual attitudes are even more appropriate and necessary when one deals with the fundamental social issues of our society.

Open Discussion

M.S.: One of the continuing criticisms of the university is that as it becomes involved in its research efforts in real problems for direct benefit to society, it loses its ability to reflect on both the progress of society on a generational time scale and on the long-term effect of the particular task on which they may be working on at the moment. Certainly this objection could be raised with regard to our involvement in military research, because at one point in time we did an evaluation and decided it was good and we just kept doing it without continual re-evaluation. The same argument can be raised regarding our involvement in urban studies: we may at some point recommend a housing project which ten years from now people will consider to be a terrible thing and will wonder how we ever did it. In an engineering school where some form of practical application of engineering is vital to the education of an engineer, how do we cope with the problem of teaching engineering in a real sense and yet remaining sufficiently separated from the society to be able to evaluate long-run implications?

[Contemporary affairs as part of the curriculum]

CHOMSKY: I don't think there's any way to do it. I think that technology can't remain separate from the question of how technology is used. It seems to me that the problem in the past has been that the question of how technology is used was not one that was raised inside the university. I think it was out of ignorance that these questions weren't raised. The kinds of commitments to technical developments that went on at MIT and other universities were based on tacit, unquestioned assumptions about what was of benefit to the society, and about public policy, and about international affairs.

We must now do something that is very unpleasant for academic people, namely, we must take seriously and thrash out political, social, and ideological issues, and let decisions about the development of technology be within the context of very explicit value judgments and commitments with respect to ideological positions. These are the kinds of things that a university has always tried to avoid, for rather good reasons. If you do get involved in them, then clearly the university becomes very heavily politicized. It becomes a place where specific historical and political judgments are made and where decisions about the development of technology are made within the context of those judgments. The only way I see to avoid this open politicization is to make such judgments tacitly and rather mindlessly as a reflection of social policies that are set elsewhere. Between these two alternatives—either making the judgments tacitly and mindlessly, or making them on the basis of open discussion and clear commitment, however questionable and difficult it may be—I prefer the latter. The idea that universities were in the past apolitical, extricated somehow from the political process, was very much an illusion. What occurred was rather, as Fulbright has said, that they simply became wedded to a particular interpretation, to a particular ideology, and to a particular concept of public process.

M.S.: Could we reduce the intensity of these arguments by withdrawing from applications of technology and working more in the pure sciences, which may have less clear political implications?
CHOMSKY: Yes, MIT could avoid a lot of these questions, but I just don't think that that would be the responsible thing to do. These are problems that just have to be faced and there's no point in our trying to withdraw from them. If we do, it just means that someone else is going to face them. In other words, I think that the real problems that are pressing on MIT are problems of American society as reflected at MIT, and I don't think that we, as American citizens or American scientists, can withdraw from those problems.

L.S.: What is your view not about the universities in the United States in general, but about this particular institution and the role it should play?

CHOMSKY: I think MIT ought to continue to be an institution with science and technology as its central component. Society needs such institutions of the highest level. However, I think that MIT is going to have to take seriously something that it never has in the past, namely, the social, political, and historical context in which scientific and technical development takes place. It is appalling that a person can come through an MIT education and say the kind of things that were quoted in the *New York Times* article on Sunday, November 9 [1969]. Perhaps the quotes were wrong, but I've heard enough of the same kind of things myself to know that the reporter got them right in spirit even if wrong in words. One student said, right along straight Nazi scientist lines: "What I'm designing may one day be used to kill millions of people. I don't care. That's not my responsibility. I'm given an interesting technological problem and I get enjoyment out of solving it."

You know perfectly well that we can name twenty faculty members who've said the same thing. In fact, one rather distinguished faculty member said about the same thing in a long speech, though not in those words, in the faculty meeting a couple of weeks ago. This is an attitude that is very widely held and very widely expressed: that we work on our problems and it's somebody else's responsibility to see what happens. Given our present state, given American power, and given the present destructive capacities of contemporary technology, that's an impossible and really antisocial attitude that has to be somehow overcome by the educational institutions.

E.M.: We have been discussing and listening to suggestions on how to give our students more opportunity to think about the implications of what they are doing, and how it affects policy. Among the suggestions we have had so far have been the need for a center for policy studies and for policy seminars on science, policy, and technology, and the need for a new kind of renaissance man, so to say, a man who understands both society and technology. We have to make some proposals for changing the life around here to give people an opportunity to think about things other than what is scheduled for them to think about. But I have a fear of the natural tendency of students to goof off when they are given disposable time (of some undergraduate policy seminars becoming kind of Mickey Mouse). We have also even heard a suggestion that the policy seminars be directed to produce legislative briefings so that the students act as legmen and prepare briefs for the legislators on various topics. Have you thought of any alternate mechanisms beyond just trying to loosen things up a little bit?

CHOMSKY: Yes. Although I think these suggestions may have some value, I'm very skeptical about them. A center for public policy, for one thing, at least according to the plans that I've heard, will be just another variant of our political science department, which happens to be a highly ideological department which takes a very particular stance on a range of public issues and represents a very specific ideological position; and that's the way it should be regarded. I don't see anything wrong with having a department of ideology in the university, but I think there ought to be many departments of ideology, not just one department of ideology expressing one point of view. I'd have the same reaction to the plan to react to things that are initiated on Capitol Hill because Congress represents a very particular perception of what American social problems are and they are far from having the only or even the most relevant perception.

I feel that there are a number of questions that are almost never studied by the social sciences but that are critical for any civilized person, and especially critical for a person who is going to have power in his hands. Any person working in technology has that power, whether he decides to use it mindlessly or consciously. These problems have to do with the nature of power in American society; there's practically nothing done concerning, for example, just how America is ruled. That's a question which is not studied in a serious way. There are very few books about it, and there are many fundamental questions about how America is ruled which are just not open to discussion. The reasons for that are not very obscure, for social knowledge is demanded by certain people and used by them for their purposes. Among their purposes is the manipulation and management of urban problems and of society, but not the change of the American power structure. That's not their problem, and consequently it's not studied. However, I think that question and the problem of the American role since the Second World War should be put in the center of study.

The American international role is, again, something which is not studied in a sufficiently serious way. I have my own views about these questions as does everyone else, and it would be very regressive and stupid if, for example, I were to be able to dominate that program, though I think my views are right, of course. What really ought to happen in such a program is that students should be exposed to a variety of views. Again, I see no point in *requiring* that they be put through this, because I don't think anybody can really learn anything unless he chooses to study it. Yet somehow or other the option of studying questions of that sort needs to be placed at the center of the curriculum. It must be done in such a way that a real variety of views, a real conflict of ideas and interpretations, is presented, in a very live way, so that anybody who has some sort of interest will be drawn into participating. There are many inherent dangers in this idea, such as loss of intellectual content, but they have to be faced.

L.S.: The Lewis Commission urged the strengthening of humanities at MIT with the idea that we might come up with a new blend of knowledgeable people, who would have an understanding both of technology and science and of its humane implications. However, I think it's commonly held by most people at the Institute that this attempt has failed singularly. We have a prospering humanities department that is essentially the same as at Harvard or anywhere else.

CHOMSKY: It seems to me that what happened in the humanities department was that it became more professionalized, and personally I was in favor of that. I think that the departments ought to be professional and meet professional standards that are set by those fields. The trouble is that professionalization has some inherent dangers. Professionalization means setting up problems that are either on the border of what you can solve or are solvable given your present technique, and letting this process determine the way intellectual tradition evolves. That is very good, and I have no objections. Yet one of the troubles is that there is another source for problems, other than the consideration of solvability given present technique, and that is the question "What is important?" Very often this can be a totally different source from the first, for quite commonly, problems that are important are not solvable by present techniques. That is not to say, however, that you shouldn't deal with them; you have to deal with them as best you can.

I don't think that there is, or will be in the near future, a profession that deals with the problems of contemporary society, and it would be a mistake to try to set up such a profession, for if it had intellectual integrity, it too would begin to follow the dynamics of professionalization and steer away from the really difficult, important problems. These questions belong to civilized man, and he must try to deal with them with whatever degree of knowledge he can bring and can acquire and with whatever degree of integrity he can muster. The fact that this responsibility lies with all of us has to be encapsulated in a program. The social inquiry program was an attempt to do this: to make a non-professional program where the problems are determined by importance rather than by availability of technique for solving them. Something of that sort really ought to be integral to the education of every person, but in particular to a scientist or someone who will be involved in technology.

L. T.: Is that the kind of programming you had in mind when you were referring to opening more options? What level were you talking about there? In other words, would you demand that university requirements be abolished?

[The two university foci: professionalism and significance]

CHOMSKY: No. I think that a proper university today has to combine these two sources of problems—those that come from professionalism, and those that arise from significance. There are a number of reasons for this. First, for a sort of human sanity an individual really ought to be a professional as well as a civilized person. I think you gain enormously by having a foot in science.

One of the real problems and weaknesses in the social sciences (economics being one of the exceptions) is that the people involved in the social sciences haven't the foggiest conception of what science is about. I think it would be very helpful to the social sciences if they were studied by scientists, by people who could compare the social sciences with the fields that have intellectual content, which in a sense the social sciences do not. This would not solve the problems of the social sciences but at least it would make it possible to deal with them from a helpful perspective, with some understanding of what it means to have evidence and a solution. Also, for these reasons, the scientific disciplines are the best possible training that I can imagine for a radical activist to learn what intellectual integrity means. In addition, this melange of history, contemporary issues, and classical social theory will help to suggest what the important problems are.

K. H.: Do you really think that the mental process used by scientists is the same as that which is involved in the kind of analyses one needs in order to understand society and the world around him?

CHOMSKY: Yes, I think it is. I don't contend that having studied physics guarantees that you'll approach social problems in a sensible fashion, that is obviously far from being true, but it gives you at least one foot up on beginning to deal with these problems. Incidentally, that's one reason why I'm delighted to have an institution of science and technology becoming involved in consideration of these fundamental social issues.

L. S.: You imply that these issues are being discussed at the university, perhaps not in the classroom, but certainly in the living quarters and in the privacy of the laboratory. Would you like this discussion brought about in some more formal way?

CHOMSKY: Not a more formal but a more integrated way. It could be rather informal; part of the curriculum might be seminars on contemporary affairs in which a great effort is made to bring in people—not necessarily university people, but maybe people involved in community organizing, or visitors from overseas—and to achieve the widest possible range of ideas and interpretations. This part of the curriculum should attempt to study just what modern industrial society is all about.

S.B.: I'm a little unclear as to who would do this study. Do you visualize that the faculty would enter into this on a temporary basis?

CHOMSKY: Actually, perhaps on a shifting basis. I would hope that this would become almost a permanent commitment of everyone at MIT. Something that I have done over the past years, which has been good for me, and I hope for students, is to teach courses in many different fields, including those I knew little about. This is a very good way to learn something about a field.

There are very few fields, math and physics being exceptions, that with a couple of months' hard work a moderately intelligent person can't get into and at least develop a feel for what kind of questions and problems there are. I don't think we should exaggerate the actual intellectual content of most academic disciplines. That's not to say, of course, that after a few months of study you can do serious research in the field—obviously not. But you can begin to give a more intelligent reaction, some sort of critical analysis, and you also learn a great deal. I think people ought to be very much encouraged to teach out of their field in this way, with the clear understanding that they're not coming forth as experts who have all the answers, but rather with the attitude that they are going to undertake an investigation of this field and that the students can join their effort. A program of that sort can be very valuable. In almost any field (again, perhaps not math and physics) a graduate student could really benefit by having a seminar taught by someone from outside the field in which the fundamental question of the seminar is, "Prove to me that what you're doing has some sense." That's the kind of question that's very rarely asked in the graduate program.

K.H.: Actually, the same thing works in physics and mathematics, at least in different parts of physics and mathematics which are quite non-communicable with one another. In fact, that's very effective at the graduate level.

In regard to another point you raised, it does seem clear that we're now entering an era of more involvement and commitment on the part of a number of faculty people. But one thing that has to be considered when thinking about institutions over a long time period is how much of a long-term commitment there

*is likely to be, and how effective you're likely to be in getting the kind of involve-
ment you're talking about. On the basis of past experience, it seems to me that you're
never going to have widespread faculty involvement. In fields such as physics,
math, and biology you're always going to have a basic group of highly committed
individuals who are rather narrow and therefore damned good in what they're
doing. At the same time, isn't one of the mistakes made by institutions in the past
that they have turned for advice on what projects to undertake to the people who
were undertaking them? It seems to me that they should have been listening to
someone else, for in fact the people already involved in the projects are almost the
least qualified to evaluate whether or not that should have been done. Do you think
that an institution develops an ability to listen to a certain core of critics within its
own institution? From personal experience, I regard the ideal of getting all kinds
of involved faculty all over the Institute as being a pretty remote possibility, assuming that you also continue to perform at a high level. Is there a way to develop this
kind of attitude or type of person?*

[The beginning of wisdom: a need to educate the faculty]

CHOMSKY: Looking back over the past fifteen years, we can see how it
might have been done. In the past fifteen or twenty years [1949/1954–1969],
there was only a very small number of people raising questions about the
character of American society, about Third World revolutions, and about the
cold war. And these people were considered pretty crazy. In fact, a lot of them
either couldn't be published or were derided in the professional journals.
Today, many of the things that these people were saying have become, if not
the conventional wisdom, at least very close to the center of what is believed
by a large number of serious people in the field.

I think that there's a lesson here, and that is that universities will need to
go out of their way to encourage this kind of outside criticism, which the faculty intuitively reacts to with derision. To give a concrete example, at the faculty meeting on Friday, the SDS [Students for a Democratic Society] critique
of defense work at MIT was read, and a number of faculty tried to put it
down. That's a very infantile attitude, actually. The fact of the matter is that
although I think that there are plenty of weaknesses in the critique which was
read, it's far from the craziest thing that's been read at a faculty meeting. The
SDS paper was at least dealing with very serious issues, and a lot of what was
said was certainly worthy of the attention of any serious person. Somehow or
other I think the faculty is going to have to be educated to the point where
they are open to ideas not within their own particular narrow framework—
this is just the beginning of wisdom. An active effort must be made to

broaden the range of ideological discussion, to bring in critical positions which some faculty members may feel don't deserve the name of rationality. This is the corrective for the ideological straitjacket you fall into if you simply react to the pressure of outside institutions.

K.H.: If something of this sense is missing in faculty people (and I have a hunch that this will remain the case because of the continued degree of specialization), what specifically can be done in the educational process of this institution, other than the general "opening up" that you've described?

CHOMSKY: If there are going to be research and study programs on urban problems, for example, I think that an effort should be made to hear people who live in urban ghettos, such as Panther members and community organizers. In fact, we should let them take part in the programs. Last year Wayne O'Neil ran a course on urban education that included half a dozen people from the local community. That's a good model for an educational course; they definitely added something. It seems to me that there is indeed an ethical question as to whether or not it's proper to develop knowledge in such a way that the weight of the knowledge is outside the community studied. It seems questionable that there should be knowledge which is not really under the control of the people who are being studied; this is a major, though rarely recognized, problem in the social sciences. A program of study or research or activism in urban problems should be put into the hands of the communities themselves, the results of that knowledge, and involve them directly in determining the way it's going. If it does not, it is ethically very questionable and dangerous, and probably a weak sort of program.

The same idea applies in international affairs, though it's harder to implement. However, any study of the American impact on the Third World that doesn't involve spokesmen for Third World revolutionary movements is just hopelessly off the beam and a virtually useless program. As a rather far-out example, but one which could be worked on, I think it would be perfectly possible for MIT to invite representatives of the NLF from Paris to come and take part in discussions and seminars on a topic such as the United States' role in Southeast Asia. This is the kind of thing which would be very valuable and ought to be done. If we are going to be in a world where our knowledge and technology are going to be related to the exercise of power, then let's face up to the fact realistically, and in a balanced fashion listen to the people at both ends of the gun.

L. T.: Don't you think that if you want a university faculty full of the kind of people you're describing, somewhere in the promotion process consideration has to be taken for people who are not only good in their profession but are also concerned individuals? What kind of trade-off are you going to make between someone who is the best mathematician and someone who is a good mathematician and also very socially aware of the important problems?

CHOMSKY: As I said, I think that the university has to have at least two separate foci, one being that they must have professional competence and work with the problems that grow out of professional involvement. On the other hand, we've got to face the fact that there is this other focus from which problems arise, namely, significance, and this requires different kinds of people.

E. G.: I agree with Noam about bringing in exogenous resources to the university, but in reference to the Humanities Department I want to say something about the use of the existing internal Institute resources.

When the Humanities Department was initiated, the fundamental failure was in stating that the aim was to bring in social scientists and humanists who, immersed in the MIT community, would come to understand the nature of this problem, and who at the same time, by introducing humanist social values at MIT, would educate technologists to be humanistic on social science issues. This is what failed. Our faculty failed to be educated, and consequently our students failed to be educated by the existing faculty. I think that the remedy for this is for professors to participate in two different ways in courses that are entirely outside their field. One is a method of cross-field participation in which faculty members teach subjects outside their field. The other would introduce a new kind of opportunity under the following semi-sabbatical arrangement: faculty members would be encouraged to register at any time as students in subjects which are very far from their own fields. This participation would count essentially as teaching. The aim here is to educate the faculty to what the issues are and to introduce the field of science into social science, and vice versa; this, I believe, should have been the aim when humanities and social science were first introduced into the MIT community.

[A social inquiry program: student-initiated courses]

CHOMSKY: One of the hopes in the social inquiry program was that it would construct a rather loose format in which student-initiated courses could develop, and that's one way to respond to a very legitimate problem. By and large, I'm in agreement with the ideas about the value of teaching outside one's field. However, it would seem to me very unlikely at this stage in the game if some students didn't raise or consider such questions. I think that the students ought to have much greater options for raising these issues and forcing their consideration, and this may mean breaking down some of the rigidity of the lecture system.

J.O.: I'd like to raise a question about your statement that there are no profession-als in ethics, aside from philosophers who are students of ethics. You may be right, but there are leaders in ethics who have a practical effect, and there are intellectual tools and theoretical studies of the process and method of analysis and reasoning used by these leaders.

CHOMSKY: Yes, there are people who try in their lives and their thinking to represent ethical values, and those people very rarely get anywhere near a university. For example, take someone like A. J. Muste, who in my opinion is one of the great men of this century. I don't think he ever got near a univer-sity campus until maybe a year or two before his death in his eighties. This is the kind of person whom a university wouldn't even dream of bringing in, but it is just this type of person who should be heard in a university and in any community that aspires to intellectual honesty and openness.

I would also agree with you that action should very definitely be com-bined with discussion of these matters, and there are a number of ways to do this. For example, there are concrete questions that arise with the whole problem of industrial democracy. For example, there is the question of bring-ing the industrial system under direct democratic control of the workforce—elimination of management, elimination of ownership, and so on. These issues are very closely related to the problems of conversion that everybody is worried about now. It's very possible that when the International Harvester plant was shut down in Chicago a couple of weeks ago, the only way to save it would have been to turn it into a worker-managed plant which would be involved in the kind of production relevant to the community in which the largely black and Puerto Rican workers live. Now these are real questions, which would require substantial resources, intellectual as well as material. The university hasn't got the material resources but, in theory at least, it does have the intellectual resources. I think it's very sad that there wasn't a lot of groundwork laid among workers in that International Harvester plant, for example, at least to raise the questions of how they might in fact proceed to develop a collectively managed plant that would do something useful with those material resources that were there.

are other possibilities which probably are related to development of some radically different means of control over the economy, in particular controls similar to those of workers' councils over industrial enterprise. These are pretty far-out ideas in the United States today, though not in many other countries, not in England, for example, where the second-largest trade union, Amalgamated Engineering Federation, is headed at the moment by a person who's thinking precisely along these lines. I think that it's a great tragedy that these are far-out ideas in the United States.

L.S.: What are your views on who should run this place and what that means?

[The faculty and students ought to run the university]

CHOMSKY: I'm rather torn there, to be perfectly honest. My own feeling is that the administrators here over the past fifteen years have been very much more liberal than the faculty. In principle, however, I think the faculty and students ought to run the place. There really ought to be a move, despite what would probably be unfortunate short-run consequences, toward real faculty and student control of the institution, and I say this without criticizing any particular decisions that have been made by the administration. In principle, having committees appointed by administrative officers is deplorable and is the wrong system, although they probably come out better that way, from my point of view, than if they had been appointed by the faculty. It should not be possible for administrators to appoint committees; administrators, after all, represent no one and were appointed from above by people outside the institution, not by those within the institution.

This question came up in the Pounds Review Panel [MIT Review Panel on Special Laboratories] over the proposal for a committee to give advisory reports on administrative positions with regard to defense research. My own feeling was (a) that it should not be an advisory committee but should be a faculty-student-staff deciding committee, and (b) that it should not be appointed but should be elected. A large number of faculty reacted by saying that it would be undemocratic to have this committee elected, and this reaction is not so crazy as it might sound. These faculty trusted the authorities to do more or less what they wanted, and they knew that in a functioning democracy the politically active people (vocal minority, I think, is the technical term) would have an inordinately large role, out of proportion to their weight.

There is something to that idea but, in effect, it amounts to an argument for a totalitarian state run by a benevolent dictator who can be trusted to do the decent thing, thus leaving us free to do our own work. That point of view has no more sense within a university than it has within a society at large. We have to move toward having the university administrators do nothing but administer, that is, carry out decisions that are arrived at from democratically elected bodies composed in some proportion of faculty, students, and staff. Simple moves can be made toward that, for example, by having committees elected and subject to referendum and recall from particular constituencies rather than having them appointed.

VISITOR: How can you impart knowledge to one who is not concerned with learning, or impart a social conscience to one who's socially apathetic? How can you educate to the importance of these problems the random student on campus who's not concerned with the political problems, or the random faculty member who's not really concerned with anything more than his research project?

CHOMSKY: From my experience the only way to do this is to keep the problem alive—by demonstrations, by picketing, and by many other means. It seems to me that that is the proper way to keep issues alive in a democratic institution. There is no way you can force anyone to learn physics if he's not really interested in it; if the study of it doesn't grow out of his interest, then he might as well not go to the course. I don't see any difference on this point between humanities and anything else, but I do want to again emphasize that humanities is not the place where a social conscience is instilled; it is a place where a study of history and literature and the arts is carried out.

[A Hippocratic oath, weapons production, and the fate of civilization]

VISITOR: Do you think the time has come for a Hippocratic oath in science?

CHOMSKY: Yes, it was due long ago. I think it would be quite important to try to organize scientists, particularly students, around some sort of Hippocratic oath, which, in my opinion, ought to involve refusal to work on such things as defensive weaponry or counterinsurgency. Such a position demands an understanding of the historic context within which the decision is made to sign one's name. That involves a lot of thinking about modern history, and about the character of American society—the kind of thinking that really ought to go on within a university.

VISITOR: If I understand you correctly, you are saying that one has to reorient priorities to some degree away from efficiency, defined as maximum output of data, or maximum publication of papers. That seems to be a real problem when the university has to interact with the outside world, at least financially. It's also a problem within a university, given that there are factions that don't agree with this idea. Specifically, it is a very personal issue to a lot of graduate students who've been active over these past couple of years, and on whom pressure is now being brought to bear to do their work and to get their theses done.

CHOMSKY: I can't suggest an absolute principle, but my own understanding of academic freedom would suggest that the universities ought to be extremely flexible about such things, although, of course, there have to be some limits. If a person at some stage of his career feels that political action is relevant to his growth as a person and to current social problems, I would think there would be an enormous burden of proof on anyone who decided otherwise. Somebody made a nice statement to the effect that no rule is worth one student, and in the university particularly, if rules can't be suspended for a particular student interest, then there's something seriously wrong.

K.H.: Certainly, but the point is that once you have undone the rules, then there's a different set of students and the same argument comes back in reverse; it is just never that simple.

CHOMSKY: I would be willing to bet that your new math department rules concerning time limits were effective because your students recognized their legitimacy in respect to their own lives. If they had been felt as an imposition or as something irrational with respect to the way in which the students saw their lives, then the rules wouldn't have been effective.

K.H.: I'm also willing to bet that if you remove these rules, the students very rapidly will go right back to their old pattern of the long delay of exams and so forth. I don't pretend to know the answer to this, but I claim it's not a trivial matter.

E.M.: One of the non-political problems at MIT is the strong collectivization of the students, in the sense that they are asked to take rather strongly programmed courses in a synchronous fashion. When we hear the proposal for other courses of study, seminars, and directed changes of attitudes, my reaction is that we are talking about another kind of collectivization. I would like your opinion on benefits of collectivization and on the issue of whether we should encourage more independent study and let students go their own way more and find out for themselves, or whether we should encourage this other kind of collectivization—meaning well-ordered, well-organized, strict programs.

CHOMSKY: It seems to me that certain well-ordered programs should be designated for anybody who has so little originality that that is what he wants. There are such people and they should have such things well laid out before them. However, I don't think people should be encouraged to do this. I don't see too much reason why college has to be a four-year affair these days. Precisely because of the affluence of the society, we really ought to be looking forward to a day when college is a thing that people move in and out of at almost any time in their lives. I think that there's plenty of latent funding around for education; in fact, education has been a real growth industry and it should be even more so.

L.S.: I think the present system is constituted such that you can really do whatever you want if you are so inclined; I have found this to be true and so have most of the people I know.
CHOMSKY: Yes, you can do whatever you want within the framework of what exists, but the point is that I think different things ought to exist.

M.S.: I think one of the reasons for having the structured system is that it forces a set pace, and there's a certain tendency to want to get as many people as possible coming to the institution and participating.
CHOMSKY: If the pattern were for students to be part time involved in academic pursuits and part time in outside work, it would also mean that more students could be handled by the same facilities. As to the question of fellowships, if a person is working on the outside, then he may be getting support from someone else, so that the amount per person of fellowships could be reduced. In any event, though, the facilities are presently only partly used, and that leaves some openings.

However, I think there's a begged question in your statement, and that is the assumption that what MIT gives is technical training and that this is what you want to give to a maximum number of people. I would like to question this assumption, for it seems to me that this is the case, and I think it's very dangerous at this stage of history, for any institution to be giving only technical training. What MIT ought to be giving is technical training within a context of social perception, and perhaps the way to do this is for students to work at a different pace and be involved in different things.

VISITOR: What puzzles me about your conception of the university is the way people become involved in socially relevant concerns. It seems to be designed only for those few remarkable individuals who are so good in their own profession that they can produce their two or three really substantial papers and make a name for themselves in their own profession and then have time to start considering other questions. It seems to me that there is a group that is equally brilliant but simply cannot see the importance of the narrow professional area and don't want to deal with it, and these people would be left out in the cold. Secondly, there are the less able who are concerned with both their own profession and with socially relevant questions, but who simply can't devote half their time to socially relevant issues and half to

their profession and still score. It seems to me that these people too are still going to
be left out in the cold and that we really haven't done much.
CHOMSKY: I think that statement is correct. It's just that the university
should design the kind of options and curriculum that could in principle produce the "ideal man," recognizing full well that every individual is going to
have to find his own way through that maze and that he's going to become
the kind of man he wants to be. I think MIT should very definitely be open
to someone who wants to do nothing but a concentrated study within a very
narrowly specialized field. At the same time, however, MIT ought to be making it easy for people to face the fact that the work that they do as professionals is related to the exercise of power in the world, and that by their
actions and their work they are making particular political judgments, which
will affect other human beings and the world at large. Now, once having
faced that problem, they may decide that is indeed not their problem, and
that someone else is going to have to worry about it. I don't think there is
much you can do if this is their decision, but what the university can do is at
least make it very hard to avoid facing that problem.

VISITOR: Would you accept the lowering of the level of competence of the faculty?
CHOMSKY: Yes, I would, but I really don't think it's necessary. I think very
few people really work fifteen hours a day at their profession, and I really
don't believe it's true, as a general rule, that if people concentrate only in a
narrow professional area, then they are much better in that area. I also feel
that investigations into the qualities that make somebody valuable as a social
critic would end up nowhere. Therefore, the alternative which is open to us
and which I think we should follow is to bring in a wide variety of people,
opening up the range of debate and questions, and trying to bring students
into discussions at a very early stage.

For example, I think it would be very valuable for anyone planning to
become an engineer to study intensively, at a very early stage of his career, the
history of the cold war presented from many different points of view. I'm
confident enough about my own interpretation of the cold war to believe that
if it were presented to others it would really win many people to the belief
that they shouldn't be involved in things like weapons production, because
involvement in weapons production is based on a complete misconception of
what the cold war is about. This kind of question never arises for most engineers now, and I think it must arise. I think that it has been a terrible tragedy
over the years that these questions have not been raised. And that, for example, a large number of engineers who testified before the Pounds Panel all

believed that they were building weapons because otherwise the United States would be overwhelmed by some enemy. Personally I think that's a myth, but that's not what is important. What is important is that they arrived at this position on the basis of extremely limited knowledge. This really shows a tremendous defect in our institutions and in particular in their own institution, MIT, for their decision was a terribly important one; in fact, the fate of civilization may depend on that decision.

Chapter 19

Two roles of the American university (1997)

I (1997)

The history of intellectuals and dissent during the cold war period must first be seen in light of the changes in the American psyche that the dramatic rise in international power created.

[The rise in international power and the intellectual climate]

During World War II, vast changes took place. For one thing, wartime spending got the United States out of the Depression. The industrial economy in the United States boomed, while much of Europe was devastated or destroyed. It was pretty clear as the early 1940s went on that the United States was going to come out of the war with an enormous degree of domination of the world on every front: industrially, diplomatically, militarily. By 1945, the United States had a level of preponderance in the international sphere which probably has no counterpart in history. It had 50 percent of the world's wealth, most of the world's industrial production, military dominance, security, control of both oceans—the opposite sides of both oceans!—and so on. Such power was simply unparalleled, and that sank in. American planners had very ambitious and sophisticated ideas about organizing the entire world, and they carried out many of those ideas.

There was a reflection of this shift in power in the cultural sphere and in the universities. It had a complicated background. Part of the reaction was against the prewar sense of inferiority, when the United States had, culturally speaking, a subordinate relationship with Europe. If you were an American artist or a writer, you would go to Paris; if you were a mathematician or a physicist, you would go to Germany; if you were a philosopher, you would go to England; and so on. The United States was thought of as a cultural backwater, somewhat like the Midwest is regarded by easterners now.

This reaction was epitomized during the war when many European scholars, scientists, and intellectuals fled the Nazis and tried to come to the United States. Many were treated pretty shabbily, partly out of fear that they would dominate if they were allowed in, and partly out of outright hostility. So when these distinguished scholars and scientists arrived, many of them could not get decent positions. For example, Roman Jakobson came to the United States in 1941 as a refugee from Sweden, where he had gone from Prague. Although he was an extremely distinguished linguist and literary scholar, one of the leading figures in these fields, a petition actually circulated by leading American linguists to universities urging that they not hire him, that it would be bad for American linguistics. He ended up, through the good offices of two linguists—Zellig Harris and Carl Voegelin—translating at Yivo Institute, and later got a position at the University of Chicago. Jakobson's case was not an anomaly; many European scholars and scientists were treated in the same manner.

By the late 1940s and early 1950s, the reaction was in full force. Throughout the world, American planners developed a kind of can-do sense. European civilization was viewed as a failure; after all, it collapsed. Planners did not want to worry about that dust anymore. Things would be done our way, the right way, the American way. There was a lot of jingoism, supported by the American victory, power, and global dominance. A recent study of the Cuban missile crisis and the attitude of the Kennedy intellectuals and planners toward the Europeans at the time, as expressed in internal discussions (since declassified), is pretty dramatic: it simply never occurred to them to consult the Europeans. To do so would be to bring in, it was supposed, people who were emotional, unserious, backward, and so on. The attitude was that we will do this ourselves and then we will tell them, including the British. That is one of the reasons Charles de Gaulle became so infuriated and attempted to move toward an independent European course. Europe's fate was certainly at stake—the planners saw a war as rather likely, and in it Europe might be smashed. But the Kennedy administration did not consult with the Europeans; it was a case of total contempt.

I remember what the feeling was like in the late 1940s and early 1950s, when I was a student. I was doing mainly linguistics and philosophy, first at Penn, then at Harvard. We were never expected to read anything on the history of the subjects. It was as if the history was nonexistent; everything serious was done by Americans and a few other people. In philosophy, we read Quine's response to Carnap in 1951; that is where philosophy started. And we had to know what they were talking about: Frege, early Russell. And we read some modern British philosophy. Then there were the pre-Socratics, and you had to know that there was somebody named Hume, but that was pretty much it.

This is a caricature, but not by much. In American linguistics, the tone of it is very clearly exhibited by a volume called *Readings in American linguistics,* published in 1955 and edited by Martin Joos, a highly respected American linguist. His comments on the articles are filled with utter contempt for anything that preceded modern American linguistics. It was considered old-fashioned European metaphysical nonsense; the attitude was that we are doing stuff so important we cannot pay any attention to that. Even classics such as Otto Jespersen, in the early part of this century, I read on my own, out of personal curiosity. It was simply not part of the canon. I had the good fortune to obtain a graduate fellowship at Harvard, at the Society of Fellows, which gave me the opportunity, for the first time, to be at a university without working on the side and so to browse in the marvelous resources of Widener Library. I found plenty of important work by linguists and philosophers. I was quite surprised to discover how much of the earlier work had been forgotten, or derided if mentioned at all.

The same was true in other disciplines. In the mid-1950s, I was teaching cram courses for Massachusetts Institute of Technology (MIT) students who had to pass doctoral exams in French and German. We read articles in their subjects, often from early in the century. Sometimes students (in engineering particularly) were shocked to discover that the "incompetent" Europeans, who had to be "rescued" by America from the consequences of their own supposed backwardness and depravity, had discovered things long ago that they were just beginning to learn about and work on in their graduate studies.

Such attitudes were stimulated by a number of factors. One was that during World War II substantial technological developments had been made; computers were coming along, and the field of electronics generally was developing significantly. There were new ways of studying things that really had not been available before. In the 1930s, a major scientific event took place when Linus Pauling analyzed the chemical bond in quantum theoretic terms, which unified chemistry and physics for the first time. Chemistry had been a separate field, which had no solid physical basis and seemed even inconsistent with physics. Through the 1940s, these developments were pursued further by Pauling and others. In the early 1950s came the unification of good parts of biology with biochemistry, which meant that you at least had a sense of unification of science. Somehow the whole range, from the new physics (quantum physics) to theoretical chemistry through at least the foundations of biology, were all part of one unitary enterprise. The next obvious place to look was the brain sciences, the mind, the behavioral sciences, and so on.

And that time, with the Macy conferences, cybernetics, communication theory, and so on, there was a feeling that the horizons were unlimited. We had gotten to biology, the next thing would be psychology, and then we take in other aspects of human life and existence. Here, the American way entered in, through behaviorism. That was the heyday of the "behavioral sciences," and that was supposed to be an American innovation, not mystical like what the Europeans did. We are serious scientists, we study behavior, and are hard-headed and operationalist—Skinner had shown this, the behavioral sciences have shown that, and so on. That was very much the mood of the 1950s— thinking of itself as innovative, very arrogant, ahistorical—part and parcel of the general sense of America taking over the world.

Now, it was not entirely uniform. For example, at Harvard, where I was, virtually no interest existed in continental philosophy, or even history of philosophy. That was virtually unknown except for Frege and early Russell, or parts of logical positivism, and they were known mainly for their influence in contemporary work. But British philosophy was still very much respected. And, in fact, something of the 1930s attitude of cultural subordination still existed, in funny ways. It was considered proper for graduate students in philosophy to adopt British manners, clothes, style—even accent. And of course everyone went to study in Oxford or Cambridge if they could, and there was a significant influence of Wittgenstein and Oxford philosophy that was intermingled with a kind of homebred, arrogant sense of "we know it all," in a very strange brew.

I believe something like this was happening across a large part of American intellectual culture in those years. This arrogance became tied up with what was called anti-communism, which also had a strong jingoistic element.

This continued right to the revival of Europe; the missile crisis was a striking and dramatic example of it. And it continues right to the present. Only the other day, the U.S. ambassador to the United Nations (UN), Madeleine Albright, said something that would be considered scandalous if it came from another country, but here it is considered perfectly normal. The UN Security Council was wavering on a U.S.-supported resolution on Iraq, and she simply said that this is a region where our interests are at stake, that we will act multilaterally if we can, unilaterally if we must. Well, that is the American way. When the World Court condemned the United States for "unlawful use of force" against Nicaragua, the general reaction here across the board—virtually with no exception, including people who write eloquently about the sanctity of international law—was contempt for the Court. The Court, it was said, had dishonored itself by daring to condemn the United States. When the UN Security Council debated a resolution, not mentioning the United States, simply calling on all states to observe international law, the United States just vetoed it. It was considered so insignificant it was barely mentioned here. When it went to the UN General Assembly and the United States voted virtually alone against it, that was not even reported. We do what we like, and in the cultural sphere that has had its analogue.

The beginnings of the Cold War increased the jingoism, the sense of self-righteousness, the narrowness of perspective, the rallying around the flag. It might well have gone on anyway, but the Cold War intensified elements that were there.

[Activism and the university]

As an intellectual, if you were critical of the developing Cold War system in those years, you were so far out of the mainstream you did not talk to anyone except your few friends—I remember that very well. So if you felt qualms about the U.S. war in Greece in the late 1940s—I had more than qualms, I thought it was horrifying—you were marginalized. I cannot remember anyone else I knew who felt the same way. The same was true of Korea. It was not until the early 1960s that this near-uniformity of subordination to domestic power, combined with arrogance and self-righteousness, began to erode significantly.

Of course it is not that in all of Cambridge in the 1950s no one shared my reservations about Greece or Korea. But it did not come out publicly very much. It was marginal at best; for example, the journal *Dissent,* which must have been started about 1953 or 1954. These people were Trotskyites—Irving Howe, Lewis Coser, and others—but left the Trotskyite organization around 1950. By the mid-1950s, it was pretty much as it has remained: social democratic, critical of extremes of American power. But it was at the time regarded as—and in a sense it was—a very courageous break with conformity. But that was very much the exception. Much more typical was, to mention only one case, the reaction to the Hungarian uprising and the brutal suppression of it by the Russians in 1956. I was once with a group of faculty at Harvard who were bitterly denouncing the Russian invasion of Hungary, which I agreed with; it was horrifying. But I remember saying, "Look, you're right about this, but it's not the only terrible thing that's going on in the world." I mentioned what the British were doing in Kenya at the same time, which was also horrifying. And there was a kind of silence. Then someone who knows better said, "Well, it's not comparable because there are very few people in Kenya, unlike Hungary." The idea that colonial atrocities could even be considered was remote from understanding.

Another example can be found by looking at the reaction to the overthrow of the government of Guatemala, which led to a real reign of terror, with thousands if not tens of thousands killed. Nobody batted an eyelash. I think perhaps the most dramatic example, specifically because of what came later, is what happened in Vietnam in 1961, what happened in Indochina altogether. In 1954 the United States took over and quickly undermined the Geneva accords, blocked a diplomatic settlement, and set up a typical Latin American–style terrorist state in South Vietnam, which had probably killed 60–70,000 people by the end of the decade—not a small amount. It was not unknown, but unimportant, simply standard Latin American–style terror, like Guatemala, no big deal. In 1961, Kennedy took over. By then the repression and violence had elicited resistance, and the U.S.-client government was going to collapse; that was clear. So Kennedy simply escalated the war. He moved from a war of terror to outright aggression against South Vietnam. And it was not secret. We know a lot of details we did not know then; but the main outlines were clear. I remember in October 1962 I read in the *New York Times*—hidden in the back pages, but it was there—that American pilots were carrying out a third of the bombing missions in South Vietnam in planes disguised with Vietnamese aircraft markings. It was known that American forces were either involved in or close to combat, that napalm and crop destruction were authorized. There were plenty of atrocity stories, but no reaction, because it was considered entirely legitimate for us to invade and attack another country and to terrorize its civilian population.

It was not until the mid-1960s that resistance on campus was mobilized, and even then, of course, the level of awareness and activity differed enormously from one university to another. In fact, I had the opportunity to observe this difference firsthand since, in those years, I worked at both Harvard and MIT.

Despite its connections to the Pentagon, MIT was in fact much more active in opposition and less hostile to dissent on campus than was Harvard. Most anti–Vietnam War efforts on the area were centered at MIT. Salvador Luria, who was at MIT, was a refugee from fascist Italy and remained a committed, militant leftist. He initiated a lot of activity. If you take a look at national faculty ads in the *New York Times,* you will find that MIT initiated most of them, with some Harvard participation, but that was much more marginal. I do not doubt that you would find the Harvard faculty to be more liberal, again by usual standards, than the MIT faculty in those years. But the freedom to be an open, outspoken, dissenting intellectual and political activist has been greater here than at Harvard, in my experience. That is why it is not only faculty peace activities but also other activities that are usually centered at MIT, even public meetings on issues of the day, at least those with grassroots initiative and participation. Take, for example, RESIST, a national funding support group for various movement activities, which got started around 1967. In large measure it grew out of MIT. If one were to look at the list of people directly involved, people on the board, you would find lots of MIT people. From the beginning up until today, there have scarcely been any Harvard faculty. That has been a fairly consistent difference. It is not 100 percent, obviously, but the tendency is real.

The general difference between MIT and Harvard was probably due to the fact that MIT was a science-based university, and hence the ideological constraints were much less. I do not think that I could have survived at Harvard. I have had no problems at MIT, never did, even though I was very visible and I am sure causing them plenty of problems—I was involved in the resistance, in and out of jail, and all sorts of things. And this was virtually a Pentagon university. Aside from two military labs that it ran, about 100 percent of the budget came from the Pentagon. But the academic freedom record was quite good by comparative standards. I never heard a word. If the administration was getting pressure from somewhere, I never heard of it. And the same was true of others; I would not say it was perfect, but one of the best in the country. Much better than other universities that I know about, where there was plenty of repression and persecution of activists and people on the left. There were things here that should not have happened, but by and large their record was quite good—and remains so.

When I came here in 1955, MIT was heavily military. The building I work in was the Research Lab of Electronics, which was funded by the three armed services. Everyone routinely underwent security clearance. I refused clearance, and I was told that I was the only person to have done that then. Nobody cared; people considered it mostly silly. All I was doing was turning down free trips on military air transport and other amenities. I simply made it clear that I refused to undergo clearance, and I do not recall anyone noticing it. I was very up-front and outspoken about my political views, but it simply was not an issue.

The undergraduate population at MIT was very passive. Until the fall of 1968, very little student activity existed. There was a small group of students who formed the Rosa Luxemburg Collective around 1965 or 1966. Louis Kampf and I were their faculty advisors, and by then we were teaching courses on our own time, big undergraduate courses on these issues with hundreds of students, so the interest was beginning to develop. But it was not until the fall of 1968 that it crystallized. A lot of these students, incidentally, are still among the most active and effective on the left up until today. One of them, Mike Albert, who was elected student body president and then was thrown out (though we were able to have him reinstated partially), went on to help found South End Press, later *Z Magazine*. A lot of writers, like Steve Shalom, come from that background, too. So it was quite a lively and very good group, still quite active—some of the best people around.

But they were very much on the margins at MIT until the fall of 1968, when this small group proposed to set up a sanctuary for an army deserter, the kind of thing that people were doing at the time. The guy in question was a working-class white deserter from downtown Boston. The students involved had talked to him. He had thought it through carefully, knew the consequences, and decided that he was going to desert publicly. It was a hard decision to make. He would announce it publicly in the sanctuary, where people would stay with him until the FBI came. I was opposed. I thought it would get no support from the student body. But the students went through with it anyway, and I was dead wrong. They had a news conference at the student center, and within no time MIT had practically shut down. Practically the whole student body was over there, thousands of people, twenty-four hours a day. There was an endless stream of everything from political seminars and meetings to rock music and the rest of what went on in those days. It just turned the whole Institute around.

After that came a lot of initiatives, including the first serious inquiry into the MIT-government relationship, the questions about the social role of science and technology and what considerations should go into it, and much else. On March 4, 1969, a big, full-day meeting took place, in which the whole Institute shut down. It had plenty of impact, which lasted. The place really has not been the same since.

The funny thing is, around that time, MIT was still thought of as entirely passive. In 1968, when there was a business-initiated decision to stop the escalation of the war and move toward negotiations and eventual withdrawal, one thing that was done was to try to calm down the universities, to say, "Okay, it is all over, we're all on the same side now." McGeorge Bundy, who had been national security advisor and a former Harvard dean, was sent on a "peace mission" around the country to tell everybody, "Let's be friends and make up, it's all over." As a trial balloon, he was sent first to a very quiet place, De Paul University, I think, simply to see how that would work. And it worked well—there was a big story in the *New York Times* about it. I think the second place on his tour was MIT, which was presumably picked because it was so quiescent and passive, and therefore it would be safe. What happened was a bit of a surprise to everyone, which I will not go into. But anyway, that ended the tour.

Going back to the question of government money, I think there is a considerable difference between the natural sciences and the social sciences. Although the natural scientists were pretty supportive of government policy, I would say, I do not think this was because of military funding. I believe my experience is quite typical in that regard. But if one were to look at the social sciences, it is different. What is now the Political Science Department at MIT was under economics until around 1960; MIT was an engineering school, it had very few departments in other fields. Not until the 1960s did it become a university in the usual sense. So around 1960, the Political Science Department separated off from the Economics Department. And at that time it was openly funded by the CIA; it was not even a secret.

No one saw any reason to keep it quiet. I do not see any reason either, frankly. In the mid-1960s, it stopped being publicly funded by the Central Intelligence Agency, but it was still directly involved in activities that were scandalous. The Political Science Department was, as far as I know, the only department on campus which had closed, secret seminars. I was once invited to talk to one, which is how I learned about it. They had a villa in Saigon where students were working on pacification projects for their doctoral dissertations and that sort of thing. In that framework, I do not doubt that relation to the government was very strong in shaping political attitudes or maybe selecting faculty and students. I do not know how long that lasted. Certainly, nothing like that is true now; it is a much more open department. But I thought there was a pretty dramatic difference between the Political Science Department and the Institute as a whole. Now if you had given people a questionnaire, you probably would have found the Political Science Department to be more liberal than the Engineering Department, by usual standards. But that is independent.

The fact of the matter is that there was very little secrecy even then. In 1969, I was on the committee that looked into the MIT budget in the aftermath of the events I mentioned. This is public, so you can find the data. My recollection is that the MIT budget was something over $200 million a year, half of it straight to big military labs that MIT ran, Lincoln Laboratories and the Instrumentation Lab, now called the Draper Lab. Of the other half, the academic budget, my recollection is that 90 percent was Pentagon-based. That shifted over the years, partly because of changes in the sciences, because biology grew and developed after that period. So by now it is nothing like 90 percent, though it has been substantial. But I think very little secret work was being done.

There was supposed to be a library somewhere of classified material in the sciences. If so, the material was marginal and unlikely to have survived this period. The decision was made at that time to cut off all classified work, and I doubt that there has been any secret work since. On the other hand, as you move away from government funding and toward corporate funding, then secrecy increases. Corporate funding is much more restricted and narrow than Pentagon funding, in general. The Pentagon funded basic science. The Pentagon, in fact, has been the cover for U.S. industrial policy. It was set up this way in the late 1940s to be a device for public funds to be used to subsidize advanced sectors of industry—that was completely public. It was in the business press; no secret was made about it at all.

So, for example, through the 1950s about 85 percent of electronics research was Pentagon-funded—by Pentagon I mean the whole system, the National Aeronautics and Space Administration, the Department of Energy, and so on, what is euphemistically called "defense." A large part of it, and one of the reasons it stays at roughly Cold War levels, is that it is the system of public funding of advanced sectors of industry. And that meant that the Pentagon was funding basic science without concern for short-term payoff. The Pentagon would fund fundamental science in the expectation that sooner or later something will come out that would be useful for private power. The history of computers is an example of such an arrangement. They were unmarketable in the 1950s, because they were too big and clumsy. So public funding was at about 100 percent through the Pentagon. By the 1960s, computers became marketable, so the Pentagon handed it over to what is called "private enterprise" (public subsidy, private profit), and then the public share gets to be about 50 percent. The story is similar in other fields.

It is hard to find a sector of the American economy that did not then and does not now live off something like this. Right through the 1980s, the Reaganites—statist reactionaries, nothing conservative about them—apart from greatly increasing protectionism, also took the initiative to fund the big development in computers and related technologies at that time. It was partially funded by the Defense Advanced Research Projects Agency, the Pentagon research agency that set up the start-up companies of the Silicon

Valley type, which became the leaders in this field. "Star Wars" was pretty much the same. That has been the case for almost fifty years.

On the other hand, business does not want to fund basic science for the same reasons Ford Motor Company does not give its technology to General Motors. Anyone can use basic science. They want to fund things they can profit from. So that means very narrow funding, short-term applied work, and secrecy, because they do not want anyone to know about it. Now, they cannot impose secrecy, but they can make it known that renewal of funding depends on it. The effects can be felt as the universities shift toward more corporate funding, away from government funding. The Pentagon was in many ways the freest of all the funding institutions. The Pentagon did not have Senator Proxmire looking over its shoulder to see what it was doing; the National Science Foundation (NSF) did. So the Pentagon was much freer in the kind of the funding it would do. It simply regarded itself as the nanny state for the rich, for advanced sectors of industry; so funding could be provided for anything that might ultimately be useful, maybe years down the road, without much supervision. The NSF was much more bureaucratic—it was being monitored—and corporations are micromanaged, they have their own short-term interests. This has reached a sufficient scale for *Science* magazine to have a news article about it recently, discussing the nationwide effects of narrowing the scope of research, and also increasing secrecy—at least unwillingness to share information—with the shift to corporate funding.

[War and the intellectuals]

To this day, the fact that the United States attacked South Vietnam has not penetrated American scholarship, intellectual life, or, indeed, most of the left. It is hard to imagine a more dramatic example of discipline and subordination of the intellectual class than the fact that we cannot recognize the elementary truth that we attacked South Vietnam—certainly in 1961—and that South Vietnam was the main target of our attack right to the end of the war. One example of how this has been treated can be illustrated with Robert McNamara's book, which is now a major phenomenon, and everybody has reviewed it and discussed it.

McNamara was involved in two major decisions. The first was in 1961, shifting from state terrorism to direct attack against South Vietnam. The second major decision of the war was in January-February 1965: not the decision to bomb North Vietnam and not to send American troops to South Vietnam, but to bomb South Vietnam at triple the scale of the bombing of North Vietnam, and at a level that no area had ever been subjected to before. That is virtually a direct quote from Bernard Fall, who was the very hawkish French military historian and expert, also a very valued U.S. advisor—he went on missions in the field and so on. McNamara does not quote him, but he cites the article from which I just quoted. In fact, Fall is the only outside expert who is cited seriously in the book. McNamara cited his articles as "encouraging news." The context is McNamara's explanation of why it made sense to escalate the attack and bomb South Vietnam. He says that we were getting encouraging news from the ground. The article of Bernard Fall's that he cites says exactly what I mentioned—that the major decision of the war was to bomb South Vietnam at a level that no area had ever been subjected to. McNamara never discusses the decision to bomb South Vietnam in 1961 or in 1965. The bombing of the South carried no cost—so it was uncontroversial and unimportant. Furthermore, Fall goes on to say that the United States is using so much military force that it cannot be militarily defeated in the short run. The United States was going way beyond anything the French ever did— so it cannot be militarily defeated any more than the French were in Algeria. But the Vietnamese will suffer the same fate, Fall says. That is McNamara's "encouraging news" from Fall. Fall was a hawk, but he cared about the Vietnamese. He goes on to describe horrible war crimes, torture, combat missions in which the United States is massacring peasants, bombing hospitals, and so on. That is the "encouraging news." It is costless to us, so irrelevant.

Then McNamara has a footnote in which he says that two years later Fall changed his mind and departed from his optimistic views, coming to think that perhaps U.S. force would not prevail. McNamara's referring to articles that Fall wrote in 1967 in which he expressed his concern that American forces might prevail. What he says in these articles is that Vietnam as a cultural and historical entity is in danger of becoming extinct under the blows of the most massive military machine ever directed against an area of this size. To McNamara, that means he changed his views from optimism to pessimism as to whether the U.S. force would prevail.

Well, the fact that McNamara interprets it that way is of no interest; he is an insignificant technocrat who barely understood what was going on. But what is of interest is the reaction to this book across the spectrum. Take a look at the reviewers. No one thought there was anything odd about McNamara citing Bernard Fall's bitter condemnation of U.S. atrocities as "encouraging news," and saying that he changed his mind on the "encouraging news" because he thought the United States was going to drive the country to absolute extinction. One would have to work pretty hard to find a counterpart to this in the Nazi archives. And that is across the spectrum!

I bring this up to show the inability of American intellectuals, including most of the dissidents on the left, to break out of the constraints of the propaganda system. To this day, we cannot face the elementary fact that the United States attacked Vietnam. In fact, the United States carried out what must be the most amazing propaganda achievement in history. They managed to transfer the blame to the Vietnamese: we were the injured party. So from the end of the war up till today, the operative question is whether Vietnamese behavior has been good enough for us to allow them to enter the civilized world. When George Bush was president, a front-page story appeared in the *New York Times* that quoted a speech he gave in which he said that Hanoi must understand that we do not seek retribution for the crimes they have committed against us; we just want them to give an honest accounting of what they have done. This article appeared next to another, one of dozens of articles, noting with a kind of amazement that the Japanese have some flaw in their character: they seem to be unable to confess to the crimes they committed during World War II. I doubt that you would find such behavior anywhere else, even in Brezhnev's Russia. There, people knew that they were invading Afghanistan, that Russia was not the injured party. Here, the reversal passes smoothly, virtually without comment, probably even without awareness.

There was a story in the *Times,* another one of Nicholas Kristof's innumerable stories about the Japanese character flaw, in which it says that the Japanese finally did express remorse, but they used a word that does not mean "apology" but means "regret." What follows is a kind of philological analysis of the characters right there on the front page. And, furthermore, when the Japanese referred to their atrocities, Kristof argues, although they did make a strong statement about the fact that Japan had caused terrible suffering to the people of Asia, they did not really come clean. They were still trying to evade their guilt by putting it in the context of other aggression and colonialism. Obviously, that is absurd—nobody but the Japanese carried out colonial atrocities or aggression in Asia. Certainly, the Dutch never did, the British never did, the French never did, and we never did. How could anyone imagine that when we conquered the Philippines and killed a couple hundred thousand people it was anything but a welcoming party? As for Vietnam, four million Indochinese may have been killed, but it is the fault of the North Vietnamese, not our fault. And this is right in the same paragraph! The report quotes *Asahi Shimbun,* sort of the *New York Times* of Japan, to show that not everyone is willing to go along with this Japanese unwillingness to apologize; *Asahi* had a strong editorial condemning the outrageous refusal of

Japan to apologize fully. Has the *New York Times* ever apologized fully or condemned the United States for not apologizing fully for the war in Vietnam, or for anything else, for that matter? If you look at McNamara's book, he does apologize—but to the American people for what was done to Americans. If you now look at the reviews, that is considered very courageous and honorable.

Big changes took place in the whole culture in the 1960s, and the university was in many ways involved in it. There were major changes in attitudes toward everything, and these changes affected the entire society: in personal relations, in attitudes toward women, toward the environment, respect for other cultures—across the board there has been a very substantial change.

Even the *Times* has changed, because any institution reflects public attitudes to some extent. Even the Kremlin reflected public attitudes to some extent. So, as a result, the *Times* is much more open than it was in the 1960s. You wouldn't have had Bob Herbert writing in the *Times*. In fact, the *Times* was very pro-war. Anthony Lewis was maybe the first person that I recall at the *Times* to criticize the war—though what it called "criticism of the war" was to say that the United States might not win at an acceptable cost. So David Halberstam was "critical," and the editorials were "critical," on the grounds that the United States was following bad tactics and probably would not win, or maybe it was costing too much, so we should try some other way. Even Lewis's belated criticism was very mild: it was that we began with bungling efforts to do good but it turned into a disaster and was costing too much. That was called "criticism" back in the 1960s and 1970s.

The students are not all that different from the general culture, nor were they at the time. But let us take something very remote from this topic—Native Americans. The original sin of American culture, after all, is what happened to the native population. That was not part of popular culture, not part of intellectual culture, not even part of academic anthropology. It was not until the late 1960s that the issue finally entered understanding and attitudes, and there was a willingness to notice that something happened to several million people who are not here anymore. That is when the scholarly research began in a serious way, some of it initiated from outside the academic profession, though it gradually got in. Public attitudes changed, too. By 1992, an attempt was made to carry off a celebratory quincentennial, liberation of the hemisphere. It was impossible. Not because of the colleges; the public would not accept it. They would not accept this as liberation of the hemisphere. And this change extends to almost every issue.

Again, you can see this dramatically with regard to Vietnam. Polls have been taken on public attitudes toward the Vietnam War since 1970 or so, and the responses are dramatic. The latest one that I know of was done in the early 1990s, I think. From the time they began in the 1970s until the early 1990s, about 70 percent of the general public describe the war as "fundamentally wrong and immoral," not "a mistake." But virtually none of the intellectuals have ever described it that way. The most they will say is "a mistake," and that is true of a good part of the left. In Charles Kadushin's *The American intellectual elite,* published in 1974, he asked two hundred "elite intellectuals," many of whom could be considered as left or left-liberal, what their attitudes were to the Vietnam War. These interviews, incidentally, were done in April 1970 or so, right after the invasion of Cambodia, which was the peak period of opposition to the war—colleges were closed down, everything was collapsing. This is from memory, so I may not have it exactly, but as I recall, he divided them into three categories. There were those he called "pragmatic" opponents of the war, such as Anthony Lewis, who basically said we are not going to get away with it, and it is costing us too much. Then there were what he called "moral opponents," who basically said, look, it is getting too bloody; napalming one hospital was okay but not ten hospitals. So that is "moral" opposition. The term is interesting. Then he had what he called the "ideological opponents," who said aggression is wrong. I think there were two out of two hundred—I'm not sure who the other one is, but every statement he quoted I recognized as my own.

Now, Kadushin did not do it, but suppose he had asked people what they thought of the Russian invasion of Czechoslovakia. That was bad enough, but they did not kill millions of people; they killed virtually no one. Well, everyone would have been an "ideological opponent," but he or she certainly would not have called it "ideological"—that would have been simply normal decency. On the other hand, among the American intellectual elite, at the peak period of opposition to the [Vietnam] war, virtually no one opposed it on principled grounds, and those few are dismissed as "ideological," not really serious folk. At that time, about two-thirds of the public were condemning the war as immoral, and in a few years you get this stable result: "fundamentally wrong and immoral and not a mistake." Now that is one of many, I should say, reflections of a cultural split between the general public and the intellectual elite, which I think is pretty noticeable.

The universities have changed because the people in them have changed. When I say that the intellectuals have not changed, I mean the *public intellectuals,* people who are in the public arena who make profound statements about the world and so on—I do not think they have changed a great deal. To the extent one can measure it, the change is less dramatic than in the general public.

In any society, the respectable intellectuals, those who will be recognized as serious intellectuals, will overwhelmingly tend to be those who are subordinated to power. Those who are not subordinated to power are not recognized as intellectuals or are marginalized as dissidents, maybe "ideological." Societies differ, however, and it is never 100 percent. But the tendency is just as obvious as the fact that corporate media serve corporate interests.

This goes back through all of history, as far as I know. An example can be found in the Bible. Who were the respectable intellectuals and who were the dissidents? The false prophets were the respectable intellectuals. Centuries later they were labeled "false" prophets, but not at the time. At the time, who were the people that were imprisoned, reviled, and driven over to the desert? They were the ones who were called "prophets" hundreds of years later. The reason was that they were giving both a moral and a geopolitical critique: that the leaders were going to drive the country to destruction, people should care about widows and orphans, and other such deranged fanaticism. Such people are going to be treated harshly; how harshly depends on the nature of the society. In Brezhnev's Eastern Europe they might be imprisoned or exiled. In a typical U.S. dependency such as El Salvador, they might have their brains blown out by U.S.-trained elite battalions or be cut to pieces with machetes, or they might simply flee for their lives. But such people are unikely to gain much respect in the respectable mainstream.

This is not something that is peculiar to our society by any means, far from it. Our own society is an unusually free and open one, and relatively privileged people—which means a lot of people—may undergo many kinds of unpleasantness, but not much by comparative standards.

The tendency to marginalize dissidents is always there and will always be there as long as grave inequalities in actual power and domination exist. When the actual power to make decisions is narrowly concentrated, then that power will be exercised in the doctrinal institutions as well.

John Dewey once described politics as the shadow cast by big business over society. The same is true of the universities and the doctrinal system generally, to no slight extent. Of course, one can struggle against that and change it, as in the 1960s and since. The situation in the universities or in the country generally is not what it was forty years ago. The change in the way blacks are treated in the South is dramatic. To mention one example: I was in Hattiesburg, Mississippi, a couple of years ago, and the difference from the early 1960s is day and night. These changes were not a gift. They came from brave and dedicated struggle. And the same is true of everything else. Furthermore, it is an ongoing struggle. Those who are trying to roll the situation back to what it was will never stop. They are always engaged in that effort; they have plenty of resources, and unless people resist, they will win.

The changes cannot be rolled back easily, but they can be rolled back. The history of the labor movement is an instructive case. In every modern society, it has been a leading force for democratization and human rights. The United States happens to have an unusual labor history. This is a business-run society, to an unusual extent, and American labor history has been unusually violent and harsh. Not until the 1930s did American workers obtain the rights that workers had gained long before even in quite reactionary industrial societies. May Day was originally a day of solidarity with American workers; it is a dramatic reflection of the prevailing culture that this is one of the few societies where hardly any people know anything about May Day, let alone participate in it.

When the United States entered the mainstream of industrial society sixty years ago, the business press warned of the "hazard facing industrialists" in "the political power of the masses" and [spoke of] the need to "direct their thinking" to more proper channels and to roll back the rights that had at last been won. After the war, the counterattack began in force. It was quite astonishing in scale and dedication, and class consciousness, with business leaders calling for a huge effort to win "the everlasting battle for the minds of men" and to "indoctrinate citizens with the capitalist story."

Forty-five years of intense propaganda has had an enormous effect. One result is that attitudes toward unions are very critical. About 80 percent of the population thinks working people ought to have more of a voice in public affairs, but about half that number think unions have too much of a voice. That is a reflection of extremely successful propaganda, everything from advertisements to the entertainment industry, where business propaganda presents the image of honest working people fighting their enemy, the union. Demonizing unions has been one consciously designed theme of business propaganda from the late 1930s, and by now it has had an effect. Another theme holds a certain picture of government, one that supports a huge welfare state for the rich through the Pentagon system and other devices, while engendering fear and dislike of those aspects of government function that reflect popular interests and concern—and of course concealing Dewey's truism. That's true quite broadly. For example, why are the deficit and the debt a big issue? Are they an issue because people are worried about the fact that the debt is well within the historic range, relative to gross national product? They are issues because it is driven into people's heads, day after day, that this is our biggest problem.

The reasons are simple: the business world, particularly financial interests, want the budget balanced, and also see that they can use that project as a device to undermine the social programs that they have always regarded as at best a tolerable luxury. As for the public, here the polls are interesting. Typically, two kinds of questions are asked: one set for the headline writers, the other for people who are fighting "the everlasting battle for the minds of men" and therefore want to keep their finger on the public pulse so that they can package their agenda properly. For the headlines, the question is: Do you want the budget balanced? The expected answer: Sure—as if you were asked whether you want your household debts magically canceled. Then comes the sensible question, on a par with Do you want your debts canceled if you lose your house, your car, your children's education?—in this case, Do you want the budget balanced if it means cutbacks in spending for health, education, environmental protection? Then support drops radically, to 20 to 30 percent, depending on just how the question is asked.

But the business-financial world has spoken, and the shadow obeys. Both political parties are adamant that the budget must be balanced, and the media ram home the message constantly, telling the public that it demands a balanced budget and it has voted for it. A fabrication, but by dint of endless repetition, it will probably come to be internalized, maybe even believed. The idea is that if you drill something into people's heads long enough, their attitudes will change, or at least what people think are their attitudes. Lacking any support in a depoliticized society in which popular organizations that might sustain a functioning democracy have largely eroded, individuals are in a difficult position, often unable to come to understand what they think, believe, and want—not an easy task under the best of circumstances. They sometimes react in irrational ways, which is no problem, as long as it does not threaten privilege.

The same is true of other propaganda campaigns. The "drug war" is just one example. Until Bush dramatically announced a "drug war" (once again—it is periodic) in September 1989, the drug problem was low on the list of public concerns. Out of curiosity, I monitored the media that month. The Associated Press wires had more on drugs than the whole international scene combined. On television and in the press, everything was drugs, drugs, drugs. By the end of the month the drug problem had shot way up to the leading issue of public concern. Was it because the problem had increased? No, simply very successful propaganda.

Again, these are natural features of a business-run society, that is, a society based on marketing and advertising—essentially, forms of manipulation and deceit. And these things have their effects, though they are sometimes slow. The United States came out of World War II as pretty much a social democratic society. Right through the 1980s, in fact, and even today, New Deal–style attitudes have remained deeply ingrained, despite half a century of intense propaganda using every available medium to drive such ideas out of people's heads. It takes time, but there can ultimately be an effect, even if it is only confusion and demoralization, which is as good as actual thought control for those who want to ensure that the shadow remains obedient to the substance that casts it, and that democratic forms do not function significantly to undermine the power of the private tyrannies.

In my opinion, one leading current tendency is an extension of the traditional effort to reduce the threat of democracy and to establish more firmly the Madisonian principle on which the country was founded: that the prime responsibility of government is "to protect the minority of the opulent against the majority," as Madison put it in the debates of the Constitutional Convention. The public is aware of the erosion of democracy. There is a regular Gallup Poll question asking people who they think the government works for. For a long time about half said "a few big interests looking out for themselves." Now over 80 percent say that the government is working for the few and the special interests—though what the public thinks the "special interests" are after years of intense propaganda is another question.

Such results, which extend rather broadly, reflect a general sense that we do not have a functioning democratic society, even if the reasons are not understood. In such a situation, a small group of dedicated fanatics with plenty of money behind them can make many changes, whatever the public prefers. A look at the Heritage Foundation budget proposals reveals such a possibility. It calls for severe cuts in social spending (in sharp opposition to the public will) and for an increase in Pentagon spending (overwhelmingly opposed by the public).

Where this will lead it is hard to say. It depends on whether, as often in the past, people can find ways to organize and respond constructively, defending at least a minimal social contract and recovering what was common understanding among a very large part of the population not too long ago: that concentration of decision making in the hands of unaccountable institutions of a basically totalitarian character is completely unacceptable, and that no decent human being should tolerate "the new spirit of the age" denounced by the popular working-class press in the mid-nineteenth century: "Gain wealth, forgetting all but self."

If they choose, privileged intellectuals in the universities and elsewhere can contribute to protecting and advancing democracy, freedom, and human rights. That is unlikely to win them many plaudits, but it brings rewards that are immeasurable.

II (FEBRUARY 1997)

The book *The Cold War and the university* isn't my accomplishment. I'm sure Howard [Zinn] will say it's not his either. It was a joint project to which we happened to contribute, as did other people. My contribution was an interview. So it's a joint enterprise, the first volume of several, on the thesis of the Cold War and the university. I'm not going to talk specifically on the book. I'll say a couple of words about the Cold War and where the universities fit into it and something about what happens now that the Cold War is technically over.

[The course of recent historical scholarship]

There's a huge amount of historical scholarship on the Cold War, and I'm not going to try to review it. There's also a standard picture, which I'll accept, of the course of that scholarship that sort of goes in the structure of thesis, antithesis, synthesis. The thesis is the original position from the origins, sometimes called the orthodox or traditional view, and that is, in a phrase, that the Cold War was the result of Soviet aggressiveness and intransigence and the U.S. played a completely defensive and reactive role. It was simply a matter of light versus dark, absolute perfection versus total evil. If you want to read it in its purest form and you haven't done it, you should read NSC [National Security Council] 68, which everyone recognizes as the standard Cold War document, declassified—and no one ever quotes it. (I think the reason it's never quoted is because the rhetoric is so outlandish and the image it gives of the culture of the period is so intolerable that it's better to refer to it indirectly rather than to actually quote it.) That's the thesis.

The antithesis is what's called "revisionist" scholarship that comes along in the mid-1960s as part of the whole ferment of that period. That took the heretical position that the Cold War was a kind of interaction, with both sides playing some role in initiating and sustaining it.

The synthesis, which is sometimes called "post-revisionism," is basically the traditional orthodox view with a few nuances. The leading figure, by common consent, is John Lewis Gaddis, sometimes called the dean of diplomatic historians, with the most authoritative studies and the leading figure in the field. I'll just refer to him.

The revisionist heresy, when it came along, caused enormous uproar and concern, which itself tells you something about the period. Arthur Schlesinger, in October 1966, wrote that "it's time to blow the whistle" on the heresy. The debate is kind of interesting, because the heresy had barely been expressed at that time. In fact, he was responding to a review by a young historian of a book about the Cold War in which the historian, Gar Alperovitz, said that "the Cold War cannot be seen simply as an American response to Soviet challenges, but rather has to be traced to a mutual interaction of insidious suspicions for which blame must be shared by all." That was the heresy. Schlesinger was so outraged that he at once wrote that it's time to blow the whistle on this before things really get out of hand and the plague spreads.

A couple of years later, Henry Kissinger lamented that "in the 1960s, the European intellectuals began to argue that the Cold War was caused by American as well as Soviet policy and a verbal and sometimes violent minority in the U.S. challenged the hitherto almost unanimous conviction that the Cold War had been caused by Soviet intransigence alone." In other words, the pillars were really collapsing. He was writing at a time of great concern about what was called the "crisis of democracy," which was the title of an important book which everyone ought to read, the first and only serious study by the Trilateral Commission in the mid-1970s. They were concerned by the fact that during the 1960s in all of the trilateral areas—Europe, Japan, and the United States—there had been sectors of the population that are normally quiescent and obedient that had become organized and tried to enter the political arena to press their demands, which created a crisis of democracy, which has to be overcome by driving them back to apathy and obedience and out of the political arena, where they have no place to be.

This was from the liberal end of the spectrum, these comments. These are the groups around the Carter administration. In fact, the whole Carter administration was drawn from this. One of the problems was that the media were becoming much too adversarial. They said it might be necessary to think about means to try to control the media, because they're also getting out of hand. Another problem had to do with what they called the institutions responsible for the indoctrination of the young. That meant the universities, the schools, the churches, and so on. They weren't doing their job of indoctrinating the young properly, and something would have to be done about that. The spread of this awful heresy, saying that maybe it wasn't just pure light versus pure darkness, was one aspect of that.

The postrevisionist synthesis was just appearing at that point to try to end this heresy. Its own framework and point of view are kind of interesting. Its main figure is John Lewis Gaddis. I basically agree with what he says, so I'll just quote him. He traces the origins of the Cold War to 1917, which I think is correct. Another phase began in 1945. As you know, right after the Bolshevik Revolution, within a couple of months, there was an invasion of Russia by the West in which the U.S. participated. It was taken pretty seriously. The documents on what I'm going to now say have been out for about fifteen years, but they have yet to enter the public record, as far as I know.

The British took the thing so seriously that they used poison gas on the northern front. Remember, this was right after World War I. That was the ultimate atrocity at the time. They weren't kidding around. Gaddis describes the Western intervention and says it was justified and in fact defensive. "It was in response to a profound and potentially far-reaching intervention by the new Soviet government in the internal affairs not just of the West but of virtually every country in the world, namely, the revolution's challenge to the very survival of the capitalist order." So the security of the U.S. was already in danger in 1917, not just 1950, and the invasion of Russia was entirely warranted in defense. In defense against what? Against an internal change in Russia and an announcement of revolutionary intentions. That justifies invasion in defense, because it's a threat to us. Notice, by the same logic, if, say, the U.S. calls for global capitalism, any country in the world that feels they want to take some different course would be entirely justified in carrying out a defensive invasion of the U.S., and if they don't have the power for that, at least carrying out international terrorism, which is like, say, blowing up the World Trade Center, which is several steps short of aggression.

The point is, Gaddis has captured the mentality exactly. By leaving the Western orbit and announcing that they wanted others to do so, too, that was an intolerable challenge and it does justify aggression in order to block it. That is the standard justification that's given all the time for intervention in the Third World.

Remember, Russia was the original Third World. It goes back to the fifteenth century. That's crucial to bear in mind when you think about the cold war. Back around the fifteenth century, Europe began to divide, with the West beginning to develop and the eastern half becoming sort of its service area: raw materials, markets, cheap labor, that kind of thing. That division continued. There is actually a fault line right down Germany. The division continued right into early this century. The East became relatively more impoverished, that is, relative to the West, until early in this century, and then in 1917 Russia adopted a course "that reduced its willingness and ability to complement the industrial economies of the West," which is the major threat of communism. I'm quoting from a very important 1955 study by a prestigious study group of the political economy of U.S. foreign policy. I think they hit it right on the nose. That was the threat of communism: the refusal to complement the industrial economies of the West, which is the job of the Third World.

It was still worse than that. Russia was what later came to be called a "virus" that was spreading the infection to others. That's what Gaddis is talking about. They were calling on others to follow that same unacceptable course, right into the 1960s, when our record runs dry. (That's where the record of declassified documents ends.) Right into the 1960s the major concern of U.S. and British planners was precisely that: Soviet success. They were going to be a model that others might follow. So, for example, Arthur Schlesinger, in a very recently declassified memo to John F. Kennedy, talking about Cuba, says that the problem is "the spread of the Castro idea of taking things into your own hands and demanding the opportunity for a decent living, all of this stimulated by the Soviet Union, which is presenting itself as a model for modernization in one generation." So not only did they refuse to complement the industrial economies of the West, violating the rules for the Third World, but they're even inducing others to do so. Incidentally, by this time the U.S. had already in secret formally determined that it would overthrow the government of Cuba.

This is the basic logic of the North-South conflict, and I think if you look at the Cold War, it applies very well. Of course, the scale was so different in this case that it took on a life of its own, but the logic is not dissimilar from the threat posed by Grenada, Nicaragua, Cuba, and lots of others. And it's not very surprising that after 1989 the region is returning pretty much to what it was. So the parts that were part of the West, like, say, Czechoslovakia, the Czech Republic at least, and western Poland, are returning to the West. They're becoming what they were, part of the industrial societies. The others are sinking into deep Third World misery, with all the standard Third World properties. Here it's all attributed to the failures of communism. It's a little hard to explain why it happened after 1989 and also why it so totally resembles everything that's gone on in the places that have continued to play their role of being complementary to the industrial economies of the West, not precisely by choice.

In brief, I think Gaddis is basically right in the postrevisionist consensus, right in dating the Cold War and also in identifying the challenge. The challenge was success and the threat that it might be a model to others. I think one interesting result of contemporary scholarship is that it's now over-whelmingly obvious, really not denied on any side, that the threat was pretty much what George Kennan said in secret in 1947: not a military challenge but a political challenge, namely the unwillingness to accept the role of being complementary to the West and even instigating others to follow this idea of trying to get a decent life and doing it your own way—the virus effect. And that goes right up to the present.

In my view, that's the essence of the Cold War and the attitudes that it engenders. I think you see it right in the orthodox scholarship. I don't think you have to go to the critical scholarship to see this. It comes right out in the mainstream. So, for example, in the fact that Gaddis's view doesn't seem strange. We have the right to invade another country if it carries out an inter-nal change and says that others should do so likewise, particularly if it seems to be succeeding and maybe offering a model that others might want to fol-low. That's a challenge, and obviously we have a right to use violence in self-defense. You might search for a critique of that view.

[The university and two related systems]

Where do universities figure in all this? Two major respects. First of all, they have to forge the doctrinal framework. They are, after all, the institutions responsible for indoctrinating the young, and they've got to make sure that the young are properly indoctrinated and that the old are indoctrinated, too. The people that do the indoctrinating have to believe it, and other people who reach a general audience through the major mechanisms [do too]. You're allowed to have hawks and doves. That's not only allowed but required. There should be very lively debate. That's very useful for a propaganda system. But it should be within an extremely narrow framework. So the debate should be, as it was, for example, over Nicaragua, the biggest issue of the 1980s, the hawks say, We should overthrow the government by violence; the doves say, No, that's going to be too costly for us. We should overthrow it in other ways and restore it to what was called the Central American mode, imposing regional standards, that is, the standards of El Salvador and Guatemala (I'm quoting Tom Wicker and other doves), and between those extreme views you should have a terrific controversy. The idea that there might be something outside that framework would be unthinkable.

Quite apart from the doctrinal side, the universities have played a very significant role within the domestic economy. That's discussed in a number of those papers. There's an extremely important role that the universities have played within the entire domestic economy. In brief, if you don't know this, you really should. It's very important. During the 1930s there was the Depression. The New Deal didn't do much. The war got us out of it. The war was extremely successful from the U.S. point of view. The U.S. had a kind of command economy. Industrial production tripled. The country was producing like mad. There was a lesson that was taught. Later it was called the lesson of Keynes, namely, that if the government mobilizes resources and pours them into the economy, it can stimulate production and maintain a sort of state capitalist economy. Furthermore, that lesson was taught to exactly the guys who had to learn it, namely, the corporate managers who were brought to Washington to run the semi-command economy that succeeded in this.

They got the message and carried it into the postwar period. It was assumed across the board (economists, industrialists, everyone else) that if the spigot was turned off, the country would go right back to the Depression. This isn't even secret. It's all in the business press in the late 1940s. In *Fortune, Business Week,* and so on, there was a lot of talk of how advanced industry cannot survive in a competitive, unsubsidized, free-enterprise economy and the government must be the savior. There was also discussion about how that should be done. For rather sensible reasons it was decided that the military was the best way to do it. It was recognized that social spending would work. Everybody knew the Keynesian stories you learn in first-year economics about hiding dollars in the sand and so on. That they understood. They knew that social spending could have the same stimulative effect, but it has a downside. Social spending has a redistributive effect and a democratizing effect. People care where there's going to be a hospital. They don't have any opinions on what kind of missile you should build. And furthermore, social spending is not a direct subsidy to the corporate sector. It's indirect.

Military spending has none of these problems. It's redistributive, but upward. It's anti-democratic. It keeps people out of policy. And it's a direct gift to corporations. And besides, it's easy to sell. That was put very frankly. Truman's first secretary of the air force, Stuart Symington, advised that the word to use is not *"subsidy"* but *"security."* And that's exactly the story from then till today. Use the word *"security"* when you mean *"subsidy."* Then people hide.

The Cold War both contributed to this and was stimulated by it. Without proceeding, take a look at any dynamic sector of the economy since then and right up till today, and you'll find it very heavily dependent on this system of the public assuming the costs and also assuming the risks, incidentally, if anything goes wrong, but the profit being privatized. That's the existing system. It comes straight out of the early Cold War period, and it interacts closely with the Cold War. And the universities play a crucial role.

First of all, say, why do I have a job? Very simple. Because MIT is part of the funnel by which public funds get poured into high-tech industry. It gives them a little luxury to have fringes around the edge, like a music department, or me. That's basically what a good part of the universities are about, as well as creating the doctrinal framework for all this, which means not only instilling Cold War ideology, but preventing people from knowing things like that. So try to find a department in the university that studies the way the American economy works, namely, this way. It's not in the economics department because they're doing models of economies in ten-dimensional space. It's not in the political science department because they're studying electoral politics. If there's a business school, it's probably taught in the business school. It's certainly not in the general curriculum. But these are the core issues of the American economy.

You read the newspapers today, the front pages, all full of the great decision of the World Trade Organization to let the U.S. telecommunications industry take over the world, which is what it amounts to, and this is supposed to show our passion for free markets and the terrific American way, the way we're exporting our values. I'm quoting. How did the telecommunications industry of the U.S. get to the point where it could take over the world? They put up the satellites and created the computers and the networking and the Arpanet and the software and the fiber-optic cables and so on? Absolutely not. This is public resources funneled in large measure through the universities, a lot of the direct organization done by the Pentagon research agency, which started up the start-up companies and initiated most of the new ideas. When it finally works you hand it over to private corporations, and then our passion for free markets, et cetera, et cetera.

Part of a good indoctrination system is not letting people see what is so obvious. It's right in front of everyone's eyes. But you're not supposed to see it, and if the system really is working, like if institutions for the indoctrination of the young and everyone else are functioning properly, so there's no crisis of democracy, then you can write about the passion for free markets and all the rest of it.

[Three nontrivial questions]

All of this raises a number of questions, and they're not trivial. One question is, How should public funds be used? How should public resources be used to lay the basis for the economy and the intellectual culture of the future? That's one question, not trivial. A second is, Should the results of whatever comes out of public funds be handed over just automatically to unaccountable private power? Third question: Who should make the decisions about this? Should it be a topic of public discussion and debate? Should the public be involved in deciding on these non-trivial questions? About the third question there shouldn't be any debate, at least among people who think that democracy might be an amusing idea, but in practice it just doesn't happen. It's not even an option.

For example, the whole business about telecommunications, including the 1996 Telecommunications Act, is not even treated as a public interest story. It's a business story. How should the system be handed over to private power? Not, Should it be handed over to private power? That's not even at issue. Just what modality should be used to take this huge public giveaway and hand it over to private power. Notice it's a little more than just giving the aircraft industry away, because this whole system is crucial for the functioning of a democratic system. But virtually no discussion.

The public is not supposed to be involved in this. That's true in practice, not just in this case, but in the whole background, and it's even a principle you can read about in standard texts on American politics. For example, one that's written a couple of years ago by a guy (Samuel Huntington) with the lovely title of professor of science of government at Harvard who explained that "the architects of power must create a force that can be felt but not seen. Power remains strong when it remains in the dark. Exposed to sunlight it begins to evaporate."

I think that statement is very accurate, just like the statements by other leading intellectuals and academics whom I quoted earlier. Part of the task of the institutions that are responsible for the indoctrination of the young and everyone else is to protect power from exposure. The Cold War provided a framework for that, but the issue is far broader, and it remains with us long after the Berlin Wall has thankfully collapsed into ruins.

Chapter 20

The universities and the corporations (May 1973)

Do you think that within our society as it is now composed there should be a direct relationship or any direct ties or responsibilities between the university and the corporations?

Under the present conditions, if there is no relationship between wealth, however expressed, and the universities, the universities will collapse. This is obvious, because the universities exist on the basis of the supply of funds that come from the government, and basically from the wealthy. So in that sense there has to be a relationship. I think that's unfortunate myself, but that's the fact of social organization.

By their very nature, it often seems that the faculty assume a liberal or radical or critical view of the society.

I don't agree. I think the faculty is a very conservative group. That is, it is considered liberal within the spectrum of American opinion, but American opinion on the whole has shifted so far to the right as compared with, say, Western Europe, that by the general standards of the Western European democracies, the faculties in American universities are really quite conservative.

[Narrow ideological controls and a failure of honesty]

Then do you think faculty are failing in a role that they might play of supplying a liberal thrust in society—one of positive criticism?

Well, I don't care what kind of opinions people have. I think the university should tolerate a large diversity of opinion, which it does not. I think there is a severe failure—the failure is one of honesty, in my opinion. That is, I don't believe that scholarship within the university attempts to come to grips with the real structure of the society. I think it is under such narrow ideological controls that it avoids any concern or investigation of central issues in our society. And this is not merely a matter of opinion; I think this is easily demonstrable.

Is it possible within the society as it is now constructed to let the faculty have a more free role?

I don't think that anyone is stopping the faculty from doing it. Because of their profound conservatism, the faculty in the ideological subjects such as history, political science, and so on find ways to avoid studying basic issues about the nature and exercise of power in our society. Or if they do study them, they do it in a perverse and confusing fashion. In fact, the very nature of academic specialization contributes to that. For example, consider the study of political economy—there's a specialization of fields which makes it very difficult to investigate the central topics in the structure of American society within some academic department.

I think the most striking example of this that I know of is the study of foreign policy. There was a recent survey that appeared in the *Annals of the American Academy of Political and Social Sciences*. The author investigated two hundred major works in what he called the respectable literature on international affairs and foreign relations, and he discovered that more than 95 percent of them make no mention whatsoever of the relationship between corporations and foreign policy, and that less than 5 percent give the subject passing mention. Now, of course it's obvious to any 10th grader that that's a central issue. And the fact that academic scholarship so systematically avoids what is a central issue is just a very dramatic indication of the ideological controls under which it operates.

From what I've read myself, that article itself seems pretty conservative in its considerations.

You see, what's striking to me is two things. First of all, the fact that he was able to unearth it; namely, that within the mainstream, everybody avoids this topic like poison. And secondly, his own attitude toward that fact. That is, having noticed that there's a mass of literature that avoids the central issue (I think there's a periphery that touches the real issue), it never occurred to him that maybe it's the periphery that's the respectable literature, and the mass, that's the literature of advocacy. He himself is so caught up in the ideological structure of the society that he can't see what his own data suggests to him.

Considering the whole nature of society, as you see it, is there a way that faculty members and corporations can try and solve some of these problems?

We're looking at it rather differently. I think faculty and corporations are communicating beautifully. The corporations plainly want academic scholarship to create a web of mystification that will avoid any public awareness of the way in which power actually functions in the society, and the faculty has caught the message and they do it magnificently. They spin confusions and mystifications beautifully, and they do things like refusing to study the questions of corporations and foreign policy. I think the communication is working excellently. Of course, never good enough. For example, Agnew is not satisfied that only 92 percent of the press supports Nixon—it's got to be 100 percent. In this respect, too, I'm sure that corporations aren't satisfied that only more than 95 percent of the major foreign policy works failed to mention this issue; they'd rather have no one mention it. But the communication is going pretty well.

What about in the political sphere? It seems to me that faculties were solidly for McGovern, at least at Princeton and the Ivy League schools. Now, I don't know if this is pervasive in the country, but it seems to me that on the political front, these faculty are not going along with your analysis. I don't think the comparison between the faculty and the press is really valid here.

I think it's a good comparison. I don't know the actual statistics, but I suspect that if you took the newspapers read by Princeton professors, you'd also find that they are atypical in the country as a whole. But if you take the faculty at large, I think you would discover that, rather like the press, it's a conservative institution—very tightly tied to the ideological controls of modern society. I should mention that supporting McGovern really doesn't prove very much; McGovern is also a conservative.

What do you think the general trend in the university community is? Is it to continue this conservative trend, or do you think that the periphery is becoming more vocal?

I think there was a brief period in the 1960s when, largely as a result of disillusionment with the Vietnam War, a student movement developed, and there was something like a mass movement of dissent. In the wake of that, there *were* some efforts at opening up the universities slightly to permit a wider expression of opinion than the conservatism that dominated the ideological subjects had allowed. But I think these controls are being reasonably effectively reestablished. I don't think that it's likely that the major universities at least will tolerate much diversity of opinion. For example, take a case in point: Harvard has just fired four of its major radical economists—refused to grant them tenure, that is. Of course, a couple of them did get jobs elsewhere, University of Massachusetts and so on. But I think that's what I'd expect.

[Missing: an integrated view of the way society functions]

This hiring policy has come up quite a bit. Conservatives often accuse universities of having hiring policies against conservative professors. Do you think this might be true?

I suspect that's true as well. I think the universities tend to be what is called liberal. It's a pretty narrow orthodoxy; how you place it in the spectrum of opinion depends on which spectrum you're using. If you use the spectrum, let's say, of a Western European democracy, it seems to me our faculty is quite conservative. If you use American opinion [in the early 1970s—CPO], it's more or less on the left. But it's still pretty narrow; it doesn't tolerate much dissent. It's not merely political constraints that are imposed; as I mentioned before, academic specialization itself, and the particular manner in which it worked, functions in such a way as to eliminate areas of research that would tend to give us some sort of integrated view of the way society functions.

About ethical investing by the university, do you think this practice will have any effect within the corporation? Will it play any role in reform or cause any sort of change?

It is very minor, although it might affect something. Right now in England, for example, there's a great turmoil over practices that have recently been exposed of British investing in South Africa, and it's possible that that will raise the level of wages slightly of black workers in South Africa—probably only temporarily, though, until people forget about it. But these are not things which can have much impact. Power and wealth is too centralized to affect. It has to respond marginally to turmoil of the periphery.

What, then, do you really think the goals of society must be?

Personally, I'm in favor of democracy, which means that the central institutions in the society have to be under popular control. Now, under capitalism we can't have democracy by definition. Capitalism is a system in which the central institutions of society are in principle under autocratic control. Thus, a corporation or an industry is, if we were to think of it in political terms, fascist; that is, it has tight control at the top and strict obedience has to be established at every level—there's a little bargaining, a little give-and-take, but the line of authority is perfectly straightforward. Just as I'm opposed to political fascism, I'm opposed to economic fascism. I think that until major institutions of society are under the popular control of participants and communities, it's pointless to talk about democracy.

In this sense, I would describe myself as a libertarian socialist—I'd love to see centralized power eliminated, whether it's the state or the economy, and have it diffused and ultimately under direct control of the participants. Moreover, I think that's entirely realistic. Every bit of evidence that exists (there isn't much) seems to show, for example, that workers' control increases efficiency. Nevertheless, capitalists don't want it, naturally; what they're worried about is control, not the loss of productivity or efficiency.

Turning to the British attempt within the system to socialize: is that still touching on the periphery or has it been effective?
The British approach was to take over marginal and defunct industries that were no longer profitable and make the public bear the cost of them. That's called socialism. It has no bearing on anything; as far as I know, the concentration of capital and the degree of control by private capital over the economy and the distribution of goods haven't changed significantly; there's merely been a little softening of the structures.

[Loyal servants of the autocratic corporate state and economic fascism]

How do you view the possible transition of the economic system to libertarian socialism?
One can imagine it happening by a series of very radical reforms, imagine it happening by social revolution, but it would be a fundamental change in the nature of social organization however it happens. I don't think it's very *likely* to happen unless there's at the very least considerable awareness of the possibility of another kind of organization and a real commitment to achieve it on the part of a large mass of the population—of course, that's nothing like the case here. And the universities and other ideological institutions are working very hard to prevent it from being the case. This is the respect in which they are very loyal servants of the corporate state. For example, the questions that I've just been discussing aren't dealt with in the university curriculum. To my knowledge, up to until about two or three years ago, I know of one book on workers' control in the United States, a very hostile one. In the last two or three years, again as a result of the activity of the 1960s, there has been a little discussion that will subside if the ferment subsides.

All the communist revolutions have been in basically non-capitalist societies.
I don't think they're communist revolutions. I think what are called communist revolutions are authoritarian—are revolutions of development that introduce structures which are politically authoritarian and socially egalitarian, and basically they take a do-it-yourself kind of approach to development. That's what we call communist. It has nothing to do with what we call communist in the tradition of Western European socialism, so I don't think there are any communist revolutions, at least in the traditional sense.

Do you think that strict Marxist development is still viable in the way capitalism has developed since the mid-nineteenth century?
Well, I think it would be very surprising if the analysis given by Marx a century ago would be directly relevant to problems of capitalism today; I think it is only marginally relevant. In some general way, though, I think his point of view is useful to our present consideration.

Is there any up-to-date analysis in any country which deals with this? Does Lenin come much closer?
No, Lenin is much farther away. Lenin was merely a kind of authoritarian, although one can say that what he said was of some validity for developing societies. But it has no bearing on the advanced industrial societies, and if anything it would be a step backward for those advanced countries.

Is there any appropriate analysis?
I think there is a very significant, if undeveloped, tradition that grew out of Marxism and anarchism. It presents a range of opinion which is important but hasn't been developed, since it's been carefully excluded. Anyone's chances of airing this viewpoint in the universities or elsewhere are pretty slight, so there's been very little advance.

[Worker and community control of industry]
What possibilities do you see for the future?
Well, for example, I think one can imagine perfectly well a movement developing for combined worker and community control of industry. I think it makes a great deal of sense. Why should workers agree to be slaves in a basically authoritarian structure? They should have control over it themselves. Why shouldn't the communities have a dominant voice in running the institutions that affect their lives? If such a movement develops, it could take a variety of forms: a parliamentary system, with a new party developing that

would be outside the structure of the Republican and Democratic consensus; or it could take direct-action forms, like simply taking over economic institutions.

So you feel it's possible to work within the parliamentary system?
Yes, theoretically. My guess is that the possibility would not be realized. Those who really have power in this society tolerate democracy only so long as it doesn't infringe on their power. If, through the parliamentary system, we ever began to expropriate industry, then the people who have wealth and power would destroy the parliamentary system. In this respect there probably wouldn't be any way within the system. But any revolutionary I've ever heard of must prefer peaceful, non-violent means if these are possible. But it's rarely been possible because of the resistance by those who want to preserve their privileges.

Part ii

Language in the classroom

Chapter 21

Some observations on the teaching of language (September 1969)

The first bit of advice that a linguist can give to the language teacher is to take his advice with a grain of salt. It must be clearly recognized that linguistics and psychology cannot support a technology of instruction in the sense in which physics supports a "technology" of nuclear reactor design or space exploration. Teachers would be well advised to pay some attention to the achievements of these disciplines, but also to preserve a healthy skepticism about the possibility of direct application to their immediate problems. One of the greatest of linguists, Wilhelm von Humboldt, once wrote that a language cannot really be taught; rather, one can present to the child the thread along which he will develop in his own way. The discoveries of linguistics or psychology are unlikely to lead to a significant modification of this judgement. Learning will take place when the child is presented with a rich and complex intellectual environment, and to the extent that he is motivated to explore it and free to do so along lines determined by his own awakening interests and mentality. The successful teacher, of language or anything else, will be the one who can provide the requisite challenge, stimulation, and freedom.

[An intelligently designed curriculum and active participation]

Other things being equal, there is no doubt that language teaching will be facilitated to some extent by an intelligently designed curriculum making use of texts that introduce new vocabulary and structures at a reasonable rate and with adequate repetition. At the same time, it is quite possible that a carefully designed curriculum, no matter how excellent, may even hamper learning if the teacher is too overawed by it, too bound to it. Both observation and experiment indicate that a primary factor in successful learning is the element of voluntary action and self-willed exploration of the environment. A child normally learns his first language in a fairly chaotic environment. A second language can also be learned, quite successfully, under similar conditions, as for example when a child learns a second language on the streets or in the schoolyard. It has been experimentally demonstrated that certain kinds of learning are literally contingent upon voluntary behavior. Under certain conditions, learning will not take place when the subject is a passive observer rather than an active participant, exploring and manipulating the environment, even though the total "range of experience" presented to the subject is the same under the two conditions. For example, in the study of visual adaptation on the part of a subject wearing distorting prisms, there are significant differences in adaptation between a subject who walks down a path and another who is pushed in a wheelchair down the same path, between one who watches his hand as he moves it and another whose hand is moved. Caution is, of course, in order in attempting to generalize from such discoveries. Nevertheless, there is an obvious lesson for the educator, a lesson that is surely known intuitively by anyone who is involved in teaching, a lesson that should be given a prominent place in his thinking and planning.

Many illustrations can be cited. To mention one, there is little doubt that from the point of view of pedagogic principles, narrowly conceived, the actual text of the Bible is far from optimal as a language text for obvious reasons. The constructions are complex, the rate of introduction of vocabulary is far too high and there is much too little repetition, and much of the content may be beyond the easy comprehension of the child. Yet a child who is captivated by the excitement of studying something real and alive, of great cultural and historical significance, may put forth a compensating effort that will lead to a high level of achievement, even with respect to language learning, which may, in this case, be a by-product of a cultural experience of independent value. This is not to suggest that the unmodified biblical text should be used for elementary language instruction. Rather, the point is that proper design of textual materials must take into account the major factors that create the conditions under which language learning will proceed in a meaningful and satisfactory way, the factors of intellectual interest, motivation, and significance in the mental and emotional world of the language learner.

It can be said with fair confidence that the worst possible conditions for language learning are those marked by rigidity and intellectual and emotional vacuity. There can be nothing more stultifying than language drill, whether it is mere memorization of paradigms or the mindless repetition of patterns divorced from any meaningful context. Unfortunately, the linguistics and psychology of a generation ago, which are now—given the familiar culture lag—achieving a certain influence in educational circles, had a tendency to influence curriculum in these directions. It was commonly assumed that language, like other forms of behavior, is a system of habits developed through drill and training, reward and punishment. The structure of language was assumed to be a system of patterns that are acquired through constant repetition and "overlearning" under proper conditions of reinforcement. As a result, so-called "pattern practice" methods came to be regarded as an essential component of the language curriculum.

[An entirely invalid inference]

Whatever the actual results of recent methods of language teaching may be—and to my knowledge they are dubious at best—it must be understood that these methods are founded not on scientific knowledge but on conceptions that derive largely from the limitations of knowledge and from certain methodological constraints that needlessly limited investigation. The belief that behavior, animal or human, is describable as a system of habits is based on certain experimental artifacts. Namely, it has been easy, and occasionally useful, to design experiments in which certain habits are inculcated and behavior is "shaped" by the control of certain contingencies of reinforcement. From this observation, surely correct, nothing follows about animal and human behavior in general. The inference from the observation that behavior can be shaped and habits formed by drill to the claim that behavior is a system of habits is an entirely invalid one, totally foreign to the method of scientific inquiry. The latter conclusion could only be based on an analysis of the structure of behavior that demonstrates that it has the character of a system of habits. But when the structure of behavior is analyzed independently of the experimental designs of behaviorist psychology, no support is found for this hypothesis. Quite the contrary.

In particular, in the case of language, it is easily demonstrated that the normal speaker's knowledge of his language cannot be described as a "plan for behavior" or a system of habits. The belief that language is a system of habits, quite commonly voiced some years ago, was based not only on illegitimate inference from the experimental artifacts of the psychologist, but also on certain limitations of modern structural linguistics. Again, it is important to recognize that the concentration on the study of sound structure in modern linguistics is the result of methodological inadequacies. It reflects the limitations of certain methods of inquiry rather than discoveries about the nature of language.

The same can be said of the claim that sentence structure is representable as a system of patterns, the hypothesis that underlies much of the current methodology of language teaching. This claim too was based not on a discovery about language but on the limitations of certain methods of inquiry. The methods of linguistic analysis, like those of behaviorist psychology, were intrinsically incapable of revealing what lies beyond the habits and patterns, which, in fact, constitute only a marginal and insignificant part of normal language use or of the speaker's knowledge of his language. When the normal speaker's knowledge of his language is subjected to an independent study, free from the artificial restrictions of certain methods of analysis that are, in the end, quite arbitrary, then it is quickly determined that his knowledge cannot be represented as a system of patterns and habits. Rather, the normal speaker has developed an abstract system of processes that he puts to use in producing and interpreting the endless variety of structures that constitute the normal flow of speech. The child who learns a language has somehow—we do not begin to understand how—succeeded in inventing for himself this underlying system of processes. He is, therefore, capable of understanding and producing linguistic forms that do not fall under any simple pattern to which he has been exposed, still less that he has overlearned. And it is characteristic of his behavior that he creates these novel structures on the appropriate occasion, and understands them when he encounters them, as he constantly does. Presumably, the ability to construct for oneself an abstract grammar of underlying principles is a unique human endowment, a fundamental characteristic of human intelligence. It is the task of the teacher to construct the conditions under which this natural human ability will be put to use.

There are few simple rules that can be relied on by one who is concerned to construct the conditions under which the child's natural curiosity will lead him to acquire knowledge of language, or of anything else. Thus I have already mentioned that memorization of paradigms, like repetition of patterns, can in general be expected to destroy the conditions for learning. But even in this case caution is necessary. A creative teacher can even use paradigms successfully, I have no doubt. For example, he can use them to demonstrate the quite fascinating principles that determine the structure and organization of these regularities, something that might be quite intriguing to many children and that might awaken rather than dull their interest in the language. Children generally enjoy language games, and even invent them spontaneously. Old-fashioned grammar, properly employed, can provide opportunities and materials for work that can capture the imagination and provide incentive for learning.

[Graded reading materials and oral practice]

It stands to reason that graded reading materials and oral practice should be central to the curriculum, if their subject matter is of independent interest and is related to other activities and studies. What this subject matter should be is, of course, an independent question. It will be chosen in terms of more general educational aims, as to which linguistics nor psychology provide any enlightenment. If the goals of an educational program are to involve the child in a tradition of which the Hebrew language is an essential element, or to create a sympathetic awareness and sense of involvement in contemporary Israeli life and culture, then it can hardly be questioned that Hebrew-language instruction ought to occupy a central place in the curriculum.

Even if the language is forgotten in later life, it need not be assumed that study of it was necessarily a waste of time and effort. It may be that experiences and understanding that are an inseparable part of meaningful language instruction will endure, and it might also be argued, with some plausibility, that these are enriched by early study of the language as part of a broader cultural experience. It is a bit too mechanical to suppose that an adult who retains no ability to use a language has not been affected by the experience of studying it, though this may well be true insofar as language study is divorced from other aspects of his educational experience and is taught by meaningless drill and repetition. And for some, at least, there will be opportunities in later life to expand and develop what is learned in childhood. An intelligently designed curriculum will be oriented toward the realization of these possibilities by those who will be so inclined, in the light of their later experience and interests.

At this level of generality, there is not much more to be said about the matter. Concrete questions arise only when more specific goals are formulated. About this topic I have no competence to speak.

APPENDIX
The irrelevance of prescriptive grammar (1954)

Any study of modern Hebrew must take account of certain realities. Hebrew was revived quite recently and quite artificially as a spoken language, and the participants in this revival have been speakers of many different linguistic backgrounds. There are at present great numbers of recent immigrants in Israel who speak Hebrew haltingly or not at all, and many first-generation speakers even of long residence still speak self-consciously and with distinct traces of their native languages. On the other hand, modern Hebrew has by now evolved as a unified language with a strong nucleus of native speakers.

This rapid development naturally poses many special problems for study, but it makes prescriptive grammar, whatever its justification might have been approximately a half century ago, approximately as irrelevant here as in the study of any other language.

That the author [of *Modern Hebrew*] is well aware of this is evident from many remarks that he makes. Thus he points out correctly that "the emergence of a unified Hebrew pronunciation is taking place at a very rapid rate," and he criticizes the attempts to impose preconceived systems on languages, at the same time proposing the project of a descriptive grammar of current usage. Unfortunately, this awareness seems to dissipate when he in fact approaches the linguistic material. Not long after reading that "the task of the grammarian is not to devise rules but to analyze and describe the structure of the language at a given period," we come upon a list and discussion of the 225 most common "errors" in spoken Hebrew. The technique by which these "errors" were collected suggests a method that a linguist might be tempted to use in constructing a linguistic corpus: "each student [of the Hebrew University School of Education] spent a week listening to the speech around him—on the street, in buses, in restaurants and cafes, etc.—and jotted down all the errors he could detect." The conclusion is then reached that "conventional Hebrew grammar does not reflect many important aspects of everyday spoken Hebrew." But now, in place of the previous suggestion that this gap be closed by the construction of a truly descriptive grammar, it is recommended that this list of "errors" be used as a guide for a correctional teaching program. "One can divide this number over a specified number of years and concentrate each year on correcting a given number of errors."

A detailed investigation of the list merely adds to the confusion. Many of the errors appearing in the list are common idioms typical of native speech, for example, *ex kor'im lxa* 'what's your name', *ani oxel hamon* 'I eat a lot', *kmuvan šehalaxti lakontsert* 'naturally I went to the concert'. Many are forms representing regular and typical morphological developments of the modern language, such as *ra'ítem* instead of *r'itém*; *habetsefer* instead of *bet-hasefer*, where a common compound noun 'school', literally 'house of a book', is treated as a single inseparable noun, a very prevalent development; *yašan* in the past tense instead of *yašan*, by analogy with all other common verbs. Many are deeply entrenched forms which no native would think of questioning, such as *tsorfat* instead of *tsarfat*, as the biblical vocalization would indicate; *bana'í* instead of *banái*; *amod* 'stop' instead of *atsor*. Others are real errors which would stamp any speaker as non-native. At the same time the recommended "correct" forms are often in fact standard usage, but are frequently stilted and pedantic forms which would be considered purely literary, or perhaps even foreign, by native speakers.

The chapter on pronunciation is equally confused. While on the one hand the author takes a stand against those who favor the reintroduction of the gutturals (as if grammarians could effect this return to the "original" pronunciation), at the same time he asserts that "comparatively few people in Israel take pains with their pronunciation, and consequently the Hebrew pronunciation one commonly hears leaves much to be desired"; "modern Hebrew pronunciation tends to be careless and little attention is paid to the esthetic aspect"; "the most important step [to improve "the esthetic quality of our speech"] would be to introduce geminated consonants and the shva," et cetera. The principal objective motivating these suggestions for the "improvement" of Hebrew pronunciation is "to achieve a common standard pronunciation in Israel and the Diaspora." But in view of the fact that modern Hebrew is a living language with a large body of native speakers, it is clear that the only significance of such a goal is that the language of this community be taught wherever modern Hebrew is proposed as a second language. The proposal that immigrants should be taught an artificially constructed language quite different from that of the speech community into which they are to be introduced seems a strange conclusion for a study intended in part to help to "shorten considerably the period of adaptation required by the masses of immigrants in Israel."

The second half of the book contains a discussion of methods in language teaching, leading up to the presentation and discussion of the "Jerusalem method," which, much more than the linguistic sections of the book, is in accord with current linguistic theory. The "Jerusalem method" is based on the aural-conversational approach, with careful attention to pronunciation, gradually decreasing amounts of translation, inductive presentation of grammar, material based on Israeli life, and a carefully controlled vocabulary. This vocabulary, based mainly on frequency counts carried out by the author and on a suggested "basic" vocabulary, is presented in detail, along with a discussion of the considerations involved in its construction.

Chapter 22
Language theory and language teaching (August 1966)

I should like to make it clear from the outset that I am participating in this conference not as an expert on any aspect of the teaching of languages, but rather as someone whose primary concern is with the structure of language and, more generally, the nature of cognitive processes. Furthermore, I am, frankly, rather skeptical about the significance, for the teaching of languages, of such insights and understanding as have been attained in linguistics and psychology.

Certainly the teacher of language would do well to keep informed of progress and discussion in these fields, and the efforts of linguists and psychologists to approach the problems of language teaching from a principled point of view are extremely worthwhile from an intellectual as well as a social point of view. Still, it is difficult to believe that either linguistics or psychology has achieved a level of theoretical understanding that might enable it to support a "technology" of language teaching.

[The principles of "learning," under challenge]

Both fields have made significant progress in recent decades, and, furthermore, both draw on centuries of careful thought and study. These disciplines are, at present, in a state of flux and agitation. What seemed to be well-established doctrine a few years ago may now be the subject of extensive debate. Although it would be difficult to document this generalization, it seems to me that there has been a significant decline, over the past ten or fifteen years, in the degree of confidence in the scope and security of foundations in both psychology and linguistics. I personally feel that this decline in confidence is both healthy and realistic. But it should serve as a warning to teachers that suggestions from the "fundamental disciplines" must be viewed with caution and skepticism.

Within psychology, there are now many who would question the view that the basic principles of learning are well understood. Long-accepted principles of association and reinforcement, gestalt principles, the theory of concept formation as it has emerged in modern investigation, all of these have been sharply challenged in theoretical as well as experimental work. To me it seems that these principles are not merely inadequate but probably misconceived—that they deal with marginal aspects of acquisition of knowledge and leave the central core of the problem untouched. In particular, it seems to me impossible to accept the view that linguistic behavior is a matter of habit, that it is slowly acquired by reinforcement, association, and generalization, or that linguistic concepts can be specified in terms of a space of elementary, physically defined "criterial attributes."

Language is not a "habit structure." Ordinary linguistic behavior characteristically involves innovation, formation of new sentences and new patterns in accordance with rules of great abstractness and intricacy. This is true both of the speaker, who constructs new utterances appropriate to the occasion, and of the hearer, who must analyze and interpret these novel structures. There are no known principles of association or reinforcement, and no known sense of "generalization" that can begin to account for this characteristic "creative" aspect of normal language use. The new utterances that are produced and interpreted in the daily use of language are "similar" to those that constitute the past experience of speaker and hearer only in that they are determined, in their form and interpretation, by the same system of abstract underlying rules. There is no theory of association or generalization capable of accounting for this fact, and it would, I think, be a fundamental misunderstanding to seek such a theory, since the explanation very likely lies along different lines. The simple concepts of ordinary language (such concepts as "human being" or "knife" or "useful," etc., or, for that matter, the concept "grammatical sentence") cannot be specified in terms of a space of physical attributes, as in the concept formation paradigm. There is, correspondingly, no obvious analogy between the experimental results obtained in studies of concept formation and the actual processes that seem to underlie language learning.

Evidently, such an evaluation of the relevance of psychological theory to language acquisition requires justification, and it is far from uncontroversial. Nor will I attempt, within the framework of this paper, to supply any such justification. My point simply is that the relevance of psychological theory to acquisition of language is a highly dubious and questionable matter, subject to much controversy and plagued with uncertainties of all sorts. The applied psychologist and the teacher must certainly draw what suggestions and hints they can from psychological research, but they would be well advised to do so with the constant realization of how fragile and tentative are the principles of the underlying discipline.

Turning to linguistics, we find much the same situation. Linguists have had their share in perpetuating the myth that linguistic behavior is "habitual" and that a fixed stock of "patterns" is acquired through practice and used as the basis for "analogy." These views could be maintained only as long as grammatical description was sufficiently vague and imprecise. As soon as an attempt is made to give a careful and precise account of the rules of sentence formation, the rules of phonetic organization, or the rules of sound-meaning correspondence in a language, the inadequacy of such an approach becomes apparent. What is more, the fundamental concepts of linguistic description have been subjected to serious critique. The principles of phonemic analysis, for example, have recently been called into question, and the status of the concept "phoneme" is very much in doubt. For that matter, there are basic, unsolved problems concerning even the phonetic representations used as a basis for analysis of form in structural linguistics. Whereas a decade ago it would have been almost universally assumed that a phonetic representation is simply a record of physical fact, there is now considerable evidence that what the linguist takes to be a phonetic transcription is determined, in nontrivial ways, by the syntactic structure of the language, and that it is, to this extent, independent of the physical signal. I think there are by now very few linguists who believe that it is possible to arrive at the phonological or syntactic structure of a language by systematic application of "analytic procedures" of segmentation and classification, although fifteen or twenty years ago such a view was not only widely accepted but also supported by significant results and quite plausible argument.

[A frightful willingness to rely on "experts"]

I would like to emphasize again that this questioning of fundamental principles is a very healthy phenomenon that has led to important advances and will undoubtedly continue to do so. It is, in fact, characteristic of any living subject. But it must be recognized that well-established theory, in fields like psychology and linguistics, is extremely limited in scope. The applications of physics to engineering may not be seriously affected by even the most deep-seated revolution in the foundations of physics, but the applications of psychology or linguistics to language teaching, such as they are, may be gravely affected by changing conceptions in these fields, since the body of theory that resists substantial modification is fairly small.

In general, the willingness to rely on "experts" is a frightening aspect of contemporary political and social life. Teachers, in particular, have a responsibility to make sure that ideas and proposals are evaluated on their merits and not passively accepted on grounds of authority, real or presumed. The field of language teaching is no exception. It is possible—even likely—that principles of psychology and linguistics, and research in these disciplines, may supply insights useful to the language teacher. But this must be demonstrated and cannot be presumed. It is the language teacher himself who must validate or refute any specific proposal. There is very little in psychology or linguistics that he can accept on faith.

[Developments with a possible impact on language teaching]

I will not try to develop any specific proposals relating to the teaching of languages—as I mentioned before, because I am not competent to do so. But there are certain tendencies and developments within linguistics and psychology that may have some potential impact on the teaching of language. I think these can be usefully summarized under four main headings: the creative aspect of language use, the abstractness of linguistic representation, the universality of underlying linguistic structure, and the role of intrinsic organization in cognitive processes. I would like to say just a few words about each of these.

The most obvious and characteristic property of normal linguistic behavior is that it is stimulus-free and innovative. Repetition of fixed phrases is a rarity; it is only under exceptional and quite uninteresting circumstances that one can seriously consider how "situational context" determines what is said, even in probabilistic terms. The notion that linguistic behavior consists of "responses" to "stimuli" is as much a myth as the idea that it is a matter of habit and generalization. To maintain such assumptions in the face of the actual facts, we must deprive the terms "stimulus" and "response" (similarly "habit" and "generalization") of any technical or precise meaning. This property of being innovative and stimulus-free is what I refer to by the term "creative aspect of language use." It is a property of language that was described in the seventeenth century and that serves as one cornerstone for classical linguistic theory, but that has gradually been forgotten in the development of modern linguistics, much to its detriment. Any theory of language must come to grips with this fundamental property of normal language use. A necessary but not sufficient step toward dealing with this problem is to recognize that the native speaker of a language has internalized a "generative grammar"—a system of rules that can be used in new and untried combinations to form new sentences and to assign semantic interpretations to new sentences. Once this fact has become clear, the immediate task of the linguist is likewise clarified. He must try to discover the rules of this generative grammar and the underlying principles on the basis of which it is organized.

The native speaker of a language has internalized a generative grammar in the sense just described, but he obviously has no awareness of this fact or of the properties of this grammar. The problem facing the linguist is to discover what constitutes unconscious, latent knowledge—to bring to light what is now sometimes called the speaker's intrinsic "linguistic competence" [linguistic knowledge—CPO]. A generative grammar of a language is a theory of the speaker's competence. If correct, it expresses the principles that determine the intrinsic correlation of sound and meaning in the language in question. It thus serves as one component of a theory that can accommodate the characteristic creative aspect of language use.

When we try to construct explicit, generative grammars and investigate their properties, we discover at once many inadequacies in traditional and modern linguistic descriptions. It is often said that no complete generative grammar has ever been written for any language, the implication being that this "newfangled" approach suffers in comparison with older and well-established approaches to language description in this respect. The statement concerning generative grammar is quite accurate; the conclusion, if intended, reveals a serious misunderstanding. Even the small fragments of generative grammars that now exist are incomparably greater in explicit coverage than traditional or structuralist descriptions, and it is important to be aware of this fact. A generative grammar is simply one that gives explicit rules that determine the structure of sentences, their phonetic form, and their semantic interpretation. The limitations of generative grammar are the limitations of our knowledge in these areas. Where traditional or structuralist descriptions are correct, they can immediately be incorporated into generative grammars. Insofar as these descriptions merely list examples of various kinds and make remarks (which may be interesting and suggestive) about them, then they cannot be directly incorporated into generative grammars. In other words, a traditional or structuralist description can be immediately incorporated into a generative grammar to the extent that it is correct and does not rely on the "intelligence of the reader" and his "linguistic intuition." The limitations of generative grammar, then, are a direct reflection of the limitations of correctness and explicitness in earlier linguistic work.

A serious investigation of generative grammars quickly shows that the rules that determine the form of sentences and their interpretations are not only intricate but also quite abstract, in the sense that the structures they manipulate are related to physical fact only in a remote way, by a long chain of interpretative rules. This is as true on the level of phonology as it is on the level of syntax and semantics, and it is this fact that has led to the questioning both of structuralist principles and of the tacitly assumed psychological theory that underlies them. It is because of the abstractness of linguistic representations that one is forced, in my opinion, to reject not only the analytic procedures of modern linguistics, with their reliance on segmentation and classification, but also principles of association and generalization that have been discussed and studied in empiricist psychology. Although such phenomena as association and generalization, in the sense of psychological theory and philosophical speculation, may indeed exist, it will be difficult to see how they have any bearing on the acquisition or use of language. If our current conceptions of generative grammar are at all accurate, then the structures manipulated and the principles operating in these grammars are not related to given sensory phenomena in any way describable in the terms that empiricist psychology offers, and what principles it suggests simply have no relation to the facts that demand explanation.

[A universal prerequisite for language acquisition]

If it is correct that the underlying principles of generative grammars cannot be acquired through experience and training, then they must be part of the intellectual organization which is a prerequisite for language acquisition. They must, therefore, be universal properties, properties of any generative grammar. These are, then, two distinct ways of approaching what is clearly the most fundamental question of linguistic science, namely, the question of linguistic universals. One way is by an investigation of a wide range of languages. Any hypothesis as to the nature of linguistic universals must meet the empirical condition that it is not falsified by any natural language, any language acquired and used by humans in the normal way. But there is also another and, for the time being, somewhat more promising way of studying the problem of universals. This is by deep investigation of a particular language, investigation directed toward establishing underlying principles of organization of great abstractness in this language. Where such principles can be established, we must account for their existence.

One plausible hypothesis is that they are innate, therefore universal. Another plausible hypothesis is that they are acquired through experience and training. Either hypothesis can be made precise; each will then be meaningful and worthy of attention. We can refute the former by showing that other aspects of this language or properties of other languages are inconsistent with it. We can refute the latter by showing that it does not yield the structures that we must presuppose to account for linguistic competence. In general, it seems to me quite impossible to account for many deep-seated aspects of language on the basis of training or experience, and that therefore one must search for an explanation for them in terms of intrinsic intellectual organization. An almost superstitious refusal to consider this proposal seriously has, in my opinion, enormously set back both linguistics and psychology. For the present, it seems to me that there is no more reason for assuming that the basic principles of grammar are learned than there is for making a comparable assumption about, let us say, visual perception. There is, in short, no more reason to suppose that a person learns that English has a generative grammar of a very special and quite explicitly definable sort than there is to suppose that the same person learns to analyze the visual field in terms of line, angle, motion, solidity, persons with faces, etc.

Turning, then, to the last of the four topics mentioned above, I think that one of the most important current developments in psychology and neurophysiology is the investigation of intrinsic organization in cognition. In the particular case of language, there is good reason to believe that even the identification of the phonetic form of a sentence presupposes at least a partial syntactic analysis, so that the rules of the generative grammar may be brought into play even in identifying the signal. This view is opposed to the hypothesis that phonetic representation is determined by the signal completely and that the perceptual analysis proceeds from formal signals to interpretation, a hypothesis which, I understand, has been widely quoted in discussion of language teaching. The role of the generative grammar in perception is paralleled by the role of the universal grammar—the system of invariant underlying principles of linguistic organization—in acquisition of language. In each case, it seems to me that the significance of the intrinsic organization is very great indeed, and that the primary goal of linguistic and psychological investigation of language must be to determine and characterize it.

I am not sure that this very brief discussion of some of the leading ideas of much current research has been sufficiently clear to be either informative or convincing. Once again, I would like to stress that the implications of these ideas for language teaching are far from clear to me. It is a rather dubious undertaking to try to predict the course of development of any field, but, for what it is worth, it seems to me likely that questions of this sort will dominate research in the coming years, and, to hazard a further guess, that this research will show that certain highly abstract and highly specific principles of organization are characteristic of all human languages, are intrinsic rather than acquired, play a central role in perception as well as in production of sentences, and provide the basis for the creative aspect of language use.

APPENDIX
Letter about the teaching of grammar (March 4, 1984)
March 4, 1984

Dear Mrs. Davis,

Thanks very much for sending me your paper and discussion comments, which I read with much interest. I hesitate to express a judgment on the main question you are addressing, simply from lack of relevant knowledge. My uninformed guess would be that the study of grammar would have little detectable effect on writing ability, but I think it should be taught for its own intrinsic interest and importance. I don't see how any person can truly be called "educated" who doesn't know the elements of sentence structure, or who doesn't understand the nature of a relative clause, a passive construction, and so on. Furthermore, if one is going to discuss literature, including here what students write themselves, and to come to understand how it is written and why, these conceptual tools are indispensable.

For these purposes, I think traditional grammar so called (say, the grammar of Jespersen) remains today a very impressive and useful basis for such teaching. I can't see any reason for teaching structural grammars of English, or for teaching transformational grammar in the manner of some instructional books that I have seen (I really don't know the literature well at all), which simply amount to memorizing meaningless formulas.

If contemporary linguistics is to be taught (I think it should be), it is in a different context. I do think it offers an incomparable avenue to understanding the nature of the human mind. It also can provide students with a way to understand how science works. There are questions that are, or should be, fascinating and puzzling: for example, why does the sentence "Who did the boys expect to see them" allow the interpretation with *them* referring to the boys, while the sentence "The boys expect to see them" does not? Or why do the sentences "John is too stubborn to talk to Bill" and "John is too stubborn to talk to" have different "understood subjects" for *talk to* (John in the first case; someone other than John in the second)? And myriad others. These are simple, but very puzzling facts. Every child has command of a huge mass of data of this sort.

It is also possible to develop explanatory theories of a rather nontrivial sort that explain some of these facts, and to do so without resort to higher mathematics or other conceptual tools not available to the student (or teacher, generally). In this way, one might be introduced into the marvelous world of inquiry in which one learns to wonder about the nature of what seem, superficially, to be obvious phenomena, and to ask why they are the way they are, and to come up with answers. This is an experience generally lacking in the study of the sciences unless the instruction is really done superlatively well. These are all reasons for studying contemporary grammar—as a branch of science, which deals with questions of central human concern and which happens to be fairly accessible, as compared, say, with quantum physics. I doubt that it will improve writing style, but it could help students learn how (and why) to think about hard and intriguing questions, and to develop the natural curiosity that is so often dulled by what we (perhaps misleadingly) call "education."

Anyway, for what it is worth, my own view is that you should go on teaching traditional grammar, even if educational research shows no effect on ability to write. That should not be the main goal of such teaching, in my view.

Sincerely,

Noam Chomsky

Letter from Noam Chomsky to the Editor

March 21, 1984

Dear Professor Berger,

In response to your letter of March 15, I suppose I would have no objection to your publishing my letter to Mrs. Davis, though I would appreciate it if you would make it clear that it was merely an informal letter, not written with an eye to publication. As indicated in the letter, I would not want people to be misled into thinking that I have any special insight into the question of grammar teaching and writing or any special competence to talk about the matter. Quite frankly, I doubt that others are in a better position, apart from teachers themselves, who really have experience in the matter.

Sincerely yours,

Noam Chomsky

Chapter 23
Our understanding of language and the curriculum (1964)

A grammar of a language aims to present in a precise and explicit form just those facts about the language that its speakers know intuitively. It attempts to account for the native speaker's ability to understand any sentence of his language and to produce sentences, appropriate to the occasion, that are immediately comprehensible to other speakers although they may never have been spoken or written before. In fact, in the normal everyday use of language, one is constantly dealing with sentences that are quite new, both as a speaker (or writer) and a hearer (or reader).

For example, the sentences of this paragraph will be new to most readers, as will most of the sentences in today's newspapers or tomorrow's conversations. From this observation we can conclude that the speaker-hearer's knowledge of his language must be represented as a system of rules, and that his linguistic competence lies precisely in his ability to arrange these rules in new and previously untried combinations in forming and interpreting sentences. These rules, in their various arrangements, specify the structure of each sentence of the language; intuitive mastery of them is what constitutes knowledge of a language. A grammar presents this system of rules.

[From a simple observation to an important conclusion]
In more technical terms, we can think of a grammar as a system of rules that specifies the class of phonetically possible utterances that are well formed in the language in question, and that assigns to each well-formed sentence (whether or not it has ever actually been produced or ever will be produced) a structural description that incorporates and expresses just the information about the sentence that is available to the person who understands it. Thus a speaker of English knows that "The puppy looks terrifying" is well formed, whereas "The puppy looks barking" and "Terrifying looks puppy the" both fail

to be well formed (though, to be sure, they differ in the degree to which they are deviant). Similarly, given the sentences

(A) *John impresses Bill as incompetent*
(B) *John regards Bill as incompetent*

any speaker of English knows that in A the word *incompetent* qualifies *John* and that in B it qualifies Bill. An adequate grammar of English must provide such information as this, with respect to each phonetically possible utterance.

When we speak of a grammar as presenting what the native speaker knows, we are referring, of course, to unconscious knowledge. The speaker of a language is, normally, no better able to state the rules of his language than to formulate the principles that enable him to recognize a physical object or to determine its distance or velocity. The principles of sentence formation and interpretation formulated in a grammar are those that must be presupposed to account for the actual use of language. Presentation of these principles to the native speaker may bring them to awareness. In part, however, these principles may be quite beyond the limits of possible introspective awareness (just as in the case of the principles that underlie visual perception). The fact that the performance of the speaker-hearer is governed by an internalized system of grammatical rules does not imply that he is conscious of the character of these rules or the manner of their operation.

[Shortcomings of traditional and structuralist grammars]

As research on the structure of language progresses, it becomes increasingly clear that the subtlety, diversity, and bewildering complexity of the skills that have been attained by the native speaker have been seriously underestimated in modern attempts to develop a theory of the nature, use, and acquisition of language. As a result, the study of linguistic structure is very much alive today. In particular, much work is being devoted to the study of syntactic structure and the role it plays in determining sound and meaning. In the context of considerable discussion and debate, certain assumptions about the nature of language are emerging which appear to be insightful and, increasingly, to be supported by empirical evidence. This book [*English syntax* by Paul Roberts] presents some of the results of recent study of linguistic structure. To appreciate more fully the motivation for the direction that it takes, it is useful to consider briefly some of the characteristic ways in which the structure of language has been studied in the past.

Traditional scholarly descriptive grammars (e.g., those of Jespersen, Poutsma, etc.) do, in a sense, attempt to provide an account of what the fluent speaker knows intuitively. An intelligent reader might be able to develop a good deal of competence in a new language from such grammars, or from pedagogical grammars based on them. We cannot, however, conclude from this that these grammars do actually present a full and explicit account of native linguistic competence. It remains to be determined what is being supplied by the grammar and what by the intelligence of the reader.

In fact, a careful analysis shows that the unanalyzed contribution of the intelligent reader is far from small. The most careful and compendious traditional grammar may give a full account of exceptions and irregularities, but it provides only examples and "paradigmatic instances" of regular constructions, together with various informal hints and remarks as to how the reader is to generalize from these instances. The basic regular processes of sentence construction remain unexpressed; it is the task of the reader to infer them from the presented material. It turns out that to fill this gap is no small task. In fact, even the best traditional descriptive studies cover only small fragments of a language, and because of their implicit appeal to the reader's intelligence and linguistic abilities, they leave fundamental questions unresolved. In other words, we do not know in any detail what constitutes "the intelligence of the reader" or what is accomplished when it is applied to the data presented in the grammar. Until these questions are answered, our descriptions of language, and of the nature of human linguistic abilities, are incomplete and defective in an essential way.

Modern structural linguistics has reached levels of rigor that often exceed those of traditional grammar, and it has revealed previously unrecognized aspects of linguistic structure. However, it provides little insight into the processes of formation and interpretation of sentences. Study of these questions has been outside of the scope of modern structuralism, which has limited itself, almost completely, to the system of inventories of elements (phonemes, morphemes) and to analytic procedures that may assist in determining these elements. There has been some discussion of syntactic patterns, but it has been fairly primitive as compared with traditional grammar.

It is, therefore, not surprising that there has recently been renewed interest in the formalization and use of techniques and devices that are more characteristic of traditional than of structuralist grammars. In fact, a reader who is acquainted with traditional grammar will find much that appears familiar in this book. Current work in grammar attempts to meet the standards of explicitness characteristic of the best structuralist work without sacrificing scope. It attempts to formulate precisely the processes of sentence formation and interpretation that constitute the linguistic competence of the fluent speaker and that underlie the actual use of language, processes that are only hinted at in traditional grammars and that are quite beyond the scope of structuralist descriptions. The goal of this work is to eliminate the reliance, characteristic of traditional grammar, on the intelligence of the reader. In other words, it attempts to present an explicit analysis of what is involved in his "application of intelligence" to the data given in the grammar.

[The basic parts of a transformational grammar]

A complete grammar should have three basic parts. Its **syntactic component** (which includes, in particular, a lexicon) provides an analysis of the sentence into minimal functional units. Thus the syntactic component of an English grammar might analyze "We began smoking" into the sequence of six units: *I, plural, begin, past tense, smoke, -ing*. Furthermore, it provides a structural description which determines the manner in which these units are interrelated and organized into larger structures of varying complexity. For example, in the case of "We began smoking" or "We enjoy smoking" the syntactic component of an English grammar would indicate that a certain grammatical relation (call it *subject–verb*) holds of the pairs (*we, begin*), (*we, enjoy*), and (*we, smoke*), whereas in the case of "We oppose smoking" it would assign this relation only to the pair (*we, oppose*), and not to (*we, smoke*). An adequate syntactic description of English would have to provide a great deal of information of this and other kinds.

The **semantic component** of a grammar (the second of its three parts) utilizes this syntactic structural description to provide a semantic interpretation of the sentence. Continuing with the last example, the semantic component of the grammar, making use of the information about grammatical relations presented to it by the syntactic component, would assign semantic descriptions to "We enjoy smoking" and "We oppose smoking" in such a way as to indicate that the former is a paraphrase of "We smoke and we enjoy it," though the latter is not a paraphrase of "We smoke and we oppose it."

The **phonological component** of the grammar utilizes the syntactic structural description to provide a phonetic representation of the sentence. In the case of a language with a conventional orthography, one might also add to the grammar an *orthographical component* that utilizes the syntactic structural description to provide a spelling of the sentence. The latter has rarely been studied in any serious way, since investigation of this output system would be fairly easy and uninformative as compared to the investigation of the phonological component of a grammar.

Clearly, the central and fundamental part of a grammar is its syntactic component. Both semantic and phonological rules require syntactic information for their proper functioning. The study of semantic and phonetic structure cannot proceed beyond the limits set by our understanding of the rules of syntax and of the structural descriptions that they provide. It is these rules that embody the essential creative aspect of linguistic competence, that is, that enable the native speaker to form and analyze new sentences. This book is an introduction to the study of the syntactic component of English grammar. In principle, it should be supplemented by studies of how these structures provide the basis for semantic and phonetic interpretation. It must be recognized, however, that in raising these highly interesting questions we reach the borders of contemporary research.

The theory of grammar that is presented in this book generally goes by the name transformational grammar. This theory is based on certain assumptions about the kinds of processes that exist in language and the manner in which they interrelate. In particular, it assumes that fundamental to the interpretation and forming of sentences are certain processes—called grammatical transformations—that relate a sentence to a set of underlying sentence-like structures of a particularly simple form. These simple underlying structures, which do not involve any grammatical transformations in their construction, express all of the grammatical relations and functions that appear in any sentence. The normal sentences of everyday life are formed, characteristically, by a complex series of transformations of underlying structures. Although the underlying structures are finite in number, the rules of transformation can be used in indefinitely many arrangements to form an unending variety of sentence types.

As in the case of any substantial theory of language, the theory of transformational grammar makes certain implicit claims concerning the nature of human intellectual capacity. It asserts that a child will seek to impose a specific kind of structure—namely, the kind formulated in this theory—on the data to which he is exposed as he grows up in a speech community. It assumes, in other words, that the person who discovers the structure of a language from presented data is utilizing the resources of the theory of transformational grammar in constructing a grammar of his language.

Although the theory of transformational grammar has deep roots in traditional grammar and in classical linguistic theory, its explicit formulation is fairly recent, and much of the material presented in this book is the product of work of the past few years. Neither the theory of transformational grammar nor the description of English structure that has been and is being developed in accordance with its principles can be regarded as a closed and fixed system.

There is an enormous amount to be learned concerning the nature of language in general and the structure of English in particular. This fact was obscured by the informality of traditional grammar, but it becomes quite evident as soon as an attempt is made to state the principles of sentence formation and interpretation exactly, without reliance on the unanalyzed contribution of the intelligent reader. As compared with the explicit coverage of traditional or structuralist grammar, the scope of this book is quite broad. It presents the main outlines of English syntax and deals explicitly with a variety of quite complicated structures by means of rules that are at best vaguely suggested in traditional grammar. Nevertheless, material of the sort that is presented here must be regarded as representing only a stage in the development of linguistic theory and the theory of English structure, a stage which surely will be surpassed as research proceeds. In brief, the study of language is a living subject, and its future growth and development are consequently unpredictable.

[A unique opportunity for studying the basis of mental development]

I think it is obvious that study of linguistic structure can provide deep insights into human intellectual capacity and mental processes. Understanding of a sentence is achieved through a perceptual process of extreme complexity; there are few, if any, other examples of processes of equal complexity that are as amenable to direct study as this. Acquisition of language involves the construction of a highly intricate, abstract, and closely integrated system of rules. This accomplishment is, nevertheless, carried out uniformly, extremely rapidly, and (to a high degree of approximation) quite independently of intelligence, on the basis of an amount of data which is not at all large, considering the character of the system that the child masters and internally represents in some form. Again, there are few aspects of complex human competence that offer a comparable opportunity for studying basic characteristics of human learning and the prerequisites for it to take place.

The structure of a language is a remarkable intellectual product, created anew, in a sense, every time the language is learned by a child, and there is little doubt that wherever real understanding of linguistic structure is achieved, it can be translated into terms of immediate relevance for the study of human intellectual activity and its underlying mechanisms. Considerations of this sort have been one main source of interest in the study of linguistic structure.

Traditionally, the goal of the grammarian has been viewed in quite a different way. As we noted above, from the fact that a person has attained a level of competence represented by a certain system of rules, it does not follow that he is aware of these rules. It is also clear that various factors may limit an individual's ability to use the skills and knowledge that he possesses. A person may, for example, have learned the rules of arithmetical computation perfectly and may still have frequent and characteristic errors even in relatively simple computations. Similarly, two speakers of a language who know the language equally well (whose knowledge is expressed by the same system of rules) may differ markedly in fluency and facility.

One of the traditional motives for teaching grammar has been to extend the range of situations in which the body of skill and knowledge that the speaker has developed can be put to effective use. Furthermore, it is important not to overlook the fact that the English-speaking student of English is being introduced, in the schools, to a variety of English (namely, the standard literary language) that may differ in some respects from the language that he knows. Thus, grammatical instruction has often been called "normative," although perhaps it would be more accurate to say that, at its best, it has been instruction in the descriptive grammar of a variety of English closely related to, but not identical with, the student's own.

In any event, pursuit of these traditional goals of grammatical instruction should, one would suppose, be facilitated by the use of a system of grammar that expresses the underlying regularities of the language as fully and explicitly as possible. To the extent that this is correct, progress in the understanding of linguistic structure should naturally be reflected in the English curriculum. But quite apart from this, the intrinsic intellectual interest of the investigation of linguistic structure, with its many and varied implications for a broad range of questions, surely provides sufficient motivation for introducing the student to the systematic study of his native language, and for doing so in a manner that is responsive to the issues that give substance and significance to current work.

APPENDIX
Comments for Project Literacy meeting (September 1964)

Morris Halle and I have been working for several years on a study of English sound structure, some aspects of which seem to me to touch on the concerns of this meeting—in particular, on questions of dialectal variation, the psychological reality of linguistic units, and the nature of conventional orthography and its relation to the sound system.

When we consider the structure of a language we are, fundamentally, concerned with a relation of sound and meaning. The rules of the language— the rules that the native speaker intuitively commands and that the linguist tries to discover and exhibit—relate certain physical signals to certain semantic interpretations; more precisely, they relate phonetic representations of sentences to their structural descriptions. Thus one level of representation that must have psychological significance, both on the perceptual and motor levels, is the level of phonetic representation; another is the level of representation that appears in structural descriptions.

The level of phonetic representation is fairly well understood. Structural descriptions are a more obscure matter. Clearly, a structural description (adequate to express the semantic content of a sentence) must contain, at least, a representation of the meaning-bearing units of which the sentence is composed and of the phrasing of the sentence (and, of course, much more which we here disregard). Thus the structural description of the Phrase "American history teacher" must contain the units *Americ, -an, histor-, -y, teach, -er*, and a bracketing indicating which of the two semantic interpretations is intended. Similarly, the word *theatricality,* for example, must be represented as a Noun derived from the Adjective *theatrical,* which is in turn derived from the Noun *theater.* Thus the grammar of a language must contain (at least) syntactic rules that determine phrasing and the placement of "grammatical" units such as *-er,* *-ity,* a lexicon that contains the semantically functioning units, and rules that convert structural descriptions to phonetic representations.

Consider now the character of the lexicon. It is easy to justify the requirement that each lexical item be represented as a sequence of *segments.* Each item, of course, has a unique such spelling—a single entry—in the lexicon. This spelling must contain all information not predictable by phonological rules (presupposing the rest of the structural description of the sentence in which the item is embedded). Thus the lexical representation of the common item of *histor-y, histor-ic-al, histor-ian,* or of *anxi-ous, anxi-ety,* or of *courage, courage-ous,* or of *tele+graph, tele+graph-ic, tele+graph-y,* et cetera, must be selected so as to contain just what is not predictable in the variant phonetic realizations of these items. The psychological reality of lexical representation, in this sense, is hardly open to question.

Observe that a lexical representation, in this sense, provides a natural orthography for a person who knows a language. It provides just the information about words that is not predictable by phonological rule or by the syntactic rules that determine the phrasing of the sentence in which the item is embedded. It provides just the information needed by a person who has command of the syntactic and phonological rules (up to ambiguity). Conventional orthography, in English, as in every case of which I have any knowledge, is remarkably close to optimal, in this sense. For example, the spellings *histor-, anxi-, courage, telegraph* are (minor notational conventions aside) essentially what would appear in the lexicon of spoken English. Conventional orthographies tend to differ *systematically* from lexical representation only in that true irregularities (e.g., *man-men, cling-clung*) are differently represented, as is quite natural. The symbols of conventional orthography correspond to feature sets in the underlying sound system of the spoken language.

It seems fairly well established that the level of lexical representation is highly resistant to change, and is highly persistent over time (and hence over a range of dialects). Correspondingly, one finds that conventional orthographies remain useful, with minor change, over long periods and for a wide range of dialects.

As a result of our work, we have come to the conclusion that there is no linguistically significant (and, presumably, no psychologically real) level of systematic representation intermediate between the level of representation to which conventional orthographies closely correspond and (broad) phonetic representation. These underlying representations we call "phonological," following Sapir, our conclusions being closely akin in many respects to his views on the nature of sound pattern and phonological rules. Following this usage, we may say that the relation between conventional spelling and phonological representation is very close, and that conventional spelling is, by and large, a highly effective system for a wide range of dialects because it corresponds to a common underlying phonological representation, relatively invariant among dialects despite wide phonetic divergence. Let me emphasize again the advantages of phonological (i.e., essentially conventional orthographic) representation *for a speaker who understands the language*. In contrast, broad phonetic (or, possibly, so-called phonemic) representation is the only kind that would be of any use for someone who knows nothing of the syntax of the language but who wishes to produce a noise which is close to the phonetic form of a sentence—for example, an actor who has to produce a sentence of a language that he does not know.

Consider, in contrast, phonemic representation in the modern (post-Sapir) sense. The phonemic system, in effect, extracts all regularities from the sound system that can be detected with no consideration (or, in some varieties, highly restricted consideration) of higher-level structure. A priori, there is no reason to suppose that such a system exists. For example, it is obvious that a child does not first construct such a phonemic system and then proceed to the problem of acquiring syntax and semantics, and there is not the slightest reason to believe that there is a level of perceptual processing (or of motor performance) that corresponds to phonemic representation, in the modern sense. Furthermore, we have offered several arguments in support of

the conclusion that there is no linguistic justification for a phonemic level—
that is, it can be incorporated in a full grammar only at the cost of otherwise
valid generalizations. Consequently, it seems to me that phonemics, in the
modern sense, is perhaps nothing more than a methodological artifact.

In considering problems of literacy, the questions of "phoneme-grapheme
correspondences" and of dialect variation naturally arise. As to the latter, this
is a problem only to the extent that dialects differ on the syntactic and lexical
level. Differences in phonological rules are irrelevant, since orthography corresponds to a deeper level of representation than (broad) phonetic. Hence the
question raised above (of uniformity of lexicon over time and dialect), and the
analogous question with respect to sameness of deeper structures in syntax,
becomes highly relevant. As to the question of "phoneme-grapheme" correspondence, it may be that this is something of a pseudo-issue, or more properly, a set of pseudo-issues, depending on how exactly it is interpreted.

If by "phoneme" is meant the unit constructed in accordance with modern principles, there is no reason to expect any significant set of phoneme-
grapheme correspondences, since it seems that phonemes are artificial units,
having no linguistic status, whereas the "graphemes" of the conventional
orthography do correspond fairly closely to a linguistically significant level of
representation. Hence it is not clear why one should investigate phoneme-
grapheme correspondence at all. (In passing, it should be noted that so far as
relevant information is now available, the same seems to be true for other languages.) If the word "phoneme" is taken in the sense of Sapir, and "phonological representation" is the level at which all predictable differences are
extracted, then the phoneme-grapheme correspondences seem quite simple—they are very close to one-one, given certain notational conventions and
disregarding a class of true exceptions. On the other hand, if we use the
phrase "phoneme-grapheme correspondences" to refer to the study of sound-
letter correspondences, we are, in effect, simply doing phonology. Or, to be
more precise, the only reasonable way to study sound-letter correspondences
seems to be to utilize the fact that orthography corresponds closely to a significant level of linguistic representation—namely, phonological representation, in the sense used above—which is, furthermore, related to sound by
general rules, namely, the rules of the phonological component. Hence the
study of sound-letter correspondences can be divided into three parts:
phonology, the systematic (nearly one-one) relations between phonological
segments and letters (or conventional letter sequences), and a residue of
exceptions (some of which exhibit subregularities of various sorts). But the
bulk of the study is simply investigation of the phonological pattern.

If this much is correct, then it would seem to follow that the rules of sound-letter correspondence need hardly be taught, particularly the most general and deepest of these rules. For these rules are in any event part of the unconscious linguistic equipment of the non-literate speaker. What he must learn (except for true irregularities) is simply the elementary correspondence between the underlying phonological segments of his internalized lexicon and the orthographic symbols.

However, there is one qualification that must be added to this remark. The conventional orthography corresponds closely to a level of representation that seems to be optimal for the sound system of a fairly rich version of standard spoken English. Much of the evidence that determines, for the phonologist, the exact form of this underlying system is based on consideration of learned words and complex derivational patterns. It is by no means obvious that a child of six has mastered this phonological system in full—he may not yet have been presented with all of the evidence that determines the general structure of the English sound pattern.

It would not be at all surprising to discover that the child's intuitive organization of the sound system continues to develop and deepen until considerably later. Furthermore, it seems that children are much more attuned to phonetic nuance than adults—they "hear phonetically" rather than phonologically, to a considerable extent. Though I have no serious evidence, I have observed quite a few cases where children developing their own alphabet or learning to read insisted on a much narrower representation than would strike the adult ear as plausible.

To take one extreme case, my oldest daughter at age five objected to using the same symbol for the two stops in *cocoa*, as it turned out on investigation, because the difference in aspiration seemed to her sufficiently significant to require a different symbolization. Though this is hardly better than a guess, it is not particularly a surprising one. Thus it is a familiar observation that children can mimic and can acquire a new pronunciation much more readily than adults, and this may correlate with a more superficial (narrower) level of organization of the phonetic material. For various reasons, then, it may turn out that the psychologically real representation for the child changes and deepens with age, approaching the adult phonology with increasing maturity and linguistic experience. Serious investigation of these questions is far from easy, but it should shed much light on problems of speech perception and production and, perhaps indirectly, on the problems of literacy as well.

Chapter 24

Language theory and language use (1981)

How far do you think the analytic methods of linguistics have really done justice to the richness and inventiveness of language use? What kinds of work are still to be done?
In one sense, the central question of linguistics is "the richness and inventiveness of language use," and work on this question has, I think, led to quite substantial understanding of the mechanisms involved in such language use and the biological endowment that makes it possible for these mechanisms to develop. But from another point of view, this research has led to very little insight into the ways in which language is used and can hardly be expected to do so, I believe. There is no paradox here. One simply has to be careful to maintain a clear understanding of the differences among several questions, in particular, the following:

(1) What is it exactly that a person knows when that person is said to "know a language," say, to know English?
(2) How does a person come to have such knowledge?
(3) How is such knowledge put to use?

These questions are crude and should be refined. When they are, I think we can see the outlines of quite reasonable answers to the first two questions, but not the third.

Roughly, the answer to the first question is that a person who knows a language has acquired knowledge of a grammar—that is, there is represented in the mind/brain a system of rules and principles that determines for each of infinitely many expressions certain basic aspects of its sound, its meaning, and other structural properties.

The answer to the second question is that the mind/brain is designed, by genetic endowment, with certain structural properties that are often referred to as "universal grammar," in a contemporary sense of a traditional notion.

This universal grammar is itself a system of rules and principles and conditions, but a system that is only partially determined. Many different grammars (though, quite probably, only finitely many) are consistent with universal grammar. One sometimes says that the principles of universal grammar have certain open parameters and that the values of the latter have to be set by experience. For example, the order of subject, verb, object in declarative sentences varies from language to language; some languages require overt expression of subject in such sentences (e.g., English), while others do not (e.g., Spanish), and so on. Language acquisition, from this point of view, is a process whereby experience determines the values of parameters in a fixed system of universal grammar. The richness of the fixed, given system makes it possible for the acquired grammar to be subtle, complex, intricate, and highly articulated, a structure only weakly determined by experience and attained with a high degree of uniformity among people with varied childhood experience—all of which is far too impoverished to yield the precise structures of the attained grammar by any inductive or conventional "learning" mechanism, as I think has been shown beyond reasonable doubt.

To the extent that questions 1 and 2 receive reasonable answers—and to a nontrivial extent, they already do, in my opinion—we can approach question 3 with the hope of gaining some real insight and understanding that goes beyond descriptive taxonomy; that is, the study of questions 1 and 2 might (and to some extent already does) provide an understanding of the mechanisms that are put to use, and the basis in innate mental endowment for the growth of these mechanisms (what is—misleadingly, I think—called "language learning"). But this hope has not been realized, and quite frankly, I do not expect it to be realized. To be a bit more explicit, I doubt very much that we can attain anything that might be called "scientific understanding" of the sources and character of human action, in particular, language use— that we can develop theoretical principles that will yield insight into how humans choose to put to use the cognitive systems, language among them, that have developed in the mind. I think one can even put forth some not implausible speculations as to why this should be the case, though I will not pursue this question here. Note that "scientific understanding," in this sense, is only one particular form of understanding and insight. My feeling is that we can approach questions 1 and 2 in these terms, with some hope (and indeed some measure of success), but probably not question 3. At least this much seems to me correct: there is no evidence now available to challenge this judgment.

[A Cartesian assumption about humans]

Many people would say that linguistics ought to be interesting and yet appears to be arid. Have these people got it wrong?

What is interesting to one person is arid to another. Modern physics or mathematics is interesting to one type of mind, arid to another type. There is no right or wrong about these matters. Suppose that someone is interested in the nature of human knowledge and the ways in which it is attained. For such a person, linguistics should, I think, prove interesting, because it offers some quite nontrivial ideas, with a degree of empirical support, bearing on these questions in one domain that is certainly central to human life. Someone who is not particularly interested in these questions will find this work arid.

To speculate again, I tend to believe that research in what we might call "cognitive psychology" and related areas of the neurosciences can yield theoretical insight into certain kinds of questions but probably not others. Among the questions that may yield to rational inquiry as we understand it are those that have to do with the ways in which information is presented to the mind: for example, the ways in which the system of visual processing works, or the mechanisms by which sound is assigned grammatical and (in part) semantic structure. Furthermore, such rational inquiry may provide real understanding of how these systems develop in the individual, and conceivably someday how they develop in the species and what their neural basis may be.

Even if these questions are completely answered (whatever that means; not much, I would say), vast numbers of other questions remain. For example, what does the mind do with the information available to it? How and why do we decide to act as we do? How do we think, solve problems, create and invent, et cetera? I see little reason to question a rather traditional Cartesian assumption: that machines are "compelled," but humans only "incited and inclined" to act in such-and-such a way, given external conditions and an internal state. Perhaps this is wrong, but we are hard put to find substantive reasons to challenge the assumption. If this traditional view contains some kernel of truth, then it may be possible to develop theories, even successful predictive theories, of motivation, and so on, but crucial elements will be missing. I do not propose that the mysteries that remain are "beyond scientific explanation" in some absolute sense of this notion (if there is one), but they may well be beyond the understanding that can be achieved by one specific biological system that has developed in the natural world, namely, the human mind.

Even if this proves wrong, there are other reasons for skepticism, I believe, about the prospects for gaining theoretical scientific understanding of these mysteries. The successes of the natural sciences can be traced to the fact that it has been possible to abstract certain (somewhat idealized) systems and to study their properties in relative isolation. But thinking, choice of action, and so on simply involve too much. There does not seem to be any way to isolate significant subsystems, or at least no such way has been found, to my knowledge. Perhaps this is a temporary state of ignorance, perhaps not. My guess is the latter.

Returning to the question, as of now, linguistics and cognitive psychology (of which linguistics, in my view, is a part) are able to deal with certain questions but not with others, perhaps for rather deep and intrinsic reasons. Whether these subjects are arid or interesting depends in the first instance on whether one finds the questions amenable to rational inquiry (now, or maybe ever) arid or interesting; and furthermore, on whether the results attained are of a sufficiently high order as to have intellectual interest in themselves. I think that in certain areas the latter question receives positive answers, and there is reason to hope for quite substantial success in the future, perhaps even the near future.

Linguistics on the whole has paid relatively little attention to texts. How much would you say linguists have contributed to our understanding of the production and reception of written texts?
There is a great deal of study of production and reception of written texts, but for reasons already mentioned, I don't anticipate that it will lead to any real theoretical understanding of a nontrivial nature, and do not believe that it does so now.

[The importance of psychology for educational practice]
Educationalists have attempted to draw from the work of linguists implications for educational practice. What is your experience of this process, particularly with reference to your own work?
This question should be posed to practitioners—to people who are faced with the problems of teaching. I don't see any reason why my opinion should be taken seriously on these matters, but if anyone wants it, my feeling is that linguistics or psychology more generally have little of value to offer with regard to educational practice, except insofar as they provide theoretical understanding of certain specific questions, such as those mentioned. If education is to include an effort to provide some understanding of the way the mind works, then linguistics and psychology are important for educational practice, in the sense in which physics is important for teachers who hope to develop

some understanding of the nature of the physical world. Beyond that, I am personally skeptical.

As for my own work and experience, it offers nothing of value, as far as I can see, apart from the particular topics mentioned.

Teachers have turned to linguists for help in understanding why working-class children and ethnic minorities have failed in school. It has become something of a growth industry. How would you assess their contribution? Can linguists contribute to a more just society?

Again, I am very skeptical. Speaking personally, a very substantial part of my time and effort is devoted to attempts to bring about a more just and decent domestic and international society. I do not see these efforts as related in any significant way to my work as a linguist, and do not see how this work in linguistics could contribute significantly to these quite different ends. Perhaps there is some possible contribution. For example, in the United States at least, perhaps in England too, one hears a good deal of nonsense about languages or dialects that are somehow "inherently impoverished" or that "lack grammar" and so on. I suppose that linguists can do something to counteract these silly and insidious ideas, but to be honest, no special expert knowledge is required for this perhaps useful task.

I might again add a more personal note. I am constantly asked how my linguistic work relates to my endeavors in other domains, say, in opposing state violence or defending human rights. No doubt one can always find some links among the various activities in which a single individual is engaged, though in my case at least, the links seem to me tenuous indeed. If there is a point of contact, it is quite abstract; perhaps at the level of some concept of human nature involving a basic need for free, creative work and self-expression. But the idea of trying to derive a system of beliefs concerning social change or social organization from principles of language, for example, seems to me too absurd to merit comment. If comment is necessary at all, it is only because the opposite is sometimes claimed. For example, a book recently published by a prestigious press in England—out of charity, I will not mention the name of the author or publisher—attributes to me the belief that one can derive the anarchist commitments that I find fairly compelling from principles of syntax. This is sheer fabrication from beginning to end; one would have to be daft to believe any such thing. It is perhaps of some interest that such a book can be published and taken seriously by reviewers, but that has to do with the pathology of our intellectual culture, not with any beliefs of mine.

[Aspects of language important for us to understand]

The study of language has recently become an explicit part of the curriculum in some schools. What aspects of language do you feel it is particularly important for people to understand?

There are many aspects of language that it is important for people to understand. I think that children should gain some understanding of how their language works, and here linguistics can be of some help, if adapted with intelligence and care. Beyond that, I think that questions concerning the nature and development of cognitive structures should be a part, maybe an important part, of the curriculum. And at another level, it is important for people to learn how to defend themselves from the devices that are employed in any society, including our own, to indoctrinate and control, and among these devices is the corruption of language in the service of power—propaganda, or what is called sometimes "the engineering of consent." But for this linguistics is irrelevant, so far as I can see. Thus I have done a great deal of work on how the media, and much of the academic and intellectual community, devote themselves to distortion of contemporary reality, an extremely serious matter in my view and one that is insufficiently studied. But this work, again, is almost totally unrelated to my work on language. Nor do I see any interesting connections, actual or potential.

Chapter 25
Language, politics, and composition (1991)

You have published an overwhelming number of works. Do you think of yourself as a writer?

No, I've never particularly thought of myself as a writer. In fact, most of what I've published is written-up versions of lectures. For example, *Syntactic structures,* the first book that actually appeared, was essentially lecture notes for an undergraduate course at MIT, revised slightly to turn them into publishable form. I would say probably 80 or 90 percent of the work I do on political issues is sort of working out notes from talks. Much of the material that ends up as professional books is based on class lectures or lectures elsewhere, so I tend to think out loud.

So you see yourself first as a speaker, a lecturer.

The fact is that most of the writing I do is probably letters. I spend about twenty hours a week, I guess, just answering letters. Many of the letters are on questions that are in response to the hundreds of letters that I receive which are thoughtful and interesting and raise important questions (here's today's batch). Hundreds go out every week, and that requires thought; some of them are rather long. Those are actually written without being spoken. Sometimes I do sit down and write a book, too, but most of the time I don't think of myself as a writer particularly.

You have had a few words to say about your writing process. In fact, you commented once, "I'm able to work in twenty-minute spurts. I can turn my attention from one topic to another without start-up time. I almost never work from an outline or follow a plan. The books simply grow by accretion." Would you tell us more about your writing process?

The reason for the twenty-minute spurts—which is a bit of an exaggeration;

maybe hour spurts would be more accurate—is just the nature of my life, which happens to be very intense. I have two full-time professional careers, each of them quite demanding, plus lots of other things. I just mentioned one—lots and lots of correspondence—and other things as well, and that doesn't leave much time. In fact, my time tends to be very chopped up. I discovered over the years that probably my only talent is this odd talent that I seem to have that other colleagues don't, and that is that I've got sort of buffers in the brain that allow me to shift back and forth from one project to the other and store one.

So you can't when writing a book, for example, concentrate for ten hours at a time.
No, I know that a lot of people don't seem to be able to do that, and it's certainly an advantage to be able to do it. I can pick up after a long stretch and be more or less where I left off. In fact, I've sometimes had to. I have friends like this. I had, in particular, one friend who just died a couple of years ago who was an Israeli logician and who'd been an old friend since I was twenty or so. We would meet every five or six years and usually pick up the conversation we had been having as if we had just had it five minutes ago and go on from there. As far as my books just sort of writing themselves, that's pretty much what happens. I don't recall ever having sat down and planned a book—except maybe for saying, "Well, I'm going to talk about X, Y, and Z, and I'll have Chapter One on X, Chapter Two on Y, and Chapter Three on Z." Then it's just a matter of getting the first paragraph, and it just goes on from there.

That's quite a talent.
Well, it's probably because I've thought about most of it before, or lectured on it before, or written a letter to someone about it, or done it twenty times in the past. Then it becomes mainly a problem of trying to fit it all in. I have discovered, if it's of any interest to you, that I write somewhat differently now that I have a computer—quite a bit differently. I don't know if it shows up any different, but I know I write differently. I was very resistant to the computer. I didn't want to use it, and finally the head of the department just stuck it in my room. My teenage son, who was—like every teenager, I guess—a super-hacker, carried me gently through the early stages, which I never would have had the patience to do. Once I was able to use the computer, I discovered that there were a lot of things that I could do that I'd never done before. For example, I'd never done much editing, simply because it was too much trouble; I didn't want to retype everything. And I never did much in the way

of inserting and rearranging and so on. Now I do a fair amount of that because it's so easy. Whether that shows up differently for the reader, I don't know. But I know I'm writing quite differently.

[Persuasion as an authoritarian practice]

As someone who is profoundly interested in the structure of language as well as the use and abuse of rhetoric in political contexts, you must have some thoughts about the nature of rhetoric. For you, what are the most important elements of rhetoric?
I don't have any theory of rhetoric, but what I have in the back of my mind is that one should not try to persuade; rather, you should try to lay out the territory as best you can so that other people can use their own intellectual powers to work out for themselves what they think is right or wrong. For example, I try, particularly in political writing, to make it extremely clear in advance exactly where I stand. In my view, the idea of neutral objectivity is largely fraudulent. It's not that I take the realistic view with regard to fact, but the fact is that everyone approaches complex and controversial questions— especially those of human significance—with an ax to grind, and I like that ax to be apparent right up front so that people can compensate for it. But to the extent that I can monitor my own rhetorical activities, which is probably not a lot, I try to refrain from efforts to bring people to reach my conclusions.

Is that because you might lose credibility or lose the audience?
Not at all. In fact, you'd probably lose the audience by not doing it. It's just kind of an authoritarian practice one should keep away from. The same is true for teaching. It seems to me that the best teacher would be the one who allows students to find their way through complex material as you lay out the terrain. Of course, you can't avoid guiding, because you're doing it a particular way and not some other way. But it seems to me that a cautionary flag should go up if you're doing it too much, because the purpose is to enable students to be able to figure out things for themselves, not to know this thing or to understand that thing but to understand the next thing that's going to come along; that means you've got to develop the skills to be able to critically analyze and inquire and be creative. This doesn't come from persuasion or forcing things on people. There's sort of a classical version of this—that teaching is not a matter of pouring water into a vessel but of helping a flower to grow in its own way—and I think that's right. It seems to me that that's the model we ought to approach as best as possible. So I think the best rhetoric is the least rhetoric.

In his critique of Western metaphysics, Jacques Derrida exposed the indeterminacy of language, showing how meaning is never fixed, always fluid, never certain. What are your thoughts on this issue?

I don't know this literature very well, and to tell you the truth, the reason I don't know it is that I don't find it interesting. I try to read it now and then but just don't find it very interesting. People have come at the question of indeterminacy from many points of view, and I think there's an element of truth to it, but there's also a respect in which it's not true. These are questions of fact, not of ideology; therefore, there's no grounds for dogmatism concerning them, and they're not a matter of pronouncements but of discovery.

To the extent that we understand things about language, the facts point rather clearly to a specific conclusion which is halfway like that, but only halfway. What we find is that there is a highly determinate, very definite structure of concepts and of meaning that is intrinsic to our nature, and that as we acquire language or other cognitive systems these things just kind of grow in our minds, the same way we grow arms and legs. To that extent, meaning is determinate. However, there's a sense in which it's not fully determinate, and that is the way we use these conceptual and, in particular, these rich semantic structures in our interactions with one another and our interactions with the world. In that domain, there's a high degree of interest-relativity, intrusion of value, relativity to purposes and intentions, modifiability often in a somewhat rather creative fashion, and so on. At that level it's true that elements of fluidity and indeterminacy do enter; however, they have their own structure. It's just that we don't understand very much about it. So I think there's an element of truth to that, but it can be carried much too far.

In the philosophical literature—those parts of it that I feel more comfortable with and where I think I understand what people are talking about—similar ideas arise in the study of what's called "meaning holism." Take Hilary Putnam as an example, someone who's extended views originally due to Quine toward a general theory of semantics which would express a viewpoint related to this—namely, that the meaning of a word is never determinate (it's certainly not something in the mind), and if it's not determinate then it depends on the place of the concept within the whole intellectual structure, and it can change, your beliefs change, the meanings change, and so forth; that is, the intentions change, the meaning may be modified, and so on.

Well, I think that this thesis is half true. In the same respect, there is a fixed structure of meaning, and it's an interesting one, a very intriguing one. In fact, contrary to what is believed by many people—for example, Richard Rorty—there are strong empirical grounds for believing that there is quite a sharp analytic/synthetic distinction that derives from intrinsic semantic structures and is just a reflection of the fact that there are probably biologically determined and quite rich and intriguing semantic structures that are basically fixed. But there's a sense in which meaning holism is correct; that is, what we describe as meaning in commonsense discourse, and in philosophical discourse, is never fixed entirely by the structures that are present in the mind, and we've gotten that way because that's the kind of creature we are. So in that sense there's some truth to meaning holism.

So you probably wouldn't agree with Bakhtin. Are you familiar with his work?
No, I'm not.

His ideas sound very similar to this concept of meaning holism.
Yes, but that's the standard view. That's the view of Derrida to the extent that I understand him, but also of a large sector of analytic philosophy and, again, Richard Rorty. Donald Davidson, for example, whom Rorty quotes, argued—actually, I should say "asserted"—that Quine's demolition of the analytic/synthetic distinction, his demonstration that this distinction doesn't hold, created the modern philosophy of language as a serious discipline.

Well, the analytic/synthetic question is a technical one, but the point is the same. If there were determinate meanings, there would be an analytic/synthetic distinction. So the domain in which this issue is fought out in philosophical terrain is over the analytic/synthetic issue, but the real question is whether there are fixed, determinate meanings. Does the word *house* have a determinate meaning or can it vary arbitrarily, depending on the way our belief systems vary? I think the answer is right in between. There's a fixed and quite rich structure of understanding associated with the concept "house," and that's going to be cross-linguistic, and it's going to arise independently of any evidence because it's just part of our nature. But there's also going to be a lot of variety in how we use that term in particular circumstances, or against the background of particular kinds of theoretical understanding, and so on.

Some thinkers draw on Rorty's work to posit that knowledge itself is a socially constructed artifact. That is, knowledge is not absolute; rather, it is the product of consensus within any given discourse community. This concept is related to Kuhn's notion of how knowledge is formed within the scientific community. What are your thoughts about this theory?
There is an element of truth to it, obviously. There is no doubt that the pur-

suit of knowledge is often, not always, but typically—a kind of communal activity. In particular, that's true of organized knowledge, say, research in the natural sciences, say, what we do in this corridor; that's obviously a social activity. For example, a graduate student will come in and inform me I was wrong about what I said in a lecture yesterday for this or that reason, and we'll discuss it, and we'll agree or disagree, and maybe another set of problems will come out. Well, that's normal inquiry, and whatever results is some form of knowledge or understanding; obviously, that's socially determined by the nature of these interactions.

On the other hand, most domains we don't understand much about—like how scientific knowledge develops, something we basically understand nothing about—but if we look more deeply at the domains where we do understand something, we discover that the development of cognitive systems, including systems of knowledge in particular, is substantially directed by our biological nature. In the case of knowledge of language, we have the clearest evidence about this. Part of my own personal interest in the study of language is that it's a domain in which these questions can be studied much more clearly, much more easily than in many others. Also, it's one intrinsic to human nature and human functions, so it's not a marginal case. There, I think, we have very powerful evidence of the directive effect of biological nature on the form of the system of knowledge that arises.

In other domains like, for example, the internalization of our moral code, or our style of dress, we just know less. But I think the qualitative nature of the problem faced strongly suggests a very similar conclusion: a highly directive effect of biological nature. When you turn to scientific inquiry, again, so little is known that everything that one says is virtually pure speculation, but I think the qualitative nature of the process of acquiring scientific knowledge again suggests a highly directive effect of biological nature.

The reasoning behind this is basically Plato's, which I think is quite valid. That's why it's sometimes called "Plato's problem." The reasoning in the Platonic dialogues, which is valid if not decisive, is that the richness and specificity and commonality of the knowledge we attain is far beyond anything that can be accounted for by the experience available, which includes interpersonal interactions. And, besides being acts of God, that leaves only the possibility that it's inner-determined.

That's the same logic that's constantly used by every natural scientist studying organic systems. So, for example, when we study, metaphorically speaking, physical growth below the neck, everything but the mind, we just take this reasoning for granted. For example, let's say I were to suggest to you that undergoing puberty is a matter of social interaction and people do it because they see other people do it, that it's peer pressure. Well, you laugh, just as you're laughing now. Why do you laugh? Everyone assumes that it's biologically determined, that you're somehow programmed to undergo puberty at a certain point. Is it that something is known about that biological program? Is that why you laugh? No, nothing's known about it. In fact, we know a lot more about the acquisition of meaning and the fixed factors in that than we do about the factors that determine puberty. Is it that social factors are irrelevant to puberty? No, not at all. Social interaction is certainly going to be relevant. Under certain conditions of social isolation, it might not even take place. Why do people laugh? That's the question.

[The Cartesian revolution in the cognitive sciences]

What about knowledge in a particular field, say linguistics? You came along with Syntactic structures *and changed the way we think of linguistics. If your colleagues and followers had not accepted and then helped champion that cause, you would simply be a kook out in the wilderness with some crazy idea. But what happened is that a large part of your discourse community accepted the ideas and worked with them and perhaps refined them, and that became the "knowledge" of the time. Well, perhaps in the future there will be some revolution within the field that turns it completely in another direction; your discourse community will have constructed new "knowledge."*

That has happened several times in the last thirty years, but that's a totally different question. In fields that have a rational nature, where the conditions of rational inquiry are observed and there's a sort of a common understanding of what it means to move toward truth (or at least a better grasp of truth), and where there's a sort of common and rational understanding of the nature of argument and evidence—and I think those things are essentially fixed—in such fields, there's a course of development. It's not perfect; all sorts of erratic things happen. Sure, changes take place and some things are accepted while others are not accepted, sometimes rightly, sometimes wrongly, and there are ways of correcting error.

But I don't understand what that has to do with the social determination of knowledge. That's a matter of how, through social interaction, each person contributing tries to advance a common enterprise. Now, this is somewhat idealized because there are all sorts of personal conflicts and somebody's trying to undercut someone else, but let's abstract away from that; let's abstract away from the vile nature of human beings and talk about it as if we're living up to the ideals that at least theoretically we hold. To that extent there's a common enterprise, and understanding will grow as people participate in this common enterprise. And it will change, and sometimes change radically.

Has your colleague down the hall, Thomas Kuhn, ever discussed the Chomskyan revolution in terms of a "paradigm shift"?
He hasn't, but other people have; I don't. My own view is that while there have been several significant changes (Tom and I kind of differ on this), there's been basically one scientific revolution: the Galilean revolution, the seventeenth-century revolution stretching over a period including Galileo. That was a real revolution, a different way of looking at things in many respects. For example, there was a very sharp shift at that point from a kind of natural-history perspective to a natural-science perspective. A different attitude toward fact developed, a different attitude toward idealization, a different concept of explanation. There was a complete breakdown, especially with Newton, of the commonsense notion of mechanical explanation, which led in new directions. Put all these things together and I think that's a radical shift in perspective. Now, there are very few fields of human endeavor where that shift of perspective has taken place. In the study of language, I think that shift did take place to an extent in the 1950s. You could call that a "paradigm shift" if you want to use the term, but it seems to me to be adapting the methods of the natural sciences to another domain; in that respect, it's not really a dramatic shift.

Furthermore, even if you look at the basic intellectual developments and changes in points of view associated with what's called the "cognitive revolution" in the mid-1950s—of which the development of generative grammar was a part and, in fact, a major contributing part—I think they're quite real; but in a number of respects, rather critical respects, they recapitulate and revise changes that took place during what I prefer to call the "first cognitive revolution," namely, in the seventeenth century. For example, a major shift in the 1950s was a shift of perspective away from concern for behavior and the products of behavior toward the inner processes that determine behavior and determine the processes of behavior. Now, that's a shift toward the natural sciences because the inner processes are real. They're part of psychology, part of biology. So that's a shift toward the natural sciences, away from behavior toward inner mechanisms and inner processes that underlie behavior. It's also a shift toward explanation rather than description.

Now, that's a big shift. But a shift like that took place in what we might call the "Cartesian revolution" in the cognitive sciences. Associated with this was a revival of interest—it wasn't a new interest—in what are sometimes called computational models of the mind, that is, theories of rules and representations, roughly. That's part of the same thing because the inner mechanisms and inner processes appear to be computational systems, mentally representative and, in some unknown manner, physically instantiated. But that again is highly reminiscent of something that took place in the seventeenth century—in particular, Descartes' theory of vision, which was a crucial breakthrough and developed a kind of a representational, computational theory of mind. It was a major shift.

Another change that took place in the 1950s, part of the cognitive revolution, had to do with things like, say, the Turing test for general intelligence. But that's just a watered-down version of a much richer and more interesting seventeenth-century notion: the Cartesian tests for the existence of other minds, which crucially used aspects of linguistic performance, the fact that normal human linguistic behavior has what I sometimes call—they didn't call it this—a creative aspect, meaning it's appropriate to situations but not caused by situations (which is a fundamental difference); it's innovative, unbounded, and not determined by internal stimuli or external causes; it's coherent, whatever that means (we recognize that but we can't characterize it); it evokes thoughts in others that they may express themselves, and so on. There's a collection of properties, and one can turn those properties into an experimental program, as in fact was suggested in the seventeenth century, to determine whether another organism has a mind like yours.

Now, in that context there's real scientific inquiry being carried out in which one tries to determine whether a machine, let's say, is a person with a mind. That's a real scientific question embedded in that rich framework of scientific inquiry dealing with real questions, noting crucial facts about human beings, which, in fact, are true facts. That all makes a lot of sense. In contrast, the twentieth-century version of this, sometimes called the Turing test, is almost totally pointless. It's just an operational test to determine whether, say, a computer program manifests intelligence, and like most operational tests, it doesn't matter how it comes out because operational tests are of no interest or significance except in some theoretical context. The reason I mention that is to indicate that in this respect the second cognitive revolution was a regression, in my view, from the first cognitive revolution.

Another question has to do with the body/mind relation. In the seventeenth century, in the Cartesian system, the body/mind relation was absolutely central. Descartes and the Cartesians had a plausible, though we now know an incorrect, argument for the existence of mind. The argument basically was that they had a conception of body based on a kind of intuitive mechanics, a sort of contact mechanics—you know, things pushing and pulling each other. Our normal intuitive, commonsense notion of mechanics was what they meant by body. They argued correctly that that concept had certain limits, and they therefore postulated a second substance, a thinking substance, to deal with things that plainly go beyond those limits, like the creative aspects of language use. Well, then a body/mind problem arises. That's a real problem, but it didn't survive Newton because Newton blew the theory of mechanics out of the water. The concept of body disappeared, and, since then, there is no concept of body and no classical body/mind problem—at least there shouldn't be, in my view. In the new version, what we really just have is different levels of understanding and they're all natural and we try to relate them as much as we can.

In the twentieth-century cognitive revolution, something like the body/mind problem reemerged but in a pernicious way, a way that's again a regression from the earlier version. The earlier version was a metaphysical problem, hence a problem of reality, and a serious one. The modern version is a kind of an epistemological dualism; that is, questions of mind are just studied differently than questions of body. The example I just mentioned is one. In the case of studying puberty, we allow our conception of rational inquiry to guide us, and it guides us right to the study of innate structure. In the case of the study of, say, meaning, people don't follow the same line of inquiry, though they should because the logic is the same. That's one of numerous examples showing that the way we study the traditional phenomena of mind departs from the way we study other aspects of physical reality. That's a very pernicious dualism, an extremely dangerous version of traditional dualism which ought to be abandoned. So that's another respect in which I think there's regression from the first cognitive revolution.

The point I'm trying to make is that there was a very substantial change in general psychology, including linguistics, in the mid-1950s, and in some ways it was a regression. There are some ways in which it was real progress. The traditional view about language, which is correct, is that, as Humboldt put it, language makes "infinite use of finite means." But nobody knew what to make of that notion because they had no concept of infinite use of finite means. By the mid-twentieth century, we had a concept of what that means. It came out of mathematics, really. Out of parts of mathematics and logic there came a sharp understanding of the notion of infinite use of finite means, and it was therefore possible to apply that to the traditional questions. That led to a huge move forward in understanding; in fact, that's generative grammar. It's looking at a lot of the classical questions in the light of the modern understanding of what it means to make infinite use of finite means. That confluence did make possible a substantial change. If one wants to call this a revolution, okay; if not, okay. I don't. It seems to me like just normal progress when new understanding arises and you can apply it to old problems.

["Teaching" or "learning" as just some kind of triggering effect]

You're talking about biological directiveness, and in your work over the last three decades you have emphasized that there is this strong element of innateness in language. What about writing, which is a learned phenomenon—something, unlike language, that not every healthy human has? Would you pursue this same line in talking about written language?

I'm sure if we look at written language we're going to find the conditions of Plato's problem arising once again. Namely, we just know too much. The basic problem that you always face when you look at human competence, or for that matter at any biological system, is that the state it has attained is so rich and specific that you cannot account for it on the basis of interactions, such as learning, for example. That's something that's found almost universally.

The case of puberty that I gave you is only one example, but it's true from the level of the cell on up. When you look at any form of human activity, whether it's speech or moral judgment or ability to read, I think you'll find exactly the same thing. When you understand the actual phenomenon, what you discover typically is that there's some kind of triggering effect from the outside—often what we call "teaching" or "learning"—that sets in motion inner directive processes. That's how you can gain such rich competence on the basis of such limited experience. It's not unlike the fact that when a child eats, it grows. The food makes it grow, if you like, but it's not the food that's determining the way it grows; the way it grows is determined by its inner nature. It won't do it without food; if you keep the food away, the child won't grow. But when you give the child the food, it's going to grow into what it's going to be, a human and not a bird, and the reason for that is the inner nature. That's basically Plato's argument.

Many feminists have argued that because language controls thought and because ours is a male-inscribed, male-dominated language, language works to reproduce patriarchal ideology and thus the oppression of women. Do you agree with these assumptions and the conclusion?

I understand the point, but I wouldn't call it a property of language. There are many properties of language use which reflect structures of authority and domination in the society in which this language is used, and that's true. However, I don't think there's anything in the language that requires that. You could use the same language without those aspects of use in it. For example, there are ways of using language which are deeply racist, but the very same language can be used without the need to be racist.

But given how language is actually used . . .
Well, given language use, it's undoubtedly correct, and it's true of all sorts of systems of authority and domination, one being the gender issue.

Here's one brief example: some feminists have argued that the term motherhood *is something like a semantic universal and that that oppresses women. Do you see any justification for that argument?*
Well, you have to ask what you mean by "semantic universal." First of all, there's the question of whether it's true, but let's say for the sake of argument that every language known has a concept like "motherhood," and let's say that every one of those languages and every one of those concepts has something that oppresses women in it. Suppose, for the sake of argument, that this were discovered to be true. We still would not have finished, because it may simply be that every culture you sample is a culture that oppresses women. That doesn't yet show that it's inherent in our nature that women be oppressed. That just shows that the cultures that exist oppress women. And therefore it'll turn out that in every language that's developed in those cultures there will be a concept which reflects this relation of authority and control. But that doesn't tell you it's a semantic universal.

In fact, there's ambiguity in the notion "semantic universal," which ought to be clarified. Some things are semantic universals in the sense that you find them in every language. Other things are semantic universals in the sense that they're part of our nature and therefore must be in every language. That's a fundamental difference. For example, it's a fact that every human society we know—I suppose this is probably close to true if not totally true—places women in a subordinate role in some fashion. But it doesn't follow from that that it's part of our nature. That just shows that it's part of the society. If that were true, it would be a "weak universal." That is, it would be a descriptive universal but not a deep universal, something that's necessarily true. Now, there are things that are necessarily true. For example, there are properties of our language which are just as much part of our nature as the fact that we have arms and not wings. But just sampling the languages of the world is not enough to establish it.

In a recent article in Mother Jones, *one of your former students was quoted as saying, "Chomsky thinks he's a feminist, but—at heart—he's an old fashioned patriarch. . . . He just has never really understood what the feminist movement is about." Do you support the goals and aspirations of the feminist movement?*

I don't think there's such a thing as *the* aspirations and goals of the feminist movement, and I don't think there's such a thing as *the* feminist movement. There are many aspirations and goals of the feminist movement—or the feminist movements, I should say—which I think are timely and proper and important and have had an enormous effect in liberating consciousness and thought and making people aware of forms of oppression that they had internalized and not noticed. I think that's all for the good. In fact, my own view, and I've said this many times, is that of all the movements that developed in what's called the 1960s—which really is not the 1960s, because the feminist movement is basically later, but what is metaphorically called the 1960s—the one that's had the most profound influence and impact is probably the feminist movement, and I think it's very important. As to the student's comment, that could very well be correct, but I'm not the person to judge.

[The propaganda function of concision]

For the last few years, the media and the political establishment have asserted that the U.S. is experiencing a literacy crisis. Do you agree?

Sure. It's just a fact. I don't think it's even questioned. There's a big degree of illiteracy and functional illiteracy. It's remarkably high. What's more, the interest in reading is declining, or it certainly looks as if it's declining. People do seem to read less and to want to read less and be able to read less. I know of colleagues, for example, academic people whose world is reading, who won't subscribe to some journals that they are sympathetic to and find important because the articles are too long. They want things to be short. That just boggles my mind.

In fact, let me report to you a personal case. I once had an interview at a radio station in which the interviewer was interested in why I don't appear on MacNeil/Lehrer, *Nightline,* and that sort of program. He began the interview by playing a short tape of an earlier interview he'd had with a producer of *Nightline.* The interviewer asked him this question: "It's been claimed that the people on your program are all biased in one direction and that you cut out critical, dissident thought. How come, for example, you never have Chomsky on your program?" The producer first went into sort of a tantrum, saying I was from Neptune, and a "wacko" and so on; but after he'd calmed down he said something which, in fact, has an element of truth to it: "Chomsky lacks concision."

Concision means you have to be able to say things between two commercials. Now, that's a structural property of our media—a very important structural property which imposes conformism in a very deep way, because if you have to meet the condition of concision, you can only either repeat conventional platitudes or else sound like you are from Neptune. That is, if you say anything that's not conventional, it's going to sound very strange. For example, if I get up on television and say, "The Soviet invasion of Afghanistan is a horror," that meets the condition of concision. I don't have to back it up with any evidence; everyone believes it already, so therefore it's straightforward, and now comes the commercial.

Suppose I get up in the same two minutes and say, "The U.S. invasion of South Vietnam is a horror." Well, people are very surprised. They never knew there was a U.S. invasion of South Vietnam, so how could it be a horror? They heard of something called the U.S. "defense" of South Vietnam, and maybe that it was wrong, but they never heard anybody talk about the U.S. "invasion" of South Vietnam. So, therefore, they have a right to ask what I'm talking about. Copy editors will ask me when I try to sneak something like this into an article what I mean. They'll say, "I don't remember any such event." They have a right to ask what I mean. This structural requirement of concision that's imposed by our media disallows the possibility of explanation; in fact, that's its propaganda function. It means that you can repeat conventional platitudes, but you can't say anything out of the ordinary without sounding as if you're from Neptune, a wacko, because to explain what you meant—and people have a right to ask if it's an unconventional thought—would take a little bit of time.

Here in the United States, to my knowledge, it's quite different from virtually every other society, maybe with the exception of Japan, which is more or less in our model. But at least in my experience,when you appear on radio and television in Europe and the Third World—first of all, you can appear on radio and television if you have dissident opinions, which is virtually impossible here—you have enough time to explain what you mean. You don't have to have three sentences between two commercials, and if it takes a few minutes to explain or, more often, an hour, you have that time. Here, our media are constructed so you don't have time; you have to meet the condition of concision. And whether anybody in the public relations industry thought this up or not, the fact is that it's highly functional to impose thought control.

Pretty much the same is true in writing, like when you've got to say

something in seven hundred words. That's another way of imposing the condition of conventional thinking and of blocking searching inquiry and critical analysis. I think one effect of this is a kind of illiteracy.

[Paulo Freire's avenue to "critical consciousness"]

*Speaking of critical analysis and literacy, Paulo Freire and others argue that writ-
ing, because it can lead to "critical consciousness," is an avenue to social and political empowerment of the disenfranchised. Do you agree?*
Absolutely. In fact, writing is an indispensable method for interpersonal
communication in a complicated society. Not in a hunter-gatherer tribe of
fifteen people; then you can all talk to one another. But in a world that's more
complicated than that, intellectual progress and cultural progress and moral
progress, for that matter, require forms of interaction and communicative
interchange that go well beyond that of speaking situations. So, sure, people
who can participate in that have ways of enriching their own thought, of
enlightening others, of entering into constructive discourse with others
which they all gain by. That's a form of empowerment. It's not the case if a
teacher tells the kid, "Write five hundred words saying this." That's just a
form of reducing; that's a form of de-education, not education.

*There's a movement within composition studies to make a kind of critical/cultural
studies based on a Freirean model the subject matter for the first-year English
course. Do you think that's a good idea?*
Doing things that will stimulate critical analysis, self-analysis, and analysis of
culture and society is very crucial. In fact, it seems to me that part of the core
of all education ought to be the development of systems of intellectual self-
defense and also stimulation of the capacity for inquiry, which means also
collective inquiry. And this is one of the domains in which it can be done. It
is done, say, in the natural sciences, but localized in those problems. It ought
to be done in a way so that people understand that this is a general need and
a general capacity; English composition courses are perfectly appropriate
places for that.

[A deeper understanding of our own moral nature]

*In 1973 [actually, in 1971—CPO] you had an extended discussion on Dutch
television with Michel Foucault, one of the most important of the French post-
structuralist philosophers. In a subsequent interview, you said that you and
Foucault found some areas of agreement, but you commented that he was much
more skeptical than you were about the possibility of developing a concept of human*

nature that is independent of social and historical conditions. How would you ground a concept of human nature beyond human capacity to acquire language?

I would study it the same way. I would apply the logic of Plato's problem. Take any domain—the domain of moral judgment, let's say. I don't think we're in a position to study it yet, but the way you would study it is clear. You'd take people and ask what is the nature of the system of moral judgment that they have. We certainly have such systems. We make moral judgments all the time, and we make them in coherent ways and with a high degree of consistency; we make them in new cases that we've not faced before. So we have some sort of a theory, or a system, or a structure that underlies probably an unbounded range of moral judgments. That's a system that can be discovered; you can find out what it is. We can then ask questions about the extent to which different systems that arise in different places are different and the extent to which they're the same. We can ask the harder, deeper question: What was the nature of the external input, the external stimulation or evidence on the basis of which the system of moral judgment arose? To the extent that you can answer that, you can determine what the inner nature was from which it began.

The logic is exactly like the problem of why children undergo puberty. You first find out what happens to them at that age; you ask what factors, what external events took place; and then you'd say what must have been the internal directive capacity that led to this phenomenon given those external events. That's a question of science, a hard question of science. In these domains it's usually not hard because you usually find that the external events are so impoverished and so unstructured and so brief, in fact, that they couldn't have had much of an effect. So qualitatively speaking, most of it is going to be internal. That's a way of finding out our entire moral nature.

You can also study other things, like moral argument, for example. Take a real case; take, say, the debate about slavery. A lot of the debate about slavery took place—or, as we reconstruct it, could have taken place—on shared moral grounds. In fact, one can understand the slave owner's arguments on our moral grounds, and one can even see that those arguments are not insignificant.

Take one case just to illustrate. Suppose I'm a slave owner, and you're opposed to slavery, and I give you the following argument for slavery: "Suppose you rent a car and I buy a car. Who's going to take better care of it?" Well, the answer is that I'm going to take better care of it because I have a capital investment in it. You're not going to take care of it at all. If you hear a rattle, you're just going to give it back to Hertz and let somebody else worry about it. If I hear a rattle, I'm going to take it to the garage because I don't want to get in trouble later on. In general, I'm going to take better care of the car I own than you're going to take of the car you rent. Suppose I own a person and you rent a person. Who's going to take better care of that person? Well, by parity of argument, I'm going to take better care of that person than you are. Consequently, it follows that slavery is much more moral than capitalism. Slavery is a system in which you own people and therefore you take care of them. Capitalism, which has a free labor market, is a system in which you rent people. If you own capital, you rent people and then you don't care about them at all. You use them up, throw them away, get new people. So the free market in labor is totally immoral, whereas slavery is quite moral.

Now, that's a moral argument, and we can understand it. We may decide that it's grotesque. In fact, we *will* decide that it's grotesque, but we have to ask ourselves why. It's not that we lack a shared moral ground with the slave owner; we *have* a shared moral ground, and we would then want to argue that ownership of a person is such an infringement on the person's fundamental human rights that the question of better or worse doesn't even arise. That's already a complex argument, but it's an argument based on shared moral understanding. Now where's that shared moral understanding coming from? I have a strong suspicion that if we understood the nature of the problem better, we might discover that that shared moral understanding comes from our inner nature.

Let's return to the feminist question. The respect in which the feminists are exactly right, I think, is that when they bring forth and make you face the facts of domination, you see that such domination is wrong. Why do you see that it's wrong? Well, because something about your understanding of human beings and their rights is being brought out and made public. You didn't see it before, but that's because you're now exploring your own moral nature and finding something there that you didn't notice before. To the extent that there's any progress in human history—and there's some, after all—it seems to me that it's partly a matter of exploring your own moral nature and discovering things that we didn't recognize before. It wasn't very far back when slavery was considered moral, in fact, even obligatory. Now it's considered grotesque. I think there are social and historical reasons for that—like the rise of industrial capitalism, and so on—but that's not the whole story. That may be something that stimulated something internal, but what it stimulated was a deeper understanding of our own moral nature. It seems to me that these are various ways in which one might hope to discover the innate basis of moral judgment. But I think anywhere you look, if there's any system that's even complex enough to deserve being studied, you're going to get roughly the same result, and basically for Plato's reasons.

In Asian societies, especially Chinese society, there's a strong patriarchal assumption. While in Singapore, one of us had this very debate on innate human moral authority, and they said, "No, the innate human moral authority is that men should be superior to women." So there's a strong cultural impasse that we seem to bring out. Do you have any insights on that? Is it that we're more advanced than Asians or Chinese society?

Well, I think we are. For example, I admit that this is a value judgment and I can't prove it, but I would suspect that there's going to be an evolution (assuming that the human race doesn't self-destruct, which it's likely to do) from rigid patriarchal societies to more egalitarian societies and not the other way around. I would suspect an asymmetry in development because, as circumstances allow, people do become more capable of exploring their own moral nature. Now, "circumstances allow" means that the conditions of freedom generally expand, either partially for economic reasons or partially for other cultural reasons. As there's an expansion of the capacity to inquire into our own cultural practices instead of just accepting them rigidly, the assumptions about the need for domination or the justice of domination are challenged and typically overthrown—like peeling away layers of an onion. If that's correct, then yes, for cultural reasons, the move away from patriarchy is a step upward, not just a change. It's a step toward understanding our true nature.

["Education" as filtering toward submissiveness and obedience]

You have suggested that "intellectuals are the most indoctrinated part of the population . . . the ones most susceptible to propaganda." You have explained that the educated classes are "ideological managers," complicit in "controlling all the organized flow of information." How and why is this so? What can be done to change this situation?

Well, there's something almost tautological about that; that is, the people we call intellectuals are those who have passed through various gates and filters and have made it into positions in which they can serve as cultural managers. There are plenty of other people just as smart, smarter, more independent, more thoughtful, who didn't pass through those gates, and we just don't call them intellectuals. In fact, this is a process that starts in elementary school.

Let's be concrete about it. You and I went to good graduate schools and teach in fancy universities, and the reason we did this is because we're obedient. That is, you and I, and typically people like us, got to the positions we're in because from childhood we were willing to follow orders. If the teacher in third grade told us to do some stupid thing, we didn't say, "Look, that's ridiculous. I'm not going to do it." We did it because we wanted to get on to fourth grade. We came from the kind of background where we'd say, "Look, do it, forget about it, so the teacher's a fool, do it, you'll get ahead, don't worry about it." That goes on all through school, and it goes on through your professional career. You're told in graduate school, "Look, don't work on that; it's a wrong idea. Why not work on this? You'll get ahead." However it's put, and there are subtle ways of putting it, you allow yourself to be shaped by the system of authority that exists out there and is trying to shape you.

Well, some people do this. They're submissive and obedient, and they accept it and make it through; they end up being people in the high places— economic managers, cultural managers, political managers. There are other people who were in your class and in my class who didn't do it. When the teacher told them in the third grade to do X, they said, "That's stupid, and I'm not going to do it." Those are people who are more independent-minded, for example, and there's a name for them: they're called "behavior problems." You've got to deal with them somehow, so you send them to a shrink, or you put them in a special program, or maybe you just kick them out and they end up selling drugs or something. In fact, the whole educational system involves a good deal of filtering of this sort, and it's a kind of filtering toward submissiveness and obedience.

This goes on through professional careers as well. You're a journalist, let's say, and you want to write a story that's going to expose people in high places, and somebody else is going to write a story that serves the needs of people in high places; you know which one is going to end up being the bureau chief. That's the way it works. So in a way there's something almost tautological about your question. Sure, the people who make it into positions in which they're respected and recognized as intellectuals are the people who are not subversive of structures of power. They're the people who in one way or another serve those structures, or at least are neutral with respect to them. The ones who would be more subversive aren't called intellectuals; they're called wackos, or crazies, or "wild men in the wings," as McGeorge Bundy put it when he said, "There are people who understand that we have to be in Indochina and just differ on the tactics, and then there are the wild men in the wings who think there's something wrong with carrying out aggression against another country." (He said that in *Foreign Affairs*—a mainstream journal.) But that's the idea. There are wild men in the wings who don't accept authority, and they remain wild men in the wings and not intellectu-als, not respected intellectuals. Of course, this isn't 100 percent. These are tendencies, actually very strong tendencies, and they're reinforced by other strong tendencies.

[Two conceptions of the intellectuals and their role]

Another strong tendency has to do with the role of intellectuals. Why are you and I called intellectuals but some guy working in an automobile plant isn't an intellectual? I don't think it's necessarily because we read more or go to better concerts or anything like that. Maybe he does; in fact, I've known such cases. I grew up in such an environment. I grew up in an environment where my aunts and uncles were New York Jewish working-class, and this was still the 1930s when there was a rich working-class culture. Lots of them had barely gone to school. I had one uncle who never got past fourth grade and an aunt who never graduated from school. But that was the richest intellec-tual environment I've ever seen. And I mean high culture, not comic book culture: Freud, Steckel, the Budapest String Quartet, and debates about any-thing you can imagine. But those people were never called intellectuals. They were called "unemployed workers" or something like that.

Now, why are they not intellectuals, whereas a lot of people in the uni-versities who are basically doing clerical work (from an intellectual point of view, a lot of scholarship is just very low-level clerical work) are respected intellectuals? First of all, it's a matter of subordination and power, and sec-ondly, it's a matter of which role you choose for yourself. The ones we call intellectuals, especially the public intellectuals—you know, the ones who make a splash or who are called upon to be the experts—are people who have chosen for themselves the role of manager. In earlier societies they would have been priests; in our societies they form a kind of secular priesthood.

In fact, in the nineteenth and twentieth centuries, intellectuals have rather typically taken one or another of two very similar paths. One is basically the Marxist/Leninist path, and that's very appealing for intellectuals because it provides them with the moral authority to control people. The essence of Marxism/Leninism is that there's a vanguard role and that's played by the rad-ical intellectuals who whip the stupid masses forward into a future they're too dumb to understand for themselves. That's a very appealing idea for intellectu-als. There's even a method: you achieve this position on the backs of people who are carrying out a popular struggle. So there's a popular struggle, you iden-tify yourself as a leader, you take power, and then you lead the stupid masses forward. That basically captures the essence of Marxism/Leninism—a tremendous appeal to the intellectuals for obvious reasons, and that's why that's one major direction in which they've gone all over the world.

There's another direction which is not all that different: a recognition that there's not going to be any popular revolution; there's a given system of power that's more or less going to stay, I'm going to serve it, I'm going to be the expert who helps the people with real power achieve their ends. That's the Henry Kissinger phenomenon or the state capitalist intellectual. Well, that's another role for the intellectuals. Actually, Kissinger put it rather nicely in one of his academic essays. He described an expert as "a person who knows how to articulate the consensus of his constituency." He didn't add the next point: "Your constituency is people with power." But that's tacit. Knowing how to articulate the consensus of unemployed workers or the homeless doesn't make you an expert. The point is that an expert is a person who knows how to artic-ulate the consensus of the people of power, who can serve the role of manager.

Those two conceptions of the intellectual are very similar. In fact, I think it's a striking fact that people find it very easy to shift from one to the other. That's called the "god-that-failed phenomenon." You see there isn't going to be a popular revolution and you're not going to make it as the vanguard driv-ing the masses forward, so you undergo this conversion and you become a servant of "state capitalism." Now, I won't say that everybody who underwent that was immoral. Some people really saw things they hadn't seen. But by now it's become a farce. You can see it happening: people perfectly con-sciously recognizing, "Well, there isn't going to be a revolution. If I want the power and prestige, I'd better serve these guys. So I suddenly undergo this conversion, and I denounce my old comrades as unregenerate Stalinists." It's a farcical move at which we should laugh at this point. I think the ease of that transition in part reflects the fact that there isn't very much difference. There's a difference in the assessment of where power lies, but there's a kind of com-monality of the conception of the intellectual's role.

Now, my point is that the people we call intellectuals are people who have passed the filters, gone through the gates, picked up these roles for themselves, and decided to play them. Those are the people we call intellec-tuals. If you ask why intellectuals are submissive, the answer is they wouldn't be intellectuals otherwise. Again, this is not 100 percent, but it's a large part.

[One purpose of the media and the educational system]

You alluded to the media a minute ago. You have written repeatedly that the state and the media collaborate to support and sustain the interests and values of the establishment. Yet we in the U.S. boast proudly of our "free press." Are our media victims of ideological indoctrination, or are they willing conspirators in suppressing truth?

I wouldn't exactly put it either way. They're not victims and they're not conspirators. Suppose, for example, you were to ask a similar question about, say, General Motors. General Motors tries to maximize profit and market share; are they victims of our system or are they conspirators in our system? Neither. They are components of the system which act in certain ways for well-understood institutional reasons. If they didn't act that way, they would not be in the game any longer.

Let's take the media. The media have a particular institutional role. We have a free press, meaning it's not state-controlled but corporate-controlled; that's what we call freedom. What we call freedom is corporate control. We have a free press because it's a corporate monopoly, or oligopoly, and that's called freedom. We have a free political system because there's one party run by business; there's a business party with two factions, so that's a free political system. The terms *freedom* and *democracy*, as used in our Orwellian political discourse, are based on the assumption that a particular form of domination—namely, by owners, by business elements—is freedom. If they run things, it's free, and the playing field's level. If they don't run things, the playing field isn't level and you've got to do something about it. So if popular organizations form or if labor unions are too important, you've got to level the playing field. If it's El Salvador, you send out the death squads; if it's at home, you do something else, but you've got to level the playing field.

Coming back to the free press: yes, our press is free. It's fundamentally a narrow corporate structure, deeply interconnected with big conglomerates. Like other corporations, it has a product which it sells to the market, and the market is advertisers, other businesses. The product, especially for the elite press, the press that sets the agenda for others that follow, is privileged audiences. That's the way to sell things to advertisers. So you have an institutional structure of major corporations selling privileged elite audiences to other corporations. Now it plays a certain institutional role: it presents the version of the world which reflects the interests and needs of the sellers and buyers. That's not terribly surprising, and there are a lot of other factors that push it in the same direction.

Well, that's not a conspiracy, any more than GM's making profit is a conspiracy. It's not that they're victims; they're part of the system. In fact, if any segment of the media, say, the *New York Times*, began to deviate from that role, they'd simply go out of business. Why should the stockholders or the advertisers want to allow them to continue if they're not serving that role? Similarly, if some journalist from the *New York Times* decided to expose the truth, let's say started writing accurate and honest articles about the way power is being exercised, the editors would be crazy to allow that journalist to continue. That journalist is undermining authority and domination and getting people to think for themselves, and that's exactly a function you don't want the media to pursue. It's not that it's a conspiracy; it's just that the media's institutional structure gives them the same kind of purpose that the educational system has: to turn people into submissive, atomized individuals who don't interfere with the structures of power and authority but rather serve those structures. That's the way the system is set up, and if you started deviating from that, those with real power, the institutions with real power, would interfere to prevent that deviation. That's the way institutions work, so it seems to me almost predictable that the media will serve the role of a kind of indoctrination.

You have said that "propaganda is to democracy what violence is to the totalitarian state," which, of course, relates to what you are saying here.
And, in fact, there's a very intriguing line of thought in democratic theory that goes back certainly to the seventeenth-century English revolutions— sort of the first major modern democratic revolutions. There's been a recognition which becomes very explicit in the twentieth century, especially in the United States, that as the capacity to control people by force declines, you have to discover other means of control. Harold Lasswell, one of the founders of the modern area of communications in the political sciences, put it this way in the 1930s in an article on propaganda in the *International Encyclopedia of Social Sciences:* "We should not succumb to democratic dogmatism about men being the best judges of their own interests." They're not. We're the best judges. In a military state or what we would now call a totalitarian state, you can control people by force; in a democratic state you can't control them by force, so you'd better control them with propaganda—for their own good. This is a standard view; in fact, I suspect this is the dominant view among intellectuals.

This, of course, relates to Walter Lippmann's concept of "the manufacture of consent," the idea that government distrusts the public's ability to make wise decisions and so it reserves real power for a "smart" elite who will make the "right decisions" and then create the illusion of public consensus.
Yes, but you really have to think considerably about the framework of thinking that that came from. Lippmann designed this notion of "manufacture of consent" as progress in the art of democracy, and he believed it was a good

thing—and that's important. It's a good thing because, as he put it, "We have to protect ourselves from the rage and trampling of the bewildered herd." So there's this mass of people out there who are the bewildered herd, and if we just let them go free—if we allow things like democracy, for example—there's just going to be rage and trampling because they're all totally incapable. The only people who are capable of running anything are we smart guys, what he called "the specialized class." He didn't add—something, again, which is tacitly understood—that we make it to the specialized class if we serve people with real power. So it's not that we're smarter; it's that we're more submissive. And we, the specialized class, the servants of power, have to save ourselves and our prestige and power from the rage and trampling of the bewildered herd. For that you need manufacture of consent because you can't shoot people down in the streets; you can't control them by force. In that respect, indoctrination is to democracy what a bludgeon is to totalitarianism.

[Preventing democracy in the form of democracy]

In fact, it's even better, much more effective.

It's certainly much more important. In a totalitarian state, let's say the Soviet Union under Stalin's direction (that's about as close as you can come), it didn't matter too much what people believed. They could more or less believe what they liked. What mattered was what they did, and what they did you control by force or by threat. In fact, rather commonly fascist and totalitarian states have been reasonably open. In Franco's Spain, for example, a lot of people were reading more widely than they were here in many respects and debating much more, and it didn't matter that much because you've got them under control: you have a bludgeon over their heads; there's not much they can do. In the Soviet Union, for example, *samizdat* were very widely read. I read some studies of this which had astonishingly high figures of distribution of *samizdat*. The authorities could have stopped it, but they probably just didn't care that much: "So people have crazy ideas. Who cares? They're not going to do anything about it because we control them."

Now, in a more free and more democratic society, it becomes very dangerous if people start thinking, because if they start thinking they might start doing, and you don't have the police to control them. If they're blacks in downtown Boston, it's not a big problem: you do have the police to control them. But if they're relatively privileged, middle-class white folk like us, then you don't have the police to control them because they're too powerful to allow that to happen. They share in the privilege of the wealthy and therefore you can't control them by force so you've got to control what they think.

Indoctrination is, therefore, a crucial element of preventing democracy in the form of democracy.

Recently, you told Bill Moyers that you'd "like to see a society moving toward voluntary organization and eliminating as much as possible the structures of hierarchy and domination, and the basis for them in ownership and control." How can this be achieved? The system that you've been describing is quite entrenched.

Different societies have different forms of domination. Patriarchy is one, and in principle we know how to overcome that—it's not too easy to do, but we know in principle. But in our kinds of society, the major forms of domination, at least the core ones, are basically ownership. Private ownership of the means of production grants owners the ultimate authority over what's produced, what's distributed, what takes place in political life, what the range of cultural freedom is, and so on. They have decisive power because they control capital, and there's no reason why that should be vested in private hands. In my view, if you take the ideals of the eighteenth century seriously, you become very anti-capitalist. If you take the ideals of classical liberalism seriously, I think it leads to opposition to corporate capitalism. Classical liberalism—as developed, for example, by Humboldt—or much of Enlightenment thought was opposed to the church and the state and the feudal system, but for a reason: because those were the striking examples of centralized power. What it was really opposed to was centralized power that's not under popular control.

Nineteenth-century corporations are another form of centralized power completely out of public control, and by the same reasoning we should be opposed to them. If you take classical liberal thought and apply it rationally to more recent conditions, you become a libertarian socialist and a kind of a left-wing anarchist. I don't mean anarchist in the American sense where it means right-wing capitalist, but anarchist in the traditional sense, meaning a socialist who's opposed to state power and in favor of voluntary association to the extent that social conditions permit and who regards the role of an honest person as one of constant struggle forever, as long as human history goes on, against any forms of authority and domination, maybe many that we don't even see now and will only discover later.

What society do you think comes closest to achieving anything like this kind of voluntary association? Do you think any society even comes close?

Well, sure, every society has aspects of it, and they differ. Sometimes you find things in very poor, backward, undeveloped societies that you don't find in advanced societies. In many ways the United States is like this. There are very positive things in the United States. In many respects, the United States is the freest country in the world. I don't just mean in terms of limits on state coercion, though that's true too, but also just in terms of individual relations. The United States comes closer to classlessness in terms of interpersonal relations than virtually any society. I'm always struck by the fact when traveling elsewhere, let's say to England, that the forms of deference and authority that people assume automatically are generally unknown here.

For example, here there's no problem with a university professor and a garage mechanic talking together informally as complete equals. But that is not true in England. That's a very positive thing about the United States. Intellectuals in the United States are always deploring the fact that intellectuals here aren't taken seriously the way they're taken seriously in Europe. That's one of the good things about the United States. There's absolutely no reason to take them seriously for the most part. I remember in the 1960s, sometimes I would sign an international statement against the war in Vietnam—signed by me here, Sartre and some other person in Europe, and so on. Well, in Paris there'd be big front-page headlines; here nobody paid any attention at all, which was the only healthy reaction. Okay, so three guys signed a statement; who cares? The statement signed by 120 intellectuals in the time of the Algerian war was a major event in Paris. If a similar thing happened here, it wouldn't even make the newspapers—correctly.

All that reflects a kind of internalized democratic understanding and freedom that's extremely important. One shouldn't underestimate it. I think that it's one of the reasons why we have the Pentagon system. Compare the United States, say, with Japan. How come we had to turn to the Pentagon system as a way to force the public to subsidize high-technology industry, whereas Japan didn't? They just get the public to subsidize high-technology industry directly, through reduction of consumption, fiscal measures, and so on. That makes them a lot more efficient than we are. If you want to build the next generation of, say, computers, the Japanese just say, "Okay, we're going to lower consumption levels, put this much into investment, and build computers." If you want to do it in the United States, you say, "Well, we're going to build some lunatic system to stop Soviet missiles, and for that you're going to have to lower your consumption level and maybe, somehow, we'll get computers out of that." Obviously, the Japanese system is much more efficient.

So why don't we adopt the more efficient system? The reason is that we're a freer society; we can't do it here. In a society that's more fascist than state capitalist, and I mean that culturally as well as in terms of economic institutions, you can just tell people what they're going to do and they do it.

Here you can't do that. No politician in the United States can get up and say, "You guys are going to lower your standard of living next year so that IBM can make more profit, and that's the way it's going to work." That's not going to sell. Here you have to fool people into it by fear and so on. We need all kinds of complicated mechanisms of propaganda and coercion which in a well-run, more fascistic society are quite unnecessary. You just give orders. That's one of the reasons fascism is so efficient.

You've even expressed fear that the U.S. is ripe for a fascist leader. You write, "In a depoliticized society with few mechanisms for people to express their fears and needs and to participate constructively in managing the affairs of life, someone could come along who was interested not in personal gain, but power. That could be very dangerous." Is this statement rhetorical, or cautionary, or do you have serious fears that the U.S. can fall victim to a charismatic, fascist dictator?

It's real. I mentioned something very good about the United States, but there are also a number of things that are very bad. One is the breakdown of independent social organization and independent thought, the atomization of people. As we move toward a society which is optimal from the point of view of the business classes—namely, that each individual is an atom, lacking means to communicate with others so that he or she can't develop independent thought or action and is just a consumer, not a producer—people become deeply alienated, and they may hate what's going on but have no way to express that hatred constructively. And if a charismatic leader comes along, they may very well follow. I think the United States is very lucky that that hasn't happened.

I think that's one of the reasons why I'm very much in favor of corruption. I think that's one of the best things there is. You'll notice that in my books I never criticize corruption. I think it's a wonderful thing. I'd much rather have a corrupt leader than a power-hungry leader. A corrupt leader is going to rob people but not cause that much trouble. For example, as long as the fundamentalist preachers—like Jim Bakker, or whatever his name is—are interested in Cadillacs, sex, and that kind of thing, they're not a big problem. But suppose one of them comes along who's a Hitler and who doesn't care much about sex and Cadillacs, who just wants power. Then we're going to be in real trouble. The more corrupt these guys are, the better off we are. I think we all ought to applaud corruption. In fact, that's true in authoritarian societies too. The more corrupt they are, the better off the people usually are because power hunger is much more dangerous than money hunger. But I think the United States is ripe for a fascist leader. It's a very good thing that everyone who's come along so far is impossible: Joe McCarthy, for example, was too much of a thug; Richard Nixon was too much of a crook; Ronald Reagan was too much of a clown; the fundamentalist preachers are ultimately too corrupt. In fact, we've escaped, but it's by luck. If a Hitler comes along, I think we might be in serious trouble.

Your political views have been called "radical," while your notions of language have been termed "conservative." Jay Parini writes, "Some colleagues take Chomsky to task for ignoring the social realities of language and, therefore, defining it too narrowly. Chomsky's work, for example, isn't concerned with showing how language is used in everyday situations to sustain inequities between men and women." Is this a fair assessment? How do you reconcile these two seemingly contradictory perspectives?

There's something to that, but let me tell you what my own choices and priorities are. Like any human being, I'm interested in a lot of things. There are things I find intellectually interesting and there are other things I find humanly significant, and those two sets have very little overlap. Maybe the world could be different, but the fact is that that's the way the world actually is. The intellectually interesting, challenging, and exciting topics, in general, are close to disjoint from the humanly significant topics. If I have X hours a day, I, like any other person, am going to distribute them somehow. I'm not saying I spend every waking moment trying to help other people: I eat, take a walk, read a book, work on problems that excite me, and so on. I do these things just for myself because I like them. I also spend a part of my time, and in fact quite a large part, doing things that I think are humanly significant.

Now, I'm going to make this much too mechanical to make a point, but suppose I say, "Okay, now it's my hour for doing something humanly significant and I have two choices: one is to study the way in which language is used to facilitate authority, and the other is to do something to help Salvadoran peasants who are getting slaughtered." Well, I'm going to do the second because that's overwhelmingly more significant than the first, by huge orders of magnitude. That's why I don't spend time on things like the use of language to impose authority. Doubtless it's true, but it's a topic that's not intellectually interesting; it has no intellectual depth to it at all, like most things in the social sciences. Also, it's of marginal human significance as compared with other problems. Therefore, I don't think it's a reasonable distribution of my own priorities.

There are people who think differently, and I think they are making a very poor moral judgment. If people want to study, say, social use of language because they find it interesting, fine; that's on a par with my reading a book. There's no moral issue involved. Similarly, I find technical problems about language structure or Plato's problem interesting, so I study them. On the other hand, if people claim they are doing that out of some moral imperative, they're making a severe error because in terms of moral imperatives that's a much lower order than others. People often argue, and I think this is a real fallacy, "Look, I'm a linguist; therefore, in my time as a linguist I have to be socially useful." That doesn't make sense at all. You're a human being, and your time as a human being should be socially useful. It doesn't mean that your choices about helping other people have to be within the context of your professional training as a linguist. Maybe that training just doesn't help you to be useful to other people. In fact, it doesn't.

I have a feeling there's a lot of careerism in this. For example, if I spend all my time working as a linguist and some fraction of it is on things of marginal social utility, I can say, "Look how moral I am," and at the same time be advancing my career. On the other hand, if I take that segment of my life and use it for going to last week's demonstration in Washington about the Romero assassination, I'm not advancing my career at all, though I may be helping people more. You have to be careful not to fall into that trap. So if people want to work on these problems—and I think they're perfectly valid problems—they simply have to ask themselves why they're doing it. Are they doing it because that's the way to help other human beings? If so, I think they're making a poor judgment. If they're doing it because that's what they're interested in, well fine, I've no objection. People have a right to do things they're interested in.

[Creative reading as the heart of the writing program]

Your discussions of creativity were influential, even inspirational, to those who developed sentence combining as a way of teaching writing. We know one teacher who began each writing course by asking students to combine four or five short sentences into one. Of course, the number of possible solutions is large, and students were always impressed that nearly all of their sentences were different. Nonetheless, anyone who has taught writing at any level can attest that many students fall into predictable patterns of language use. Do you think creativity in language can be fostered so that more of a student's innate potential is used?

I'm sure it can be fostered. Creative reading, for example, surely is a way of fostering it; getting people to wrestle with complex ideas and to find ways of expressing them ought to be at the heart of the writing program. Frankly, I doubt very much that linguistics has anything to contribute to this. Perhaps it can suggest some things, but I don't suspect it can really be applied.

My own feeling is that teaching is mostly common sense. I taught children when I was a college student. I worked my way through college in part by teaching Hebrew school. I've taught graduate students across the range, and just from my own experience or anything I've read, it seems to me that 99 percent of good teaching is getting people interested in the task or problem and providing them with a rich enough environment in which they can begin to pursue what they find interesting in a constructive way.

I don't know of any methods for doing that other than being interested in it yourself, being interested in the people you are teaching, and learning from the experience yourself. In that kind of environment, something good happens, and I suppose that's true with writing as much as auto mechanics. I often quote a famous statement from one of MIT's great physicists, Victor Weisskopf, but it's a standard comment. He was often asked by students, "What are we going to cover this semester?" His standard answer was supposed to have been "It doesn't matter what we cover; it matters what we *discover*." That's basically it: that's good teaching. It doesn't matter what you cover; it matters how much you develop the capacity to discover. You do that and you're in good shape.

In College English *in 1967, you wrote that "a concern for the literary standard language—prescriptivism in its more sensible manifestations—is as legitimate as an interest in colloquial speech." Do you still believe that a sensible prescriptivism is preferable to linguistic permissiveness? If so, how would you define a sensible prescriptivism?*

I think sensible prescriptivism ought to be part of any education. I would certainly think that students ought to know the standard literary language with all its conventions, its absurdities, its artificial conventions, and so on because that's a real cultural system, and an important cultural system. They should certainly know it and be inside it and be able to use it freely. I don't think people should give them any illusions about what it is. It's not better, or more sensible. Much of it is a violation of natural law. In fact, a good deal of what's taught is taught because it's wrong. You don't have to teach people their native language, because it grows in their minds, but if you want people to say, "He and I were here" and not "Him and me were here," then you have to teach them because it's probably wrong. The nature of English probably is the other way, "Him and me were here," because the so-called nominative form is typically used only as the subject of the tense sentence; grammarians who misunderstood this fact then assumed that it ought to be, "He and I were here," but they're wrong. It should be "Him and me were here," by that rule. So they teach it because it's not natural. Or if you want to teach the so-called proper use of *shall* and *will*—and I think it's totally wild—you have to teach it because it doesn't make any sense.

On the other hand, if you want to teach people how to make passives, you just confuse them because they already know, because they already follow these rules. So a good deal of what's taught in the standard language is just a history of artificialities, and they have to be taught because they're artificial. But that doesn't mean that people shouldn't know them. They should know them because they're part of the cultural community in which they play a role and in which they are part of a repository of a very rich cultural heritage. So, of course, you've got to know them.

The standard literary language, what's called "standard English," is an object of great controversy in some parts of the Third World now. For example, there's a debate in India over whether people should still be taught the colonial language to give them greater access to technology or whether there should be just a few people who are very active translators into the local languages. What's your sense of the desirability of the spread of world English? First of all, do you think that it is continuing to spread now that American economic hegemony has been broken? Also, is it desirable that it spread?

I've never seen a real study, but my strong impression is that it's continuing to spread and that U.S. cultural hegemony is growing even while U.S. economic hegemony is declining. Take the relations between the United States and Europe. Europe is becoming relatively more powerful economically and will soon be absolutely more powerful. On the other hand, my strong impression is that it's much more culturally colonized by the United States in terms of ways of thinking, the sources of news, and so on. This is not an unusual phenomenon. Look at the relations between England and the United States, say, around 1950. England was declining as a power sharply relative to the United States, but that was combined with a high degree of Anglophilia and often a rather childish imitation of British cultural styles and modes on the part of the intellectual classes here. These things aren't necessarily parallel, but my strong impression is that the hegemony of U.S. English and U.S. culture in general is extending in everything from the sciences to pop music.

Now, what should they do in places like India? Well, that's a hard problem. It's like what should you do with Black English? I don't think there are simple answers to that. There are good reasons to preserve and develop national languages and national cultures because they enrich human life for the participants and for others. On the other hand, the people who are in them may suffer. For example, if people in Wales learn Welsh, the way the world is they're going to be worse off in many respects than if they had learned English. You might want the world to be some other way, but this is the way it is. The same kinds of questions arise in the case of Black English and in the case of teaching English as a second language in India. How you balance those values is tricky, and I don't think there's any general answer to it. I think there are particular answers in particular places. In the case of India, the answer being pursued is that people ought to learn English, and I think that's probably reasonable.

In 1979, you gave a series of lectures in Pisa which were later published and which many linguists think introduced the most important development of the 1980s: the principles and parameters approach. Yet, unlike your earlier work in the Aspects *phase, it's not known outside of linguistics, and it hasn't had the same impact. Do you think people outside of linguistics should know about the principles and parameters approach?*

I think it's more important than the *Aspects*-type approach. In fact, if anything deserves to be called a revolution, that's probably it. It leads to a conception of language which is, in fact, radically different from anything in the historical tradition. Early transformational grammar, early generative grammar, say in the 1950s and 1960s, had a kind of a traditional feel to it. In many ways, it was more acceptable to traditional grammarians than to structural linguists because in a lot of ways it had a traditional look. It was more like Jespersen than it was like Bloomfield, for example, and traditional grammarians recognized that. They may not have understood the details or liked the way it was being done, but they could kind of see the point. For example, there were particular rules for particular constructions, and just as a traditional grammar had a chapter on the passive or on the imperative and so on, the early generative grammars were like that in structure: there was a passive rule and a question rule and a chapter on what verb phrases look like, and so on.

The post-1980s theories are radically different. There are no constructions; there are no rules. Things like traditional constructions—say, relative clauses—are just taxonomic artifacts. They're like "large mammal." A large mammal is a real thing, but it has no meaning in the sciences. It's just something that results from a lot of different things interacting. The same seems to be true of the passive. It's not a real thing; it's just a taxonomic phenomenon. So there's no meaning to the question, "Is Japanese passive the same as

English passive?" Furthermore, there don't seem to be any rules—that is, language-specific rules. In fact, you can speculate without being thought absurd that there may be only one computational system and in that sense only one language. The variety of languages may be a matter of a number of lexical options, where those lexical options probably leave out a large part of the substantive vocabulary, meaning nouns and verbs and so on. So it looks as if the variety of languages is very narrowly circumscribed and the apparent radical difference among languages derives from the fact that in quite complicated systems, if you make small changes here and there, the output may look very different at the end, even though they're basically the same. That's all work of the 1980s, and I think if it's right, it's very rich in its implications. I don't think it's going to be so easily assimilated elsewhere because you have to understand it. In the work of the 1960s, you could have a rough feel for what it was like and misunderstand it but apply it nonetheless. And a lot of the apparent impact of this linguistics was kind of casual misunderstanding of things that look more or less familiar. This new work is quite different. You have to understand what it's about, and that means some work.

What would you suggest people read—people who are out of the field who want to understand this new approach?
Well, there are some pretty good relatively introductory books. It depends on what level they want to understand it. I've tried myself. I have a book called *Language and problems of knowledge*, which is a collection of lectures given in Managua to a public audience of non-linguists. This was just a general audience and they seemed to find it intelligible, and other people have told me they find it intelligible. At a somewhat more technical level, there's a book by Howard Lasnik and a student of his, Juan Uriagereka, called *A course in GB syntax: lectures on binding and empty categories*, which is actually first-year graduate lectures from the University of Connecticut. Now, those are very lucid and carry it much further into the technical intricacies. But for the general points, at least as I understand them, I'd recommend the first book.

What readership did you target in your 1986 book, Knowledge of language?
That's a funny sort of book. One chapter is pretty technical linguistics; one chapter is about thought control; the rest is sort of philosophy of language. I had an original idea for that book, but it just turned out to be too encyclopedic to carry off; it's sort of described in the Preface. It was going to be about two problems in the theory of knowledge: Plato's problem, or how we know

so much given so little evidence; and Orwell's problem, or how we know so little given so much evidence. I still think that would be a nice book to write. It went too far.

Well, you did sketch out Orwell's problem in the last chapter. What's your sense of the treatment of your work in popularizations such as Neil Smith's The twitter machine?
That's a very good book. I think he knows what he's doing; he's very sophisticated. I don't agree with him on everything, but I think it's an intelligent presentation not just on my work but on lots of things in the field, including lots of interesting work done on relevance theory and pragmatics and so on.

Well, he does deal quite extensively with your work.
That's a mistake people make: they call it "mine" because I sometimes write about it. Take the Pisa lectures. They weren't "mine." They were the result of years of very interesting work. There's a reason why they were given in Pisa: a lot of the best work was being done by Italian and European linguists. So I happened to give some summer lectures there. These things don't have individual names attached to them.

[Language and interpretation]
Earlier in the interview you raised the issue of semantics and your interest in it, but you've also consistently reiterated over your career, most recently in The generative enterprise, *that linguists' chief concern should not be semantics. We were surprised to hear that you're now teaching a course in semantics.*
It's not surprising. Part of this is terminological. In my view, most of what's called semantics is syntax. I just call it syntax; other people call the same thing semantics. *Syntactic structures,* in my view, is pure syntax, but the questions dealt with there are what other people call semantics. I was interested in the question "Why does 'John is easy to please' have a different meaning from 'John is eager to please'?" I wanted to find a theory of language structure that would explain that fact. Most people call that semantics; I call it syntax because I think it has to do with mental representations.

Take a point we discussed earlier: the word *house,* the concept "house," and the use of the word *house* in real situations to refer to things. There are two relations there, and I don't think you can turn them into one, as is commonly done. The common idea is that there's one relation, the relation of reference, and I don't believe that. I think there's a relation that holds between the word *house* and a very rich concept that doesn't only hold of *house* but of all sorts of other things. That relation most people would call semantics. I call it syntax because it has to do with mental representations and the structure of mental representations.

Then there's the relationship between that rich semantic representation and things in the world, like someplace I'm going tonight after class. Now, that relationship is what is real semantics, and about that there is almost nothing to say. That's the part that's subject to holism and interest relativity and values and so on, and you can sort of assemble Wittgensteinian particulars about it, but there doesn't seem to be anything general to say. Where I depart from Wittgenstein is that I think there is something very general and definite to say about the relation between words and concepts. I call that syntax because it has to do with mental representations, things inside the skin, rules and computations and representations and so on, going all the way into intrinsic semantic properties, analytic/synthetic distinctions, and most problems of the theory of meaning that can be dealt with.

Now, there are plenty of people who call their work semantics who in my view are not dealing with semantics at all. Take "all possible world semantics." In my view, that's just straight syntax. It's either right or wrong (and I think it's right), but if it's right, it's right in the sense in which some other theory of phonology is right. It's a form of syntax. Problems of semantics will arise when you begin to tell me how a possible world relates to things, and the people who work with this topic don't deal with it. When you start dealing with the relation of mental constructions to the world, you discover that there's very little to say other than Wittgensteinian-type questions about ways of life. At that level, I think he's basically right; you can discuss ways of life. So this is largely illusion. I do think that syntax and semantics should deal with what I call syntax, mostly, because that's where the richness in the field is.

In your famous review in 1959 of Skinner's verbal behaviorist psychology, you argued convincingly that terms such as reinforcement, *which have well-defined meanings in experiments using rats, become meaningless when extended to the complexity of human behavior. Many of your terms have also been metaphorically extended. Can you think of any instances in which metaphorical extensions of a concept like "deep structure" might be justified, or should such extensions always be avoided?*

I think you've got to be careful. In the case of "deep structure," I simply stopped using the term because it was being so widely misunderstood. "Deep structure" was a technical term. It didn't have any sense of "profundity," but it was understood to mean "profound," or "far-reaching," or something like that. It might turn out that what I call "surface structure" is much more profound in its implications. Most invariably in the secondary literature, "deep structure" has been confused with what I would call "universal grammar." So "deep structure" is identified as kind of the innate structure, and that's not correct. The term was so widely misunderstood that I decided—I think it was in *Knowledge of language*—to drop the word and just make it an obvious technical term so nobody would be confused; nowadays I just refer to it as "D-structure." I figure that's not going to confuse anybody. It looks technical and it is technical.

It's very rare that you ever get a free ride from some other field. People who think they're talking about free will because they mention Heisenberg usually don't know what's going on. Or people who say, "Well, people aren't computers. Remember Gödel." That's too easy. Life isn't that easy. You'd better understand it before you start drawing conclusions from it. Sometimes people who do understand what they're talking about can make plausible suggestions or even inferences or guesses from outside the field. That's not impossible, but first you've got to understand what you're talking about. These topics are not like political science. I mean, they're not just there on the surface; there's some intellectual structure and some degree of intellectual depth. It's not quantum physics either, so I think any person who's interested can figure it out without too much trouble. But you've got to take the trouble. I've been appalled by what I've read on how "deep structure" is used.

Some of your work both in linguistics and in political analysis has generated considerable controversy. Are you aware of any specific misunderstanding or criticism of your work that you'd like to take issue with at this time?
We could go on forever. On the linguistics side, there's plenty of misunderstanding, but I think it's resolvable. I'm enough of a believer in the rational side of human beings to think that if you sit down and talk these questions through and you think them through, you can reach a resolution.

On the political side, I don't think it's resolvable because I think there's a deep functional need not to understand. The problem is that if what I'm saying is correct, then it's also subversive and, therefore, it'd better not be understood. Let me put it this way: if I found that I did have easy access to systems of power like journals and television, then I'd begin to be worried. I'd think I'm doing something wrong because I ought to be trying to subvert those systems of power, and if I am doing it and I'm doing it honestly, they shouldn't want to have me around. In those areas, misunderstanding (if you want to call it that) is almost an indication that you may well be on the right track. It's not proof that you're on the right track, but it's an indication you may be. If you're understood and appreciated, it's almost proof that you're not on the right track.

Editor's Notes

Editor's notes to Prologue ("Democracy and education")

This selection, which overlaps with Selection 15, is placed here as a Prologue because it lucidly sets the stage. It is a slightly edited version of a transcript of Chomsky's Mellon Lecture, delivered at Loyola University, Chicago, on October 19, 1994, and published here in full for the first time. (A tape recording of the oral version is available from Alternative Radio, P.O. Box 551, Boulder, CO, 800–444–1977.) It can also be seen as a supplement to Selection 7. The 1995 Jeffrey and Kitty Cole Honors College Lecture Chomsky gave on March 28, 1995, at Michigan State University, under the title "Education and democracy," was apparently quite similar in content.

Chomsky begins by contrasting two completely different traditions of Western thought about the ideas of "freedom," "justice," and "democracy" that have developed since the Enlightenment. One tradition stems from the nineteenth-century working-class press and organizations, evolves through libertarian and socialist movements, and underlies the education-for-democracy conceptions of John Dewey and Bertrand Russell—and that of Chomsky (for the reasons why Dewey had "a strong influence" on Chomsky in his formative years, and for differences between the philosophies of Dewey and Russell, and between both and Chomsky's, see the Introduction). The other tradition develops in association with emergent state capitalism, especially in its twentieth-century corporate form (the intellectual soil of which can be, revealingly, traced back to Hegel), and finds cultural expression in contemporary educational institutions and the media. See Selection 15 and the Introduction, Section 3, for more on this theme and its implications and ramifications.

Broader discussions of some of the topics can be found in other publications by Chomsky, in particular recent ones such as *Deterring democracy* (1991,

1992), in particular Ch. 12, *Year 501* (1993), *World orders old and new* (1994, 1996), *The umbrella of U.S. power: the Universal Declaration of Human Rights and the contradictions of U.S. policy* (1994, 1999), *Powers and prospects* (1996), Chs. 4ff., and in several of other recent writings of his, including "'Consent without consent': reflections on the theory and practice of democracy" (1996), "Market democracy in a neoliberal order: doctrine and reality" (1997), "Power in the global arena" (1998), *Profits over people: neoliberalism and global order* (1999), *The new military humanism* (1999), *Rogue states: the rule of force in world affairs* (2000), and *A new generation draws the line: Kosovo, East Timor and the standards of the West* (2000), as well in a number of interviews, among them "Human nature, freedom and political community" (1998), "There is no limits to what can be done" (1998), and those collected in *Keeping the rabble in line* (1994), *Secrets, lies and democracy* (1994), *Class warfare* (1996), *The common good* (1998), and *Propaganda and the public mind* (2001).

It is enlightening to compare Chomsky's discussion with other writings on the topic, in particular recent ones, e.g., those in *Challenges facing higher education at the millennium* (1999), ed. W. Z. Hirsch and Luc E. Weber, or Nussbaum, *Cultivating humanity: a classical defense of reform in liberal education* (1997).

Editor's notes to Selection 1 ("Things no amount of learning can teach")

As indicated in the Foreword, the writings collected in this book fall into two different categories: interviews and articles (some originally talks, later written up). The advantages of the interviews are two: they are easier to read, and they address questions raised by an interviewer from an individual perspective, some of which Chomsky never addresses in his writings.

This interview, reprinted from Chomsky's *Language and politics*, ed. by C. P. Otero (1988), is a good example of both advantages, its focus being a fundamental question prior to any serious discussion of democracy or education. It was conducted by an interviewer with a background helpful for the occasion: psychologist and science journalist John Gliedman ("who studied Chomsky's theories in the late Sixties at MIT, [and] discussed ideas about language and mind in the linguist's austere campus office"). It first appeared in *Omni* 6, 11 (1983), pp. 113–14, 116, 118, and 171–74, under the title "The revolutionary linguist who believes we have a 'language organ' in our brain also thinks there are some things no amount of learning can teach." It was also included, under the title "How language is shaped: an interview," in Richard-Amato, *Making it happen* (1988), pp. 283–90, and in part (approximately the first two-thirds), in *Language: introductory readings*, ed. by Clark et al., 4th ed. (1985), pp. 366–75, preceded by a brief introductory note by the editors and followed by five questions for discussion and review. It was not included, however, in *The Omni interviews*, ed. by P. Weintraub (1984), even though what Chomsky has to say in this interview does not seem less plausible or less interesting or informative than what B. F. Skinner says in his— or perhaps because Chomsky has nothing to say about such topics as the complexity of a dolphin's brain, the nature of "altered states," the future of "cosmic colonies," and so on.

In the preliminary note to the interview when it first appeared it is pointed out that "before Chomsky's breakthrough in the mid-Fifties, American linguists did not believe that brain structure played any significant role in shaping language" and that his "rise to scientific prominence was meteoric": in scarcely a decade he became "the world-renowned leader of an intellectual revolution in the field of linguistics." "Aside from the originality of his ideas," the note continues, "Chomsky owes his success to his awesome ability as a debater; he's famous for surgically dissecting the logical flaws in rival views. . . . His widely recognized gifts as a teacher also helped him." (For a hint of his awesome ability, see R. Botha's convoluted *Challenging Chomsky: the generative garden game*, 1989; for his gifts as a teacher, see the Introduction.)

We are also given the following statistics: after achieving national recognition as a critic of the Vietnam War, "he sometimes made eight speeches a day while producing a torrent of documented critiques of American policy, as well as numerous technical books and papers in linguistics and philosophy. . . . Since 1958 he has written 21 books and about 100 articles on linguistics, philosophy and psychology. He has also found time to author or coauthor an additional 11 books and perhaps 1,000 articles on political and social themes." (By 1983, that is. A recent publication puts the number of books at eighty, and the number of articles is becoming harder and harder to count.) Mention is also made of the fact that he "withheld half of his federal income taxes as a protest against the war" for years.

On the "crisis of modernism," see Chomsky, *Reflections on language* (1975), pp. 124ff. (Stent's paper has been reprinted as Ch. 9 in his *Paradoxes of progress*, 1978.)

Editor's notes to Selection 2 ("Language as a key to human nature and society")

This interview, also reprinted from Chomsky's *Language and politics*, ed. by C. P. Otero (1988), was first published in English in *Contrasts: Soviet and American thinkers discuss the future*, ed. by Osiatynski (1984), pp. 95–101. The book, which was apparently conceived as a bridge between the natural sciences and the humanities, contains eleven pairs of interviews (one with a Soviet thinker and one with an American thinker) divided in three parts: (1) on the universe and life, (2) on man and his environment (which includes Chomsky's), (3) on the future of science. Chomsky is paired with Guram Ramishvili, who was born five years before Chomsky (in 1923), and, like Chomsky, is interested in the linguistic ideas of Wilhelm von Humboldt (the topic of Ramishvili's doctoral dissertation, published in German in 1970). The two interviews are grouped under the title "On language and culture." It is enlightening to compare Chomsky's views with those of each of the other interviewees, not just with Ramishvili's.

The interview, conducted by Osiatynski, took place in 1975; a Polish translation was apparently included in a book he published shortly afterward. An English transcription he prepared eight years later was edited on or before September 24, 1983, by Chomsky, who "made some changes and corrections for clarity" (letter to Osiatynski). The text reproduced here follows this corrected transcription.

The first sentence of the first question is based on a wrong assumption: contrary to what the interviewer assumes, Chomsky's approach to language is psychological (ultimately, biological—see the Introduction, Sect. 2). Less surprising is Osiatynski's statement (p. 95) that Chomsky's books "offer an insight into Chomsky's radical, though not revolutionary, approach to contemporary politics," since the people who are incapable of recognizing a truly revolutionary approach for what it is are legion—a clear sign of cultural underdevelopment (cf. the Introduction, Section 3). Compare Chomsky, *American power* (1969), p. 22; interviews 4, 7, 13, 23, 24, and particularly 45, among others, in Chomsky, *Language and politics*, ed. by C. P. Otero (1988); and, above all, his commissioned but not published (it later appeared in a different journal and was subsequently collected in a book) "The Soviet Union versus socialism" (1985). See Chomsky, *Deterring democracy* (1992), 12.2.

On the matter of "learning," see also Selections 1 and the Introduction. On "communication," see Chomsky, "Human language and other semiotic systems" (1978).

On thought without language, see also Chomsky's introduction to Schaff, *Language and cognition* (1973).

Editor's Notes to Selection 3 ("A really new way of looking at language")
This interview, reprinted from Chomsky's *Language and politics*, ed. by C. P. Otero (1988) by permission of the author and Black Rose Books, first

appeared as "Interview with Noam Chomsky," *The Reading Instruction Journal* (1988), pp. 2–7 (placed there "as a prologue" to the special issue—a thematic one on "New directions in reading instruction"). Lillian Putnam, professor and director of the Reading Clinic, Kean College, Union, New Jersey, spoke with Chomsky in November 1987, while she was a visiting scholar at the Harvard Graduate School of Education, eliciting one of the clearest brief expositions of Chomsky's conception of language.

The answer to the last question deserves to be pondered by people with a position on the controversial issue, which has numerous ramifications. The approach suggested by Chomsky in this interview was adopted, wittingly or unwittingly, by at least one school board (in Oakland, California) in 1996, immediately giving rise to intense controversy. California state senator Barbara Lee was quoted at the time as saying that she thought that the senator who was attempting to legislate what teachers should do in the classroom was "misinformed and grossly misguided." She might have been right. After all, no one has ever argued that the double negative constructions used by Spanish speakers (both the powerful and the powerless) are "bad speech patterns," or that the "good" speech patterns of so-called standard American English should be imposed on British speakers.

But of course more than language is at stake here, as any student of the Spanish Inquisition is well aware. The "bad speech patterns" go hand in hand with recent discussions of "bad genes," which tend to be just as muddleheaded. Nor is the current spurt of this type of *über alles* meanness anything new. See, for example, "'English-only' breeding bigotry in the U.S.," *RESIST* Newsletter 208 (Aug.-Sep. 1988), pp. 3–5, by Edward M. Chen, staff counsel for the American Civil Liberties Union of Northern California. (See the editor's notes to Selection 19.) Information about groups working against English-only initiatives is provided by the ACLU, 1663 Mission St., Suite 460, San Francisco, CA 94103; EPIC, 227 Massachusetts Ave., NE, Suite 120, Washington, DC 20002; or MALDEFF, 1430 K St., NW, Suite 700, Washington, DC, 20005. For an overview, see *The real Ebonics debate,* ed. by Perry and Delpit (1998), in particular the article by Wayne O'Neil, and O'Neil's "Linguistics for everyone" (1998) and references. ("Ebonics" is sometimes used to mean "Black English.")

As many people are aware, it is no more difficult for a child to learn several languages than to learn one—under appropriate conditions. See Strozer, *Language acquisition under puberty* (1994).

A helpful complement to the interview is Chomsky's discussion of "The development of grammar in child language" by Wick Miller and Susan Ervin (first published in *The acquisition of language*, ed. by Bellugi and Brown [1964], pp. 35–39), which was reprinted in *Readings in applied transformational grammar*, ed. by M. Lester (1970), pp. 41–50, and in *Child language: a book of readings*, ed. by Bar-Adon and Leopold (1971); a more technical discussion is found in Chomsky, *Aspects of the theory of syntax* (1965), Ch. 1. For the evidence "presented elsewhere in fair detail," see Chomsky and Halle, *The sound pattern of English* (1968, 1991); on the investigation of the stage in which children produced so-called "telegraphic speech," see Chomsky, *Rules and representations* (1980), pp. 53f.

Editor's notes to Selection 4 ("Perspectives on language and mind")

This is Chomsky's Galileo Lecture, given in the Scuola Normale Superiore, Pisa, in October 1999, on the occasion of his honorary doctorate. It will appear in a new series that will include all "lectiones magistrales" of SNS's "honoris causa" degrees. It is closely related to several of his recent lectures, in particular "Linguistics and brain science" (Tokyo, November 15, 1998), "New horizons in the study of language and mind" (University of Maryland, November 30, 1998), and "Language and the brain" (Siena, October 27–30, 1999). Some of its themes are further developed in his recent collection of philosophical papers, *New horizons in the study of language and mind* (2000).

Since his *Cartesian linguistics* (1966) it has been clear that Chomsky is a superb intellectual historian—a historian of philosophy in the case of his 1966 book, his earliest incursion in the field; later writings (e.g., *Year 501*) extended the coverage to world history. The lectures just mentioned and other writings take on highly significant and sometimes not properly appreciated, and often misunderstood, developments in the history of science. See the Introduction, in particular Section 2.

Editor's notes to Selection 5 ("Rationality/science and post-this-or-that")

This essay first appeared in *Z Papers* 1, 4 (Oct.-Dec. 1992), pp. 52–57, under the title "Rationality/science," with other papers presenting a range of views on the subject; see also "Chomsky replies," *Z Papers* 2, 3 (Jul.-Sep. 1993), pp. 11–12, about a reaction to his essay. The general topic is touched upon in *Year 501* (1992), pp. 285–86. For a fairly detailed study of a particular case, see C. P. Otero, "Chomsky v. Foucault: pursue justice or grab power?" in *The essential Chomsky*, vol. 1.

The appendix is Chomsky's answer when on September 6, 1999, via Internet (in the Znet Sustainer's Forum System), he was asked whether he was "perturbed" by the Kansas school curriculum decision against teaching natural selection. For some relevant background, see note 8 of the Introduction and related text.

Editor's notes to Selection 6 ("Equality")

This paper, which elaborates on one of the questions which are central for the following one (Selection 7) and can serve as an excellent example of a type of philosophical analysis advocated by Chomsky elsewhere ("Philosophers and public policy," *Ethics; an international journal of social, political and legal philosophy* 79, 1 [1968], pp. 1–9), was read at the "Conference on the Promise and Problems of Human Equality" held at the University of Illinois (Urbana) in March 1976, and was included in the proceedings (*Equality and social policy,* edited by Walter Feinberg [Champaign: University of Illinois Press, 1978]), and later in *The Chomsky reader* (1987), from which it is reprinted here. It was first published in *Philosophy and Social Action* (an interdisciplinary international quarterly of concerned philosophers for social action, New Delhi, India) 2, 3 (1976), pp. 1–20.

The importance of the question of equality in any vision of democracy and education in a culturally advanced society can hardly be exaggerated. "We can have a democratic society or we can have great concentrated wealth in the hands of a few. We cannot have both," wrote Justice Louis Brandeis (the first Jewish justice of the U.S. Supreme Court, perhaps not a sheer coincidence), consciously or unwittingly echoing Jefferson (see Prologue and Selection 15; also, Chomsky, *Powers and prospects,* [1996], Ch. 4), who in turn was echoing Aristotle; the real case on which the recent film *Erin Brockovich* is based provides one type of illustration. The quote suggests that at least on this question Brandeis had already reached, or at least was not far from reaching, the cultural level of "that dangerous radical Aristotle" (see Chomsky, *The common good* [1998]), something which cannot be said of many "educated" people many years later. (A bumper sticker of the 1960s comes to mind: "Don't let schools interfere with your education.")

There are several enlightening recent studies of the topic, differently focused. In *Sovereign virtue: the theory and practice of equality* (2000), one of the most recent, Ronald Dworkin argues, along Aristotelian lines, that true equality means equality in the value of the resources that people command, not in the success they achieve, and that equality is not in conflict with freedom and individual responsibility, but the three flow from and into one another as facets of the same humanist conception of democracy.

Other recent studies are Freeman, *The new inequality* (1999); Collins et al., *Shifting fortunes: the perils of the growing American wealth gap* (1999);

Wilkinson, *Unhealthy societies: the afflictions of inequality* (1996); and *Dying for growth: global inequality and the health of the poor* (2000), ed. by Kim et al. (cf. the special issue of the *Boston Review*, Feb.-Mar. 2000, "Is equality good medicine?"); and Spring, *Deculturalization and the struggle for equality: a brief history of the education of dominated cultures in the United States* (1994) and Arrow et al., *Meritocracy and economic inequality* (2000); see also Jencks et al., *Inequality: a reassessment of the effect of family and schooling in America* (1972) and Edsall, *The new politics of inequality* (1984). For a historical overview of successive speculations on "social justice," see Boucher and Kelly, eds., *The social contract from Hobbes to Rawls* (1994); for critiques of Rawls's view that indirectly shed light on Chomsky's, see Sandel, *Liberalism and the limits of justice* (1998) and Alejandro, *The limits of Rawlsian justice* (1998).

It is always instructive to compare Chomsky's analysis of egalitarianism with other contemporary analyses, in particular with that of the much admired and sometimes extravagantly praised British philosopher Isaiah Berlin ("Equality" [1956]).

The passing comment that in "a complex and intricate system, small differences in initial condition may have major consequences" brings of course to mind the "principles and parameters" approach briefly explained in Chomsky, "Human language and other semiotic systems" (1978) and more technically and extensively in his *Lectures on government and binding* (1981).

For more on IQ and race, see Chomsky, "Psychology and ideology" (1972), in his *For reasons of state,* reprinted in part in *The Chomsky reader.* On the restraining role of the state in preventing "the destructive forces of capitalism" from "demolish[ing] social existence and the physical environment," see also Selection 7.

The quote from Adam Smith, whose ideas and commitments are standardly disfigured nowadays, should be placed in the context of the Prologue and several other selections, in particular 15, and, more generally, of the more extended comments on his work by Chomsky (for example, in *Year 501* [1992], Ch. 1, and in *The common good* [1998]), which may be enough to see why he's said to be an exceptionally perceptive intellectual historian.

The "combination of attributes" for success suggested in this essay may be less idiosyncratic than it might seem at first. To mention just a very recent piece of likely supporting evidence: a recent biography paints a "billionaire entertainment mogul" (the term is not without interest) as a "ruthless entrepreneur who bullied his way to the top of Hollywood's power structure." The "sheer robbery backed by state power" referred to in the context of the "combination of attributes" brings to mind the often-repeated observation that behind every big fortune (the "great concentrated wealth" of Justice Brandeis) there are major crimes.

"Some elementary comments on the rights of freedom of expression" (October 11, 1980), published here in English for the first time, as an appendix, appeared as an "avis" to Robert Faurisson's *Mémoire en défense* (1980)—and unintendedly served as a litmus test for the commitment to freedom of a good number of intellectuals, particularly in the "City of Lights." Cf. Rai, *Chomsky's politics* (1995), pp. 131–32.

Editor's notes to Selection 7 ("Two conceptions of social organization")

This lecture, perhaps the most self-contained, straightforward, and comprehensive overview of Chomsky's ideas about the organization of advanced industrial societies, develops the theme of the sharp contrast between the two traditions outlined in the Prologue. (See the Introduction, Section 3, for more on this theme and its implications and ramifications.) Transcribed by the editor and published here for the first time under a new title, it was first presented as a sound seminar at the Poetry Center of the New York YMCA on Feb. 16, 1970, and recorded and made available by Jeffrey Norton Publishers under the title "Government in the future." (The present transcription was checked against two subsequent ones: one by Sandy Adler for Alternative Radio, and one by Mark Alonzo, both of whom generously put them at my disposal. I'm indebted to both of them, and to Mark also for having made a copy of the recording for me—among other things.) At the beginning it overlaps with a lecture given in Chicago a month earlier ("Language and freedom," reprinted in *The Chomsky reader*), and toward the end with the first part of Ch. 1 of Chomsky's *At war with Asia* (1970). Precise references to the quotes can be found in those two books and in his *Cartesian linguistics* (1966). (On the "permanent war economy," see the writings by Seymour Melman.) A number of the topics are discussed further in Chomsky's *Problems of knowledge and freedom* (1971), Ch. 2, and in *Deterring democracy* (1992), 1.2. (Wilhelm von Humboldt's *Limits of state action*, written in 1791–1792, to some extent under the stimulus of the French Revolution, experienced two years earlier, was not published in full until 1851—the reason apparently being that Humboldt anticipated trouble with the Prussian censorship—except for Chapter II and parts of Chapter III, which appeared in Schiller's journal *Neue Thalia*, and Chapters V–VI and VIII, published in the *Berlinische Monatsschrift* in the fall of 1792. The title of Karl Polanyi's book is *The great transformation: the political and economic origins of our time* [1944, paperback 1957].)

In the background of these writings is "the insight of the 18th century

European Enlightenment that the value and meaning of freedom are learned through its exercise, and that the instinctive desire of 'all free peoples to guard themselves from oppression' (Rousseau) may be repressed among a subordinated population, effectively removed from the political system disengaged from the struggle against state and other authority, and in general, objects rather than agents," ideas which are "important for understanding modern Western society as well as the early stages when oppressed people break their bonds" (Chomsky, *The culture of terrorism* [1988], Ch. 10).

To properly appreciate what Chomsky has to say on the general topic, it might help to compare his writings with more recent ones (which in principle had the advantage of benefiting from earlier efforts), as recently exemplified in, e.g., *The origins of modern freedom in the West* (1995), ed. by R. W. Davis.

The appendix, "On the national interest," written on Jan. 28, 1977, at the request of *Partisan Review* but published for the first time in Chomsky's *Radical priorities*, ed. by C. P. Otero (1981, rev. 1984), from which it is reprinted here as an extension of the discussion of one of the topics of the main selection, is one of the briefest and most direct statements of Chomsky's view of the contemporary world of nation-states, and, together with the main part of the selection, of "the deep structures of the American state" (to borrow a phrase from Doug Henwood in the latest (no. 97) issue of the *Left Business Observer*). Cf. Laswell, *Politics: who gets what, when, how* (1936), keeping in mind that "if we follow Harold Lasswell's famous definition of politics as a social process determining 'who gets what, when, and how,' there is no doubt that chimpanzees engage in it," as a distinguished primatologist points out (de Waal, *Chimpanzee politics* [1989], p. 214).

Editor's notes to Selection 8 ("Some tasks for responsible people")

This essay, which in a way is the practice counterpart to the analysis of Selection 7 (and like it and "Language and freedom" [January 1970] provides one of the keys to Chomsky's thinking on these matters), first appeared in *Liberation* 14, 5–6 (Aug.-Sept. 1969), pp. 38–43, under the title "Some tasks for the left," and it was included in his *Radical priorities*, ed. by C. P Otero (1981, 1984), from which it is reprinted here (with the title slightly modified, since in contemporary discourse the terms "left," "right," or "center" are largely meaningless and often misleading). Much in it is "prophetic," sometimes in one sense of the term, sometimes in the other. It seems "to have lost none of [its] power or persuasiveness" (to borrow a phrase from Chomsky's *American power*, p. 323).

In a paper already referred to in the editor's notes to Selection 6, "Philosophers and public policy," written in May 1968 (not your average month, by any measure), Chomsky had written (echoing Marx) that "the task that faces the responsible citizen is to work to change the world." In this essay, which opens with the reference to Senator Fulbright's "extremely important speech on the Senate floor" that closes the May 1968 paper, he provides some specifics that may contribute considerably to raising "the level of intellectual culture and moral perception of the society in general." Among them are these truths, which reasonable people will hold to be self-evident:

> A movement of the left has no chance of success, and deserves none, unless it develops an understanding of contemporary society and a vision of a future social order that is persuasive to a large majority of the population. Its goals and organizational forms must take shape through their active participation in political struggle and social reconstruction. A genuine radical culture can be created only through the spiritual transformation of great masses of people, the essential feature of any social revolution that is to extend the possibilities for human creativity and freedom [and so on, down to "a central goal of any revitalized left with a working-class base"].

"The particular form of state-subsidized capitalism evolving in the United States," sometimes referred to as "neo-liberal," can be seen as a contemporary form of "mercantilism," the older system Adam Smith (an authentic liberal) argued against in his *Wealth of nations* (1776), hence neither truly "liberal" in the sense of Smith's "liberalism" nor really "new" (see Selection 7). The topic is insightfully discussed in Chomsky, *Profits over people: neoliberalism and global order* (1999), in particular pp. 34f.

Needless to say, the "wave of repression" of 1969 is still very much with us, in a way, and so is the "criminal police violence," as recent trials (e.g., those in New York and Los Angeles) attest—additional evidence in support of Chomsky's prophetic analysis.

For an important discussion of the "revisionist" work on the Cold War, see Chomsky's *For reasons of state* (1973), I.v.

Editor's notes to Selection 9 ("Toward a humanistic conception of education")

This paper, which also expands on a theme of Selection 7 and the already referred-to "Language and freedom" (in this case a little more than a year later), overlaps with the Prologue. It is a slightly revised version of a talk given at the University of Illinois at Urbana-Champaign on Apr. 1, 1971, under the sponsorship of the College of Education and the G. E. Miller Lecture Committee. A revised version was included in *Work, technology, and education,* ed. by Feinberg and Rosemont (1975), pp. 204–20. Cf. Veblen, *The instinct of workmanship, and the state of industrial arts* (1914), on the nature of work.

The "null hypothesis" Chomsky defends here underlies also his attitude toward persuasion and preachiness (see Selection 25; also "Helping people persuade themselves," the last interview in Chomsky, *Language and politics*).

His criticism of behaviorism and the related "cult of the expert" presents, in a nutshell, one aspect of his epoch-making contribution to cognitive psychology, discussed more at length and with emphasis on different ramifications in "Psychology and ideology" (1972), already referred to.

The remark about the need to be trained to resist indoctrination is expanded on in Selection 16. A comparison between the 1961 social science reader (referred to also in Selections 16 and 25) and, e.g., Hine and Faragher's *The American West* (2000) gives at least the flavor of a difference between then (i.e., the 1960s) and now.

Editor's notes to Selection 10 ("The function of the university in a time of crisis")

This essay, first published in Robert M. Hutchins and Mortimer J. Adler, eds., *The Great Ideas Today Nineteen Sixty-nine* (Chicago: Encyclopedia Britannica, 1969), pp. 41–61, was included in Chomsky's *For reasons of state* (1973), from which it is reprinted here (with the Russell quote in note 12 restored). It is closely related to Selections 17, 18, and 19. All four lead to the conclusion, if anything truer today, that "it is a matter of great urgency, for ourselves and for world society, that our institutions and ideology be subjected to serious critical analysis," for which the universities "must provide the 'institutional form' within which it can be freely conducted" (their "primary object").

In the tradition of Thoreau, the literary critic and essayist Randolph Bourne (1886–1918), also referred to in Selection 16, opposed and indicted the "pragmatic" ideas of the "liberal" intellectuals of his time who supported World War I (including Dewey, whose writings on education he greatly admired), thus becoming a sort of spokesperson for the young people of his generation (not enthralled with the rise of the new corporate order—see the editor's Introduction, Section 3). A regular contributor to the weekly *The New Republic* since it was founded in 1914, he was unceremoniously dropped when the United States entered the war. On the other hand, when disillusion with the war set in in the 1920s, he became (posthumously) larger than life (he appears in John Dos Passos's *1919* as a ghost haunting the American conscience with the refrain "war is the health of the state," one of Bourne's most celebrated statements, often repeated since then as a self-evident truth). He believed and hoped that the youth of his day would sweep away much that was anachronistic and wrong in his country—no wonder interest in his work was revived in the 1960s, in part because of the attention it received in Chomsky's writings. See Chomsky's introduction to his *American power* (1969), pp. 5–8; also, 240 and 317, a page also part of Selection 16. (It is important not to miss note 4.)

Editor's notes to Selection 11 ("Scholarship and commitment, then and now")

This is Chomsky's address at the Presidential Forum of the Modern Language Association (MLA) in Dec. 1999 (the president in 1999 was Edward Said, the well-known Columbia University professor), thirty-one years after the memorable meeting of December 1968 described in Chomsky, *Radical priorities* (1981), p. 198. The title has been supplied. A different version, with references, appeared in the MLA's *Profession 2000*, pp. 32–39, under the title "Paths taken, tasks ahead." Among the relevant references, two that are especially enlightening are *Propaganda* (1928), by Edward L. Bernays, the founder of the public relations industry (notice that in 1928, the year Chomsky was born, he still referred to propaganda by that name; later it was rebaptized, as in his 1952 book *Public relations*), and *The crisis of democracy: report on the governability of democracies by the Trilateral Commission* (1975). (See the editor's notes to Selection 19.) Both works deserve to have a place in the curriculum, particularly in the United States.

The Dec. 26–29, 1968, meeting of the MLA was one of a kind in more ways than one—and evidently not without consequences. For one thing, it was far from business as usual. Not for nothing did an editorial in the *New York Times* of Jan. 1, 1969, complain about "the irresponsible behavior of a noisy fringe group of academics" on that occasion.

One of those academics was Chomsky. He, with his MIT colleague Louis Kampf, Paul Lauter of Antioch-Putney, Florence Howe of Goucher, and Richard Ohmann of Wesleyan—where he was, at different moments, associate provost, acting provost, or chancellor, in addition to alumnus, professor, and editor of *College English*—all of which were on the RESIST board, had originally planned to form a caucus of the just-launched New University Conference (NUC) at the 1968 meeting of the MLA, just a few months after the well-known events at Columbia University and in Paris. (See the editor's notes to Selection 19.)

The first, preparatory meeting at Columbia on Thursday, Dec. 28, 1968, out of which the group that was to do the work of the caucus emerged, drew several hundred people, a much larger number than had been expected. Also unexpected was the harassment (by the hotel security police) and arrest (by the city police) of Kampf and two young instructors on Friday morning for trying to prevent Americana Hotel house detectives from ripping down NUC posters in the lobby. That Friday evening even more people attended a meeting that was virtually unanimous in condemning the structure and functioning of the MLA. On Saturday morning, NUC sponsored workshops on high school teaching, on curriculum change, on teaching assistants, on racism, and on women in the profession. Later in the day, the NUC caucus, in about two hours, gathered some five hundred people (about a thousand for some) at the Hilton's Trianon Room for a teach-in on Vietnam led by Chomsky (who had that day been named as a co-conspirator in the "Boston Five" case).

The next day (Sunday, Dec. 29), at the business meeting (the climax of the convention), all but one of the resolutions put forward by the caucus, though not in the official agenda (they had been arbitrarily shelved by the Resolution Committee of the MLA) passed overwhelmingly. To top it all off, the caucus ultimately succeeded in electing Kampf, chair of the literature department at MIT, second vice president of the MLA, which virtually meant he would become president two years later, as he did. "What then was accomplished . . . ? . . . no more than a beginning: a very small dent in a huge structure . . . What matters is . . . the new sense of freedom and interest on the part of so many members, to change, to reform, to improve their profession" (Howe and Cantarow, "What happened at MLA: the radical perspective" [1969], pp. 486–87). See also Ohmann, "An informal and perhaps unreliable account of the Modern Language Association of America" (1969), much of it included in his *English in America: a radical view of the profession* (1976), Ch. 2; *The politics of literature: dissenting essays on the teaching of English,* edited by Kampf and Lauter (1972), pp. 34f., and Kampf's "Introduction," *Radical Teacher,* March 1979, pp. 1–2 (the issue on "The Academic Profession, 1968–1978"). Cf. *Left politics and the literary profession* (1990), ed. by Davis and Mirabella, pp. 2f.

In his talk Chomsky does not go into the "significant changes that have taken place in the intervening years," which "perhaps merit some reflection." But he would be the first to agree with Kampf's closing remark in *Radical Teacher:* "No, we'll not sink into the slime of the 1950s."

Editor's notes to Selection 12 ("The mechanisms and practices of indoctrination")

This selection is adapted from a long excerpt (roughly the second half) of a talk given on Sunday, Dec. 9, 1984, at the Community Church of Boston ("a free community of human beings united for the study and practice of universal religion, seeking to apply ethical ideas to individual life and the democratic and cooperative principle to all forms of social and economic life"). A written version of the talk was published in Apr. 1985 under the title "The manufacture of consent" on pp. 1–21 of a thirty-two-page pamphlet that launched their 1985–86 Fund Drive. Two selections from it were included in *The Chomsky reader* (1987), pp. 121–36 and 223–26.

Since, in the view of this Community Church, Chomsky shows in his talk how "consent is manufactured not merely by the state but by its (mainstream) critics, who determine the limits of the debate and thus the voices that are heard," the venue was not inappropriate: as stated in the opening pages of the pamphlet, "the Community Church of Boston's overriding commitment is to 'A Free Pulpit in Action,'" a commitment which has led this Church, "oppressed at times by those who would silence and suppress any voice or view that differs from their own," "to provide a platform for countless men and women who were barred from speaking elsewhere because of the alternatives they offered to the status quo, because they dared to lead public opinion rather than follow it." Their efforts go back to 1920, when it was founded "to provide an alternative . . . to bland, innocuous preachments," to seek higher ends "by involvements that shape liberation and justice." To continue to quote from the pamphlet:

> The precipitating influence was World War I and the prevailing response of most churches, whose sanctuaries were turned into recruiting stations with cries to arms and prayers for victory. Their response was seen as a betrayal of a fundamental religious belief: the universal ethic of brotherhood and sisterhood that transcends nationality and race and reveres all people as members of one human family. It was this universal ethic that led men and women of diverse political, economic, social and religious backgrounds to come together and form a new—and non-sectarian— church.
>
> The non-sectarian nature of Community Church helps one to better understand the alternative it offers. Community Church defines non-sectarianism in its most inclusive sense. There is no creedal conformity, no test of sect, class, nation, race or political ideology. It seeks to be truly a community church—a church representative of the whole *human* community.

A version of a similar talk by the author appeared in *The Thoreau Quarterly* 16, 1–2 (1984), pp. 14–21, under the title "1984: Orwell's and ours," followed (pp. 22–49) by the transcription of numerous questions from the audience and Chomsky's answers (p. 49 is of particular interest). For a less informal and fuller discussion, see "Notes on Orwell's problem," the last chapter (pp. 276–87) of Chomsky's *Knowledge of language: its nature, origin and use*, also written in 1984 (though published in 1986). A considerably edited and revealingly sanitized version of essentially the same excerpt included below appeared under the title "The bounds of thinkable thought" in *The Progressive* 49, 10 (1985), pp. 28–31, which was reprinted in *Blueprint for Social Justice* 42, 8 (1989) and in *Voices of Dissent*, ed. by Grover and Peschak (1993), pp. 49–53.

The immediate background for all these 1984 writings is, of course, *1984*, Orwell's much-celebrated novel. Not surprisingly, they provide vivid illustrations of what Chomsky calls "Orwell's problem," which he contrasts with "Plato's problem," as discussed in the Introduction. (See Selection 19.) For a more nuanced exposition of Orwell's view of indoctrination, see Chomsky, *World orders old and new* (1994, 1996), Section 2.1.

"The media as a mirror of society" (editor's title), included as an appendix, appeared in *Comity* 6 (1985), pp. 18–20—"a magazine of international affairs and opinion" published by the Albany Student Press, State University of New York—and it was included in Chomsky, *Language and politics*, ed. by C. P. Otero (1988), from which it is reprinted here. It was one of three interviews conducted by Brian Jacobs and published under the title "Cover story—Network television news: Perspectives on the medium" followed by this note: "Network news is the primary source of information for most Americans. But the limits of the medium prevent viewers from being truly informed. CBS personnel, Edwin Diamond and Noam Chomsky lend their perspective." Chomsky was interviewed on Oct. 21, 1984. A caption under his photograph states that "the subject of the interview was the print media, which is what he felt most comfortable discussing, but as is apparent from what follows, his comments apply to all forms of the establishment media."

For more on Thomas Friedman (twice a Pulitzer Prize winner for balanced and informed coverage), particularly on his racism and megalomania, see *Language and politics*, interview 36. See also Chomsky's "Middle East terrorism and the American ideological system," in *Blaming the Victims*, 1988, p. 118; *World orders old and new* (updated edition, 1996); and *Fateful triangle: the United States, Israel and the Palestinians* (updated edition, 1999).

On David MacMicael's testimony at the World Court Hearings, see Chomsky, *The culture of terrorism* (1988), p. 121.

Editor's note to Selection 13 ("The task of the media")

This essay first appeared in *Nicaraguan Perspectives* 17 (1989), pp. 28–29, 33–36, under the title "Controlling the public mind," a pointed use of "the terminology of the Public Relations industry" (Chomsky, *The culture of terrorism* [1988], p. 201). See the Prologue, p. 34, Selection 14 and the immediately following editor's note.

On the general topic, see also his *Necessary illusions: thought control in democratic societies* (1989) and Alex Carey, *Taking the risk out of democracy* (1995, 1997). For an illuminating reaction to a solicited copy of "hundreds of opinion pieces surveyed" (by Chomsky), see the editor's Introduction to *Language and politics* (1988), n. 48.

Editor's note to Selection 14 ("Propaganda and control of the public mind")

The following remarks, excerpted from a talk with the same title given at the Harvard University Trade Union Program, Cambridge, Massachusetts, on Feb. 7, 1997, first appeared in McChesney, ed., *Capitalism and the Information Age: The political economy of the global communication revolution* (1998), pp. 179–89. (The complete talk is available on two cassettes from Alternative Radio, P.O. Box 551, Boulder, CO, 800–444–1977.) A closely related discussion is found in Selection 15. For the background, and in particular for Chomsky's use of the terminology of the public relations industry in the title, see the editor's notes to Selection 13.

The full titles of two of the books referred to are *The fall of the house of labor: the workplace, the state and American labor activism, 1865–1925* (1987) by David Montgomery (Farnam Professor of History at Yale) and *Selling free enterprise: the business assault on labor and liberalism, 1945–60* (1994) by Elizabeth A. Fones-Wolf (professor of history at West Virginia University). The first one is a sweeping study of American labor activism from the first embryonic trade unions in the mid-nineteenth century to the emergence of an insurrectionary force during the first two decades of the twentieth and its temporary defeat in the early 1920s; the second one offers a comprehensive analysis of corporate America's ideological crusade to undermine popular support for unions and other democratic organizations concerned with the welfare of the majority of the population. See also Carey's book (referred to in the editor's notes to Selection 13).

Editor's notes to Selection 15 ("Prospects for democracy")

This is the transcription of a talk given at MIT, Cambridge, Massachusetts, on Mar. 8, 1994. It is published here for the first time. (A tape recording of the oral version is available from Alternative Radio, P.O. Box 551, Boulder, CO, 800–444–1977.)

For more on the main themes of this talk and sources, see Chomsky, *World orders old and new* (1994, rev. 1996), 2.1, and for quotes from Carothers, Ch. 1, n. 19 and text. On the unsuccessful "battle for the control of U.S. broadcasting, 1928–1935" and the subsequent "gift of radio to corporations under the guise of democracy" (Chomsky, *Powers and prospects* [1996], p. 226), see McChesney's *Telecommunications, mass media, and democracy* (1993); see also his *Corporate media and the threat of democracy* (1997), and *Rich media, poor democracy* (1999) about the new records in decline of public participation into communications policy making (a measure of the level of democracy), and a review and analysis of emerging technologies, respectively.

On Bolshevism and the modern corporation as subcases of the very same kind of absolutism, see the Introduction, Sect. 3.

Editor's notes to Selection 16 ("Some thoughts on intellectuals and the schools")

This essay, written in Jun. 1966, first appeared in a special issue of the *Harvard Educational Review* 36, 4 (1966) devoted to a symposium on the topic "American intellectuals and the schools" (pp. 484–91). It is included, with the addition of the footnotes, in Chomsky's first "non-professional" book, *American power* (1969), pp. 309–21 (see pp. 5–8, 240 for more on Bourne's critique of the support of World War I by the "liberal" public intellectuals—cf. the editor's notes to Selection 10), from which it is reprinted here. It also appeared in *Starting over: a college reader*, edited by Frederick Crews and Orville Schell (1970), pp. 359–65—with questions and comments by Crews in the accompanying *Guide*, pp. 61–63.

On the similarities between fascism and "liberal" imperialism, see the Introduction, section 3.

A central idea of this essay is the need for a program of intellectual self-defense, one of Chomsky's leitmotifs, particularly in recent years (see, e.g., Selection 9). The teach-in can be seen as an attempt to meet the gap. It originated at the University of Michigan, after anti-war students staged a protest sit-in at the offices of the local draft board. The first one took place on Mar. 24–25, 1965, at four auditoriums, and went on all night (see Rudy, *The campus and a nation in crisis* [1996], pp. 155f.; cf. Lasch's 1965 article in *The Nation*.)

A now-pressing issue, undreamed of in the 1960s, is the current attempt to privatize the educational system, that is, the attempt of the corporations to take over the educational system as they took over the health system and the prison system in order to make it a source of large profits. In other words, the educational analogue of HMOs will be EMOs. See the Introduction, n. 16.

The appendix, "On staying informed and intellectual self-defense," appeared as a Znet post (www.zmag.org) of Mar. 8, 1999. (The book with "far more detailed analyses" is *Letters from Lexington* [1993]).

Editor's notes to Selection 17 ("The responsibility of a university community")

This "Personal Addendum to the Panel Report [of May 31, 1969] by Noam A. Chomsky," the first of the "Personal Statements by Panel members" (section IV of the document), pp. 33–43, published here, with a new title, for the first time, is of one piece with his remarks before the MIT Commission on MIT Education, included immediately after this as Selection 18. A note on p. 33 states that "Since the First Report of the Panel was published, Professor Chomsky, in a letter dated September 10, 1969, has asked that his statement be modified as described in Section IV of this report." The letter, which appears on p. 88 of the document under the title "Noam A. Chomsky— Comment on Personal Addendum in May 31 Report," simply states that he "would like to add the following introductory paragraph to [his] personal addendum." This new paragraph is inserted in its place (i.e., as a first paragraph) in the present reprint of the addendum.

An important part of the background for both the present selection and the following one (Selection 18) is the research stoppage of Mar. 4, 1969, organized by students and faculty at MIT to express the concern of scientists with the "misuse of scientific and technical knowledge." See *March 4*, ed. by Jonathan Allen (1970), "a historical record of a series of talks and panel discussions that were sponsored by the Union of Concerned Scientists at MIT and held on March 3 and 4, 1969," which includes "Responsibility," a talk given by Chomsky at Rindge High School on Mar. 4, 1970 (in his "historical introduction" Allen notes [p. xiii] that "Chomsky is held in high regard by many student activists at MIT, for both his political attitudes and his intellectual integrity"); see also Nelkin, *The university and military research: moral politics at M.I.T.* (1972). Nelkin writes (p. 67) that "at first [Howard W.] Johnson [president of MIT] appointed eighteen members to the panel; but in response to pressures from SACC for broader representation, Noam Chomsky, professor of linguistics, and Jerome Lerman, a graduate student and SACC activist, were added. Though Chomsky was giving a series of lectures at Oxford during this time, his presence on the panel was considered so important that he was flown back to M.I.T. each week to attend the meetings." (SACC was a Science Action Coordinating Committee, formed by students to deal specifically with the issue of defense research and other military-related activities on campus with the purpose of generating research, action, self-education, and greater social consciousness.)

Also of interest is the fact that in late Sept. 1969, "twenty-four nationally prominent professors signed a public statement endorsing a nation-wide student boycott of classes for 15 October as a condemnation of the war," and that "among the signatories were Kenneth Galbraith of Harvard, Noam Chomsky of MIT, and Hans Morgenthau of the University of Chicago" (Rudy, *The campus and a nation in crisis* [1996], p. 170, with reference to the *New York Times*, Sept. 23, 1969, p. 7; see also Lasch's 1965 article in *The Nation*).

Editor's notes to Selection 18 ("Remarks before the MIT Commission on MIT Education")

These "Abridged Version of Remarks by Noam A. Chomsky, Professor of Modern Languages and Linguistics, to the Commission on MIT Education" on Nov. 11, 1969, published here for the first time, is of one piece with his "Personal Addendum to the Panel Report [of May 31, 1969]," included immediately before as Selection 17. See the editor's notes to that selection.

Some of the crucial questions discussed in the two selections, which are at the core of Chomsky's conception of democracy and education, have rarely, if ever, been addressed by him in the available written record, to my knowledge.

On A. J. Muste, see Chomsky, *American power and the new mandarins* (1969), Ch. 2.

Editor's notes to Selection 19 ("Two roles of the American university")

Part I, "extracted from an interview with Professor Chomsky," appeared in *The cold war and the university: toward an intellectual history of the postwar years* (1997), pp. 171–94, "the first of several volumes discussing the ramifications of the [Cold War]," "the most important fact in all of our lives during most of the second half of the century," to quote from the "Editor's note" by André Schiffrin. One of its outstanding features is that Chomsky expands on a theme evidently of great importance for him: the impact of American power after World War II on the intellectual climate and his feelings about it "in the late 1940s and early 1950s when [he] was a student." He had already touched on the subject in his 1973 introduction (pp. 39–40) to the published version of his first monumental work, *The logical structure of linguistic theory* (1975 [1955–56]), and again in a interview conducted by the present editor in Apr. 1986, a Spanish version of which appeared in a Madrid newspaper at the time.

On *The crisis of democracy*, see Chomsky, "Intellectuals and the state" (1977), reprinted as Ch. 1 of *Towards a new cold war* (1982), in particular pp. 67–69. (See the editor's notes to Selection 11.) On "the basic logic of the North-South conflict," see Chomsky, *Radical priorities* (1981, 1984), pp. 121f., and his comments on the World Trade Organization (WTO) in *Profit over people* (1999), in particular pp. 65f.

The reference to RESIST can benefit from some additional context. Because he had been a national sponsor of a citizens' committee to publicize tax refusal as protest against the war in Vietnam since 1965 and had been trying to organize a national tax resistance movement with Harold Tovish, a well-known sculptor, his would-be friend Paul Lauter asked Chomsky to join him and others in supporting draft resistance. In a few months the draft resistance initiative led to the first "Call to Resist Illegitimate Authority," signed by thousands, which was published in *The New York Review of Books* on Oct. 12, 1967, and figured prominently in the conspiracy trial of the "Boston Five" (one of whom was Dr. Benjamin Spock), who on Jul. 12, 1968, had been found guilty of "conspiring" to counsel, aid, and abet evasion of the draft, a decision reversed one year later by the U.S. Court of Appeals. However, the substantive questions (the legality of the government's prosecution of the war and the validity of the statement of the "Call" quoted above) were never addressed, a clear indication of how little war resisters could expect from the courts at the present level of civilization. See N. Chomsky, P. Lauter, and F. Howe, "Reflections on a political trial," *The New York Review of Books*, Aug. 22, 1968, pp. 23–30, reprinted, followed by a comment by Arlene Siegel, in N. Chomsky, P. Lauter, and F. Howe, *Trials of the resistance* (1970), pp. 74–105. (Siegel's comment had appeared in the RESIST Newsletter of Aug. 7, 1969) In contrast with some of the "Boston Five," Chomsky had been deeply involved in the elaboration and promotion of the first "Call to Resist Illegitimate Authority," which figured prominently in the trial. Surprisingly, he escaped being indicted as a main participant (not just a co-conspirator), apparently because the FBI did not have a clue of what was actually going on. Cf. Selection 8.

The signers of this first "Call" (now available at www.resistinc.org) considered it important to bring out the fact that the behavior of the U.S. government was illegitimate within the legal terms that it formally accepted, including the United Nations Charter, the Nuremberg Principles, and the Constitution itself, which together provide a fairly reasonable framework within which the citizens can seek to determine their own proper role and responsibility. The "Call" in turn led to the founding of RESIST (by Chomsky, Lauter, Louis Kampf, Mitchell Goodman, Hans Koning, and others, among them several linguists, including Ken Hale and Wayne O'Neil, like Kampf Chomsky's colleagues at MIT), perhaps the only national organization of the 1960s that has survived to this day and continues to be very much alive, in Boston as always, and as always with Chomsky's unwavering support (he is still on its board). (RESIST's current address is 259 Elm Street, Suite 201, Somerville, MA 02144, www.resistinc.org.; cf. Chomsky, *Radical priorities,* ed. by C. P. Otero [1981, 1984], p. 62. See also the editor's notes to Selection 11.)

The success of "a good indoctrination system" in "not letting people see what is so obvious" is part of what he calls "Orwell's problem," on which see his *Knowledge of language* (1986 [1984]), Preface and Ch. 5, and his "Mental constructions and social reality," paper presented at the Groningen Conference on Knowledge and Language in May 1989 and included in the first volume of the proceedings of the conference (*Knowledge and language: From Orwell's problem to Plato's problem* [1992]). See the editor's notes to Selection 12.

The second part is a transcription of a brief talk on the same general topic given by Chomsky at Boston University (on the occasion of the publication of the New Press book, on Feb. 2, 1997), published here for the first time. A tape recording of the oral version, together with a talk by Howard Zinn on the same occasion, and answers by one of the two to questions from the floor (Noam Chomsky/Howard Zinn, "The Cold War and the University"), is available from AR, P.O. Box 551, Boulder, CO, 800–444–1977.

Editor's notes to Selection 20 "The universities and the corporations"
This interview first appeared as "One man's view: Noam Chomsky. Are universities too conservative? Do they collude with corporations to obscure the way power works in our society? Noam Chomsky thinks so and explains why," *Business Today,* May 1973, pp. 13–15, and it was included in Chomsky, *Language and politics,* ed. by C. P. Otero (1988), from which it is reprinted here. For more on fascism and, more generally, totalitarianism, see Selections

7, 15, 16, and 25, and the corresponding editor's notes; also, the editor's Introduction, Section 3.

Editor's notes to Selection 21 ("Some observations on the teaching of language")

This article first appeared in *The Pedagogic Reporter* 21, 1 (1969), pp. 5–6, 13. It was written "in response to an invitation extended by the editor" for Chomsky to write an article on the place of Hebrew in elementary Jewish education. The quote is from the editor's preliminary note, which includes the following:

> The author was asked to address himself to the following questions:
>
> What, in his opinion, are the conditions, psychological and social, essential to the success of learning a second language on the elementary school level?
>
> What, in his view, should and could the role of Hebrew play in the elementary Jewish education of the American-Jewish child?
>
> Can the American-Jewish school as it is presently organized—orientation, program, time schedule, etc.—achieve his objectives for Hebrew instruction?
>
> What changes, in his opinion, are needed in the Jewish school in order to realize his proposed goals for Hebrew instruction?
>
> While Dr. Chomsky's discussion is directed only to the first question, it is, nonetheless, of sufficient intellectual interest and challenge to merit the serious attention of the profession of Jewish education. . . .
>
> . . . Incidentally, Prof. Chomsky is the son of the renowned Hebrew scholar and author, Dr. William Chomsky, Gratz College, Philadelphia.

The appendix, a review of Emezer Rieger, *Modern Hebrew* (New York: Philosophical Library, 1953), published in *Language* 30 (1954), pp. 180–81, was written when Chomsky was still a pre-doctoral student at the Society of Fellows, Harvard University, and it is his earliest publication in a linguistics journal. (His very first published article had appeared just a few months earlier in *Journal of Symbolic Logic* 18, 3 [1953].) See also the transcript of his "statement delivered informally in a debate with Professor Peter Geach" at the University of Birmingham (School of Education) in 1969, "Should traditional grammar be ended or mended?" (1969).

Editor's notes to Selection 22 ("Language theory and language teaching")

This written version of a talk at the Northeast Conference on the Teaching of Foreign Languages of Aug. 1, 1966, first appeared, under the title

"Linguistic theory," in *Northeast conference on the teaching of foreign languages* (1966), working committee reports, ed. by Robert G. Mead Jr., pp. 43–49. It was reprinted in *Readings in applied transformational grammar*, ed. by Lester (1970), pp. 51–60 (rev. edition, 1973, pp. 36–45), and in *Focus on the learner: pragmatic perspectives for the language teacher*, ed. by Oller and Richards (1973), pp. 29–35. It was also included in *Chomsky: selected readings* (1971), pp. 152–29, under the title "Implications for language teaching." It is a paper that can easily be misunderstood, and often has been. Reading it together with the appendix that follows it should help.

This appendix is a brief but highly significant letter Chomsky wrote to Mrs. Frederica Davis, dated Mar. 4, 1984, together with his reply to Prof. Berger, dated Mar. 21, 1984. They were first published in *English Education* 16, 3 (1984), pp. 165–66, under the title "Noam Chomsky writes to Mrs. Davis about grammar and education," immediately following Mrs. Davis's article "In defense of grammar." See also Honda, *Linguistic inquiry in the science classroom* (1994) and other writings by her and by Wayne O'Neil listed in the References.

Editor's notes to Selection 23 ("Our understanding of language and the curriculum")

This essay first appeared as an introduction to Roberts, *English syntax* (1964), pp. ix–xv. Shortly afterward (Nov. 1965) Chomsky returned briefly to "the matter of the teaching of grammar in the schools" and, after outlining how the students often "miss both the challenge and the accomplishments in the study of language," went on to close his talk with the following words:

> This seems to me a pity, because both are very real. Perhaps as the study of language returns gradually to the full scope and scale of its rich tradition, some way will be found to introduce students to the tantalizing problems that language has always posed for those who are puzzled and intrigued by the mysteries of human intelligence. ("The current scene in linguistics: present directions," *College English* 27, 8 [1966], p. 595)

The appendix, "Comments for Project Literacy meeting," first appeared in *Project Literacy Reports* 2 (1964), pp. 1–8. It was reprinted in *Readings in applied transformational grammar*, ed. by Lester (1970), pp. 279–83. (For more extended discussion, see his "Phonology and reading" [1970]. For some empirical results, see Carol Chomsky, "Stages in language development and reading exposure" [1972] and "Approaching reading through invented spelling" [1979], both reprinted in *Noam Chomsky: critical assessments*, ed. by

C. P. Otero [1994].) The study referred to at the very beginning of the appendix is Chomsky and Halle, *The sound pattern of English* (1968, 1991).

Editor's notes to Selection 24 ("Language theory and language use")

This interview first appeared as part of "Mark these linguists," *The English Magazine*, summer 1981, pp. 4–6. On the "engineering of consent," see Chomsky, *Deterring democracy* (1992), 1.2, and references. See the editor's notes to Selections 4, 7, and 11.

Editor's notes to Selection 25 ("Language, politics, and composition")

"Language, politics, and composition: a conversation with Noam Chomsky" was published in *Journal of Advanced Composition* 11, 1 (1991), pp. 4–35, with an introduction by the interviewers (Gary A. Olson, member of the faculty of the University of South Florida and editor of the journal—with Jacques Derrida, mentioned in the interview, as a member of the board—and Lester Faigley). The introduction begins as follows:

> Ever since the publication in 1957 of *Syntactic structures*, Noam Chomsky has been a towering eminence in linguistics and the philosophy of language; and since the 1960s, he has remained and astute and outspoken social critic. Compositionists familiar with Chomsky's work only through his transformational grammar and its compositional application, sentence combining, may not be aware of how profoundly Chomsky has influenced modern thought on language. It would be fair to say that Chomsky's scholarship over the last three decades [1960–1990] has forever altered our notions of the integral relationship between language and the human mind.
>
> Especially noteworthy about Chomsky's position as recorded in the interview below is that in this age of social construction, meaning relativity, and Derridean indeterminacy, Chomsky tenaciously contends that at the heart of most human cognitive operations is a fixed, structured, biological directiveness.

The Israeli logician referred to at the beginning is Yehoshua Bar-Hillel. The remarks about "infinite use of finite means" should be qualified, and were qualified by Chomsky in recent lectures. The need for the qualification derives from the fact that the notion of "use" brings in free will and choice, questions about which hardly more is understood now than before the breakthrough in mathematics and logic he refers to in the interview. See *New horizons in the study of language and mind* (2000), p. 6.

On the 1971 discussion on Dutch television with Michel Foucault, see C. P. Otero, "Chomsky v. Foucault: pursue justice or grab power?," in *The essential Chomsky*, vol. 1.

For more on Chomsky's attitude toward persuasion and preachiness, see "Helping people persuade themselves" (the last interview in his *Language and politics*), and Selection 9.

References

Achbar, Mark, ed. 1994. *Manufacturing consent: Noam Chomsky and the media*. Montreal, New York, London: Black Rose.

Alejandro, Roberto. 1998. *The limits of Rawlsian justice*. Baltimore, London: The Johns Hopkins University Press.

Allen, JoBeth, ed. 1999. *Class actions: teaching for social justice in elementary and middle school*. Foreword by Carole Edelsky. New York, London: Teachers College Press.

Allen, Jonathan, ed. 1970. *March 4: scientists, students and society*. Cambridge: MIT Press.

Appleman, P., ed. 1979. *Darwin*. 2nd ed. New York: W. W. Norton.

Arrow, Kenneth, Samuel Bowles, and Steven Burlauf, eds. 2000. *Meritocracy and economic inequality*. Princeton, N.J.: Princeton University Press.

Ayers, William, Jean Ann Hunt, and Therese Quinn, eds. 1998. *Teaching for social justice: a Democracy and education reader*. With an introduction by Maxine Greene. New York: The New Press.

Bar-Adon, Aaron, and Werner F. Leopold, eds. 1971. *Child language: a book of readings*. Englewood Cliffs, N.J.: Prentice-Hall.

Barsky, Robert. 1997. *Noam Chomsky: a life of dissent*. Cambridge, MA: MIT Press. (Paperback, 1998.)

——— Forthcoming. "Noam Chomsky's approach: radical assessments of education, language, law, and the social sciences." Ms., University of Western Ontario, Canada.

Beakley, Brian, and Oeter Ludlow, eds. *The philosophy of mind: classical problems, contemporary issues*. Cambridge: The MIT Press.

Beehler, Rodger, and Alan R. Drengson, eds. 1978. *The philosophy of society*. London: Methuen.

Bellamy, Edward, 1928. *Equality*. New York: D. Appleton-Century. (First published in 1897.)

Bellugi, Ursula, and Roger Brown, eds. 1964. *The acquisition of language*. Lafayette, Ind.: Child Development Publications of the Society for Research in Child Development. (Reprint, Chicago: University of Chicago Press, 1971.)

Benson, Robert W. 1999. *Challenging corporate rule: the petition to revoke Unocal's charter as a guide to citizen action*. Foreword by Ronnie Dugger. Croton-on-Hudson, N.Y.: Apex Press.

Bentley, Tom. 1998. *Learning beyond the classroom: education for a changing world*. London, New York: Routledge.

Berelson, Bernard, and Morris Janowitz, eds. 1950. *Reader in public opinion and communication*. Glencoe, Ill.: Free Press. (Reprinted in 1953 and 1966.)

Berlin, Isaiah. 1956. "Equality." *Proceedings of the Aristotelian Society* 56: 301–26. (Reprinted in Berlin 1979.)

——— 1979. *Concepts and categories: philosophical essays*. New York: The Viking Press. (Penguin ed., 1981.)

Bernays, Edward L. 1928. *Propaganda*. New York: H. Liveright.

——— 1928a. "Manipulating public opinion: the why and the how." *American Journal of Sociology* 33: 958–71.

——— 1952. *Public relations*. Norman: University of Oklahoma Press.

Bérubé, Michael, and Cary Nelson, eds. 1995. *Higher education under fire: politics, economics, and the crisis of the humanities*. New York: Routledge.

Blackstock, Nelson. 1976. *COINTELPRO: the FBI's secret war on political freedom*. Introduction by Noam Chomsky. New York: Vintage Books. (3rd ed., New York: Anchor Foundation, 1988.)

Block, Ned, ed. 1980–81. *Readings in philosophy of psychology*. 2 vols. Cambridge: Harvard University Press.

Blumberg, Paul. 1969. *Industrial democracy: the sociology of participation*. New York: Schocken Books.

Blumenfeld, Samuel L. 1984. *NEA: Trojan horse in American education*. Boise, Id.: The Paradigm Company.

Botha, Rudolf P. 1989. *Challenging Chomsky: the generative garden game*. Oxford: Basil Blackwell.

Boucher, David, and Paul Kelly, eds. 1994. *The social contract from Hobbes to Rawls*. London, New York: Routledge.

Boudreau, Thomas. 1998. *Universitas: the social restructuring of American undergraduate education*. Foreword by John M. Carfora. Westport, Conn.: Praeger.

Bourne, Randolph. 1965. *The world of Randolph Bourne*. Edited and with an introduction by Lillian Schlissel. New York: Dutton.

Bowden, Charles. 1997. *Juarez: the laboratory of our future*. New York: Aperture, 1997. (Reprinted, not in full, in 1998.)

Bowles, Samuel, and Herbert Gintis. 1976. *Schooling in capitalist America: educational reform and the contradictions of economic life*. New York: Basic Books.

———. 1986. *Democracy and capitalism: property, community, and the contradictions of modern social thought*. New York: Basic Books.

Boyd, William. 1995. *The history of Western education*. 12th ed., revised and enlarged by Edmund J. King. Lanham, Md.: Barnes and Noble Books. (First published in 1921.)

Brady, Robert A. 1943. *Business as a system of power*. Columbia University Press. (Paperback edition, with a new introduction by Douglas Dowd, New Brunswick and London: Transaction Publishers, 2001.)

Bracken, Harry. 1984. *Mind and language: essays on Descartes and Chomsky*. Dordrecht: Foris.

Brooks, Ron. 1991. *Contemporary debates in education: an historical perspective.* London: Longman.

Brubacher, John Seiler. 1968. *Modern philosophies of education.* 4th ed. New York: McGraw-Hill. (First published in 1939.)

———— and Willis Rudy. 1997. *Higher education in transition: a history of American colleges and universities.* With new chapters by Willis Rudy. 4th ed. New Brunswick, N.J.: Transaction Publishers. (First published in 1958.)

Buderi, Robert. 2000. "From the ivory tower to the bottom line." *Technology Review,* Jul.-Aug., 82–86.

Caetano da Silveira, Jane Rita, ed. 1999. *Anais do 3 seminario internacional de lingüística.* Porto Alegre, Brasil: Universidade Católica do Rio Grande do Sul.

Calvin, William H., and Derek Bickerton. 2000. *Lingua ex machina: reconciling Darwin and Chomsky with the human brain.* Cambridge: The MIT Press.

Campbell, James. 1995. *Understanding John Dewey: nature and cooperative intelligence.* Chicago: Open Court.

Carey, Alex. 1995. *Taking the risk out of democracy: Propaganda in the US and Australia.* Edited by Andrew Lohrey. Foreword by Noam Chomsky. Sydney: University of South Wales Press. (Reprinted by the University of Illinois Press in 1997 with the subtitle *Corporate propaganda versus freedom and liberty.*)

Chomsky, Carol. 1972. "Stages in language development and reading exposure." *Harvard Educational Review* 42: 1–33. Reprinted in Otero, ed., 1994, 4: 518–547.

———— 1979. "Approaching reading through invented spelling," in Resnick and Weaver, eds., 1979, 2: 43–65. Reprinted in Otero, ed., 1994, 4: 620–42.

Chomsky, Noam. 1951. "Morphophonemics of modern Hebrew." Master's thesis, University of Pennsylvania. (Published in 1979 by Garland Publications in its series "Outstanding Dissertations.")

———— 1954. Review of Emezer Rieger, *Modern Hebrew. Language* 30: 180–81. (Included in this volume as an appendix to Selection 21.)

———— 1955–56. *The logical structure of linguistic theory.* Chicago: University of Chicago, 1975. (Paperback edition, 1985, with an index by Jan van Voorst.)

———— 1956. "Three models for the description of language." *I.R.E. Transactions on Information Theory* IT-2: 113–24. Reprinted, with corrections, in Luce, Bush, and Galanter, eds., 1965, vol. 2.

———— 1957. *Syntactic structures.* The Hague: Mouton.

———— 1959. Review of Skinner, *Verbal Behavior. Language* 35, 1: 26–58. (Reprinted as no. A-34 in the reprint series in the social sciences by Bobbs-Merrill, Inc.; in Fodor and Katz (eds.) 1964; in Jakobovits and Miron, eds., 1967, with an important preliminary note by Chomsky; in De Cecco, ed., 1969 (abridged); in Hollander and Hunt, eds., 1972; and in Block 1980–81, vol. 1.)

———— 1964a. Introduction to Roberts, *English syntax* (1964), pp. ix–xv. (Included in this volume as Selection 23.)

———— 1964b. "Comments for Project Literacy meeting." *Project Literacy Reports* 2: 1–8. (Included in this volume as an appendix to Selection 23.)

———— 1966. *Cartesian linguistics: a chapter in the history of rationalist thought.* New York: Harper and Row.

———— 1966a. "The responsibility of intellectuals." *Mosaic* 7, 1: 2–16. (An expanded version appeared in the *New York Review of Books,* Feb. 23, 1967, pp. 16–26, and was reprinted, as a separate publication, by the Inter-University Committee for Debate on Foreign Policy, Ithaca, N.Y., 1967. It is included in Roszak, ed., 1968, 254–98; in Chomsky 1969; in Chomsky 1987; in Robbins, ed., 1999, 76–99, 309–14, and in Chomsky, forthcoming a.)

———— 1966b. "Some thoughts on intellectuals and the schools." *Harvard Educational Review* 36: 484–91. (Special issue devoted to a symposium on the topic "American intellectuals and the schools.") (Reprinted in Chomsky 1969, in Crews and Schell, eds., 1970, 359–65, with questions and comments by Crews in the accompanying *Guide,* 61–63. Included in this volume as Selection 16.)

———— 1966c. "Linguistic theory." Talk at the Northeast Conference on the Teaching of Foreign Languages, Aug. 1, 1966. It first appeared in *Northeast Conference on the Teaching of Foreign Languages* (1966), Working Committee Reports, ed. by Robert G. Mead Jr., 43–49. Reprinted in Lester, ed., 1970, 51–60 (rev. edition, 1973, 36–45); in Oller and Richards, eds., 1973, 29–35; and in *Chomsky* 1971c, 152–59, under the title "Implications for language teaching." (Included in this volume as Selection 22.)

———— 1967. "Recent contributions to the theory of innate ideas." *Synthese* 17: 2–11. (Reprinted in Cohen and Wartofsky, eds., 1967, 3: 81–90; in Strain, ed., 1971, 332–41 [with "Recent" replaced by "Some"]; in Morick, ed., 1980, 230–40; and in Cohen and Wartofsky, eds., 1985, 31–40.)

———— 1968. *Language and mind.* New York: Harcourt, Brace and World. (Enlarged edition with three additional chapters, 1972.)

———— 1968a. "Noam Chomsky's view of language: Noam Chomsky and Stuart Hampshire discuss the study of language." *The Listener* (London), May 30, 1968, 686–91. (Reprinted in Chomsky 1988b.)

———— 1968b. "Philosophers and public policy." *Ethics* 79, 1: 1–9.

———— 1968c. "The menace of liberal scholarship." *New York Review of Books,* Jan. 2, 1969. (Included, together with "An exchange on liberal scholarship" (four letters to the editor and Chomsky's reply), in the *Congressional Record*: 91st Congress, first session, vol. 115, part 3 (Feb. 5, 1969, to Feb. 21, 1969, 3644–56, at the initiative of Senator Mark Hatfield.)

———— 1969. *American power and the new mandarins.* New York: Pantheon.

———— 1969a. "Intellectuals and the war lords." *The Activist* 24: 26–33, 40. (Talk Chomsky gave in a forum at Oberlin College on Feb. 6, 1969. Reprinted in Chomsky 1981 under the title "The politicization of the university.")

———— 1969b. "Responsibility." In Allen, ed., 1970. 8–14. (Speech at Rindge High School, Mar, 4, 1969, regarding Mar. 4 research stoppage at MIT.)

———— 1969c. "Personal Addendum to the Panel Report [of May 31, 1969] by Noam A. Chomsky." (First published in this volume as Selection 17.)

———— 1969d. "Remarks before the M.I.T. Commission on M.I.T. Education." (First published in this volume as Selection 18.)

—— 1969e. "The function of the university in a time of crisis." *The great ideas today nineteen sixty-nine,* ed. by Robert M. Hutchins and Mortimer Adler. Chicago: Encyclopedia Britannica, pp. 40–61. (Reprinted in Chomsky 1973. Included in this volume as Selection 10.)

—— 1969f. "Some tasks for the left," *Liberation* 14:5–6 (Aug-Sept. 1969), pp. 38–43. (Reprinted in *Radical priorities* (1981), 219–31. (Included in this volume as Selection 8.)

—— 1969g. "Some observations on the teaching of language," *The Pedagogic Reporter* 21:1 (September 1969), pp. 5–6 and 13. (Included in this volume as Selection 21.)

—— 1969h. "Should traditional grammar be ended or mended?, *Educational Review* 22 (November 1969), pp. 5–17 (=*The state of language,* edited by Andrew Wilkinson). (Reprinted in Wade, ed. 1982, 10–22.)

—— 1970. *At war with Asia: essays on Indochina.* New York: Pantheon.

—— 1970a. Language and freedom, *Abraxas: A journal for the theoretical study of philosophy, the humanities and the social sciences* 1:1, 9–24; also in White and Newman, eds. 1972. (Reprinted in Chomsky 1973 and in Chomsky 1987.)

—— 1970b. "Government in the future." Sound seminar at the Poetry Center of the New York YMCA on Feb. 16, 1970, recorded and made available by Jeffrey Norton Publishers at the time, and now by Alternative Radio, P.O. Box 551, Boulder, CO, 800–444–1977. (Included in this volume as Selection 7.)

—— 1970c."Revolt in the academy: some thoughts on the student movement." *Modern Occasions* 1, 1: 50–75.

—— 1970d. "The creative experience" (interview). In Rosner and Abt, eds., 1970, 71–87. (Reprinted in Chomsky 1981.)

—— 1970e. "Phonology and reading." In Levin and Williams, eds., 1970, pp. 3–18.

—— 1971. *Problems of knowledge and freedom: the Russell lectures.* New York: Pantheon Books.

—— 1971a. "Toward a humanistic conception of education." Lecture, University of Illinois (Urbana). Revised version in Feinberg and Rosemont, eds., 1975, 204–20. (Included in this volume as Selection 9.)

—— 1971b. "The case against B. F. Skinner." *New York Review of Books* 17, 11. (Reprinted in *Without/Within Behaviorism and Humanism,* edited by F. W. Matson. Belmont, Calif.: Wadsworth, 1973, pp. 58–79.)

—— 1971c. *Chomsky: selected readings.* Edited by J. P. B. Allen and Paul van Buren. London, New York: Oxford University Press, 1971.

—— 1972a. "The fallacy of Richard Hernstein's IQ." *Cognition* 1: 285–98. Reprinted in part in Appleman, ed., 1979, 499–504.

—— 1972b. Psychology and ideology. *Cognition* 1: 11–46 (see also 407–18). (Reprinted in Chomsky 1973; Beehler and Drengson, eds., 1978, 110–55.)

—— 1972c. "Science and ideology." Talk delivered at Jawaharlal Nehru University on Nov. 13, 1972, as the Nehru Memorial Lecture. (Published in *Jawaharlal Nehru memorial lectures, 1967–1972,* edited by P. M. S. Blackett et al. Bombay: Bharatiya Vidya Bhavan, 1973, 170–208; parts appear in Chomsky 1973.)

——— 1972d. "Scholarship and ideology: American historians as 'experts in legitimation.'" Talk delivered at Jawaharlal Nehru University on Nov. 14, 1972 (a counterpart to Chomsky 1972a). (Published in *Social Scientist* 7, 1: 20–37, and in *UAG Magazine* [University Action Group] 2, 1: 31–43; parts appear in Chomsky 1973.)

——— 1973. *For reasons of state*. New York: Pantheon.

——— 1973a. "Comments on Herrnstein's Response." *Cognition* 1, 4: 407–18.

——— 1973b. Introduction to Schaff, *Language and cognition*.

——— 1973c. "One man's view: Noam Chomsky. Are universities too conservative? Do they collude with corporations to obscure the way power works in our society? Noam Chomsky thinks so and explains why," *Business Today*, May 1973, 13–15." (Reprinted in Chomsky 1988. Included in this volume as Selection 20.)

——— 1974. "Conversation with Noam Chomsky." In Oltmans, ed., 1974, 285–91.

——— 1975. *Reflections on language*. New York: Pantheon. (See Chomsky 1998f.)

——— 1975a. "On cognitive structures and their development: a reply to Piaget." In Piattelli-Palmarini, ed., 1980, 35–52.

——— 1975b. "Language as a key to human nature and society." In Osiatynski, ed., 1984, 95–101. (Reprinted in Chomsky 1988. Included in this volume as Selection 2.)

——— 1976a. Introduction to Blackstock 1976.

——— 1977a. "On the national interest," written on Jan. 28, 1977, at the request of *Partisan Review*. First published in Chomsky 1981, 59–61. (Included in this volume as an appendix to Selection 7.)

——— 1976b. "Equality: language development, human intelligence, and social organization." *Philosophy and Social Action* 2, 3: 1–20. (Reprinted in Feinberg, ed., 1978, and in Chomsky 1987. Included in this volume as Selection 6.)

——— 1977. "The ideas of Chomsky" (interview). In Magee, ed., 1979, 202–23.

——— 1978. "Human language and other semiotic systems." Delivered on Feb. 16, 1978, in a symposium on "The Emergence of Language: Continuities and Discontinuities," at the annual meeting of the American Association for the Advancement of Science. (Published in *Semiotica*, 25 1–2 (1979): 31–44; reprinted in Sebeok and J. Umiker-Sebeok, eds., 1980.)

——— 1979. *Language and responsibility*. (Based on Conversations in December 1975 and January 1976 with Mitsou Ronat.) New York: Pantheon. (See 1998f.)

——— 1980. *Rules and representations*. New York: Columbia University Press.

——— 1980a. "The new organalogy." *The Behavioral and Brain Sciences* 3: 42–61.

——— 1980b. "Some elementary comments on the rights of freedom of expression" (October 11), Ms., MIT. (Published in this volume for the first time as an appendix to Selection 6. A French translation appeared as an "avis" to Faurisson 1980.)

——— 1981. *Radical priorities*. Edited by C. P. Otero. Montreal: Black Rose. (Enlarged ed., 1984.)

——— 1981a. Interview. In "Mark these linguists," *The English Magazine*, summer 1981, 4–6. (Included in this volume as Selection 24.)

——— 1982. *Towards a new cold war: essays on the current crisis and how we got there*. New York: Pantheon.

——— 1983. *The fateful triangle: the United States, Israel, and the Palestinians*. Boston: South End Press. (Updated ed., 1999, with a foreword by Edward Said.)

———— 1983a. "The revolutionary linguist who believes we have a 'language organ' in our brain also thinks there are some things no amount of learning can teach" (interview by John Gliedman) *Omni* 6, 11: 113–14, 116, 118, 171–74. (Reprinted in Chomsky 1988. Included in this volume as Selection 1.)

———— 1984. *Knowledge of language: its nature, origin, and use.* New York: Praeger, 1986.

———— 1984a. Letter of March 4, 1984, to Mrs. Davis (about the teaching of grammar). (Included in this volume as an appendix to Selection 22.)

———— 1984b. Interview conducted by Brian Jacobs on October 21, one of three published as "Cover story—Network television news: Perspectives on the medium." *Comity* (6: 1985, 18–20). (Reprinted in Chomsky 1988 under the title "The media as a mirror of society." Included in this volume as an appendix to Selection 12.)

———— 1984c. "The manufacture of consent." Talk given on Dec. 9, 1984, at the Community Church of Boston. (Included in *The manufacture of consent*, a 32–page pamphlet published by the church to launch its 1985–86 fund drive. Two selections from it were reprinted in Chomsky 1987, 121–36 and 223–26. An excerpt including, but not limited to, these two selections is included in this volume as Selection 12.)

———— 1985. *Turning the tide: U.S. intervention in Central America and the struggle for peace.* Boston: South End Press. (2nd ed., enlarged, *Turning the tide: the U.S. and Latin America.* Montreal: Black Rose Books, 1987.)

———— 1985a. "The Soviet Union versus socialism." *Our Generation* 17, 2 (1986): 47–52. (Reprinted in Roussopoulos, ed., 1987, 47–52.)

———— 1985b. "The bounds of thinkable thought." *The Progressive* 49 10, 28–31. (Reprinted in *Blueprint for Social Justice* 42:8 [1989] and in Grover and Peschak, eds., 1993, 49–53. Edited excerpt from Chomsky 1984b.)

———— 1986a. *Language and problems of knowledge.* Cambridge: The MIT Press, 1988.

———— 1986b. *On power and ideology.* Cambridge: The MIT Press, 1988.

———— 1987. *The Chomsky reader.* Edited by James Peck. New York: Pantheon.

———— 1987a. "Interview with Noam Chomsky." *The Reading Instruction Journal* (New Jersey Reading Association) 31, 3 (Spring 1988), 2–7. Reprinted in Chomsky 1988. Included in this volume as Selection 3.

———— 1988a. *The culture of terrorism.* Boston: South End Press.

———— 1988b. *Language and politics.* Ed. by C. P. Otero. Montreal: Black Rose.

———— 1988c. "Helping people persuade themselves." Interview by David Barsamian (on Feb. 15). (Included in Chomsky 1988b. Also in Chomsky 1992b, in a somewhat different form, under the title "Elite power and the responsibility of intellectuals.")

———— 1988d. "One man's view: Noam Chomsky—Are Universities too conservative? Do they collude with explorations to obscure the way power in our society? Noam Chomsky thinks so and explains why," *Business Today*, May 1973, 13–15." (Reprinted in Chomsky 1988. Included in this volume a Selection 20.)

———— 1988e. "Images of the Cold War." *Educational Leadership* 46, 4: 75–78.

———— 1988f. "Middle East Terrorism and the American Ideological System." In Said and Hitchens, eds., 97–147.

———— 1989. *Necessary illusions: thought control in democratic societies.* Boston: South End Press.

———— 1989a. Mental constructions and social reality. Paper presented at the Groningen

conference on "Knowledge and Language," May 1989. Included in Reuland and
Abraham, eds., 1992.

———— 1989b. "Controlling the public mind." *Nicaraguan Perspectives* 17: 28–29, 33–36.
(Included in this volume as Selection 13.)

———— 1989c. [Letter to historian Carolyn Eisenberg.] *Radical History Review* 44: 138–144.

———— 1989d. "Society, the university and language: an interview with Noam Chomsky."
Conducted by Sol Saporta, *Critica* 2, 2: 19–42.

———— 1991. *Deterring democracy*. London: Verso, 1991. (Paperback ed., with a new after-
word, New York: Hill and Wang, 1992.)

———— 1991a. "Language, politics, and composition: a conversation with Noam
Chomsky." Conducted by Gary A. Olson and Lester Faigley, *Journal of Advanced
Composition* 11, 1: 4–35. (Included in this volume as Selection 25.)

———— 1992a. *What Uncle Sam really wants*. Berkeley, Calif.: Odonian Press.

———— 1992b. *Chronicles of dissent*. Interviews with David Barsamian. Monroe, Me.:
Common Courage Press.

———— 1992c. "Rationality/science." *Z Papers* 1, 4: 52–57. (Included in this volume as
Selection 5. See also "Chomsky replies," *2 Papers* 2, 3: 11–12. An excerpt was translated into French as "Le vrai visage de la critique post-moderne, "*Agone* 18–19: 47–48,
a monographic double issue on the theme "Neutralité et engagement du savoir.")

———— 1993a. *Year 501: The conquest continues*. Boston: South End Press.

———— 1993b. *Rethinking Camelot: JFK, the Vietnam War, and the US political culture*.
Boston: South End Press.

———— 1993c. *Letters from Lexington: reflections on propaganda*. Monroe, Me.: Common
Courage Press; Edinburgh, Scotland: AK Press.

———— 1993d. *The prosperous few and the restless many*. Interview by David Barsamian.
Berkeley, Calif.: Odonian Press.

———— 1993e. *Language and thought*. Wakefield, R.I., London: Moyer Bell, 1994.
(Paperback, 1995.)

———— 1993f. "World order and its rules: variations on some themes," *Journal of Law and
Society* (Cardiff Law School), summer.

———— 1993g. "The masters of mankind." *The Nation*, March 29, 412–16. (Excerpted as
"A New Deal for the New Imperial Age," in *Toronto Star*, April 14, 1993, A14; translated as "I padroni dell' umanità," *L'Unita*, May 24, 1993, 13; reprinted for educational
use at the University of Western Ontario, Canada; excerpted as "Notes on NAFTA,"
in *Open Magazine Pamphlet* 29 and in Ruggiero and Sahulka, eds., 1995, 61–65;
reprinted as "Les maîtres de l'humanities: commentaires sur l'ALENA," *Un monde
completement surréel* [Quebec: EDAM, 1996], 13–20; reprinted as preface to Bowden
1997; excerpted as Preface to Bowden 1998.)

———— 1994. *World orders old and new*. Columbia University Press. (Rev. ed., "with an
update on the Palestinian predicament," 1996.)

———— 1994a. *The umbrella of U.S. power: the Universal Declaration of Human Rights and
the contradictions of U.S. policy*. New York: Seven Stories Press, 1999.

———— 1994b. "Prospects for democracy." Talk given at MIT, Cambridge, Mass., on Mar.

8, 1994. (Published here for the first time, as Selection 15. A tape recording of the oral version is available from Alternative Radio, P.O. Box 551, Boulder, CO, 800–444–1977.)

———— 1994c. "21st century: democracy or absolutism." Talk in Chicago, on October 17. (Available from Alternative Radio, P.O. Box 551, Boulder, CO, 800–444–1977.)

———— 1994d. "Democracy and education." Mellon Lecture, Loyola University, Chicago, October 19. (First published in full in this book as the Prologue.)

———— 1994e. *Keeping the rabble in line.* Monroe, Me.: Common Courage Press.

———— 1994f. *Secrets, lies and democracy.* Interview by David Barsamian. Berkeley, Calif.: Odonian Press.

———— 1995. *The minimalist program.* Cambridge, MA: The MIT Press.

———— 1995a. "Rollback." Four parts. Z, Jan., Feb., Apr., and May. (Reprinted in Ruggiero and Sahulka, eds., 1995, 11–30, with "March," mistakenly, for "May.")

———— 1995b. "Education and democracy." The 1995 Jeffrey and Kitty Cole Honors College Lecture at Michigan State University, given on March 28, 1995.

———— 1995c. Foreword to Carey 1995, 1997.

———— 1996. *Powers and prospects: reflections on human nature and the social order.* Boston: South End Press.

———— 1996a. "Language and evolution." (Reply to J. Maynard Smith.) *New York Review of Books,* February 1, 41.

———— 1996b. "'Consent without consent': reflections on the theory and practice of democracy." Lecture delivered on March 28. An edited and updated version appeared in the *Cleveland State Law Review* 44: 4.

———— 1996c. *Class warfare.* Interview with David Barsamian. Monroe, Me.: Common Courage Press.

———— 1996d. "The system is weak." Talk, June 7, Woods Hole, Mass. (Available from Alternative Radio, P.O. Box 551, Boulder, CO, 800–444–1977.)

———— 1997a. "The Cold War and the university." In Schiffrin, ed. *The Cold War and the university: toward an intellectual history of the postwar years.* New York: The New Press, 1997, 171–94. (Included in this volume as the first part of Selection 19.)

———— 1997b. "The Cold War and the university." Talk at Boston University on Feb. 2, 1997, on the occasion of the publication of the collection of essays mentioned in the preceding entry. (First published in this book as the second part of Selection 19. A tape recording of the oral version, together with a talk by Howard Zinn on the same occasion, and answers to questions from the floor [Noam Chomsky/Howard Zinn, "The Cold War and the University"], is available from Alternative Radio, P.O. Box 551, Boulder, CO, 800–444–1977.)

———— 1997c. "Propaganda and control of the public mind." Talk at Harvard Trade Union Program, Cambridge, Mass., Feb. 7, 1997. (Available in full from Alternative Radio, P.O. Box 551, Boulder, CO, 800–444–1977. Selection 14 is an excerpt from this talk. Included in McChesney, ed., 1998, 179–89.)

———— 1997d. "Market democracy in a neoliberal order: doctrine and reality." Davie Lecture, University of Cape Town, May 1997. (Published in *Pretexts: Studies in writing and culture* 7, 1 [1998]: 9–33. Reprinted in Chomsky 2000e, 135–72.)

—— 1998a. *The common good.* Interview by David Barsamian. Compiled and edited by Arthur Naiman. Berkeley, Calif.: Odonian Press.

—— 1998b. "Minimalist inquiries: the framework." Ms., MIT. In Martin, Michaels, and vriageraka, eds., 2000, 89–155.

—— 1998c. "Jubilee 2000." Published in *The Guardian,* May 15, as "Debt: the people." (Reprinted in *Guardian Weekly* as "The poor always pay debts of the rich," May 24, 15.)

—— 1998d. "Hordes of Vigilantes." *Z,* July-August.

—— 1998e. "Power in the global arena." *New Left Review* 230, 3–27.

—— 1998f. "Linguistics and brain science." Lecture at the first Mind Articulation Project symposium, Tokyo, Japan, Nov. 15. (Included in Marantz, Miyashita, and O'Neal, eds., 2000, 13–28.)

—— 1998g. "New horizons in the study of language and mind." Lecture at the University of Maryland, College Park, Nov. 30, 1998.

—— 1998h. *On language.* New York: The New Press. ("Chomsky's classic works *Language and responsibility* [1977, actually 1976] and *Reflections on language* [1975] in one volume.")

—— 1998i. "There is no limits to what can be done" (interview). In South End Collective, eds., 14–25.

—— 1998j. "Human nature, freedom and political community: an interview with Noam Chomsky." Conducted by Scott Burchill, *Citizenship Studies* 2, 1: 5–21.

—— 1999a. *Profits over people: neoliberalism and global order.* Introduction by Robert W. McChesney. New York, Toronto, London: Seven Stories Press.

—— 1999b. *The new military humanism: lessons from Kosovo.* Monroe, Me.: Common Courage Press.

—— 1999c. "U.S. to World: Get Out of the Way." Interview by David Barsamian on Feb. 1–2, 1999. (Available from Alternative Radio, P.O. Box 551, Boulder, CO, 800–444–1977.)

—— 1999d. "Comment regarding Darwinism controversy." Znet Sustainer's Forum System, www.zmag.org. (Web post first published in this volume as an appendix to Selection 5.)

—— 1999e. "Perspectives on language and mind." Galileo Lecture, Pisa, October. (Included in this volume as Selection 4.)

—— 1999f. "Language and the brain." Address at European Conference on Cognitive Science, Siena, Oct. 27–30.

—— 1999g. "An interview on minimalism." Conducted by Adriana Belletti and Luigi Rizzi, University of Siena, Nov. 8–9, 1999; revised Mar. 16, 2000. (Included in Chomsky 2001c and Chomsky 2002.)

—— 1999h. Address at the Presidential Forum of the Modern Language Association (MLA). (Included in this volume as Selection 11. An edited version appeared in the MLA's *Profession 2000,* 32–39, under the title "Paths taken, tasks ahead.")

—— 1999j. "Derivation by phase." In Kenstowicz, ed., 2001, 1–52.

—— 2000a. *New horizons in the study of language and mind.* Cambridge University Press.

———— 2000b. *The architecture of language.* Edited by N. Mukherji, B. N. Patnaik, and R. K. Agnihotri. New Delhi: Oxford University Press.

———— 2000c. *Rogue states: the rule of force in world affairs.* Boston: South End Press.

———— 2000d. *A new generation draws the line: Kosovo, East Timor and the standards of the West.* London, New York: Verso.

———— 2000e. *Chomsky on miseducation.* Edited and introduced by Donaldo Macedo. Lanham, Md.: Rowman and Littlefield.

———— 2000g. "Control of our lives." Talk, Kiva Auditorium, Albuquerque, New Mexico, on Feb. 26. Available at www.zmag.org/chomskyalbaq.htm.

———— 2000h. "Liberating the mind from orthodoxies." Interview by David Barsamian in Lexington, Mass., Mar. 10. (Available from Alternative Radio, P.O. Box 551, Boulder, CO, 800–444–1977.)

———— 2000i. "Assaulting solidarity—privatizing education." ZNet Commentary, May 12, 2000. Available at www.zmag.org/Commentaries/donorform.htm.

———— 2001a. *Propaganda and the public mind.* Interviews by David Barsamian. Boston: South End Press.

———— 2001b. *Su natura e linguaggio.* A cura di A. Belletti e L. Rizzi. Trad. di S. Trovato e C. Cechetto. Siena: Edizione dell'Università degli Studi di Siena. (It includes original English versions of the three lectures and the interview.)

———— 2001c. "Beyond explanatory adequacy." Ms., MIT.

———— 2001d. "The new war against terror." Talk given for The Technology and Culture Forum, MIT, Cambridge, Mass., Oct. 18, 2001. (Videotape.)

———— 2001e. *9–11.* New York: Seven Stories Press. (Published simultaneously in several languages.)

———— 2001f. *De la guerre comme politique etrangère des Etats-Unis.* Marseilles: Agone; Montreal: Comeau and Nadequ.

———— 2001g. *Deux heures de lucidité: Entretiens avec Denis Robert et Weronika Zarachowicz.* Paris: Editions des Arènes.

———— 2002. *On nature and language.* Ed. by L. Rizzi and A. Belletti. Cambridge: Cambridge University Press. (It includes the original English versions of Chomsky 2001b, but not only those.)

———— Forthcoming a. *The essential Chomsky,* vol. 1. Monroe, Me.: Common Courage Press.

———— Forthcoming b. *U.S.A.: the Noam Chomsky discussions.* Ed. by Peter Mitchell and John Shoeffel.

Chomsky, Noam, and M. Halle. 1968. *The sound pattern of English.* New York: Harper and Row. (Paperback ed., MIT Press, 1991, with a preface dated August 1990.)

Chomsky, Noam, and E. Herman. 1973. *Counter-revolutionary violence: Bloodbaths in fact and propaganda.* Preface by Richard A. Falk. Module no. 57. Andover, Mass.: Warner Modular Publications. (Suppressed by the publisher. See next item, pp. xiv-xvii.)

————. 1979. *The political economy of human rights.* 2 vols. Boston: South End Press. (A greatly expanded version of the previous item. See also Herman and Chomsky 1988.)

————. 1998. *The myth of the liberal media: the propaganda model of news.* Northampton, Mass.: Media Education Foundation, www.igc.org/mef. (Single 60-min. video in three parts—"The Filters of News," "Domestic Issues," "International Issues"—with background and contextual information by Professor Justin Lewis, Univ. of Massachusetts, Amherst.)

Chomsky, Noam, Paul Lauter, and Florence Howe. 1968. "Reflections on a political trial." *The New York Review of Books*, Aug. 22, 23–30. (Reprinted, with a comment by Arlene Siegel [first published in the *RESIST* Newsletter of Aug. 7, 1969], in Chomsky, Lauter, and Howe 1970.)

———. 1970. *Trials of the resistance.* New York: New York Review of Books.

Chomsky, William. 1946. *How to teach Hebrew in the elementary grades.* New York: The United Synagogue Commission on Jewish Education.

——— 1947. *Hebrew, the story of a living language.* New York: Education Dept., Zionist Organization of America. (1956 printing.)

——— 1956. *Teaching Hebrew.* New York: Jewish Education Committee Press.

——— 1957. *Hebrew: the eternal language.* Philadelphia: The Jewish Publication Society of America, 1957. (8th printing, 1986.)

——— 1959. *Teaching and learning: an introduction to Jewish education.* New York: Jewish Education Committee Press. (*Apprendre et enseigner.* Traduit et adapté par L. Lazare. Paris: AJDC, 1963.)

———, ed. and tr. 1952. *David Kimhi's Hebrew grammar (Mikhlol).* New York: Published for the Dropsie College for Hebrew and Cognate Learning by Bloch Publishing Co. (Originally prepared as a doctoral dissertation, published in part in 1933.)

Clark, Virginia P., Paul A. Eschholz, and Alfred F. Rosa, eds. 1985. *Language: introductory readings.* 4th ed. New York: St. Martin's Press.

Cogswell, David. 1996. *Chomsky for beginners.* New York: Writers and Readers Publishing, Inc.; London: Writers and Readers Limited.

Cohen, Joshua, and Joel Rogers. 1983. *On democracy.* New York: Penguin Books.

Cohen, Joshua, and Joel Rogers, eds. 1995. *Associations and democracy.* London; New York: Verso.

Cohen, Mitchell, and Dennis Hale, eds. 1967. *The new student left.* Boston: Beacon Press. (Italian translation, *Gli studenti a la nuova sinistra in America.* Antologia a cura di Enrico Forni, Mitchell Cohen and Dennis Hale. Introduzione di Noam Chomsky. Bari: De Donato Editore, 1968.)

Cohen, Robert S., and M. Wartofsky, eds. 1967. *Boston Studies in the Philosophy of Science,* vol. III. New York: Humanities Press.

———. 1985. *A portrait of twenty-five years: Boston Studies in the Philosophy of Science.* Dordrecht, Boston, Lancaster: Reidel.

Collins, Chuck, Betsy Leondar-Wright, and Holly Sklar. 1999. *Shifting fortunes: the perils of the growing American wealth gap.* Forewords by Juliet Schor and Lester Thurow. Boston: United for a Fair Economy.

Connor, Walter D. 1996. *Tattered banners: labor, conflict, and corporatism in postcommunist Russia.* Boulder, Colo.: Westview Press.

Corson, David J. 1980. "Chomsky on education." *The Australian Journal of Education* 24: 164–85. (Reprinted in Otero, ed., 1994, 3: 176–198.)

Cowan, Rich, et al., eds. 1997. *Uncovering the right on campus*. Houston, Tex.: Public Search, Inc.

Cox, Andrew, and Noel O'Sullivan, eds. 1988. *The corporate state: corporatism and the state tradition in Western Europe*. Aldershot, Hants, England: Edward Elgar; Brookfield, Vt.: Gower.

Crews, Frederick, and Orville Schell, eds. 1970. *Starting over: a college reader*. New York: Random House. (With a very helpful accompanying *Guide to Starting over: a college reader*, prepared by Crews.)

Darder, Antonia. 1991. *Culture and power in the classroom: a critical foundation for bicultural education*. New York: Bergin and Garvey.

Darder, Antonia, and Rodolfo D. Torres, eds. 1998. *The Latino studies reader: culture, economy, and society*. Malden, Mass.: Blackwell.

Darder, Antonia, Rodolfo D. Torres, and Henry Gutiérrez, eds. 1997. *Latinos and education: a critical reader*. New York: Routledge, 1997.

Davis, Lennard J., and M. Bella Mirabella, eds. 1990. *Left politics and the literary profession*. New York: Columbia University Press.

Davis, R. W., ed. 1995. *The origins of modern freedom in the West*. Stanford, Calif.: Stanford University Press.

De Cecco, John P., ed. 1969. *Psychology of language, thought and instruction: readings*. New York: Holt.

De Leon, David, ed. 1994. *Leaders from the 1960s: a biographical sourcebook of American activism*. Westport, Conn./London: Greenwood Press.

Denning, Michael. 1997. *The cultural front: the laboring of American culture in the twentieth century*. London, New York: Verso.

Dewey, John. 1899. *The school and society*. Chicago: University of Chicago Press. (Three lectures, supplemented by a statement of the university elementary school.) (Reprinted in 1907, 1909; rev. ed., 1915; reprinted in 1942, 1961, 1980, and, with *The child and the curriculum*, 1943, with introduction by Leonard Carmichael, and in 1990, with an introduction by Philip W. Jackson. See the following item.)

—— 1902. *The child and the curriculum*. Chicago: University of Chicago Press.

—— 1909. *Moral principles in education*. Boston: Houghton.

—— 1910. *How we think*. Boston: D. C. Heath. (Reprinted as *How we think: a restatement of the relation of reflective thinking to the educative process*, Boston: Houghton Mifflin, 1998, with a foreword by Maxine Greene.)

—— 1913. *Interest and effort in education*. Boston: Houghton Mifflin.

—— 1916. *Democracy and education: an introduction to the philosophy of education*. New York: Macmillan, 1923. (Free Press paperback ed., New York: The Free Press; London: Collier-Macmillan, 1966.)

—— 1922. *Human nature and conduct; an introduction to social psychology*. New York: H. Holt. (Modern Library ed., 1957.)

—— 1929. *Impressions of soviet Russia and the revolutionary world, Mexico—China—Turkey*. New York: New Republic.

—— 1938. *Experience and education*. New York: Macmillan.

—— 1939. *Freedom and culture*. New York: G. P. Putnam's Sons.

———— 1946. *Problems of men.* New York: Philosophical Library. (Reprinted as *Philosophy of education* in 1958.)

———— 1993. *Philosophy and education in their historic relations.* Transcribed from his lectures by Elsie Ripley Clapp; edited and with an introduction by J. J. Chambliss. Boulder, Colo.: Westview Press.

Dewey, John, and Horace M. Kallen, eds. 1941. *The Bertrand Russell case.* New York: Viking Press.

Dillon, John. 1997. *Turning the tide: confronting the money traders.* Toronto, Ont.: Ecumenical Coalition for Economic Justice; Ottawa, Ont.: Canadian Centre for Policy Alternatives.

Drèze, Jean, and Amartya Sen. 1995. *India: economic development and social opportunity.* Oxford: Clarendon Press. (Paperback ed., 1998.)

Driver, Rosalind, John Leach, Robin Millar, and Phil Scott. 1996. *Young people's images of science.* Buckingham, Philadelphia: Open University Press.

Dworkin, Ronald. 2000. *Sovereign virtue: the theory and practice of equality.* Harvard University Press.

Edsall, Thomas Byrne. 1984. *The new politics of inequality.* New York: W. W. Norton.

Faurisson, Robert. 1980. *Mémoire en défense.* Paris: Vieille Taupe.

Featherstone, Liza. 2000. "The new student movement." *The Nation,* May 15, 11–16.

Feinberg, Walter, ed. 1978. *Equality and social policy.* Urbana, Chicago, London: University of Illinois Press.

Feinberg, W., and H. Rosemont, eds. 1975. *Work, technology and education: dissenting essays in the intellectual foundations of American education.* Urbana: University of Illinois Press.

Fodor, Jerry A., and Jerrold J. Katz, eds. 1964. *The structure of language.* New York: Prentice-Hall.

Fones-Wolf, Elizabeth. 1995. *Selling free enterprise: the business assault on business and liberalism, 1945–1960.* Urbana: University of Illinois Press.

Freeman, Eugene, ed. 1976. *The abdication of philosophy: philosophy and the public good.* La Salle, Ill.: Open Court.

Freeman, Richard B. 1999. *The new inequality: creating solutions for poor America.* Boston: Beacon Press.

Freire, Paulo. 1969. *Educaçao como pratica da liberdade.* Rio de Janeiro: Editora Paz e Terra. (English translation by Myra Bergman Ramos in *Education for critical consciousness,* New York: The Seabury Press, 1973, 1–84.)

———— 1970. *Pedagogy of the oppressed.* New York: The Seabury Press.

Gardner, Howard. 2000. *The disciplined mind: beyond facts and standardized tests, the K-12 education that every child deserves.* New York: Penguin Books.

Gardner, Martin. 1957. *Fad and fallacies in the name of science.* New York: Ballantine Books.

Gartner, Alan, Colin Greer, and Frank Riessman, eds. 1973. *After deschooling, what?* New York: Harper and Row.

George, Henry. 1981. *Progress and poverty: an inquiry into the cause of industrial depressions and of increase of want with increase of wealth . . . the remedy.* Centennial ed. New York: Robert Schalkenbach Foundation.

————— 1928. *Significant paragraphs from Henry George's* Progress and poverty. With an introduction by John Dewey. Garden City, N.Y.: Doubleday, Doran.

————— 1941. *Guide for teaching the principles of political economy*. Based on the text of *Progress and poverty* by Henry George. New York: Robert Schalkenbach Foundation.

Ghiselin, Brewster. 1952. *The creative process*. New York: New American Library, 1952. (Reprint, Berkeley: University of California Press, 1954.)

Giroux, Henry A., and Peter McLaren. 1992. "Education for democracy." Foreword to J. Goodman. 1992.

Goodman, Jesse. 1992. *Elementary schooling for critical democracy*. Albany: State University of New York Press.

Goodman, Paul. 1957. *Growing up absurd: problems of youth in the organized system*. New York: Random House.

————— 1962. *The community of scholars*. New York: Random House.

————— 1963. *The society I live in is mine*. New York: Horizon Press.

————— 1964. *Compulsory mis-education*. New York: Horizon Press.

————— 1965. *Seeds of liberation*. New York: G. Braziller.

————— 1977. *Drawing the line: the political essays of Paul Goodman*. Edited by Taylor Stoehr. New York: Free Life Editions.

Goodman, Robert. 1971. *After the planners*. New York: Simon and Schuster.

Greider, W. 1992. *Who will tell the people: the betrayal of American democracy*. New York: Simon and Schuster.

Grover, William F., and Joseph G. Peschak, eds. 1993. *Voices of Dissent*. New York, Harper Collins.

Gross, Beatrice and Ronald, eds. 1971. *Radical school reform*. New York: Simon and Schuster.

————— 1974. *Will it grow in a classroom?* New York, Delacorte Press.

————— 1977. *The children's rights movement: overcoming the oppression of young people*. Garden City, N.Y.: Anchor Books.

————— 1985. *The great school debate : which way for American education?* New York: Simon and Schuster.

Gutmann, Amy. 1999. *Democratic education*. With a new preface and new epilogue. Princeton, N.J.: Princeton University Press. (First published in 1987.)

Hale, Kenneth, and Samuel Jay Keyser, eds. 1993. *The view from Building 20: essays in linguistics in honor of Sylvain Bromberger*. Cambridge: MIT Press.

Haley, Michael C., and Ronald L. Lundsford. 1994. *Noam Chomsky*. New York: Twayne.

Hendley, Brian. 1986. *Dewey, Russell, Whitehead: philosophers as educators*. Carbondale: Southern Illinois University Press.

Herman, Edward. 1992. *Beyond democracy: decoding the news in an age of propaganda*. Boston: South End Press.

————— 1998. "The propaganda model revisited," *Monthly Review*, Jul.-Aug.

Herman, Edward, and Chomsky, N. 1988. *Manufacturing consent: The political economy of the mass media*. New York: Pantheon.

Herman, Edward, and Robert W. McChesney. 1997. *The global media: the new missionaries of corporate capitalism*. London, Washington, D.C.: Cassell.

Hertz, Noreena. 2001. *The silent takeover: Global capitalism and the death of democracy.* New York: The Free Press.

Hewlett, Sylvia Ann. 1991. *When the bough breaks: the cost of neglecting our children.* New York: Basic Books. (HarperPerennial, 1992.)

———— 1993. *Child neglect in rich societies.* New York: UNICEF.

Hewlett, Sylvia Ann, and Cornel West. 1998. *The war against parents: what we can do for America's beleaguered moms and dads.* Boston: Houghton Mifflin.

Hine, Robert V., and John Mack Faragher. 2000. *The American West: a new interpretive history.* New Haven, London: Yale University Press.

Hirsch, Werner Z., and Luc E. Weber, eds. 1999. *Challenges facing higher education at the millennium.* Phoenix, Ariz.: Oryx Press.

Hollander, Edwin P., and Raymond G. Hunt, eds. 1972. *Classic contribution to social psychology: readings with commentary.* New York: Oxford University Press.

Hollis, Martin, and Edward J. Nell. 1975. *Rational economic man: a philosophical critique of neo-classical economics.* London, New York: Cambridge University Press.

Holt, John. 1969. *The underachieving school.* New York: Dell.

———— 1972. *Freedom and beyond.* New York : Dell.

———— 1982. *How children fail.* Rev. ed. New York: Delta/Seymour Lawrence.

———— 1989. *Learning all the time.* New York: Addison-Wesley.

Holton, Gerald. 1960. "Modern science and the intellectual tradition." *Science* 131: 1187–93. (Reprinted, slightly abbreviated, in Holton 1973.)

———— 1963. "Physics and culture: criteria for curriculum design." *Bulletin of the Institute of Physics and the Physical Society,* 321–29. (Reprinted in Holton 1973.)

———— 1973. *Thematic origins of scientific thought: Kepler to Einstein.* Cambridge: Harvard University Press.

———— 1976. "The Project Physics Course: notes on its educational philosophy." *Physics Education* 11: 330–35. (Reprinted, with the title reordered, in Holton 1978.)

———— 1978. *The scientific imagination: case studies.* Cambridge: Cambridge University Press.

Honda, Maya. 1994. "Linguistic inquiry in the science classroom: 'it *is* science, but it's not like a science problem in a book.'" MIT Occasional Paper in Linguistics no. 6. (mitwpl@mit.edu)

Honda, Maya, and W. O'Neil. 1993. "Triggering science-forming capacity through linguistic inquiry." In Hale and Keyser, eds., 1993, 229–55.

———— and W. O'Neil. 1994. "Constructing and evaluating theories using linguistics in the school science curriculum," in Otero, ed., 1994, 4: 643–656.

Horvat, Branko, Mihailo Markovic, and Rudi Supek, eds., 1975. *Self-governing socialism.* 2 vols. White Plains, N.Y.: International Arts and Sciences Press.

Horwitz, Morton. 1992. *The transformation of American law, 1870–1960: the crisis of legal orthodoxy.* New York, Oxford: Oxford University Press. (Paperback, 1994.)

Howe, Florence, and Ellen Cantarow. 1969. "What happened at MLA: the radical perspective." *College English* 30: 484–87.

Humboldt, Wilhelm von. 1792. *The limits of state action.* Edited with an introduction and notes by J. W. Burrow. Cambridge: Cambridge University Press.

———— 1963. *Humanist without porfolio*. Edited by Marianne Cowan. Detroit: Wayne State University Press.

Hyman, Larry M., and C. N. Li, eds. 1988. *Language, speech and mind: studies in honour of Victoria Fromkin*. London, New York: Routledge.

Illich, Ivan. 1971. *Deschooling society*. New York: Harper and Row.

———— 1978. *Toward a history of needs*. New York: Pantheon Books.

Illich, Ivan, and Barry Sanders. 1988. *ABC: the alphabetization of the popular mind*. San Francisco: North Point Press.

Jacob, François. 1973. *The logic of life*. New York: Pantheon Books.

Jakobovits, Leon A., and Murray S. Miron, eds. 1967. *Readings in the psychology of language*. Englewood Cliffs, N.J.: Prentice-Hall.

Jasper, James M., and Dorothy Nelkin. 1992. *The animal rights crusade: the growth of a moral protest*. New York: Free Press/Maxwell Macmillan International; Toronto: Maxwell Macmillan Canada.

Jencks, Christopher, et al. 1972. *Inequality: a reassessment of the effect of family and schooling in America*. New York: Basic Books.

Jencks, Christopher, and David Riesman. 1968. *The academic revolution*. New York: Doubleday.

Jenkins, Lyle. 2000. *Biolinguistics: exploring the biology of language*. Cambridge: Cambridge University Press.

———— 2001. Review of Calvin and Bickerton 2000. *Mind and Language* 16, 4.

Jennings, Francis. 1975. *The invasion of America: Indians, colonialism, and the cant of conquest*. Chapel Hill: University of North Carolina Press.

———— 1988. *Empire of fortune: crowns, colonies, and tribes in the Seven Years' War in America*. New York: Norton.

Jones, Ken. 1983. *Beyond progressive education*. London: Macmillan.

Kampf, Louis. 1969. "Statement." *College English* 30: 489–90.

———— 1979. "Introduction." *Radical Teacher*, March, 1–2.

Kampf, Louis, and Paul Lauter, eds. 1972. *The politics of literature: dissenting essays on the teaching of English*. New York: Pantheon.

Kanpol, Barry. 1999. *Critical pedagogy: an introduction*. 2nd ed. Westport, Conn.: Bergin and Garvey.

Kapp, K. William. 1971. *The social cost of private enterprise*. New York: Schocken Books.

Kauffman, Stuart. 1995. *At home in the universe: the search for the laws of self-organization and complexity*. New York, Oxford: Oxford University Press.

Kenstowicz, Michael, ed. 2001. *Ken Hale: a life in language*. Cambridge: The MIT Press.

Kim, Jim Yong, Joyce V. Millen, Alec Irwin, and John Gershman, eds. 2000. *Dying for growth: global inequality and the health of the poor*. Monroe, Me.: Common Courage Press.

Kinsman, Clare D., ed. 1975–78. *Contemporary authors, permanent series: a bio-bibliographical guide to current authors and their works*. 2 vols. Detroit, Mich.: Gale Research Co.

Kirp, David L. 2000. "The new U." *The Nation*, April 17, 25–29.

Klinkner, Philip A. 2000. "Affirmative retraction." *The Nation*, July 3, 32–34.

References

Klinkner, Philip A., with Rogers M. Smith. 1999. *The unsteady march: the rise and decline of racial equality in America.* Chicago: University of Chicago Press.

Koerner, E. F. Konrad, and M. Tajima, comps. 1986. *Noam Chomsky: a personal bibliography, 1951–1986.* Amsterdam, Philadelphia: John Benjamins.

Koerner, James D. 1963. *The miseducation of American teachers.* Boston: Houghton Mifflin. (Penguin Books ed., 1965; reprinted in 1971.)

Kohen, Arnold, and John Taylor. 1979. *An act of genocide: Indonesia's invasion of East Timor.* Foreword by Noam Chomsky. London: TAPOL.

Kohl, Herbert R. 1967. *36 children.* Illustrated by Robert George Jackson III. New York: New American Library. (Reprinted, with a new introduction, in 1988.)

―――― 1970. *The open classroom: a practical guide to a new way of teaching.* New York: New York Review.

―――― 1994. *I won't learn from you: and other thoughts on creative maladjustment.* New York: New Press.

―――― 1998. *The discipline of hope: learning from a lifetime of teaching.* New York: Simon and Schuster.

Kohn, Alfie. 1986. *No contest: the case against competition (why we lose in our race to win).* Boston: Houghton Mifflin.

―――― 1993. *Punished by rewards: the trouble with gold stars, incentive plans, A's, praise, and other bribes.* Boston: Houghton Mifflin.

Konig, Hans. 1991. *Columbus: his enterprise. Exploding the myth.* With a 1991 introduction. Including "Columbus in the classroom" by Bill Bigelow. New York: Monthly Review Press. (First published in 1976.)

Kozol, Jonathan. 1967. *Death at an early age: the destruction of the hearts and minds of Negro children in the Boston public schools.* Boston: Houghton Mifflin. (Bantam ed., 1968.)

―――― 1972. *Free schools.* Boston: Houghton Mifflin. (Rev. ed., *Alternative schools: a guide for educators and parents,* New York: Continuum, 1982.)

―――― 1980. *Prisoners of silence: breaking the bonds of adult illiteracy in the United States.* New York: Continuum.

―――― 1981. *On being a teacher.* New York: Continuum. (Rev. ed., Oxford: Oneworld, 1993.)

―――― 1985. *Illiterate America.* Garden City, N.Y.: Anchor Press/Doubleday.

―――― 1991. *Savage inequalities: children in America's schools.* New York: Crown.

―――― 1995. *Amazing grace: the lives of children and the conscience of a nation.* New York: Crown.

Landauer, Carl. 1883. *Corporate state ideologies: historical roots and philosophical origins.* Berkeley, Calif.: Institute of International Studies, University of California.

Laqueur, Thomas. 1976. *Religion and respectability: Sunday schools and working class culture, 1780–1850.* New Haven: Yale University Press.

Lasch, Christopher. 1965. *The new radicalism in America, 1889–1963: the intellectual as a social type.* New York: Knopf.

―――― 1965a. "New curriculum for the teach-ins." *The Nation,* May 31, 239–40.

―――― 1969. *The agony of the American left.* New York: Knopf.

―――― 1977. *Haven in a heartless world: the family besieged.* New York: Basic Books.

Lasswell, Harold D. 1935. "Propaganda," *Encyclopedia of Social Sciences.* New York: Macmillan. (Reprinted in 1954.)

———— 1936. *Politics: who gets what, when, how.* New York, P. Smith, 1950. (Paperback ed., with postscript, New York: Meridian Books, 1958.)

———— 1939. "The propagandist bids for power." *American Scholar* 8, 350–357.

———— 1950. "The theory of political propaganda." In Berelson and Janowitz, eds.

Lauter, Paul. 1965. *Teaching about peace issues; a collection of materials assembled.* Philadelphia: National Peace Literature Service of the Peace Education Division, American Friends Service Committee.

Lauter, Paul, and Florence Howe. 1970. *The conspiracy of the young.* New York, Cleveland: World Publishing.

————. 1978. *The women's movement: impact on the campus and curriculum.* Washington, D.C.: American Association for Higher Education.

Leach, Penelope. 1994. *Children first: what society must do—and is not doing—for children today.* New York: Alfred A. Knopf. (Vintage Books ed., 1995.)

Leiber, Justin. 1975. *Noam Chomsky: a philosophic overview.* New York: St. Martin's Press.

Lester, Mark, ed. 1970. *Readings in transformational grammar.* New York: Holt.

Levin, Harry, and Joanna P. Williams, eds. 1970. *Basic studies in reading.* New York: Basic Books.

Lewin, Roger. 1992. *Complexity: life at the edge of chaos.* New York: Macmillan. (2nd ed., University of Chicago Press, 1999.)

Lightfoot, David. 1983. *The language lottery: toward a biology of grammars.* Cambridge: The MIT Press.

Lippmann, Walter. 1963. *The essential Lippmann: a political philosophy for liberal democracy.* Edited by Clinton Rossiter and James Lare. New York: Random House. (Reprinted in 1982 by Harvard University Press.)

Luce, R. Duncan, Robert R. Bush, and Eugene Galanter, eds. 1963–65. 3 vols. *Handbook of mathematical psychology.* New York: Wiley.

————. 1963–65. *Readings in mathematical psychology.* 2 vols. New York: Wiley.

Luria, Salvador E. 1973. *Life: the unfinished experiment.* New York: Scribner's Sons.

Luria, Salvado E., and Zella Luria. 1970. "The role of the university: ivory tower, service station, or frontier post?" *Daedalus* 99 (Part I): 75–83.

Lyons, John. 1970. *Noam Chomsky.* New York: Viking. (2nd ed., 1977; reprinted, Penguin, 1978; 3rd ed., Fontana, 1991.)

MacIntyre, Alasdair. 1966. *A short history of ethics: a history of moral philosophy from the Homeric age to the twentieth century.* New York: Macmillan.

MacIntyre, Alasdair, Anthony Quinton and Bernard Williams. 1987. *Education and values.* Edited and with an introduction by Graham Haydon. Foreword by Paul H. Hirst. London: Institute of Education, University of London.

Magee, B., ed. 1979. *Men of ideas: face to face with fifteen of the world foremost philosophers.* New York: The Viking Press.

Maher, John, and Judy Groves. 1997. *Introducing Chomsky.* New York: Totem Books.

Marantz, Alec, Yasushi Miyashita, and Wayne O'Neil, eds. 2000. *Image, language, brain: papers from the first Mind Articulation Project symposium.* Cambridge: The MIT Press.

Martin, Roger, David Michaels, and Juan Uriagereka, eds. 2000. *Step by step*. Cambridge: The MIT Press.

McChesney, Robert W. 1989. "The battle for America's ears and minds: the debate over the control and structure of American radio broadcasting, 1930–1935." University of Washington doctoral dissertation. (See next item for revised version.)

——— 1993. *Telecommunications, mass media, and democracy: the battle for the control of U.S. broadcasting, 1928–1935*. New York: Oxford University Press.

——— 1997. *Corporate media and the threat of democracy*. New York: Seven Stories Press.

——— ed., 1998. *Capitalism and the Information Age: The political economy of the global communications revolution*. New York: Monthly Review Press.

——— 1999. *Rich media, poor democracy: communication politics in dubious times*. Champaign: University of Illinois Press.

McGilvray, James. 1999. *Chomsky: language, mind, politics*. Cambridge: Polity Press.

Meade, J. E. 1965. *Efficiency, equality and the ownership of property*. Cambridge: Harvard University Press.

Melman, Seymour. 1958. *Decision-making and productivity*. Oxford: Blackwell.

——— 1970. *Pentagon capitalism*. New York: McGraw-Hill.

——— 1974. *The permanent war economy: American capitalism in decline*. New York: Simon and Schuster. (Revised and updated, 1985.)

——— 1981. *From military to civilian economy: issues and options*. Los Angeles: Center for the Study of Armament and Disarmament.

——— 1983. *Profits without production*. New York: Knopf. (University of Pennsylvania Press ed., 1987.)

Mittal, Anuradha, and Peter Rosset, eds. 1999. *America* needs *human rights*. Oakland, Calif.: Food First Books.

Miyoshi, Masao. 2000. "Ivory tower in escrow." *Boundary 2*, 27, 1: 7–50.

Monod, Jacques. 1971. *Chance and necessity*. New York: Alfred A. Knopf.

Monson, Charles H., ed. 1970. *Education for what? Readings in the ends and means of education*. Boston: Houghton Mifflin.

Montagu, Ashley, ed. 1984. *Science and creationism*. Oxford, New York: Oxford University Press.

Montgomery, David. 1987. *The fall of the house of labor: the workplace, the state, and American labor activism, 1865–1925*. Cambridge University Press. (Paperback ed., 1989. Reprinted in 1989, 1991, 1993, 1995, 1996.)

——— 1993. *Citizen worker: the experience of workers in the United States with democracy and the free market during the nineteenth century*. Cambridge, New York: Cambridge University Press.

Morick, Harold, ed. 1980. *Challenges to empiricism*. Indianapolis, Cambridge: Hackett.

Mouradian, Wendy E., ed. 1998. *Children, our future: ethics, health policy, medical/dental care for children*. Foreword by Jonathan Kozol. Seattle: Washington State Department of Health.

Muscatine, Charles, et al. 1968. *Education at Berkeley*. Berkeley, Los Angeles: University of California Press.

Nelkin, Dorothy. 1972. *The university and military research: moral politics at M.I.T.* Ithaca, N.Y.: Cornell University Press.

——— 1984. *Science as intellectual property: who controls research?* New York: Macmillan.

———— 1995. *Selling science: how the press covers science and technology.* Rev. ed. New York: W.H. Freeman.

Nelkin, Dorothy, and M. Susan Lindee. 1995. *The DNA mystique: the gene as a cultural icon.* New York: Freeman.

Nelkin, Dorothy, and Laurence Tancredi.1994. *Dangerous diagnostics: the social power of biological information.* With a new preface. Chicago: University of Chicago Press.

Nelson, Jack L., Kenneth Carlson, and Stuart B. Palonsky. 1990. *Critical issues in education: a dialectic approach.* New York: McGraw-Hill. (2nd ed., 1993.)

Nelson, Jack L., Kenneth Carlson, and Thomas E. Linton, eds. 1972. *Radical ideas and the schools.* New York: Holt, Rinehart and Winston.

Niebuhr, Reinhold. 1944. *The children of light and the children of darkness: a vindication of democracy and a critique of its traditional defence.* New York: C. Scribner's sons.

Niebuhr, Reinhold, and Paul E. Sigmund. 1969. *The democratic experience: past and prospects.* New York: Praeger.

Nielsen, H. Dean, and William K. Cummings, eds. 1997. *Quality education for all: community oriented approaches.* New York, London: Garland.

Noble, David F. 1977. *America by design: science, technology, and the rise of corporate capitalism.* New York: Knopf. (Oxford University Press ed., 1979.)

———— 1984. *Forces of production: a social history of industrial automation.* New York: Knopf. (Oxford University Press ed., 1986.)

———— 1992. *A world without women: the Christian clerical culture of Western science.* New York: Knopf.

———— 1993. *Progress without people: in defense of Luddism.* Chicago: Charles H. Kerr.

———— 1997. *The religion of technology: the divinity of man and the spirit of invention.* New York: Knopf.

———— 2002. *Digital diploma mills: The automation of higher education.* New York: Monthly Review Press.

———— 2002a. "Technology and commodification of higher education." *Monthly Review*, March, 26–40. (Overview of Noble 2002.)

Noll, Roger G., ed. 1998. *Challenges to research universities.* Washington, D.C.: Brookings Institution Press.

Northrop, F. S. C., and Mason W. Gross, eds. 1961. *Alfred North Whitehead: an anthology.* New York: Macmillan.

Nussbaum, Martha C. 1996. *For love of country: debating the limits of patriotism.* Edited by Joshua Cohen. Boston: Beacon Press. (With comments by respondents and author's reply.)

———— 1997. *Cultivating humanity: a classical defense of reform in liberal education.* Cambridge: Harvard University Press.

O'Brien, Conor Cruise, ed. 1969. *Power* and *consciousness.* New York: New York University Press.

Ohanian, Susan. 1992. *Garbage pizza, patchwork quilts, and math magic: stories about teachers who love to teach and children who love to learn.* New York: W. H. Freeman

———— 1999. *One size fits few: the folly of educational standards.* Portsmouth, N.H.: Heinemann.

Ohmann, Richard. 1969. "An informal and perhaps unreliable account of the Modern Language Association of America." *The Antioch Review* 29, 3: 329–47. (Much of it included in Ohmann 1976, Ch. 2.)

——— 1976. *English in America: a radical view of the profession.* New York: Oxford University Press.

Oller, John W., and Jack C. Richards, eds. 1973. *Focus on the learner: pragmatic perspectives for the language teacher.* Rowley, Mass.: Newbury House.

Oltmans, Willem L., ed. 1974. *On growth: the crisis of exploding population and resource depletion.* New York: Capricorn Books.

——— 1975. *On growth II.* New York: Capricorn Books.

O'Neil, Wayne A. 1976. "An alternative to U.S. education: teaching minority people to study their own cultures." In Feinberg, ed., 1978, 129–42.

——— 1998. "Linguistics for everyone." On-line proceedings of the 1998 meetings of the Applied Linguistics Association of Australia and the Australian Linguistics Society. Brisbane: The University of Queensland. (http://www.cltr.uq.edu.au/als98/oneil.html)

——— 1999a. "Tests and the media: An interview with FairTest." *Radical Teacher* 54: 18–22.

——— 1999b. "Linguistics in the science classroom: progress and problems." In Caetano da Silveira, ed., 1999, 7–16.

Osiatynski, Wiktor, ed. 1984. *Contrasts: Soviet and American thinkers discuss the future.* Translated by Ewa Woydyllo. New York: Macmillan.

Otero, C. P. 1986. "Background and publication history of the dissertations written under the supervision of Noam Chomsky, 1964–1986." In Koerner and Tajima, eds., 1986, 181–204.

——— 1988. "The third emancipatory phase of history." Introduction to Chomsky 1988.

——— 1994. "Background and publication history of the dissertations written under the supervision of Noam Chomsky, 1964–1994." In Otero, ed., 1994, 1:819–839. (Updated version of Otero 1986.)

——— Forthcoming a. *Chomsky for everyone.*

——— Forthcoming b. *Chomsky's revolution: cognitivism and anarchism.* Oxford: Blackwell.

——— Forthcoming c. "Chomsky v. Foucault: pursue justice or grab power?" In *Chomsky,* forthcoming a, vol. 1.

———, ed. 1994. *Noam Chomsky: critical assessments.* 4 vols. London, New York: Routledge.

Pauling, Linus. 1958. *No more war!* London: Gollanz. (25th anniversary edition, New York: Dodd, Mead, 1983.)

Perlman, Fredy. 1968. *Essay on commodity fetishism.* Somerville, Mass.: New England Free Press.

Perry, Theresa, and Lisa Delpit, eds. 1998. *The real ebonics debate: power, language, and the education of African-American children.* Boston: Beacon Press.

Peters, R. S., ed. 1973. *The philosophy of education.* Oxford: Oxford University Press.

Piattelli-Palmarini, Massimo, ed. 1980. *Language and learning: the debate between Jean Piaget and Noam Chomsky.* Cambridge: Harvard University Press. (First published in French in 1979.)

Polanyi, K. 1944. *The great transformation: the political and economic origins of our time.* Foreword by R. M. MacIver. Boston: Beacon Press. (Paperback edition, 1957.)

Popkin, Richard H. 1979. *The history of scepticism from Erasmus to Spinoza.* Rev. and expanded ed. Berkeley, Los Angeles: University of California Press. (First published in 1960 as *The history of scepticism from Erasmus to Descartes.*)

Postman, Neil, and Charles Weingartner.1969. *Teaching as a subversive activity.* New York: Delacorte Press.

Puette, William. 1992. *Through jaundiced eyes: how the media view organized labor.* Ithaca, N.Y.: Cornell University Press.

Purpel, David E., and H. Svi Shapiro, eds. 1985. *Schools and meaning: essays on the moral nature of schooling.* Lanham, Md.: University Press of America.

Rai, Milan. 1995. *Chomsky's politics.* London: Verso.

Raywid, Mary Anne. 1980. "The discovery and rejection of indoctrination." *Education Theory* 30: 1–10.

Resnick, Lauren B., and Phyllis A.Weaver, 1979. *Theory and practice of early reading.* 2 vols. Hillsdale, N.J.: Lawrence Erlbaum Associates.

Reuland, Eric, and W. Abraham, eds. 1992. *Knowledge and language, vol. 1: From Orwell's problem to Plato's problem.* Norwell, Mass.: Kluwer Academic Publishers.

Richard-Amato, Patricia A. 1988. *Making it happen: interaction in the second language classroom (from theory to practice).* New York, London: Longman.

Richelle, Marc N. 1993. *B. F. Skinner: a reappraisal.* Hillsdale, N.J.: Lawrence Erlbaum Associates.

Richie, Robert, and Steven Hill. 1999. *Reflecting all of us: the case for proportional representation.* Foreword by Lani Guinier. Boston: Beacon Press.

Ridgeway, James. 1968. *The closed corporation.* New York: Random House.

Rippa, S. Alexander. 1967. *Education in a free society: an American history.* New York: D. McKay. (5th ed., Longman, 1984.)

———, ed. 1969. *Educational ideas in America: a documentary history.* New York: D. McKay.

Ritz, Dean, ed. 2001. *Defying corporations, defining democracy: A book of history and strategy.* New York: The Apex Press.

Robbins, Mary Susannah, ed. 1999. *Against the Vietnam War: writings by activists.* Syracuse: Syracuse University Press.

Roberts, Paul. 1964. *English syntax: a programmed introduction to transformational grammar.* Alternate edition. New York: Harcourt, Brace and World.

Rocker, R. 1937. *Nationalism and culture.* Translated by Ray E. Chase. St. Paul, Minnesota: Coughlin, 1978. (Reprint of the second, expanded edition [Los Angeles, 1947], with an important epilogue by Rocker. The publisher contributed a preface and an additional bibliography of works by and about Rocker.)

——— 1989. *Anarcho-syndicalism.* Preface by Noam Chomsky. Introduction by Nicolas Walter. London: Pluto Press. (A complete facsimile reproduction of the 1938 edition as well as a corrected transcript of the epilogue to the Indian edition of 1947.)

Rosenberg, Arthur. 1939. *A history of Bolshevism: from Marx to the first five years' plan.* Tr.

from the German by Ian F. D. Morrow. London: Oxford University Press. (First published April 1934.)

Rosner, Stanley, and Lawrence E. Abt, eds. 1970. *The creative experience.* New York: Grossman Publishers.

Roszak, Theodore, ed. 1968. *The dissenting academy.* New York: Pantheon.

Rousseau, G. S., ed. 1972. *Organic form: the life of an idea.* London, Boston: Routledge and Kegan Paul.

Roussopoulos, Dimitrios I., ed. 1987. *The radical papers.* Montreal, New York: Black Rose Books.

Rubinstein, Annette T. 1970. *Schools against children: the case for community control.* New York, London: Monthly Review Press.

Rudy, Willis. 1960. *The evolving liberal arts curriculum; a historical review of basic themes.* New York: Teachers College, Columbia University.

———— 1991. *Total war and twentieth-century higher learning: universities of the Western world in the First and Second World Wars.* Rutherford, N.J.: Fairleigh Dickinson University Press; London, Cranbury, N.J.: Associated University Presses.

———— 1996. *The campus and a nation in crisis: from the American Revolution to Vietnam.* Madison, N.J.: Fairleigh Dickinson University Press; London: Associated University Presses.

Ruggiero, Greg, and Stuart Sahulka, eds. 1995. *The new American crisis.* New York: The New Press.

Russell, Bertrand. 1920. *The theory and practice of Bolshevism.* London: Allen and Unwin.

———— 1926. *Education and the good life.* New York: Horace Liveright, Inc. (Introduction and Part II reprinted as *Education of character,* New York: Philosophical Library, 1961.)

———— 1932. *Education and the social order.* London: Unwin.

———— 1938. *Power.* New York: W. W. Norton.

———— 1945. *A history of Western philosophy and its connection with political and social circumstances from the earliest times to the present day.* New York: Simon and Schuster.

Said, Edward and C. Hitchens, eds., 1988. *Blaming the Victims.* London and New York: Verso, 1988.

Salkie, Raphael. 1990. *The Chomsky update: linguistics and politics.* London: Unwin Hyman.

Sandel, Michael J. 1996. *Democracy's discontents: America in search of a public philosophy.* Cambridge: Harvard University Press.

———— 1998. *Liberalism and the limits of justice.* 2nd ed. Cambridge: Cambridge University Press.

Sarason, Seymour B. 1996. *Revisiting "The culture of the school and the problem of change."* New York: Teachers College Press.

———— 1997. *How schools might be governed and why.* New York: Teachers College Press.

———— 1998. "Some features of a flawed educational system." *Daedalus* 127, 4: 1–12.

———— 1999. *Teaching as a performing art.* Foreword by Maxine Greene. New York: Teachers College Press

Schaff, Adam. 1973. *Language and cognition.* Introduction by Noam Chomsky. New York: McGraw-Hill.

Schiffrin, André., ed. 1997. *The Cold War and the university: toward an intellectual history of the postwar years.* New York: The New Press.

Sebeok, Thomas A., and J. Umiker-Sebeok, eds. 1980. *Speaking apes.* New York: Plenum.

Sen, Amartya. 1992. *Inequality reexamined.* Cambridge: Harvard University Press. (Paperback ed., 1995).

Sellers, Charles. 1991. *The market revolution: Jacksonian America, 1815–1846.* New York: Oxford University Press.

Shapiro, Svi. 1990. *Between capitalism and democracy: educational policy and the crisis of the welfare state.* Introduction by Henry A. Giroux and Paulo Freire. New York: Bergin and Garvey.

Shapiro, Svi, and David E. Purpel, eds. 1993. *Critical social issues in American education: toward the 21st century.* New York: Longman.

———. 1998. *Critical social issues in American education: transformation in a postmodern world.* 2nd ed. Mahwah, N.J.: L. Erlbaum Associates, 1998.

Simon, Brian. 1991. *Education and the social order, 1940–1990.* New York: St. Martin's Press.

Sizer, Theodore R., and Nancy Faust Sizer. 1999. *The students are watching: schools and the moral contract.* Boston: Beacon Press.

Skinner, B. F. 1966. "The phylogeny and ontogeny of behavior." *Science* 153: 1205–13.

Sklar, Martin. 1988. *The corporate reconstruction of American capitalism, 1890–1916: the market, the law, and politics.* New York: Cambridge University Press.

——— 1992. *The United States as a developing country: studies in U.S. history in the progressive era and the 1920s.* Cambridge: Cambridge University Press.

Snow, C. P. 1995. *The two cultures.* New York: Cambridge University Press. (Part I, The Rede Lecture, was first published in 1959.)

Soley, Lawrence C. 1989. *Radio warfare: OSS and CIA subversive propaganda.* New York: Praeger.

——— 1995. *Leasing the ivory tower: the corporate takeover of academia.* Boston: South End Press.

Soley, Lawrence C., and John S. Nichols. 1987. *Clandestine radio broadcasting: a study of revolutionary and counterrevolutionary electronic communication.* New York: Praeger.

Solomon, Robert C., and Jon Solomon. 1993. *Up the university: recreating higher education in America.* Reading, Mass.: Addison-Wesley.

Smith, David N. 1974. *Who rules the universities?: an essay in class analysis.* New York: Monthly Review Press.

Smith, Neil. 1999. *Chomsky: ideas and ideals.* Cambridge: Cambridge University Press.

South End Press Collective, eds. 1998. *Talking about a revolution.* Cambridge: South End Press.

Spring, Joel. 1971. *Education and the rise of the corporate state.* Cuernavaca, Mexico: Centro Intercultural de Documentación. (Beacon Press ed., 1973.)

——— 1975. *A primer of libertarian education,* New York: Free Life Editions.

——— 1978. *American education: an introduction to social and political aspects.* New York: Longman. (8th ed., *American education,* Boston: McGraw-Hill, 1998.)

——— 1986. *The American school, 1642–1985: varieties of historical interpretation of the foundations and development of American education.* New York: Longman. (*The American school, 1642–1996,* 4th ed., New York: McGraw-Hill, 1997.)

———— 1988. *Conflict of interests: the politics of American education.* New York: Longman. (3rd ed., Boston: McGraw-Hill, 1998.)

———— 1989. *The sorting machine revisited: national educational policy since 1945.* Updated ed. New York: Longman. (First published in 1976.)

———— 1992. *Images of American life: a history of ideological management in schools, movies, radio, and television.* Albany: State University of New York Press.

———— 1994a. *Wheels in the head: educational philosophies of authority, freedom, and culture from Socrates to Paulo Freire.* New York: McGraw-Hill.

———— 1994b. *Deculturalization and the struggle for equality: a brief history of the education of dominated cultures in the United States.* New York: McGraw-Hill. (2nd ed., 1997.)

———— 1995. *The intersection of cultures: multicultural education in the United States.* New York: McGraw-Hill.

———— 1997. *Political agendas for education: from the Christian Coalition to the Green Party.* Mahwah, N.J.: L. Erlbaum Associates.

———— 1998. *Education and the rise of the global economy.* Mahwah, N.J.: L. Erlbaum Associates.

Stanford, John. 1999. *Victory in our schools: we can give our children excellent public education.* New York: Bantam.

Stannard, D. E. 1992. *American holocaust: Columbus and the conquest of the world.* New York: Oxford University Press.

Stasz, Clarice. 1981. *The American nightmare: why inequality persists.* New York: Schocken Books.

Stent, Gunther. 1978. *Paradoxes of progress.* San Francisco: Freeman.

Stone, Lawrence, ed. 1976. *Schooling and society: studies in the history of education.* Baltimore, London: The Johns Hopkins University.

Strauss, Gerald. 1976. "The state of pedagogical theory c. 1530: what Protestant reformers knew about education." In Stone, ed., 1976, 69–94.

Strain, John P. 1971. *Modern philosophies of education.* New York: Random House.

Strozer, Judith R. 1994. *Language acquisition after puberty.* Washington, D.C.: Georgetown University Press.

Sweet, Paul R. 1978–80. *Wilhelm von Humboldt: a biography.* 2 vols. Columbus, Oh.: Ohio University Press.

Torrance, E. Paul. 1977a. *Creativity in the classroom.* Washington, D.C.: National Education Association.

———— 1977b. *Discovery and nurturance of giftedness in the culturally different.* Reston, Va.: Council for Exceptional Children.

Torrance, E. Paul, and R. E. Myers. 1970. *Creative learning and teaching.* New York: Dodd, Mead.

Uriagereka, Juan. 1998. *Rhyme and reason: an introduction to minimalist syntax.* Cambridge: The MIT Press.

Veblen, Thorstein. 1914. *The instinct of workmanship, and the state of industrial arts.* New York: Macmillan.

———— 1918. *The higher learning in America: a memorandum on the conduct of universities by business men.* New York: B. W. Huebsch. (Reprinted, New York: Sagamore Press, 1957, with an introd. by Louis M. Hacker.)

Vickerstaff, Sarah, and John Sheldrake. 1989. *The limits of corporatism: British experience in the twentieth century.* Aldershot, Hants, England: Avebury; Brookfield, Vt.: Gower.

Viertel, John. 1973. "The concept of 'diversity' in Humboldt's thought." Lingua e Stile 8: 83–105.

de Waal, Frans. 1982. *Chimpanzee politics: power and sex among apes.* New York: Harper and Row.

Wade, B., ed. 1982. *Language perspectives.* London: Heinemann Educational Books.

Waldrop, M. Mitchell. 1992. *Complexity.* New York: Simon and Schuster. (Paperback ed., 1993.)

Ware, Norman. 1924. *The industrial worker, 1840–1860: the reaction of American industrial society to the advance of the Industrial Revolution.* With an introduction by Thomas Dublin. Boston, New York: Houghton Mifflin. (Reprinted, in 1959 by Peter Smith in Gloucester, Mass.; reprinted in 1990 by I. R. Dee in Chicago.)

——— 1929. *The labor movement in the United States, 1860–1895: a study in democracy.* New York, London: D. Appleton and Company. (Reprinted in 1959.)

——— 1935. *Labor in modern industrial society.* Boston, New York: D. C. Heath and Company.

Weiler, Kathleen, and Candace Mitchell, eds. 1992. *What schools can do: critical pedagogy and practice.* Albany: State University of New York Press.

Weintraub, Pamela, ed. 1984. *The Omni interviews.* New York: Ticknor and Fields.

Werhane, Patricia. 1985. *Persons, rights, and corporations.* Englewood Cliffs, N.J.: Prentice-Hall.

Wesson, Robert. 1991. *Beyond natural selection.* Cambridge: The MIT Press. (Paperback ed., 1993.)

Westbrook, Robert B. 1991. *John Dewey and American democracy.* Chicago: University of Chicago Press.

White, G. A., and Newman, C., eds. 1972. *Literature in revolution.* New York: Holt.

Whitehead, Alfred North. 1917. "The aims of education." Presidential Address to the Mathematical Association of England. (Reprinted in Northrop and Gross, eds., 1961.)

——— 1925. *Science and the modern world.* New York: Macmillan. (Free Press paperback edition, 1967.)

Wiarda, Howard J. 1997. *Corporatism and comparative politics: the other great "ism."* Armonk, N.Y.: M. E. Sharpe.

Wilkin, Peter. 1997. *Noam Chomsky: on power, knowledge and human nature.* London: Macmillan; New York: St. Martin's Press.

Wilkinson, Richard G. 1996. *Unhealthy societies: the afflictions of inequality.* London, New York: Routledge.

Williamson, Peter J. 1989. *Corporatism in perspective: an introductory guide to corporatist theory.* London: Sage.

Wolk, Steven. 1998. *A democratic classroom.* Portsmouth, N.H.: Heinemann.

Wood, Ellen. 1972. *Mind and politics.* Berkeley: University of California Press.

Yeo, Frederick, and Barry Kanpol, eds. 1999. *From nihilism to possibility: democratic trans-formations for the inner city.* Cresskill, N.J.: Hampton Press.

Zabel, Gary, ed. 1993. *Art and society: lectures and essays by William Morris.* Boston: George's Hill.

Zacks, Rebecca. 2000. "The TR university research scorecard." *Technology Review,* Jul.-Aug., 88–90.

Zepezauer, Mark, and Arthur Naiman. 1996. *Take the rich off welfare.* Tucson, Ariz.: Odonian Press.

Zinn, Howard. 1980. *A people's history of the United States.* New York: Harper and Row. (HarperPerennial ed., 1990.)

———— 1998. *The twentieth century, a people's history.* Revised and updated edition. New York: HarperPerennial.

———— 1999. *The future of history.* Interviews with David Barsamian. Monroe, Me.: Common Courage Press.

Zwick, J., ed. 1992. *Mark Twain's weapons of satire: Anti-imperialist writings on the Philippine-American war.* Syracuse: Syracuse University Press.

Index